The A to Z
of
Plant Names

A Quick Reference Guide to 4000 Garden Plants

ALLEN J. COOMBES

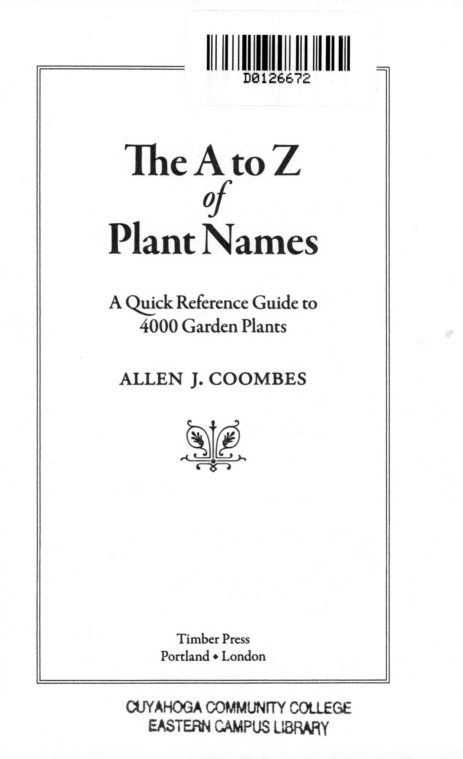

Timber Press
Portland ◆ London

Published in 2012 by Timber Press, Inc.

The Haseltine Building
133 S.W. Second Avenue, Suite 450
Portland, Oregon 97204-3527
timberpress.com

2 The Quadrant
135 Salusbury Road
London NW6 6RJ
timberpress.co.uk

Printed in the United States of America

Library of Congress Cataloging-in-Publication Data
Coombes, Allen J.
    The A to Z of plant names : a quick reference guide to 4000 garden plants
/ Allen J. Coombes. — 1st ed.
        p. cm.
    Includes bibliographical references.
    ISBN 978-1-60469-196-2
    1. Plants—Great Britain—Nomenclature—Dictionaries. 2. Plants—
North America—Nomenclature—
Dictionaries. 3. Botany—Great Britain—Dictionaries. 4. Botany—North
America—Dictionaries. I. Title.
    QK96.C78 2012
    635.03—dc23
                                                                    2011029271

A catalogue record for this book is also available from the British Library.

To Piers Trehane,
a good friend as well as a
valued mentor and critic,
sorely missed.

Contents

Acknowledgements

I would like to thank my wife for her continued patience, support and encouragement throughout this work.

Thanks to the editorial team at Timber Press, especially Franni Bertolino and Anna Mumford, who have been a joy to work with.

Lastly I would like to thank all those institutions worldwide that have made their herbarium records freely available to all, and without which this book would have taken many more years, and miles, to complete.

Introduction

AS PLANTS ARE ESSENTIAL to man's existence, providing food, medicine and shelter, plant names are surely as old as language itself, and we can imagine that early man needed names for the plants and plant products that he used or traded. Although plants were documented soon after the earliest written languages appeared, several thousand years BCE, the first systematic documentation of known plants is owed to the Greek scholar Theophrastus in the 4th century BCE. Many of the names he used (as well as those given by later Greeks, such as Dioscorides, and Romans, such as Pliny the Elder) are still in use today, though not necessarily for the same plants.

The rest of the world was slow to take advantage of what the Greeks and Romans had accomplished, and it was not until the 16th and 17th centuries that serious efforts were made to name plants. This was a particularly important time as many new discoveries were being made in various parts of the world. The plant names used at this time were in the form of a descriptive phrase starting with the name of the genus and listing key characters that would distinguish a species from its relatives, with different authors providing different phrase names for the same plant. It was not until the publication of *Species Plantarum* by Linnaeus in 1753 that plant names existed in the form we know them today. In this, Linnaeus listed the phrase names applied by himself and others but, as well as the name of the genus, also gave a single word to denote the species. These were originally regarded as trivial names, a sort of aide-memoire to the full names that, as more species were described, were becoming increasingly lengthy. For example, Linnaeus called common holly *Ilex foliis ovatis acutis spinosis*, i.e., the holly with ovate, sharply spiny leaves, and added after this the word *Aquifolium*.

These trivial names were quickly adopted as the standard way to write plant names, and this binomial (two-name) system is the method in use today. The beauty of this system lies in its simplicity, making plant names instantly recognisable as such and while at first glance they can appear strange, each has its own story to tell.

What makes a plant name

The scientific name of any plant consists of the name of the genus followed by the species epithet, which together with the genus makes the name of the species. The epithet is not regarded as a name as it is meaningless without the name of a genus. Finally comes the name of the author or authors, usually abbreviated, who described the species. A subspecies or variety is a botanically recognised division of a species and will also include an additional epithet and author. The genus and epithets are written in italics, the genus starting with a capital letter, the species and other epithets with a low-case letter.

While the name of a genus is a noun, the species epithet is usually an adjective, so *Quercus rubra* is literally 'the red oak'. As Latin is one of the languages, that, unlike English, assigns gender to nouns, the adjectival species epithet needs to agree with the genus. As *Quercus* is feminine, the female form of the adjective is used. With genera of different genders, the ending would change: neuter, *Acer rubrum*; masculine, *Centranthus ruber*. Not all epithets are subject to change. When a plant is named after a person and the epithet is the person's name in the genitive, the ending agrees with the gender of the person, so the *-ii* ending applies only to plants named after men. The epithets of plants named after women have a different ending, e.g., *Kniphofia northiae*, after Marianne North. If, however the ending is the name as an adjective, the epithet does agree with the genus. Examples of these are *Acer davidii*, named after Armand David, and *Forsythia giraldi-*

ana, named after Giuseppe Giraldi. As noun and adjective, these give the names subtly different meanings, with the first translating as David's maple, the second as Giraldi forsythia. Occasionally the epithet is a noun and is not altered by gender. For example, *Styrax* is masculine and the adjectival epithets end in *-us*, as in *S. americanus*. However, the epithet of *S. obassia* is a noun derived from the Japanese name, so retains its original form.

Cultivars are selections maintained in horticulture by means that retain their distinguishing characteristics. They are capitalised, are not written in italics and are enclosed in single quotation marks (e.g., *Magnolia* ×*soulangeana* 'Lennei'). Many cultivars have epithets in Latin form, but any named since 1959 must have names in a modern language. Some of the more popular cultivars with names in Latin form are treated here.

A group can be regarded as similar to a cultivar in that it is only recognised in gardens but can contain many variants that share the same characters and often includes cultivars. The cabbage, for example, is a group within the species *Brassica oleracea* (*Brassica oleracea* Capitata Group), and all cabbage cultivars belong here. Species or divisions within species no longer recognised as botanically distinct can be regarded as groups if they are distinct in gardens. For example, *Celosia cristata* and *C. plumosa*, formerly recognised as species, are now regarded as falling within the variation of *C. argentea*. Their distinctness in gardens, however, can continue to be recognised by calling them *C. argentea* Cristata Group and *C. argentea* Plumosa Group.

Hybrids that are recognised botanically have a multiplication sign immediately preceding the epithet.

The origin and meaning of plant names

Plant names are of diverse origin. They can be formed from the classical languages, from personal names, the name of a country where they grow or from one of their common names. This is why they should be referred to as scientific, rather than Latin, names; and the term Latin name used here refers to names used in Classical Latin. Whatever their origin, plant names are regarded as being in Latin form. The name of the genus is often from mythology or named for an eminent person, not necessarily connected with the plants in question. The species epithet is more likely to have a direct association with the plant it represents. It could relate to a particular character of the plant or the part of the world it comes from, or it may commemorate a person who had some association with the species. Species can be named for someone who provided assistance to the author or collector, or in some cases someone who recognised it as distinct but gave it another name, but are more often named for the person who collected what is referred to as the type specimen. This is a herbarium specimen that was used to prepare the original description of the species.

Whatever the origin of a name or epithet, knowledge of its meaning gives it added significance and often makes it easier to associate with a plant. Knowing the meaning of a name is only one step in this process. To link the name to a plant, it is more important to know why that name was chosen. Commemorative epithets may do little to help with recognition, but they often add a great deal of historical interest by linking a plant to its discoverer or the person who first collected it. Descriptive epithets on the other hand often make it easy to link the name to the plant. It is only necessary to know that *pardalis* is Latin for a leopard, to link the name to the leopard-like spots on the flowers of *Lilium pardalinum*. However, names can also give the wrong impression of a plant.

When a plant is named, the author may have had very little material to go on. The chosen name, therefore, may not represent a state that is typical of that genus or species. When Linnaeus named the genus *Arenaria*, for example, he had relatively few species available to him. The generic name is derived from the fact that several of these grow in sandy soils. It cannot be assumed, however, that this applies to all species and some even grow in marshes. *Dictamnus albus*, commonly grown in gardens and named for its white flowers, is often seen with flowers in shades of pink to purple. Names can also be misleading, as with *Pinus palustris*, the name of which implies that it grows in marshes, while it prefers well-drained soils. Occasionally the country of origin is wrongly identified. *Simmondsia chinensis*, for example, was thought to be a native of China but is, in fact, from California.

In addition, the meaning of many place names have changed with time; for example, in the time of Linnaeus, Canada would have included much of the northeastern USA, and plants with the specific epithet *canadensis* cannot be assumed to have been described from Canada, although they may well occur there. *Glandularia canadensis*, for example, is not a native of Canada. Spellings can also change with time so that some plant names can appear misspelled. For example, 'Pensylvania' was a commonly used 18th-century spelling for Pennsylvania, and so plant names that use the single *n* are not considered incorrect. Chinese place names have also changed a great deal, and so we come across the epithet *hupehensis* for plants described from Hubei (previously Hupeh), or *cantoniense* for plants from Guangzhou (previously Canton).

Occasionally an epithet may have a meaning that seems strange for the genus it is in. *Crocosmia* ×*crocosmiiflora* and *C.* ×*crocosmioides*, for example, mean, respectively, 'the *Crocosmia* with flowers like *Crocosmia*' and 'the *Crocosmia* like a *Crocosmia*'. The reason for this is that the first was originally named as a species of *Montbretia* and the second as a species of *Antholyza*. Therefore the original meanings were 'the *Montbretia* with flowers like *Crocosmia*' and 'the *Antholyza* like a *Crocosmia*'. When a species is moved to another genus, the characters that distinguished it in the first genus, and gave rise to its name, may not be as meaningful in the current genus. For example the epithet of *Vancouveria hexandra* means 'having six stamens', which all species in this genus have. The epithet was more meaningful when it was originally named as a species of *Epimedium*, the species of which have four stamens.

Although scientific names are regarded as being in Latin form, they are far from the Latin spoken by the Romans and incorporate words that the Romans never knew or words given a different meaning for the purpose of botany. Many scientific names use place names that were used in Roman times, many more use the names of modern countries, regions or cities unfamiliar to the Romans, or the modern names for regions. The epithet *sinense/sinensis*, for example, is derived from *Sina*, the Latin name for China. The epithet *chinense/chinensis*, which has the same meaning ('from China'), is a Latinised version of the country's English name. Such words could be described as modern Latin. Often, the names of plant parts have been adapted from Latin words that were originally used in a different sense. For example, the spathe—the conspicuous bract around the inflorescence in *Arum* and its relatives—derives from the Latin word (from the Greek) for a broadsword.

Common names

Common, or vernacular, names have been with us for much longer than scientific names; their origins are often steeped in history and their meanings can be fascinating. They have the advantage of being easier to pronounce, spell and remember for most people than scientific names and often contain words that can be related to, immediately conveying an impression of a plant. While common names are generally sufficient for everyday language, they do have some disadvantages. One plant may have several or many common names, which can be specific to different regions, languages or countries. While some foreign common names have been adopted in English, such as edelweiss (German for 'noble white'), these are the exception. While common names often tell us something about the plant, they may not always indicate its true relations. Plants from several different genera are referred to as 'cedar' or 'pine', for example, and *Symphyotrichum novi-belgii* is known as Michaelmas daisy, or New York aster, in spite of being neither a daisy nor an aster.

In addition, the same common name can have different meanings. To illustrate the confusion that can occur, in North

America the common name 'sycamore' is applied to members of the genus *Platanus*, which in Europe are called 'planes'. In Europe the name 'sycamore' applies to a maple, *Acer pseudoplatanus*, which in Scotland is referred to as 'plane'. A sycamore mentioned in the Bible, however, is a type of fig.

Scientific names have the advantage over common names in that they have the same meaning in any part of the world. In addition they are documented, and it is always possible go back to the original to discover exactly what the author meant, something that is not always possible with common names. Knowing the correct scientific name of a plant allows access to a much wider range of information about it, in sources that may not use common names.

Name changes

Changes to the scientific name of plants are part of life, though often frustrating. However, names are only changed for good reasons, and changes aim to give an accurate representation, not only of the true identity of a plant but also of its relationships. Some examples of why names are changed are given here.

1. Plants can be wrongly identified. For many years, a bedding plant was commonly grown under the name *Helichrysum microphyllum*. Its correct name, however, is *Plecostachys serpyllifolia*. Both species are in cultivation. The spider plant commonly referred to in the literature and grown in gardens as *Cleome spinosa*, is, in fact, a different species, *C. hassleriana*, now known as *Tarenaya hassleriana*. The author 'hort.' (Latin *hortulanorum*, 'of gardeners') is often used to denote plants that are grown in gardens under the incorrect name. In the example just given, *Helichrysum microphyllum* hort. (or at least hort. in part) is different *to H. microphyllum* (Willd.) Cambess.

2. Names can change for nomenclatural reasons. Nomenclature decides if the name used for a plant is the correct one—for

example, if it was published correctly, or if there is an earlier name for the same plant. The rules of nomenclature state that the earliest validly published name takes priority, even if this is obscure. Since the adoption of their use, many genera have been found to have earlier names, which should have been used. However, as changing the names of many familiar and important genera would cause considerable disruption, it has been possible to conserve these later names and allow their use. *Pittosporum* is an example of a conserved generic name. Without conservation, the earlier name *Tobira* would have to be used.

The names of species can also be conserved, an important point when talking about those plants with a high profile in horticulture. As an example of this, *Zinnia violacea* is an earlier name applied to the same species as *Z. elegans*. Under the rules of nomenclature, if they are regarded as the same species then *Z. violacea* must take priority, as it was published first. However, as *Z. elegans* is a much more widely used name, it has been proposed for conservation. Many of these possible changes can therefore be avoided.

3. Names can change for taxonomic reasons. Taxonomy deals with the relationships between plants—for example, which genus does a particular plant belong in, or should it be regarded as a species, or maybe as a subspecies of a different species. There have always been name changes of this sort, but recent molecular work has made considerable advances in the understanding of plant relationships, resulting in many changes. It has been found, for instance, that most American species of *Aster* are not closely related to the Old World species, thus resulting in the splitting of the genus into several smaller ones.

Are these changes avoidable? In this example, it is not wrong to retain all species in the genus *Aster*, if, with good reason, it is believed that is where they should be, but the new classification shows better the relationships of the species involved, which can help gardeners and plant breeders. In addition, new species named may not have a useable name in the old genus. For example, new species of *Veronica* have already been described from New Zealand and Australia with no name available for them in *Hebe* or *Parahebe*, or whichever genus they would have been assigned to in the past.

While conservation is a considerable help in promoting name stability, sometimes it comes at a price. When the genus *Chrysanthemum* was split into smaller genera, the generic name should have stayed with *C. segetum* (corn marigold) and its relatives, necessitating a new genus for the florists' 'mums'. As this would have caused considerable horticultural disruption, the genus *Chrysanthemum* was conserved so that the 'mums' would not have to change their name. This, however, necessitated moving the corn marigold and its relatives to another genus, *Glebionis*.

Pronunciation

Pronunciation is one of the most controversial aspects of plant names, and although there are strict rules on how to form and spell plant names, there are no rules on how to pronounce them. They are derived from, or at least regarded as being, Latin, but that does not mean they have to be pronounced as such. As a language, Latin is very rarely spoken in the way the Romans used it. As it spread across Europe, used as an international language, its pronunciation was heavily influenced by the native language; even church Latin, at least today, is strongly influenced by Italian. The original Latin pronunciation is not known for certain, and much of what is known would make it inappropriate, difficult and incomprehensible for English speakers.

It is surprising how infrequently plant names are actually spoken; they are much more likely to be encountered when reading or writing. One simple rule to follow is to pronounce every vowel separately, except for diphthongs (two vowels together pronounced as one) such as ae, ai, au, oe and eu), so *Abies* is ab-ee-ayz, not ay-beez. The most important aspect to take into consideration when saying a plant name is to be understood, that the person listening knows which plant is being referred to. It therefore makes sense to adopt a traditional pronunciation, one that is widely used and understood, and I have based the suggested pronunciations used here on what I have heard and what I know people recognise. Of course, there is a considerable variety of ways that plant names are pronounced, often depending on regional accent. There is also a great deal of leeway in how names can be pronounced and still be understood. For example, it does not matter if you say uh-me-ri-*kah*-nuh or uh-me-ri-*kay*-nuh; both will be understood, and the difference between the two is very small. Some may prefer to use pur-*poo*-ree-oos, while most will say pur-*pew*-ree-oos. Pronunciation can clarify which is meant of two similar-sounding names—for example, *Dahlia* and *Dalea*, both commonly pronounced *day*-lee-uh.

One of the most difficult parts of a name to decide how to pronounce is the *-ii* found at the end of many species epithets. By far the most common pronunciation of this, in my experience, is 'ee-ie' (e.g, wil-*son*-ee-ie, but *wil*-son-ie or wil-*son*-ee-ee are also found). I have opted for '-ee-ee' here because it is more likely to be accepted by non-English speakers (who would not use the '-ie' sound for the letter *i*) and emphasises the spelling, thus differentiating between epithets ending *-ii* and those ending *-iae*. However, all are likely to be understood, and in every case, it is better to use a pronunciation with which you are familiar and confident.

The pronunciation of names derived from personal names can be problematic. If we were to pronounce the plant name in the same way as the person's name, some names would not be understood, at least in English-speaking countries. *Magnolia*, for example, would be pronounced man-*yol*-ee-uh. In addition, when a Latin ending is added to a name it changes the stressed syllable, so in the earlier example only *wil*-son-ie (not recommended) would come close to the original pronunciation.

How to use this book

The aim of this book is to give the correct name as well as its derivation and pronunciation for the most commonly grown plants in the UK and in temperate areas of North America. Most of the plants included will be grown out of doors, but also listed is a wide range of plants that are grown either indoors or with protection in many areas.

Entries are arranged alphabetically by genus, then by species. Information given for the genus includes the name of the genus followed by the author and then, parenthetically, the family, which links the genus to related plants. The suggested pronunciation, with the stressed syllable in italics, is followed by the common name, if there is one, and the derivation of the scientific name. Finally, the number of species currently accepted, the type of plant and the distribution is given. The number of species should be regarded as approximate. Some plants are known only in cultivation. This may be because they are hybrids that arose in gardens; species now extinct in the wild; so widely grown that their native origin has become obscured; or because the plants in cultivation have changed so much from the original species by selection in cultivation over a long period that they are sufficiently distinct to be regarded as a different species.

Entries for species include the specific epithet followed by the author, the suggested pronunciation, common name, derivation of the epithet, and the distribution (unless this is the same as that given for the genus) and the parentage (if it is a hybrid). Information for the derivation of the epithet given in parentheses is implied and is derived from knowledge of the meaning together with knowledge of the plant. Common names and synonyms (previously used names) are cross referenced.

Words commonly used as cultivar epithets

While some cultivars that have epithets in Latin form are included in the text, to avoid repetition a list is included here of those that are most commonly used together with their pronunciation and meaning. As with the epithets of species, the ending often varies depending on the gender of the genus to which they are assigned, and they are presented here in the order masculine/feminine/neuter. Two or more words are often used in combination to form an epithet. They may be joined by a connecting vowel, for example 'Albiflora', meaning white-flowered, or 'Roseopicta', meaning variegated with pink, or retained as separate words, e.g., 'Alba Plena', meaning double white.

albus/alba/album. *al*-boos/buh/boom. Lat. white.

atro-. *at*-roh. Lat. dark (used in combination).

aureus/aurea/aureum. *aw*-ree-oos/uh/oom. Lat. golden.

compactus/compacta/compactum. kom-*pak*-toos/tuh/toom. Lat. compact.

crispus/crispa/crispum. *kris*-poos/puh/poom. Lat. finely wavy.

elegans. *el*-i-ganz. Lat. elegant, slender.

fastigiatus/fastigiata/fastigiatum. fas-tig-ee-*ah*-toos/tuh/toom. Lat. pointed (fastigate, narrow upright).

-florus/-flora/-florum. *flaw*-roos/ruh/room. Lat. flower (used in combination).

-folius/-folia/-folium. *foh*-lee-oos/uh/oom. Lat. leaf (used in combination).

glaucus/glauca/glaucum. *glaw*-koos/kuh/koom. Lat. bluish white.

grandi-. *gran*-di-. Lat. large (used in combination).

laciniatus/laciniata/laciniatum. la-sin-ee-*ah*-toos/tuh/toom. Lat. deeply cut.

maculatus/maculata/maculatum. mak-ew-*lah*-toos/tuh/toom. Lat. spotted.

macrophyllus/macrophylla/macrophyllum. mak-*rof*-i-loos/luh/loom. Gk. large-leaved.

major/major/majus. *may*-juh/juh/joos. Lat. larger.

marginatus/marginata/marginatum. mar-jin-*ah*-toos/tuh/toom. Lat. margined.

maximus/maxima/maximum. *max*-i-moos/muh/moom. Lat. largest.

microphyllus/microphylla/microphyllum. mik-*rof*-i-loos/luh/loom. Gk. small-leaved.

minimus/minima/minimum. *min*-i-moos/muh/moom. Lat. smallest.

minor/minor/minus. *mie*-nuh/nuh/noos. Lat. smaller.

monstrosus/monstrosa/monstrosum. mon-*stroh*-soos/suh/ soom. Lat. monstrous.

nanus/nana/nanum. *nah*-noos/nuh/noom. Lat. dwarf.

nigrus/nigra/nigrum. *nie*-groos/gruh/groom. Lat. black.

niveus/nivea/niveum. *niv*-ee-oos/uh/oom. Lat. snow-white.

pendulus/pendula/pendulum. *pen*-dew-loos/luh/loom. Lat. pendulous, weeping.

pictus/picta/pictum. *pik*-toos/tuh/toom. Lat. painted (variegated).

plenus/plena/plenum. *pleen*-oos/uh/oom. Lat. full (used particularly for double flowers).

plumosus/plumosa/plumosum. plue-*moh*-soos/suh/soom. Lat. feathery.

prostratus/prostrata/prostratum. pro-*strah*-toos/tuh/ toom. Lat. prostrate.

purpureus/purpurea/purpureum. pur-*pew*-ree-oos/uh/ oom. Lat. purple.

roseus/rosea/roseum. *roh*-zee-oos/uh/oom. Lat. pink or rose.

ruber/rubra/rubrum. *rue*-ber/bruh/broom. Lat. red.

splendens. *splen*-duhnz. Lat. splendid.

striatus/striata/striatum. stree-*ah*-toos/tuh/toom. Lat. striped.

sulphureus/sulphurea/sulphureum. sul-*few*-ree-oos/uh/ oom. Lat. sulphur-coloured.

tortuosus/tortuosa/tortuosum. tort-ew-*oh*-soos/suh/soom. Lat. twisted.

tricolor. *tri*-ko-lor. Lat. three-coloured.

undulatus/undulata/undulatum. un-dew-*lah*-toos/tuh/ toom. Lat. wavy-edged.

variegatus/variegata/variegatum. va-ree-uh-*gah*-toos/tuh/ toom. Lat. variegated.

Abbreviations

Am.	America	**N**	north(ern)
ann.	annual	**N.I.**	North Island
B.C.	Baja California	**nothosubsp.**	nothosubspecies (a hybrid involving subspecies)
bienn.	biennial		
C	central		
ca.	approximately	**NSW**	New South Wales
cult.	cultivated	**NZ**	New Zealand
E	east(ern)	**perenn.**	perennial
Eur.	Europe	**reg(s).**	region(s)
f.	forma	**S**	south(ern)
Gk.	Greek	**S.I.**	South Island
hemisph.	hemisphere	**sp.**	species (singular)
Himal.	Himalaya	**spp.**	species (plural)
Is.	island(s)	**subsp.**	subspecies
Lat.	Latin	**subtrop.**	subtropical
med.	medicinal	**temp.**	temperate
Medit.	Mediterranean	**trop.**	tropical
Mex.	Mexico	**var.**	variety
myth.	mythology	**W**	west(ern)

Aaron's beard *Hypericum calycinum*
Aaron's rod *Verbascum thapsus*

Abelia R. Br. (Linnaeaceae). uh-*bee*-lee-uh. After Clarke Abel (1780– 1826), British surgeon and naturalist who discovered and introduced *A. chinensis*. 5 spp. shrubs. China, Japan.
  chinensis R. Br. chin-*en*-sis. Of China. China.
  engleriana (Graebn.) Rehder = *A. uniflora*
  floribunda (M. Martens & Galeotti) Decne. = *Vesalea floribunda*
  ×***grandiflora*** Rehder. gran-di-*flaw*-ruh. Glossy abelia. Lat. large-flowered. *A. chinensis* × *A. uniflora*. Cult.
  mosanensis T. H. Chung ex Nakai = *Zabelia mosanensis*
  parvifolia Hemsl. = *A. uniflora*
  schumannii (Graebn.) Rehder = *A. uniflora*
  triflora R. Br. ex Wall. = *Zabelia triflora*
  uniflora R. Br. ew-nee-*flaw*-ruh. Lat. one-flowered (the flowers are borne singly). China.

abelia, fragrant *Zabelia mosanensis*.
  glossy *Abelia* ×*grandiflora*

Abeliophyllum Nakai (Oleaceae). uh-bee-lee-oh-*fil*-um. Gk. with leaves like *Abelia*. 1 sp., deciduous shrub. Korea.
  distichum Nakai. *dis*-tik-oom. White forsythia. Lat. arranged in two rows (the leaves).

Abelmoschus Medik. (Malvaceae). a-buhl-*mosk*-oos. Arabian, father or source of musk, from the scented seeds. 15 spp. herbs. Trop. Asia.
  esculentus (L.) Moench. esk-ew-*lent*-oos. Lady's fingers, okra. Lat. edible (the fruit). Tropics.
  manihot (L.) Medik. *man*-ee-hot. Sunset hibiscus. From the resemblance of the leaves to those of *Manihot*, from Brazilian Portuguese *mandioca*. SE Asia.
  moschatus Medik. mos-*kah*-toos. Musk okra/mallow. Arabian, musk-scented (the seeds). S Asia.

Abies Mill. (Pinaceae). *a*-bee-ayz. Firs. From Lat. to rise, for their height. 48 spp. conifers. N hemisph.
  alba Mill. *al*-buh. Silver fir. Lat. white (the bark). Eur.
  amabilis Douglas ex J. Forbes. uh-*mah*-bi-lis. Pacific silver fir, red silver fir. Lat. beautiful. W N Am.
  balsamea (L.) Mill. ball-*sam*-ee-uh. Balsam fir, balm of Gilead fir. Lat. balsam-scented. N Am.
  cephalonica Loudon. kef-uh-*lon*-i-kuh. Greek fir. Lat. of Cephalonia. S Greece.
  concolor (Gordon & Glend.) Lindl. ex Hildebr. *kon*-ko-lor. White fir. Lat. of similar colour (both leaf surfaces). W USA, Mex. (B.C.). var. ***lowiana*** (Gordon & Glend.) Lemmon.

low-ee-*ah*-nuh. After Messrs Low, to
whose Clapton nursery William
Lobb sent seed from California in
1851.

delavayi Franch. del-uh-*vay*-ee. After
French missionary Jean Marie
Delavay (1834–1895), who collected
the type specimen in Yunnan in
1884. SW China, N Myanmar.

forrestii Coltm.-Rog. fo-*rest*-ee-ee.
After Scottish botanist George
Forrest (1873–1932), who collected
the type specimen in Yunnan in
1910. SW China.

fraseri (Pursh) Poir. *fray*-zuh-ree.
Fraser fir. After Scottish botanist
John Fraser (1750–1811), who discovered it and introduced it to cultivation ca. 1807. SE USA.

grandis (Dougl. ex D. Don) Lindl.
gran-dis. Giant fir, grand fir. Lat.
large. W N Am.

homolepis Sieb. & Zucc. ho-moh-
lep-is. Nikko fir. Gk. with equal
scales (on the cone). Japan.

koreana E. H. Wilson. ko-ree-*ah*-nuh.
Korean fir. Of Korea. S Korea.

lasiocarpa (Hook.) Nutt. laz-ee-oh-
kar-puh. Subalpine fir. Gk. with
rough cones. W N Am. var. ***arizonica*** (Merriam) Lemmon. a-ri-*zon*-i-
kuh. Corkbark fir. Of Arizona.
SW USA.

magnifica A. Murray. mag-*ni*-fi-kuh.
California red fir. Lat. magnificent.
W USA.

nordmanniana (Steven) Spach.
nord-man-ee-*ah*-nuh. Nordmann fir.
After its discoverer Alexander von
Nordmann (1803–1866), Finnish
zoologist. Caucasus, N Turkey.

numidica de Lannoy ex Carrière.

new-*mid*-i-kuh. Algerian fir. Of
Numidia (now Algeria). Algeria.

pinsapo Boiss. pin-*sah*-poh. Spanish
fir. The Spanish name, from *pino*
(pine) and *sapino* (fir). S Spain.

procera Rehder. *pro*-suh-ruh. Noble
fir. Lat. tall. W USA.

veitchii Lindl. *veech*-ee-ee. Veitch fir.
After John Gould Veitch (1839–
1870), British plant collector and
nurseryman who discovered it in
1860. Japan.

absinthe *Artemisia absinthium*

Abutilon Mill. (Malvaceae). uh-*bew*-
ti-lon. From the Arabic name for one
species or a similar plant. 150 spp.,
trees, shrubs, herbs. Tropics and subtropics.

×***hybridum*** hort. ex Voss. *hib*-rid-
oom. Lat. hybrid. *A. darwinii* × *A.
pictum*. Cult.

megapotamicum (Spreng.) St. Hil. &
Naud. meg-uh-po-*tam*-i-koom. Gk.
large river (referring to the Rio
Grande). Brazil.

pictum (Gillies ex Hook. & Arn.)
Walp. *pik*-toom. Lat. painted (the
flowers, with branched veins). Brazil.

×***suntense*** C. D. Brickell = *Corynabutilon* ×*suntense*

vitifolium (Cav.) Presl = *Corynabutilon vitifolium*

Acacia Mill. (Fabaceae). uh-*kay*-see-
uh. Wattles. From Gk. for thorn.
1000 spp., trees, shrubs. Australia,
Pacific Is., SE Asia, Madagascar.

baileyana F. Muell. bay-lee-*ah*-nuh.
After British-born Australian botanist Frederick Manson Bailey (1827–

1915), who collected the type specimen in Bowen Park, Brisbane, in 1876. Australia (NSW).

cultriformis A. Cunn. ex G. Don. kul-tri-*form*-is. Knife-leaf wattle. Lat. knife-shaped (the phyllodes). Australia (NSW, Queensland).

dealbata Link. dee-al-*bah*-tuh. Mimosa, silver wattle. Lat. whitened (the shoots). SE Australia.

longifolia (Andrews) Willd. long-gi-*foh*-lee-uh. Sallow wattle, Sydney golden wattle. Lat. long-leaved (the phyllodes). SE Australia.

melanoxylon R. Br. mel-uhn-*ox*-i-lon. Blackwood, black wattle. Gk. black wood. SE Australia.

paradoxa DC. pa-ruh-*dox*-uh. Hedge wattle, kangaroo wattle. Lat. unusual. E Australia.

pataczekii D. I. Morris. pat-uh-*chek*-ee-ee. Wally's wattle. After Tasmanian forester Wolfgang (Wally) Pataczek, who collected the type specimen in 1972. Tasmania.

pravissima F. Muell. pra-*vis*-i-muh. Ovens wattle. Lat. very crooked (the phyllodes). SE Australia.

retinodes Schltdl. ret-in-*oh*-deez. Swamp wattle. Gk. resinous (it produces gum). SE Australia.

verticillata (L'Hér.) Willd. vur-ti-si-*lah*-tuh. Prickly Moses. Lat. whorled (the phyllodes). SE Australia.

Acaena Mutis ex L. (Rosaceae). uh-*see*-nuh. From Gk. spine, referring to the spiny fruit. 100 spp., perenn. herbs, subshrubs. S hemisph., Americas.

buchananii Hook.f. bew-*kan*-uhn-ee-ee. After Scottish-born NZ botanist and artist John Buchanan

(1819–1898), who, with James Hector, collected the type specimen. NZ (S.I.).

caesiiglauca (Bitter) Bergm. see-zee-i-*glaw*-kuh. Lat. grey-blue, bluish white (the foliage). NZ (S.I.).

inermis Hook.f. in-*urm*-is. Lat. spineless (the fruit). NZ (S.I.).

magellanica (Lam.) Vahl. ma-juh-*lan*-i-kuh. Of the Magellan reg. Chile, Argentina, Antarctic and Subantarctic Is.

microphylla Hook.f. mik-*rof*-i-luh. Gk. with small leaves (leaflets). NZ (N.I.).

novae-zelandiae Kirk. *noh*-vie-zee-*land*-ee-ie. Of New Zealand. NZ, SE Australia.

saccaticupula Bitter. suh-kat-ee-*kup*-ew-luh. Lat. with a pouch-shaped cupule (receptacle). NZ (S.I.).

Acalypha L. (Euphorbiaceae). a-kuh-*lee*-fuh. From the Gk. name for nettle or a similar plant. 450 spp., herbs, shrubs, trees. Tropics and subtropics.

hispida Burm.f. *his*-pid-uh. Chenille plant, red-hot cat tail. Lat. bristly (the fruit). Papua New Guinea.

wilkesiana Müll. Arg. wilk-see-*ah*-nuh. Beefsteak plant, copperleaf. After American admiral and explorer Charles Wilkes (1798–1877), on whose expedition the type specimen was collected on Fiji ca. 1840. Pacific Is. 'Godseffiana'. god-sef-ee-*ah*-nuh. After Joseph Godseff (1846–1921), plant collector and manager of Sander's orchid nursery.

Acanthopanax sieboldianus = *Eleutherococcus sieboldianus*

Acanthus L. (Acanthaceae). uh-*kan*-thoos. Bear's breeches. From Gk. for thorn and spiny plants. 30 spp., perenn. herbs, subshrubs. Medit., Asia, Africa.

balcanicus Heywood & I. Richardson = *A. hungaricus*

dioscoridis L. dee-os-ko-*ree*-dis. After Gk. physician Pedanius Dioscorides (ca. 40–90), who wrote about another species. E Turkey, SW Asia. var. *perringii* (Siehe) E. Hossain. pe-*ring*-ee-ee. After Wilhelm Perring (1838–1907), technical director of Berlin Botanic Garden.

hirsutus Boiss. hir-*sue*-toos. Lat. hairy. Turkey, Greece (Rhodes).

hungaricus (Borbás) Baenitz. hun-*ga*-ri-koos. Of Hungary. SE Eur.

mollis L. *mol*-is. Lat. soft (i.e., not spiny as other species). SW Eur., NW Africa.

sennii Chiov. *sen*-ee-ee. After Italian botanist Lorenzo Senni (1879–1954), who collected the type specimen in Ethiopia in 1937. E Africa.

spinosissimus Pers. = *A. spinosus* Spinosissimus Group

spinosus L. spin-*oh*-soos. Lat. spiny (the leaves). SE Eur., W Turkey. **Spinosissimus Group**. spin-oh-*sis*-i-moos. Lat. most spiny.

Acca O. Berg (Myrtaceae). *ak*-uh. From a native Peruvian name for *A. macrostema*. 3 spp. shrubs. S Am.

sellowiana (O. Berg) Burrett. sel-oh-wee-*ah*-nuh. Pineapple guava, guavasteen. After German botanist Friedrich Sellow (Sello) (1798–1831), who collected the type specimen in Brazil. Brazil, Uruguay.

Acer L. (Sapindaceae). *ay*-suh. Maples. The Lat. name for the maple, from Lat. sharp (wood was used to make spears). 150 spp., trees, shrubs. Mainly N hemisph.

buergerianum Miq. bur-guh-ree-*ah*-noom. Trident maple. After Heinrich Bürger (1806–1858), German botanist who studied the Japanese flora. China, Japan, Korea.

campestre L. kam-*pes*-tree. Field maple, hedge maple. Lat. growing in fields. Eur., W Asia. **'Postelense'**. pos-tel-*en*-see. Of Postolin (Postel), Poland, where it was found. **'Pulverulentum'**. pul-ve-rue-*len*-toom. Lat. dusty (leaves dotted white).

capillipes Maxim. ka-*pil*-i-peez. Kyushu maple. Lat. hair, foot (the slender flower stalks). Japan.

cappadocicum Gled. kap-uh-*doh*-si-koom. Cappadocian maple. Of Cappadocia (now part of Turkey). W Asia. subsp. *sinicum* (Rehder) Hand.-Mazz. *sin*-i-koom. Lat. of China. China.

carpinifolium Sieb. & Zucc. kar-pin-i-*foh*-lee-oom. Hornbeam maple. Lat. with leaves like *Carpinus*. Japan.

circinatum Pursh. sur-sin-*ah*-toom. Vine maple. Lat. rounded (the leaves). W N Am.

cissifolium (Sieb. & Zucc.) K. Koch. sis-i-*foh*-lee-oom. Ivyleaf maple. Lat. with leaves like *Cissus*. Japan.

×*conspicuum* van Gelderen & Oterdoom. kon-*spik*-ew-oom. Lat. conspicuous (the bark). *A. davidii* × *A. pensylvanicum*. Cult.

crataegifolium Sieb. & Zucc. kruh-tee-gi-*foh*-lee-oom. Hawthorn maple. With leaves like *Crataegus*. Japan.

davidii Franch. da-*vid*-ee-ee. David's maple. After French missionary, botanist and zoologist Armand David (1826–1900), who collected the type specimen in Sichuan in 1869. China.

forrestii Diels. fo-*rest*-ee-ee. Forrest's maple. After Scottish botanist George Forrest (1873–1932), who collected the type specimen in 1906. SW China, NW Myanmar.

×*freemanii* A. E. Murray. free-*man*-ee-ee. Freeman maple. After Oliver Myles Freeman (1891–1969), botanist and plant breeder at the US National Arboretum, who raised it. *A. rubrum* × *A. saccharinum*. E USA.

glabrum Torr. *glab*-room. Rock maple. Lat. glabrous (the leaves). W N Am. subsp. *douglasii* (Hook.) Wesm. dug-*las*-ee-ee. After Scottish botanist David Douglas (1799–1834), who collected it in 1830.

griseum (Franch.) Pax. *griz*-ee-oom. Paperbark maple. Lat. grey (the leaf undersides). China.

grosseri Pax. *groh*-suh-ree. After Wilhelm Carl Heinrich Grosser (1869–1942), German botanist. China.

japonicum Thunb. juh-*pon*-i-koom. Fullmoon maple. Of Japan. Japan. **'Aconitifolium'**. a-kon-ee-ti-*foh*-lee-oom. Lat. with leaves like *Aconitum*. **'Vitifolium'**. vi-ti-*foh*-lee-oom. Lat. with leaves like *Vitis*.

macrophyllum Pursh. mak-*rof*-i-loom. Oregon maple. Gk. large-leaved. W N Am.

maximowiczianum Miq. max-im-oh-vich-ee-*ah*-noom. Nikko maple. After Russian botanist Carl Johann Maximowicz (1827–1891). Japan, China.

micranthum Sieb. & Zucc. mik-*ranth*-oom. Gk. with small flowers. Japan.

miyabei Maxim. my-*ab*-ee-ee. After Japanese botanist Kingo Miyabe (1860–1951), who collected the type specimen. Japan.

mono Maxim. = *A. pictum*

monspessulanum L. mon-spes-ew-*lah*-noom. Montpelier maple. Of Montpelier. S Eur., N Africa, W Asia.

negundo L. ne-*goon*-doh. Ash-leaved maple, box elder. From the Malay name for *Vitex negundo*, for the similar leaves. N Am., Guatemala.

nikoense hort. = *A. maximowiczianum*

palmatum Thunb. pahl-*mah*-toom. Japanese maple. Lat. hand-like (the leaves). Japan, China, Korea. **Dissectum Group**. dis-*sek*-toom. Finely divided (the leaves).

pentaphyllum Diels. pent-uh-*fil*-oom. Gk. with five leaves (leaflets). China.

pictum Thunb. *pik*-toom. Painted maple. Lat. painted (the leaves; it was described from a variegated plant). Japan, China, Korea.

platanoides L. plat-uh-*noy*-deez. Norway maple. Like *Platanus* (the leaves). Eur., Caucasus. **'Drummondii'**. drum-*ond*-ee-ee. After Messrs Drummond, Stirling, Scotland, who first distributed it.

pseudoplatanus L. sue-doh-*plat*-uh-noos. Sycamore, sycamore maple. Gk. false *Platanus*. Eur., W Asia. **'Brilliantissimum'**. bril-yuhn-*tis*-i-moom. Lat. most brilliant. **'Leopoldii'**. lee-oh-*pohld*-ee-ee. After King Leopold I of Belgium (1790–1865).

pseudosieboldianum (Pax) Kom. sue-doh-see-bold-ee-*ah*-noom. False *A. sieboldianum*. China, Korea, E Russia.

rubrum L. *rue*-broom. Red maple. Lat. red (the flowers). E N Am.

rufinerve Sieb. & Zucc. roof-i-*nur*-vee. Honshu maple. Lat. with red hairs on the (leaf) veins. Japan.

saccharinum L. sak-uh-*rie*-noom. Silver maple. Lat. sugary (the sap). E N Am.

saccharum Marshall. *sak*-uh-room. Sugar maple. Lat. sugary (the sap). N Am. subsp. *grandidentatum* (Nutt. ex Torr. & A. Gray) Desmarais. grand-i-den-*tah*-toom. Bigtooth maple. Lat. with large teeth (the leaves). SW USA. subsp. *nigrum* (F. Michx.) Desmarais. *nie*-groom. Black maple. Lat. black (the bark).

sempervirens L. sem-puh-*vie*-ruhnz. Cretan maple. Lat. evergreen. E Medit.

shirasawanum Koidz. shi-raz-uh-*wah*-noom. After Japanese dendrologist Miho Shirasawa (1868–1947). Japan.

sieboldianum Miq. see-bold-ee-*ah*-noom. After Philip Franz von Siebold (1796–1866), who studied the flora and fauna of Japan and collected the type specimen. Japan.

spicatum Lam. spi-*kah*-toom. Mountain maple. Lat. in spikes (the flowers). NE N Am.

tataricum L. tuh-*ta*-ri-koom. Tatarian maple. From the reg. of C and E Asia once called Tartary. SE Eur., W Asia. subsp. *ginnala* (Maxim.) Wesm. jin-*ah*-luh. Amur maple. From the native name in N China. China, Korea, Japan.

tegmentosum Maxim. teg-men-*toh*-soom. Lat. covering (possibly referring to the white bloom that covers the shoots). NE Asia.

triflorum Kom. trie-*flaw*-room. Lat. with three flowers (in each cluster). N China, Korea.

truncatum Bunge. trun-*kah*-toom. Shantung maple. Lat. truncate (the leaf base). N China.

×*zoeschense* Pax. zur-*shen*-see. Of Zöschen (Zoeschen), Germany. *A. campestre* × *A. lobelii*. Cult.

Achillea L. (Asteraceae). uh-*kil*-ee-uh. Yarrow. After Achilles of Gk. myth., who is said to have used it to treat wounds. 85 spp. herbs. Mainly N temp. regs.

ageratifolia (Sibth. & Sm.) Boiss. uh-ge-ruh-ti-*foh*-lee-uh. Greek yarrow. With leaves like *Ageratum*. SE Eur.

ageratum L. uh-*ge*-ruh-toom. Sweet Nancy. Like *Ageratum*. SE Eur.

chrysocoma Friv. krie-soh-*koh*-muh. Gk. golden head of hair (referring to the flowers). SE Eur.

clavennae L. kluh-*ven*-ie. After Nicholas Clavena (d. 1617), apothecary in Bellune, Italy. SE Eur.

clypeoplata Sm. klie-pee-oh-*lah*-tuh. Gk. shield-shaped (the flowerheads). SE Eur.

filipendulina Lam. fil-i-pen-dew-*lee*-nuh. Like *Filipendula*. W and C Asia.

grandifolia Friv. gran-di-*foh*-lee-uh. Lat. large-leaved. SE Eur.

×*kellereri* Sünd. *kel*-uh-ruh-ree. After Johann Kellerer (b. 1859). *A. ageratifolia* × *A. clypeolata*. Cult.

×*kolbiana* Sünd. kohl-bee-*ah*-nuh.
After Max Kolb (1829–1915). *A.*
clavennae × *A. umbellata*. Cult.

×*lewisii* Ingw. lue-*is*-ee-ee. After Mr
Lewis, in whose garden it originated.
Cult.

millefolium L. mil-ee-*foh*-lee-oom.
Common yarrow. Lat. 1000 leaves
(the leaves are finely divided). Eur.,
W Asia.

nobilis L. *noh*-bi-lis. Lat. renowned.
Eur., W Asia. subsp. *neilreichii* (A.
Kerner) Formánek. niel-*riek*-ee-ee.
After Austrian botanist August
Neilreich (1803–1871). SE Eur.

ptarmica L. *tar*-mi-kuh. Sneezewort.
From Gk. for sneeze (it was used as
snuff). Eur.

sibirica Ledeb. si-*bi*-ri-kuh. Of Siberia.
Russia.

tomentosa L. to-men-*toh*-suh. Lat.
tomentose. SW Eur.

Achimenes Pers. (Gesneriaceae). uh-
kim-en-eez. Hot water plant. Possibly
from Gk. for cold-sensitive (they are
tender). 25 spp. herbs. Trop. Am.

grandiflora (Schltdl.) DC. gran-di-
flaw-ruh. Lat. large-flowered. Mex.,
C Am.

longiflora DC. long-gi-*flaw*-ruh. Lat.
long-flowered. Mex., C and S Am.

Achlys DC. (Berberidaceae). *ak*-lis.
Gk. goddess of night and mist (it
grows in shade). 3 spp. herbs. N Am.,
Japan.

triphylla (Sm.) DC. trie-*fil*-uh. Deerfoot, vanilla leaf. Gk. with three
leaves (leaflets). W N Am.

Achnatherum P. Beauv. (Poaceae).
ak-*nath*-uh-room. From Gk. scale

awn, referring to the awned lemma.
50 spp. grasses. N temp. regs.

calamagrostis (L.) P. Beauv. kal-uh-
muh-*grost*-is. Gk. reed grass. C and
S Eur.

hymenoides (Roem. & Schult.) Barkworth. hie-muhn-*oy*-deez. Indian
rice grass. Lat. membrane-like (the
lemma). W Canada, W and C USA,
N W Mex.

Acidanthera bicolor Hochst. = *Glad-*
iolus murielae

Acinos Mill. (Lamiaceae). uh-*see*-nos.
From the Gk. name used by Dioscorides for an aromatic herb. 10 spp.
herbs. Eur., Asia.

alpinus (L.) Moench. al-*pie*-noos.
Alpine calamint. Lat. alpine. Eur.

Aciphylla J. R. & G. Forst. (Apiaceae).
a-si-*fil*-uh. Gk. sharp-pointed leaf.
40 spp. herbs. Australia, NZ.

aurea W. R. B. Oliv. *aw*-ree-uh.
Golden Spaniard. Lat. golden (the
foliage). NZ (S.I.).

Acis Salisb. (Amaryllidaceae). *a*-kis.
Gk. myth., after the spirit of the
River Acis in Sicily. 9 spp. bulbous
herbs. Medit.

autumnalis (L.) Herb. aw-toom-*nah*-
lis. Autumn snowflake. Lat. of
autumn (flowering).

Acmella Rich. (Asteraceae). ak-*mel*-
uh. From the Sinhalese name for *A.*
oleracea. 30 spp. herbs. Warm and
trop. Am.

oleracea (L.) R. K. Jansen. ol-uh-*ray*-
see-uh. Para-cress. Lat. vegetable-
like. S Am.

aconite *Aconitum*. **winter** *Eranthis hyemalis*

Aconitum L. (Ranunculaceae). a-kon-*ee*-toom. Aconite, monkshood. Gk. name for one species, used by Theophrastus and Dioscorides. 100 spp. herbs. Temp. N hemisph.

×*cammarum* L. ka-*mar*-room. From Lat. for lobster or crayfish (from the tail-like shape of the upper part of the flower). *A. napellus* × *A. variegatum*. Eur. **'Bicolor'**. *bi*-ko-lor. Two-coloured (the flowers).

carmichaelii Debeaux. kar-mie-*kel*-ee-ee. After J. R. Carmichael (1838–1870), English physician, plant collector and missionary in China. China, N Vietnam.

columbianum Nutt. ko-lum-bee-*ah*-noom. Of the Columbia River. W N Am.

fischeri Rchb. *fish*-uh-ree. After Friedrich Ernst Ludwig Fischer (1782–1854), German-born Russian botanist. N China, Korea, E Russia.

hemsleyanum E. Pritz. hemz-lee-*ah*-noom. After English botanist William Botting Hemsley (1843–1924), who worked on Chinese plants at Kew. China, N Myanmar.

japonicum Thunb. juh-*pon*-i-koom. Of Japan. Japan.

lycoctonum L. lie-kok-*toh*-noom. Wolfsbane. From the Gk. name, from Gk. wolf. Eur., N Africa. subsp. *neapolitanum* (Ten.) Nyman. nee-uh-pol-i-*tah*-num. Lat. of Naples (Lat. *Neapolis*).

napellus L. nuh-*pel*-oos. Lat. a small turnip, referring to the root. Eur., Asia. subsp. *vulgare* (DC.) Rouy & Foucaud. vul-*gar*-ree. Lat. common. Pyrenees, Alps.

Acorus L. (Acoraceae). *a*-ko-roos. Lat. name (from Gk.) for *Iris pseudacorus*. 3 spp. herbs. N hemisph.

americanus (Raf.) Raf. = *A. calamus* var. *americanus*

calamus L. *ka*-luh-moos. Sweet flag. Gk. name for a reed, from Kalamos of Gk. myth., who drowned in the Meander River and turned into a reed. Asia. var. *americanus* Raf. uh-me-ri-*kah*-noos. Of America. N Am.

gramineus Sol. gra-*min*-ee-oos. Lat. grass-like (the foliage). E Asia.

Acradenia Kippist (Rutaceae). ak-ruh-*deen*-ee-uh. Gk. at the tip, gland, referring to glands at the tips of the carpels. 2 spp. shrubs. Australia.

frankliniae Kippist. frank-*lin*-ee-ie. After Jane Griffin, Lady Franklin (1791–1875), wife of Sir John Franklin, governor of Tasmania. W Tasmania.

Acroclinium roseum Hook. = *Rhodanthe chlorocephala* subsp. *rosea*

Actaea L. (Ranunculaceae). ak-*tee*-uh. Gk./Lat. name for elder (*Sambucus*), from the similar leaves. 27 spp. perenn. herbs. Temp. N hemisph.

cimicifuga L. sim-i-si-*few*-guh. Bugbane. Lat. repelling bugs (from its use as an insect repellent). E Asia.

cordifolia DC. kord-i-*foh*-lee-uh. Lat. heart-shaped (the leaflets). SE USA.

dahurica (Turcz. ex Fisch. & C. A. Mey.) Franch. dah-*hew*-ri-kuh. Of Dahuria, Siberia. NE Asia.

japonica Thunb. juh-*pon*-i-kuh. Of
Japan. China, Korea, Japan.
pachypoda Elliott. pak-ee-*poh*-duh.
White baneberry. Gk. thick-stalked
(the fruit). N Am.
racemosa (L.) Nutt. ras-i-*moh*-suh.
Black snakeroot. Lat. in racemes (the
flowers). N Am.
rubra (Aiton) Willd. *rue*-bruh. Red
baneberry. Lat. red (the fruit). N
hemisph.
simplex (DC.) Wormsk. ex Prantl.
sim-plex. Lat. unbranched (the inflorescence). E Asia.

Actinidia Lindl. (Actinidiaceae).
ak-tin-*id*-ee-uh. From Gk. ray (the
styles). 55 spp. woody climbers.
E Asia.
arguta (Sieb. & Zucc.) Planch. ex Miq.
ar-*gew*-tuh. With sharp teeth (the
leaves). China, Korea, Japan.
deliciosa C. S. Liang & A. R. Ferguson.
de-lis-ee-*oh*-suh. Chinese gooseberry,
kiwi fruit. Lat. delicious (the fruit).
China.
kolomikta (Maxim. & Rupr.) Maxim.
ko-loh-*mik*-tuh. From the native
name. China, Korea, E Russia, Japan.
pilosula (Finet. & Gagnep.) Stapf ex
Hand.-Mazz. pi-*lohz*-ew-luh. Lat. a
little hairy (the leaves). China.
polygama (Sieb. & Zucc.) Maxim.
po-*lig*-uh-muh. Silver vine. Lat.
polygamous (i.e., having flowers of
different sexes on the same plant).
Japan.

Adenophora Fisch. (Campanulaceae).
ad-en-*of*-o-ruh. Gk. gland-bearing,
referring to the tubular nectary. 40
spp. herbs. Eur., Asia.
bulleyana Diels. boo-lee-*ah*-nuh.

After Arthur Kiplin Bulley (1861–
1942), Liverpool cotton merchant
and founder of Bees Nursery, who
sponsored plant collecting expedi-
tions. China.
liliifolia (L.) Ledeb. ex A. DC. lil-ee-i-
foh-lee-uh. With leaves like *Lilium*.
potaninii Korsh. po-tan-*in*-ee-ee.
After Russian explorer Grigory
Nikolayaevich Potanin (1835–1920).
China.

Adiantum L. (Adiantaceae). ad-ee-*an*-
toom. Maidenhair fern. From Gk.
unwettable (the fronds repel water).
200 spp. ferns. Worldwide.
aleuticum (Rupr.) Paris. uh-*lue*-ti-
koom. Of the Aleutian Is. N Am., N
Mex. 'Imbricatum'. Lat. overlapping
(the pinnae).
capillus-veneris L. ka-*pil*-oos-*ven*-e-
ris. Lat. hair of Venus (referring to
the fine foliage).
hispidulum Sw. his-*pid*-ew-loom.
Roughly hairy (the rachis). S Asia,
E Africa, Pacific Is.
pedatum L. ped-*ah*-toom. Lat. resembling a bird's foot (the fronds).
E N Am.
raddianum C. Presl. rad-ee-*ah*-num.
After Italian botanist Giuseppe
Raddi (1770–1829), who collected
the type specimen in Brazil. Trop.
Am.
tenerum Sw. *ten*-e-room. Brittle
maidenhair fern. Lat. delicate (the
foliage). Florida to S Am.
venustum D. Don. ven-*oos*-toom.
Evergreen maidenhair fern. Lat.
handsome. Himal., W China.

Adonis L. (Ranunculaceae). uh-*doh*-
nis. After Adonis of Gk. myth., who

is said to have been turned into one of these when he died. 20 spp. herbs. Eur., Asia.

aestivalis L. ees-ti-*vah*-lis. Lat. of summer (flowering). Eur.

amurensis Regel & Radde. am-ew-*ren*-sis. Of the Amur River. NE China, E Russia, Korea, Japan.

annua L. *an*-ew-uh. Pheasant's eye. Lat. annual. S Eur., W Asia.

vernalis L. vur-*nah*-lis. Lat. of spring (flowering). Eur.

Adromischus Lem. (Crassulaceae). ad-roh-*mis*-koos. From Gk. stout, stalk, referring to the flower stalks. 29 spp. succulents. S Africa.

cooperi (Baker) A. Berger. *kue*-puh-ree. Plover eggs. After British plant collector Thomas Cooper (1815–1913), who introduced many species from S Africa.

cristatus (Haw.) Lem. kris-*tah*-toos. Lat. crested (the foliage).

maculatus (Salm-Dyck) Lem. mak-ew-*lah*-toos. Lat. spotted (the leaves).

Aechmea Ruiz & Pav. (Bromeliaceae). eek-*mee*-uh. From Gk. pointed, referring to the sharp-pointed sepals and bracts. 180 spp. herbs. Trop. Am.

fasciata (Lindl.) Baker. fas-ee-*ah*-tuh. Lat. striped (the leaves). Brazil.

fulgens Brongn. *fool*-genz. Lat. shining (the bracts). Brazil.

miniata (Beer) Baker. min-ee-*ah*-tuh. Lat. coloured with red (the bracts). Brazil.

Aegopodium L. (Apiaceae). ee-goh-*poh*-dee-oom. From Gk. a goat's foot, referring to the leaf shape. 7 spp. herbs. Eur., Asia.

podagraria L. pod-uh-*grair*-ree-uh. Goutweed, ground elder. Gk. foot pain (it was considered a remedy for gout). Eur.

Aeonium (L.) Webb & Berth. (Crassulaceae). ie-*oh*-nee-oom. From Gk. eternal (they appear to live for ever). 35 spp. succulents. Canary Is., Madeira, N Africa.

arboreum (L.) Webb & Berth. ar-*bor*-ree-oom. Lat. tree-like. Canary Is.

balsamiferum Webb & Berth. bal-suhm-*i*-fe-room. Lat. bearing balsam (it is balsam-scented). Canary Is.

haworthii Salm-Dyck ex Webb & Berth. ha-*wurth*-ee-ee. After English botanist and entomologist Adrian Hardy Haworth (1767–1833). Canary Is.

tabuliforme (Haw.) Webb & Berth. tab-ew-li-*form*-ee. Lat. table-shaped (the flat-topped rosettes). Canary Is.

undulatum Webb & Berth. un-dew-*lah*-toom. Lat. wavy (the leaves). Canary Is.

Aesculus L. (Sapindaceae). *ees*-kew-loos. Buckeyes, horse chestnuts. Lat. name for an oak (*Quercus*) with edible acorns. 12 spp., trees, shrubs. N Am., SE Eur., E Asia.

californica (Spach) Nutt. kal-i-*for*-ni-kuh. California buckeye. Of California. Calif.

×***carnea*** Hayne. *kar*-nee-uh. Red horse chestnut. Lat. flesh-pink (the flowers). *A. hippocastanum* × *A. pavia*. Cult.

flava Sol. *flah*-vuh. Yellow buckeye. Lat. yellow (the flowers). SE USA.

glabra Willd. *glab*-ruh. Ohio buckeye. Lat. glabrous (the leaves). E USA.

hippocastanum L. hip-oh-kas-*tah*-num. Horse chestnut. Gk. horse chestnut. Balkans. **'Baumannii'**. bow-*man*-ee-ee. After A. N. Baumann, who found the original sport in 1820 in a garden near Geneva.
indica (Wall. ex Cambess.) Hook. *in*-di-kuh. Indian horse chestnut. Lat. of India. Himal.
×*mutabilis* (Spach) Schelle. mew-*tab*-i-lis. Lat. changing (the flower colour). *A. pavia* × *A. sylvatica*. Cult.
×*neglecta* Lindl. neg-*lek*-tuh. Lat. neglected, overlooked. *A. flava* × *A. sylvatica*. SE USA. **'Erythroblastos'**. e-rith-roh-*blast*-os. Gk. red, bud or sprout (young growth is pink).
octandra Marshall = *A. flava*
pavia L. *pah*-vee-uh. Red buckeye. After Dutch surgeon and botanist Peter Paaw (Lat. *Pavius*) (1564–1617). SE USA. **'Atrosanguinea'**. at-roh-san-*gwin*-ee-uh. Lat. dark red (the flowers).

Aethionema R. Br. (Brassicaceae). ee-thee-oh-*nee*-muh. Gk. unusual, thread, referring to the appearance of the filaments. 40 spp., herbs, subshrubs. Eur., SW Asia.
grandiflorum Boiss. & Hohen. grandi-*flaw*-room. Lat. large-flowered. Caucasus, SW Asia.

African violet *Saintpaulia ionantha*

Agapanthus L'Hér. (Amaryllidaceae). a-guh-*panth*-oos. Gk. love flower. 10 spp. herbs. S Africa.
africanus (L.) Hoffmanns. af-ri-*kah*-noos. African.
campanulatus F. M. Leight. kam-pan-ew-*lah*-toos. Lat. bell-shaped (the flowers). subsp. *patens* (F. M. Leight.) F. M. Leight. *pay*-tuhnz. Lat. spreading widely (the perianth lobes).
caulescens Spreng. kawl-*es*-uhnz. Lat. developing a stem.
inapertus Beauverd. in-uh-*purt*-oos. Lat. not open (the flowers are narrow-mouthed). subsp. *pendulus* (L. Bolus) F. M. Leight. *pen*-dew-loos. Lat. pendulous (the flowers).
praecox Willd. prie-kox. Lat. early (the flowers). subsp. *minimus* (Lindl.) F M. Leight. *min*-i-moos. Lat. smallest. subsp. *orientalis* (F. M. Leight.) F. M. Leight. o-ree-en-*tah*-lis. Lat. eastern.

Agarista D. Don ex G. Don (Ericaceae). ag-uh-*rist*-uh. After Agarista of Gk. myth., the beautiful daughter of Cleisthenes, referring to the attractive flowers. 31 spp., trees, shrubs. SE USA to S Am., Africa.
populifolia (Lam.) Judd. pop-ew-li-*foh*-lee-uh. Florida hobblebush. Lat. with leaves like *Populus*. SE USA.

Agastache Clayton ex Gronov. (Lamiaceae). uh-*ga*-stuh-kee. From Gk. admirable spikes, referring to the flowers. 20 spp. herbs. N Am., E Asia.
aurantiaca (A. Gray) Lint & Epling. aw-rant-ee-*ah*-kuh. Lat. orange (the flowers). Mex.
cana (Hook.) Wooton & Standl. *kah*-nuh. Mosquito plant. Lat. grey (the foliage). S USA.
foeniculum (Pursh) Kuntze. fee-*nik*-ew-loom. Giant blue hyssop. Like *Foeniculum*, fennel (the scent). N Am.
mexicana (Kunth) Lint & Epling. mex-i-*kah*-nuh. Of Mexico. Mex.

nepetoides (L.) Kuntze. ne-pe-*toy*-deez. Yellow giant hyssop. Like *Nepeta*. E N Am.

pallidiflora (A. Heller) Rydb. pa-li-di-*flaw*-ruh. Lat. with pale flowers. SW USA.

rugosa (Fisch. & C. A. Mey.) Kuntze. rue-*goh*-suh. Lat. rugose (the leaves). E Asia.

rupestris (Greene) Standl. rue-*pes*-tris. Lat. growing on rocks. SW USA, N Mex.

scrophulariifolia (Willd.) Kuntze. skrof-ew-lah-ree-i-*foh*-lee-uh. Purple giant hyssop. Lat. with leaves like *Scrophularia*. E N Am.

urticifolia (Benth.) Kuntze. ur-ti-ki-*foh*-lee-uh. Nettleleaf giant hyssop. Lat. with leaves like *Urtica*. W N Am.

Agathis Salisb. (Araucariaceae). *ag*-uh-this. Gk. a ball of thread, referring to the female cones. 21 spp. coniferous trees. Malaysia to NZ.

australis Lindl. os-*trah*-lis. Kauri pine. Lat. southern. NZ (N.I.).

Agave L. (Asparagaceae). uh-*gah*-vee. Gk. noble, referring to the tall inflorescence. 220 spp. succulents. S USA to N S Am.

americana L. uh-me-ri-*kah*-nuh. Century plant. Of America. S USA, Mex.

attenuata Salm-Dyck. uh-ten-ew-*ah*-tuh. Lat. long-tapered (the inflorescence). Mex.

chrysantha Peebles. kris-*anth*-uh. Gk. golden-flowered. Arizona.

deserti Engelm. dez-*urt*-ee. Lat. of the desert. Calif., Mex. (B.C.).

filifera Salm-Dyck. fi-*li*-fuh-ruh. Lat. thread-bearing (the leaf margins). Mex.

geminiflora (Tagl.) Ker Gawl. jem-in-i-*flaw*-ruh. Lat. twin-flowered. Mex.

lechuguilla Torr. le-chue-*gee*-yuh. The native name. New Mexico, Mex.

lophantha Schiede ex Kunth = *A. univittata*

montana Villareal. mon-*tah*-nuh. Lat. of mountains. Mex.

neomexicana Wooton & Standl. = *A. parryi* subsp. *neomexicana*

palmeri Engelm. *pahl*-muh-ree. After Edward Palmer (1829–1911), English-born botanist and archaeologist who lived in the USA and in 1869 collected one of the specimens from which it was described. Arizona, N Mex.

parryi Engelm. *pa*-ree-ee. After Charles Christopher Parry (1823–1890), English-born botanist who collected plants in SW USA. SW USA, Mex. subsp. *neomexicana* (Wooton & Standl.) B. Ullrich. nee-oh-mex-i-*kah*-nuh. Of New Mexico.

potatorum Zucc. pot-uh-*tor*-rum. Lat. of the drinkers (it is used to make alcoholic drinks, including mezcal). Mex.

salmiana Otto ex Salm-Dyck. sal-mee-*ah*-nuh. After German botanist and artist Joseph Salm-Reifferscheid-Dyck (1773–1861). Mex. var. *ferox* (K. Koch) Gentry. *fe*-rox. Lat. spiny.

stricta Salm-Dyck. *strik*-tuh. Lat. upright (the leaves). NE Mex.

tequilana F. A. C. Weber. te-kee-*lah*-nuh. Of Tequila, Jalisco. The only species from which tequila can be made. Mex.

univittata Haw. ew-nee-vi-*tah*-tuh. Lat. with one stripe (the leaves). Texas, N and C Mex.

utahensis Engelm. ew-tah-*en*-sis. Of Utah. SW USA.

victoriae-reginae T. Moore. vik-*tor*-ree-ie-re-*jeen*-ie. After Queen Victoria (1819–1901). NE Mex.

virginica L. = *Manfreda virginica*

Ageratina Spach (Asteraceae). uh-ge-ruh-*tee*-nuh. Diminutive of *Ageratum*. 250 spp., herbs, shrubs. Americas.

altissima (L.) R. M. King & H. Rob. al-*tiss*-i-muh. White snakeroot. Lat. tallest. E N Am.

ligustrina (DC.) R. M. King & H. Rob. lig-oos-*tree*-nuh. Like *Ligustrum*. Mex., C Am.

Ageratum L. (Asteraceae). uh-*ge*-ruh-toom. From Gk. not ageing, referring to the everlasting flowers. 40 spp. herbs. Americas.

corymbosum Zuccagni. ko-rim-*boh*-soom. Flat-top whiteweed. Lat. corymbose (the inflorescence). SW USA, Mex.

houstonianum Mill. hew-stone-ee-*ah*-noom. After William Houston (1695–1733), Scottish surgeon and botanist who collected the type specimen and sent seeds to England. Mex., C Am.

Aglaonema Schott (Araceae). uh-glay-oh-*nee*-ma. From Gk. bright thread, referring to the stamens. 21 spp. herbs. Trop. Asia.

commutatum Schott. kom-ew-*tah*-toom. Lat. changing. Malesia.

modestum Schott. ex Engl. mo-*dest*-oom. Lat. modest (it is not variegated). SE Asia.

nitidum (Jacq.) Kunth. *ni*-ti-doom. Lat. glossy (the leaves). Indo-China, Malesia.

pictum (Roxb.) Kunth. *pik*-toom. Lat. painted (the leaves). Sumatra.

Agrostemma L. (Caryophyllaceae). ag-roh-*stem*-uh. From Gk. field garland (it decorates the fields, or used to). 2 spp. ann. herbs. Medit.

githago L. gi-*thah*-goh. Corn cockle. Lat. name used by Pliny for a species of *Nigella*.

Aichryson Webb & Berth. (Crassulaceae). ie-*kris*-on. From Gk. always gold, referring to the flower colour. 15 spp. succulents. Canary Is., N Africa.

×*aizoides* (Lam.) E. C. Nelson. ie-*zoid*-eez. Like *Aizoon*. *A. punctatum* × *A. tortuosum*. Cult.

×*domesticum* Praeger = *A.* ×*aizoides*

tortuosum (Aiton) Praeger. tort-ew-*oh*-soom. Lat. tortuous (the stems). Canary Is.

Ailanthus Desf. (Simaroubaceae). ie-*lanth*-oos. Tree of heaven, from the Malay name for one species. 10 spp. trees. E Asia to Australia.

altissima (Mill.) Swingle. al-*tis*-i-muh. Tree of heaven. Lat. tallest. China.

air plant *Kalanchoe pinnata*

Ajania Poljakov (Asteraceae). uh-*jah*-nee-uh. Of Ajan, E Russia. 34 spp., herbs, shrubs. Asia.

pacifica (Nakai) K. Bremmer &
Humphries. puh-*si*-fi-kuh. Of the
Pacific. Japan (coast).

Ajuga L. (Lamiaceae). uh-*jue*-guh.
Bugle. Lat. name used by Pliny for a
related plant. 50 spp. herbs. Eur.,
Asia.
pyramidalis L. pi-ram-i-*dah*-lis. Pyramidal bugle. Lat. pyramidal (the
inflorescence). Eur.
reptans L. *rep*-tanz. Common bugle.
Lat. creeping. Eur., W Asia.

Akebia Decne. (Lardizabalaceae).
uh-*kee*-bee-uh. From Akebi, the Japanese name for *A. quinata*. 5 spp.
woody climbers. E Asia.
quinata (Houtt.) Decne. kwin-*ah*-
tuh. Lat. in fives (the leaflets). China,
Japan, Korea.
trifoliata (Thunb.) Koidz. trie-foh-lee-
ah-tuh. Lat. with three leaves (leaflets). China, Taiwan, Japan.

Albizia Durazz. (Fabaceae). al-*biz*-ee-
uh. After Florentine nobleman
Filippo del Albizzi, who introduced
A. julibrissin to Eur. in 1749. 130
spp., trees, shrubs. Tropics and subtropics.
julibrissin Durazz. jue-lee-*bris*-in. Silk
tree, pink siris. From the Persian
name. SW Asia to China.

Alcea L. (Malvaceae). al-*see*-uh. From
the Gk. name used by Dioscorides
for a type of mallow. 60 spp., herbs,
shrubs. SE Eur. to China.
ficifolia L. feek-i-*foh*-lee-uh. Lat. with
leaves like *Ficus*. C Asia.
pallida (Willd.) Waldst. & Kit. *pa*-li-

duh. Lat. pale (the flowers). SE Eur.,
Turkey.
rosea L. *roh*-zee-uh. Hollyhock. Lat.
pink (the flowers). Cult.
rugosa Alef. rue-*goh*-suh. Lat. rough
(the leaves). SE Eur., Caucasus.

Alchemilla L. (Rosaceae). al-kem-
il-uh. Lady's mantle. From Arabic for
alchemy (the way the leaves repel
water was considered magical). 300
spp. herbs. Eur., Asia, Africa,
Americas.
alpina L. al-*pie*-nuh. Alpine lady's
mantle. Lat. alpine. Eur.
conjuncta Bab. kon-*joonk*-tuh. Lat.
joined (the leaf lobes).
ellenbeckii Engl. el-uhn-*bek*-ee-ee.
After German physician Hans
Ellenbeck, who collected the type
specimen in Ethiopia in 1900. NE
Africa.
erythropoda Juz. e-rith-roh-*poh*-duh.
Gk. red-stalked (the leaves). SE Eur.,
Caucasus.
mollis (Buser) Rothm. *mol*-is. Lat. soft
(the leaves). E Eur., Caucasus.
xanthochlora Rothm. zanth-oh-*klor*-
ruh. Gk. yellow-green (the flowers).
Eur.

alder *Alnus*. **European** *A. glutinosa*.
grey *A. incana*. **green** *A. viridis*.
hazel *A. serrulata*. **Italian** *A. cor-*
data. **Japanese** *A. japonica*. **red** *A.*
rubra. **Sitka** *A. viridis* subsp. *sinuata*.
thinleaf *A. incana* subsp. *tenuifolia*.
white *A. rhombifolia*
alecost *Tanacetum balsamita*
Alexanders *Smyrnium olusatrum*

Alisma L. (Alismataceae). uh-*liz*-muh.
Water plantain. Gk. name for a water

plant. 8 spp. aquatic herbs. Worldwide.
plantago-aquatica L. plan-*tay*-goh-
uh-*kwat*-i-kuh. Water plantain. Lat.
water plantain. var. **americanum**
Schult. & Schult.f. = *A. subcordatum*
subcordatum Raf. sub-kor-*dah*-toom.
Lat. slightly heart-shaped (the leaves).
N Am.
triviale Pursh. tri-vee-*ah*-lee. Lat.
ordinary, common. N Am.

Allamanda L. (Apocynaceae). al-uh-
man-duh. After Swiss naturalist
Frederick-Louis Allamand (1736–
1803), who studied the Brazilian
flora and sent seeds to Linnaeus. 14
spp., shrubs, climbers. Trop. Am.
cathartica L. kuh-*thar*-ti-kuh. Golden
trumpet. Lat. purging. S Am.

Allium L. (Amaryllidaceae). *al*-ee-
oom. Lat. garlic. 750 spp. bulbous
herbs. N hemisph.
aflatunense B. Fedtsch. af-luh-tun-*en*-
see. Of Aflatun, Kyrgyzstan. C Asia.
See *A. hollandicum*.
ampeloprasum L. am-pel-oh-*prah*-
soom. Wild leek. Gk. vine, leek (it is
often found in vineyards). S Eur., N
Africa, W Asia. **Porrum Group**.
po-room. Garden leek. The Lat.
name.
atropurpureum Waldst. & Kit.
at-roh-pur-*pew*-ree-oom. Lat. dark
purple (the flowers). S Eur.
beesianum W. W. Sm. beez-ee-*ah*-
noom. After Bees Nursery, Cheshire,
which introduced it to cultivation.
W China.
bulgaricum (Janka) Prodán = *A.
siculum* subsp. *dioscoridis*

caeruleum Pall. kie-*rue*-lee-oom. Lat.
blue (the flowers). C Asia.
canadense L. kan-uh-*den*-see. Of
Canada. N Am.
carinatum L. ka-ri-*nah*-toom. Keeled
garlic. Lat. keeled. Eur. subsp. *pulchellum* (G. Don) Bonnier &
Layens. pool-*kel*-oom. Lat. beautiful.
cepa L. *see*-puh. Onion. Lat. onion.
Cult. **Aggregatum Group**. ag-ree-
gah-toom. Shallot. Lat. clustered (the
bulbs).
cernuum Roth. *surn*-ew-oom. Lat.
nodding (the flowers). N Am.
cristophii Trautv. kris-*tof*-ee-ee. After
the physician Cristoph, who collected the type specimen in 1883.
C Asia.
cyaneum Regel. sie-*an*-ee-oom. Lat.
blue (the flowers). China.
cyathophorum Bureau & Franch.
sie-uh-*thof*-uh-room. Gk. bearing
cups (the flowers). China. var. *farreri*
(Stearn) Stearn. *fa*-ruh-ree. After
English plant collector and author
Reginald John Farrer (1880–1920).
It was described from plants grown
at Cambridge Botanic Garden that
he introduced from China in 1914.
fistulosum L. fis-tew-*loh*-sum. Welsh
onion. Lat. hollow (the scape). Cult.
flavum L. *flah*-voom. Lat. yellow (the
flowers). Eur., W Asia.
giganteum Regel. jie-*gan*-tee-oom.
Lat. very large. C Asia.
hollandicum R. M. Fritsch. ho-*land*-i-
koom. Of Holland, where it was
widely grown as *A. aflatunense*. Iran.
karataviense Regel. ka-ruh-tah-vee-
en-see. Of Karatau, Kazakhstan.
C Asia.
lusitanicum Lam. lue-si-*tan*-i-koom.
Lat. of Portugal. Eur.

moly L. *mol*-ee. Gk. a plant mentioned by Homer in the Odyssey. S Eur.

neapolitanum Cirillo. nee-uh-pol-i-*tah*-noom. Naples garlic. Lat. of Naples (Lat. *Neapolis*). S Eur., N Africa, W Asia.

nigrum L. *nie*-groom. Lat. black (the ovary in the centre of the flower). Eur., N Africa, W Asia.

oreophilum C. A. Mey. o-ree-oh-*fil*-oom. Gk. mountain-loving. C Asia.

porrum L. = *A. ampeloprasum* Porrum Group

×*proliferum* (Moench) Schrad. ex Willd. proh-*lif*-uh-room. Tree onion. Lat. bearing offspring (the bulbils in the flowerhead). *A. cepa* × *A. fistulosum*. Cult.

rosenbachianum Regel. roh-zuhn-bahk-ee-*ah*-noom. After Nikolai Ottonowitsch Rosenbach (1836–1901), governor-general of Turkestan 1884–89. C Asia.

roseum L. *roh*-zee-um. Lat. pink (the flowers). S Eur., N Africa, SW Asia.

sativum L. sa-*tee*-voom. Garlic. Lat. cultivated. Cult.

schoenoprasum L. skeen-oh-*prah*-soom. Chives. Gk. rush leek. N hemisph.

schubertii Zucc. shue-*burt*-ee-ee. Tumbleweed onion. After German physician and plant collector Gotthilf Heinrich von Schubert (1780–1860). SW Asia, Libya.

senescens L. sen-*e*-suhnz. Lat. becoming white or dying off. N Asia. subsp. *glaucum* (Regel) Dostál. *glaw*-koom. Lat. bluish white (the foliage). subsp. *montanum* (Schrank) Holub. = *A. lusitanicum*

siculum Ucria. *sik*-ew-loom. Lat. of Sicily. France, Italy. subsp. *dioscori-dis* (Sm.) K. Richt. dee-os-ko-*ree*-dis. After Gk. physician Pedanius Dioscorides (ca. 40–90). Romania, Bulgaria, NW Turkey.

sikkimense Baker. si-kim-*en*-see. Of Sikkim. Himal., W China.

sphaerocephalon L. sfair-roh-*kef*-uh-lon. Round-headed garlic. Gk. with a spherical head. Eur., N Africa, W Asia.

thunbergii G. Don. thun-*berg*-ee-ee. After Swedish botanist and physician Carl Peter Thunberg (1743–1828), who collected in Japan and S Africa. E Asia.

triquetrum L. trie-*kweet*-room. Three-cornered leek. Lat. three-angled (the scapes). S Eur.

tuberosum Rottler ex Spreng. tew-buh-*roh*-soom. Chinese chives. Lat. bearing tubers. SE Asia.

unifolium Kellogg. ew-ni-*foh*-lee-oom. Lat. with one leaf. W USA.

ursinum L. ur-*see*-noom. Lat. of bears (which eat it). Eur., W Asia.

allspice, California *Calycanthus occidentalis*. **Carolina** *C. floridus*

almond *Prunus dulcis*. **dwarf Russian** *P. tenella*

Alnus Mill. (Betulaceae). *al*-noos. Alders. Lat. for the alder. 35 spp., trees, shrubs. N hemisph., N Andes.

cordata (Loisel.) Duby. kor-*dah*-tuh. Italian alder. Lat. heart-shaped (the leaves). S Italy, Corsica.

glutinosa (L.) Gaertn. glue-ti-*noh*-suh. European alder. Lat. sticky (the young shoots and leaves). Eur., W Asia.

incana (L.) Moench. in-*kah*-nuh. Grey alder. Lat. grey (the leaf undersides).

Eur., W Asia. subsp. *tenuifolia*
(Nutt.) Breitung. ten-ew-i-*foh*-lee-uh.
Thinleaf alder. Lat. with slender
leaves. W N Am.
japonica (Thunb.) Steud. juh-*pon*-i-
kuh. Japanese alder. Of Japan.
NE Asia.
rhombifolia Nutt. rom-bi-*foh*-lee-uh.
White alder. Lat. with rhombic
(diamond-shaped) leaves. W USA.
rubra Bong. *rue*-bruh. Red alder. Lat.
red (the wood). W N Am.
serrulata (Aiton) Willd. se-rue-*lah*-
tuh. Hazel alder. Lat. finely toothed
(the leaves). E N Am.
sinuata (Regel) Rydb. = *A. viridis*
subsp. *sinuata*
tenuifolia Nutt. = *A. incana* subsp.
tenuifolia
viridis (Chaix) DC. *vi*-ri-dis. Green
alder. Lat. green. Eur. subsp. *sinuata*
(Regel) Á. Löve & D. Löve. sin-ew-
ah-tuh. Sitka alder. Lat. wavy (the
leaves). W N Am., E Asia.

Alocasia (Schott) G. Don (Araceae).
al-oh-*kay*-see-uh. Gk. not, *Colocasia*
(a related genus). 65 spp. herbs.
China, SE Asia to Australia.
'**Amazonica**'. am-uh-*zon*-i-kuh. Of the
Amazon Nursery, Florida. *A. longil-
oba* × *A. sanderiana*.
macrorrhizos (L.) G. Don. mak-roh-
ree-zos. Gk. with large roots. China,
SE Asia.

Aloe L. (Xanthorrhoeaceae). *a*-loh-ee.
From Arabic *alloeh* (bitter) from the
substance found in the leaves. 400
spp. succulents. Mainly Africa.
arborescens Mill. ar-bor-*res*-enz. Lat.
becoming tree-like. S Africa.

aristata Haw. a-ris-*tah*-tuh. Lat. with
a bristle tip (the leaves). S Africa.
brevifolia Mill. brev-i-*foh*-lee-uh. Lat.
short-leaved. S Africa.
ferox Mill. *fe*-rox. Lat. spiny. S Africa.
hemmingii Reynolds & Bally.
he-*ming*-ee-ee. After Christopher
Francis Hemming, English ecologist
in E Africa. N Somalia.
humilis (L.) Mill. *hew*-mi-lis. Lat. low
(growing). S Africa.
juvenna P. Brandham & S. Carter. jue-
ven-uh. From a misreading of a label
on a cultivated plant, which stated
that it was "possibly a juvenile form."
Kenya.
striatula Haw. stree-*at*-ew-luh. Lat.
with fine stripes (the leaf bases). S
Africa.
variegata L. va-ree-uh-*gah*-tuh. Lat.
variegated (the leaves). Southern
Africa.
vera (L.) Burm.f. *veer*-ruh. Lat. true.
SW Arabia.

Aloysia Juss. (Verbenaceae). a-loh-*is*-
ee-uh. After Maria Luisa of Parma
(1751–1819), wife of King Charles
IV of Spain. 37 spp. shrubs. S USA to
S Am.
citrodora Palau. sit-roh-*dor*-ruh.
Lemon verbena. Lat. lemon-scented.
Chile, Argentina.
triphylla (L'Hér.) Britt. = *A. citrodora*

Alpinia Roxb. (Zingiberaceae).
al-*pin*-ee-uh. Ginger lily. After Italian physician and botanist Prospero
Alpini (1553–1617). 200 spp. herbs.
Trop. Asia.
japonica (Thunb.) Miq. juh-*pon*-i-kuh.
Of Japan. S China, Taiwan, Japan.

purpurata (Vieill.) K. Schum. pur-pew-*rah*-tuh. Lat. dressed in purple (the inflorescence). Pacific Is.
zerumbet (Pers.) B. L. Burtt & R. M. Sm. ze-*room*-bet. Shell ginger. From the name of an Indian spice. SE Asia.

Alstroemeria L. (Alstroemeriaceae). ahl-strurm-*e*-ree-uh. After Swedish baron Clas (Claus) Alströmer (1736–1794), who sent seed from plants grown in Spain to his friend Linnaeus. 125 spp. perenn. herbs. S Am.
aurea Graham. *aw*-ree-uh. Lat. golden (the flowers). Chile, Argentina.
brasiliensis Spreng. bra-zil-ee-*en*-sis. Of Brazil. Brazil.
hookeri Sweet. *hook*-uh-ree. After Sir William Jackson Hooker (1785–1865), English botanist and first director of RBG Kew, who illustrated it as *A. rosea*. Chile.
ligtu L. *lig*-tue. From *liutu*, the native name in Chile. S Am.
psittacina Lehm. = *A. pulchella*
pulchella L.f. pool-*kel*-uh. Lat. beautiful. Brazil, Argentina.

Alternanthera Forssk. (Amaranthaceae). awl-turn-an-*the*-ruh. Chaff flower, joyweed. Lat. alternate, anthers (are sterile). 80 spp. herbs. Tropics and subtropics.
brasiliana (L.) Kuntze. bra-zil-ee-*ah*-nuh. Brazilian joyweed. Of Brazil. S Am., Caribb.
dentata (Moench) Stuchlik ex R. E. Fr. = *A. brasiliana*
ficoidea (L.) P. Beauv. fee-*koid*-ee-uh. Like *Ficus* (the leaves). Trop. Am.

Althaea L. (Malvaceae). al-*thee*-uh. From Gk. to heal, referring to med. properties. 12 spp. herbs. Eur., Asia.
cannabina L. kan-uh-*been*-uh. Hemp marsh mallow. Like *Cannabis* (the leaves). Eur. to C Asia.
ficifolia (L.) Cav. = *Alcea ficifolia*
officinalis L. o-fis-i-*nah*-lis. Marsh mallow. Lat. sold as a med. herb. Eur.

alum root *Heuchera*. **American** *H. americana*. **crevice** *H. micrantha*. **hairy** *H. villosa*. **poker** *H. cylindrica*
aluminium plant *Pilea cadierei*

Alyogyne Alef. (Malvaceae). al-ee-oh-*gy*-nee. From Gk. united, female, referring to the undivided style. 6 spp. shrubs. Australia.
huegelii (Endl.) Fryxell. hew-*gel*-ee-ee. After Austrian botanist Charles von Hügel (1795–1870), who collected the type specimen. S and W Australia.

Alyssum L. (Brassicaceae). *a*-lis-oom, uh-*lis*-oom. Gk. not, rage (it was said to cure rabies). 190 spp., herbs, subshrubs. Eur., N Africa, W Asia.
maritimum (L.) Lam. = *Lobularia maritima*
montanum L. mon-*tah*-noom. Lat. of mountains. Eur.
murale Waldst. & Kit. mew-*rah*-lee. Yellow tuft. Lat. of walls. SE Eur.
saxatile L. = *Aurinia saxatilis*
spinosum L. spi-*noh*-soom. Lat. spiny. SW Eur.
wulfenianum Schltdl. wool-fen-ee-*ah*-num. After German baron Franz Xaver von Wulfen (1728–1805), botanist and mineralogist. W Asia.

alyssum, golden *Aurinia saxatilis*
amaranth, purple *Amaranthus*
 cruentus

Amaranthus L. (Amaranthaceae).
 am-uh-*ranth*-oos. Gk. unfading,
 referring to the long-lasting flowers.
 70 spp. herbs. Widespread.
caudatus L. kaw-*dah*-toos. Love-lies-
 bleeding. Lat. with a tail, referring to
 the slender inflorescence. Tropics.
cruentus L. krue-*en*-toos. Purple amaranth, prince's feather. Lat. stained
 with blood (referring to the flowers).
 C Am.
hypochondriacus L. hie-poh-kon-
 dree-*ah*-koos. Prince's feather. Melancholy, from Gk. below the carti-
 lage, where the seat of melancholy
 was thought to be. N Am.
tricolor L. *tri*-ko-lor. Joseph's coat.
 Lat. three-coloured (the leaves).
 Tropics.

Amaryllis L. (Amaryllidaceae).
 am-uh-*ril*-is. The name of a shepherd-
 ess in Gk. myth. 1 sp., bulbous herb.
 S Africa.
belladonna L. bel-uh-*don*-uh. Belladonna lily, Jersey lily. Ital. beautiful
 woman.

Amberboa Vaill. (Asteraceae).
 am-bur-*boh*-uh. From the Turkish
 name. 6 spp. herbs. S Eur. to C Asia.
moschata (L.) DC. mos-*kah*-tuh.
 Sweet sultan. Lat. musk-scented (the
 flowers). SW Asia.

Amelanchier Medik. (Rosaceae).
 am-uh-*lang*-kee-uh. Provençal name
 for the fruit of *A. ovalis*, from Lat.

malum (apple). 20 spp., shrubs, trees.
 Eur., N and C Am.
alnifolia (Nutt.) Nutt. ex M. Roem.
 al-ni-*foh*-lee-uh. Lat. with leaves like
 Alnus. USA, Canada.
arborea (F. Michx.) Fernald. ar-*bor*-
 ree-uh. Lat. tree-like. E USA, E
 Canada.
canadensis (L.) Medik. kan-uh-*den*-
 sis. Of Canada. E USA, E Canada.
×*grandiflora* Rehder. gran-di-*flaw*-
 ruh. Lat. large-flowered. Cult.
laevis Wiegand. *lee*-vis. Lat. smooth
 (the leaves). E USA, E Canada.
lamarckii Schröd. la-*mar*-kee-ee.
 After Jean-Baptiste Lamarck (1744–
 1829), French naturalist. Eur.

American bugleweed *Lycopus*
 americanus

Ammi L. (Apiaceae). *am*-ee. Name
 used by Dioscorides for probably a
 different plant, from Gk. sand, referring to the habitat. 4 spp. herbs. S
 Eur., N Africa, W Asia.
majus L. *may*-joos. Lat. larger.
visnaga (L.) Lam. viz-*nah*-guh. From
 an old word for parsnip, referring to
 the roots. S Eur., W Asia.

Ammophila Host (Poaceae). uh-*mo*-
 fil-uh. Gk. sand-loving. 3 spp. grasses.
 Eur., N Africa, E USA, E Canada,
 SW Asia.
arenaria (L.) Link. a-ruh-*nair*-ree-uh.
 Marram grass. Lat. growing in sand.
 Eur., N Africa, SW Asia.
breviligulata Fernald. bre-vee-lig-ew-
 lah-tuh. American beach grass.
 Lat. with a short ligule. E USA, E
 Canada.

Amorpha L. (Fabaceae). uh-*mor*-fuh. Gk. shapeless (the corolla has only one petal, unlike related genera). 15 spp. shrubs. N Am.

canescens Pursh. kan-*es*-uhnz. Lead plant. Lat. grey (the foliage).

fruticosa L. frue-ti-*koh*-suh. False indigo. Lat. shrubby.

ouachitensis Wilbur. wosh-ee-*ten*-sis. Of the Ouachita Mts. USA (Arkansas, Oklahoma).

Amorphophallus Blume ex Decne. (Araceae). uh-mor-foh-*fa*-loos. Gk. shapeless phallus. 150 spp. cormous herbs. Old World tropics.

bulbifer (Roxb.) Blume. *bul*-bi-fuh. Voodoo lily. Lat. bearing bulbs (on the leaves). NE India, Myanmar.

Ampelaster carolinianus (Walter) G. L. Nesom = *Symphyotrichum carolinianum*

Ampelopsis Michx. (Vitaceae). am-pel-*op*-sis. Gk. like a grape vine. 25 spp. climbers. N Am., Asia.

aconitifolia Bunge. a-kon-ie-ti-*foh*-lee-uh. Lat. with leaves like *Aconitum*.

brevipedunculata (Maxim.) Trautv. = *A. glandulosa* var. *brevipedunculata*

glandulosa (Wall.) Momiy. gland-ew-*loh*-suh. Lat. glandular. E Asia. var. *brevipedunculata* (Maxim.) Momiy. brev-ee-pe-dunk-ew-*lah*-tuh. Lat. with a short peduncle. var. *heterophylla* (Thunb.) Momiy. het-e-*rof*-i-luh. Gk. with variable leaves.

megalophylla Diels & Gilg. meg-uh-loh-*fil*-uh. Gk. with large leaves. W China.

Amsonia Walter (Apocynaceae). am-*soh*-nee-uh. Bluestar. After Charles Amson, 18th-cent. physician of Virginia. 20 spp. herbs. N Am., Japan, SE Eur., Turkey.

ciliata Walter. sil-ee-*ah*-tuh. Lat. ciliate (the young shoots and leaves, sometimes). SE USA.

hubrichtii Woodson. hew-*brikt*-ee-ee. After American naturalist Leslie Hubricht (1908–2005), who discovered it in 1942. Ouachita Mts. USA (Arkansas, Oklahoma).

illustris Woodson. il-*us*-tris. Lat. shining (the leaves). SE USA.

orientalis Decne. o-ree-en-*tah*-lis. Lat. eastern. Greece, NW Turkey.

tabernaemontana Walter. tab-ur-nie-mon-*tah*-nuh. Originally named as a species of the related genus *Tabernaemontana*. E USA.

Anacyclus L. (Asteraceae). an-uh-*sike*-loos. From Gk. without, flower and ring, referring to the outer florets lacking petals. 12 spp. herbs. Medit.

pyrethrum (L.) Link. pie-*reeth*-room. From the Gk. name of a plant. var. *depressus* (Ball) Maire. dee-*pres*-oos. Lat. low-growing. Spain, N Africa.

Anagallis L. (Primulaceae). uh-*nag*-uh-lis, an-uh-*gah*-lis. The Gk. name, from Gk. to laugh (it was said to make people happy). 30 spp. herbs. Widespread.

arvensis L. ar-*ven*-sis. Scarlet pimpernel. Lat. of fields. Eur.

monelli L. mon-*el*-ee. Blue pimpernel. After French doctor Jean Monnell (Lat. *Monellus*) de Bouverix. Medit.

tenella (L.) L. ten-*el*-uh. Bog pimpernel. Lat. slender (the stems). W Eur.

Ananas Mill. (Bromeliaceae). uh-*nan*-uhs. From a native S American name meaning excellent fruit. 8 spp. herbs. S Am.

comosus (L.) Merr. ko-*moh*-soos. Pineapple. Lat. with a head of long hair, referring to the apical tuft of leaves. Cult.

Anaphalis DC. (Asteraceae). uh-*na*-fuh-lis. Gk. name for a similar plant. 50 spp. herbs. E Asia, N Am.

margaritacea (L.) Benth. & Hook.f. mar-guh-ri-*tay*-see-uh. Pearly everlasting. Lat. like pearls (the flowerheads). USA, Canada, Mex. (B.C.), E Asia.

triplinervis (Sims) C. B. Clarke. tri-pli-*nerv*-is. Lat. with three veins (the leaves). Himal., Tibet.

Anchusa L. (Boraginaceae). an-*chue*-suh. Gk. name of a plant mentioned by Dioscorides as used for dyeing. 35 spp. herbs. Eur., Africa, W Asia.

azurea Mill. uh-*zewr*-ree-uh. Lat. blue (the flowers). Eur., N Africa, W Asia.

Andromeda L. (Ericaceae). an-*drom*-i-duh. After Andromeda of Gk. myth. 2 spp. shrubs. N temp. regs.

polifolia L. pol-i-*foh*-lee-uh. Bog rosemary. An old name used for this plant.

Andropogon L. (Poaceae). an-*drop*-oh-gon. From Gk. man, beard, referring to the hairy spikelets. 100 spp. grasses. Widespread.

gerardii Vitman. je-*rard*-ee-ee. Big bluestem. After Louis Gerard (1733–1819), French physician and botanist. N and C Am.

glomeratus (Walter) Britton et al. glom-uh-*rah*-toos. Bushy bluestem. Lat. clustered (the inflorescence). USA to Colombia and Caribb.

hallii Hack. *hawl*-ee-ee. After American author and plant collector Elihu Hall (1822–1882), who, with J. P. Harbour, collected the type specimen in Nebraska in 1862. N Am.

scoparius Michx. = *Schizachyrium scoparium*

virginicus L. vir-*gin*-i-koos. Of Virginia. N Am. to Colombia and Caribb.

Androsace L. (Primulaceae). an-*dros*-uh-see. Rock jasmines. Gk. name used by Dioscorides for another plant, from Gk. man, shield, referring to the shape of the anthers. 150 spp. herbs. N temp. regs.

carnea L. *kar*-nee-uh. Lat. flesh-pink (the flowers). Alps. subsp. *brigantiaca* (Jord. & Fourr.) I. K. Ferguson. brig-an-tee-*ah*-kuh. Of Briançon, SE France. SW Alps. subsp. *laggeri* (A. Huet) Nyman. *lag*-uh-ree. After Franz Joseph Lagger (1799–1870), German doctor and botanist, friend of the author Huet. Pyrenees.

cylindrica DC. si-*lin*-dri-kuh. Lat. cylindrical (the shape of a leafy shoot). Pyrenees.

himalaica (Knuth) Hand.-Mazz. him-uh-*lay*-i-kuh. Himalayan. Himal.

lanuginosa Wall. lan-ue-jin-*oh*-suh. Lat. woolly (the foliage). W Himal.

primuloides Duby = *A. studiosorum*

sarmentosa Wall. sar-men-*toh*-suh. Lat. producing stolons. Tibet, Himal.

sempervivoides Jacquem. ex Duby. sem-pur-vie-*voy*-deez. Like *Sempervivum*. NW Himal.

studiosorum Kress. stew-dee-oh-*sor*-oom. Lat. of students (it was dedicated to amateur botanists). Himal.

vitaliana (L.) Lapeyr. vi-tal-ee-*ah*-nuh. After Italian doctor and botanist Vitaliano Donati (1717–1762). Alps.

Anemanthele Veldkamp (Poaceae). uh-nem-uhn-*thee*-lee. Gk. wind, small flower. 1 sp., grass. NZ.

lessoniana (Steud.) Veldkamp. les-oh-nee-*ah*-nuh. After French botanist René Primevère Lesson (1794–1849), who, with d'Urville, collected the type specimen.

Anemone L. (Ranunculaceae). uh-*nem*-uh-nee. From Gk. wind. 150 spp. herbs. Widespread.

acutiloba (DC.) G. Lawson. uh-kew-ti-*loh*-buh. Lat. with pointed lobes (the leaves). SE Canada, E USA.

americana (DC.) H. Hara. uh-me-ri-*kah*-nuh. Of America. SE Canada, E USA.

apennina L. a-pen-*ie*-nuh. Of the Apennines. Medit.

blanda Schott & Kotschy. *blan*-duh. Lat. alluring. SE Eur., SW Asia.

canadensis L. kan-uh-*den*-sis. Of Canada. N Am.

coronaria L. ko-ro-*nair*-ree-uh. Lat. of garlands. S Eur., N Africa, SW Asia.

flaccida F. Schmidt. *flak*-si-duh. Lat. drooping. E Asia.

hepatica L. huh-*pat*-i-kuh. From Gk. liver (the shape and colour of the leaves). Eur., E Asia.

hupehensis (Lemoine) Lemoine. hew-pee-*hen*-sis. Of Hubei (Hupeh), China. var. *japonica* (Thunb.) Bowles & Stearn. juh-*pon*-i-kuh. Of Japan. China, Taiwan.

×*hybrida* Paxton. *hib*-ri-duh. Japanese anemone. Lat. hybrid. *A. hupehensis* × *A. vitifolia*. Cult.

×*lesseri* H. R. Wehr. *les*-uh-ree. After Ludwig Lesser (1869–1957), German landscape architect. *A. multifida* × *A. sylvestris*. Cult.

leveillei Ulbr. lay-*vay*-ee-ee. After French botanist Augustin Hector Léveillé (1863–1918). China.

×*lipsiensis* Beck. lip-see-*en*-sis. Of Lipsi, Greece. *A. nemorosa* × *A. ranunculoides*. Eur.

×*media* (Simonk.) Kárpáti. *mee*-dee-uh. Lat. intermediate (between the parents). *A. hepatica* × *A. transsilvanica*. Romania.

multifida Poir. mul-ti-*fee*-duh. Lat. divided many times (the leaves). N and S Am.

nemorosa L. nem-o-*roh*-suh. Wood anemone. Lat. of woods. Eur.

pavonina Lam. pav-oh-*neen*-uh. Lat. like a peacock. S Eur.

pulsatilla L. puls-uh-*til*-uh. Pasque flower. From Lat. to agitate (referring to the movement of the flowers by the wind). Eur.

ranunculoides L. ruh-nunk-ew-*loy*-deez. Like *Ranunculus*. Eur.

rivularis Buch.-Ham. ex DC. riv-ew-*lah*-ris. Lat. of riverbanks. Himal. to China.

sylvestris L. sil-*ves*-tris. Snowdrop anemone/windflower. Lat. of forests. Eur., Asia.

transsilvanica (Fuss) Heuff. trans-sil-*van*-i-kuh. Of Transylvania (historical reg. of NW Romania). Romania.

virginiana L. vir-jin-ee-*ah*-nuh. Of Virginia. N Am.

vitifolia Buch.-Ham. ex DC. vi-ti-*foh*-lee-uh. Lat. with leaves like *Vitis*. Himal., W China.

anemone, Japanese *Anemone* ×*hybrida*. **rue** *Thalictrum thalictroides*. **snowdrop** *Anemone sylvestris*. **wood** *A. nemorosa*

Anemonella thalictroides (L.) Spach = *Thalictrum thalictroides*

Anemonopsis Sieb. & Zucc. (Ranunculaceae). uh-nem-uh-*nop*-sis. Gk. like *Anemone*. 1 sp., herb. Japan.
macrophylla Sieb. & Zucc. mak-*ro*-fil-uh. Gk. large-leaved.

Anemopsis Hook. & Arn. (Saururaceae). an-uh-*mop*-sis. Gk. like *Anemone*. 1 sp., herb. W USA, NW Mex.
californica (Nutt.) Hook. & Arn. kal-i-*for*-ni-kuh. Hierba mansa. Of California.

Anethum L. (Apiaceae). uh-*nee*-thoom. From the Gk. name. 1 sp., herb. S Asia.
graveolens L. grav-ee-*oh*-luhnz. Dill. Lat. strong-smelling.

Angelica L. (Apiaceae). an-*jel*-i-kuh. Lat. angelic (from the med. properties). 50 spp. herbs. N hemisph.
archangelica L. ark-an-*jel*-i-kuh. After Archangel Michael, with whom it has been associated. Eur., W and C Asia.

atropurpurea L. at-roh-pur-*pew*-ree-uh. Lat. dark purple (the stems). E USA, SE Canada.
gigas Nakai. *jee*-guhs. Lat. giant. China, Korea, Japan.
pachycarpa Lange. pak-ee-*kar*-puh. Gk. thick fruit. Spain, Portugal.
sylvestris L. sil-*vest*-ris. Lat. of woods. Eur.

Angelonia Bonpl. (Plantaginaceae). an-gel-*oh*-nee-uh. From *angelon*, the native name. 30 spp., herbs, subshrubs. Mex. to S Am.
angustifolia Benth. an-gus-ti-*foh*-lee-uh. Lat. narrow-leaved. Mex., W Indies.
gardneri Hook. *gard*-nuh-ree. After English botanist George Gardner (1812–1849), who collected the type specimen in 1838. Brazil.

angel's fishing rod *Dierama*
angel's wings *Caladium*

Angraecum Bory (Orchidaceae). an-*greek*-oom. From *angurek*, the Malay name. 200 spp. orchids. Trop. Africa, SE Asia.
leonis (Rchb.f.) Veitch. lee-*oh*-nis. Lion's moustache orchid. From Lat. lion (from its resemblance to a lion's mane). Madagascar.
sesquipedale Thouars. ses-kwee-ped-*ah*-lee. Star of Bethlehem orchid. Lat. one and a half feet (referring to the long spur). Madagascar.

anise, Florida *Illicium floridanum*. **Japanese star** *I. anisatum*. **swamp star** *I. parviflorum*

Anomatheca laxa (Thunb.) Goldblatt
= *Freesia laxa*

Antennaria Gaertn. (Asteraceae).
an-ten-*air*-ree-uh. Cat's ears, pussy
toes. From Lat. antenna (the pappus
bristles of the male flower resemble
an insect's antenna). 45 spp. alpine
herbs. N and S Am., Eur., Asia.
dioica (L.) Gaertn. die-*oy*-kuh. Gk.
dioecious. Eur., Asia, Aleutian Is.
neglecta Greene. neg-*lek*-tuh. Lat.
neglected (it had been confused with
another species for many years).
N Am.
plantaginifolia (L.) Hook. plan-taj-i-
ni-*foh*-lee-uh. With leaves like *Plantago*. E USA, SE Canada.
rosea Greene. *roh*-zee-uh. Lat. pink
(the flowerheads). N Am.

Anthemis L. (Asteraceae). *an*-them-is.
The Gk. name. 175 spp. herbs. Eur. to
W Asia.
marschalliana Willd. mar-shal-ee-*ah*-
nuh. After German botanist
Friedrich August Marschall von
Bieberstein (1768–1826). NE Turkey, Caucasus.
nobilis L. = *Chamaemelum nobile*
punctata Vahl. punk-*tah*-tuh. Lat.
spotted (with glands, the leaves).
Sicily, N Africa. subsp. *cupaniana*
(Tod. ex Nyman) R. R. Fern. kew-
pan-ee-*ah*-nuh. After Francesco
Cupani (1657–1710), Italian monk
and botanist.
sancti-johannis Turrill. sank-tee-yoh-
han-is. After St. John the Baptist, on
whose feast day (June 24) it flowers.
Bulgaria.
tinctoria L. tink-*tor*-ree-uh. Dyers'
chamomile. Lat. of dyers. Eur.

Anthericum L. (Asparagaceae).
an-*the*-ri-koom. From the Gk. name.
6 spp. perenn. herbs. S Eur., Turkey,
Africa.
liliago L. li-lee-*ah*-go. St. Bernard's
lily. Lat. like *Lilium*. S Eur.
ramosum L. ra-*moh*-soom. Lat.
branched (the flower spikes). S Eur.

Anthoxanthum L. (Poaceae). an-thox-
anth-oom. Gk. yellow flower. 50 spp.
herbs. Widespread.
nitens (Weber) Schouten & Veldkamp
= *Hierochloe odorata*
odoratum L. oh-do-*rah*-tum. Sweet
vernal grass. Lat. scented (the foliage). Eur., Asia.

Anthriscus Pers. (Apiaceae). an-*thris*-
koos. Gk. name for a similar plant.
9 spp. herbs. Eur., Asia, N Africa.
cerefolium (L.) Hoffm. ke-ree-*foh*-lee-
oom. Chervil. Lat. wax-leaved. Eur.,
W Asia.
sylvestris (L.) Hoffm. sil-*ves*-tris. Cow
parsley, Queen Anne's lace. Lat. of
woods. Eur., W Asia, N Africa.

Anthurium Schott (Araceae). an-*thur*-
ree-oom. Flamingo flower. Gk.
flower, tail, referring to the slender
flower spikes. 1000 spp. perenn.
herbs. Trop. Am.
andraeanum Linden ex André.
on-dray-*ah*-noom. After Édouard
François André (1840–1911), French
nurseryman and landscape architect.
Colombia, Ecuador.

Anthyllis L. (Fabaceae). an-*thil*-is. Gk.
name of a plant used by Dioscorides.
20 spp., herbs, shrubs. Eur., Medit.

montana L. mon-*tah*-nuh. Lat. of
mountains. Medit.
vulneraria L. vul-nuh-*rair*-ree-uh.
Kidney vetch, lady's fingers. From
Lat. wound (it was classically used to
dress wounds).

Anticlea Kunth (Melanthiaceae).
an-*tik*-lee-uh. Death camus. After
Anticlea of Gk. myth., mother of
Odysseus. 10 spp. bulbous herbs. N
and C Am., E Eur., temp. Asia.
elegans (Pursh) Rydb. *el*-i-ganz. Alkali
grass. Lat. elegant. N Am., N Mex.

Antirrhinum L. (Plantaginaceae).
an-tee-*rie*-noom. Gk. like a nose,
referring to the flowers. 20 spp.,
herbs, subshrubs. Eur., Medit.
majus L. *may*-joos. Snapdragon. Lat.
large. Medit.
molle L. *mol*-ee. Lat. softly hairy.
Spain, Portugal.

Aphelandra R. Br. (Acanthaceae).
af-uh-*lan*-druh. Gk. simple, male,
referring to the one-celled anthers.
170 spp. shrubs. Trop. Am.
squarrosa Nees. skwo-*roh*-suh. Zebra
plant. Lat. with projecting tips (on
the inflorescence). Brazil.

Apios Fabr. (Fabaceae). *ay*-pee-os. Gk.
pear, from the shape of the tubers.
10 spp. herbs. N Am., E Asia.
americana Medik. uh-me-ri-*kah*-nuh.
Potato bean. Of America. N Am.

Apium L. (Apiaceae). *ay*-pee-oom.
Lat. celery, parsley. 25 spp. herbs.
Widespread.
graveolens L. grav-ee-*oh*-luhnz.
Celery. Lat. strong-smelling. var.

rapaceum (Mill.) DC. ra-*pay*-see-
oom. Celeriac. Lat. like a turnip.

apple *Malus.* orchard *M. pumila*
apple of Peru *Nicandra physalodes*
apricot *Prunus armeniaca.* **Japanese**
P. mume

Aquilegia L. (Ranunculaceae). ak-wi-
lee-*juh*. Columbine. From Lat. eagle,
referring to the shape of the flowers.
80 spp. herbs. N temp. regs.
alpina L. al-*pie*-nuh. Lat. alpine. Alps.
atrata W. D. J. Koch. uh-*trah*-tuh.
Lat. black (the dark flowers). S Eur.
bertolonii Schott. bur-to-*loh*-nee-ee.
After Italian botanist Antonio
Bertoloni (1775–1869). SW Eur.
canadensis L. kan-uh-*den*-sis.
Meetinghouses, honeysuckle. Of
Canada. E USA, S Canada.
chrysantha A. Gray. kris-*anth*-uh.
Golden columbine. Gk. golden-
flowered. S USA.
coerulea E. James. suh-*rue*-lee-uh.
Colorado blue columbine. Lat. blue
(the flowers). W USA.
ecalcarata Maxim. ee-kal-suh-*rah*-
tuh. Lat. without a spur (the flower).
China.
flabellata Sieb. & Zucc. flab-uh-*lah*-
tuh. Lat. fan-like (the leaflets). Japan.
formosa Fisch. ex DC. for-*moh*-suh.
Western columbine. Lat. beautiful.
W USA, W Canada.
fragrans Benth. *fray*-gruhnz. Lat. fragrant (the flowers). Himal.
longissima A. Gray ex S. Watson.
long-*gis*-i-muh. Longspur columbine.
Lat. longest (the spur). SW USA.
saximontana Rydb. sax-ee-mon-*tah*-
nuh. Rocky Mountain blue

columbine. Of the Rocky Mountains. USA (Colorado).
scopulorum Tidestr. skop-ew-*lor*-room. Utah columbine. Lat. of rocky places or cliffs. W USA.
skinneri Hook. *skin*-uh-ree. Skinner's columbine. After George Ure Skinner (1804–1867), English merchant. It was described from plants grown at Woburn Abbey that he sent from Guatemala. Mex., Guatemala.
vulgaris L. vul-*gar*-ris. Common columbine. Lat. common. Eur.

Arabis L. (Brassicaceae). *a*-ruh-bis. Rockcress. Gk. Arabian. 100 spp. herbs. N temp. regs.
alpina L. al-*pie*-nuh. Lat. alpine. Eur. subsp. *caucasica* (Willd.) Briq. kaw-*kas*-i-kuh. Of the Caucasus.
blepharophylla Hook. & Arn. blef-uh-roh-*fil*-uh. Rose rockcress. Gk. with fringed leaves. Calif.
caucasica Willd. = *A. alpina* subsp. *caucasica*
ferdinandi-coburgii Kellerer & Sünd. fer-di-*nan*-dee-koh-*burg*-ee-ee. After King Ferdinand of Bulgaria (1861–1948). Bulgaria.
procurrens Waldst. & Kit. pro-*ku*-ruhnz. Lat. running (spreads by stolons). E Eur.

Aralia L. (Araliaceae). uh-*rah*-lee-uh. From the French-Canadian name. 70 spp., herbs, shrubs, climbers, trees. E Asia, N Am.
cachemirica Decne. kash-*mi*-ri-kuh. Of Kashmir. W and C Himal.
californica S. Watson. kal-i-*for*-ni-kuh. California spikenard. Of California. Calif., Oregon.

cordata Thunb. kor-*dah*-tuh. Lat. heart-shaped (the leaflets, sometimes). E Asia.
elata (Miq.) Seem. ee-*lah*-tuh. Japanese angelica tree. Lat. tall. E Asia.
racemosa L. ras-i-*moh*-suh. American spikenard. Lat. in racemes (the flowers). E USA, E Canada.
spinosa L. spi-*noh*-suh. Devil's walking stick, Hercules' club. Lat. spiny. E USA, E Canada.

Araucaria Juss. (Araucariaceae). a-row-*kah*-ree-uh. From the Araucanos (now Mapuche), Spanish name for inhabitants of the region where *A. araucana* grows. 18 spp. trees. New Caledonia, Chile, Brazil.
araucana (Molina) K. Koch. a-row-*kah*-nuh. Monkey puzzle. Deriv. as for genus. Chile.
columnaris (J. R. Forst.) Hook. ko-loom-*nah*-ris. New Caledonia pine. Lat. columnar (the habit). New Caledonia.
heterophylla (Salisb.) Franco. het-e-*rof*-i-luh. Norfolk Island pine. Lat. variably leaved. Norfolk Is.

Araujia Brot. (Apocynaceae). uh-*row*-jee-uh. After António de Araújo e Azevedo (1754–1817), Portuguese botanist and statesman. 3 spp. climbers. S Am.
sericifera Brot. se-ri-*ki*-fuh-ruh. Cruel plant. Lat. silky (the young foliage).

arborvitae *Thuja*. **American** *T. occidentalis*. **Chinese** *Platycladus orientalis*

Arbutus L. (Ericaceae). ar-*bew*-toos. Lat. name for *A. unedo*. 10 spp. trees. Eur., W Asia, N and C Am.

×*andrachnoides* Link. an-drak-*noy*-deez. Like *A. andrachne*. *A. andrachne* × *A. unedo*. S Eur., W Asia.

menziesii Pursh. men-*zeez*-ee-ee. Pacific madrone. After Scottish surgeon and naturalist Archibald Menzies (1754–1842), who collected the type specimen. W USA, SW Canada.

texana Buckley = *A. xalapensis*

unedo L. ew-*nee*-doh. Strawberry tree. Lat. I eat one (referring to the bland taste, *unum edo*, words of Pliny the Elder). Medit., Turkey, SW Ireland.

xalapensis Kunth. hal-uh-*pen*-sis. Of Xalapa. Mex., C Am., SW USA.

Arctostaphylos Adans. (Ericaceae). ark-toh-*staf*-i-los. Gk. bear, bunch of grapes (see *A. uva-ursi*). 60 spp., shrubs, trees. W N Am., Eur., N Asia.

columbiana Piper. ko-lum-bee-*ah*-nuh. Hairy manzanita. Of the Columbia River area. W USA, SW Canada.

nevadensis A. Gray. nev-uh-*den*-sis. Pinemat manzanita. Of the Sierra Nevada. W USA.

uva-ursi (L.) Spreng. ue-vuh-*ur*-see. Bearberry. Lat. bear grape. N temp. regs.

Arctotis L. (Asteraceae). ark-*toh*-tis. African daisy. Gk. bear's ear (the ear-like pappus scales). 50 spp., herbs, subshrubs. S Africa.

fastuosa Jacq. fas-tew-*oh*-suh. Cape daisy. Lat. proud (the showy flowers).

×*hybrida* hort. *hib*-ri-duh. Lat. hybrid. Cult.

Ardisia Sw. (Myrsinaceae). ar-*dis*-ee-uh. From Gk. point or arrow point, referring to the pointed anthers. 120 spp., shrubs, trees. Mainly trop. Asia and Am.

crenata Sims. kre-*nah*-tuh. Coral-berry. Lat. finely way (the leaf edge). E Asia.

japonica (Thunb.) Blume. juh-*pon*-i-kuh. Of Japan. China, Japan.

Arenaria L. (Caryophyllaceae). a-ruh-*nair*-ree-uh. Sandwort. From Lat. sand, referring to the habitat of many. 210 spp. herbs. N temp. regs.

montana L. mon-*tah*-nuh. Lat. of mountains. SW Eur.

purpurascens DC. pur-pew-*ras*-uhnz. Lat. purplish (the flowers). Pyrenees, N Spain.

Argemone L. (Papaveraceae). ar-*gem*-on-ee. Prickly poppy. Gk. name for a poppy-like plant, from Gk. for cataract (supposed med. properties). 25 spp. herbs. S USA to S Am.

grandiflora Sweet. gran-di-*flaw*-ruh. Lat. large-flowered. Mex.

polyanthemos (Fedde) G. B. Ownbey. pol-ee-*an*-thuh-mos. Crested prickly poppy. Gk. many-flowered. W USA.

Argyranthemum Webb (Asteraceae). ar-gi-*ranth*-uh-moom. Gk. silver flower. 24 spp. subshrubs. Macaronesia.

frutescens (L.) Sch. Bip. frue-*tes*-uhnz. Marguerite. Lat. somewhat shrubby. Canary Is.

Arisaema Mart. (Araceae). a-ri-*see*-muh. Gk. arum, blood, referring to the spotted leaves of some. 170 spp. herbs. Asia, E Africa, N Am.

candidissimum W. W. Sm. kan-di-*dis*-i-moom. Lat. most white (the spathe). W China.

ciliatum H. Li. sil-ee-*ah*-toom. Lat. edged with fine hairs (the spathe). China (Sichuan, Yunnan).

consanguineum Schott. kon-san-*gwin*-ee-oom. Lat. related to (another species). Himal.

costatum (Wall.) Mart. kos-*tah*-toom. Lat. ribbed (the tube of the spathe). Nepal, Tibet.

dracontium (L.) Schott. dra-*kon*-tee-oom. Green dragon. Lat. dragon-like. E USA, E Canada.

fargesii Buchet. far-*jee*-zee-ee. After French missionary and plant collector Paul Guillaume Farges (1844–1912), who collected the type specimen in Sichuan. China.

flavum (Forssk.) Schott. *flah*-voom. Lat. yellow (the spathe). Africa to W China.

griffithii Schott. gri-*fith*-ee-ee. After William Griffith (1810–1845), English botanist and doctor. E Himal.

jacquemontii Blume. jak-*mont*-ee-ee. After French botanist and geologist Victor Jacquemont (1801–1832), who collected the type specimen in NE India. Himal.

nepenthoides (Wall.) Mart. nep-enth-*oy*-deez. Cobra plant. Like *Nepenthe*. E Himal., SW China.

propinquum Schott. proh-*pink*-woom. Lat. close to (another species). Himal.

ringens (Thunb.) Schott. *ring*-uhnz. Lat. wide open (the spathe). China, Taiwan, Japan, Korea.

sikokianum Franch. & Sav. shi-koh-kee-*ah*-noom. Of Shikoku. Japan.

speciosum (Wall.) Mart. spee-see-*oh*-soom. Lat. showy. E Himal., SW China.

tortuosum (Wall.) Schott. tor-tew-*oh*-soom. Lat. twisted (the spadix). Himal.

triphyllum (L.) Schott. trie-*fil*-oom. Jack in the pulpit. Lat. with three leaves (leaflets). E USA, E Canada.

utile Hook.f. ex Engl. *ew*-ti-lee. Lat. useful (edible leaves and inflorescence). Himal., SW China.

Arisarum Mill. (Araceae). uh-*ris*-uh-room, a-ris-*ah*-room. Gk. name for *A. vulgare*. 3 spp. perenn. herbs. Medit.

proboscideum (L.) Savi. pro-bos-*kid*-ee-oom. Mouse plant. Gk. like an elephant's trunk (the spathe). SW Eur.

vulgare O. Targ. Tozz. vul-*gar*-ree. Friar's cowl. Lat. common. SW Eur.

Aristea Sol. ex Aiton (Iridaceae). uh-*ris*-tee-uh. Gk. awn, referring to the pointed bracts. 50 spp. herbs. Africa.

ecklonii Baker. ek-*lon*-ee-ee. After Danish apothecary Christian Friedrich Ecklon (1795–1868), who collected the type specimen. E and S Africa.

Aristolochia L. (Aristolochiaceae). uh-rist-oh-*lok*-ee-uh. Gk. best, childbirth, referring to supposed med. properties (flower shape resembles birth canal). 300 spp., herbs, shrubs, climbers. Widespread.

durior Hill = *A. macrophylla*

gigantea Mart. & Zucc. jie-*gan*-tee-uh. Lat. very large (the flowers). C and S Am.

littoralis D. Parodi. li-to-*rah*-lis. Calico flower. Lat. coastal. C and S Am., Caribb.

macrophylla Lam. mak-*ro*-fil-uh. Dutchman's pipe, pipevine. Gk. large-leaved. E USA, SE Canada.

Aristotelia L'Hér. (Elaeocarpaceae). uh-rist-oh-*tee*-lee-uh. After Aristotle (384–322 BCE), Gk. philosopher. 5 spp., shrubs, trees. S Am., Australia, NZ.

chilensis (Molina) Stutz. chil-*en*-sis. Of Chile. Chile.

Armeria Willd. (Plumbaginaceae). ar-*meer*-ree-uh. Lat. for *Dianthus*. 100 spp. perenn. herbs. N temp. regs., S Am.

caespitosa (Cav.) Boiss. = *A. juniperifolia*

juniperifolia (Vahl) Hoffmanns. jue-nip-uh-ri-*foh*-lee-uh. Lat. with leaves like *Juniperus*. Spain.

maritima (Mill.) Willd. muh-*ri*-ti-muh. Thrift. Lat. of the sea. N temp. regs.

pseudarmeria (Murray) Mansf. sued-ar-*meer*-ree-uh. Gk. false *Armeria*. Spain, Portugal.

Armoracia P. Gaertn., B. Mey. & Scherb. (Brassicaceae). ar-mo-*ray*-see-uh. The Lat. name. 3 spp. herbs. Eur., SW Asia.

rusticana P. Gaertn., B. Mey. & Scherb. rus-ti-*kah*-nuh. Horseradish. Lat. of the country.

Arnica L. (Asteraceae). *ar*-ni-kuh. Gk. lambskin, for the soft leaves. 30 spp. herbs. N temp. and arctic regs.

chamissonis Less. kam-i-*soh*-nis. After Adelbert von Chamisso (1781–1838), German botanist and poet. N Am.

montana L. mon-*tah*-nuh. Lat. of mountains. Eur., W Asia.

Arnoglossum Raf. (Asteraceae). ar-noh-*glos*-oom. Indian plantain. Gk. name for plantain, meaning lamb's tongue. 7 spp. herbs. E USA, SE Canada.

atriplicifolium (L.) H. Rob. at-ri-plis-i-*foh*-lee-oom. Pale Indian plantain. E USA.

Aronia Medik. (Rosaceae). uh-*roh*-nee-uh. Chokeberry. Gk. name for medlar (*Mespilus*). 2 spp. shrubs. E USA, E Canada.

arbutifolia (L.) Pers. ar-bew-ti-*foh*-lee-uh. Red chokeberry. Lat. with leaves like *Arbutus*.

melanocarpa (Michx.) Elliott. me-luh-noh-*kar*-puh. Black chokeberry. Gk. black-fruited.

×*prunifolia* (Marshall) Rehder. prue-ni-*foh*-lee-uh. Purple chokeberry. Lat. with leaves like *Prunus*. *A. arbutifolia* × *A. melanocarpa*.

Arrhenatherum P. Beauv. (Poaceae). a-ruh-*nath*-uh-room. Oat grass. Gk. male, bristle, referring to awns on the male flowers. 6 spp. herbs. Eur., Asia.

elatius J. & C. Presl. ee-*lah*-tee-oos. False oat grass. Lat. tall. Eur. var.

bulbosum (Willd.) Spenner. bul-*boh*-soom. Lat. bulbous (the swollen stem bases).

arrowhead *Sagittaria*
arrowwood *Viburnum dentatum*

Artemisia L. (Asteraceae). art-ee-*mis*-ee-uh. The Lat. name, from the Gk. goddess Artemis. 400 spp., herbs, shrubs. Widespread.
abrotanum L. uh-*brot*-uh-noom. Lad's love, southernwood. The Lat. name. S Eur., Turkey.
absinthium L. ab-*sinth*-ee-oom. Absinthe. The Lat. name. Eur., N Africa, Asia.
alba Turra. *al*-buh. Lat. white (the plant). S Eur., N Africa.
annua L. *an*-ew-uh. Sweet wormwood. Lat. annual. SE Eur., W Asia.
arborescens L. ar-bor-*res*-uhnz. Lat. becoming tree-like. Medit.
cana Pursh. *kah*-nuh. Lat. grey (the foliage). SW Canada, W USA.
caucasica Willd. kaw-*kas*-i-kuh. Of the Caucasus. Eur., W Asia.
dracunculus L. druh-*kunk*-ew-loos. Tarragon. Lat. a little dragon (from the shape of the roots). SE Russia.
filifolia Torr. fi-li-*foh*-lee-uh. Sand sagebrush. Lat. with thread-like leaves. C USA, N Mex.
frigida Willd. *fri*-ji-duh. Prairie sagewort. Lat. cold (it can be found in cold places). N Am.
lactiflora Wall. ex DC. lak-ti-*flaw*-ruh. Lat. with milky flowers. Himal., China, SE Asia.
ludoviciana Nutt. lue-doh-vis-ee-*ah*-nuh. White sagebrush. Of St. Louis, from near where it was described. N Am.
nova A. Nelson. *noh*-vuh. Black sagebrush. Lat. new (it long escaped detection). W USA.

pontica L. *pon*-ti-kuh. Roman wormwood. Of Pontus (now NE Turkey). Eur., Turkey.
schmidtiana Maxim. shmit-ee-*ah*-nuh. After German botanist Carl Friedrich Schmidt (1811–1890), who worked on the genus. Japan.
stelleriana Besser. stel-uh-ree-*ah*-nuh. Beach wormwood, dusty miller. After Georg Wilhelm Steller (1709–1746), German naturalist and explorer. NE Asia, Alaska.
tridentata Nutt. trie-den-*tah*-tuh. Big sagebrush. Lat. three-toothed (the leaves). W USA. subsp. *wyomingensis* Beetle & A. M. Young. wie-oh-ming-*en*-sis. Of Wyoming.
vulgaris L. vul-*gar*-ris. Mugwort. Lat. common. Eur., N Africa, W Asia.

Arthropodium R. Br. (Asparagaceae). arth-roh-*poh*-dee-oom. Gk. jointed (flower) stalk. 9 spp. herbs. Madagascar, New Caledonia, Australia, NZ.
candidum Raoul. *kan*-di-doom. Lat. white (the flowers). NZ.
cirrhatum (G. Forst.) R. Br. si-*rah*-toom. Gk. curled (the anthers). NZ.

artichoke, globe *Cynara cardunculus* Scolymus Group. **Jerusalem** *Helianthus tuberosus*
artillery plant *Pilea microphylla*

Arum L. (Araceae). *a*-room. Gk. name for this or a similar plant. 28 spp. perenn. herbs. Eur., N Africa, Asia.
creticum Boiss. & Heldr. *kret*-i-koom. Lat. of Crete. Crete, SW Turkey.
cyrenaicum Hruby. si-ruh-*nay*-i-koom. Of Cyrenaica (E Libya). Crete, Libya.

dioscoridis Sm. dee-os-ko-*ree*-dis. After Gk. physician Pedanius Dioscorides (ca. 40–90), who wrote about it. E Medit.

italicum Mill. i-*tal*-i-koom. Of Italy. Eur., N Africa, SW Asia.

maculatum L. mak-ew-*lah*-toom. Cuckoo pint, lords and ladies. Lat. spotted (the leaves). Eur., W Asia.

pictum L.f. *pik*-toom. Lat. painted (the leaves). W Medit.

arum, bog *Calla palustris*

Aruncus L. (Rosaceae). uh-*run*-koos. Lat. name used by Pliny the Elder, from Gk. goat's beard. 3 spp. perenn. herbs. N temp. regs.

aethusifolius (H. Lév.) Nakai. ee-thew-zi-*foh*-lee-oos. Lat. with leaves like *Aethusa*. Korea.

dioicus (Walter) Fernald. die-*oy*-koos. Goat's beard. Gk. dioecious. Eur., Asia, N Am.

Arundinaria Michx. (Poaceae). uh-run-di-*nair*-ree-uh. Lat. like *Arundo*. 1 sp., bamboo. E USA.

gigantea (Walter) Muhl. jie-*gan*-tee-uh. Giant cane. Lat. very large. subsp. *tecta* (Walter) McClure. *tek*-tuh. Switch cane. Lat. a covering (the large sheaths covering the inflorescence). SE USA.

Arundo L. (Poaceae). uh-*run*-doh. Lat. reed. 3 spp. grasses. Medit.

donax L. *doh*-naks. Giant reed. Gk. name for a kind of reed.

asarabacca *Asarum europaeum*

Asarina Mill. (Plantaginaceae). az-uh-*ree*-nuh. Spanish name for an antirrhinum, meaning like *Asarum*. 1 sp., perenn. herb. SW Eur.

procumbens Mill. proh-*kum*-buhnz. Lat. creeping.

Asarum L. (Aristolochiaceae). az-uh-room. Lat. name, from Gk. 80 spp. perenn. herbs. N temp. regs.

arifolium Michx. a-ri-*foh*-lee-oom. Littlebrownjug. Lat. with leaves like *Arum*. SE USA.

canadense L. kan-uh-*den*-see. Wild ginger. Of Canada. E USA, SE Canada.

caudatum Lindl. kaw-*dah*-toom. Lat. with a tail-like point (the calyx lobes). W USA, SW Canada.

caulescens Maxim. kaw-*les*-uhnz. Lat. developing a stem. China.

europaeum L. ew-roh-*pee*-oom. Asarabacca. Of Europe. W Eur.

maximum Hemsl. *max*-i-moom. Lat. largest. China (Hubei, Sichuan).

naniflorum hort. nahn-i-*flaw*-room. Lat. with small flowers. SE USA (Carolinas).

shuttleworthii Britten & Bak.f. shut-uhl-*wurth*-ee-ee. After English naturalist Robert James Shuttleworth (1810–1874), who first recognised it as distinct. SE USA.

splendens (F. Maekawa) C. Y. Cheng & C. S. Yang. *splen*-duhnz. Lat. splendid. China.

Asclepias L. (Apocynaceae). uh-*sklee*-pee-uhs. Milkweed. Classical name, from Asklepios, Gk. god of medicine, for their med. properties. 120 spp., herbs, shrubs. Americas, Africa.

asperula (Decne.) Woodson. uh-*spe*-rue-luh. Spider milkweed. Lat. somewhat rough (the shoots). W USA.

curassavica L. koo-ruh-*sav*-i-kuh. Blood flower, swallowwort. Of Curaçao (Netherlands Antilles). S Am.

exaltata L. ex-awl-*tah*-tuh. Poke milkweed. Lat. very tall. E USA, E Canada.

incarnata L. in-kar-*nah*-tuh. Swamp milkweed. Lat. flesh-coloured (the flowers). USA, E Canada.

physocarpa (E. Mey.) Schltr. fie-soh-*kar*-puh. Balloon plant. Gk. bladder, fruit. S Africa.

purpurascens L. pur-pew-*ras*-uhnz. Purple milkweed. Purplish (the flowers). E USA, E Canada.

speciosa Torr. spee-see-*oh*-suh. Showy milkweed. Lat. showy. W USA, W Canada.

sullivantii Engelm. ex A. Gray. sul-i-*van*-tee-ee. Prairie milkweed. After American bryologist William Starling Sullivant (1803–1873), who collected the type specimen. SE Canada, C USA.

syriaca L. si-ree-*ah*-kuh. Common milkweed. Of Syria, where it was thought to originate. N Am.

tuberosa L. tew-buh-*roh*-suh. Butterfly milkweed. Lat. bearing tubers. USA, E Canada.

verticillata L. vur-ti-si-*lah*-tuh. Whorled milkweed. Lat. whorled (the leaves). N Am.

ash *Fraxinus*. **Arizona** *F. velutina*. **black** *F. nigra*. **blue** *F. quadrangulata*. **European** *F. excelsior*. **green** *F. pennsylvanica*. **Manchurian** *F. mandshurica*. **manna** *F. ornus*. **narrow-leaved** *F. angustifolia*.

Oregon *F. latifolia*. **red** *F. pennsylvanica*. **velvet** *F. velutina*. **white** *F. americana*

Asimina Adans. (Annonaceae). uh-*sim*-i-nuh. From *assimin*, the Native American name. 8 spp., shrubs, trees. E USA, SE Canada.

triloba (L.) Dunal. trie-*loh*-buh. Pawpaw. Lat. three-lobed (the calyx).

Asparagus Tourn. ex L. (Asparagaceae). uh-*spa*-ruh-goos. The Lat. name. 120 spp., herbs, climbers. Eur., Africa, Asia.

aethiopicus L. ee-thee-*op*-i-koos. Asparagus fern. Of Ethiopia (originally applied to all Africa). C and S Africa. **Sprengeri Group**. *spreng*-uh-ree. After Carl Ludwig Sprenger (1846–1917), German botanist and nurseryman who introduced it.

asparagoides (L.) Druce. uh-spa-ruh-*goy*-deez. Like *Asparagus* (originally named in another genus). S Africa.

densiflorus hort. = *A. aethiopicus*

officinalis L. o-fis-i-*nah*-lis. Garden asparagus. Lat. sold as a med. herb. Eur., N Africa.

plumosus Baker = *A. setaceus*

setaceus (Kunth) Jessop. see-*tay*-see-oos. Lat. bristly. Africa.

sprengeri Regel = *A. aethiopicus* Sprengeri Group

asparagus, garden *Asparagus officinalis*

aspen *Populus tremula*. **bigtooth** *P. grandidentata*. **quaking** *P. tremuloides*

Asperula odorata L. = *Galium odoratum*

asphodel *Asphodelus*. **yellow** *Asphode-line lutea*. **white** *Asphodelus albus*

Asphodeline Rchb. (Xanthorrhoea-ceae). as-fod-uh-*lee*-nee. Like *Aspho-delus*. 17 spp. herbs. Medit., W Asia.
liburnica (Scop.) Rchb. li-*burn*-i-kuh. Of Liburnia, now part of Croatia. SE Eur.
lutea (L.) Rchb. *lue*-tee-uh. Yellow asphodel. Lat. yellow (the flowers). Medit.
taurica (Pall.) Endl. *tow*-ri-kuh. Of the Taurus Mts. S Turkey.

Asphodelus L. (Xanthorrhoeaceae). as-*fod*-uh-loos. Asphodel. From the Gk. name. 17 spp. ann. and perenn. herbs. Eur. to Himal., N Africa.
albus Mill. *al*-boos. White asphodel. Lat. white (the flowers). C and S Eur.
ramosus L. ra-*moh*-soos. Lat. branched (the inflorescence). S Eur., N Africa.

Aspidistra Ker Gawl. (Asparagaceae). as-pi-*dis*-truh. From Gk. a small round shield, from the shape of the stigma. 95 spp. herbs. E Asia.
elatior Blume. ee-*lay*-tee-or. Cast-iron plant. Lat. tall. China.
lurida hort. = *A. elatior*

Asplenium L. (Aspleniaceae). uh-*splee*-nee-oom. Spleenwort. Gk. name used by Dioscorides, not, spleen, referring to med. properties. 700 spp. ferns. Widespread.
nidus L. *nee*-doos. Bird's nest fern. Lat. nest. Trop. Asia.
platyneuron (L.) Oakes. plat-ee-*new*-ron. Ebony spleenwort. Gk. broad-veined. Tropics.

scolopendrium L. skol-oh-*pen*-dree-oom. Hart's tongue fern. Gk. centi-pede (from the arrangement of the sori on the fronds). Eur., E USA, E Canada.
trichomanes L. trie-koh-*may*-neez. Maidenhair spleenwort. Gk. name for a fern.

Astelia Banks & Sol. ex R. Br. (Asteli-aceae). uh-*steel*-ee-uh. Gk. without a trunk (stemless). 25 spp. herbs. Pacific Is., NZ, Australia, Chile.
banksii A. Cunn. *banks*-ee-ee. After Sir Joseph Banks (1743–1820), Eng-lish botanist and explorer who col-lected the type specimen on Cook's first voyage. NZ.
chathamica (Skottsb.) L. B. Moore. chuh-*tam*-i-kuh. Of the Chatham Is. NZ.
nervosa Banks & Sol. ex Hook.f. ner-*voh*-suh. Bush flax. Lat. veined (con-spicuously, the leaves). NZ.

Aster L. (Asteraceae). *as*-tuh. Lat. star (the flowerheads). 180 spp., perenn. herbs, shrubs. Eur., Asia, 1 sp. in N Am.
acris L. = *A. sedifolius*
alpinus L. al-*pie*-noos. Alpine aster. Lat. alpine. Asia, with a subsp. in N Am.
amellus L. uh-*mel*-oos. Italian aster. Lat. name for this or a similar plant. Eur., W Asia.
azureus Lindl. = *Symphyotrichum ool-entangiense*
bigelovii A. Gray = *Dieteria bigelovii*
carolinianus Walter = *Symphyotri-chum carolinianum*
chilensis Nees = *Symphyotrichum chilense*

coloradoensis A. Gray = *Xanthisma coloradoense*

cordifolius L. = *Symphyotrichum cordifolium*

diplostephioides (DC.) C. B. Clarke. dip-loh-stef-ee-*oy*-deez. Gk. like a double crown (the flowerheads). Himal., China.

divaricatus L. = *Eurybia divaricata*

drummondii Lindl. = *Symphyotrichum drummondii*

dumosus L. = *Symphyotrichum dumosum*

ericoides L. = *Symphyotrichum ericoides*

×*frikartii* Silva Tar. & C. K. Schneid. fri-*kar*-tee-ee. After Swiss nurseryman Carl Ludwig Frikart (1879–1964), who raised it. *A. amellus* × *A. thomsonii*. Cult.

glaucodes S. F. Blake = *Eurybia glauca*

×*herveyi* A. Gray = *Eurybia* ×*herveyi*

horizontalis Desf. = *Symphyotrichum lateriflorum* var. *horizontale*

laevis L. = *Symphyotrichum laeve*

lanceolatus Willd. = *Symphyotrichum lanceolatum*

lateriflorus (L.) Britton = *Symphyotrichum lateriflorum*

linariifolius L. = *Ionactis linariifolia*

macrophyllus L. = *Eurybia macrophylla*

novae-angliae L. = *Symphyotrichum novae-angliae*

novi-belgii L. = *Symphyotrichum novi-belgii*

oblongifolius Nutt. = *Symphyotrichum oblongifolium*

oolentangiensis Riddel = *Symphyotrichum oolentangiense*

pilosus Willd. = *Symphyotrichum pilosum*

prenanthoides Muhl. ex Willd. = *Symphyotrichum prenanthoides*

ptarmicoides Torr. & A. Gray = *Solidago ptarmicoides*

puniceus L. = *Symphyotrichum puniceum*

pyrenaeus Desf. ex DC. pi-ruh-*nay*-oos. Lat. of the Pyrenees. France (Pyrenees).

radula Aiton = *Eurybia radula*

sagittifolius Wedem. ex Willd. = *Symphyotrichum cordifolium*

sedifolius L. sed-i-*foh*-lee-oos. Lat. with leaves like *Sedum*. Eur., W and C Asia.

sericeus Vent. = *Symphyotrichum sericeum*

shortii Lindl. = *Symphyotrichum shortii*

simplex Willd. = *Symphyotrichum lanceolatum*

spectabilis Aiton = *Eurybia spectabilis*

tanacetifolius Kunth = *Machaeranthera tanacetifolia*

tataricus L.f. tuh-*ta*-ri-koos. From the reg. of C and E Asia once called Tartary. E Russia, China, Korea, Japan.

thomsonii C. B. Clarke. tom-*soh*-nee-ee. After Thomas Thomson (1817–1878), British surgeon and botanist with the East India Company. Himal.

tongolensis Franch. ton-go-*len*-sis. Of Tongolo (Dong'eluo), Sichuan. W China, Himal.

tradescantii L. = *Symphyotrichum tradescantii*

umbellatus Mill. = *Doellingeria umbellata*

aster, alpine *Aster alpinus*. **aromatic** *Symphyotrichum oblongifolium*.

beach *Erigeron glaucus*. **bigleaf** *Eurybia macrophylla*. **calico** *Symphyotrichum lateriflorum*. **China** *Callistephus chinensis*. **climbing** *Symphyotrichum carolinianum*. **common blue wood** *S. cordifolium*. **crooked stem** *S. prenanthoides*. **Drummond's** *S. drummondii*. **eastern showy** *Eurybia spectabilis*. **flat top white** *Doellingeria umbellata*. **flaxleaf white top** *Ionactis linariifolia*. **grey** *Eurybia glauca*. **Italian** *Aster amellus*. **low rough** *Eurybia radula*. **New England** *Symphyotrichum novae-angliae*. **New York** *S. novi-belgii*. **oldfield** *S. pilosum*. **Pacific** *S. chilense*. **Pringle's** *S. pilosum* var. *pringlei*. **purplestem** *S. puniceum*. **rice button** *S. dumosum*. **seaside purple** *Eurybia spectabilis*. **shore** *Symphyotrichum tradescantii*. **Short's** *S. shortii*. **silky** *S. sericeum*. **sky blue** *S. oolentangiense*. **smooth blue** *S. laeve*. **white heath** *S. ericoides*. **white panicle** *S. lanceolatum*. **white wood** *Eurybia divaricata*

Asteranthera Hanst. (Gesneriaceae). uh-ste-ruhn-*the*-ruh. Gk. star-shaped flowers. 1 sp., woody climber. Chile. *ovata* (Cav.) Hanst. oh-*vah*-tuh. Lat. ovate (the leaves).

Astilbe Buch.-Ham. ex G. Don (Saxifragaceae). uh-*stil*-bee. Gk. without brilliance (the individual flowers are very small). 12 spp. perenn. herbs. E Asia, SE USA.
×*arendsii* Arends. uh-*rend*-zee-ee. After German nurseryman Georg Arends (1863–1952), who raised it. Cult.

chinensis (Maxim.) Franch. & Sav. chin-*en*-sis. Of China. China, NE Asia. var. *davidii* Franch. da-*vid*-ee-ee. After French missionary, botanist and zoologist Armand David (1826–1900), who collected the type specimen in Mongolia in 1864. **'Pumila'.** *pew*-mi-luh. Lat. dwarf. var. *taquetii* (H. Lév.) Vilm. ta-*ket*-ee-ee. After French missionary E. J. Taquet, who collected the type specimen. Korea.
×*crispa* (Arends) Bergmans. *kris*-puh. Lat. wrinkled (the leaves). Cult.
glaberrima Nak. gluh-*be*-ri-muh. More or less glabrous. Japan. var. *saxatilis* Nakai. sax-*a*-ti-lis. Lat. growing on rocks.
japonica (C. Morren & Decne.) A. Gray. juh-*pon*-i-kuh. Of Japan. Japan.
rivularis Buch.-Ham. ex D. Don. riv-ew-*lah*-ris. Lat. of riverbanks. Himal., China, SE Asia. var. *myriantha* (Diels) J. T. Pan. mi-ree-*an*-thuh. Lat. many-flowered. China.
simplicifolia Makino. sim-pli-si-*foh*-lee-uh. Lat. with simple (undivided) leaves. Japan.
thunbergii (Sieb. & Zucc.) Miq. thun-*berg*-ee-ee. After Swedish botanist and physician Carl Peter Thunberg (1743–1828), who collected in Japan and S Africa. Japan.

Astilboides (Hemsl.) Engl. (Saxifragaceae). a-stil-*boy*-deez. Lat. like *Astilbe*. 1 sp., herb. China.
tabularis (Hemsl.) Engl. tab-ew-*lah*-ris. Lat. table-like (the leaves).

Astrantia L. (Apiaceae). uh-*stran*-tee-uh. Masterwort. Poss. from Gk. star (the flowerheads). 8 spp. herbs. Eur., W Asia.

carniolica Wulf. kar-nee-*o*-li-ka. Of
Carniola (now part of Slovenia).
SE Alps.

major L. *may*-juh. Greater masterwort. Lat. large. C and E Eur. subsp.
involucrata (W. D. J. Koch) Ces.
in-vo-lue-*krah*-tuh. Lat. with an
involucre.

maxima Pall. *max*-i-muh. Lat. largest.
Caucasus.

minor L. *mie*-nuh. Lesser masterwort.
Lat. small. S Eur.

Astrolepis Benham (Pteridaceae).
as-troh-*lee*-pis. Gk. star scale, referring to the star-shaped scales on the
fronds. 8 spp. ferns. USA to S Am.

sinuata (Lag. ex Sw.) Benham &
Windham. sin-ew-*ah*-tuh. Wavy
cloak fern. Lat. wavy-edged (the
fronds). S USA to S Am.

Astrophytum Lem. (Cactaceae).
as-troh-*fie*-toom. Gk. star plant,
referring to the shape. 6 spp. cacti.
Texas, Mex.

asterias (Zucc.) Lem. uh-*ste*-ree-oos.
Silver dollar cactus. Gk. like a star
(the plant). Texas, NE Mex.

capricorne (A. Dietr.) Britton & Rose.
kap-ree-*kor*-nee. Goat's horn cactus.
Lat. goat's horn. N Mex.

myriostigma Lem. mi-ree-oh-*stig*-
muh. Bishop's cap cactus. Gk. with
many stigmas. NE Mex.

ornatum (DC.) F. A. C. Weber.
or-*nah*-toom. Star cactus. Lat. ornamental. Mex.

Athrotaxis D. Don (Cupressaceae).
ath-roh-*tax*-is. Gk. crowded arrangement, from the densely arranged
leaves. 2 spp. trees. Tasmania.

cupressoides D. Don. kew-pres-*oy*-
deez. Tasmanian pencil pine. Lat.
like *Cupressus*.

×*laxifolia* Hook. lax-i-*foh*-lee-uh. Lat.
open, leaves (loosely arranged foliage). *A. cupressoides* × *A. selaginoides*.

selaginoides D. Don. se-la-ji-*noy*-deez.
King William pine. Like *Lycopodium
selago* (the foliage).

Athyrium Roth (Woodsiaceae).
uh-*thi*-ree-oom. Gk. without, door
(the sporangia appear not to open).
180 spp. ferns. N hemisph.

filix-femina (L.) Roth. *fi*-lix-*fem*-i-
nuh. Lady fern. Lat. female fern. N
temp. regs.

niponicum (Mett.) Hance. ni-*pon*-i-
koom. Of Japan. E Asia. '**Pictum**'.
pik-toom. Japanese painted fern. Lat.
painted (the fronds).

otophorum (Miq.) Koidz. oh-*to*-fo-
room. Gk. bearing ears (the auricles
on the fronds). E Asia. var. *okanum*
Sa. Kurata. oh-*kah*-noom. After Japanese botanist K. Oka (b. 1918), who
collected the type specimen.

Atriplex L. (Amaranthaceae). *at*-ri-
plex. Lat. name for *A. hortensis*. 250
spp., herbs, shrubs. Widespread.

canescens (Pursh) Nutt. kan-*es*-uhnz.
Four-wing saltbush. Lat. grey (the
foliage). W and C USA, W Canada,
N Mex.

confertifolia (Torr. & Frém.) S.
Watson. kon-fer-ti-*foh*-lee-uh. Spiny
saltbush. Lat. with crowded leaves.
W and C USA, N Mex.

gardneri (Moq.) D. Dietr. *gard*-nuh-
ree. Gardner's saltbush. Intended to
honor the collector of the type
specimen, thought to be Gardner but

who actually was Alexander Gordon.
W and C USA, W Canada.
halimus L. *hal*-i-moos. Sea orache.
Gk. of the sea (it grows on coasts).
S Eur., W Asia, Africa.
hortensis L. hor-*ten*-sis. Orache. Lat.
of gardens. Asia.
lentiformis (Torr.) S. Watson. lent-i-
form-is. Big saltbush, quailbush. Lat.
lens-shaped (the fruit). SW USA,
Mex.
polycarpa (Torr.) S. Watson. pol-ee-
kar-puh. Cattle saltbush. Gk. with
many fruits. SW USA, NW Mex.

Atropa L. (Solanaceae). *a*-tro-puh.
After the Gk. goddess Atropa, who
was said to cut the thread of life.
3 spp. herbs. Eur., Asia.
belladonna L. bel-uh-*don*-uh. Deadly
nightshade. Lat. beautiful woman
(it was used to dilate pupils). Eur.,
W Asia.

aubergine *Solanum melongena*

Aubrieta Adans. (Brassicaceae).
aw-*bree*-shuh. After Claude Aubriet
(1665–1742), French botanical artist.
15 spp. herbs. Eur., W Asia.
deltoidea (L.) DC. del-*toy*-dee-uh. Gk.
deltoid (i.e., triangular, the petals).
SE Eur.

Aucuba Thunb. (Garryaceae). aw-*kew*-
buh. From the Japanese name, which
means green leaf. 5 spp. shrubs.
E Asia.
japonica Thunb. juh-*pon*-i-kuh. Of
Japan. China, Taiwan, Korea, Japan.
'**Crotonifolia**'. kroh-ton-i-*foh*-lee-
uh. Lat. with leaves like croton
(*Codiaeum*). '**Picturata**'. pik-tew-

rah-tuh. Lat. painted (the variegated
leaves).

auricula *Primula auricula*

Aurinia Desv. (Brassicaceae). aw-*rin*-
ee-uh. From Lat. golden (the flowers).
13 spp. herbs. Eur., W Asia.
saxatilis (L.) Desv. sax-*a*-ti-lis. Basket
of gold, golden alyssum. Lat. growing
in rocky places. C and SE Eur.

Austrocedrus Florin & Boutelje
(Cupressaceae). os-troh-*seed*-roos.
Lat. southern cedar. 1 sp., conifer.
Chile, Argentina.
chilensis (D. Don) Pic. Serm. &
Bizzarri. chi-*len*-sis. Chilean cedar.
Of Chile.

Avena L. (Poaceae). uh-*vee*-nuh. The
Lat. name. 25 spp. grasses. Eur., W
Asia, E Africa.
sativa L. sa-*tee*-vuh. Oats. Lat. cultivated. Cult.

avens *Geum*. **alpine** *G. montanum*.
mountain *Dryas octopetala*. **water**
Geum rivale

Averrhoa L. (Oxalidaceae). a-vee-*roh*-
uh. After Averroes, 12th-cent. Moor-
ish philosopher. 2 spp., trees, shrubs.
SE Asia.
carambola L. kuh-*ram*-bo-luh. Starfruit. Portuguese name, from San-
skrit, appetiser.

avocado *Persea americana*

Azara Ruiz & Pav. (Salicaceae).
uh-*zar*-ruh. After José Nicolás de

Azara (1730–1804), Spanish diplomat. 10 spp., shrubs, trees. S Am.

dentata Ruiz & Pav. den-*tah*-tuh. Lat. toothed (the leaves). Chile.

integrifolia Ruiz & Pav. in-teg-ri-*foh*-lee-uh. Lat. entire (the leaves). Chile, Argentina.

lanceolata Hook.f. lahn-see-oh-*lah*-tuh. Lat. lance-shaped (the leaves). Chile, Argentina.

microphylla Hook.f. mik-*rof*-i-luh. Gk. small-leaved. Chile, Argentina.

serrata Ruiz & Pav. se-*rah*-tuh. Lat. saw-toothed (the leaves). Chile.

azarole *Crataegus azarolus*

Azolla Lam. (Azollaceae). uh-*zol*-uh. Gk. to dry, to kill (they are drought sensitive). 5 spp. ferns. Widespread.

caroliniana Willd. ka-ro-lin-ee-*ah*-nuh. Mosquito fern. Of the Carolinas. E USA, trop. Am.

filiculoides Lam. fi-lik-ew-*loy*-deez. Lat. like a little fern. N and S Am.

Babiana Ker Gawl. (Iridaceae).
bab-ee-*ah*-nuh. Baboon flower. 90
spp. herbs. S Africa.
stricta (Aiton) Ker Gawl. *strik*-tuh.
Lat. upright (the stems).

baboon flower *Babiana*
baby blue-eyes *Nemophila menziesii*
baby's breath *Gypsophila paniculata*.
annual *G. elegans*
baby's tears *Soleirolia soleirolii*

Baccharis L. (Asteraceae). *bak*-uh-ris.
After Bacchus, Roman god of wine.
400 spp., herbs, shrubs, trees.
Americas.
halimifolia L. ha-li-mi-*foh*-lee-uh. Lat.
with leaves like *Atriplex halimus*. Sea
myrtle, tree groundsel. E USA, Mex.,
W Indies.
patagonica (Lam.) Pers. pat-uh-*gon*-i-
kuh. Of Patagonia. Chile, Argentina.
pilularis DC. pil-ew-*lah*-ris. Coyotebrush. Lat. bearing little balls (the
flowerheads). W USA.

baldmoney *Meum athamanticum*
balloon flower *Platycodon grandiflorus*
balloon plant *Asclepias physocarpa*

balloon vine *Cardiospermum halicacabum*

Ballota L. (Lamiaceae). buh-*lot*-uh.
Gk. name for *B. nigra*. 30 spp., herbs,
shrubs. Eur., Medit., Africa.
nigra L. *nie*-gruh. Black horehound.
Lat. black. Eur., N Africa.
pseudodictamnus (L.) Benth.
sue-doh-dik-*tam*-noos. Gk. false
Dictamnus. SE Eur.

balmony *Chelone glabra*
balsam, garden *Impatiens balsamina*

Balsamita major Desf. = *Tanacetum
balsamita*
vulgaris Willd. = *Tanacetum
balsamita*

bamboo, black *Phyllostachys nigra*.
candy stripe *Himalayacalamus falconeri*. **heavenly** *Nandina domestica*.
Himalayan blue *Himalayacalamus
hookerianus*. **lucky** *Dracaena
braunii*. **marbled** *Chimonobambusa
marmorea*. **sacred** *Nandina domestica*. **walking stick** *Chimonobambusa tumidissinoda*
baneberry, red *Actaea rubra*. **white**
A. pachypoda

Banksia L.f. (Proteaceae). *banks*-ee-
uh. After Sir Joseph Banks (1743–
1820), English botanist and explorer
who collected the first specimens at
Botany Bay, Australia, in 1770 on the
voyage with Cook. 80 spp., trees,
shrubs. Australia.
integrifolia L.f. in-teg-ri-*foh*-lee-uh.
Coast banksia. Lat. with entire
leaves. E Australia.

marginata Cav. mar-ji-*nah*-tuh. Silver banksia. Lat. edged (the leaves with teeth). SE Australia.
serrata L.f. se-*rah*-tuh. Saw leaf banksia. Lat. saw-toothed (the leaves). SE Australia.

banksia, coast *Banksia integrifolia.* **saw leaf** *B. serrata.* **silver** *B. marginata*

Baptisia Vent. (Fabaceae). bap-*tiz*-ee-uh. From Gk. to dye, as some were used in dyeing. 15 spp. herbs. N Am.
alba (L.) Vent. *al*-buh. White wild indigo. Lat. white (the flowers). E USA. var. *macrophylla* (Larisey) Isely. mak-*rof*-i-luh. Gk. large-leaved.
australis (L.) R. Br. os-*trah*-lis. Blue wild indigo. Lat. southern. E USA, SE Canada. var. *minor* (Lehm.) Fernald. *mie*-nuh. Lat. small.
leucantha Torr. & A. Gray = *B. alba* var. *macrophylla*
minor Lehm. = *B. australis* var. *minor*
sphaerocarpa Nutt. sfair-roh-*kar*-puh. Yellow wild indigo. Gk. spherical fruit. S USA.
tinctoria (L.) R. Br. tink-*tor*-ree-uh. Horsefly weed. Lat. of dyers. E USA, SE Canada.

Barbarea R. Br. (Brassicaceae). bar-*bair*-ree-uh. After St. Barbara (4th cent.), perhaps because it was the only food available on that saint's day (Dec 4). 20 spp. herbs. N temp. regs.
praecox (Sm.) R. Br. = *B. verna*
verna (Mill.) Asch. *ver*-nuh. Land cress. Lat. of spring. SW Eur.
vulgaris R. Br. vul-*gar*-ris. Yellow rocket. Lat. common. Eur.

barberry *Berberis.* **common** *B. vulgaris.* **netleaf** *B. dictyophylla*
barley *Hordeum vulgare.* **foxtail** *H. jubatum*
barrenwort *Epimedium*
basil *Ocimum basilicum.* **African** *O. americanum.* **American** *O. americanum*
basket flower *Centaurea americana*
basket of gold *Aurinia saxatilis*

Bassia All. (Amaranthaceae). *bas*-ee-uh. After Italian botanist Ferdinando Bassi (1710–1774). 25 spp. herbs. Widespread.
scoparia (L.) A. J. Scott. skoh-*pair*-ree-uh. Burning bush, summer cypress. Lat. broom-like. Eur., Asia.

basswood *Tilia americana*
bastard balm *Melittis melissophyllum*
bay, bull *Magnolia grandiflora.* **California** *Umbellularia californica.* **swamp** *Magnolia virginiana.* **sweet** *Laurus nobilis, Magnolia virginiana*
bay laurel *Laurus nobilis*
bayberry, northern *Morella pensylvanica.* **southern** *M. cerifera*
bead plant *Nertera granadensis*
bead tree *Melia azedarach*
bean *Phaseolus.* **broad** *Vicia faba.* **butter** *Phaseolus lunatus.* **dwarf** *P. vulgaris.* **French** *P. vulgaris.* **Lima** *P. lunatus.* **runner** *P. coccineus*
bear's breeches *Acanthus*
bear's paws *Cotyledon tomentosa*
bearberry *Arctostaphylos uva-ursi*

Beaucarnea Lem. (Asparagaceae). boh-*kar*-nee-uh. After Jean-Baptiste Beaucarne, 19th-cent. Belgian plant collector. 9 spp. herbs. Mex., C Am.

recurvata Lem. ree-kur-*vah*-tuh. Lat. recurved (the leaves). Mex.

beauty berry *Callicarpa*
beauty bush *Kolkwitzia amabilis*
bedstraw *Galium.* **lady's** *G. verum*
bee balm *Monarda.* **lemon** *M. citriodora.* **spotted** *M. punctata*
beech *Fagus.* **American** *F. grandifolia.* **Antarctic** *Nothofagus antarctica.* **blue** *Carpinus caroliniana.* **European** *Fagus sylvatica.* **roble** *Nothofagus obliqua.* **southern** *Nothofagus*
beefsteak plant *Acalypha wilkesiana, Iresine herbstii*
beetleweed *Galax urceolata*
beetroot *Beta vulgaris*
beggarticks *Desmodium.* **Arizona** *Bidens aurea.* **devil's** *B. frondosa.* **nodding** *B. cernua*

Begonia L. (Begoniaceae). bee-*goh*-nee-uh. After Michel Bégon (1638–1710), French official and plant collector. 1400 spp., herbs, subshrubs. Tropics and subtropics.
boliviensis A. DC. bo-liv-ee-*en*-sis. Of Bolivia. Bolivia, NW Argentina.
dregei Otto & Dietr. *dreg*-ee-ee. After Johann Franz Drège (1794–1881), German plant collector. The type specimen was taken from plants at Berlin Botanic Garden grown from his introduction. S Africa.
evansiana Andrews = *B. grandis*
foliosa Kunth. foh-lee-*oh*-suh. Lat. leafy. NW S Am. var. *miniata* (A. DC.) L. B. Sm. & Schub. = *B. fuchsioides*
fuchsioides Hook. fue-shee-*oy*-deez. Like *Fuchsia.* Colombia, Venezuela.
grandis Dryand. *gran*-dis. Lat. large. S China.

×*hiemalis* Fotsch. heem-*ah*-lis. Lat. of winter. *B. socotrana* × *B.* ×*tuberhybrida.* Cult.
luxurians Scheidw. lux-*ewr*-ree-anz. Lat. extravagant, profuse. SE Brazil.
masoniana Irmsch. ex Ziesenh. may-son-ee-*ah*-nuh. Iron cross begonia. After English plant collector Maurice Mason, who introduced it from Singapore in 1952. S China, Malaysia.
palmata D. Don. pahl-*mah*-tuh. Lat. palmate (the leaves). Himal. to SE Asia.
Rex-cultorum Group. rex-kul-*tor*-room. Lat. *B. rex* of cultivation, mainly hybrids. Cult.
Semperflorens-cultorum Group. sem-per-*flaw*-ruhnz. Lat. *B. semperflorens* of cultivation, mainly hybrids. Cult.
serratipetala Irmsch. se-rah-tee-*pet*-uh-luh. Lat. with toothed petals. New Guinea.
solananthera A. DC. sol-uhn-*an*-the-ruh. Lat. with *Solanum*-like anthers. SE Brazil.
sutherlandii Hook.f. su-tHuh-*land*-ee-ee. After Peter Cormack Sutherland (1822–1900), Scottish doctor who collected the type specimen in 1861. S Africa.
×*tuberhybrida* Voss. tew-buh-*hib*-rid-uh. Lat. tuberous hybrid. *B. boliviensis* × *B. pearcei* × *B. veitchii.* Cult.

Belamcanda chinensis (L.) DC. = *Iris domestica*

Bellevalia Lapeyr. (Asparagaceae). bel-*val*-ee-uh. After French physician and botanist Pierre Richer de Belleval (1564–1632), who founded the

Jardin des Plantes in Montpellier in 1593. 64 spp. bulbous herbs. Medit. to C Asia.

paradoxa (Fisch. & C. A. Mey.) Boiss. pa-ruh-*dox*-uh. Lat. unusual. W Asia.

romana (L.) Sweet. roh-*mah*-nuh. Roman hyacinth. Lat. Roman. S Eur., N Egypt.

bellflower *Campanula*. **Adriatic** *C. garganica*. **Aleutian** *C. chamissonis*. **American** *C. americana*. **bearded** *C. barbata*. **chimney** *C. pyramidalis*. **clustered** *C. glomerata*. **creeping** *C. rapunculoides*. **Dalmatian** *C. portenschlagiana*. **giant** *C. latifolia*. **Italian** *C. isophylla*. **Korean** *C. takesimana*. **milky** *C. lactiflora*. **nettle-leaved** *C. trachelium*. **peach-leaved** *C. persicifolia*. **spotted** *C. punctata*. **trailing** *C. poscharskyana*. **tussock** *C. carpatica*

Bellis L. (Asteraceae). *bel*-is. The Lat. name, from Lat. pretty. 8 spp. herbs. Eur., Medit., W Asia.

perennis L. pe-*ren*-is. Daisy. Lat. perennial. Eur., W Asia.

bells of Ireland *Moluccella laevis*
bellwort *Uvularia*

Beloperone guttata Brandegee = *Justicia brandegeeana*

Benincasa Savi (Cucurbitaceae). ben-in-*kas*-uh. After Giuseppe Benincasa, 16th-cent. Flemish botanist. 1 sp., herb. SE Asia.

hispida (Thunb.) Cogn. *his*-pid-uh. Wax gourd. Lat. with rough hairs.

Berberidopsis Hook.f. (Berberidopsidaceae). ber-be-ri-*dop*-sis. Lat. resembling *Berberis*. 2 spp. woody climbers. Chile, Australia.

corallina Hook.f. ko-ruh-*leen*-uh. Coral plant. Lat. coral-red (the flowers). Chile.

Berberis L. (Berberidaceae). *ber*-buh-ris. Barberry. From the Arabic name. 500 spp. shrubs. N hemisph., S Am.

buxifolia Lam. = *B. microphylla*

calliantha Mulligan. kal-ee-*anth*-uh. Gk. beautiful flower. Tibet.

candidula C. K. Schneid. kan-*did*-ewluh. Lat. bright white (the leaf underside). China.

×*carminea* Ahrendt. kar-*min*-ee-uh. Medieval Lat. carmine (the fruit). *B. aggregata* × *B. wilsoniae*. Cult.

darwinii Hook. dar-*win*-ee-ee. After English naturalist Charles Darwin (1809–1882), who collected the type specimen in 1835 during the voyage of the *Beagle*. Chile.

dictyophylla Franch. dik-tee-oh-*fil*-uh. Netleaf barberry. Gk. net-leaved. W China.

×*frikartii* C. K. Schneid. ex Van de Laar. fri-*kar*-tee-ee. After Swiss nurseryman Carl Ludwig Frikart (1879–1964), who raised it. *B. candidula* × *B. verruculosa*. Cult.

gagnepainii C. K. Schneid. gan-yuh-*pan*-ee-ee. After François Gagnepain (1866–1952), French botanist. China. var. *lanceifolia* Ahrendt. lahn-see-i-*foh*-lee-uh. Lat. with lance-shaped leaves.

×*gladwynensis* E. Anders. glad-win-*en*-sis. Of Gladwyne, Pennsylvania, where it was raised. *B. gagnepainii* × *B. verruculosa*. Cult.

×*hybridogagnepainii* Suringar. hib-ri-doh-gan-yuh-*pan*-ee-ee. Hybrid of *B. gagnepainii. B. candidula* × *B. gagnepainii.* Cult.

×*interposita* Ahrendt. in-ter-*poz*-i-tuh. Lat. put between (the parents). *B. hookeri* × *B. verruculosa.* Cult.

julianae C. K. Schneid. jue-lee-*ah*-nee. After Juliana, wife of author Camillo Schneider. China.

linearifolia Phil. = *B. trigona*

×*lologensis* Sandwith. lo-log-*en*-sis. Of Lago (lake) Lolog, where the type specimen was collected in 1927. *B. darwinii* × *B. trigona.* Argentina.

×*media* Groot. *mee*-dee-uh. Lat. inter-mediate (between the parents). *B.* ×*chenaultii* × *B. thunbergii.* Cult.

'Mentorensis'. men-to-*ren*-sis. Of Mentor, Ohio, where it was raised. *B. julianae* × *B. thunbergii.*

microphylla G. Forst. mik-*rof*-i-luh. Gk. small-leaved. Chile, Argentina.

×*ottawensis* C. K. Schneid. ot-uh-*wen*-sis. Of Ottawa, where it was raised. *B. thunbergii* × *B. vulgaris.* Cult.

×*stenophylla* Lindl. sten-*of*-i-luh. Gk. narrow-leaved. *B. darwinii* × *B. empetrifolia.* Cult.

thunbergii DC. thun-*berg*-ee-ee. After Swedish botanist and physician Carl Peter Thunberg (1743–1828), who collected in Japan and S Africa. Japan.

trigona Kunze ex Poepp. & Endl. tri-*goh*-nuh. Gk. three-angled (the shoots). Chile, Argentina.

valdiviana Phil. val-div-ee-*ah*-nuh. Of Valdivia. Chile.

verruculosa Hemsl. & E. H. Wilson. ve-rue-kew-*loh*-suh. Lat. warty (the shoots). China.

vulgaris L. vul-*gar*-ris. Common barberry. Lat. common. Eur., N Africa, W Asia.

wilsoniae Hemsl. wil-*son*-ee-ie. After Ellen Wilson (ca. 1872–1930), whose husband, E. H. Wilson, collected the type specimen in 1903. W China.

Bergenia Moench (Saxifragaceae). ber-*gen*-ee-uh. After Karl August von Bergen (1704–1759), German botanist. 10 spp. perenn. herbs. E Asia.

ciliata (Haw.) Sternb. sil-ee-*ah*-tuh. Lat. edged with fine hairs (the leaves). Himal.

cordifolia (Haw.) Sternb. = *B. crassifolia*

crassifolia Fritsch. kras-i-*foh*-lee-uh. Lat. with thick leaves. NE Asia.

delavayi (Franch.) Engl. = *B. purpurascens*

purpurascens (Hook.f. & Thomson) Engl. pur-pew-*ras*-uhnz. Lat. becoming purple (the leaves). Himal., W China.

×*schmidtii* (Regel) Silva Tar. *shmit*-ee-ee. After Carl Schmidt of the Haage & Schmidt nursery, Erfurt, Germany, whence it was described. *B. ciliata* × *B. crassifolia.* Cult.

stracheyi (Hook.f. & Thomson) Engl. *stray*-kee-ee. After Lt.-Gen. Sir Richard Strachey (1817–1908), English army officer in India, who, with J. E. Winterbottom, collected the type specimen. Himal.

Bessera Schult.f. (Asparagaceae). *bes*-uh-ruh. After Wilbald von Besser (1784–1842), Austrian botanist. 3 spp. herbs. Mex.

elegans Schult.f. *el*-i-ganz. Coral drops. Lat. elegant.

Beta L. (Amaranthaceae). *bee*-tuh. The Lat. name. 12 spp. herbs. Eur., Medit.
vulgaris L. vul-*gar*-ris. Beetroot, sugarbeet. Lat. common.

betony *Stachys officinalis*

Betula L. (Betulaceae). *bet*-ew-luh. Birch. From the Lat. name. 35 spp., trees, shrubs. N hemisph.
albosinensis Burkill. al-boh-sin-*en*-sis. Lat. white, of China (i.e., the Chinese white birch). W China. var. *septentrionalis* C. K. Schneid. sep-ten-tree-oh-*nah*-lis. Lat. northern.
alleghaniensis Britton. al-ee-gan-ee-*en*-sis. Yellow birch. Of the Allegheny Mts. E USA, E Canada.
ermanii Cham. er-*man*-ee-ee. Erman birch. After German physicist Georg Adolf Erman (1806–1877), who collected it in Kamchatka. NE Asia.
fontinalis Sarg. = *B. occidentalis*
jacquemontii Spach = *B. utilis* var. *jacquemontii*
lenta L. *len*-tuh. Cherry birch, sweet birch. Lat. flexible (the shoots). E USA, E Canada.
lutea Michx. = *B. alleghaniensis*
maximowicziana Reg. max-im-oh-vich-*ee*-ah-nuh. Monarch birch. After Carl Johann Maximowicz (1827–1891), Russian botanist. Japan.
nana L. *nah*-nuh. Dwarf birch. Lat. dwarf. N Eur., NE Canada, Greenland.
nigra L. *nie*-gruh. Red birch, river birch. Lat. black (bark of mature trees). E USA.

occidentalis Hook. ok-si-den-*tah*-lis. Water birch. Lat. western. W USA, W Canada.
papyrifera Marshall. pa-pi-*ri*-fe-ruh. Paper birch. Lat. bearing paper (the bark). N USA, Canada.
pendula Roth. *pen*-dew-luh. Silver birch. Lat. pendulous (the shoots). Eur., N Asia.
platyphylla Suk. plat-ee-*fil*-uh. Gk. broad-leaved. NE Asia.
populifolia Marshall. pop-ew-li-*foh*-lee-uh. Grey birch. Lat. with leaves like *Populus*. NE USA, SE Canada.
pubescens Ehrh. pew-*bes*-uhnz. Downy birch. Lat. hairy. Eur., N Asia.
utilis D. Don. *ew*-ti-lis. Himalayan birch. Lat. useful (the bark and wood). Himal., China. var. *jacquemontii* (Spach) H. J. P. Winkl. jak-*mont*-ee-ee. After French botanist and geologist Victor Jacquemont (1801–1832), who collected the type specimen.

Bidens L. (Asteraceae). *bee*-duhnz. Lat. with two teeth, referring to the fruit. 200 spp., herbs, shrubs, climbers. Widespread.
aurea (Aiton) Sherff. *aw*-ree-uh. Arizona beggarticks. Lat. golden (the flowers). S USA, Mex., C Am.
cernua L. *sern*-ew-uh. Nodding beggarticks. Lat. nodding. Eur., W Asia.
frondosa L. fron-*doh*-suh. Devil's beggarticks. Lat. leafy. USA, E Canada.
heterophylla Ortega = *B. aurea*

Bignonia L. (Bignoniaceae). big-*noh*-nee-uh. After Jean-Paul Bignon (1662–1743), librarian to King Louis

XIV of France. 28 spp. climbers.
Warm and trop. Am.
capreolata L. kap-ree-oh-*lah*-tuh.
Crossvine. Lat. bearing tendrils.
SE USA.

Billardiera Sm. (Pittosporaceae).
bil-ar-dee-*e*-ruh. After French botanist Jacques-Julien Houtou de La
Billardiere (1755–1834). 24 spp.
climbers. Australia.
heterophylla (Lindl.) L. Cayzer &
Crisp. het-uh-*rof*-i-luh. Bluebell
creeper. Gk. with variable leaves.
SW Australia.
longiflora Lab. long-gi-*flaw*-ruh. Lat.
long-flowered. Tasmania.

birch *Betula*. **cherry** *B. lenta*. **downy**
B. pubescens. **dwarf** *B. nana*. **Erman**
B. ermanii. **grey** *B. populifolia*.
Himalayan *B. utilis*. **monarch** *B.
maximowicziana*. **paper** *B. papyrifera*. **red** *B. nigra*. **river** *B. nigra*.
silver *B. pendula*. **sweet** *B. lenta*.
water *B. occidentalis*. **yellow** *B.
alleghaniensis*
bird of paradise flower *Strelitzia
reginae*
bird of paradise shrub *Caesalpinia
gilliesii*
bird's eyes *Gilia tricolor*
bird's foot trefoil *Lotus corniculatus*
bishop's mitre *Epimedium*
bistort *Persicaria bistorta*
bitterbrush *Purshia tridentata*
bittercress *Cardamine*. **coral-root**
C. bulbifera
bitternut *Carya cordiformis*
bitterroot *Lewisia rediviva*
bittersweet, American *Celastrus
scandens*. **oriental** *C. orbiculatus*

black cumin *Nigella sativa*
black-eyed Susan *Rudbeckia hirta*,
Thunbergia alata
black horehound *Ballota nigra*
black sarana *Fritillaria camschatcensis*
blackberry *Rubus fruticosus*
blackthorn *Prunus spinosa*
blackwood *Acacia melanoxylon*
bladder senna *Colutea arborescens*
bladdernut *Staphylea*. **American** *S.
trifolia*
blanket flower *Gaillardia*
blazing star *Chamaelirium luteum*,
Liatris, *Mentzelia*
bleeding heart *Lamprocapnos spectabilis*. **Pacific** *Dicentra formosa*
bleeding heart vine *Clerodendrum
thomsoniae*

Blechnum L. (Blechnaceae). *blek-
noom*. From Gk. name of a fern. 180
spp. ferns. Widespread.
chilense (Kaulf.) Mett. chi-*len*-see. Of
Chile. Chile, Argentina.
discolor (G. Forst.) Keys. *dis*-ko-lor.
Crown fern. Lat. two-coloured (the
fronds). NZ.
fluviatile (R. Br.) Salom. flue-vee-*a*-ti-
lee. Lat. of rivers. SE Australia, NZ.
magellanicum (Hook.) Mett. maj-uh-
lan-i-koom. Of the Magellan reg.
Tierra del Fuego, Falklands.
novae-zelandiae T. C. Chambers &
P. A. Farrant. *noh*-vie-zee-*lan*-dee-ie.
Of New Zealand. NZ.
nudum (Labill.) Mett. ex Luerss. *new*-
doom. Fishbone water fern. Lat.
naked (the frond stalks). Australia.
penna-marina (Poir.) Kuhn. *pen*-uh-
ma-ri-nuh. Dwarf hard fern. Lat. sea
pen (which the fronds resemble).
Australia, S Am., NZ.

spicant (L.) Roth. *spee*-kuhnt. Deer fern, hard fern. Lat. tufted. Eur., Asia, W USA, W Canada.
tabulare (Thunb.) Kuhn. tab-ew-*lah*-ree. Lat. of Table Mt., where it was first collected. S Africa.

Bletilla Rchb.f. (Orchidaceae). blet-*il*-uh. Diminutive of the related *Bletia* (after Louis Blet, 18th-cent. Spanish apothecary). 5 spp. orchids. E and SE Asia.
striata (Thunb.) Rchb.f. stree-*ah*-tuh. Lat. striped (the pleated leaves). China, Korea, Japan.

bloodflower *Asclepias curassavica*
bloodroot *Sanguinaria canadensis*
blue mistflower *Conoclinium coelestinum*
blue star creeper *Lobelia pedunculata*
blue thimble flower *Gilia capitata*
bluebell *Hyacinthoides non-scripta*.
   California *Phacelia campanularia*.
   Scottish *Campanula rotundifolia*.
   Spanish *Hyacinthoides hispanica*
bluebell creeper *Billardiera heterophylla*
blueberry *Vaccinium corymbosum*.
   lowbush *V. angustifolium*. **New Zealand** *Dianella nigra*
blueblossom *Ceanothus thyrsiflorus*.
   creeping *C. thyrsiflorus* var. *repens*
blue-eyed grass *Sisyrinchium bermudiana*
blue-eyed Mary *Omphalodes verna*
bluejoint *Calamagrostis canadensis*
bluestar *Amsonia*
bluestem, big *Andropogon gerardii*.
   bushy *A. glomeratus*. **little** *Schizachyrium scoparium*

bluets *Houstonia caerulea*

Boenninghausenia Rchb. ex Meissn. (Rutaceae). bur-ning-how-*zen*-ee-uh. After Clemens Maria Franz Freiherr (Baron) von Bönninghausen (1785–1864), Dutch lawyer and botanist. 1 sp., shrub. E Asia.
albiflora (Hook.) Meissn. al-bi-*flaw*-ruh. Lat. white-flowered.

bog arum *Calla palustris*
bog myrtle *Myrica gale*
bogbean *Menyanthes trifoliata*

Bolboschoenus (Asch.) Palla (Cyperaceae). bol-boh-*skeen*-oos. Bulrushes. Gk. bulb reed, referring to the corms. 14 spp. perenn. herbs. Widespread.
fluviatilis (Torr.) Soják. flue-vee-*at*-i-lis. Lat. of rivers. N Am., N Mex., E Australia, NZ.
maritimus (L.) Palla. muh-*rit*-i-moos. Lat. of the sea (it often grows on coasts).

Boltonia L'Hér. (Asteraceae). bowl-*toh*-nee-uh. After James Bolton (1758–1799), English botanist. 6 spp. herbs. N Am.
asteroides (L.) L'Hér. as-tuh-*roy*-deez. White doll's daisy. Lat. like *Aster*.

Bongardia C. A. Mey. (Berberidaceae). bon-*gard*-ee-uh. After August Gustav Heinrich von Bongard (1786–1839), German botanist. 1 sp., herb. E Medit.
chrysogonum (L.) Spach. kris-*og*-on-oom. Gk. golden, knee (yellow flowers, jointed stems).

bonnet bellflower *Codonopsis clematidea*

borage *Borago officinalis.* **dwarf** *B. pygmaea*

Borago L. (Boraginaceae). bo-*rah*-goh. Possibly from Lat. hairy garment, referring to the hairy shoots and leaves. 3 spp. herbs. Eur., Africa, Asia.
officinalis L. o-fis-i-*nah*-lis. Borage. Lat. sold as a med. herb. S Eur., N Africa, W Asia.
pygmaea (DC.) Chater & Greuter. *pig*-mee-uh. Dwarf borage. Lat. dwarf. S Eur.

Boston ivy *Parthenocissus tricuspidata*
bottlebrush *Callistemon.* **weeping** *C. viminalis*

Bougainvillea Comm. ex Juss. (Nyctaginaceae). bue-guhn-*vil*-ee-uh. After French explorer Louis-Antoine, Comte de Bougainville (1729–1811). 18 spp. climbers. Trop. Am.
×***buttiana*** Holttum & Standl. but-ee-*ah*-nuh. After Mrs R. V. Butt, who brought it from Cartagena, Colombia, to Trinidad in 1910. *B. glabra* × *B. peruviana.* Cult.
glabra Choisy. *glab*-ruh. Lat. glabrous (the leaves). Brazil.
spectabilis Willd. spek-*tab*-i-lis. Lat. spectacular. Brazil.

bouncing Bet *Saponaria officinalis*

Bouteloua Lag. (Poaceae). bue-tuh-*lue*-uh. After Esteban Boutelou (1776–1813), Spanish botanist. 40 spp. grasses. Americas.
curtipendula (Michx.) Torr. kurt-ee-*pen*-dew-luh. Sideoats grama grass.

Lat. short, drooping (the flower spikes). N and S Am.
dactyloides (Nutt.) J. T. Columbus. dak-til-*oy*-deez. Buffalo grass. Like *Dactylis.* Canada, USA, Mex.
gracilis (Kunth) Lag. ex Griffiths. *gras*-i-lis. Blue grama grass. Lat. slender (the stems). Canada, USA, Mex.

Bouvardia Salisb. (Rutaceae). bue-var-dee-uh. After Charles Bouvard (1572–1658), French chemist and physician to Louis XIII. 20 spp. shrubs. Trop. Am.
ternifolia (Cav.) Schltdl. tern-i-*foh*-lee-uh. Lat. with leaves in threes. SW USA, Mex.

bower plant *Pandorea jasminoides*
box, Balearic *Buxus balearica.*
Christmas *Sarcococca.* **common** *Buxus sempervirens.* **sweet** *Sarcococca*
box elder *Acer negundo*

Brachyscome Cass. (Asteraceae). brak-i-*skoh*-mee. Gk. a short head of hair, from the short pappus. 80 spp. herbs. Australia, NZ.
iberidifolia Benth. i-be-ri-di-*foh*-lee-uh. Swan River daisy. Lat. with leaves like *Iberis.* W and S Australia.

Brachyglottis J. R. & G. Forst. (Asteraceae). brak-ee-*glot*-is. Gk. short tongue (referring to the short ray florets). 40 spp. shrubs. Australia, NZ.
compacta (Kirk) B. Nord. kom-*pak*-tuh. Lat. compact. NZ (N.I.).
monroi (Hook.f.) B. Nord. mon-*roh*-ee. After Sir David Monro (1813–1877), Scottish-born NZ politician. A shepherd, Roderick

McDonald, collected the type specimen for him. NZ (S.I.).

bramble *Rubus fruticosus*
brass buttons *Cotula coronopifolia*

Brassica L. (Brassicaceae). *bras*-i-kuh. Lat. name of the cabbage. 40 spp. herbs. Eur., N Africa, Asia.
hirta Moench. *hur*-tuh. White mustard. Lat. hairy. Medit., W Asia.
juncea (L.) Czerniak. *jun*-see-uh. Chinese mustard. Lat. rush-like. E Asia.
napus L. *nah*-poos. Rape. Lat. turnip. Cult. **Napobrassica Group**. nah-poh-*bras*-i-kuh. Swede. Lat. turnip cabbage.
nigra (L.) W. D. J. Koch. *nie*-gruh. Black mustard. Lat. black (the seeds).
oleracea L. ol-uh-*ray*-see-uh. Wild cabbage. Lat. vegetable-like. Eur. **Acephala Group**. ay-*kef*-uh-luh. Kale. Lat. without a head. **Botrytis Group**. bo-*trie*-tis. Broccoli, cauliflower. Gk. like a bunch of grapes. **Capitata Group**. kap-i-*tah*-tuh. Cabbage. Lat. with a head. **Gemmifera Group**. gem-*i*-fe-ruh. Brussels sprouts. Lat. bearing buds. **Gongylodes Group**. gon-gil-*oh*-deez. Kohlrabi. Gk. swollen (the tuber). **Italica Group**. i-*tal*-i-kuh. Sprouting broccoli. Lat. Italian.
rapa L. *rah*-puh. Lat. turnip. N Africa. **Rapifera Group**. ra-*pi*-fuh-ruh. Turnip. Lat. bearing turnips. **Pekinensis Group**. pee-kin-*en*-sis. Chinese cabbage. Of Peking.

Brazilian plume *Justicia carnea*
briar, Austrian *Rosa foetida*. **Austrian copper** *R. foetida* 'Bicolor'. **sweet** *R. rubiginosa*

bridal wreath *Francoa sonchifolia*

Brimeura Salisb. (Asparagaceae). brie-*mew*-ruh. After Marie de Brimeur, 16th-cent. French gardener. 3 spp. bulbous herbs. SW Eur.
amethystina (L.) Chouard. am-uh-this-*tee*-nuh. Lat. violet (the flowers). Pyrenees, N Spain.

Briza L. (Poaceae). *bree*-zuh. Quaking grass. Gk. name for rye. 20 spp. grasses. Eur., Asia, Mex. to S Am.
maxima L. *max*-i-muh. Great quaking grass. Lat. largest. Medit.
media L. *mee*-dee-uh. Common quaking grass. Lat. medium. Eur., Asia.
subaristata Lam. sub-a-ris-*tah*-tuh. Lat. somewhat aristate (the lemmas). Mex. to S Am.

broccoli *Brassica oleracea* Botrytis Group. **sprouting** *B. oleracea* Italica Group

Brodiaea Sm. (Asparagaceae). broh-dee-*ie*-uh. After James Brodie (1724–1844), Scottish botanist. 16 spp. cormous herbs. W N Am.
californica Lindl. ex Lem. kal-i-*for*-ni-kuh. Of California. Calif.
coronaria (Salisb.) Jeps. ko-ro-*nair*-ree-uh. Lat. of garlands. W USA, SW Canada.
elegans Hoover. *el*-i-ganz. Lat. elegant. W USA.

brome *Bromus*

Bromus L. (Poaceae). *broh*-moos. Brome. From Gk. name of an edible grass. 150 spp. grasses. Widespread.

inermis Leysser. in-*er*-mis. Lat. unarmed (the awnless lemmas). Eur., Asia.

broom *Cytisus, Genista.* **common** *Cytisus scoparius.* **Mount Etna** *Genista aetnensis.* **pineapple** *Cytisus battandieri.* **pink** *Carmichaelia carmichaeliae* **purple** *Chamaecytisus purpureus.* **Spanish** *Genista hispanica, Spartium junceum*
broombush *Hypericum prolificum*

Broussonetia L'Hér. ex Vent. (Moraceae). brue-son-*et*-ee-uh. After Pierre Marie Auguste Broussonet (1761–1807), French naturalist. 8 spp., trees, shrubs. Asia, Madagascar.
papyrifera (L.) Vent. pa-pi-*rif*-uh-ruh. Paper mulberry. Lat. bearing paper. E Asia.

Browallia L. (Solanaceae). broh-*wah*-lee-uh. After Johan Browall (1707–1755), Swedish botanist. 5 spp., herbs, shrubs. S USA to S Am.
americana L. uh-me-ri-*kah*-nuh. Jamaican forget-me-not. Of America. Trop. Am.
speciosa Hook. spee-see-*oh*-suh. Sapphire flower. Lat. showy. Trop. Am.

brown-eyed Susan *Rudbeckia triloba*

Brugmansia Pers. (Solanaceae). broog-*man*-zee-uh. After Sebald Justinus Brugmans (1763–1819), Dutch botanist. 5 spp. shrubs. S Am.
arborea (L.) Lagerh. ar-*bor*-ree-uh. Lat. tree-like.
×*candida* Pers. *kan*-di-duh. Lat. white (the flowers). *B. aurea* × *B. versicolor.* Cult.

×*insignis* (Barb. Rodr.) Lockw. in-*sig*-nis. Lat. notable. *B. suaveolens* × *B. versicolor.* Cult.
sanguinea (Ruiz & Pav.) D. Don. san-*gwin*-ee-uh. Lat. bloody (the flowers).
suaveolens (Humb. & Bonpl. ex Willd.) Bercht. & C. Presl. sway-vee-*oh*-luhnz. Lat. sweet-smelling.
versicolor Lagerh. ver-*si*-ko-lor. Lat. variably coloured (the flowers).

Brunfelsia L. (Solanaceae). brun-*fel*-see-uh. After Otto Brunfels (1488–1534), German botanist. 45 spp., shrubs, trees. Trop. Am.
pauciflora (Cham. & Schltdl.) Benth. paw-si-*flaw*-ruh. Yesterday, today and tomorrow. Lat. few-flowered.

Brunnera Steven (Boraginaceae). *broon*-uh-ruh. After Samuel Brunner (1790–1844), Swiss botanist and plant collector. 3 spp. herbs. E Eur., W Asia.
macrophylla (Adams) I. M. Johnst. mak-*rof*-i-luh. Gk. large-leaved. Caucasus.

Brussels sprouts *Brassica oleracea* Gemmifera Group
buckbrush *Ceanothus cuneatus*
buckeye *Aesculus.* **California** *A. californica.* **Ohio** *A. glabra.* **red** *A. pavia.* **yellow** *A. flava*
buckthorn *Rhamnus cathartica.* **alder** *Frangula alnus.* **cascara** *F. purshiana.* **Italian** *Rhamnus alaternus*
buckwheat *Fagopyrum esculentum.* **green** *F. tataricum.* **tall** *F. dibotrys*

Buddleja Houston ex L. (Scrophulariaceae). *bud*-lee-uh. After Rev. Adam Buddle (1662–1715), English botanist. 90 spp., herbs, shrubs, trees. Americas, Asia, Africa.

alternifolia Maxim. al-ter-ni-*foh*-lee-uh. Lat. with alternate leaves. China.

asiatica Lour. ay-see-*a*-ti-kuh. Asian. E and SE Asia.

auriculata Benth. o-rik-ew-*lah*-tuh. Lat. with small, ear-like lobes (at the leaf bases). S Africa.

colvilei Hook.f. & Thomson. kol-*vil*-ee-ee. After Sir James William Colvile (1810–1880), a judge in India. Himal.

crispa Benth. *kris*-puh. Lat. curled (the leaf edge). Himal., China.

davidii Franch. da-*vid*-ee-ee. After French missionary, botanist and zoologist Armand David (1826–1900), who collected the type specimen in Sichuan in 1869. China.

fallowiana Balf.f. fa-low-ee-*ah*-nuh. After George Fallow, gardener at RBG Edinburgh, who was killed in Egypt in 1917. W China.

globosa Hope. glo-*boh*-suh. Lat. spherical (the flowerheads). Chile, Argentina.

lindleyana Fortune. lind-lee-*ah*-nuh. After John Lindley (1799–1865), English botanist. China.

loricata Leeuwenb. lo-ri-*kah*-tuh. Lat. armoured (referring to the tough leaves). S Africa.

nivea Duthie. *niv*-ee-uh. Lat. snow-white (the leaf undersides). China.

salviifolia (L.) Lam. sal-vee-i-*foh*-lee-uh. Lat. with leaves like *Salvia*. S and E Africa.

×*weyeriana* Weyer ex Rehder. way-er-ree-*ah*-nuh. After Van de Weyer, who raised it in 1914. *B. davidii* × *B. globosa*. Cult.

buffalo berry *Shepherdia argentea*
bugbane *Actaea cimicifuga*
bugle *Ajuga*. **common** *A. reptans*.
pyramidal *A. pyramidalis*

Buglossoides Moench (Boraginaceae). boog-los-*oy*-deez. Like *Buglossum* (*Anchusa*). 15 spp. herbs. Eur., Asia.

purpurocaerulea (L.) I. M. Johnst. pur-pew-roh-kie-*rue*-lee-uh. Purple gromwell. Lat. purple-blue (the flowers). E Eur., W Asia.

Bulbine Wolf (Asphodelaceae). bul-*bee*-nee. Gk. name for a bulbous plant. 50 spp., herbs, shrubs. Africa.

frutescens (L.) Willd. frue-*tes*-uhnz. Lat. somewhat shrubby. S Africa.

Bulbinella Kunth (Asphodelaceae). bul-bi-*nel*-uh. Diminutive of *Bulbine*. 20 spp. herbs. S Africa, NZ.

hookeri (Colenso ex Hook.) Cheesem. *hook*-uh-ree. After Joseph Dalton Hooker (1817–1911), English botanist, plant collector, and director of RBG Kew. The name was suggested by William Colenso, when he sent plants from NZ to W. J. Hooker, "in honour of my good friend and your dear son." NZ.

Bulbocodium vernum L. = *Colchicum bulbocodium*

bulrush *Bolboschoenus, Schoenoplectus, Scirpus*
bunchberry *Cornus canadensis*

Buphthalmum L. (Asteraceae). boof-*thal*-moom. Ox-eye. Gk. ox eye. 2 spp. herbs. Eur., W Asia.

salicifolium L. sal-i-si-*foh*-lee-oom. Lat. with leaves like *Salix*. Eur.
speciosum Schreb. = *Telekia speciosa*

Bupleurum L. (Apiaceae). bew-*plur*-room. Hare's ear, thorow wax. From the Gk. name, meaning ox rib. 180 spp., herbs, shrubs. Widespread.
fruticosum L. frue-ti-*koh*-soom. Shrubby hare's ear. Lat. shrubby. S Eur.
longifolium L. long-gi-*foh*-lee-oom. Lat. long-leaved. Eur., W Asia.
rotundifolium L. roh-tun-di-*foh*-lee-oom. Lat. round-leaved. Eur., Asia.

bur reed *Sparganium*
burnet, Canadian *Sanguisorba canadensis*. **great** *S. officinalis*. **salad** *S. minor*
burning bush *Bassia scoparia, Dictamnus albus*
burro's tail *Sedum morganianum*
bush flax *Astelia nervosa*
bush honeysuckle *Diervilla*
busy lizzie *Impatiens walleriana*
butcher's broom *Ruscus aculeatus*

Butomus L. (Butomaceae). bew-*toh*-moos. Gk. ox cutting, from the sharp-edged leaves. 1 sp., herb. Eur., Asia.
umbellatus L. um-buhl-*ah*-toos. Flowering rush. Lat. in umbels (the flowers).

butter and eggs *Linaria vulgaris*
butterbur *Petasites*
buttercup *Ranunculus*. **creeping** *R. repens*. **meadow** *R. acris*
butterfly flag *Diplarrena moraea*
butternut *Juglans cinerea*

Buxus L. (Buxaceae). *bux*-uhs. The Lat. name. 30 spp., shrubs, trees. Eur., Asia, Africa, Mex., C Am.
balearica Lam. bal-ee-*a*-ri-kuh. Balearic box. Of the Balearics. Balearic Is., SW Spain.
microphylla Sieb. & Zucc. mik-*rof*-i-luh. Gk. small-leaved. Cult. var.
japonica (Müll.-Arg.) Rehder. juh-*pon*-i-kuh. Of Japan. Japan.
sempervirens L. sem-per-*vie*-ruhnz. Common box. Lat. evergreen. Eur., N Africa, W Asia.

cabbage *Brassica oleracea* Capitata Group. **Chinese** *B. rapa* Pekinensis Group. **wild** *B. oleracea*
cabbage tree *Cordyline australis*

Cacalia atriplicifolia L. = *Arnoglossum atriplicifolium*

cactus, **Arizona barrel** *Ferocactus wislizeni*. **bishop's cap** *Astrophytum myriostigma*. **California barrel** *Ferocactus cylindraceus*. **Christmas** *Schlumbergera* ×*buckleyi*. **devil's tongue** *Ferocactus latispinus*. **Easter** *Hatiora gaertneri*. **goat's horn** *Astrophytum capricorne*. **old man** *Cephalocereus senilis*. **silver dollar** *Astrophytum asterias*. **star** *A. ornatum*. **Texas barrel** *Ferocactus hamatacanthus*. **thanksgiving** *Schlumbergera truncata*

Caesalpinia L. (Fabaceae). see-zuhl-*pin*-ee-uh. After Andrea Cesalpino (1519–1603), Italian botanist. 40 spp., shrubs, trees, climbers. Tropics.
gilliesii (Wall. ex Hook.) D. Dietr. gi-*leez*-ee-ee. Bird of paradise shrub. After Scottish doctor John Gillies (1792–1834), who collected in S Am.

and sent details of this plant to Hooker. Argentina, Uruguay.
pulcherrima (L.) Sw. pool-*ke*-ri-muh. Pride of Barbados. Lat. very beautiful. Trop. Am.

calabaza *Cucurbita moschata*

Caladium Vent. (Araceae). kuh-*lay*-dee-oom. Angel's wings, elephant ears. From a native name for the plant. 12 spp. herbs. Trop. S Am.
bicolor (Aiton) Vent. *bi*-ko-lor. Of two colours (the leaves).
esculentum (L.) Vent. = *Colocasia esculenta*
×*hortulanum* Birdsey = *C. bicolor*

Calamagrostis Adans. (Poaceae). kal-uh-muh-*gros*-tis. Gk. reed grass. 250 spp. grasses. Temp. N hemisph.
×*acutiflora* (Schrad.) DC. uh-kew-ti-*flaw*-ruh. Lat. with pointed flowers. *C. arundinacea* × *C. epigejos*. Cult.
arundinacea (L.) Roth. uh-run-di-*nay*-see-uh. Lat. reed-like. Eur., W Asia.
brachytricha Steud. brak-ee-*trie*-kuh. Gk. with short hairs. E Asia.
canadensis (Michx.) P. Beauv. kan-uh-*den*-sis. Bluejoint. Of Canada. N Am., Greenland.
emodensis Griseb. em-o-*den*-sis. Of the Himalaya (Lat. *Emodus*). Himal., China.

calamint *Calamintha*. **alpine** *Acinos alpinus*. **large-flowered** *Calamintha grandiflora*. **lesser** *C. nepeta*

Calamintha Mill. (Lamiaceae). kal-uh-*min*-thuh. Calamint. Gk.

name, meaning beautiful mint. 7 spp.
herbs. Eur., W Asia.
alpina (L.) Lam. = *Acinos alpinus*
grandiflora (L.) Moench. gran-di-
flaw-ruh. Large-flowered calamint.
Lat. large-flowered. S Eur., W Asia.
nepeta (L.) Savi. *ne*-pe-tuh. Lesser calamint. Gk. name for a plant. S Eur.
subsp. *glandulosa* (Req.) P. W. Ball.
glan-dew-*loh*-suh. Lat. glandular (the
leaves).

calamondin *Citrus ×microcarpa*

Calandrinia Kunth (Portulacaceae).
kal-uhn-*drin*-ee-uh. Redmaids. After
Jean-Louis Calandrini (1703–1758),
Swiss scientist. 150 spp. herbs. Widespread.
ciliata (Ruiz & Pav.) DC. sil-ee-*ah*-
tuh. Fringed redmaids. Lat. edged
with hairs (the leaves and sepals). W
USA, SW Canada.
grandiflora Lindl. gran-di-*flaw*-ruh.
Lat. large-flowered. Chile.
umbellata (Ruiz & Pav.) DC. um-
buhl-*ah*-tuh. Rock purslane. Lat. in
umbels (the flowers are in umbel-like
clusters). Chile, Peru.

Calanthe R. Br. (Orchidaceae). kuh-
lan-thee. Gk. beautiful flower. 100
spp. orchids. Asia, Pacific, Africa,
Mex., C Am.
nipponica Makino. ni-*pon*-i-kuh.
Of Japan. Japan, China.
reflexa Maxim. ree-*flex*-uh. Lat.
turned back (the sepals and petals).
Japan, S China.
sieboldii Decne. ex Regel. see-*bold*-ee-
ee. After German physician and botanist Philip Franz von Siebold
(1796–1866). China, Taiwan.

striata R. Br. ex Lindl. stree-*ah*-tuh.
Lat. striped (the flowers). Korea,
Japan.

Calathea G. Mey. (Marantaceae). kal-
uh-*thee*-uh. From Gk. basket (the
flowers are held among coloured
bracts). 300 spp. herbs. Mex., trop.
Am.
burle-marxii H. A. Kenn. burl-*marx*-
ee-ee. After Brazilian landscape
architect Roberto Burle Marx (1909–
1994), who collected the plant from
which it was described. Brazil.
makoyana E. Morren. mak-oy-*ah*-nuh.
After Lambert Jacob-Makoy (1790–
1873), Belgian nurseryman. SE
Brazil.
picturata K. Koch & Linden. pik-tew-
rah-tuh. Lat. embroidered (the leaves
appear). Brazil.
roseopicta (Linden) Regel. roh-zee-oh-
pik-tuh. Lat. painted pink (the leaves
appear). S Am.

Calceolaria L. (Calceolariaceae).
kal-see-oh-*lah*-ree-uh. Lat. like a little
slipper (the flowers). 300 spp., herbs,
shrubs. Mex. to S Am.
integrifolia Murr. in-teg-ri-*foh*-lee-uh.
Lat. with untoothed leaves. Chile.

Calendula L. (Asteraceae). ka-*len*-
dew-luh. From Lat. first day of the
month, referring to the long flowering period. 12 spp. herbs. Eur., W
Asia.
officinalis L. o-fis-i-*nah*-lis. Pot marigold. Lat. sold as a med. herb. Cult.

Calia Térean & Berland. ex Yakovlev
(Fabaceae). *kal*-ee-uh. Gk. beauty. 4
spp., shrubs, trees. SW USA, Mex.

secundiflora (Ortega) Yakovlev. se-kun-di-*flaw*-ruh. Mescal bean. Lat. with flowers on one side.

Calibrachoa Cerv. (Solanaceae). kal-ee-brak-*oh*-uh. After Antonio de la Cal y Bracho (1766–1833), Mexican botanist and pharmacologist. 32 spp., perenn. herbs, subshrubs. S USA to S Am.
parviflora (Juss.) D'Arcy. par-vi-*flaw*-ruh. Seaside petunia. Lat. small-flowered. SW USA to S Am.

calico bush *Kalmia latifolia*
calico flower *Aristolochia littoralis*
California fuchsia *Epilobium canum*
California rosebay *Rhododendron macrophyllum*

Calla L. (Araceae). *kal*-uh. Gk. beautiful. 1 sp., perenn. herb. N temp. regs.
palustris L. puh-*lus*-tris. Bog arum. Lat. of marshes.

Callicarpa L. (Lamiaceae). kal-i-*karp*-uh. Beauty berry. Gk. beautiful fruit. 140 spp., shrubs, trees. Tropics and subtropics.
americana L. uh-me-ri-*kah*-nuh. Of America. USA, N Mex., Caribb. '**Lactea**'. *lak*-tee-uh. Lat. milky (the fruit).
bodinieri H. Lév. bod-in-ee-*e*-ree. After French missionary Emile Marie Bodinier (1842–1901), who collected some of the original material from which it was described. China, Laos, Cambodia, Vietnam. var. ***giraldii*** (Rehder) Rehder = *C. bodinieri*
dichotoma (Lour.) K. Koch. di-*ko*-to-muh. Gk. dividing in two (the shoots.). E Asia.

japonica Thunb. juh-*pon*-i-kuh. Of Japan. China, Taiwan, Korea, Japan.
kwangtungensis Chun. kwang-tung-*en*-sis. Of Guangdong (Kwangtung), S China. China.

Callirhoe Nutt. (Malvaceae). kal-i-*roh*-ee. Poppy mallow. Gk. beautiful poppy, and a nymph in myth. 9 spp. herbs. USA, Mex.
digitata Nutt. di-ji-*tah*-tuh. Winecup. Lat. finger-like (the leaf lobes). C and SE USA.
involucrata (Torr. & A. Gray) A. Gray. in-vo-lue-*krah*-tuh. Purple poppy mallow. With an involucre (of bracts). USA, N Mex.
triangulata (Leavenw.) A. Gray. trie-ang-ew-*lah*-tuh. Clustered poppy mallow. Lat. triangular (the leaves). E USA.

Callisia Loefl. (Commelinaceae). ka-*lis*-ee-uh. From Gk. beauty. 20 spp. herbs. Trop. Am.
elegans Alexander ex H. E. Moore = *C. gentlei* var. *elegans*
gentlei Matuda. *gen*-tuhl-ee. After Belizean botanist Percival Hildebart Gentle (1892–1958), who collected the type specimen in Belize in 1938. Mex., C Am. var. ***elegans*** (Alexander ex H. E. Moore) D. R. Hunt. *el*-i-ganz. Striped inchplant. Lat. elegant.
navicularis (Ortgies) D. R. Hunt. na-vik-ew-*lah*-ris. Chainplant. Lat. like a small boat (the folded leaves). Mex.
repens (Jacq.) L. *ree*-puhnz. Creeping inchplant. Lat. creeping. Mex., C and S Am.

Callistemon R. Br. (Myrtaceae). kal-ee-*stem*-on. Bottlebrushes. Gk.

beautiful stamens. 34 spp., shrubs, trees. Australia, New Caledonia.

citrinus (Curtis) Skeels. sit-*ree*-noos. Lat. lemon-scented (the leaves). E Australia.

linearis DC. lin-ee-*ah*-ris. Lat. linear (the leaves). SE Australia.

pallidus DC. *pa*-li-doos. Lat. pale (the flowers). SE Australia.

rigidus R. Br. *rij*-i-doos. Lat. rigid (the leaves). E Australia.

salignus DC. sa-*lig*-noos. Lat. willow-like (the leaves). SE Australia.

sieberi DC. *see*-buh-ree. After Prague-born botanist Franz Wilhelm Sieber (1798–1844), who collected the type specimen. SE Australia.

speciosus (Sims) Sweet. spee-see-*oh*-soos. Lat. showy. W Australia.

subulatus Cheel. sub-ew-*lah*-toos. Lat. awl-shaped (the leaves). SE Australia.

viminalis (Gaertn.) Cheel. vi-mi-*nah*-lis. Weeping bottlebrush. Lat. willow-like (the leaves). E Australia.

viridiflorus (Sims) Sweet. vi-ri-dee-*flaw*-roos. Lat. green-flowered. Tasmania.

Callistephus Cass. (Asteraceae). kal-ee-*stee*-foos. Gk. beautiful crown (the flowerheads). 1 sp., herb. China.

chinensis (L.) Nees. chin-*en*-sis. China aster. Of China.

Calluna Salisb. (Ericaceae). kuh-*lue*-nuh. From Gk. to make beautiful (the twigs were used as brushes). 1 sp., shrub. Eur., N Africa, N and W Asia.

vulgaris (L.) Hull. vul-*gar*-ris. Heather, ling. Lat. common.

Calocedrus Kurz (Cupressaceae). kal-oh-*seed*-roos. Gk. beautiful cedar. 3 spp. coniferous trees. E Asia, W N Am.

decurrens (Torr.) Florin. dee-*ku*-ruhnz. Incense cedar. Lat. decurrent (the leaf base continuing along the stem). W N Am.

Calochortus Pursh (Liliaceae). kal-oh-*kor*-toos. Gk. beautiful grass (referring to the slender leaves). 70 spp. bulbous herbs. W N Am. to C Am.

albus (Benth.) Douglas ex Benth. *al*-boos. White fairy lantern. Lat. white (the flowers). Calif., Mex. (B.C.).

concolor (Baker) Purdy & L. H. Bailey. *kon*-ko-lor. Goldenbowl mariposa lily. Lat. of the same colour. S Calif., Mex. (B.C.).

luteus Douglas ex Lindl. *lue*-tee-oos. Yellow mariposa lily. Calif.

splendens Douglas ex Benth. *splen*-duhnz. Splendid mariposa lily. Lat. splendid. Calif., Mex. (B.C.).

superbus Purdy ex Howell. sue-*per*-boos. Lat. superb. Calif.

venustus Douglas ex Benth. ven-*oos*-toos. Butterfly mariposa lily. Lat. handsome. Calif.

Caltha L. (Ranunculaceae). *kal*-thuh. From Gk. goblet, from the shape of the flowers. 10 spp. perenn. herbs. Widespread.

leptosepala DC. lep-toh-*sep*-uh-luh. White marsh marigold. Gk. with narrow sepals. W USA, W Canada.

palustris L. puh-*lus*-tris. Marsh marigold. Lat. of marshes. Eur., Asia, N Am.

polypetala Hochst. ex Lorent = *C. palustris*

Calycanthus L. (Calycanthaceae). kal-ee-*kan*-thoos. Gk. calyx flower, refer-ring to the similar petals and sepals. 3 spp. shrubs. China, USA.
chinensis W. C. Cheng & S. Y. Chang. chin-*en*-sis. Of China. China.
fertilis Walter = *C. floridus* var. *laevigatus*
floridus L. *flo*-ri-doos. Carolina all-spice. Lat. flowering. E USA. var. *laevigatus* (Willd.) Torr. & A. Gray. lee-vi-*gah*-toos. Lat. smooth (the leaves).
occidentalis Hook. & Arn. ok-si-den-*tah*-lis. California allspice. Lat. west-ern. Calif.

Calylophus serrulatus (Nutt.) P. H. Raven = *Oenothera serrulata*

Camassia Lindl. (Asparagaceae). kuh-*mas*-ee-uh. From the Native American name. 6 spp. bulbous herbs. N Am.
cusickii S. Watson. kew-*zik*-ee-ee. After American botanist William Conklin Cusick (1842–1922), who collected the type specimen in Ore-gon in 1886. W USA (Oregon, Idaho).
esculenta (Nutt.) Lindl. = *C. quamash*
leichtlinii (Baker) S. Watson. liekt-*lin*-ee-ee. After German horticultur-ist Max Leichtlin (1831–1910), who grew it. W USA, SW Canada. subsp. *suksdorfii* (Greenm.) Gould. sooks-*dorf*-ee-ee. After American botanist William Nikolaus Suksdorf (1850–1932), who collected specimens in

Washington State in 1880, 1883 and 1900 from which it was described.
quamash (Pursh) Greene. *ka*-mash. From the Native American name. W Canada, W USA.
scilloides (Raf.) Cory. sil-*oy*-deez. Like *Scilla*. SE Canada, E and C USA.

Camellia L. (Theaceae). kuh-*me*-lee-uh. After Georg Josef Kamel (Lat. *Camellus*) (1661–1706), Brno-born missionary and botanist. 120 spp., shrubs, trees. E and SE Asia.
hiemalis Nakai. hee-*mah*-lis. Lat. of winter (flowering). Cult.
japonica L. juh-*pon*-i-kuh. Of Japan. Japan, Korea, Taiwan.
oleifera Abel. oh-lee-*if*-uh-ruh. Lat. oil-bearing (the seeds). China, N Laos, N Myanmar, N Vietnam.
reticulata Lindl. re-tik-ew-*lah*-tuh. Lat. net-veined (the leaves). SW China.
saluenensis Stapf ex Bean. sal-ween-*en*-sis. Of the Salween River. SW China.
sasanqua Thunb. suh-*sang*-kwuh. From the Japanese name. Japan.
sinensis (L.) Kuntze. sin-*en*-sis. Tea plant. Lat. of China. China, N W India, SE Asia.
×*williamsii* W. W. Sm. wil-*yamz*-ee-ee. After John Charles (J. C.) Williams (1861–1939) of Caerhays Castle, Cornwall, who raised many forms. *C. japonica* × *C. saluenensis*. Cult.

Campanula L. (Campanulaceae). kam-*pan*-ew-luh. Bellflower. Lat. a little bell (the flowers). 300 spp. ann. and perenn. herbs. N temp. regs.

alliariifolia Willd. al-ee-ah-ree-i-*foh*-lee-uh. Ivory bells. With leaves like *Alliaria petiolata*. NE Turkey, Caucasus.

americana L. uh-me-ri-*kah*-nuh. American bellflower. Of America. E N Am.

arvatica Lag. ar-*vat*-i-kuh. Of Arbás. NW Spain.

barbata L. bar-*bah*-tuh. Bearded bellflower. Lat. bearded (the mouth of the flower). Eur.

bellidifolia Adams. bel-i-di-*foh*-lee-uh. Lat. with leaves like *Bellis*. Caucasus.

carpatica Jacq. kar-*pat*-i-kuh. Tussock bellflower. Of the Carpathian Mts. C and E Eur.

chamissonis Fed. kam-i-*soh*-nis. Aleutian bellflower. After Adelbert von Chamisso (1781–1838), German botanist and poet. Japan, NE Russia, Alaska.

cochlearifolia Lam. kok-lee-ah-ri-*foh*-lee-uh. Fairies' thimbles. Lat. with spoon-shaped leaves. Eur.

garganica Ten. gar-*gan*-i-kuh. Adriatic bellflower. Of Monte Gargano, Italy. SE Eur.

glomerata L. glom-uh-*rah*-tuh. Clustered bellflower. Lat. clustered (the flowers). Eur., Asia.

×*haylodgensis* hort. hay-loj-*en*-sis. Of Hay Lodge, Edinburgh, where it was raised. *C. carpatica* × *C. cochlearifolia*. Cult.

hofmannii (Pant.) Greuter & Burdet. hof-*man*-ee-ee. After Florian Hofmann (1834–1889), plant collector in Bosnia. SE Eur.

incurva Aucher ex A. DC. in-*kur*-vuh. Lat. incurved. Greece.

isophylla Moretti. ie-*so*-fil-uh. Italian bellflower. Gk. with equal (sized) leaves. NW Italy.

lactiflora M. Bieb. lak-ti-*flaw*-ruh. Milky bellflower. Lat. with milky flowers. Caucasus, NE Turkey, NW Iran.

latifolia L. lat-i-*foh*-lee-uh. Giant bellflower. Lat. broad-leaved. Eur., W and C Asia, Himal.

latiloba A. DC. lat-i-*loh*-buh. Lat. broad-lobed (the flowers). NW Turkey.

makaschvilii E. A. Busch. mak-ash-*vil*-ee-ee. After Russian botanist A. K. Makaschvili. Caucasus.

medium L. *mee*-dee-oom. Canterbury bells. From a name used by Dioscorides for a plant from Media (Azerbaijan). S Eur.

ochroleuca (Kem.-Nath.) Kem.-Nath. ok-roh-*lue*-kuh. Gk. yellowish white (the flowers). Caucasus.

persicifolia L. per-si-ki-*foh*-lee-uh. Peach-leaved bellflower. Lat. with peach-like leaves. Eur., Caucasus, C Asia.

portenschlagiana Schult. por-tuhn-shlahg-ee-*ah*-nuh. Dalmatian bellflower. After Austrian botanist Franz von Portenschlag-Ledermayer (1772–1822), who first recognised it as distinct. SE Eur.

poscharskyana Degen. posh-ar-skee-*ah*-nuh. Trailing bellflower. After Gustav Adolf Poscharsky (1832–1915), inspector of the Royal Botanic Garden, Dresden. SE Eur.

primulifolia Brot. prim-ew-li-*foh*-lee-uh. Lat. with leaves like *Primula*. SW Eur.

pulla L. *pool*-uh. Lat. dark (the flowers). Austria.

×*pulloides* hort. pool-*oy*-deez. Like C. *pulla*. *C. carpatica* × *C. pulla*. Cult.

punctata Lam. punk-*tah*-tuh. Spotted bellflower. Lat. spotted (the flowers). E Asia.

pyramidalis L. pi-ram-i-*dah*-lis. Chimney bellflower. Lat. pyramidal (the inflorescence). SE Eur.

raineri Perpent. *ray*-nuh-ree. Probably after Joseph Rainer (1783–1853), archduke of Austria. Italy.

rapunculoides L. ruh-punk-ew-*loy*-deez. Creeping bellflower. Lat. like a little turnip (the roots). Eur., W Asia.

rotundifolia L. roh-tun-di-*foh*-lee-uh. Harebell, Scottish bluebell. Lat. round-leaved.

sarmatica Ker Gawl. sar-*ma*-ti-kuh. Lat. of Sarmatia (in Roman times comprised parts of E Eur. to the Caspian Sea). Caucasus.

takesimana Nakai. tak-esh-ee-*mah*-nuh. Korean bellflower. Of Takeshima (Dokdo Is.). Korea.

trachelium L. tra-*kee*-lee-oom. Nettle-leaved bellflower, throatwort. From Gk. neck (supposed med. properties). Eur., N Africa, W Asia.

zangezura (Lipsky) Kolak. & Serdyuk. zan-ge-*zoo*-ruh. Of the Zangezur Mts. (Armenia/Azerbaijan). Caucasus, Iran.

Campanulastrum americanum (L.) Small = *Campanula americana*

campion *Silene*. moss *S. acaulis*. red *S. dioica*. rose *S. coronaria*. sea *S. uniflora*. white *S. latifolia*

Campsis Lour. (Bignoniaceae). *kamp*-sis. From Gk. curved (the stamens). 2 spp. woody climbers. China, USA.

grandiflora (Thunb.) K. Schum. gran-di-*flaw*-ruh. Chinese trumpet creeper. Lat. large-flowered. China.

radicans (L.) Seem. ex Bureau. *rad*-i-kanz. Trumpet creeper. Lat. rooting (the shoots). E and C USA.

×*tagliabuana* (Vis.) Rehder. tag-lee-ab-ew-*ah*-nuh. Of the Tagliabue Bros. nursery, Milan, where the hybrid first occurred. *C. grandiflora* × *C. radicans*. Cult.

canary creeper *Tropaeolum peregrinum*
candle plant *Senecio articulatus*
candytuft *Iberis*
cane, giant *Arundinaria gigantea*. switch *A. gigantea* subsp. *tecta*

Canna L. (Cannaceae). *kan*-uh. Indian shot plant. From Gk. reed. 10 spp. herbs. Trop. and subtrop. Am.

×*generalis* L. H. Bailey. gen-uh-*rah*-lis. Lat. general (normal). *C. indica* × *C. iridiflora*. Cult.

glauca L. *glaw*-kuh. Louisiana canna. Lat. bluish white (the leaves). S USA to S Am.

indica L. *in*-di-kuh. Of the (E) Indies (it was named from imported plants). Mex. to S Am.

cantaloupe *Cucumis melo* Cantalupensis Group
Canterbury bells *Campanula medium*

Cantua Lam. (Polemoniaceae). *kant*-ew-uh. From the Peruvian name. 12 spp., shrubs, trees. S Am.

buxifolia Juss. bux-i-*foh*-lee-uh. Magic tree. Lat. with leaves like *Buxus*. Andes.

cape leadwort *Plumbago auriculata*

Capsicum L. (Solanaceae). *kap*-si-koom. From Gk. bite (the hot taste). 10 spp., herbs, subshrubs. Trop. Am.
annuum L. *an*-ew-oom. Lat. annual. **Cerasiforme Group**. ke-ruh-si-*form*-ee. Cherry pepper. Lat. cherry-shaped (the fruit). **Conoides Group**. kon-*oy*-deez. Cone pepper. Lat. cone-like (the fruit). **Fasciculatum Group**. fa-sik-ew-*lah*-toom. Red cone pepper. Lat. clustered (the fruit). **Grossum Group**. *groh*-soom. Bell pepper. Lat. large (the fruit). **Longum Group**. *lon*-goom. Cayenne pepper, chili pepper. Lat. long (the fruit).
frutescens L. froo-*tes*-uhnz. Bird pepper, red chili pepper. Lat. somewhat shrubby.

Caragana Lam. (Fabaceae). ka-ruh-*gah*-nuh. From the Mongol name of *C. arborescens*. 75 spp., shrubs, trees. E Eur. to China.
arborescens Lam. ar-bor-*res*-uhnz. Pea tree. Lat. becoming tree-like. C and N Asia.

caraway *Carum carvi*

Cardamine L. (Brassicaceae). kar-*da*-mi-nee. Bittercress. Name used by Dioscorides for a similar plant, from Gk. tame, heart. 200 spp. ann. and perenn. herbs. Widespread, mainly temp. regs.
bulbifera (L.) Crantz. bul-*bi*-fe-ruh. Coral-root bittercress. Lat. bearing bulbs (in the leaf axils). Eur.
glanduligera O. Schwarz. glan-dew-li-*juh*-ruh. Lat. bearing glands (on the leaves). C and E Eur.

heptaphylla (Vill.) O. Schulz. hep-tuh-*fil*-uh. Gk. with seven leaves (leaflets). W and C Eur.
pentaphylla (L.) Crantz. pen-tuh-*fil*-uh. Gk. with five leaves (leaflets). W and C Eur.
pratensis L. pruh-*ten*-sis. Cuckoo flower, lady's smock. Lat. of meadows. N temp. regs.
quinquefolia (M. Bieb.) Schmalh. kwink-wi-*foh*-lee-uh. Lat. with five leaves (leaflets). E Eur., W Asia.
raphanifolia Pourr. ra-fuh-ni-*foh*-lee-uh. Lat. with leaves like *Raphanus*. S Eur.
trifolia L. trie-*foh*-lee-uh. Lat. with three leaves (leaflets). C and S Eur.
waldsteinii Dyer. wold-*stien*-ee-ee. After Count Franz Waldstein-Wartenburg (1759–1823), Austrian botanist. E Eur.

cardinal flower *Lobelia cardinalis*

Cardiocrinum (Endl.) Lindl. (Liliaceae). kar-dee-oh-*krie*-noom. 3 spp. bulbous herbs. Himal. to E Asia.
cathayanum (E. H. Wilson) Stearn. kath-ay-*ah*-noom. Of Cathay (an old name for China). China.
cordatum (Thunb.) Makino. kor-*dah*-toom. Lat. heart-shaped (the leaves). Japan.
giganteum (Wall.) Makino. jie-*gan*-tee-oom. Lat. very large. Himal., China. var. ***yunnanense*** (Leichtlin ex Elwes) Stearn. yue-nan-*en*-see. Of Yunnan. China.

Cardiospermum L. (Sapindaceae). kar-dee-oh-*sperm*-oom. Gk. heart seed, from the white heart-shaped spot on the seeds. 12 spp. climbers. Trop. Am., Africa.

halicacabum L. hal-ee-*kak*-uh-boom. Balloon vine. Gk. name for a species of *Physalis*. Trop. Am., Africa.

cardoon *Cynara cardunculus*

Carex L. (Cyperaceae). *kair*-rex. Sedges. The Lat. name. 1800 spp. perenn. herbs. Widespread.

acuta L. uh-*kew*-tuh. Slender tufted sedge. Lat. pointed. Eur., N Africa, W and C Asia.

aquatilis Wahlenb. uh-*kwat*-i-lis. Water sedge. Lat. living in water. Eur., N Asia, USA, E Canada.

bebbii Olney ex Britton. *beb*-ee-ee. Bebb's sedge. After Michael Schuck Bebb (1833–1895), US botanist. Canada, N USA.

bicknellii Britton & A. Br. bik-*nel*-ee-ee. Bicknell's sedge. After Eugene Pintard Bicknell (1859–1925), US naturalist who named several species in the genus. USA, S Canada.

brunnea Thunb. *broon*-ee-uh. Greater brown sedge. Lat. brown (the flower spikes). SE Asia, trop. Africa, Australia.

buchananii Berggr. bew-*kan*-uhn-ee-ee. Buchanan's sedge. After Scottish-born NZ botanist and artist John Buchanan (1819–1898). NZ.

comans Berggr. *koh*-muhnz. Lat. long-haired (foliage likened to hair). NZ.

comosa Boott. ko-*moh*-suh. Long hair sedge. Lat. long-haired. S Canada, USA, Mex.

conica Boott. *kon*-i-kuh. Lat. conical. S Korea, Japan.

crinita Lam. *krin*-i-tuh. Fringed sedge. Lat. long-haired (the long awns). E N Am.

dipsacea Berggr. dip-*say*-see-uh. Like *Dipsacus* (the inflorescence). NZ.

elata All. ee-*lah*-tuh. Tufted sedge. Lat. tall. Eur. to C Asia.

flacca Schreb. *flak*-uh. Glaucous sedge. Lat. drooping (the inflorescence). Eur., Medit., W and C Asia.

flagellifera Colenso. fla-je-*li*-fe-ruh. Lat. bearing whips (the whip-like stems). Tasmania, NZ.

grayi J. Carey. *gray*-ee. Gray's sedge. After Asa Gray (1810–1888), US botanist who named it as a variety of another species. E USA, E Canada.

lacustris Willd. luh-*kus*-tris. Hairy sedge. Lat. growing in lakes. N Am.

lupulina Muhl. ex Willd. lup-ew-*lee*-nuh. Hop sedge. Lat. hop-like (the inflorescence). E N Am., N Mex.

morrowii Boott. mo-*roh*-ee-ee. After James Morrow (1820–1865), US agriculturist. Japan.

muskingumensis Schwein. mus-king-uhm-*en*-sis. Muskingum sedge. Of the Muskingum River, Ohio. E USA, E Canada.

oshimensis Nakai. osh-ee-*men*-sis. Of Oshima Is. Japan.

pendula Huds. *pen*-dew-luh. Pendulous sedge. Lat. pendulous (the flowerheads). Eur., Medit., W Asia.

pensylvanica Lam. pen-sil-*van*-i-kuh. Pennsylvania sedge. Of Pennsylvania. USA, E and C Canada.

phyllocephala T. Koyama. fil-oh-*kef*-uh-luh. Gk. with a leafy head. SE China, Japan.

plantaginea Lam. plahn-tuh-*jin*-ee-uh. Plantainleaf sedge. Lat. like *Plantago*. E N Am.

pseuodocyperus L. sue-doh-*sip*-uh-roos. Gk. false *Cyperus.*

scoparia Willd. skoh-*pair*-ree-uh. Broom sedge. Lat. broom-like. N Am.

siderosticta Hance. sid-uh-roh-*stik*-tuh. Gk. iron-spotted (rusty spots on the leaf veins). E Asia.

stipata Muhl. ex Willd. stie-*pah*-tuh. Awlfruit sedge. Lat. crowded (the inflorescence). E Asia, N Am.

stricta Lam. *strik*-tuh. Upright sedge. Lat. upright (the shoots). E USA, E Canada.

tenuiculmis (Petrie) Heenan & de Lange. ten-ew-ee-*kul*-mis. Lat. slender-stemmed. NZ.

testacea Sol. ex Boott. test-*ay*-see-uh. Orange sedge. Lat. with a shell. NZ.

trifida Cav. *tri*-fi-duh. Muttonbird sedge. Lat. divided into three (the three stigmas). NZ, Tasmania (Macquarie Is.), S Chile, Subantarctic Is.

vulpinoidea Michx. vul-pin-*oy*-dee-uh. Fox sedge. Like *C. vulpina*, Lat. fox(tail)-like (the inflorescence). S Canada, USA, Mex.

Carlina L. (Asteraceae). kar-*lie*-nuh. After Charlemagne, whose army was said to be cured of plague by it. 28 spp. ann. and perenn. herbs. Eur., N Africa, Asia.

acaulis L. ay-*kaw*-lis. Stemless carline thistle. Lat. stemless. Eur. subsp. *simplex* (Waldst. & Kit.) Nyman. *sim*-plex. Lat. undivided (the stem).

carline thistle, stemless *Carlina acaulis*

Carmichaelia R. Br. (Fabaceae). kar-mie-*kee*-lee-uh. After Capt. Dugald Carmichael (1772–1827),

Scottish surgeon and naturalist. 24 spp., shrubs, trees. NZ, Australia (Lord Howe Is.).

australis R. Br. os-*trah*-lis. Lat. southern. NZ.

carmichaeliae (Hook.f.) Heenan. kar-mie-*kee*-lee-ie. Pink broom. Like *Carmichaelia* (originally named in another genus, *Notospartium*). NZ.

glabrescens (Petrie) Heenan. glab-*res*-uhnz. Lat. becoming glabrous. NZ.

×*hutchinsii* (M. D. Griffiths) Heenan. huch-*inz*-ee-ee. After English nurseryman Graham Hutchins, who raised it. *C. astonii* × *C. glabrescens*. Cult.

odorata Benth. oh-do-*rah*-tuh. Lat. fragrant (the flowers). NZ.

petriei Kirk. *pet*-ree-ee. After Scottish-born botanist Donald Petrie (1846–1925), who collected the type specimen. NZ.

×*Carmispartium hutchinsii* M. D. Griffiths = *Carmichaelia* ×*hutchinsii*

carnation *Dianthus caryophyllus*

Carpenteria Torr. (Hydrangeaceae). kar-pen-*te*-ree-uh. After William Marbury Carpenter (1811–1848), physician and naturalist of Louisiana, USA. 1 sp., subshrub. Calif.

californica Torr. kal-i-*for*-ni-kuh. Tree anemone. Of California.

Carpinus L. (Betulaceae). kar-*pie*-noos. Hornbeams. Lat. name for *C. betulus*. 40 spp., trees, shrubs. N temp. regs., C Am.

betulus L. *bet*-ew-loos. European hornbeam. Like *Betula* (birch). Eur., W Asia.

caroliniana Walter. ka-ro-lin-ee-*ah*-nuh. American hornbeam, blue beech, ironwood. Of the Carolinas. E Canada, C and E USA.

cordata Blume. kor-*dah*-tuh. Lat. heart-shaped (the leaves). E Russia, China, Japan.

fangiana Hu. fang-ee-*ah*-nuh. After Chinese botanist Fang Wenpei (1899–1983), who collected the type specimen in Sichuan in 1928. SW China.

japonica Blume. juh-*pon*-i-kuh. Japanese hornbeam. Of Japan. Japan.

turczaninowii Hance. tur-chan-i-*nov*-ee-ee. After Russian botanist Porphir Kiril Nicolai Stepanowitsch Turczaninow (1796–1863). N China, Korea, Japan.

Carpobrotus N. E. Br. (Aizoaceae). kar-poh-*broh*-toos. Gk. fruit, edible. 12 spp. succulents. S Africa, Australia, Chile.

edulis (L.) L. Bolus. *ed*-ew-lis. Hottentot fig. Lat. edible (the fruit). S Africa.

carrot *Daucus carota*

Carum L. (Apiaceae). *ka*-room. Gk. name for *C. carvi*. 30 spp. herbs. Temp. and subtrop. regs.

carvi L. *kar*-vee. Caraway. The Lat. name. Medit.

Carya Nutt. (Juglandaceae). *ka*-ree-uh. Hickories. From the Gk. name of *Juglans regia* (walnut). 18 spp. trees. N and C Am., E Asia.

cordiformis (Wangenh.) K. Koch. kor-di-*form*-is. Bitternut. Lat. heart-shaped (the nuts). SE Canada, E and C USA.

glabra (Mill.) Sweet. *glab*-ruh. Pignut. Lat. smooth (the shoots). SE Canada, E and C USA.

illinoinensis (Wangenh.) K. Koch. il-i-noh-in-*en*-sis. Pecan. Of Illinois. E and C USA, Mex.

laciniosa (F. Michx.) G. Don. luh-sin-ee-*oh*-suh. Big shellbark hickory, kingnut. Lat. with flaps (the bark). SE Canada, E and C USA.

ovata (Mill.) K. Koch. oh-*vah*-tuh. Shagbark hickory, shellbark hickory. Lat. ovate (the leaflets). SE Canada, E and C USA, Mex.

Caryopteris Bunge (Lamiaceae). ka-ree-*op*-te-ris. Gk. nut wing, referring to the winged fruit. 7 spp., herbs, shrubs. E Asia.

×*clandonensis* A. Simmonds. klan-don-*en*-sis. Of (West) Clandon, Surrey, UK, where it was found by Arthur Simmonds in his garden. *C. incana × C. mongholica*. Cult.

divaricata Maxim. di-va-ri-*kah*-tuh. Lat. wide-spreading (the branches). China, Japan, Korea.

incana (Thunb. ex Houtt.) Miq. in-*kah*-nuh. Lat. grey-hairy (the leaves). China, Taiwan, Korea, Japan.

Cassinia leptophylla (G. Forst.) R. Br. = *Ozothamnus leptophyllus*

Cassiope D. Don (Ericaceae). kas-*ee*-o-pee. After Cassiope of Gk. myth., mother of Andromeda. 12 spp. shrubs. N hemisph.

lycopodioides (Pall.) D. Don. lie-koh-poh-dee-*oy*-deez. Like *Lycopodium*. NW USA, W Canada.

mertensiana (Bong.) D. Don. mer-
ten-zee-*ah*-nuh. After Karl Heinrich
Mertens (1796–1830), German naturalist. W USA, W Canada.
tetragona (L.) D. Don. tet-ruh-*goh*-
nuh. Gk. four-angled (the shoots).

cast-iron plant *Aspidistra elatior*
castor oil plant *Ricinus communis*

Castanea Mill. (Fagaceae). kas-*tan*-ee-
uh. Chestnuts. Lat./Gk. name, probably from a locality in Greece. 8 spp.,
trees, shrubs. N temp. regs.
dentata (Marshall) Borkh. den-*tah*-
tuh. American chestnut. Lat.
toothed (the leaves). SE Canada, E
and C USA.
mollissima Blume. mol-*is*-i-muh. Chinese chestnut. Lat. softest (the hairs
of the shoots and leaf undersides).
China, Taiwan, Korea.
pumila (L.) Mill. *pew*-mi-luh.
Chinkapin, chinquapin. Lat. dwarf.
E and C USA.
sativa Mill. sa-*tee*-vuh. Spanish chestnut, sweet chestnut. Lat. cultivated.
E Eur., N Africa, W Asia.

Catalina ironwood *Lyonothamnus*
floribundus

Catalpa Scop. (Bignoniaceae). kuh-
tal-puh. The Native American name.
12 spp. trees. USA, E Asia.
bignonioides Walter. big-noh-nee-*oy*-
deez. Indian bean tree. Lat. like *Big-*
nonia. SE USA.
bungei C. A. Mey. *bunj*-ee-ee. Manchurian catalpa. After Russian botanist Alexander von Bunge (1803–
1890). China.
×*erubescens* Carrière. e-rue-*bes*-uhnz.

Lat. blushing (the young foliage).
C. bignonioides × *C. ovata*. Cult.
fargesii Bureau. far-*jee*-zee-ee. After
French missionary and plant collector Paul Guillaume Farges (1844–
1912). China.
ovata G. Don. oh-*vah*-tuh. Chinese
catalpa. Lat. ovate (the leaves). China.
speciosa (Warder) Engelm. spee-see-
oh-suh. Northern catalpa, western
catalpa. Lat. beautiful. E and C USA.

catalpa, Chinese *Catalpa ovata*. **Man-**
churian *C. bungei*. **northern** *C. spe-*
ciosa. **western** *C. speciosa*

Catananche L. (Asteraceae). kat-uh-
nan-kee. From Gk. strong force (it
was used as a love potion). 5 spp.
herbs. Medit.
caerulea L. kie-*rue*-lee-uh. Cupid's
dart. Lat. sky-blue (the flowers).
S Eur.

Catharanthus G. Don (Apocynaceae).
kath-uh-*ran*-thoos. Gk. pure flower.
8 spp. herbs. Madagascar, India, Sri
Lanka.
roseus (L.) G. Don. *roh*-zee-oos. Madagascar periwinkle. Lat. pink (the
flowers). Madagascar.

cat's ears *Antennaria*
catmint *Nepeta*, *N. cataria*
catnip *Nepeta cataria*

Cattleya Lindl. (Orchidaceae). *kat*-lee-
uh. After William Cattley (1788–
1835), who flowered *C. labiata*,
which was included as packing material in a shipment of other plants
from Brazil. 110 spp. orchids. C and
S Am.

cauliflower *Brassica oleracea* Botrytis Group

Cautleya (Benth.) Hook.f. (Zingiberaceae). *kawt*-lee-uh. After Sir Proby Thomas Cautley (1802–1871), English engineer and palaeontologist. 4 spp. tuberous herbs. Himal., China, Thailand, Vietnam.
gracilis (Sm.) Dandy. *gras*-i-lis. Lat. slender (the stems).
robusta Baker = *C. spicata*
spicata (Sm.) Baker. spi-*kah*-tuh. Lat. in a spike (the flowers). Himal., S China.

Ceanothus L. (Rhamnaceae). see-uh-*noh*-thoos. Gk. name used by Theophrastus for a spiny plant. 55 spp., shrubs, trees. Canada to C Am.
americanus L. uh-me-ri-*kah*-noos. New Jersey tea. Of America. SE Canada, E and C USA.
arboreus Greene. ar-*bor*-ree-oos. Feltleaf ceanothus. Lat. tree-like. Calif.
'Burkwoodii'. burk-*wood*-ee-ee. After the Burkwood & Skipwith nursery, where it was raised. *C.* ×*delileanus* 'Indigo' × *C. floribundus*.
cordulatus Kellogg. kor-dew-*lah*-toos. Mountain whitethorn. Lat. a little heart-shaped. W USA, NW Mex. (B.C.).
cuneatus (Hook.) Nutt. kew-nee-*ah*-toos. Buckbrush. Lat. wedge-shaped (the leaf base). W USA, NW Mex. (B.C.).
×*delileanus* Spach. duh-lil-ee-*ah*-noos. After French botanist Alire Raffeneau Delile (1778–1850). *C. americanus* × *C. coeruleus*. Cult.

gloriosus J. T. Howell. glor-ree-*oh*-soos. Point Reyes ceanothus. Lat. glorious. Calif.
griseus (Trel.) McMinn. *griz*-ee-oos. Carmel ceanothus. Lat. grey (the leaf undersides). Calif. var. *horizontalis* McMinn. ho-ri-zon-*tah*-lis. Lat. spreading horizontally.
impressus Trel. im-*pres*-oos. Santa Barbara ceanothus. Lat. impressed (the leaf veins). Calif.
integerrimus Hook. & Arn. in-tuh-ge-ri-moos. Deerbrush ceanothus. Lat. entire, untoothed (the leaves). Calif.
×*pallidus* Lindl. *pa*-li-doos. Lat. pale (the flowers). Cult.
prostratus Benth. pro-*strah*-toos. Squawcarpet. Lat. prostrate (the habit). Calif.
sanguineus Pursh. san-*gwin*-ee-oos. Redstem ceanothus. Lat. bloody (the red stems). SW Canada, W USA.
thyrsiflorus Eschsch. thur-si-*flaw*-roos. Blueblossom. Lat. with flowers in a thyrse. W USA. var. *repens* McMinn. *ree*-puhnz. Creeping blueblossom. Lat. creeping.
×*veitchianus* Hook. vee-chee-*ah*-noos. After Messrs Veitch & Sons, through which nursery it was introduced to gardens. *C. rigidus* × *C. thyrsiflorus*. Cult.
velutinus Douglas. vel-ew-*tee*-noos, vel-*ue*-ti-noos. Snowbrush. Lat. velvety (the leaf undersides). SW Canada, W USA.

ceanothus, Carmel *Ceanothus griseus*. **deerbrush** *C. integerrimus* **feltleaf** *C. arboreus*. **Point Reyes** *C. gloriosus*. **redstem** *C. sanguineus*. **Santa Barbara** *C. impressus*

cedar *Cedrus*. **Atlas** *C. atlantica*.
Chilean *Austrocedrus chilensis*.
Cyprian *Cedrus brevifolia*. **incense**
Calocedrus decurrens. **Japanese**
Cryptomeria japonica. **pencil** *Juniperus virginiana*. **western red** *Thuja plicata*. **white** *Chamaecyparis thyoides*
cedar of Goa *Cupressus lusitanica*
cedar of Lebanon *Cedrus libani*

Cedrela sinensis A. Juss. = *Toona sinensis*

Cedrus Trew (Pinaceae). *seed*-roos.
Cedars. Gk./Lat. name. 4 spp. conifers. N Africa, SW Asia, Himal.
atlantica (Endl.) Carr. at-*lan*-ti-kuh.
Atlas cedar. Lat. of the Atlas Mts.
N Africa. **Glauca Group**. *glaw*-kuh.
Lat. bluish white (the foliage).
brevifolia (Hook.f.) A. Henry.
bre-vi-*foh*-lee-uh. Cyprian cedar. Lat.
short-leaved. Cyprus.
deodara (Roxb.) G. Don. dee-oh-*dah*-ruh. Deodar. The Indian name. W
Himal.
libani A. Rich. li-*bah*-nee. Cedar of
Lebanon. Lat. of Lebanon (Lat. *Libanus*). SW Asia.

celandine, greater *Chelidonium majus*. **lesser** *Ficaria verna*

Celastrus L. (Celastraceae). sel-*as*-troos. 30 spp. climbers. N Am., E
Asia, Africa, Australia.
orbiculatus Thunb. or-bik-ew-*lah*-toos. Oriental bittersweet. Lat. orbicular (the leaves). E Asia.
scandens L. *skan*-duhnz. American
bittersweet. Lat. climbing. N Am.

celeriac *Apium graveolens* var.
rapaceum
celery *Apium graveolens*

Celosia L. (Amaranthaceae). sel-*oh*-zee-uh. 60 spp., herbs, shrubs. Trop.
Am., Africa, Asia.
argentea L. ar-*jen*-tee-uh. Lat. silvery
(the flowers). India. **Cristata Group**.
kris-*tah*-tuh. Cockscomb. Lat.
crested (the inflorescence). **Plumosa
Group**. plue-*moh*-suh. Plume flower.
Lat. feathery (the inflorescence). **Spicata Group**. spi-*kah*-tuh. Lat. in
spikes (the flowers).

Celtica F. M. Vázquez & Barkworth
(Poaceae). *kelt*-i-kuh. Lat. of the
Celts (in the Iberian peninsula).
1 sp., grass. SW Eur., N Africa.
gigantea (Link) F. M. Vázquez &
Barkworth. jie-*gan*-tee-uh. Lat. very
large.

Celtis L. (Cannabaceae). *kel*-tis. Hackberry, nettle tree. Gk. name of a tree
with edible fruit. 60 spp., trees,
shrubs. N temp. regs., tropics.
australis L. os-*trah*-lis. Mediterranean
hackberry. Lat. southern. S Eur., N
Africa, W Asia.
laevigata Willd. lee-vi-*gah*-tuh.
Southern hackberrry, sugarberry.
Lat. smooth (the leaves). E and C
USA, NE Mex.
occidentalis L. ok-si-den-*tah*-lis.
Common hackberry. Lat. western.
E and C USA, S Canada.
reticulata Torr. re-tik-ew-*lah*-tuh.
Netleaf hackberry. Lat. net-veined
(the leaves). SW USA, N Mex.

sinensis Pers. sin-*en*-sis. Chinese hackberry. Lat. of China. China, Taiwan, Japan.

Centaurea L. (Asteraceae). sen-*tor*-ree-uh. Knapweed. After the centaurs of Gk. myth., which are said to have discovered its med. properties. 650 spp. herbs. Widespread, mainly Medit., SW Asia.

americana Nutt. uh-me-ri-*kah*-nuh. Basket flower. Of America. USA.

atropurpurea Waldst. & Kit. at-roh-pur-*pew*-ree-uh. Lat. dark purple (the flowers). SE Eur.

bella Trautv. *bel*-uh. Lat. beautiful. Caucasus.

cyanus L. sie-*an*-oos. Cornflower. Gk. blue, also a youth in Gk. myth., said to be turned into one. SE Eur., W Asia.

dealbata Willd. dee-al-*bah*-tuh. Lat. whitened (the leaf undersides). Caucasus.

jacea L. *jay*-see-uh. From a Spanish name for a centaury. Eur., W Asia.

macrocephala Muss. Pusck. ex Willd. mak-roh-*kef*-uh-luh. Giant knapweed. Gk. with a large head. Caucasus, W Asia.

montana L. mon-*tah*-nuh. Perennial cornflower. Lat. of mountains. Eur.

moschata L. = *Amberboa moschata*

nigra L. *nie*-gruh. Black knapweed, lesser knapweed. Lat. black (the dark involucral bracts). Eur.

orientalis L. o-ree-en-*tah*-lis. Lat. eastern. SE Eur., W Asia.

ruthenica Lam. rue-*then*-i-kuh. Of Ruthenia (old name for part of E Eur). E Eur.

scabiosa L. skay-bee-*oh*-suh. Greater knapweed. From Lat. scabies (from med. properties). Eur., W Asia.

simplicicaulis Boiss. & Huet. simplis-ee-*kaw*-lis. Lat. with a simple (unbranched) stem. Caucasus.

triumfettii All. trie-uhm-*fet*-ee-ee. After Giovanni Battista Triumfetti (1656–1708), Italian botanist. Eur., N Africa, W Asia.

Centranthus DC. (Valerianaceae). sen-*tranth*-oos. Gk. spur flower, referring to the spur on the corolla. 10 spp., herbs, subshrubs. Eur., Medit.

ruber (L.) DC. *rue*-ber. Red valerian. Lat. red (the flowers). Medit.

century plant *Agave americana*

Cephalaria Roem. & Schult. (Dipsacaceae). kef-uh-*lah*-ree-uh. From Gk. head (the flowers are borne in dense heads). 65 spp. herbs. Eur., W and C Asia, Africa.

alpina (L.) Roem. & Schult. al-*pie*-nuh. Alpine scabious. Lat. alpine. C and S Eur.

dipsacoides Boiss. & Bal. dip-suh-*koy*-deez. Lat. like *Dipsacus*. Syria.

gigantea (Ledeb.) Bobrov. jie-*gan*-tee-uh. Giant scabious. Lat. very large. Turkey, Caucasus.

leucantha (L.) Roem. & Schult. lue-*kanth*-uh. Gk. white-flowered. S Eur., Algeria.

Cephalocereus Pfeiff. (Cactaceae). kef-uh-loh-*seer*-ree-oos. Gk. head, *Cereus*. 3 spp. cacti. Mex.

senilis (Haw.) Pfeiff. *sen*-i-lis. Old man cactus. Lat. old, of an old man (referring to the long white hairs).

Cephalotaxus Sieb. & Zucc. ex Endl. (Taxaceae). kef-uh-loh-*tax*-oos. Plum yew. Gk. head, *Taxus* (the strobili are in dense heads). 6 spp., shrubs, trees. Himal. to E Asia.

fortunei Hook. for-*tewn*-ee-ee. Chinese plum yew. After Scottish botanist Robert Fortune (1812–1880), who collected the type specimen and introduced it to gardens.

harringtonii (Knight ex Forbes) K. Koch. ha-ring-*toh*-nee-ee. Japanese plum yew. After Charles Stanhope, 4th Earl of Harrington (1780–1851), who grew it. Japan. var. ***drupacea*** (Sieb. & Zucc.) Koidz. drue-*pay*-see-uh. Lat. plum-like (the fruit).

Cerastium L. (Caryophyllaceae). ke-*ras*-tee-oom. Mouse-ear chickweed. From Gk. horn, from the shape of the capsule. 100 spp. herbs. Widespread.

alpinum L. al-*pie*-noom. Alpine mouse-ear chickweed. Lat. alpine. Canada, Greenland, N Eur.

tomentosum L. tom-en-*toh*-soom. Snow-in-summer. Lat. hairy (the foliage). Italy, Sicily.

Ceratophyllum L. (Ceratophyllaceae). ke-ruh-*tof*-i-loom. Hornwort. Gk. horn leaf, from the horn-like leaves. 4 spp. aquatic herbs. Widespread.

demersum L. dee-*mer*-soom. Lat. submerged.

Ceratostigma Bunge (Plumbaginaceae). ke-rat-oh-*stig*-muh. Gk. horn, stigma (the stigma bears horn-like structures). 8 spp., herbs, shrubs. NE Africa, E Asia.

griffithii C. B. Clarke. gri-*fith*-ee-ee.
After William Griffith (1810–1845), English botanist and doctor who collected the type specimen. Himal., W China.

plumbaginoides Bunge. plum-baj-in-*oy*-deez. Like *Plumbago*. W China.

willmottianum Stapf. wil-mot-ee-*ah*-noom. After Ellen Ann Willmott (1858–1934), English gardener who grew it at Warley Pace, Essex, from the first introduction in 1908 by E. H. Wilson. W China.

Cercidiphyllum Sieb. & Zucc. (Cercidiphyllaceae). ser-sid-i-*fil*-oom. Gk. with leaves like *Cercis*. 2 spp. trees. China, Japan.

japonicum Sieb. & Zucc. juh-*pon*-i-koom. Katsura tree. Of Japan.

Cercis L. (Fabaceae). *ser*-sis. Gk. a weaver's shuttle, referring to the shape of the pods. 10 spp., trees, shrubs. Eur., W and C Asia, Canada, USA, Mex., China.

canadensis L. kan-uh-*den*-sis. Redbud. Of Canada. E and C USA, Mex. var. ***texensis*** (S. Watson) Hopkins. tex-*en*-sis. Texas redbud. Of Texas. S USA.

chinensis Bunge. chin-*en*-sis. Chinese redbud. Of China. China.

occidentalis A. Gray. ok-si-den-*tah*-lis. California redbud, western redbud. Lat. western. SW USA.

reniformis S. Watson = *C. canadensis* var. *texensis*

siliquastrum L. si-li-*kwas*-troom. Judas tree. Lat. somewhat like a pod (the fruit). E Medit.

Ceropegia L. (Apocynaceae). ke-roh-*pee*-jee-uh. Gk. wax fountain, referring to the flowers. 160 spp. herbs, often succulent. Mainly S Africa.

linearis E. Mey. lin-ee-*ah*-ris. Lat. linear (the leaves). S Africa. subsp. **woodii** (Schltr.) H. Huber. *wood*-ee-ee. Sweetheart vine, hearts on a string. After John Medley Wood (1827–1915), English-born South African botanist who discovered it.

woodii Schltr. = *C. linearis* subsp. *woodii*

Cestrum L. (Solanaceae). *kes*-troom. Gk. name of a plant. 175 spp. shrubs. Trop. Am.

×*cultum* Francey. *kul*-toom. Lat. cultivated. *C. elegans* × *C. parqui*. Cult.

elegans (Brogn.) Schltdl. *el*-i-ganz. Lat. elegant. Mex.

'**Newellii**'. new-*el*-ee-ee. After Mr Newell of Downham Market, Norfolk, UK, who raised it.

nocturnum L. nok-*tur*-noom. Lady of the night. Lat. of night (when the flowers open). W Indies.

chainplant *Callisia navicularis*

Chaenomeles L. (Rosaceae). kie-*nom*-i-leez. Flowering quince. Gk. gaping apple, from a belief that the fruit splits when ripe. 3 spp. shrubs. E Asia.

cathayensis (Hemsl.) C. K. Schneid. kath-ay-*en*-sis. Of Cathay. China.

japonica (Thunb.) Spach. juh-*pon*-i-kuh. Of Japan. Japan.

speciosa (Sweet) Nakai. spee-see-*oh*-suh. Lat. showy. China.

×*superba* (Frahm) Rehder. sue-*per*-buh. Lat. superb. *C. japonica* × *C. speciosa*. Cult.

Chaenorhinum (DC.) Rchb. (Plantaginaceae). kie-noh-*reen*-oom. Gk. gaping nose, referring to the flowers. 20 spp. ann. and perenn. herbs. Medit., SW Asia.

origanifolium (L.) Kostel. o-ri-gahn-i-*foh*-lee-oom. Lat. with leaves like *Origanum*. SW Eur.

Chaenostoma Benth. (Scrophulariaceae). kie-noh-*stoh*-muh. Gk. gaping mouth, referring to the flowers. 45 spp. herbs. S Africa.

cordatum (Thunb.) Benth. kor-*dah*-toom. Lat. heart-shaped (the leaves).

chaff flower *Alternanthera*

Chamaecyparis Spach (Cupressaceae). kam-ee-*sip*-uh-ris. Gk. dwarf, cypress. 5 spp. conifers. N Am., E Asia.

lawsoniana (A. Murray) Parl. law-soh-nee-*ah*-nuh. Lawson cypress. After Charles Lawson (1794–1873) of the Lawson Nursery, Edinburgh, which raised and distributed plants from the first introduction in 1854. Calif., Oregon. '**Ellwoodii**'. el-*wood*-ee-ee. After G. Ellwood, gardener at Swanmore Park, Hampshire, UK, where it was raised. '**Gimbornii**'. gim-*born*-ee-ee. After Dutchman Max Von Gimborn (1872–1964), on whose estate (now the Von Gimborn Arboretum) it was raised. '**Wisselii**'. vis-*el*-ee-ee. After F. van der Wissel, the Dutch nurseryman who raised it.

nootkatensis (D. Don) Spach = *Xanthocyparis nootkatensis*

obtusa (Sieb. & Zucc.) Endl. ob-*tew*-suh. Hinoki cypress. Lat. blunt (the leaves). Japan.

pisifera (Sieb. & Zucc.) Endl. pi-*si*-fuh-ruh. Sawara cypress. Lat. pea-bearing (the cones). Japan. **'Filifera'**. fi-*lif*-uh-ruh. Lat. bearing threads (the slender shoots). **'Plumosa'**. ploo-*moh*-suh. Lat. feathery (the foliage). **'Squarrosa'**. skwo-*roh*-suh. Lat. with spreading tips (the juvenile foliage).

thyoides (L.) Britton, Sterns & Poggenb. tie-*oy*-deez. White cedar/cypress. Lat. like *Thuja*. E USA. **'Andelyensis'**. an-duh-lee-*en*-sis. Of Les Andelys, France, where it was raised.

Chamaecytisus Link (Fabaceae). kam-ee-*sit*-i-soos. Gk. dwarf, *Cytisus*. 30 spp. shrubs. Eur., W Asia.

purpureus (Scop.) Link. pur-*pew*-ree-oos. Purple broom. Lat. purple (the flowers). C and SE Eur.

Chamaedaphne Moench (Ericaceae). kam-ee-*daf*-nee. Gk. dwarf, *Daphne*. 1 sp., shrub. Canada, E and C USA, Eur., N Asia.

calyculata (L.) Moench. ka-lik-ew-*lah*-tuh. Leatherleaf. Lat. with a small calyx.

Chamaedorea Willd. (Arecaceae). kam-ee-*do*-ree-uh. Gk. dwarf, gift. 105 spp. palms. Mex., C and S Am.

elegans Mart. *el*-i-ganz. Parlour palm. Lat. elegant. Mex., Belize, Guatemala.

erumpens H. E. Moore = *C. seifrizii*

metallica O. F. Cook ex H. E. Moore. me-*tal*-i-kuh. Metallic palm. Lat. of metal (the foliage appears to be). S Mex.

microspadix Burret. mik-roh-*spa*-dix.

Gk. with a small spadix (flower spike). E Mex.

seifrizii Burret. sie-*frits*-ee-ee. Bamboo palm, reed palm. After German botanist William Seifriz, who collected the (since destroyed) type specimen. SE Mex., C Am.

Chamaelirium Willd. (Melanthiaceae). kam-ee-*li*-ree-oom. Gk. dwarf, lily. 1 sp., tuberous herb. E USA, SE Canada.

luteum (L.) A. Gray. *lue*-tee-oom. Blazing star, fairywand. Lat. yellow (the flowers age to).

Chamaemelum Mill. (Asteraceae). kam-ee-*mel*-oom. Gk. dwarf, apple, from the scent. 2 spp. herbs. Eur., Medit.

nobile (L.) All. *noh*-bi-lee. Chamomile. Lat. renowned (healing properties). W Eur.

Chamaerops L. (Arecaceae). *kam*-ee-rops. Gk. dwarf, bush, referring to its shrubby habit. 1 sp., palm. W Medit.

humilis L. *hew*-mil-is. Dwarf fan palm. Lat. low (growing). var. ***argentea*** André. ar-*jen*-tee-uh. Lat. silvery (the foliage). N Africa.

Chamerion (Raf.) Raf. (Onagraceae). ka-*me*-ree-on. From Gk. dwarf, *Nerium*. 8 spp. herbs. N temp. regs.

angustifolium (L.) Holub. an-gus-ti-*foh*-lee-oom. Rose-bay willow herb. Lat. narrow-leaved.

chamomile *Chamaemelum nobile*.
dyers' *Anthemis tinctoria*
chaste tree *Vitex agnus-castus*
checkerberry *Gaultheria procumbens*

Cheilanthes Sw. (Pteridaceae).
kie-*lanth*-eez. Gk. lip or edge, flower,
referring to the marginal sporangia.
150 spp. ferns. Widespread.
lanosa (Michx.) D. C. Eaton. lan-*oh*-
suh. Hairy lip fern. Lat. woolly (the
fronds). E USA.
sinuata (Lag. ex Sw.) Domin = *Astrolepis sinuata*
tomentosa Link. to-men-*toh*-suh.
Woolly lip fern. Lat. hairy (the
fronds). S USA.

Cheiranthus cheiri L. = *Erysimum
cheiri*

Chelidonium L. (Papaveraceae).
kel-i-*doh*-nee-oom. From Gk. swal-
low (it was said to restore their sight).
1 sp., herb. Eur., N Asia.
majus L. *may*-joos. Greater celandine,
swallowwort. Lat. large.

Chelone L. (Plantaginaceae). kee-*loh*-
nee. Turtlehead. Gk. turtle, tortoise,
from the resemblance of the flowers
to a turtle's head. 4 spp. herbs. SE
Canada, E USA.
barbata Cav. = *Penstemon barbatus*
glabra L. *glab*-ruh. Balmony, white
turtlehead. Lat. smooth (the leaves).
lyonii Pursh. lie-*on*-ee-ee. Pink turtlehead. After John Lyon (1765–1814),
Scottish plant collector in the E
USA, who discovered it. SE USA.
obliqua L. o-*bleek*-wuh. Red turtlehead. Lat. oblique (the mouth of the
corolla). E USA.

chenar tree *Platanus orientalis*
chenille plant *Acalypha hispida*

Chenopodium L. (Amaranthaceae).
kee-noh-*poh*-dee-oom. Gk. goose
foot, referring to the shape of the
leaves. 100 spp., herbs, subshrubs.
Widespread.
album L. *al*-boom. Fat hen, goosefoot.
Lat. white (the leaves).
ambrosioides L. = *Dysphania ambrosioides*
bonus-henricus L. *boh*-noos-*hen*-ri-
koos. Good King Henry. Lat. good
Henry, from the German name
Guter Heinrich, possibly a corruption
of *heimrich* (German, home, good to
eat). Eur.
botrys L. = *Dysphania botrys*
capitatum (L.) Ambrosi. kap-i-*tah*-
toom. Indian paint, strawberry blite.
Lat. in a head (the flowers). N Am.

chequer tree *Sorbus torminalis*
cherry, bird *Prunus padus*. **black** *P.
serotina*. **Carolina laurel** *P. caroliniana*. **choke** *P. virginiana*. **cornelian**
Cornus mas. **downy** *Prunus tomentosa*. **Fuji** *P. incisa*. **Jerusalem** *Solanum pseudocapsicum*. **Manchurian**
Prunus maackii. **pin** *P. pensylvanica*.
rum *P. serotina*. **sand** *P. pumila*.
sour *P. cerasus*. **sweet** *P. avium*.
western choke *P. virginiana* var.
melanocarpa. **western sand** *P.
pumila* var. *besseyi*
cherry pie *Heliotropium arborescens*
chervil *Anthriscus cerefolium*
chestnut *Castanea*. **American** *C. dentata*. **Chinese** *C. mollissima*. **Spanish** *C. sativa*. **sweet** *C. sativa*

Chiastophyllum oppositifolium
(Ledeb.) A. Berger = *Umbilicus
oppositifolius*

chicory *Cichorium intybus*
Chilean bellflower *Lapageria rosea*
Chilean firebush *Embothrium coccineum*

Chimonanthus Lindl. (Calycanthaceae). kim-on-*anth*-oos. Gk. winter flower (they flower in winter). 6 spp. shrubs. China.
praecox (L.) Link. *prie*-koks. Wintersweet. Lat. early (flowering).

Chimonobambusa Makino (Poaceae). ki-mo-noh-bam-*bew*-suh. Gk. winter, *Bambusa*. In some, the shoots appear in winter. 37 spp. bamboos. E Asia, mainly China.
marmorea (Mitf.) Makino. mar-*mor*-ree-uh. Marbled bamboo. Lat. marbled (the young culm sheaths). Japan.
quadrangularis (Fenzi) Makino. kwod-rang-ew-*lah*-ris. Lat. four-angled (the shoots). China.
tumidissinoda D. Ohrnb. tew-mi-dis-i-*noh*-duh. Walking stick bamboo. Lat. with very swollen nodes. China.

Chinese gooseberry *Actinidia deliciosa*
Chinese houses *Collinsia heterophylla*
Chinese lantern *Physalis alkekengi*
chinkapin *Castanea pumila*
chinquapin *Castanea pumila*

Chionanthus L. (Oleaceae). kee-on-*an*-thoos. Gk. snow flower, referring to the white flowers. 60 spp., shrubs, trees. E Asia, USA, Africa.
retusus Lindl. ree-*tew*-soos. Chinese fringe tree. Lat. blunt with a shallow notch (the leaf tip). E Asia.
virginicus L. vir-*jin*-i-koos. Fringe tree. Of Virginia. E and C USA.

Chionodoxa forbesii Baker = *Scilla forbesii*
gigantea Whittall = *Scilla luciliae*
luciliae Boiss. = *Scilla luciliae*
sardensis Whittall ex Barr & Sayden = *Scilla sardensis*

×***Chitalpa*** T. S. Elias & Wisura (Bignoniaceae). chi-*tal*-puh. From the names of the parents (*Catalpa* × *Chorisia*). Shrubs, trees. Cult.
taschkentensis T. S. Elias & Wisura. tash-kent-*en*-sis. Of Tashkent, Uzbekistan, where it was raised. *Catalpa bignonioides* × *Chorisia linearis*.

chittamwood *Cotinus obovatus*
chives *Allium schoenoprasum*. **Chinese** *A. tuberosum*

Chlidanthus Herb. (Amaryllidaceae). kli-*dan*-thoos. Gk. luxury flower. 4 spp. bulbous herbs. Bolivia, Peru.
fragrans Herb. *fray*-gruhnz. Lat. fragrant (the flowers). Peru.

Chlorophytum Ker Gawl. (Asparagaceae). klo-roh-*fie*-toom. Gk. green plant. 150 spp. herbs. Trop. and S Africa.
comosum (Thunb.) Jacq. ko-*moh*-soom. Spider plant. Lat. long-haired (the drooping leaves).

chocolate cosmos *Cosmos atrosanguineus*
chokeberry *Aronia*. **black** *A. melanocarpa*. **red** *A. arbutifolia*. **purple** *A.* ×*prunifolia*

Choisya Kunth (Rutaceae). choy-zee-uh. After Jacques Denis Choisy

(1799–1859), Swiss botanist. 7 spp. shrubs. SW USA, Mex.

×*dewitteana* Geerinck. duh-wit-ee-*ah*-nuh. After French nurseryman Dominique de Witte. *C. dumosa* var. *arizonica* × *C. ternata*. Cult.

ternata Kunth. ter-*nah*-tuh. Mexican orange blossom. Lat. in threes (the leaflets). Mex.

Christmas rose *Helleborus niger*

Chrysanthemum L. (Asteraceae). kris-*an*-thuh-moom. Gk. golden flower, referring to *C. coronarium* (now *Glebionis coronaria*), the original type species. 30 spp., herbs, subshrubs. E Eur., Asia.

alpinum L. = *Leucanthemopsis alpina*

balsamita L. = *Tanacetum balsamita*

carinatum Schousb. = *Glebionis carinata*

cinerariifolium (Trevir.) Vis. = *Tanacetum cinerariifolium*

coccineum Willd. = *Tanacetum coccineum*

coronarium L. = *Glebionis coronaria*

frutescens L. = *Argyranthemum frutescens*

hosmariense = *Rhodanthemum hosmariense*

leucanthemum L. = *Leucanthemum vulgare*

maximum Ramond = *Leucanthemum maximum*

×*morifolium* Ramat. mo-ri-*foh*-lee-oom. Lat. with leaves like *Morus*. Cult.

nipponicum (Franch. ex Maxim.) Matsum. = *Nipponanthemum nipponicum*

pacificum Nakai = *Ajania pacifica*

parthenium (L.) Bernh. = *Tanacetum parthenium*

segetum L. = *Glebionis segetum*

vulgare (L.) Bernh. = *Tanacetum vulgare*

weyrichii (Maxim.) Miyabe. way-*rich*-ee-ee. After Heinrich Weyrich (1828–1863), Russian naval surgeon. E Russia (Sakhalin), Japan (Hokkaido).

Chrysogonum L. (Asteraceae). kris-*og*-on-oom. Gk. name for another plant, Gk. golden knee, from the yellow flowers and jointed stems. 1 sp., herb. E USA.

virginianum L. vir-jin-ee-*ah*-noom. Green and gold. Of Virginia.

Cicerbita Wallr. (Asteraceae). si-*ser*-bi-tuh. From the Italian name for sow thistle (*Sonchus oleraceus*). 20 spp. herbs. Eur., temp. Asia.

alpina (L.) Wallr. al-*pie*-nuh. Mountain sow thistle. Lat. alpine. Eur.

plumieri (L.) Kirschl. plue-mee-*e*-ree. After Charles Plumier (1646–1704), French monk, botanist and explorer. C and S Eur.

Cichorium L. (Asteraceae). ki-*chor*-ree-oom. Lat./Gk. name, originally from Arab. 6 spp. herbs. Eur., N Africa, SW Asia.

endivia L. en-*div*-ee-uh. Endive. Deriv. as for *C. intybus*. Cult.

intybus L. *in*-ti-boos. Chicory. Probably originally from Egyptian for January, when the plant grows. Medit.

cigar flower *Cuphea ignea*

Cimicifuga acerina (Sieb. & Zucc.)
Tanaka = *Actaea japonica*
americana Michx. = *Actaea pachypoda*
ramosa Nakai = *Actaea simplex*

Cineraria ×*hybrida* Willd. = *Pericallis* ×*hybrida*

Cissus L. (Vitaceae). *sis*-oos. Gk. name for ivy (*Hedera helix*). 200 spp., mainly climbers. Tropics and subtropics.
antarctica Vent. an-*tark*-ti-kuh. Kangaroo vine. Of the Antarctic. E Australia.
discolor Blume. *dis*-ko-lor. Rex begonia vine. Lat. of different colours (the leaves). SE Asia to Australia.
quadrangularis L. kwod-rang-ew-*lah*-ris. Lat. four-angled (the stems). Trop. Africa, SE Asia.
rhombifolia Vahl. rom-bi-*foh*-lee-uh. Lat. with diamond-shaped leaves. Trop. Am.
striata Ruiz & Pav. stree-*ah*-tuh. Miniature grape ivy. Lat. striped (the shoots). Chile, Argentina, Brazil.

Cistus L. (Cistaceae). *sis*-toos. From the Gk. name. 20 spp. shrubs. Medit.
×**aguilarii** Pau. ag-wil-*ah*-ree-ee. After Spanish doctor Romualdo Aguilar Blanch, mine owner and friend of the author of the name. *C. ladanifer* × *C. populifolius*. Spain.
×**argenteus** Dans. ar-*jen*-tee-oos. Lat. silvery (the foliage). *C.* ×*canescens* × *C. laurifolius*. Cult.
×**corbariensis** Pourr. = *C.* ×*hybridus*
creticus L. *kre*-ti-koos. Lat. of Crete. E Medit.

×*cyprius* Lam. *sip*-ree-oos. Lat. of Cyprus. *C. ladanifer* × *C. laurifolius*. W Medit.
×*dansereaui* P. Silva. don-suh-*roh*-ee. After Canadian botanist Pierre Mackay Dansereau (b. 1911). *C. inflatus* × *C. ladanifer*. Portugal.
×*hybridus* Pourr. *hib*-ri-doos. Lat. hybrid. *C. populifolius* × *C. salviifolius*. SW Eur.
ladanifer L. luh-*dah*-ni-fuh. Gum cistus. Lat. producing ladanum, a fragrant exudate used in perfumes. SW Eur., N Africa.
laurifolius L. lo-ri-*foh*-lee-oos. Lat. with leaves like *Laurus*.
×*laxus* Aiton. *lax*-oos. Lat. loose, open (the inflorescence). *C. laurifolius* × *C. monspeliensis*. Spain, Portugal.
monspeliensis L. mon-spel-ee-*en*-sis. Lat. of Montpelier, France. SW Eur.
populifolius L. pop-ew-li-*foh*-lee-oos. Lat. with leaves like *Populus*. SW Eur.
×*pulverulentus* Pourr. pul-ve-rue-*len*-toos. Lat. dusty (the foliage). *C. albidus* × *C. crispus*. SW Eur.
×*purpureus* Lam. pur-*pew*-ree-oos. Lat. purple (the flowers). *C. creticus* × *C. ladanifer*. Cult.
×*rodiaei* Verg. roh-dee-*ie*-ee. After J. Rodié, who collected the type specimen in Le Var, France. *C. albidus* × *C. ladanifer*. Cult.
salviifolius L. sal-vee-i-*foh*-lee-oos. Lat. with leaves like *Salvia*. S Eur.
×*skanbergii* Lojac. skan-*berg*-ee-ee. After A. Skanberg of Stockholm, botanist and friend of the author of the name. *C. monspeliensis* × *C. parviflorus*. Greece, Sicily.

×*Citrofortunella microcarpa*
(Bunge) Wijnands = *Citrus* ×*micro-carpa*
mitis (Blanco) J. Ingram & H. E.
Moore = *Citrus* ×*microcarpa*

citron *Citrus medica*

Citrullus Schrad. (Cucurbitaceae). sit-*rool*-oos. From the resemblance of
the fruit to *Citrus*. 4 spp. herbs. Trop.
and S Africa.
lanatus (Thunb.) Matsum. & Nakai.
luh-*nah*-toos. Watermelon. Lat.
woolly (the shoots and leaves). Trop.
Africa.

Citrus L. (Rutaceae). *sit*-roos. Lat.
name for *C. medica*. 25 spp., trees,
shrubs. China, SE Asia, Australia.
×*aurantiifolia* (Christm.) Swingle.
o-ran-tee-i-*foh*-lee-uh. Lime. Lat.
with leaves like *C.* ×*aurantium*. *C.*
maxima × *C.* sp. Cult.
×*aurantium* L. o-*ran*-tee-oom.
Grapefruit, orange. Lat. golden. *C.*
maxima × *C. reticulata*. Cult.
grandis (L.) Osbeck = *C. maxima*
hystrix DC. *his*-trix. Kaffir lime. Gk.
porcupine (the shoots are spiny).
Trop. Asia.
japonica Thunb. juh-*pon*-i-kuh. Kum-quat. Of Japan. S China.
×*limon* (L.) Osbeck. *lee*-mon. Lemon.
C. medica × *C.* sp. Cult.
maxima (Burm.) Merr. *max*-i-muh.
Pomelo. Lat. largest (the fruit).
SE Asia.
medica L. *med*-i-kuh. Citron. Lat. of
medicine. N India?
×*microcarpa* Bunge. mik-roh-*kar*-puh. Calamondin. Gk. small-fruited.
C. japonica × *C. reticulata*. Cult.

×*paradisi* Macfad. = *C.* ×*aurantium*
reticulata Blanco. re-tik-ew-*lah*-tuh.
Clementine, mandarin, satsuma,
tangerine. Lat. net-veined. S China.
×*sinensis* (L.) Osbeck = *C.*
×*aurantium*
trifoliata L. trie-foh-lee-*ah*-tuh. Lat.
with three leaves (leaflets). China.

Cladrastis Raf. (Fabaceae). kla-*dras*-tis. From Gk. shoot, fragile, referring
to the brittle shoots. 7 spp. trees.
USA, E Asia.
delavayi (Franch.) Prain. del-uh-*vay*-ee. Chinese yellowwood. After
French missionary Jean Marie
Delavay (1834–1895), who collected
the type specimen in 1888. China,
Bhutan.
kentukea (Dum. Cours.) Rudd.
ken-*tew*-kee-uh. Yellowwood. Of
Kentucky. E and C USA.
lutea (F. Michx.) K. Koch = *C.*
kentukea
sinensis Hemsl. = *C. delavayi*

Clarkia Pursh (Onagraceae). *klark*-ee-uh. After American explorer
William Clark (1770–1838), of the
Lewis and Clark Expedition. 40 spp.
herbs. SW Canada, W USA, S Am.
amoena (Lehm.) A. Nelson & J. F.
Macbr. uh-*mee*-nuh. Farewell to
spring, satin flower. Lat. delightful,
showy. SW Canada, W USA.
unguiculata Lindl. un-gwik-ew-*lah*-tuh. Lat. with a claw (on the petals).
Calif.

clary *Salvia sclarea*. **annual** *S. viridis*.
meadow *S. pratensis*. **whorled** *S.*
verticillata

Clematis L. (Ranunculaceae). *klem*-uh-tis. Gk. name of a climbing plant. 320 spp., climbers, herbs. N and S temp. regs., trop. mts.

alpina (L.) Mill. al-*pie*-nuh. Lat. alpine. Eur.

armandii Franch. ar-*man*-dee-ee. After French missionary, botanist and zoologist Armand David (1826–1900), who collected the type specimen in 1870. China, N Myanmar.

×*aromatica* Lenné & K. Koch. a-roh-*ma*-ti-kuh. Lat. aromatic (the flowers). *C. flammula* × *C. integrifolia*. Cult.

campaniflora Brot. kam-pan-i-*flaw*-ruh. Lat. with bell-shaped flowers. Spain, Portugal.

×*cartmanii* hort. kart-*man*-ee-ee. After Joe Cartman of New Zealand, from whose seed it was raised. *C. marmoraria* × *C. paniculata*. Cult.

cirrhosa L. si-*roh*-suh. Lat. with tendrils (the curling leaf stalks). Medit. var. *balearica* (Rich.) Willk. & Lange. bal-ee-*a*-ri-kuh. Of the Balearic Is.

crispa L. *kris*-puh. Lat. curled, wavy (the corolla lobes). SE USA.

×*diversifolia* DC. die-vers-i-*foh*-lee-uh. Lat. with variable leaves. *C. integrifolia* × *C. viticella*. Cult.

×*durandii* T. Durand ex Kuntze. due-*rand*-ee-ee. After the French nursery of Durand Frères, where it was raised. Cult.

fasciculiflora Franch. fa-sik-ew-li-*flaw*-ruh. Lat. with clustered flowers. S China, N Myanmar, N Vietnam.

flammula L. *flam*-ew-luh. Lat. a little flame (referring to a flame-like pain caused by smelling a crushed leaf). S Eur., N Africa, W Asia.

florida Thunb. *flo*-ri-duh. Lat. flowering. S China. '**Sieboldii**'. see-*bold*-ee-ee. After German physician and botanist Philip Franz von Siebold (1796–1866), who introduced it to gardens in 1862.

fremontii S. Watson. free-*mont*-ee-ee. After American explorer John Charles Frémont (1813–1890), who collected the type specimen in 1843. NC USA.

heracleifolia DC. he-rak-lee-i-*foh*-lee-uh. Lat. with leaves like *Heracleum*. China.

hirsutissima Pursh. hir-sue-*tis*-i-muh. Lat. most hairy. W and C USA. var. *scottii* (Porter) R. O. Erickson. *skot*-ee-ee. For the Hon. John Scott, who collected it in 1872. C USA.

integrifolia L. in-teg-ri-*foh*-lee-uh. Lat. with undivided leaves. C Eur. to C Asia.

'**Jackmanii**'. jak-*man*-ee-ee. After the nursery of George Jackman and Son, where it was raised.

macropetala Ledeb. mak-roh-*pet*-uh-luh. Gk. with large petals. N China, E Russia.

montana Buch.-Ham. ex DC. mon-*tah*-nuh. Lat. of mountains. Himal., China, Taiwan. var. *rubens* E. H. Wilson. *rue*-buhnz. Lat. red (the flowers).

napaulensis DC. na-pawl-*en*-sis. Of Nepal. Himal., SW China.

orientalis L. o-ree-en-*tah*-lis. Lat. eastern. SE Eur. to W China.

paniculata J. F. Gmel. pan-ik-ew-*lah*-tuh. Lat. in panicles (the flowers). NZ.

patens C. Morren & Decne. *pay*-tuhnz. Lat. spreading (the tepals). E China, Korea, Japan.

pitcheri Torr. & A. Gray. *pich*-uh-ree. After American army surgeon Zina Pitcher (1797–1872), who collected the type specimen in Arkansas. E and C USA, N Mex.

recta L. *rek*-tuh. Lat. upright. S and C Eur.

rehderiana Craib. ray-duh-ree-*ah*-nuh. After Alfred Rehder (1863–1949), American botanist of the Arnold Arboretum, who, together with E. H. Wilson (who collected the type specimen), described it as a variety of another species. W China, Nepal.

scottii Porter = *C. hirsutissima* var. *scottii*

serratifolia Rehder. se-rah-ti-*foh*-lee-uh. Lat. with toothed leaves (leaflets).

spooneri Rehder & E. H. Wilson. *spue*-nuh-ree. After Wilson's friend Herman Spooner (1878–1976), botanist at the Veitch nursery. W China.

stans Sieb. & Zucc. *stanz*. Lat. standing still (i.e., not climbing). Japan.

tangutica (Maxim.) Korsh. tan-*gew*-ti-kuh. Of Gansu. W China, C Asia, N India.

terniflora DC. ter-ni-*flaw*-ruh. Lat. with flowers in threes. Japan, E China, Korea.

tibetana Kuntze. ti-bet-*ah*-nuh. Of Tibet. Himal., W China. subsp. *vernayi* (C. E. C. Fisch.) Grey-Wilson. *ver*-nay-ee. After Arthur Stannard Vernay (1877–1960), English-born American antique dealer who, with Charles Suydam Cutting, collected the type specimen in Tibet in 1935.

×*triternata* DC. trie-ter-*nah*-tuh. Lat. three times divided into three (the leaves). *C. flammula* × *C. viticella*. Cult. '**Rubromarginata**'. rue-broh-mar-jin-*ah*-tuh. Lat. edged with red (the tepals).

tubulosa Turcz. tew-bew-*loh*-suh. Lat. tubular (the flowers). China, Korea.

virginiana L. vir-jin-ee-*ah*-nuh. Virgin's bower. Of Virginia. N Am.

vitalba L. vit-*al*-buh. Lat. white vine. Old man's beard, traveller's joy. Eur., W Asia.

viticella L. vit-i-*sel*-uh. Lat. little vine. S Eur., W Asia.

clementine *Citrus reticulata*

Cleome hassleriana Chodat = *Tarenaya hassleriana*

serrulata Pursh = *Peritoma serrulata*

speciosa Raf. = *Cleoserrata speciosa*

spinosa hort. non Jacq. = *Tarenaya hassleriana*

Cleoserrata Iltis (Cleomaceae). klee-oh-se-*rah*-tuh. From *Cleome* and Lat. toothed, referring to the leaf margins. 5 spp. herbs. Mex. to S Am.

speciosa (Raf.) Iltis. spee-see-*oh*-suh. Showy spiderflower. Lat. showy.

Clerodendrum L. (Lamiaceae). kle-roh-*den*-droom. Gk. chance tree, from the varied med. properties. 250 spp., trees, shrubs, climbers. Asia, Africa.

bungei Steud. *bunj*-ee-ee. Glory flower. After Russian botanist Alexander von Bunge (1803–1890). China, Taiwan, Vietnam.

thomsoniae Balf. tom-*soh*-nee-ie. Bleeding heart vine. After the wife of the Rev. William Cooper Thomson, 19th-cent. missionary and linguist in W Africa. It was described from a plant he sent to RBG Edinburgh from Nigeria. W Africa.

trichotomum Thunb. tri-*kot*-o-moom. Harlequin glorybower. Gk. divided into three (the inflorescence). E Asia.
var. *fargesii* (Dode) Rehder. far-*jee*-zee-ee. After French missionary and plant collector Paul Guillaume Farges (1844–1912), who collected the specimens from which it was described.

Clethra L. (Clethraceae). *kleth*-ruh. Gk. name for alder (*Alnus*), from the similar leaves of some species. 65 spp., shrubs, trees. Americas, E Asia, Madeira.

acuminata Michx. uh-kew-min-*ah*-tuh. Mountain sweet pepperbush. Lat. taper-pointed (the leaves). E USA.

alnifolia L. al-ni-*foh*-lee-uh. Sweet pepperbush, summersweet. Lat. with leaves like *Alnus*. E USA.

arborea Aiton. ar-*bor*-ree-uh. Lily of the valley tree. Lat. tree-like. Madeira.

barbinervis Sieb. & Zucc. bar-bi-*ner*-vis. Lat. with bearded veins (hairs on the veins). E China, S Korea, Japan.

delavayi Franch. del-uh-*vay*-ee. After French missionary Jean Marie Delavay (1834–1895), who collected the type specimen in Yunnan in 1888. SW China.

fargesii Franch. far-*jee*-zee-ee. After French missionary and plant collector Paul Guillaume Farges (1844–1912), who collected the type specimen in Sichuan in 1892. China.

pringlei S. Watson. *pring*-uhl-ee. After American horticulturist Cyrus Guernsey Pringle (1838–1911), who collected the type specimen in San Luis Potosi in 1890. Mex.

tomentosa Lam. to-men-*toh*-suh. Downy sweet pepperbush. Lat. tomentose (the leaves and shoots). SE USA.

Cleyera Thunb. (Pentaphylacaceae). *klay*-uh-ruh. After Andreas Cleyer (1634–1698), German botanist and physician with the Dutch East India Co. 8 spp., trees, shrubs. E Asia, Mex., C Am.

japonica Thunb. juh-*pon*-i-kuh. Of Japan. Himal., China, Japan.

Clianthus Sol. ex Lindl. (Fabaceae). klie-*anth*-oos. From Gk. glory flower. 2 spp. shrubs. NZ.

formosus (G. Don) Ford & Vickery = *Swainsona formosa*

puniceus (G. Don) Lindl. pew-*nis*-ee-oos. Lobster claw, parrot's bill. Lat. red (the flowers).

cliff rose *Purshia mexicana*

Clivia Lindl. (Amaryllidaceae). *klive*-ee-uh. After Lady Charlotte Florentia Clive, Duchess of Northumberland (1787–1866), granddaughter of Robert Clive (of India). The genus was described from a plant of *C. nobilis* that flowered in her garden at Syon House in 1827. 6 spp. herbs. S Africa.

miniata Regel. min-ee-*ah*-tuh. Kaffir lily. Lat. coloured with red (the flowers).

nobilis Lindl. *noh*-bi-lis. Lat. renowned.

clover *Trifolium*. **crimson** *T. incarnatum*. **purple prairie** *Dalea purpurea*. **red** *Trifolium pratense*. **sulphur** *T.*

ochroleucum. **white** *T. repens.* **white prairie** *Dalea candida*

Cobaea Cav. (Polemoniaceae). *koh*-bee-uh. After Barnabas (Bernabé) de Cobo (1582–1657), Spanish Jesuit missionary. 18 spp. climbers. Trop. Am.

pringlei (House) Standl. *pring*-uhl-ee. After American horticulturist Cyrus Guernsey Pringle (1838–1911), who collected the type specimen near Monterrey in 1903. Mex.

scandens Cav. *skan*-duhnz. Cup and saucer vine. Lat. climbing. Mex.

cobra plant *Arisaema nepenthoides*
cockscomb *Celosia argentea* Cristata Group
cocksfoot *Dactylis glomerata*
cockspur thorn *Crataegus crus-galli*

Codiaeum Rumph. ex A. Juss. (Euphorbiaceae). koh-dee-*ie*-oom. From the local Moluccan name. 16 spp. shrubs. Indonesia, Malaysia, Pacific Is.

variegatum (L.) Rumph. ex A. Juss. va-ree-uh-*gah*-toom. Croton. Lat. variegated (the leaves). Indonesia, Pacific Is. var. *pictum* (Lodd.) Müll. Arg. = *C. variegatum*

Codonopsis Wall. (Campanulaceae). koh-don-*op*-sis. Gk. like a bell (the flowers). 30 spp. herbs. C, E and SE Asia.

clematidea (Schrenk) C. B. Clarke. klem-uh-*tid*-ee-uh. Bonnet bell-flower. Gk. resembling *Clematis*. C Asia, Himal.

convolvulacea Kurz. kon-vol-vew-*lay*-see-uh. Lat. like *Convolvulus*.

Himal., SW China. subsp. *vinciflora* (Kom.) D. Y. Hong. ving-ki-*flaw*-ruh. Lat. with flowers like *Vinca*. W China.

grey-wilsonii J. M. H. Shaw. gray-wil-*soh*-nee-ee. After Christopher Grey-Wilson (b. 1944), English botanist, author and plant collector, who described it as *C. nepalensis*. Nepal.

pilosula (Franch.) Nannf. pil-*oh*-zew-luh. Lat. slightly hairy. China, Korea, E Russia.

vinciflora Kom. = *C. convolvulacea* subsp. *vinciflora*

Coix L. (Poaceae). *koh*-ix. Gk. name used by Theophrastus for a reed-like plant. 4 spp. grasses. Trop. Asia.

lacryma-jobi L. *lak*-ri-muh-*joh*-bee. Job's tears. Lat. the tears of Job (the shape of the seeds). SE Asia.

Colchicum L. (Colchicaceae). *kol*-chik-oom. Autumn crocus. Lat. of Colchis on the Black Sea, where many grow (now part of Georgia). 100 spp. cormous herbs. Eur., N Africa, W and C Asia, W Himal.

×*agrippinum* Baker. uh-*grip*-i-noom. After Julia Agrippina (15–59), Roman empress and mother of Nero. *C. autumnale* × *C. variegatum*. Cult.

autumnale L. aw-toom-*nah*-lee. Lat. of autumn (flowering). Eur.

bornmuelleri Freyn = *C. speciosum*

bulbocodium Ker Gawl. bul-boh-*koh*-dee-oom. Gk. bulb wool, from the covering on the bulb. Eur., Caucasus.

×*byzantinum* Ker Gawl. biz-uhn-*tee*-noom. Of Byzantium (now Istanbul). *C. autumnale* × *C. cilicium*. SW Asia.

cilicicum (Boiss.) Dammer. si-*li*-si-koom. Lat. of Cilicia (now S Turkey). SW Asia.
speciosum Steven. spee-see-*oh*-soom. Lat. showy. Turkey, Iran.
tenorei Parl. = *C. cilicicum*

Coleus blumei Benth. = *Plectranthus scutellarioides*

colicroot *Liatris squarrosa*

Colletia Comm. ex Juss. (Rhamnaceae). ko-*let*-ee-uh. After Philibert Collet (1643–1718), French botanist. 5 spp. shrubs. S Am.
armata Miers = *C. hystrix*
cruciata Gillies & Hook. = *C. paradoxa*
hystrix Clos. *his*-trix. Lat. porcupine (it is very spiny). Chile, Argentina.
paradoxa (Spreng.) Escal. pa-ruh-*dox*-uh. Lat. unusual. Argentina, Uruguay, Brazil.

Collinsia Nutt. (Plantaginaceae). kol-*in*-zee-uh. After Zaccheus Collins (1764–1831), American naturalist. 20 spp. herbs. N Am.
bicolor Benth. = *C. heterophylla*
heterophylla G. Buist ex Graham. he-te-roh-*fil*-uh. Chinese houses. Lat. with variable leaves. Calif., Mex. (B.C.).

Colocasia Schott (Araceae). kol-oh-*kay*-zee-uh. The Gk. name, from Arabic. 7 spp. perenn. herbs. NE India, SE Asia.
esculenta (L.) Schott. esk-ew-*lent*-uh. Taro. Lat. edible (the tubers). Cult.

Colquhounia Wall. (Lamiaceae). kuh-*huen*-ee-uh. After Sir Robert David Colquhoun (1786–1838), who collected many plants in N India. 6 spp. shrubs. Himal., China, SE Asia.
coccinea Wall. kok-*sin*-ee-uh. Lat. scarlet (the flowers).

columbine *Aquilegia.* **Colorado blue** *A. coerulea.* **common** *A. vulgaris.* **golden** *A. chrysantha.* **longspur** *A. longissima.* **Rocky Mountain blue** *A. saximontana.* **Skinner's** *A. skinneri.* **Utah** *A. scopulorum.* **western** *A. formosa*

Columnea L. (Gesneriaceae). ko-*loom*-nee-uh. After Fabius Columna (1567–1650), Italian botanist. 75 spp. climbers, often epiphytic. Trop. Am.
schiedeana Schltdl. shee-dee-*ah*-nuh. After German botanist Christian Julius Wilhelm Schiede (1798–1836), who, with colleague Ferdinand Deppe, collected the type specimen in Veracruz in 1836. Mex.

Colutea L. (Fabaceae). ko-*lue*-tee-uh. From the Gk. name. 28 spp., shrubs, trees. Eur., Africa, W and C Asia.
arborescens L. ar-bor-*res*-uhnz. Bladder senna. Lat. becoming tree-like. S Eur.
×*media* Willd. *mee*-dee-uh. Lat. intermediate (between the parents). *C. arborescens* × *C. orientalis.* Cult.

comfrey *Symphytum officinale*

Commelina L. (Commelinaceae). ko-mel-*ee*-nuh. After Dutch botanists Jan (1629–1692) and Caspar (1668–1731) Commelijn, represented by the

two showy large petals. 170 spp.
herbs. Mainly tropics and subtropics.
coelestis Willd. = *C. tuberosa* Coelestis Group
dianthifolia Delile. die-anth-i-*foh*-lee-
uh. Lat. with leaves like *Dianthus*. C
USA, N Mex.
tuberosa L. tew-buh-*roh*-suh. Lat.
bearing tubers. S Mex., C and S Am.
Coelestis Group. see-*les*-tis. Lat.
sky-blue (the flowers).

compass plant *Silphium laciniatum*

Comptonia L'Hér. ex Aiton (Myricaceae). komp-*toh*-nee-uh. After Henry
Compton (1632–1713), bishop of
London 1675–1713. 1 sp., shrub.
USA, Canada.
peregrina (L.) J. M. Coult. pe-re-*gree*-
nuh. Sweetfern. Lat. travelling (it
spreads by suckers).

coneflower *Rudbeckia*. **cut-leaf** *R.*
laciniata. **drooping prairie** *Ratibida*
pinnata. **great** *Rudbeckia maxima*.
orange *R. fulgida*. **prairie** *Ratibida*
columnifera. **purple** *Echinacea*.
showy *Rudbeckia fulgida* var. *speci-*
osa. **sweet** *R. subtomentosa*. **western**
R. occidentalis

Conoclinium DC. (Asteraceae).
kon-oh-*klin*-ee-oom. Gk. cone bed,
referring to the conical receptacles.
4 spp. herbs. Canada, USA, Mex.
coelestinum (L.) DC. see-lest-*ee*-
noom. Blue mistflower. Lat. sky-blue
(the flowers). SE Canada, E and
C USA.

Convallaria L. (Asparagaceae). kon-
vuh-*lair*-ree-uh. From Lat. valley,

referring to the habitat. 1 sp., perenn.
herb. N temp. regs.
majalis L. muh-*jah*-lis. Lily of the
valley. Lat. of May (flowering). Eur.,
W Asia. var. *montana* (Raf.) H. E.
Ahles. mon-*tah*-nuh. American lily
of the valley. Lat. of mountains.
SE USA.
montana Raf. = *C. majalis* var.
montana

Convolvulus L. (Convolvulaceae).
kon-*vol*-vew-loos. Lat. to twine
(many are climbers). 125 spp., herbs,
shrubs. Widespread.
althaeoides L. al-thee-*oy*-deez. Like
Althaea. Medit.
cneorum L. nee-*or*-room. From the
Gk. name of an olive-like shrub. SE
Eur., N Africa.
mauritanicus Boiss. = *C. sabatius*
sabatius Viv. suh-*bah*-tee-oos. Of
Savona (Sabbatia), NW Italy. Italy,
N Africa.
tricolor L. *tri*-ko-lor. Lat. three-
coloured (the flowers). Medit.

copperleaf *Acalypha wilkesiana*

Coprosma J. R. & G. Forst. (Rubiaceae). ko-*proz*-muh. Gk. dung smell,
referring to the foliage. 90 spp.,
shrubs, trees. Indonesia to Australia,
NZ, Pacific Is.
acerosa A. Cunn. a-suh-*roh*-suh. Lat.
needle-like (the leaves). NZ.
brunnea (Kirk) Cockayne ex Cheesem. *broon*-ee-uh. Lat. brown (the
foliage). NZ.
cheesemanii W. R. B. Oliv. cheez-
man-ee-ee. After Thomas Frederick
Cheeseman (1845–1923), English-
born NZ botanist. NZ.

×*kirkii* Cheesem. *kirk*-ee-ee. After English-born botanist Thomas Kirk (1828–1898), who collected the type specimen in 1868. *C. acerosa* × *C. repens*. NZ.

petriei Cheesem. *pet*-ree-ee. After Scottish-born botanist and plant collector Donald Petrie (1846–1925). NZ.

propinqua A. Cunn. proh-*ping*-kwuh. Lat. close to (another species). NZ.

repens A. Rich. *ree*-puhnz. Lat. creeping (sometimes). NZ.

robusta Raoul. roh-*bus*-tuh. Lat. robust. NZ.

coral bean *Erythrina herbacea*
coral drops *Bessera elegans*
coral pea *Hardenbergia violacea*
coral plant *Berberidopsis corallina*
coral tree *Erythrina crista-galli*
coralbells *Heuchera sanguinea*
coralberry *Ardisia crenata, Symphoricarpos orbiculatus*

Cordyline Comm. ex R. Br. (Asparagaceae). kor-di-*lie*-nee. From Gk. club, referring to the thick, fleshy roots. 24 spp., shrubs, trees. SE Asia to Australia, Pacific Is.

australis (G. Forst.) Endl. os-*trah*-lis. Cabbage tree. Lat. southern. NZ.

'Albertii'. al-*bert*-ee-ee. After Albert I (1875–1934), king of Belgium 1909–34.

fruticosa (L.) A. Chev. frue-ti-*koh*-suh. Lat. shrubby. Papua New Guinea, W Pacific Is.

stricta (Sims) Endl. strik-tuh. Lat. upright. E Australia.

terminalis (L.) Kunth = *C. fruticosa*

Coreopsis L. (Asteraceae). ko-ree-*op*-sis. Tickseed. Gk. like a bug (the seeds resemble ticks). 35 spp., herbs, subshrubs. Americas.

alternifolia L. = *Verbesina alternifolia*

auriculata L. o-rik-ew-*lah*-tuh. Lobed tickseed. Lat. with small lobes (the leaves, sometimes). E USA.

basalis (A. Dietr.) S. F. Blake. buh-*sah*-lis. Goldenmane tickseed. Lat. from the base (branching, in the type specimen). SE USA.

grandiflora Hogg ex Sweet. gran-di-*flaw*-ruh. Large flower tickseed. Lat. large-flowered. SE Canada, E and C USA.

lanceolata L. lahn-see-oh-*lah*-tuh. Lanceleaf tickseed. Lat. lance-shaped (the leaves). SE Canada, E and C USA.

palmata Nutt. pahl-*mah*-tuh. Stiff tickseed. Lat. hand-like (the leaf lobing). E and C USA.

rosea Nutt. *roh*-zee-uh. Pink tickseed. Lat. pink (the flowers). E N Am.

tinctoria Nutt. tink-*tor*-ree-uh. Golden tickseed. Lat. of dyers (the flowers give a yellow dye). Canada, USA, N Mex.

tripteris L. *trip*-te-ris. Tall tickseed. Lat. three-winged (the three-lobed leaves). SE Canada, E and C USA.

verticillata L. vur-ti-si-*lah*-tuh. Whorled tickseed. Lat. whorled (the leaves). E USA.

coriander *Coriandrum sativum*

Coriandrum L. (Apiaceae). ko-ree-*an*-droom. The Lat. name, from Gk. 3 spp. herbs. SW Asia.

sativum L. sa-*tee*-voom. Coriander. Lat. cultivated. Cult.

Coriaria L. (Coriariaceae). ko-ree-*air*-ree-uh. From Lat. leather (*C. myrtifolia* was used in tanning). 15 spp., herbs, shrubs, trees. Mex. to S Am., W Medit., E and SE Asia, NZ.
japonica A. Gray. juh-*pon*-i-kuh. Of Japan. Japan.
terminalis Hemsl. ter-mi-*nah*-lis. Lat. terminal (the inflorescence). Himal., W China. var. *xanthocarpa* Rehder & E. H. Wilson. zanth-oh-*kar*-puh. Gk. yellow-fruited.

cork tree *Phellodendron*. **Amur** *P. amurense*
corn *Zea mays*
corn cockle *Agrostemma githago*
cornel *Cornus*
cornflower *Centaurea cyanus*. **perennial** *C. montana*

Cornus L. (Cornaceae). *kor*-noos. Cornel, dogwood. Lat. name for *C. mas*. 60 spp., trees, shrubs, herbs. Mainly N temp. regs.
alba L. *al*-buh. Siberian dogwood. Lat. white (the fruit). E Eur., N Asia. **'Gouchaultii'**. gue-*sholt*-ee-ee. After French nurseryman Auguste Gouchault (1851–1936), who raised it. **'Sibirica'**. si-*bi*-ri-kuh. Lat. of Siberia. **'Spaethii'**. *spayth*-ee-ee. After the Späth nursery, Germany, where it was raised.
alternifolia L.f. al-ter-ni-*foh*-lee-uh. Pagoda dogwood. Lat. with alternate leaves. SE Canada, E USA.
amomum Mill. uh-*moh*-moom. Silky dogwood. Lat. name of an aromatic shrub. SE Canada, E USA. subsp. *obliqua* (Raf.) J. S. Wilson. o-*bleek*-wuh. Lat. oblique (possibly referring to the leaf base).

angustata (Chun) T. R. Dudley = *C. elliptica*
canadensis L. kan-uh-*den*-sis. Bunchberry. Of Canada. N Am., E Asia.
capitata Wall. kap-i-*tah*-tuh. Lat. in a head (the flowers). Himal., China.
controversa Hemsl. ex Prain. kon-truh-*ver*-suh. Lat. controversial (unlike most species, it has alternate leaves). E Asia.
drummondii C. A. Mey. drum-*on*-dee-ee. After Scottish naturalist and explorer Thomas Drummond (ca. 1790–1835), who collected in Texas. SE Canada, E and C USA.
elliptica (Pojark.) Q. Y. Yang & Boufford. el-*ip*-ti-kuh. Lat. elliptic (the leaves). China.
florida L. *flo*-ri-duh. Flowering dogwood. Lat. flowering. SE Canada, E and C USA, Mex.
kousa Hance. *kue*-suh. Chinese dogwood, Japanese dogwood. From the Japanese name. China, Korea, Japan. var. *chinensis* Osborn. chin-*en*-sis. Of China.
macrophylla Wall. mak-*rof*-i-luh. Gk. large-leaved. Himal., E Asia.
mas L. *mas*. Cornelian cherry. Lat. masculine. Eur., W Asia.
nuttallii Audubon. nut-*al*-ee-ee. Pacific dogwood. After English botanist and ornithologist Thomas Nuttall (1786–1859), who collected in the USA. SW Canada, W USA.
obliqua Raf. = *C. amomum* subsp. *obliqua*
officinalis Sieb. & Zucc. of-is-i-*nah*-lis. Lat. sold as a med. herb. China.
pumila Koehne. *pew*-mi-luh. Lat. dwarf. Cult.

racemosa Lam. ras-i-*moh*-suh. Grey dogwood. Lat. in racemes (the flowers). Canada, E and C USA.

sanguinea L. san-*gwin*-ee-uh. Common dogwood. Lat. bloody (the red autumn colour). Eur., W Asia.

sericea L. suh-*rik*-ee-uh. Red osier dogwood. Lat. silky (the leaf undersides). Canada, USA, N Mex.

'Flaviramea'. flav-i-*rahm*-ee-uh. Lat. with golden yellow shoots. 'Kelseyi'. *kel*-see-ee. Of Kelsey Highlands Nursery, Massachusetts, USA, which introduced it in 1939.

stolonifera Michx. = *C. sericea*

Corokia A. Cunn. (Argophyllaceae). ko-*roh*-kee-uh. From the Maori name. 3 spp. shrubs. NZ.

buddlejoides A. Cunn. bud-lee-*oy*-deez. Lat. like *Buddleja*. NZ (N.I.).

cotoneaster Raoul. ko-toh-nee-*as*-ter. From the resemblance of the habit to a cotoneaster.

macrocarpa Kirk. mak-roh-*kar*-puh. Gk. large-fruited. Chatham Is.

×*virgata* Turrill. vir-*gah*-tuh. Lat. twiggy. *C. buddlejoides* × *C. cotoneaster*. Cult.

Coronilla L. (Fabaceae). ko-ro-*nil*-uh. Lat. a little crown (the arrangement of the flowers). 9 spp., herbs, shrubs. Eur., Medit.

emerus L. = *Hippocrepis emerus*

valentina L. val-en-*tee*-nuh. Of Valencia (originally Valentia). Medit. subsp. *glauca* (L.) Batt. *glaw*-kuh. Lat. bluish white (the leaves). 'Citrina'. sit-*ree*-nuh. Lat. lemon-yellow (the flowers).

Correa Andrews (Rutaceae). *ko*-ree-uh. After José Francisco Correia da Serra (1750–1823), Portuguese botanist. 12 spp. shrubs. Australia.

alba Andrews. *al*-buh. Lat. white (the flowers). SE Australia, Tasmania.

backhouseana Hook. bak-hows-ee-*ah*-nuh. After English nurseryman and missionary James Backhouse (1794–1869), who collected the type specimen in 1833. Tasmania.

lawrenceana Hook. lo-*rens*-ee-*ah*-nuh. After English botanist Robert William Lawrence (1807–1833), who worked in Tasmania and sent many specimens to Hooker. SE Australia, Tasmania.

'Mannii'. *man*-ee-ee. After Sir Frederick Wollaston Mann (1869–1958), Australian barrister and chief justice, in whose Melbourne garden it originated. *C. pulchella* × *C. reflexa*.

pulchella Sweet. pool-*kel*-uh. Lat. beautiful. S Australia.

reflexa (Labill.) Vent. ree-*flex*-uh. Lat. reflexed (the corolla lobes). S and E Australia.

Cortaderia Stapf (Poaceae). kor-tuh-de-ree-uh. From the Argentine name, from Spanish to cut. 24 spp. grasses. S Am., NZ.

fulvida (Buchanan) Zotov. *fool*-vi-duh. Lat. tawny (the inflorescence). NZ.

richardii (Endl.) Zotov. rich-*ard*-ee-ee. After French botanist Achille Richard (1794–1852), who called it *Arundo australis*, a name that had already been used. NZ.

selloana Schult. & Schult.f. sel-oh-*ah*-nuh. Pampas grass. After German botanist Friedrich Sellow (Sello)

(1798–1831), who collected in Brazil and Uruguay. S Am.

Corydalis DC. (Papaveraceae). ko-*rid*-uh-lis. From Gk. crested lark, from the resemblance of the spur of the flower to a lark's crest. 400 spp. herbs. N temp. regs.
buschii Nakai. *boosh*-ee-ee. After Nicolaï Adolfowitsch Busch (1869–1941), Russian botanist. E Russia, Korea.
cashmeriana Royle. kash-me-ree-*ah*-nuh. Of Kashmir. Himal., S Tibet.
cava (L.) Schweigg. & Körte. *kah*-vuh. Lat. hollow (the root). Eur., W Asia.
cheilanthifolia Hemsl. kie-lan-thi-*foh*-lee-uh. Lat. with leaves like *Cheilanthes*. China.
elata Bureau & Franch. ee-*lah*-tuh. Lat. tall. W China.
flexuosa Franch. flex-ew-*oh*-suh. Lat. curved, wavy (the spur of the flower). W China.
leucanthema C. Y. Wu. lue-*kanth*-e-muh. Gk. white-flowered (sometimes). W China.
lutea (L.) DC. = *Pseudofumaria lutea*
malkensis Galushko. mal-*ken*-sis. Of the Malka River valley. N Caucasus.
nobilis (L.) Pers. *noh*-bi-lis. Lat. renowned. C Asia.
ochroleuca W. D. J. Koch = *Pseudofumaria alba*
ophiocarpa Hook.f. & Thomson. of-ee-oh-*karp*-uh. Gk. snake fruit (the fruits are slender and twisted). Himal., China, Japan.
quantmeyeriana Fedde. kwont-may-uh-ree-*ah*-nuh. After Wilhelm Quantmeyer of Dahlem, Germany. W China.

sempervirens (L.) Pers. sem-per-*vie*-ruhnz. Lat. evergreen. N Am.
solida (L.) Clairv. *so*-li-duh. Lat. solid (the root). Eur., N Africa, W Asia.

Corylopsis Sieb. & Zucc. (Hamamelidaceae). ko-ril-*op*-sis. Gk. like *Corylus*, from the similar leaves. 7 spp. shrubs. Himal., China, Taiwan, Korea, Japan.
glabrescens Franch. & Sav. glab-*res*-uhnz. Lat. becoming glabrous. Japan, S Korea.
gotoana Makino. goh-toh-*ah*-nuh. After Suekichi Goto, of the Imperial University of Tokyo, who collected one of the specimens from which it was described. Japan, Korea.
pauciflora Sieb. & Zucc. paw-si-*flaw*-ruh. Lat. few-flowered (the inflorescence). Japan, Taiwan.
sinensis Hemsl. sin-*en*-sis. Lat. of China. China. var. ***calvescens*** Rehder & E. H. Wilson. kal-*ves*-uhnz. Lat. becoming hairless. f. ***veitchiana*** (Bean) B. D. Morley & J. M. Chao. veech-ee-*ah*-nuh. After the nursery of Messrs Veitch, which introduced it.
spicata Sieb. & Zucc. spi-*kah*-tuh. Lat. in spikes (the flowers). Japan.
veitchiana Bean = *C. sinensis* f. *veitchiana*

Corylus L. (Betulaceae). *ko*-ril-oos. From the Gk. name, from Gk. helmet, from the shape of the husk. 16 spp., trees, shrubs. N temp. regs.
americana Marshall. uh-me-ri-*kah*-nuh. American hazel. Of America. SC Canada, E USA.
avellana L. av-uh-*lah*-nuh. Common hazel. Named used by Pliny, from

Abellina, an old name for Damascus.
Eur., W Asia. **'Contorta'.** kon-*tor*-
tuh. Corkscrew hazel, Harry
Lauder's walking stick. Lat. twisted
(the shoots).

colurna L. ko-*lurn*-uh. Turkish hazel.
The Lat. name. SE Eur., W Asia.

cornuta Marshall. kor-*new*-tuh.
Beaked hazel. Lat. horned (the
beaked husk). S Canada, USA. subsp.

californica (A. DC.) E. Murr. kal-i-
for-ni-kuh. California hazel. Of California. W USA, SW Canada.

maxima Mill. *max*-i-muh. Filbert.
Lat. largest. SE Eur., W Asia.

Corymbia K. D. Hill & L. A. S.
Johnson (Myrtaceae). ko-*rim*-bee-
uh. From Lat. cluster, referring to the
corymbose flower clusters. 100 spp.
trees. Australia to New Guinea.

citriodora (Hook.) K. D. Hill &
L. A. S. Johnson. sit-ree-oh-*dor*-ruh.
Lemon-scented gum. Lat. lemon-
scented. E Australia.

Corynabutilon (K. Schum.) Kearney
(Malvaceae). ko-rien-uh-*bew*-ti-lon.
Gk. club, *Abutilon*, referring to the
shape of the stigma. 6 spp. shrubs.
Chile, Argentina.

×*suntense* (C. D. Brickell) Fryxell.
sun-*ten*-see. Of Sunte House, West
Sussex, England, where it was raised.
C. ochsenii × *C. vitifolium.* Cult.

vitifolium (Cav.) Kearney. vi-ti-*foh*-
lee-oom. Lat. with leaves like *Vitis.*
Chile.

Cosmos Cav. (Asteraceae). *koz*-mos.
Gk. ornament. 26 spp. herbs. Warm
and trop. Am.

atrosanguineus (Hook.) Voss.
at-roh-san-*gwin*-ee-oos. Chocolate
cosmos. Mex. (extinct).

bipinnatus Cav. bie-pin-*ah*-toos.
Lat. twice pinnate (the leaves). S
USA, Mex.

sulphureus Cav. sul-*few*-ree-oos. Lat.
like sulphur (the yellow flowers).
Mex. to N S Am.

Cotinus Mill. (Anacardiaceae). *kot*-i-
noos, kot-*ee*-noos. From Gk. name of
the wild olive. 6 spp., shrubs, trees.
Eur., W Asia, Himal., China, S USA,
Mex.

coggygria Scop. ko-*gig*-ree-uh. Smoke
tree. From the Gk. name. Eur. to
China.

obovatus Raf. ob-oh-*vah*-toos. American smoke tree, chittamwood. Lat.
obovate (the leaves). SC USA.

Cotoneaster Medik. (Rosaceae).
kot-oh-nee-*as*-ter. Gk./Lat. wild
quince. 400 spp., shrubs, trees. Eur.,
W and C Asia, Himal., China,
Taiwan.

adpressus Bois. ad-*pres*-oos. Lat. press-
ing against (the ground), referring to
its low, spreading habit. SW China.
var. *praecox* Bois & Berth. = *C.*
nanshan

atropurpureus Flinck & B. Hylmö.
at-roh-pur-*pew*-ree-oos. Lat. dark
purple (the base of the petals). W
China (Hubei).

bullatus Bois. bool-*ah*-toos. Lat. bul-
late (puckered, the leaves). China
(Sichuan).

cochleatus (Franch.) G. Klotz.
kok-lee-*ah*-toos. Lat. shell-like (the
leaves). W China.

congestus Baker. kon-*jes*-toos. Lat. congested (the habit). Himal.

conspicuus J. B. Comber ex Marquand. kon-*spik*-ew-oos. Lat. conspicuous (the fruit). Tibet.

dammeri C. K. Schneid. *dam*-uh-ree. After German botanist Carl Lebrecht Udo Dammer (1860–1920), who named the related *C. radicans*. China (Hubei).

dielsianus E. Pritz. deel-zee-*ah*-noos. After German botanist Friedrich Ludwig Emil Diels (1874–1945), who described several species in the genus. W China.

divaricatus Rehder & E. H. Wilson. di-va-ri-*kah*-toos. Lat. wide-spreading (the branches). China (Hubei).

franchetii Bois. fran-*shet*-ee-ee. After French botanist Adrien René Franchet (1834–1900), who described many new species from China. China (Yunnan).

frigidus Wall. ex Lindl. *frij*-i-doos. Lat. cold (the regions where it grows). Himal.

horizontalis Decne. ho-ri-zon-*tah*-lis. Lat. spreading horizontally. W China.

'Hybridus Pendulus'. *hib*-ri-doos *pen*-dew-loos. Lat. weeping hybrid.

integrifolius (Roxb.) G. Klotz. in-teg-ri-*foh*-lee-oos. Lat. with entire (untoothed) leaves (it was originally described as a species of *Crataegus*). Himal.

lacteus W. W. Sm. *lak*-tee-oos. Lat. milky (the flowers). SW China.

lucidus Schltdl. *lue*-si-doos. Lat. shiny (the leaves). Siberia, Mongolia.

microphyllus Wall. ex Lindl. mik-*rof*-i-loos. Gk. small-leaved. Nepal.

nanshan Vilm. ex Mottet. *nan*-shan. From Nanshan. SW China.

procumbens G. Klotz. proh-*kum*-buhnz. Lat. creeping. SW China.

salicifolius Franch. sal-i-si-*foh*-lee-oos. Lat. with leaves like *Salix*. W China.

simonsii Baker. sie-*monz*-ee-ee. After Charles Simons, apothecary in India, who introduced it to cultivation. Sikkim, Bhutan.

sternianus (Turrill) Boom. stern-ee-*ah*-noos. After Sir Frederick Stern (1884–1967), of Highdown, W Sussex, from whose garden the type specimen was collected. China (Yunnan).

×*suecicus* G. Klotz. *swes*-i-koos. Lat. of Sweden. *C. conspicuus* × *C. dammeri*. Cult.

×*watereri* Exell. *war*-tuh-ruh-ree. After the nursery of John Waterer Sons & Crisp, where it originated. *C. frigidus* × *C. salicifolius*. Cult.

---

cotton grass *Eriophorum*. **common** *E. angustifolium*

cottonwood *Populus*. **black** *P. trichocarpa*. **eastern** *P. deltoides*. **narrow-leaf** *P. angustifolia*

Cotula L. (Asteraceae). *kot*-ew-luh. Gk. a small cup (the flowerheads). 50 spp. herbs. Africa, Mex., S Am.

coronopifolia L. ko-ro-noh-pi-*foh*-lee-uh. Brass buttons. With leaves like *Coronopus*. S Africa.

hispida (DC.) Harv. *his*-pi-duh. Lat. with bristly hairs (the foliage). S Africa.

minor (Hook.f.) Hook.f. = *Leptinella minor*

squalida (Hook.f.) Hook.f. = *Leptinella squalida*

Cotyledon L. (Crassulaceae). kot-i-*lee*-don. Gk. a cup-shaped hollow, referring to the leaves of some species. 10 spp. succulent shrubs. E and S Africa, Arabia.
ladismithensis Poelln. = *C. tomentosa* subsp. *ladismithensis*
orbiculata L. or-bik-ew-*lah*-tuh. Lat. orbicular (the leaves, sometimes). S Africa.
tomentosa Harv. to-men-*toh*-suh. Bear's paws. Lat. hairy (the leaves). S Africa. subsp. *ladismithensis* (Poelln.) Toelken. lay-dee-smith-*en*-sis. Of Ladysmith, S Africa.

courgette *Cucurbita pepo*
cow parsley *Anthriscus sylvestris*
cow parsnip, American *Heracleum maximum*

Cowania mexicana D. Don = *Purshia mexicana*

cowberry *Vaccinium vitis-idaea*
cowslip *Primula veris*
coyotebrush *Baccharis pilularis*
crab (apple), European *Malus sylvestris*. garland *M. coronaria*. Japanese *M. floribunda*. Oregon *M. fusca*. prairie *M. ioensis*. Siberian *M. baccata*. sweet *M. coronaria*

Crambe L. (Brassicaceae). *kram*-bee. Lat./Gk. name for cabbage, from the similar leaves. 35 spp. herbs. Eur., W and C Asia, Africa.
cordifolia Steven. kor-di-*foh*-lee-uh. Lat. with heart-shaped leaves. Caucasus.
maritima L. muh-*ri*-ti-muh. Sea kale. Lat. of the sea (it grows on coasts). Eur., W Asia.

cranberry *Vaccinium macrocarpon*. European *V. oxycoccus*
cranesbill *Geranium*. Armenian *G. psilostemon*. bloody *G. sanguineum*. dusky *G. phaeum*. Himalayan *G. himalayense*. meadow *G. pratense*. spotted *G. maculatum*. wood *G. sylvaticum*
crape myrtle *Lagerstroemia indica*

Crassula L. (Crassulaceae). kras-ew-luh. From Lat. thick, referring to the succulent leaves. 200 spp., herbs, shrubs, mainly succulent. Widespread.
arborescens (Mill.) Willd. ar-bor-*res*-uhnz. Lat. becoming tree-like. S Africa.
argentea Thunb. = *C. ovata*
ovata (Mill.) Druce. oh-*vah*-tuh. Jade plant. Lat. ovate (the leaves). S Africa.

Crataegus L. (Rosaceae). kruh-*tee*-goos. Hawthorn. From Gk. strength, referring to the hard wood. 140 spp., trees, shrubs. N temp. regs.
aestivalis (Walter) Torr. & A. Gray. ees-ti-*vah*-lis. Mayhaw. Lat. of summer (flowering). SE USA.
arnoldiana Sarg. = *C. mollis*
azarolus L. az-uh-*rol*-oos. Azarole. The Italian name, from the Arabic name of the fruit. SE Eur., W and C Asia, N Africa.
coccinea L. kok-*sin*-ee-uh. Scarlet hawthorn. Lat. scarlet (the fruit). E Canada, E and C USA.
columbiana Howell = *C. douglasii*
crus-galli L. kroos-*gal*-ee. Cockspur thorn. Lat. a cock's spur (referring to the long spines). E Canada, E and C USA.

douglasii Lindl. dug-*las*-ee-ee. After Scottish botanist and plant collector David Douglas (1799–1834), who introduced it to cultivation in England in 1828. S Canada, W and C USA.

×*durobrivensis* Sarg. dew-roh-briv-*en*-sis. Of Rochester (New York), from Durobriva, Roman name for Rochester, England. USA (New York).

×*grignonensis* Mouill. green-yon-*en*-sis. Of Grignon, France, where it was found. *C. mexicana* × *C.* sp. Cult.

laevigata (Poir.) DC. lee-vi-*gah*-tuh. Midland hawthorn. Lat. smooth (the leaves). Eur.

×*lavalleei* Hérincq ex Lavallée. lah-*val*-ay-ee. After Alphonse Lavallée (1836–1881), founder of the Arboretum Segrez, France, where it was raised. *C. crus-galli* × *C. mexicana*. Cult. 'Carrièrei'. ka-ree-*e*-ree-ee. After French botanist Élie-Abel Carrière (1818–1896).

×*media* Bechst. *mee*-dee-uh. Lat. intermediate (between the parents). *C. laevigata* × *C. monogyna*. Eur.

mollis (Torr. & A. Gray) Scheele. *mol*-is. Downy hawthorn. Lat. soft (the hairy leaves). SE Canada, E and C USA.

monogyna Jacq. mon-oh-*gie*-nuh. Common hawthorn. Gk. with one ovary. Eur., W Asia, N Africa. 'Biflora'. bie-*flaw*-ruh. Glastonbury thorn. Lat. flowering twice.

×*mordenensis* Boom. mor-duhn-*en*-sis. Of Morden (Agriculture Canada Research Station, Morden, Manitoba, Canada), where it was raised. *C. laevigata* × *C. succulenta*. Cult.

orientalis Pall. ex M. Bieb. o-ree-en-*tah*-lis. Oriental hawthorn. Lat. eastern. E Eur., W Asia.

persimilis Sarg. per-*si*-mi-lis. Lat. very similar (to *C. crus-galli*). SE Canada, NE USA.

phaenopyrum (L.f.) Medik. feen-oh-*pie*-room. Washington thorn. Gk. pear-like. E USA.

pinnatifida Bunge. pin-at-i-*feed*-uh. Chinese hawthorn. Lat. pinnately cut (the leaves). E Russia, China, Korea. var. *major* N. E. Br. *may*-juh. Lat. large (the fruit). Cult.

tanacetifolia (Lam.) Pers. tan-uh-see-ti-*foh*-lee-uh. Tansy-leaved thorn. Lat. with leaves like *Tanacetum*. Turkey.

viridis L. *vi*-ri-dis. Green hawthorn. Lat. green (the leaves, on both sides). E and C USA.

creeping Jenny *Lysimachia nummularia*. **dwarf** *L. japonica* var. *minutissima*

Crepis L. (Asteraceae). *krep*-is. Gk. name of another plant, from Gk. slipper, possibly referring to the shape of the fruit. 200 spp. herbs. Widespread in N hemisph.

incana Sibth. & Sm. in-*kah*-nuh. Pink dandelion. Lat. grey (the leaves). Greece.

Cretan brake *Pteris cretica*

Crinodendron Molina (Elaeocarpaceae). krin-oh-*den*-dron. Gk. lily tree. 5 spp., shrubs, trees. S Am.

hookerianum Gay. hook-uh-ree-*ah*-noom. Lantern tree. After Sir William Jackson Hooker (1785–

1865), English botanist and first director of RBG Kew, who had a particular interest in Chilean plants. Chile.

patagua Mol. puh-*tag*-wuh. The Chilean name. Chile.

Crinum L. (Amaryllidaceae). *krie*-noom. From Gk. lily. 100 spp. bulbous herbs. Widespread in trop. and subtrop. regs.

americanum L. uh-me-ri-*kah*-noom. Florida swamp lily. Of America. SE USA, Mex., Caribb.

bulbispermum (Burm.f.) Milne-Redh. & Schweick. bulb-i-*sperm*-oom. Lat. with bulbous seeds. S Africa.

moorei Hook.f. *mor*-ree-ee. After Scottish botanist David Moore (1808–1879), curator of the National Botanic Gardens, Glasnevin, Dublin, where it was first grown. S Africa.

×***powellii*** Baker. *powl*-ee-ee. After C. Baden Powell, who raised it ca. 1885. *C. bulbispermum* × *C. moorei*. Cult.

Crocosmia Planch. (Iridaceae). kroh-*koz*-mee-uh. Montbretia. From Gk. saffron scent, referring to the fragrant flowers. 8 spp. herbs. Trop. and S Africa.

×***crocosmiiflora*** (Lemoine) N. E. Br. kroh-koz-mee-i-*flaw*-ruh. Lat. with flowers like *Crocosmia* (it was originally described as a species of *Montbretia*). *C. aurea* × *C. pottsii*. S Africa.

×***crocosmioides*** (Leichtlin ex J. N. Gerard) Goldblatt. kroh-koz-mee-*oy*-deez. Lat. like *Crocosmia* (it was originally described as a species of *Antholyza*). *C. aurea* × *C. paniculata*. Cult.

masoniorum (L. Bolus) N. E. Br. may-son-ee-*or*-room. After Marianne

Harriet Mason (1845–1932) and her brother Canon George Edward Mason (d. 1928), who collected it and introduced it to cultivation. S Africa.

paniculata (Klatt) Goldblatt. pan-ik-ew-*lah*-tuh. Lat. in panicles (the flowers). S Africa.

pottsii (Baker) N. E. Br. *pot*-see-ee. After George Honington Potts (1830–1907), who distributed it from his Scottish garden. The type specimen was taken from plants cultivated from his introduction. S Africa.

Crocus L. (Iridaceae). *kroh*-koos. From Gk. saffron. 80 spp. cormous herbs. Eur., N Africa, W and C Asia to China.

angustifolius Weston. an-gus-ti-*foh*-lee-oos. Lat. narrow-leaved. E Eur., Caucasus.

banaticus J. Gay. buh-*nat*-i-koos. Of Banat (now divided between Romania, Serbia and Hungary). E Eur.

biflorus Mill. bie-*flaw*-roos. Lat. two-flowered. SE Eur., SW Asia.

cartwrightianus Herb. kart-rite-ee-*ah*-noos. After its discoverer, John Cartwright, British consul-general in Constantinople (Istanbul) in the early 19th cent. Greece, Crete.

chrysanthus (Herb.) Herb. kris-*anth*-oos. Gk. golden-flowered. SE Eur., Turkey.

etruscus Parl. ee-*troos*-koos. Lat. of Etruria (now roughly equivalent to Tuscany). N Italy.

flavus Weston. *flah*-voos. Lat. yellow (the flowers). SE Eur., W Turkey.

goulimyi Turrill. gue-*lim*-ee-ee. After Greek lawyer and amateur botanist

Constantine N. Goulimy (1886–1963), who collected the type specimen in 1954. Greece.

hadriaticus Herb. had-ree-*at*-i-koos. Lat. of the Adriatic reg. Greece.

korolkowii Maw & Regel. ko-rol-*kov*-ee-ee. After General Nicolai Iwanawitsch Korolkow (b. 1837), who collected the type specimen. C Asia to N Pakistan.

kotschyanus K. Koch. kot-shee-*ah*-noos. After Carl Georg Theodor Kotschy (1813–1866), Austrian botanist. Turkey, Caucasus, Lebanon.

longiflorus Raf. long-gi-*flaw*-roos. Lat. long-flowered. S Italy, Sicily, Malta.

luteus Lam. = *C. flavus*

pulchellus Herb. pool-*kel*-oos. Lat. beautiful. SE Eur., Turkey.

sativus L. sa-*tee*-voos. Saffron. Lat. cultivated. E Medit.

serotinus Salisb. se-*rot*-i-noos, se-ro-*teen*-oos. Lat. late (flowering). Portugal, Spain, Morocco.

sieberi J. Gay. *zee*-buh-ree. After Prague-born botanist and plant collector Franz Wilhelm Sieber (1789–1844), who collected the type specimen on Crete in 1825. SE Eur.

speciosus M. Bieb. spee-see-*oh*-soos. Lat. showy. SW Asia.

tommasinianus Herb. tom-uh-sin-ee-*ah*-noos. After Muzio Giuseppe Spirito de Tommasini (1794–1879), Italian botanist. SE Eur.

vernus (L.) Hill. *ver*-noos. Lat. of spring (flowering). Eur.

versicolor Ker Gawl. ver-*si*-ko-lor. Lat. variably coloured (the flowers). S France, N Italy.

crocus, autumn *Colchicum*
crossvine *Bignonia capreolata*

croton *Codiaeum variegatum*
crown imperial *Fritillaria imperialis*
crown of thorns *Euphorbia milii*
cruel plant *Araujia sericifera*

Cryptogramma R. Br. (Pteridaceae). krip-toh-*gram*-uh. Gk. hidden line, the line of spore-bearing sori at the frond edge are hidden under the revolute margin. 10 spp. ferns. N hemisph., S Am.

crispa (L.) R. Br. *kris*-puh. Parsley fern. Lat. curled, wavy (the frond margin). Eur., W Asia.

Cryptomeria D. Don (Cupressaceae). krip-toh-*me*-ree-uh. Gk. hidden parts, referring to the reproductive structures. 1 sp., conifer. Japan.

japonica D. Don. juh-*pon*-i-kuh. Japanese cedar. Of Japan.

cuckoo flower *Cardamine pratensis*
cuckoo pint *Arum maculatum*
cucumber *Cucumis sativus*
cucumber tree *Magnolia acuminata*

Cucumis L. (Cucurbitaceae). kew-*kew*-mis. Lat. name for cucumber. 50 spp. herbs. Trop. Africa, trop. Asia.

melo L. *mee*-loh. Melon. Lat. name of an apple-shaped melon. Cult. **Cantalupensis Group**. kan-tuh-lue-*pen*-sis. Cantaloupe. Of Cantalupo, near Rome. **Inodorus Group**. in-oh-*dor*-roos. Honeydew melon. Lat. without scent. **Reticulatus Group**. re-tik-ew-*lah*-toos. Musk melon. Lat. net-veined (the fruit).

sativus L. sa-*tee*-voos. Cucumber, gherkin. Lat. cultivated. Cult.

Cucurbita L. (Cucurbitaceae). kew-*kur*-bit-uh. Lat. name for a gourd used as a drinking vessel. 14 spp. herbs. Trop. and subtrop. Am.

argyrosperma C. Huber. ar-gi-roh-*sperm*-uh. Silver-seed gourd. Gk. with silvery seeds. Mex., C Am.

maxima Duchesne. *max*-i-muh. Pumpkin, squash. Lat. largest. Argentina, Uruguay.

moschata Duchesne. mos-*kah*-tuh. Calabaza, pumpkin, squash. Lat. musk-scented (the fruit). Cult.

pepo L. *pee*-poh. Courgette, marrow, pumpkin, zucchini. Lat. name for a kind of melon. Cult.

Culver's root *Veronicastrum virginicum*

Cunninghamia R. Br. ex Rich. (Cupressaceae). kun-ing-*ham*-ee-uh. After James Cunningham, a surgeon with the East India Company, who discovered it in 1701. 2 spp. conifers. China, Taiwan.

lanceolata (Lamb.) Hook. lahn-see-oh-*lah*-tuh. Chinese fir. Lat. lance-shaped (the leaves). China.

cup and saucer vine *Cobaea scandens*
cup flower *Nierembergia linariifolia*
cup plant *Silphium perfoliatum*

Cuphea P. Browne (Lythraceae). *kew*-fee-uh. Gk. curved, referring to the seed pods. 260 spp., herbs, sub-shrubs. SE USA, Mex., C and S Am.

cyanea DC. sie-*an*-ee-uh. Gk. dark blue (two of the petals). Mex.

hyssopifolia Kunth. hi-sop-i-*foh*-lee-uh. Lat. with leaves like *Hyssopus*. S Mex., C Am.

ignea A. DC. *ig*-nee-uh. Cigar flower, firecracker plant. Lat. fiery (the flowers). S Mex.

Cupid's dart *Catananche caerulea*

×*Cupressocyparis leylandii* (Dallim. & A. B. Jacks.) Dallim. = ×*Cuprocyparis leylandii*

Cupressus L. (Cupressaceae). kew-*pres*-oos. Cypresses. Lat. name for *C. sempervirens*. 14 spp. conifers. Medit., SW Asia, Himal., China, N and C Am.

arizonica Greene. a-ri-*zon*-i-kuh. Arizona cypress. Of Arizona. SW USA, N Mex. var. *glabra* (Sudw.) Little. *glab*-ruh. Smooth Arizona cypress. Lat. smooth (the bark).

cashmeriana Royle ex Carrière. kash-me-ree-*ah*-nuh. Of Kashmir. Bhutan.

lusitanica Mill. lue-si-*tan*-i-kuh. Cedar of Goa, Mexican cypress. Lat. of Portugal (Lat. *Lusitania*), to where it was introduced. Mex., C Am.

macrocarpa Hartw. ex Gord. mak-roh-*kar*-puh. Monterrey cypress. Gk. large-fruited. Calif.

sempervirens L. sem-per-*vie*-ruhnz. Italian cypress. Lat. evergreen. Medit., W Asia.

×*Cuprocyparis* Farjon (Cupressaceae). kew-proh-*si*-pa-ris. From the names of the parents (*Cupressus* × *Xanthocyparis*). Coniferous trees. Cult.

leylandii (A. B. Jacks. & Dallim.) Farjon. lay-*land*-ee-ee. Leyland cypress. After Christopher John Leyland (Naylor) (1849–1926), who planted some of the first trees at Haggerston

Hall, Northumbria, England. *C. macrocarpa* × *X. nootkatensis.*

currant, alpine *Ribes alpinum.* **black** *R. nigrum.* **buffalo** *R. aureum* var. *villosum.* **clove** *R. aureum* var. *villosum.* **flowering** *R. sanguineum.* **golden** *R. aureum.* **red** *R. rubrum.* **wax** *R. cereum*
curry plant *Helichrysum italicum* subsp. *serotinum*

Cyananthus Wall. ex Benth. (Campanulaceae). sie-uhn-*anth*-oos. Gk. blue flower. 23 spp. herbs. SW China, Himal.
lobatus Wall. ex Benth. loh-*bah*-toos. Lat. lobed (the leaves). Himal.
microphyllus Edgew. mik-*rof*-i-loos. Gk. small-leaved. Himal.
sherriffii Cowan. she-*rif*-ee-ee. After Major George Sherriff (1898–1967), Scottish botanist and plant collector, who, with Frank Ludlow, collected the type specimen in 1936. Tibet.

Cycas L. (Cycadaceae). *sie*-kas. From Gk. name of a palm. 90 spp., palm-like shrubs, trees. Australia, SE Asia, Pacific Is., E Africa.
circinalis L. sir-sin-*ah*-lis. Lat. a spiral, referring to the arrangement of leaf-lets in expanding leaves. S India.
revoluta Thunb. rev-o-*lue*-tuh. Lat. revolute (the leaflet margins). S Japan.
rumphii Miq. *rumf*-ee-ee. After Georg Eberhard Rumpf (Lat. *Rumphius*) (1628–1702), German-born botanist and officer of the Dutch East India Co., whose illustration is the type of the species. Borneo and Java to Papua New Guinea.

Cyclamen L. (Primulaceae). *sik*-luh-muhn. From the Gk. name, from Gk. circle, perhaps referring to its use in garlands. 20 spp. tuberous herbs. Eur., Medit., N Africa, SW Asia.
africanum Boiss. & Reut. af-ri-*kah*-noom. Of Africa. Algeria.
alpinum hort. Damman ex Spreng. al-*pie*-noom. Lat. alpine. SW Turkey.
cilicium Boiss. & Heldr. si-*lis*-ee-oom. Lat. of Cilicia. S Turkey.
coum Mill. *koh*-oom. Lat. of Kos. SE Eur. to N Iran.
europaeum L. = *C. purpurascens*
graecum Link. *greek*-oom. Lat. of Greece. S Greece, S Turkey.
hederifolium Aiton. hed-uh-ri-*foh*-lee-oom. Lat. with leaves like *Hedera.* S Eur., Turkey.
mirabile Hildebr. mi-*rah*-bi-lee. Lat. wonderful. SW Turkey.
neapolitanum Ten. = *C. hederifolium*
persicum Mill. *per*-si-koom. Lat. of Persia (Iran), where it does not grow. Greek Is., N Africa, SW Asia.
pseudibericum Hildebr. sued-i-*be*-ri-koom. The false *C. ibericum.* S Turkey.
purpurascens Mill. pur-pew-*ras*-uhnz. Lat. purplish (the flowers). Eur.
repandum Sibth. & Sm. ree-*pan*-doom. Lat. wavy-edged (the leaves). S Eur.

Cydonia Mill. (Rosaceae). sie-*doh*-nee-uh. From the Gk. name, from Gk. Kydonia, now Chania, Crete. 1 sp., tree. SW Asia.
oblonga Mill. ob-*long*-uh. Quince. Lat. oblong (the fruit).

Cymbalaria Hill (Plantaginaceae). sim-buh-*lair*-ree-uh. Gk. like a cym-

bal (the leaf shape). 9 spp. herbs. Eur.,
Medit., SW Asia.
muralis Gaertn.f. mew-*rah*-lis. Ivy-
leaved toadflax. Lat. of walls (where
it often grows). Eur.
pallida (Ten.) Wettst. *pa*-li-duh. Lat.
pale (the flowers). Italy.

Cymbidium Sw. (Orchidaceae).
sim-*bid*-ee-oom. From Gk. boat-
shaped, from the shape of the lip. 65
spp. orchids. Trop. Asia to Australia.

Cynara L. (Asteraceae). sie-*nah*-ruh.
From the Gk. name, after the Island
of Cinara, now Kinaros. 8 spp. herbs.
Medit.
cardunculus L. kar-*dunk*-ew-loos.
Cardoon. Lat. a small thistle. SW
Eur., N Africa. **Scolymus Group**.
skol-i-moos. Globe artichoke. Lat.
name for golden thistle (*Scolymus
hispanicus*).
scolymus L. = *C. cardunculus* Scolymus Group

Cynoglossum L. (Boraginaceae).
sie-noh-*glos*-oom. Hound's tongue.
Gk. dog tongue, referring to the
shape of the leaves. 60 spp. herbs.
Widespread, mainly temp. regs.
amabile Stapf & J. R. Drumm.
uh-*mah*-bi-lee. Chinese forget-me-
not/hound's tongue. Lat. beautiful.
China, Bhutan.
nervosum Benth. ex C. B. Clarke.
ner-*voh*-soom. Himalayan hound's
tongue. Lat. (prominently) veined
(the leaves). Himal.

Cyperus L. (Cyperaceae). *sip*-uh-roos.
Gk. name for *C. longus*. 600 spp.
herbs. Widespread.

albostriatus Schräd. al-boh-stree-*ah*-
toos. Lat. white-striped (the leaves
and bracts). S Africa.
alternifolius hort. = *C. involucratus*.
subsp. ***flabelliformis*** Kük.= *C.
involucratus*
eragrostis Lam. e-ruh-*gros*-tis. After
the genus *Eragrostis* (grasses). USA,
temp. S Am., Easter Is.
involucratus Rottb. in-vol-ue-*krah*-
toos. Umbrella sedge. Lat. with an
involucre (of bracts around the inflorescence). E Africa.
longus L. *long*-oos. Galingale. Lat.
long (the stems). Eur., Africa, W and
C Asia, Himal.
papyrus L. *pa*-pi-roos. Papyrus. From
Gk. paper, which is made from this
plant. Africa.

cypress *Cupressus*. **Arizona** *C. arizo-
nica*. **bald** *Taxodium distichum*.
Hinoki *Chamaecyparis obtusa*.
Italian *Cupressus sempervirens*.
Lawson *Chamaecyparis lawsoniana*.
Leyland ×*Cuprocyparis leylandii*.
Mexican *Cupressus lusitanica*.
Monterrey *C. macrocarpa*. **Nootka**
Xanthocyparis nootkatensis. **pond**
Taxodium distichum var. *imbricar-
ium*. **Sawara** *Chamaecyparis pisifera*.
smooth Arizona *Cupressus arizonica*
var. *glabra*. **summer** *Bassia scoparia*.
swamp *Taxodium distichum*. **white**
Chamaecyparis thyoides

Cypripedium L. (Orchidaceae).
sip-ri-*pee*-dee-oom. Lady's slipper,
moccasin flower. From Gk. Venus
slipper. 55 spp. orchids. Temp. and
subalpine N hemisph., Mex., C Am.

acaule Aiton. ay-*kaw*-lee. Stemless lady's slipper. Lat. without a stem. SE Canada, E USA.

×*andrewsii* Fuller. an-*drewz*-ee-ee. After Edward Palmer Andrews (d. 1954), a medical doctor and orchid lover of Portage, Wisconsin, who discovered it in 1930. *C. candidum* × *C. parviflorum* var. *pubescens*. E Canada, NC and NE USA.

calceolus L. kal-see-*oh*-loos. Lady's slipper. Lat. a little shoe (from the flower shape). Eur., temp. Asia.

candidum Muhl. ex Willd. *kan*-di-doom. Small white lady's slipper. Lat. white (the flowers). S Canada, N USA.

kentuckiense C. F. Reed. ken-tuk-ee-*en*-see. Kentucky lady's slipper. Of Kentucky. SC and SE USA.

montanum Douglas ex Lindl. mon-*tah*-noom. Mountain lady's slipper. Lat. of mountains. W Canada, W USA.

parviflorum Salisb. par-vi-*flaw*-room. Small yellow lady's slipper. Lat. small-flowered. N Am. var. *pubescens* (Willd.) O. W. Knight. pew-*bes*-uhnz. Large yellow lady's slipper. Lat. hairy.

pubescens Willd. = *C. parviflorum* var. *pubescens*

reginae Walter. re-*jeen*-ie. Showy lady's slipper. Lat. of the queen. S Canada, E USA.

Cyrtanthus Aiton (Amaryllidaceae). kurt-*anth*-oos. Gk. curved flower, referring to the curved perianth tube. 55 spp. bulbous herbs. Trop. and S Africa.

elatus (Jacq.) Traub. ee-*lah*-toos. Scarborough lily. Lat. tall. S Africa.

mackenii Hook. muh-*ken*-ee-ee. Ifafa lily. After Scottish horticulturist and plant collector Mark Johnston McKen (1823–1872), the first curator of Durban Botanic Garden. S Africa.

Cyrtomium C. Presl (Dryopteridaceae). kur-*toh*-mee-oom. From Gk. arch, referring to the arching veins. 15 spp. ferns. Widespread.

caryotideum (Wall. ex Hook. & Grev.) C. Presl. ka-ree-oh-*tid*-ee-oom. Asiatic holly fern. Like *Caryota* (fishtail palm; the leaves). E and SE Asia, Hawaii.

falcatum (L.f.) C. Presl. fal-*kah*-toom. Japanese holly fern. Lat. sickle-shaped (the pinnae). E Asia. '**Rochfordianum**'. roch-ford-ee-*ah*-noom. After Rochford's nursery.

fortunei J. Sm. for-*tewn*-ee-ee. After Robert Fortune (1812–1880), Scottish botanist and plant collector who introduced it to gardens. E and SE Asia. var. *clivicola* (Makino) Tagawa. kli-*vi*-ko-luh. Lat. living on slopes. China, Japan.

macrophyllum (Makino) Tagawa. mak-*rof*-i-loom. Gk. large-leaved. China, Japan, Taiwan.

Cystopteris Bernh. (Woodsiaceae). sis-*top*-te-ris. Bladder fern. Gk. bladder fern, referring to the bladder-like indusium that covers the spore-producing bodies. 20 spp. ferns. Widespread.

bulbifera (L.) Bernh. bul-*bi*-fuh-ruh. Bulblet bladder fern. Lat. bearing bulbs (in the axils of the pinnae). SE Canada, E and C USA.

dickieana Sim = *C. fragilis*

fragilis (L.) Bernh. *fra*-ji-lis. Brittle bladder fern. Lat. fragile (the frond stalks).

Cytisus Desf. (Fabaceae). *si*-ti-soos. Broom. Gk. name for this or a related plant. 60 spp. shrubs. Eur., Medit., W Asia.

battandieri Maire. ba-tan-dee-*e*-ree. Pineapple broom. After French botanist Jules Aimé Battandier (1848–1922), an authority on the N African flora. Morocco.

×***beanii*** Dallim. *been*-ee-ee. After English botanist William Jackson Bean (1863–1947), curator of RBG Kew 1922–29. It was raised at Kew in 1900, when he became assistant curator. *C. ardoinoi* × *C. purgans*. Cult.

'Burkwoodii'. burk-*wood*-ee-ee. After the Burkwood & Skipwith nursery, where it was raised.

×***kewensis*** Bean. kew-*en*-sis. Of Kew, where it was raised in 1891. *C. ardoinoi* × *C. multiflorus*. Cult.

nigricans L. *nig*-ri-kanz. Lat. becoming black (the flowers, when dry). C and SE Eur.

×***praecox*** Wheeler ex Bean. *prie*-kox. Lat. early (flowering). *C. multiflorus* × *C. purgans*. Cult.

purpureus Scop. = *Chamaecytisus purpureus*

scoparius (L.) Link. skoh-*pair*-ree-oos. Common broom. Lat. broom-like. W Eur. **'Andreanus'**. an-dree-*ah*-noos. After Édouard François André (1840–1911), French horticulturist and botanist.

Daboecia D. Don (Ericaceae). da-*bee*-see-uh. After St. Dabeoc of Wales, who founded a monastery on an island in Lough Derg in the 5th or 6th cent. 1 sp., shrub. W Eur.
cantabrica (Huds.) K. Koch. kan-*tab*-ri-kuh. St. Dabeoc's heath. Of Cantabria, N Spain. nothosubsp. **scotica** (D. C. McClint.) E. C. Nelson. *skot*-i-kuh. Of Scotland (it was first raised in Glasgow). *D. cantabrica* subsp. *azorica* × *D. cantabrica* subsp. *cantabrica*. Cult.
×**scotica** D. C. McClint. = *D. cantabrica* nothosubsp. *scotica*

Dacrydium Sol. ex G. Forst. (Podocarpaceae). da-*krid*-ee-oom. From Gk. a small tear, referring to the exuded drops of resin. 25 spp. trees. SE Asia to Australasia.
cupressinum Sol. ex G. Forst. kew-pres-*ee*-noom. Red pine. Lat. like *Cupressus*. NZ.

Dactylicapnos Wall. (Papaveraceae). dak-til-ee-*kap*-nos. Gk. finger, smoke, referring to the fruits and the smoke-like appearance of related plants. 10 spp. ann. and perenn. climbing herbs. Himal., China, SE Asia.

scandens (D. Don) Hutch. *skan*-duhnz. Lat. climbing.

Dactylis L. (Poaceae). *dak*-til-is. Lat. name, from Gk. for a kind of grass. 1 sp., grass. Eur., N Africa, Asia.
glomerata L. glom-uh-*rah*-tuh. Cocksfoot. Lat. clustered (the inflorescence).

Dactylorhiza Necker ex Nevski (Orchidaceae). dak-til-oh-*rie*-zuh. Gk. finger root, from the shape of the tubers. 50 spp. orchids. Eur., Asia, Alaska.
elata (Poir.) Soó. ee-*lah*-tuh. Robust marsh orchid. Lat. tall. Medit.
foliosa (Sol. ex Verm.) Soó. foh-lee-*oh*-suh. Madeiran orchid. Lat. leafy. Madeira.
fuchsii (Druce) Soó. *fook*-see-ee. Common spotted orchid. After Leonhart Fuchs (1501–1566), German physician. Eur.
maculata (L.) Soó. mak-ew-*lah*-tuh. Heath spotted orchid. Lat. spotted (the flowers). Eur.
majalis (Rchb.) P. F. Hunt & Summerh. muh-*jah*-lis. Broad-leaved marsh orchid. Lat. of May (flowering). C and E Eur.
praetermissa (Druce) Soó. prie-ter-*mis*-uh. Southern marsh orchid. Lat. neglected. NW Eur.
purpurella (T. & T. A. Stephenson) Soó. pur-pew-*rel*-uh. Northern marsh orchid. Lat. pale purple (the flowers). NW Eur.

daffodil *Narcissus*. **hoop-petticoat** *N. bulbocodium*. **paper white** *N. papyraceus*. **poet's** *N. poeticus*. **Tenby** *N. obvallaris*. **wild** *N. pseudonarcissus*

Dahlia Cav. (Asteraceae). *dah*-lee-uh.
After Anders Dahl (1751–1789),
Swedish botanist and student of
Linnaeus. 35 spp. tuberous herbs.
Mex., C Am., Colombia.
coccinea Cav. kok-*sin*-ee-uh. Lat. scarlet (the flowers). Mex.
imperialis Roezl ex Ortgies. im-peer-
ree-*ah*-lis. Lat. imperial (the size of
the plant and the flowers). Mex.
merckii Lehm. *merk*-ee-ee. After H. J.
Merck, who collected the type specimen from a plant grown in Hamburg
Botanic Garden from Mexican seed.
Mex.

daisy *Bellis perennis*. **African** *Arctotis*.
alpine moon *Leucanthemopsis
alpina*. **Barberton** *Gerbera jamesonii*. **blue** *Felicia amelloides*. **Cape**
Arctotis fastuosa. **crown** *Glebionis
coronaria*. **globe** *Globularia*. **Michaelmas** *Symphyotrichum novi-belgii*.
ox-eye *Leucanthemum vulgare*.
painted *Glebionis carinata*. **Shasta**
Leucanthemum ×*superbum*. **Swan
River** *Brachyscome iberidifolia*. **white
doll's** *Boltonia asteroides*
daisy bush *Olearia*

Dalea L. (Fabaceae). *day*-lee-uh. After
Samuel Dale (1659–1739), English
apothecary, physician, botanist and
geologist. 160 spp., herbs, shrubs.
Americas.
candida Michx. ex Willd. *kan*-di-duh.
White prairie clover. Lat. white (the
flowers). Canada, USA, N Mex.
purpurea Vent. pur-*pew*-ree-uh. Purple prairie clover. Lat. purple (the
flowers). W Canada, USA.

dame's violet *Hesperis matronalis*
damson *Prunus domestica* subsp.
insititia

Danae Medik. (Asparagaceae).
dan-uh-ee. After Danaë of Gk.
myth., daughter of King Acrisius
and mother of Perseus by Zeus. 1 sp.,
evergreen herb. W Asia.
racemosa (L.) Moench. ras-i-*moh*-suh.
Alexandrian laurel. Lat. in racemes
(the flowers).

dandelion, pink *Crepis incana*

Danthonia DC. (Poaceae). dan-*thoh*-
nee-uh. After French botanist
Etienne Danthoine (1739–1794),
who wrote on grasses. 20 spp. grasses.
Medit., Himal., China, Canada,
USA, Mex.
spicata (L.) P. Beauv. ex Roem. &
Schult. spi-*kah*-tuh. Poverty oat
grass. Lat. in spikes (the flowers).
Canada, USA, Mex.

Daphne L. (Thymelaeaceae). *daf*-nee.
Gk. name for bay laurel (*Laurus
nobilis*), from the nymph Daphne of
myth., who was turned into one. 95
spp. shrubs. Eur., Asia.
bholua Buch.-Ham. ex D. Don.
bol-ew-uh. From Bholu Swa, a local
Nepalese name. E Himal.
×*burkwoodii* Turrill. burk-*wood*-
ee-ee. After Albert Burkwood (b.
1890), of the Burkwood & Skipwith
nursery, who raised it. *D. caucasica* ×
D. cneorum. Cult.
cneorum L. nee-*or*-room. Garland
flower. From the Gk. name of an
olive-like shrub. C and S Eur.

×*hendersonii* Hodgkin ex C. D. Brickell & B. Mathew. hen-der-*soh*-nee-ee. After Mr W. Scott Henderson, who with Arthur W. Hill discovered it near Lake Garda in 1930. *D. cneorum* × *D. petraea*. N Italy.

laureola L. lo-ree-*oh*-luh. Spurge laurel. Lat. a little laurel. Eur., W Asia. subsp. *philippei* (Gren.) Nyman. fil-*ip*-ee-ee. After French botanist Xavier Philippe (1802–1866), who gave it another name. Pyrenees.

mezereum L. mez-*e*-ree-oom. Mezereon. From the Lat. name. Eur., W and C Asia.

×*napolitana* Lodd. na-pol-i-*tah*-nuh. Of Naples (Napoli). *D. cneorum* × *D. sericea*. S Italy.

odora Thunb. oh-*dor*-ruh. Lat. scented (the flowers). China, Japan.

pontica L. *pon*-ti-kuh. Gk. of Pontus (now NE Turkey). SE Eur., W Asia.

retusa Hemsl. = *D. tangutica* Retusa Group

tangutica Maxim. tan-*gew*-ti-kuh. Of Gansu (Terra Tangutorum). China. **Retusa Group**. ree-*tew*-suh. Lat. notched at the tip (the leaves).

Daphniphyllum Blume (Daphniphyllaceae). daf-nee-*fil*-oom. Gk. with leaves like *Daphne*. 30 spp., trees, shrubs. China, SE Asia to Australia.

macropodum Miq. mak-roh-*poh*-doom. Gk. with a large stalk (the inflorescence). Himal., W China.

Darmera Voss (Saxifragaceae). *dar*-muh-ruh. After Karl Darmer (1843–1918), German botanist and horticulturist. 1 sp., perenn. herb. Calif., Oregon.

peltata (Benth.) Voss. pel-*tah*-tuh. Umbrella plant. Lat. peltate (the leaves).

Dasylirion Zucc. (Asparagaceae). das-ee-*li*-ree-on. Gk. dense lily. 20 spp. tree-like herbs. SW USA, Mex.

longissimum Lem. long-*gis*-i-moom. Lat. longest (the inflorescence). Mex.

wheeleri S. Watson ex Rothr. *wee*-luh-ree. After George Montague Wheeler (1842–1905), American army surveyor who carried out surveys of the W USA during which the type specimen was collected in the 1870s. SW USA, N Mex.

date plum *Diospyros lotus*

Datisca L. (Datiscaceae). da-*tis*-kuh. Roman name for a catananche, possibly from Gk. to heal, from med. properties. 2 spp. herbs. W N Am., SW Asia to Himal.

cannabina L. kan-uh-*been*-uh. Like *Cannabis* (the leaves). SW and C Asia, Himal.

Datura L. (Solanaceae). da-*tew*-ruh. From an Indian name. 13 spp. ann. herbs. USA to S Am.

discolor Bernh. *dis*-ko-lor. Lat. two-coloured (the flowers). SW USA, Mex.

inoxia Mill. in-*ox*-ee-uh. Lat. harmless. S USA to S Am.

metel L. *met*-el. From the Arabic name of a plant.

meteloides DC. ex Dunal = *D. discolor*

stramonium L. struh-*moh*-nee-oom. Jimson weed. Gk. name used by Theophrastus.

wrightii Regel. *rie*-tee-ee. After American botanist Charles Wright (1811–1885), who collected the type specimen in Texas in 1849. W and C USA, NW Mex.

Daucus L. (Apiaceae). *daw*-koos. Lat. name of the carrot. 22 spp. herbs. Eur. to C Asia, Africa, Australia, NZ. *carota* L. *kuh*-roh-tuh. Carrot. From the Gk. name. Eur. to C Asia.

Davidia Baill. (Nyssaceae). duh-*vid*-ee-uh. After French missionary, botanist and zoologist Armand David (1826–1900), who collected the type specimen of *D. involucrata* in Sichuan in 1869. 1 sp., tree. W China.
involucrata Baill. in-vo-lue-*krah*-tuh. Dove tree, handkerchief tree. Lat. with an involucre (of bracts around the flowerhead). var. *vilmoriniana* (Dode) Wangerin. vil-mo-rin-ee-*ah*-nuh. After French nurseryman Maurice Lévêque de Vilmorin (1849–1918), to whom the first seeds were sent.

dawn redwood *Metasequoia glyptostroboides*
dead-nettle *Lamium.* **Pyrenean** *Horminum pyrenaicum.* **spotted** *Lamium maculatum*
deadly nightshade *Atropa belladonna*
death camus *Anticlea*

Decaisnea Hook.f. & Thomson (Lardizabalaceae). de-*kayz*-nee-uh. After Joseph Decaisne (1807–1882), French botanist and director of the Jardin des Plantes in Paris. 1 sp., shrub. China, Himal.

fargesii Franch. = *D. insignis*
insignis (Griff.) Hook.f. & Thomson. in-*sig*-nis. Lat. notable.

Decumaria L. (Hydrangeaceae). dek-ew-*mah*-ree-uh. From Lat. ten (the parts of the flower are in tens). 2 spp. climbers. China, SE USA.
barbara L. *bar*-buh-ruh. Wood vamp. Lat. foreign (it was thought to be introduced). SE USA.
sinensis Oliv. sin-*en*-sis. Lat. of China. China.

deerfoot *Achlys triphylla*

Delosperma N. E. Br. (Aizoaceae). del-oh-*sperm*-uh. Gk. visible seed (when the capsule opens, the seeds are not covered with a membrane, as in related genera). 160 spp. succulent herbs and shrubs. S Africa to Arabia.
cooperi (Hook.f.) L. Bolus. *koo*-puh-ree. After English botanist Thomas Cooper (1815–1913), who sent material to England, plants from which provided the type specimen. S Africa.
nubigenum (Schltr.) L. Bolus. nue-bi-*jee*-noom. Lat. born in the clouds (referring to its habitat). S Africa.

Delphinium L. (Ranunculaceae). del-*fin*-ee-oom. From Gk. dolphin, from the supposed resemblance of the flowers. 300 spp. herbs. N temp. regs., trop. mts.
Belladonna Group. bel-uh-*don*-uh. Lat. beautiful woman. Cult.
grandiflorum L. gran-di-*flaw*-room. Lat. large-flowered. E Asia.

Dendromecon Benth (Papaveraceae). den-*drom*-i-kon. Gk. tree poppy.

2 spp., shrubs, trees. Calif., Mex.
(B.C.).
rigida Benth. *ri*-ji-duh. Tree poppy.
Lat. rigid (the leaves).

deodar *Cedrus deodara*

Deschampsia P. Beauv. (Poaceae).
des-*champ*-see-uh. After French naturalist and surgeon Louise Auguste
Deschamps (1765–1842). 30 spp.
grasses. N temp. regs.
cespitosa (L.) P. Beauv. ses-pi-*to*-suh.
Tussock grass. Lat. tufted (the habit).

Desfontainia Ruiz & Pav. (Columelli-
aceae). des-fon-*tayn*-ee-uh. After
French botanist René Louiche
Desfontaines (1750–1833). 1 sp.,
shrub. C and S Am.
spinosa Ruiz & Pav. spi-*noh*-suh. Chilean holly. Lat. spiny (the leaves).

Desmanthus Willd. (Fabaceae). dez-
manth-oos. Gk. bundle flower from
the clustered flowers. 25 spp., herbs,
subshrubs. USA to S Am.
illinoensis (Michx.) MacMill. ex B. L.
Rob. & Fernald. il-i-noh-*en*-sis.
Prairie mimosa, prickleweed. Of Illinois. USA.

Desmodium Desf. (Fabaceae).
dez-*moh*-dee-oom. Beggarticks, tick
trefoil. From Gk. chain (the fruits
break into link-like segments). 275
spp., herbs, shrubs. Widespread.
canadense (L.) DC. kan-uh-*den*-see.
Canadian tick trefoil. Of Canada.
Canada, USA.

Deutzia Thunb. (Hydrangeaceae).
doyt-see-uh. 60 spp. shrubs. E and SE
Asia, Mex.
×*elegantissima* (Lemoine) Rehder. el-
i-gan-*tis*-i-muh. Lat. most elegant. *D.
purpurascens* × *D. sieboldiana*. Cult.
gracilis Sieb. & Zucc. *gras*-i-lis. Lat.
slender (the stems). Japan.
×*hybrida* Lemoine. *hib*-ri-duh. Lat.
hybrid. *D. discolor* × *D. longifolia*.
Cult.
×*kalmiiflora* Lemoine. kal-mee-i-
flaw-ruh. Lat. with flowers like *Kalmia*. *D. parviflora* × *D. purpurascens*.
Cult.
pulchra Vidal. *pool*-kruh. Lat. beautiful. Taiwan, Philippines.
scabra Thunb. *skay*-bruh. Lat. rough
(the leaves). Japan.
setchuenensis Franch. sech-wen-*en*-sis.
Of Sichuan. China. var. *corymbi-
flora* (Lemoine) Rehder. ko-rim-bi-
flaw-ruh. Lat. with flowers in corymbs. China (Hubei, Sichuan).

devil's backbone *Kalanchoe daigremontiana*
devil's walking stick *Aralia spinosa*
devilwood *Osmanthus americanus*

Dianella Lam. ex Juss. (Xanthorrhoeaceae). die-uh-*nel*-uh. Flax lily. Diminutive of Diana, Roman goddess of
the hunt. 20 spp. herbs. E Africa, SE
Asia, Pacific Is., Australia, NZ.
caerulea Sims. kie-*rue*-lee-uh. Blue flax
lily, Paroo lily. Lat. blue (the flowers).
SE Australia.
nigra Colenso. *nie*-gruh. New Zealand
blueberry. Lat. black (the seeds). NZ.
revoluta R. Br. rev-o-*lue*-tuh. Blueberry lily. Lat. rolled under (the leaf
margins). SE Australia.

tasmanica Hook.f. taz-*man*-i-kuh.
Tasman flax lily. Of Tasmania. SE
Australia.

Dianthus L. (Caryophyllaceae).
die-*anth*-oos. Pink. Gk. name used
by Theophrastus meaning flower of
Zeus. 320 spp., herbs, subshrubs.
Eur., Asia, Africa, NW N Am.
alpinus L. al-*pie*-noos. Lat. of the Alps.
E Alps.
barbatus L. bar-*bah*-toos. Sweet
William. Lat. bearded (the petals).
S Eur.
carthusianorum L. kar-thew-zee-uh-
nor-room. Carthusian pink. Of the
monks of the Carthusian monastery,
Grenoble, who cultivated it. S and
C Eur.
caryophyllus L. ka-ree-*of*-i-loos. Carnation, clove pink. Gk. walnut-leaved
(the scent). Medit.
chinensis L. chin-*en*-sis. Of China.
China.
deltoides L. del-*toy*-deez. Maiden
pink. Gk. shaped like the Greek
uppercase letter delta (the petals).
Eur. to C Asia and N India.
gratianopolitanus Vill. grat-ee-ah-
noh-po-li-*tah*-noos. Cheddar pink.
Lat. of Grenoble (Lat. *Gratianopolis*).
W and C Eur.

Diascia Link & Otto (Scrophulariaceae). die-*ask*-ee-uh. Twinspur. Gk.
two sacs, referring to the pair of
translucent yellow windows in the
corolla. 70 spp. herbs. S Africa.
barberae Hook.f. *bar*-buh-rie. After
Mrs Barber, who sent seeds to Kew
in 1870.
fetcaniensis Hilliard & B. L. Burtt.
fet-kah-nee-*en*-sis. Of the Fetcani

Pass, E Cape, S Africa, where the
type specimen was collected.
rigescens E. Mey. ex Benth. ree-*ges*-
uhnz. Lat. rather stiff (the shoots).
vigilis Hilliard & B. L. Burtt. *vij*-i-lis.
Lat. of the sentinel, referring to a
large basalt rock in the Royal Natal
National Park, near which the type
specimen was collected in 1979.

Dicentra Benth. (Papaveraceae).
die-*sen*-truh. From Gk. two spurs,
referring to the spurs on the outer
petals. 20 spp. herbs. N Am., E Asia.
canadensis (Goldie) Walp. kan-uh-
den-sis. Squirrel corn. Of Canada. SE
Canada, NE USA.
cucullaria (L.) Bernh. kuk-ew-*lair*-
ree-uh. Dutchman's breeches. Lat.
like a hood (the flowers). SE Canada,
USA.
eximia (Ker Gawl.) Torr. ex-*im*-ee-uh.
Turkey corn. Lat. distinguished. E
USA.
formosa (Haw.) Walp. for-*moh*-suh.
Pacific bleeding heart. Lat. beautiful.
W USA, SW Canada.
macrantha Oliv. = *Ichtyoselmis
macrantha*
scandens (D. Don) Walp. = *Dactylicapnos scandens*
spectabilis (L.) Lem. = *Lamprocapnos
spectabilis*

Dichelostemma Kunth (Asparagaceae). di-kel-oh-*stem*-uh. From Gk.
bifid garland, referring to the divided
appendages that form a crown on the
perianth. 5 spp. cormous herbs.
W N Am.
ida-maia (Alph. Wood) Greene.
ee-duh-*mie*-uh. Firecracker flower.
After Ida May Burke (1862–1871),

whose father showed the flowers to Alphonso Wood, who described the species, and of the Ides of May, when it flowers. Calif., Oregon.

Dichroa Lour. (Hydrangeaceae). die-*kroh*-uh. From Gk. two-coloured (the flowers). 12 spp., shrubs, sub-shrubs. E Asia.
febrifuga Lour. feb-ri-*few*-guh. Lat. reducing fever (it is used medicinally). Himal., China, SE Asia.

Dicksonia L'Hér. (Dicksoniaceae). dik-*soh*-nee-uh. After Scottish nurseryman and botanist James Dickson (1738–1822). 20 spp. tree ferns. SE Asia to Australasia, trop. Am.
antarctica Labill. an-*tark*-ti-kuh. Soft tree fern. Of the Antarctic. SE Australia.

Dicliptera Juss. (Acanthaceae). di-*klip*-tuh-ruh. Gk. two-fold wing, referring to the wing-like divisions of the capsule. 150 spp. herbs. Widespread in trop. and warm regs.
sericea Nees = *D. squarrosa*
squarrosa Nees. skwo-*roh*-suh. Lat. with projecting tips (the flowers). S Am.
suberecta (André) Bremek. = *D. squarrosa*

Dictamnus L. (Rutaceae). dik-*tam*-noos. Gk. name for *Origanum dictamnus*. 1 sp., herb. Eur. to China.
albus L. *al*-buhs. Burning bush, false dittany. Lat. white (the flowers, sometimes).

Dieffenbachia Schott (Araceae). dee-fuhn-*bahk*-ee-uh. Dumb cane. After

Johann Karl Ernst Dieffenbach (1811–1855), German physician and naturalist. 57 spp. herbs. Mex. to trop. S Am.
amoena hort. = *D. seguine*
maculata (Lodd.) Sweet = *D. seguine*
picta Schott = *D. seguine*
seguine (Jacq.) Schott. se-*gee*-nee. A local name in the French Antilles for this and other members of the family. Trop. S Am., Caribb.

Dierama K. Koch (Iridaceae). die-uh-*rah*-muh. Angel's fishing rod, wandflower. Gk. funnel, referring to the shape of the flowers. 42 spp. cormous herbs. Trop. and S Africa.
argyreum L. Bolus. ar-gi-*ree*-oom. Gk. silvery (the flowers).
dracomontanum Hilliard. drak-oh-mon-*tah*-noom. Of the Drakensberg Mts.
erectum Hilliard. ee-*rek*-toom. Lat. upright (the flowers).
galpinii N. E. Br. gal-*pin*-ee-ee. After South African watchmaker and banker Ernest Edward Galpin (1858–1941), who collected the type specimen in 1889.
igneum Klatt. *ig*-nee-oom. Lat. fiery (the flowers).
mossii (N. E. Br.) Hilliard. *mos*-ee-ee. After Charles Edward Moss (1870–1930), English botanist and first professor of botany at the University of Witwatersrand, who collected the type specimen in 1917.
pauciflorum N. E. Br. paw-si-*flaw*-room. Lat. few-flowered.
pendulum (L.f.) Baker. *pen*-dew-loom. Lat. pendulous (the flowers).
pulcherrimum (Hook.f.) Baker. pool-*ke*-ri-moom. Lat. very beautiful.

reynoldsii Verd. re-*nold*-zee-ee. After South African optometrist Gilbert Westacott Reynolds (1895–1967), who collected the type specimen in 1939.

trichorhizum (Baker) N. E. Br. trik-oh-*ree*-zoom. Gk. hairy root (referring to the fibres on the corm).

Diervilla Mill. (Diervillaceae). die-uh-*vil*-uh. Bush honeysuckle. After French surgeon N. Diereville (b. 1670), who introduced *D. lonicera* to Europe from Canada. 3 spp. shrubs. USA, Canada.

lonicera Mill. lo-ni-*se*-ruh. After the genus *Lonicera*.

sessilifolia Buckley. se-si-li-*foh*-lee-uh. Lat. with sessile (unstalked) leaves.

×*splendens* (Carrière) Kirchn. *splen*-duhnz. Lat. splendid. *D. lonicera* × *D. sessilifolia*. Cult.

Dieteria Nutt. (Asteraceae). dee-et-*e*-ree-uh. Gk. two years, referring to their life cycle. 3 spp., herbs, sub-shrubs. W USA, N Mex.

bigelovii (A. Gray) D. R. Morgan & R. L. Hartman. big-uh-*lov*-ee-ee. After John Milton Bigelow (1804–1878), American surgeon and botanist to the expedition on which the type specimen was collected in New Mexico in 1853. W USA.

Dietes Salisb. ex Klatt (Iridaceae). die-*ee*-teez. Gk. two relatives, indicating its closeness to *Iris* and *Moraea*, in the same family. 6 spp. herbs. E and S Africa, Australia (Lord Howe Is.).

bicolor (Steud.) Sweet ex Klatt. *bi*-ko-lor. Peacock flower. Lat. two-coloured (the flowers). S Africa.

grandiflora N. E. Br. gran-di-*flaw*-ruh. Fairy iris. Lat. large-flowered. S Africa.

iridioides (L.) Sweet. i-rid-ee-*oy*-deez. Cape iris. Like *Iris*. E and S Africa.

Digitalis L. (Plantaginaceae). di-ji-*tah*-lis. Foxgloves. From Lat. finger, referring to the shape of the flowers. 22 spp., herbs, shrubs. Eur., Medit. to C Asia.

ferruginea L. fe-rue-*jin*-ee-uh. Rusty foxglove. Lat. rust-coloured (the flowers). S Eur., W Asia.

grandiflora Mill. gran-di-*flaw*-ruh. Large yellow foxglove. Lat. large-flowered. Eur.

laevigata Waldst. & Kit. lee-vi-*gah*-tuh. Lat. smooth (the leaves). SE Eur.

lanata Ehrh. lan-*ah*-tuh. Grecian foxglove. Lat. woolly (the inflorescence). SE Eur., W Asia.

lutea L. *lue*-tee-uh. Straw foxglove. Lat. yellow (the flowers). Eur.

×*mertonensis* Buxton & C. Darl. mer-ton-*en*-sis. Of Merton, Greater London, UK, where it was raised at the John Innes Institute (then in Surrey). *D. grandiflora* × *D. purpurea*. Cult.

obscura L. ob-*skew*-ruh. Lat. dusky (the flowers). Spain.

parviflora Jacq. par-vi-*flaw*-ruh. Lat. small-flowered. N Spain.

purpurea L. pur-*pew*-ree-uh. Common foxglove. Lat. purple (the flowers). Eur., Morocco.

dill *Anethum graveolens*

Dionaea Sol. ex Ellis (Droseraceae). die-on-*ee*-uh. After Dione of Gk. myth., mother by Zeus of Aphrodite

(the Roman Venus). 1 sp., carnivorous herb. SE USA (Carolinas).
muscipula Ellis. mus-*kip*-ew-luh. Venus's fly trap. Lat. fly-catching.

Diospyros L. (Ebenaceae). die-*os*-pi-ros. Gk. divine wheat, referring to the edible fruit. 550 spp., trees, shrubs. Mainly trop. Am., Asia, Africa.
kaki Thunb. *kah*-kee. Japanese persimmon, kaki. The Japanese name. China.
lotus L. *loh*-toos. Date plum. A reference to the lotus tree of Gk. myth., mentioned in Homer's Odyssey. W Asia to China and Korea.
virginiana L. vir-jin-ee-*ah*-nuh. American persimmon. Of Virginia. E and C USA.

Dipelta Maxim. (Linnaeaceae). di-*pel*-tuh. Gk. two shields, referring to the two large bracts around the fruit. 3 spp. shrubs. China.
floribunda Maxim. flo-ri-*bun*-duh. Lat. flowering profusely.
ventricosa Hemsl. = *D. yunnanensis*
yunnanensis Franch. yue-nan-*en*-sis. Of Yunnan, China.

Diplarrena Labill. (Iridaceae). dip-luh-*ree*-nuh. Gk. double male, referring to the two fertile stamens. 2 spp. herbs. SE Australia.
moraea Labill. mo-*ree*-uh. Butterfly flag. From the resemblance to the South African *Moraea*.

Dipsacus L. (Dipsacaceae). *dip*-suh-koos. From Gk. thirst, referring to the water that collects in the leaf bases in some species. 15 spp. herbs. Eur., Africa, Asia.

fullonum L. fool-*oh*-noom. Teasel. Lat. of fullers (those that raised the nap of cloth by 'teasing' it with heads of teasel). Eur., N Africa, W Asia.

Disanthus Maxim. (Hamamelidaceae). dis-*anth*-oos. Gk. two flowers (the flowers are borne in pairs). 1 sp., shrub. China, Japan.
cercidifolius Maxim. ser-sid-i-*foh*-lee-oos. Lat. with leaves like *Cercis*.

Disporopsis Hance (Asparagaceae). dis-po-*rop*-sis. Gk. like *Disporum*, a related genus. 6 spp. herbs. SE China to Philippines.
aspersa (Hua) Engler. uh-*sper*-suh. Lat. a sprinkling (the flowers are spotted). China.
pernyi (Hua) Diels. *per*-nee-ee. After French missionary Paul Hubert Perny (1818–1907), who collected the type specimen in Guizhou in 1858. China.

Disporum Salisb. ex D. Don (Asparagaceae). *dis*-po-room. Gk. two seeds (there are often two ovules in each locule of the ovary). 20 spp. herbs. E Asia.
cantoniense (Lour.) Merr. kan-toh-nee-*en*-see. Of Guangzhou (Canton). China, Himal., SE Asia.
hookeri (Torr.) Nichols. = *Prosartes hookeri*
smithii (Hook.) Piper = *Prosartes smithii*
uniflorum Baker. ew-ni-*flaw*-room. Lat. one-flowered (the inflorescence, sometimes). China, Korea.

dittany, Cretan *Origanum dictamnus.*
false *Dictamnus albus*

dock *Rumex.* **bloody** *R. sanguineus.*
prairie *Silphium terebinthinaceum*
dockmackie *Viburnum acerifolium*

Dodecatheon jeffreyi hort. ex Van
Houtte = *Primula jeffreyi*
meadia L. = *Primula meadia*
pulchellum (Raf.) Merr. = *Primula
pauciflora*

Dodonaea Mill. (Sapindaceae).
doh-do-*nee*-uh. After Flemish botanist Rembert Dodoens (Lat. *Dodo-
naeus*) (1517–1585). 65 spp., shrubs,
trees. Widespread in trop. and warm
regs., mainly Australia.
viscosa Jacq. vis-*koh*-suh. Hop bush.
Lat. sticky (the foliage).

Doellingeria Nees (Asteraceae).
dur-lin-*ge*-ree-uh. For Ignaz
Döllinger (1770–1842), German
professor of anatomy and botany. 3
spp. herbs. Canada, USA.
umbellata (Mill.) Nees. um-buhl-*ah*-
tuh. Parasol whitetop, flat top white
aster. Lat. in umbels (the flowers are
in umbel-like corymbs).

dog's tooth violet *Erythronium
dens-canis*
doghobble, coastal *Leucothoe axillaris.* **mountain** *L. fontanesiana*
dogwood *Cornus.* **Chinese** *C. kousa.*
common *C. sanguinea.* **flowering** *C.
florida.* **grey** *C. racemosa.* **Japanese**
C. kousa. **Pacific** *C. nuttallii.* **pagoda**
C. alternifolia. **red osier** *C. sericea.*
Siberian *C. alba.* **silky** *C. amomum*

Doronicum L. (Asteraceae). do-*ron*-i-
koom. From an Arabic name. 26 spp.
herbs. Eur. and N Africa to China.

×***excelsum*** (N. E. Br.) Stace. ex-*sel*-
soom. Lat. tall. *D. columnae* × *D. pardalianches* × *D. plantagineum.* Cult.
orientale Hoffm. o-ree-en-*tah*-lee.
Lat. eastern. SE Eur., W Asia.
pardalianches L. par-dal-ee-*an*-keez.
Leopard's bane. Gk. strangling
leopards; originally used by Dioscorides for a poisonous plant, possibly
this. Eur.

Douglasia vitaliana (L.) Hook.f. ex
Pax = *Androsace vitaliana*

dove tree *Davidia involucrata*

Dracaena Vand. ex L. (Asparagaceae).
druh-*see*-nuh. From Gk. dragon (a red
resin from the bark of *D. draco* is
known as dragon's blood). 100 spp.,
shrubs, trees. Widespread, trop. and
subtrop. regs.
braunii Engl. *brown*-ee-ee. Lucky
bamboo. After German botanist
Johannes Braun (1859–1893), who
sent plants to the Berlin Botanic Garden in 1888. W Africa. **'Sanderiana'**.
zahn-duh-ree-*ah*-nuh. After German-
born nurseryman Henry Frederick
Conrad Sander (1847–1920), who
established a prominent orchid nursery in St. Albans, England.
fragrans (L.) Ker Gawl. *fray*-gruhnz.
Lat. fragrant (the flowers). Trop.
Africa.
marginata Lam. = *D. reflexa* var.
angustifolia
reflexa Lam. ree-*flex*-uh. Lat. reflexed
(the inflorescence). W Indian Ocean
Is. var. ***angustifolia*** Baker. an-gus-ti-
foh-lee-uh. Lat. narrow-leaved.
sanderiana Sander = *D. braunii*
'Sanderiana'

Dracunculus Mill. (Araceae).
druh-*kunk*-ew-loos. Gk. a little
dragon, from the shape of the spathe.
2 spp. herbs. Canary Is., Madeira, S
Eur., SW Turkey.
vulgaris Schott. vul-*gar*-ris. Dragon
arum. Lat. common. S Eur. to W
Turkey.

dragon arum *Dracunculus vulgaris*

Dregea E. Mey. (Apocynaceae).
dree-gee-uh. After German botanist
Johann Franz Drège (1794–1891),
who collected the type species, *D.
floribunda*. 12 spp. climbers. S Asia,
Africa.
sinensis Hemsl. sin-*en*-sis. Lat. of
China. China.

Drimys J. R. & G. Forst. (Wintera-
ceae). *drim*-is. Gk. pungent, from the
taste of the bark. 6 spp., shrubs, trees.
Mex. to S Am.
andina (Reiche) R. A. Rodr. & Quez.
an-*dee*-nuh. Of the Andes. Chile,
Argentina.
lanceolata (Poir.) Baill. = *Tasmannia
lanceolata*
winteri J. R. & G. Forst. *win*-tuh-ree.
Winter's bark. After Admiral Sir
William Wynter (1519–1589), who
sailed with Francis Drake and in S
Am. used the bark to spice food and
combat scurvy. var. *andina* Reiche =
D. andina

dropwort *Filipendula vulgaris*

Dryas L. (Rosaceae). *drie*-uhs. After
Dryas of Gk. myth., a nymph of oak
woods (from Gk. oak, referring to

the shape of the leaves). 3 spp. subshrubs. Arctic and alpine N hemisph.
octopetala L. ok-toh-*pet*-uh-luh.
Mountain avens. Lat. with eight
petals. Eur., Asia, N Am.
×*suendermannii* Keller ex Sünd.
suen-duh-*man*-ee-ee. After Franz
Sündermann (1864–1946), in whose
alpine plant nursery in Germany it
was raised. *D. drummondii* × *D.
octopetala*. Cult.

Dryopteris Adans. (Dryopteridaceae).
drie-*op*-te-ris. Wood fern. Gk. oak
fern, from the habitat. 150 spp. ferns.
Widespread.
affinis (Lowe) Fraser-Jenk. *af*-i-nis.
Scaly male fern. Lat. related to
(another species). Eur., Turkey.
×*australis* (Wherry) Small. os-*trah*-
lis. Lat. southern. *D. celsa* × *D.
ludoviciana*. SE USA.
carthusiana (Vill.) H. P. Fuchs.
kar-thew-zee-*ah*-nuh. Narrow buckler fern. Lat. of Grande Chartreuse
(Cartusia), near Grenoble, France,
where it was collected. Canada,
USA, Eur., Turkey.
championii (Benth.) C. Chr. ex King.
champ-ee-*on*-ee-ee. After English
botanist John George Champion
(1815–1854), who collected in
China. China, Korea, Japan.
cycadina (Franch. & Sav.) C. Chr.
sie-kad-*ee*-nuh. Shaggy wood fern.
Like a cycad. China, Taiwan, Japan.
dilatata (Hoffm.) A. Gray. di-luh-*tah*-
tuh. Broad buckler fern. Lat. spreading (the fronds). Eur., W Asia.
erythrosora (D. C. Eaton) Kuntze.
e-rith-roh-*sor*-ruh. Japanese shield
fern. Gk. with red sori. China,

Taiwan, Korea, Japan, Philippines. **'Prolifica'**. proh-*li*-fi-kuh. Lat. prolific (it produces bulbils on the fronds).

filix-mas (L.) Schott. *fi*-lix-*mas*. Male fern. Lat. male fern. Canada, USA, Eur., W and C Asia. **'Barnesii'**. *barnz*-ee-ee. After Mr J. M. Barnes, who discovered it in Lancashire, UK.

goldieana (Hook. ex Goldie) A. Gray. gold-ee-*ah*-nuh. Goldie's fern. After Scottish botanist John Goldie (1793–1886), who collected the type specimen in Montreal in 1823. E N Am.

marginalis (L.) A. Gray. mar-jin-*ah*-lis. Marginal wood fern. Lat. of the margin (the sori are borne on the margin of the fronds). E Canada, E and C USA, Greenland.

remota (A. Braun ex Döll) Druce. ree-*moh*-tuh. Lat. scattered (the distribution). Eur., W Asia.

sieboldii (T. Moore) Kuntze. see-*bold*-ee-ee. After Philip Franz von Siebold (1796–1866), who studied the flora and fauna of Japan. China, Taiwan, Japan.

tokyoensis (Matsum. ex Makino) C. Chr. toh-kee-oh-*en*-sis. Of Tokyo. China, Korea, Japan.

wallichiana (Spreng.) Hyl. wol-ik-ee-*ah*-nuh. After Nathaniel Wallich (1786–1854), Danish botanist and surgeon with the East India Company, who collected plants in India and Nepal. E Asia, Mex., C and S Am.

Duke of Argyll's tea tree *Lycium barbarum*

dumb cane *Dieffenbachia*

dusty miller *Artemisia stelleriana, Jacobaea maritima, Silene coronaria*

Dutchman's breeches *Dicentra cucullaria*

Dutchman's pipe *Aristolochia macrophylla*

dyer's greenweed *Genista tinctoria*

Dysosma Woodson (Berberidaceae). dis-*oz*-muh. Gk. a disagreeable odor, after observations made by British botanist Henry Fletcher Hance (1827–1886). 7 spp. perenn. herbs. China, Vietnam.

delavayi (Franch) Hu. del-uh-*vay*-ee. After French missionary Jean Marie Delavay (1834–1895), who collected the type specimen in Yunnan in 1894. SW China.

versipellis (Hance) M. Cheng ex T. S. Ying. ver-*si*-pel-is. Lat. variable, skin (it has been used to treat skin complaints). China.

Dysphania R. Br. (Amaranthaceae). dis-*fahn*-ee-uh. From Gk. obscure (the inconspicuous flowers). 32 spp. herbs. Widespread, warm temp. to trop. regs.

ambrosioides (L.) Mosyakin & Clemants. am-broh-zee-*oy*-deez. Mexican tea. Like *Ambrosia*. N and S Am.

botrys (L.) Mosyakin & Clemants. *bot*-ris. Jerusalem oak. Gk. like a bunch of grapes (the inflorescence). N Am., Eur., Asia.

Eccremocarpus Ruiz & Pav. (Bignoniaceae). ek-ree-moh-*kar*-poos. Gk. hanging fruit, referring to the pendulous fruit. 3 spp. climbers. Chile, Peru.
scaber Ruiz & Pav. *skay*-ber. Lat. rough (the leaves). Chile.

Echeveria DC. (Crassulaceae). e-ki-*veer*-ree-uh. After Atanasio Echeverría y Godoy, 18th-cent. Mexican botanical artist. 150 spp. succulents. Mex. to S Am.
agavoides Lem. a-gah-*voy*-deez. Like *Agave*. Mex.
elegans Rose. *el*-i-ganz. Lat. elegant. Mex.
secunda Booth. se-*kun*-duh. Lat. borne on one side (flowers on the inflorescence). Mex. var. *glauca* (Baker) Otto. *glaw*-kuh. Lat. bluish white (the leaves).

Echinacea Moench (Asteraceae). ek-i-*nay*-see-uh. Purple coneflower. From Lat. sea urchin, referring to the spine-tipped receptacle scales. 9 spp. herbs. USA.
pallida (Nutt.) Nutt. *pa*-li-duh. Lat. pale (the flowers). E USA.

paradoxa (Norton) Britton. pa-ruh-*dox*-uh. Lat. unusual (the only sp. with yellow flowers). SC USA.
purpurea (L.) Moench. pur-*pew*-ree-uh. Lat. purple (the flowers). E USA.

Echinops L. (Asteraceae). *ek*-i-nops. Globe thistle. Gk. like a hedgehog or sea urchin (the flowerheads). 120 spp. herbs. Eur. to C Asia, Africa.
bannaticus Rochel ex Schrad. buh-*nat*-i-koos. Of Banat (now divided between Romania, Serbia and Hungary). E Eur.
ritro L. *rit*-roh. A S Eur. name for this plant. Eur. to C Asia.

Echium L. (Boraginaceae). *ek*-ee-oom. From the name used by Dioscorides, who likened the seeds to a snake's head and recommended it as an antivenom, from Gk. viper. 60 spp., herbs, shrubs. Canary Is., Eur., Africa, W Asia.
pininana Webb & Berth. pin-in-*ah*-nuh. A local name on the island of La Palma. Canary Is.
vulgare L. vul-*gar*-ree. Viper's bugloss. Lat. common. Eur.

edelweiss *Leontopodium nivale* subsp. *alpinum*

Edgeworthia Meissn. (Thymelaeaceae). ej-*wurth*-ee-uh. After Michael Pakenham Edgeworth (1812–1881), Irish botanist. 4 spp. shrubs. China, Himal.
chrysantha Lindl. kris-*anth*-uh. Gk. golden-flowered. China.
papyrifera Sieb. & Zucc. = E. *chrysantha*

Elaeagnus L. (Elaeagnaceae). el-ee-*ag*-noos. From Gk. olive, pure. 45 spp., shrubs, trees. Eur., N Am., Asia to N Australia.
angustifolia L. an-gus-ti-*foh*-lee-uh. Russian olive. Lat. narrow-leaved. W Asia.
commutata Bernh. kom-ew-*tah*-tuh. Silver berry. Lat. changeable (the green leaves turn to silver). USA, Canada.
×*ebbingei* Boom. eb-*ing*-ee-ee. After Dutch nurseryman Johan Wilhelm Everhard Ebbinge (1870–1948), who raised it. *E. macrophylla* × *E. pungens*. Cult.
pungens Thunb. *pun*-guhnz. Lat. sharp-pointed (the spines). Japan.
umbellata Thunb. um-buhl-*ah*-tuh. Lat. in umbels (the flowers are in umbel-like clusters). Himal., China, Korea, Japan.

elder *Sambucus nigra*. **American** *S. nigra* subsp. *canadensis*. **red-berried** *S. racemosa*
elecampane *Inula helenium*
elephant ears *Caladium*

Eleutherococcus Maxim. (Araliaceae). e-lue-thuh-roh-*kok*-oos. Gk. free seed. 40 spp., shrubs, trees. Himal., E Asia.
sieboldianus (Makino) Koidz. see-bold-ee-*ah*-noos. After Philip Franz von Siebold (1796–1866), who studied the flora and fauna of Japan, where it is cultivated and naturalised. China.

elm *Ulmus*. **American** *U. americana*. **Caucasian** *Zelkova carpinifolia*. **Chinese** *U. parvifolia*. **Dutch** *U.*

×*hollandica*. **field** *U. minor*. **red** *U. rubra*. **Scotch** *U. glabra*. **Siberian** *U. pumila*. **slippery** *U. rubra*. **wych** *U. glabra*

Elymus L. (Poaceae). *el*-i-moos. From Gk. name of a grain-producing grass. 150 spp. grasses. N temp. regs.
arenarius L. = *Leymus arenarius*
hystrix L. *his*-trix. Bottlebrush grass. Gk. porcupine or hedgehog (referring to the spiky inflorescence). S Canada, E and C USA.
magellanicus (E. Desv.) A. Löve. maj-uh-*lan*-i-koos. Of the Magellan reg. Argentina, Chile, Falkland Is.

Embothrium J. R. & G. Forst. (Proteaceae). em-*both*-ree-oom. From Gk. in a small pit (the anthers are borne in pits on the perianth segments). 8 spp., trees, shrubs. Andes of S Am.
coccineum J. R. & G. Forst. kok-*sin*-ee-oom. Chilean firebush. Lat. scarlet (the flowers).

Empress tree *Paulownia tomentosa*
endive *Cichorium endivia*

Enkianthus Lour. (Ericaceae). en-kee-*anth*-oos. Gk. pregnant flower (the pink bracts around the flowers of *E. quinqueflorus* appear to be a flower with another inside it). 12 spp., shrubs, trees. Himal. to E and SE Asia.
campanulatus (Miq.) G. Nicholson. kam-pan-ew-*lah*-toos. Lat. bell-shaped (the flowers). Japan. var. *palibinii* (Craib) Bean. pal-i-*bin*-ee-ee. After Russian botanist Ivan Vladimirovich Palibin (1872–1949), who studied the genus.

cernuus (Sieb. & Zucc.) Makino. *sern*-ew-oos. Lat. nodding (the flowers). Japan. f. *rubens* (Maxim.) Ohwi. *rue*-buhnz. Lat. red (the flowers).
perulatus (Miq.) C. K. Schneid. pe-rue-*lah*-toos. Lat. bearing bud scales. Japan, Taiwan.

Eomecon Hance (Papaveraceae). ee-*o*-mee-kon. Gk. eastern poppy. 1 sp., herb. E China.
chionantha Hance. kee-on-*anth*-uh. Dawn poppy, snow poppy. Gk. snow flower (the flowers are white).

Epilobium L. (Onagraceae). ep-i-*loh*-bee-oom. Gk. upon a pod, referring to the position of the flowers at the tip of the ovary. 165 spp., ann. and perenn. herbs, subshrubs. Widespread.
angustifolium L. = *Chamerion angustifolium*
canum (Greene) Raven. *kah*-noom. California fuchsia. Lat. grey (the foliage). W USA, N Mex.

Epimedium L. (Berberidaceae). ep-i-*mee*-dee-oom. Barrenwort, bishop's mitre. From Gk. name used by Dioscorides, possibly for *E. alpinum*. 50 spp. herbs. S Eur., N Africa to China and Japan.
acuminatum Franch. uh-kew-min-*ah*-toom. Lat. taper-pointed (the leaflets). China.
×*cantabrigiense* Stearn. kan-tuh-brig-ee-*en*-see. Lat. of Cambridge, where it was raised. *E. alpinum* × *E. pubigerum*. Cult.
davidii Franch. da-*vid*-ee-ee. After French missionary, botanist and zoologist Armand David (1826–

1900), who collected the type specimen in 1870. China (Sichuan, Yunnan).
epsteinii Stearn. ep-*stien*-ee-ee. After American rock gardener Harold Epstein (1903–1997), who had a particular interest in the genus. China (Hunan).
grandiflorum C. Morren. gran-di-*flaw*-room. Lat. large-flowered. Japan.
leptorrhizum Stearn. lep-toh-*ree*-zoom. Gk. with slender rhizomes. China.
ogisui Stearn. oh-gi-*sue*-ee. After Japanese plant collector Mikinori Ogisu, who discovered it and collected the type specimen in 1992. China (Sichuan).
×*omeiense* Stearn. om-ay-*en*-see. Of Emei Shan (Mt. Omei). *E. acuminatum* × *E. fangii*. China (Sichuan).
×*perralchicum* Stearn. pe-*ral*-chi-koom. From the names of the parents. *E. perralderianum* × *E. pinnatum* subsp. *colchicum*. Cult.
perralderianum Coss. pe-ral-duh-ree-*ah*-noom. After Henri Rene le Tourneux de la Perraudière (1831–1861), French naturalist. N Africa.
pinnatum Fisch. ex DC. pin-*ah*-toom. Lat. pinnate (the leaves). Caucasus, N Iran. subsp. *colchicum* (Boiss.) N. Busch. *kol*-chi-koom. Lat. of Colchis on the Black Sea (now part of Georgia).
pubigerum (DC.) C. Morren & Decne. pew-*bij*-uh-room. Lat. bearing hairs (the leaves). SE Eur., W Asia.
stellulatum Stearn. stel-ew-*lah*-toom. Lat. bearing little stars (referring to the flowers). China (Hubei, Sichuan).

×*versicolor* C. Morren. ver-*si*-ko-lor. Lat. variably coloured (the flowers). *E. grandiflorum* × *E. pinnatum* subsp. *colchicum*. Cult.

×*warleyense* Stearn. wor-lee-*en*-see. Of Warley Place, Essex, UK, the garden of Ellen Willmott, who raised it. *E. alpinum* × *E. pinnatum* subsp. *colchicum*. Cult.

wushanense T. S. Ying. wue-shan-*en*-see. Of Wu Shan. China (Sichuan).

×*youngianum* Fisch. & C. A. Mey. yung-ee-*ah*-noom. After Mr Young of Epsom, Surrey, who sent it to RBG Edinburgh in 1838. *E. diphyllum* × *E. grandiflorum*. Cult.

Epipactis Zinn. (Orchidaceae). ep-ee-*pak*-tis. Helleborine. From Gk. name used by Dioscorides for a plant used to curdle milk, from Gk. upon, curdled. 50 spp. orchids. Eur., Africa, Asia, N Am.

gigantea Douglas ex Hook. jie-*gan*-tee-uh. Giant helleborine. Lat. very large. SW Canada, W USA, N Mex.

palustris (L.) Crantz. puh-*lus*-tris. Marsh helleborine. Lat. of marshes. Eur. to Caucasus and Mongolia.

Epipremnum Scott (Araceae). ep-ee-*prem*-noom. Gk. upon a tree trunk, referring to their epiphytic habit. 15 spp. climbers. Trop. Asia, Pacific Is.

aureum (Linden & André) G. S. Bunting. *aw*-ree-oom. Devil's ivy, golden pothos. Lat. golden (the leaves are blotched with yellow). Moorea (Society Is.).

pinnatum (L.) Engl. pin-*ah*-toom. Lat. pinnate (the adult foliage). SE Asia, Pacific Is. to Queensland, Australia.

Equisetum L. (Equisetaceae). ek-wi-*see*-toom. Horsetails. Lat. horse hair (they are likened to a horse's tail). 15 spp. herbs. Widespread.

hyemale L. hee-*mah*-lee. Scouring rush. Lat. of winter (the evergreen stems persist in winter). N Am., Eur., Asia. subsp. *affine* (Engelm.) Calder & Roy L. Taylor. *af*-i-nee. Lat. related to (*E. hyemale*; it was originally described as a var. of *E. robustum*).

scirpoides Michx. skirp-*oy*-deez. Dwarf scouring rush. Like *Scirpus* (those species now placed in *Eleocharis*). Canada, NE USA, Greenland, Eur., Asia.

Eragrostis Wolf (Poaceae). e-ruh-*gros*-tis. Love grass. Gk. love grass, from the heart-shaped spikelets. 350 spp. grasses. Widespread.

curvula (Schrad.) Nees. *kurv*-ew-luh. African love grass, weeping love grass. Lat. a little curved (the leaves). S Africa.

elliottii S. Watson. el-ee-*ot*-ee-ee. Elliott's love grass. After American banker and botanist Stephen Elliott (1771–1830), who described it under another name. N and S Am.

spectabilis (Pursh) Steud. spek-*tab*-i-lis. Purple love grass. Lat. spectacular. Canada to Mex.

Eranthis Salisb. (Ranunculaceae). e-*ranth*-is. Gk. spring flower. 8 spp. tuberous herbs. Eur., Asia.

cilicica Schott & Kotschy. si-*li*-si-kuh. Lat. of Cilicia (now S Turkey). E Medit.

hyemalis (L.) Salisb. hee-*mah*-lis. Winter aconite. Lat. of winter (flowering). S Eur.

Eremurus M. Bieb. (Xanthorrhoeaceae). e-re-*mew*-roos. Foxtail lily.
From Gk. desert, tail, referring to
their habitat, and the long, slender
inflorescence. 58 spp. herbs. W Asia
to China.
himalaicus Baker. him-uh-*lay*-i-koos.
Of the Himalaya. Afghanistan, W
Himal.
×*isabellinus* R. Vilm. iz-a-bel-*ee*-noos.
Lat. brownish yellow (the flowers).
E. olgae × *E. stenophyllus*. Cult.
robustus (Regel) Regel. roh-*bus*-toos.
Lat. robust (the inflorescence). C
Asia.
stenophyllus (Boiss. & Buhse) Baker.
sten-*o*-fil-oos. Gk. narrow-leaved.
Iran to C Asia, W Pakistan.

Erica L. (Ericaceae). *e*-ri-kuh. Heath.
Lat. name for *E. arborea*, from the
Gk. name. 860 spp., shrubs, small
trees. Eur., W Asia, Africa.
arborea L. ar-*bor*-ree-uh. Tree heath.
Lat. tree-like. Medit., Africa.
australis L. os-*trah*-lis. Spanish heath.
Lat. southern. SW Eur., N Africa.
carnea L. *kar*-nee-uh. Winter heath.
Lat. flesh-pink (the flowers). C and
SE Eur.
cinerea L. sin-*e*-ree-uh. Bell heather.
Lat. grey (the foliage of some forms).
W Eur.
×*darleyensis* Bean. dar-lee-*en*-sis. Of
Darley (it was raised at the nursery of
James Smith, Darley Dale, Derby-
shire, England). *E. carnea* × *E. erigena*. Cult.
×*hyemalis* Nicholson. hee-*mah*-lis.
Lat. of winter (flowering). Cult.
erigena R. Ross. e-ri-*jee*-nuh. Irish
heath. Lat. of Ireland. W Eur., N
Africa.

tetralix L. *tet*-ruh-lix. Cross-leaved
heath. Gk. name for a species of
heath. N and W Eur.
vagans L. *vay*-guhnz. Cornish heath.
Lat. wandering (from its wide-
spreading habit). W Eur.

Erigeron L. (Asteraceae). e-*rig*-uh-ron.
Gk. name of a plant used by
Dioscorides, probably for groundsel
(*Senecio vulgaris*), from Gk. early, old
man (the white seedheads appear
soon after flowering). 390 spp., herbs,
shrubs, trees. Widespread.
glaucus Ker Gawl. *glaw*-koos. Beach
aster, seaside fleabane. Lat. bluish
white (the foliage). Calif., Oregon.
karvinskianus DC. kar-vin-skee-*ah*-
noos. Mexican fleabane. After
German botanist Wilhelm Friedrich
von Karwinsky von Karwin (1780–
1855), who collected the type specimen. Mex., C Am.

Erinus L. (Plantaginaceae). *e*-ri-noos.
Gk. named used by Dioscorides for
another plant. 2 spp. herbs. Eur., N
Africa.
alpinus L. al-*pie*-noos. Fairy foxglove.
Lat. of the Alps. S and C Eur.

Eriobotrya Lindl. (Rosaceae). e-ree-
oh-*bot*-ree-uh. From Gk. wool, a
bunch of grapes (the inflorescence is
covered in woolly hairs). 30 spp.,
trees, shrubs. E Asia.
japonica (Thunb.) Lindl. juh-*pon*-i-
kuh. Loquat. Of Japan. China, Taiwan, Japan.

Eriophorum L. (Cyperaceae). e-ree-*of*-
o-room. Cotton grass. Gk. wool-
bearing, referring to the fruiting

heads. 25 spp. herbs. N temp. and arctic regs., S Africa.

angustifolium Honck. an-gus-ti-*foh*-lee-oom. Common cotton grass. Lat. narrow-leaved. N Am., Eur., Asia.

Erodium L'Hér. (Geraniaceae). e-*roh*-dee-oom. Stork's bill. From Gk. heron, comparing the elongated fruit to a heron's beak. 60 spp. herbs. Eur., N Africa, W and C Asia, Australia, S Am.

chrysanthum L'Hér. ex DC. kris-*anth*-oom. Gk. golden-flowered. Greece.

manescavii Coss. man-es-*kah*-vee-ee. After André Manescau, mayor of Pau, France, 1843–48. Pyrenees.

reichardii (Murray) DC. riek-*ard*-ee-ee. After Johann Jacob Reichard (1743–1832), German botanist. Balearic Is.

×***variabile*** A. C. Leslie. va-ree-*ab*-i-lee. Lat. variable (the leaves). *E. corsicum* × *E. reichardii.* Cult.

Eruca Mill. (Brassicaceae). e-*rue*-kuh. Lat. name for this or a similar plant, which gave the English name. 1 sp., herb. Medit.

vesicaria (L.) Cav. vee-si-*kair*-ree-uh. Lat. bladder-like (the fruit). subsp. *sativa* (Mill.) Thell. sa-*tee*-vuh. Rocket. Lat. cultivated. Cult.

Eryngium L. (Apiaceae). e-*ring*-gee-oom. From the Gk. named used by Theophrastus for *E. campestre.* 250 spp. herbs. Eur., N Africa, W and C Asia, N and S Am.

agavifolium Griseb. uh-gah-vi-*foh*-lee-oom. Lat. with leaves like *Agave.* Argentina.

alpinum L. al-*pie*-noom. Lat. of the Alps. Eur.

bourgatii Gouan. boor-*gat*-ee-ee. After M. Bourgat, 18th-cent. French doctor who collected in the Pyrenees with the author, Antoine Gouan, 1766–67. SW Eur., Morocco.

eburneum Decne. ee-*burn*-ee-oom. Lat. ivory-like (the flowers). Brazil, Argentina, Uruguay.

giganteum M. Bieb. jie-*gan*-tee-oom. Lat. very large. W Asia.

maritimum L. muh-*rit*-i-moom. Sea holly. Lat. of the sea (it grows on coasts). Eur., N Africa, W Asia.

pandanifolium Cham. & Schltdl. pan-dan-i-*foh*-lee-oom. Lat. with leaves like *Pandanus.* S Am.

planum L. *play*-noom. Lat. flat (the leaves). C and E Eur., W and C Asia, NW China.

proteiflorum F. Delaroche. proh-tee-i-*flaw*-room. Lat. with flowers like *Protea.* Mex.

yuccifolium Michx. yook-i-*foh*-lee-oom. Lat. with leaves like *Yucca.* E USA.

×***zabelii*** Christ ex Bergmans. za-*bel*-ee-ee. After German botanist Hermann Zabel (1832–1912). *E. alpinum* × *E. bourgatii.* Cult.

Erysimum L. (Brassicaceae). e-*ris*-i-moom. From the Gk. name. 180 spp., herbs, subshrubs. Eur., N Africa, Asia, N Am., Australia.

cheiri (L.) Crantz. *kie*-ree. Wallflower. From the Arabic name written in Gk., which means hand (it was carried in bouquets). S Eur.

Erythrina L. (Fabaceae). e-rith-*ree*-nuh. From Gk. red, referring to the flowers and seeds. 120 spp., shrubs, trees, herbs. Tropics to warm temp. regs.

crista-galli L. *krist*-uh-*gal*-ee. Coral tree. Lat. cock's comb (the arrangement of the red flowers). S Am.

herbacea L. her-*bay*-see-uh. Coral bean, red cardinal. Lat. herbaceous. SE USA, NE Mex.

Erythronium L. (Liliaceae). e-rith-*roh*-nee-oom. Fawn lily, trout lily. From the Gk. name of another plant, thought to be an orchid, from Gk. red. 29 spp. bulbous herbs. Eur., Asia, N Am.

americanum Ker Gawl. uh-me-ri-*kah*-noom. Yellow trout lily. Of America. E N Am.

californicum Purdy. kal-i-*for*-ni-koom. California fawn lily. Of California. Calif.

dens-canis L. *dens-kan*-is. Dog's tooth violet. Lat. dog's tooth (the shape of the bulbs). Eur., W Asia.

japonicum Decne. juh-*pon*-i-koom. Of Japan. China, Korea, Japan.

revolutum Sm. rev-o-*lue*-toom. Pink fawn lily. Lat. revolute (curved backward, referring to the tepals). W USA, SW Canada.

tuolumnense Applegate. tue-ol-uhm-en-see. Tuolumne fawn lily. Of Tuolomne County. Calif.

Escallonia Mutis ex L.f. (Escalloniaceae). es-kuh-*loh*-nee-uh. After Spanish student Antonio José Escallón y Flóres (1739–1818), a companion of Mutis in Colombia. 40 spp., shrubs, trees. S Am.

laevis (Vell.) Sleumer. *lee*-vis. Lat. smooth (the leaves). Brazil.

'Langleyensis'. lang-lee-*en*-sis. Of Langley, Bucks., UK, where it was raised at the Veitch nursery in 1893. *E. rubra* × *E. virgata*.

rubra (Ruiz & Pav.) Pers. *rue*-bruh. Lat. red (the flowers). Chile. var.

macrantha (Hook. & Arn.) Reiche. mak-*ranth*-uh. Gk. large-flowered.

Eschscholzia Cham. (Papaveraceae). esh-*olt*-see-uh. After Russian physician and naturalist Johann Friedrich von Eschscholtz (1793–1831), born in what is now Estonia, who accompanied the author, Chamisso, when *E. californica* was discovered. 10 spp. herbs. W USA, N Mex.

californica Cham. kal-i-*for*-ni-kuh. California poppy. Of California.

Eucalyptus L'Hér. (Myrtaceae). ew-kuh-*lip*-toos. Gums. Gk. well-covered, referring to the cap on the flower buds formed from the calyx and/or the corolla. 800 spp., trees, shrubs. Australia, New Guinea, Indonesia, Philippines.

archeri Maiden & Blakely. *arch*-uh-ree. Alpine cider gum. After Australian botanist William Archer (1820–1874), who collected the type specimen in 1848. Tasmania.

citriodora Hook. = *Corymbia citriodora*

coccifera Hook.f. kok-*si*-fuh-ruh. Tasmanian snow gum. Lat. bearing coccids (some of the first collected specimens were infested with these scale insects). Tasmania.

dalrympleana Maiden. dal-rim-plee-*ah*-nuh. Mountain gum. After Richard Dalrymple-Hay (1861–

1943), the first commissioner of forests in NSW. SE Australia.

glaucescens Maiden & Blakely. glaw-*kes*-uhnz. Tingiringi gum. Lat. bluish white (the foliage). SE Australia.

globulus Labill. *glob*-ew-loos. Tasmanian blue gum. Lat. spherical (the fruit). SE Australia.

gunnii Hook.f. *gun*-ee-ee. Cider gum. After South African–born Australian botanist Ronald Campbell Gunn (1808–1881), who collected the type specimen in the early 1840s. Tasmania.

nicholii Maiden & Blakely. ni-*kol*-ee-ee. Narrow-leaved black peppermint. After Richard Nichol (1866–1947), Irish-born secretary to author Joseph Henry Maiden at Sydney Botanic Gardens herbarium. SE Australia (NSW).

parvifolia Cambage = *E. parvula*

parvula L. A. S. Johnson & K. D. Hill. *parv*-ew-luh. Lat. small. SE Australia (NSW).

pauciflora Sieber ex Spreng. paw-si-*flaw*-ruh. Snow gum. Lat. few-flowered (the type specimen). SE Australia. subsp. ***debeuzevillei*** (Maiden) L. A. S. Johnson & Blaxell. duh-boh-zuh-*vil*-ee-ee. After Wilfrid Alexander Watt de Beuzeville (1884–1954), assistant forester with the Australian Forestry Commission, who collected the type specimen in 1919. subsp. ***niphophila*** (Maiden & Blakely) L. A. S. Johnson & Blaxell. ni-*fof*-i-luh. Gk. snow-loving.

perriniana F. Muell. ex Rodway. pe-rin-ee-*ah*-nuh. Spinning gum. After George Samuel Perrin (1849–1900), Tasmania's first conservator of forests in the 1880s, who recognised it as distinct. SE Australia.

Eucomis L'Hér. (Asparagaceae). ew-*kom*-is. Pineapple lily. From Gk. well, head of hair, referring to the tuft of leafy bracts above the inflorescence. 10 spp. bulbous herbs. Trop. and S Africa.

autumnalis (Mill.) Chitt. aw-toom-*nah*-lis. Lat. of autumn (flowering). Malawi to S Africa.

bicolor Baker. *bi*-ko-lor. Lat. two-coloured (the flowers). S Africa.

comosa (Houtt.) Wehrh. ko-*moh*-suh. Lat. long-haired, referring to the leafy bracts. S Africa.

pallidiflora Baker. pa-li-di-*flaw*-ruh. Lat. pale-flowered. S Africa. subsp. ***pole-evansii*** (N. E. Br.) Reyneke ex J. C. Manning. *pohl*-e-*van*-zee-ee. After Illtyd Buller Pole-Evans (1879–1968), Welsh-born South African botanist who collected the type specimen in 1919.

pole-evansii N. E. Br. = *E. pallidiflora* subsp. *pole-evansii*

Eucryphia Cav. (Cunoniaceae). ew-*krif*-ee-uh. Gk. well-hidden (the joined sepals form a cap over the petals). 7 spp., trees, shrubs. E Australia, Chile.

cordifolia Cav. kor-di-*foh*-lee-uh. Ulmo. Lat. with heart-shaped leaves. Chile.

glutinosa (Poepp. & Endl.) Baill. glue-ti-*noh*-suh. Lat. sticky (the buds). Chile.

×***intermedia*** Bausch. in-ter-*mee*-dee-uh. Lat. intermediate (between the parents). *E. glutinosa* × *E. lucida*. Cult.

lucida (labill.) Baill. *lue*-si-duh. Leatherwood. Lat. shining (the leaves). Tasmania.

milliganii Hook.f. mi-li-*gan*-ee-ee. Dwarf leatherwood. After Scottish surgeon Joseph Milligan (1807–1884), who collected it. Tasmania.

×*nymansensis* Bausch. nie-muhnz-*en*-sis. Of Nymans, West Sussex, UK, where it was raised. *E. cordifolia* × *E. lucida*. Cult.

Euonymus L. (Celastraceae). ew-*on*-i-moos. Lat. name used by Pliny for a tree that grew on Lesbos, from Gk. well-named. 130 spp., shrubs, trees. Eur., Asia, N Am., Madagascar, Australasia.

alatus (Thunb.) Siebold. uh-*lah*-toos. Lat. winged (the shoots). China, Korea, Japan.

americanus L. uh-me-ri-*kah*-noos. Strawberry bush. Of America. E and C USA.

cornutus Hemsl. kor-*new*-toos. Lat. horned (the fruit wings). China, N India, N Myanmar.

europaeus L. ew-roh-*pee*-oos. Spindle tree. European. Eur., W Asia.

fortunei Hand.-Mazz. for-*tewn*-ee-ee. After Scottish botanist Robert Fortune (1812–1880), who collected the type specimen. E and SE Asia.

hamiltonianus Wall. ha-mil-toh-nee-*ah*-noos. After Scottish botanist Francis Buchanan-Hamilton (1762–1829), who studied and collected plants of India and Nepal. Afghanistan to Japan.

japonicus Thunb. juh-*pon*-i-koos. Of Japan. E and SE Asia.

nanus M. Bieb. *nah*-noos. Lat. dwarf. E Eur., W and C Asia, W China.

oxyphyllus Miq. ox-ee-*fil*-oos. Gk. sharp-leaved. China, Taiwan, Korea, Japan.

phellomanus Loes. fel-oh-*man*-oos. Gk. thinly corky (the shoots). China.

planipes (Koehne) Koehne. *plan*-i-peez. Lat. flat-stalked (the leaves). Korea, Japan.

Eupatorium L. (Asteraceae). ew-puh-*tor*-ree-oom. From the Gk. name, after Mithridates Eupator, king of Pontus (132–63 BCE). 40 spp. herbs. Mainly N temp. regs.

cannabinum L. kan-uh-*bie*-noom. Hemp agrimony. Like *Cannabis* (the leaves). Eur., N Africa, Asia.

capillifolium (Lam.) Small. kap-i-li-*foh*-lee-oom. Dog fennel. Lat. with hair-like leaves. E USA, Caribb.

coelestinum L. = *Conoclinium coelestinum*

ligustrinum DC. = *Ageratina ligustrina*

maculatum L. = *Eutrochium maculatum*

purpureum L. = *Eutrochium purpureum*

rugosum Houtt. = *Ageratina altissima*

Euphorbia L. (Euphorbiaceae). ew-*forb*-ee-uh. Spurges. Gk. name of a tree, used by Dioscorides, after Euphorbus, physician to King Juba of Numidia (N Africa). 2000 spp., herbs, shrubs, trees, succulents. Widespread.

amygdaloides L. uh-mig-duh-*loy*-deez. Wood spurge. Lat. almond-like (the leaves). Eur., SW Asia. subsp. *robbiae* (Turrill) Stace. *rob*-ee-ie. Mrs Robb's bonnet. After English plant collector Mary Anne Robb

(1829–1912), who introduced it from Turkey in her hatbox. Turkey.

characias L. kuh-*ray*-see-oos. From the Gk. name used by Dioscorides. Medit. subsp. ***wulfenii*** (Hoppe ex W. D. J. Koch) Radcl.-Sm. wool-*fen*-ee-ee. After Franz Xaver von Wulfen (1728–1805), Belgrade-born priest and botanist. SE Eur., Turkey.

cornigera Boiss. kor-*ni*-juh-ruh. Horned spurge. Lat. horned (referring to the warts on the fruit). Himal.

cyathophora Murray. sie-uh-*tho*-fuh-ruh. Fire on the mountain. Gk. bearing (conspicuous) cyathea (the flower-bearing structures, from Gk. cup). USA to S Am.

cyparissias L. sip-uh-*ris*-ee-oos. Cypress spurge. From the Gk. name used by Dioscorides for another species, from Gk. cypress. Eur., Turkey.

dulcis L. *dul*-sis. Sweet spurge. Lat. sweet. Eur.

epithymoides L. ep-ee-tiem-*oy*-deez. Lat. like *Cuscuta epithymum* (dodder). C and SE Eur., Libya, NW Turkey.

griffithii Hook.f. gri-*fith*-ee-ee. After William Griffith (1810–1845), English botanist and doctor with the East India Company, who collected plants in India and the Himalaya. Himal. to S China.

lathyris L. *la*-thi-ris. Caper spurge. From the Gk. name used by Dioscorides for a spurge. C and E Asia.

marginata Pursh. mar-jin-*ah*-tuh. Snow on the mountain. Lat. edged (the bracts are edged with white). USA, Mex.

×***martinii*** Rouy. mar-*tin*-ee-ee. After French doctor and botanist

Bernardin-Antoine Martin (1813–1897), who described it in 1886 from plants found in 1884 near Aumessas, S France. *E. amygdaloides* × *E. characias*. France.

mellifera Aiton. mel-*if*-uh-ruh. Honey spurge. Lat. bearing honey (the flowers are honey-scented). Madeira, Canary Is.

milii Des Moul. *mil*-ee-ee. Crown of thorns. After Baron Pierre Bernard de Milius (1773–1829), French governor of Île Bourbon (now Réunion), who introduced it to cultivation in France. Madagascar.

palustris L. puh-*lus*-tris. Lat. of marshes. Eur. to NW China.

×***pasteurii*** T. Walker. past-*ur*-ree-ee. After Oxford student George Pasteur, who worked on the hybrid. *E. mellifera* × *E. stygiana*. Cult.

polychroma A. Kern. = *E. epithymoides*

pulcherrima Willd. ex Klotzsch. pool-*ke*-ri-muh. Poinsettia. Lat. most beautiful. Mex., Guatemala.

rigida M. Bieb. *ri*-ji-duh. Lat. stiff (the leaves). S Eur., N Africa, SW Asia.

schillingii Radcl.-Sm. shi-*ling*-ee-ee. After English plant collector Tony Schilling, who discovered it and introduced it to cultivation in 1975. Nepal.

sikkimensis Boiss. si-kim-*en*-sis. Of Sikkim. Nepal to S China.

stygiana H. C. Watson. stig-ee-*ah*-nuh. Lat. of the River Styx of Gk. myth., the gateway to the Underworld (it grows on volcanic craters). Azores.

Eurybia (Cass.) Cass. (Asteraceae). ew-*rib*-ee-uh. From Gk. wide, few (the few wide-spreading ray florets). 23 spp. herbs. N America, Eur., Asia.

divaricata (L.) G. L. Nesom. di-va-ri-*kah*-tuh. White wood aster. Lat. wide-spreading (the branches). E N America.

glauca (Nutt.) G. L. Nesom. *glaw*-kuh. Grey aster. Lat. bluish white (the foliage). Rocky Mts.

×***herveyi*** (A. Gray) G. L. Nesom. *herv*-ee-ee. After US army surgeon E. (Eliphalet) Williams Hervey (1834–1925), who collected the type specimen in Massachusetts in 1866. *E. macrophylla* × *E. spectabilis.* NE USA.

macrophylla (L.) Cass. mak-*ro*-fil-uh. Bigleaf aster. Gk. large-leaved. E N Am.

radula (Aiton) G. L. Nesom. *rad*-ew-luh. Low rough aster. Lat. a scraper (the rough leaves). E N Am.

spectabilis (Aiton) G. L. Nesom. spek-*tab*-i-lis. Eastern showy aster, seaside purple aster. Lat. spectacular. E USA.

Euryops (Cass.) Cass. (Asteraceae). *ew*-ree-ops. From Gk. large eye (the showy flowerheads). 100 spp., herbs, shrubs. S Africa, Arabia.

chrysanthemoides (DC.) B. Nord. kris-anth-uh-*moy*-deez. Lat. like *Chrysanthemum.* S Africa.

pectinatus (L.) Cass. pek-ti-*nah*-toos. Lat. comb-like (the leaves). S Africa.

Euthamia (Nutt.) Cass. (Asteraceae). ew-*tham*-ee-uh. Gk. well-crowded, referring to the branching pattern. 5 spp., perenn. herbs, subshrubs. Canada, USA, Mex.

graminifolia (L.) Nutt. gram-i-ni-*foh*-lee-uh. Common goldentop. Lat. with grass-like leaves. Canada, USA.

Eutrochium Raf. (Asteraceae). ew-*troh*-kee-oom. Joe Pye weed. From Gk. well, wheel-like, referring to the whorled leaves. 5 spp. herbs. Canada, USA.

maculatum (L.) E. E. Lamont. mak-ew-*lah*-toom. Spotted Joe Pye weed. Lat. spotted (the stems).

purpureum (L.) E. E. Lamont. pur-*pew*-ree-oom. Sweetscented Joe Pye weed. Lat. purple (the flowers). SE Canada, E and C USA.

evening primrose *Oenothera biennis.* **white** *O. speciosa*

everlasting, golden *Xerochrysum bracteatum.* **pearly** *Anaphalis margaritacea.* **pink and white** *Rhodanthe chlorocephala* subsp. *rosea*

Exochorda Lindl. (Rosaceae). ex-oh-*kord*-uh. From Gk. external cord, referring to fibres on the ovary wall. 1 sp., deciduous shrub. C Asia to China, Korea.

giraldii Hesse = *E. racemosa* subsp. *giraldii*

×***macrantha*** (Lemoine) C. K. Schneid. = *E. racemosa*

racemosa (Lindl.) Rehder. ras-i-*moh*-suh. Pearlbush. Lat. with flowers in racemes. subsp. *giraldii* (Hesse) F. Y. Gao & Maesen. ji-*ral*-dee-ee. After Italian missionary Giuseppe Giraldi, who collected the type specimen in China and introduced it to cultivation in 1897.

Fabiana Ruiz & Pav. (Solanaceae).
fab-ee-*ah*-nuh. After Francisco
Fabián y Fuero (1719–1801), arch-
bishop of Valencia, who promoted
the study of plants. 15 spp. shrubs.
S Am.
imbricata Ruiz & Pav. im-bri-*kah*-tuh.
Lat. overlapping (the leaves). Chile,
Argentina.

Fagopyrum Mill. (Polygonaceae).
fay-goh-*pie*-room. From Gk. beech
wheat, from the beech-like edible
seeds. 16 spp. herbs. Eur., Asia, E
Africa.
dibotrys (L.) Gaertn. die-*bot*-ris. Tall
buckwheat. Gk. two bunches of
grapes (the inflorescences are paired).
Himal., China, Vietnam.
esculentum Moench. es-kew-*len*-toom.
Buckwheat. Lat. edible (the seeds).
China.
tataricum (L.) Gaertn. tuh-*ta*-ri-
koom. Green buckwheat. From the
reg. of C and E Asia once called
Tartary. C Asia, China.

Fagus L. (Fagaceae). *fay*-goos. Beeches.
Lat. name of the beech, from Gk. edi-
ble, for the edible nuts. 10 spp. trees.
SE Canada to E Mex., Eur., Asia.

grandifolia Ehrh. gran-di-*foh*-lee-uh.
American beech. Lat. large-leaved.
E N Am.
sylvatica L. sil-*vat*-i-kuh. European
beech. Lat. of woods. Eur., W Asia.
'**Aspleniifolia**'. uh-splee-nee-i-*foh*-
lee-uh. Lat. with leaves like *Asple-
nium*. '**Riversii**'. ri-*verz*-ee-ee. After
Messrs Rivers of Sawbridgeworth,
Herts., England, in whose nursery it
was raised. '**Rohanii**'. roh-*han*-ee-ee.
After Prince Camille de Rohan of
Sychrov, Bohemia (now Czech
Republic), on whose estate it was
raised. '**Zlatia**'. *zlah*-tee-uh. From
Serbian, gold (the yellow leaves).

fairies' thimbles *Campanula
cochlearifolia*
fairy bells *Prosartes*
fairy fan flower *Scaevola aemula*
fairy lantern, white *Calochortus albus*
fairywand *Chamaelirium luteum*

Fallopia Adans. (Polygonaceae).
fuh-*loh*-pee-uh. After Italian anatomist Gabriele Fallopio (1523–1562),
who described the Fallopian tube.
12 spp., herbs, woody climbers. Eur.,
Asia, N Am.
aubertii (L. Henry) Holub = *F.
baldschuanica*
baldschuanica (Regel) Holub. bald-
shoo-*an*-i-kuh. Mile-a-minute, Russian vine. Of Baldshuan, Tajikistan.
Afghanistan to China.
japonica (Houtt.) Ronse Decr. juh-
pon-i-kuh. Japanese knotweed. Of
Japan. China, Taiwan, Korea, Japan.

farewell to spring *Clarkia amoena*

Farfugium Lindl. (Asteraceae).
far-*few*-gee-oom. Lat. name used by
Pliny, probably for coltsfoot (*Tussil-
ago farfara*). 3 spp. herbs. China,
Japan.
japonicum (L.) Kitam. juh-*pon*-i-
koom. Of Japan.

Fargesia Franch. (Poaceae). far-*jee*-zee-
uh. After French missionary Paul
Guillaume Farges (1844–1912), who
collected the type specimen of *F.
spathacea*, the first species described.
90 spp. bamboos. E Himal., China,
Vietnam.
apicirubens Stapleton. ay-pi-si-*rue*-
buhnz. Lat. red at the tip (the sheaths
and internodes). China (Shaanxi,
Sichuan).
denudata T. P. Yi. dee-new-*dah*-tuh.
Lat. naked. China (Gansu, Sichuan).
dracocephala hort. = *F. apicirubens*
dracocephala T. P. Yi. drak-oh-*kef*-uh-
luh. Lat. a dragon's head (from the
resemblance of the auricles). China.
murielae (Gamble) T. P. Yi. mew-ree-
el-ie. After Muriel Primrose Wilson
(1906–1976), whose father, English
plant collector E. H. Wilson, introduced it to gardens in 1907 and asked
that it be named after her. China
(Hubei, Sichuan).
nitida (Mitford) Keng f. ex T. P. Yi.
ni-ti-duh. Lat. glossy (the leaves).
China.
robusta T. P. Yi. roh-*bus*-tuh. Lat.
robust. China (Sichuan).
rufa hort. = *F. dracocephala* T. P. Yi
utilis T. P. Yi. *ew*-ti-lis. Lat. useful (the
shoots are edible and the canes are
used for furniture). China (Yunnan).

Fascicularia Mez (Bromeliaceae).
fa-sik-ew-*lah*-ree-uh. Lat. like a small
bundle, referring to the clustered
habit. 1 sp., evergreen herb. Chile.
bicolor (Ruiz & Pav.) Mez. *bi*-ko-lor.
Lat. two-coloured (the leaves).

fat hen *Chenopodium album*

×***Fatshedera*** Guillaumin (Araliaceae). fats-*hed*-uh-ruh. From the
names of the parents (*Fatsia* ×
Hedera). Cult.
lizei Guillaumin. *lee*-zay-ee. After
the nursery of Lizé Frères, Nantes,
France, where it was raised ca. 1910.
F. japonica × *H. hibernica*.

Fatsia Decne. & Planch. (Araliaceae).
fat-see-uh. From an incorrect reading
of the Japanese name, *yatsude*, which
means eight hands. 3 spp. shrubs.
Japan, Korea, Taiwan.
japonica (Thunb.) Decne. & Planch.
juh-*pon*-i-kuh. Of Japan. Korea,
Japan.

fawn lily *Erythronium*. **California** *E.
californicum*. **pink** *E. revolutum*.
Tuolumne *E. tuolumnense*
feathertop *Pennisetum villosum*

Feijoa sellowiana O. Berg = *Acca
sellowiana*

Felicia Cass. (Asteraceae). fel-*is*-ee-uh.
After Herr Felix (d. 1846) of
Regensburg, Germany. 85 spp.,
herbs, shrubs. S and E Africa, Arabia.
amelloides (L.) Voss. am-uh-*loy*-deez.
Blue daisy. Lat. like *Aster amellus*.
S Africa.

fennel *Foeniculum vulgare*. dog *Eupatorium capillifolium*. Florence *Foeniculum vulgare* Azoricum Group. giant *Ferula communis* fennel flower *Nigella hispanica* fern, Asiatic holly *Cyrtomium caryotideum*. asparagus *Asparagus aethiopicus*. beech *Phegopteris connectilis*. bird's nest *Asplenium nidus*. bladder *Cystopteris*. Boston *Nephrolepis exaltata* 'Bostoniensis'. brittle bladder *Cystopteris fragilis*. brittle maidenhair *Adiantum tenerum*. broad buckler *Dryopteris dilatata*. bulblet bladder *Cystopteris bulbifera*. chain *Woodwardia radicans*. Christmas *Polystichum acrostichoides*. cinnamon *Osmundastrum cinnamomeum*. crown *Blechnum discolor*. deer *B. spicant*. dwarf hard *B. penna-marina*. evergreen maidenhair *Adiantum venustum*. fishbone water *Blechnum nudum*. giant chain *Woodwardia fimbriata*. Goldie's *Dryopteris goldieana*. hairy lip *Cheilanthes lanosa*. hard *Blechnum spicant*. hard shield *Polystichum aculeatum*. hart's tongue *Asplenium scolopendrium*. interrupted *Osmunda claytoniana*. Japanese holly *Cyrtomium falcatum*. Japanese painted *Athyrium niponicum* 'Pictum'. Japanese shield *Dryopteris erythrosora*. Korean rock *Polystichum tsussimense*. lady *Athyrium filix-femina*. maidenhair *Adiantum*. male *Dryopteris filix-mas*. marginal wood *D. marginalis*. marsh *Thelypteris palustris*. mosquito *Azolla caroliniana*. narrow buckler *Dryopteris carthusiana*. New York *Thelypteris noveboracensis*. oak *Gymnocarpium dryopteris*. ostrich *Matteuccia stru-*

thiopteris. parsley *Cryptogramma crispa*. rigid holly *Polystichum rigens*. royal *Osmunda regalis*. scaly male *Dryopteris affinis*. sensitive *Onoclea sensibilis*. shaggy wood *Dryopteris cycadina*. soft shield *Polystichum setiferum*. soft tree *Dicksonia antarctica*. sword *Polystichum munitum*. tassel *P. polyblepharum*. wavy cloak *Astrolepis sinuata*. wood *Dryopteris*. woolly lip *Cheilanthes tomentosa*

Ferocactus Britton & Rose (Cactaceae). fe-roh-*kak*-toos. Lat. fierce, cactus, from Gk. name for *Cynara cardunculus*. 25 spp. cacti. S USA, Mex.

cylindraceus (Engelm.) Orcutt. si-lin-*dray*-see-oos. California barrel cactus. Lat. cylindrical (the shape). SW USA, NW Mex.

emoryi (Engelm.) Orcutt. e-*mo*-ree-ee. After William Hemsley Emory (1811–1887), American soldier and explorer. SW USA, NW Mex.

glaucescens (DC.) Britton & Rose. glaw-*kes*-uhnz. Lat. bluish white (the colour). Mex.

haematacanthus (Salm-Dyck) Bravo ex Backeb. & F. M. Knuth. hee-mat-uh-*kan*-thoos. Gk. with red spines. Mex.

hamatacanthus (Muehlenpf.) Britton & Rose. ham-at-uh-*kan*-thoos. Texas barrel cactus. Gk. with hooked spines. SC USA, N Mex.

latispinus (Haw.) Britton & Rose. lat-i-*spee*-noos. Devil's tongue cactus. Lat. with broad spines. Mex.

pilosus (Galeotti ex Salm-Dyck) Werderm. pi-*loh*-soos. Lat. hairy (some of the spines are reduced to hairs). Mex.

pringlei (J. M. Coult.) Britton & Rose = *F. pilosus*

wislizeni (Engelm.) Britton & Rose. wiz-li-*zen*-ee. Arizona barrel cactus. After German doctor and explorer Friedrich Adolph Wislizenus (1810– 1889), who collected the type specimen. SW USA, N Mex.

Ferula L. (Apiaceae). *fe*-rue-luh. The Lat. name used by Pliny. 130 spp. herbs. Medit. to C Asia.

communis L. *kom*-ew-nis. Giant fennel. Lat. common. Medit. subsp. ***glauca*** (L.) Rouy & E. G. Camus. *glaw*-kuh. Lat. bluish white (the foliage).

tingitana L. ting-i-*tah*-nuh. Lat. of Tangier (Lat. *Tingis*). SW Eur., N Africa, SW Asia.

fescue *Festuca*. **blue** *F. glauca*. **Idaho** *F. idahoensis*. **red** *F. rubra*. **sheep's** *F. ovina*. **tufted** *F. amethystina*

Festuca L. (Poaceae). fes-*tue*-kuh. Fescue. Lat. straw or the stem of a grass. 500 spp. grasses. Widespread.

amethystina L. am-uh-this-*tee*-nuh. Tufted fescue. Lat. amethyst-coloured (the foliage). C Eur.

eskia Ramond ex DC. *es*-kee-uh. From *esquia*, a local name in the French Pyrenees. France, Spain (Pyrenees).

glauca Vill. *glaw*-kuh. Blue fescue. Lat. bluish white (the foliage). Eur.

idahoensis Elmer. ie-duh-hoh-*en*-sis. Idaho fescue. Of Idaho. W Canada, W USA.

ovina L. oh-*vee*-nuh. Sheep's fescue. Lat. of sheep (which eat it). Eur., Asia.

rubra L. *rue*-bruh. Red fescue. Lat. red (the inflorescence, sometimes). Eur., Asia, N Am.

feverfew *Tanacetum parthenium*. **American** *Parthenium integrifolium*

Ficaria Schaeff. (Ranunculaceae). fi-*kair*-ree-uh. Lat. resembling *Ficus* (fig), referring to the tubers. 5 spp., perenn. herbs. Eur., N Africa, W and C Asia.

verna Huds. *vern*-uh. Lesser celandine. Lat. of spring (flowering). Eur., N Africa, W Asia.

Ficus L. (Moraceae). *fee*-koos. Figs. Lat. name for *F. carica* and its fruit. 750 spp., trees, shrubs, climbers. Widespread, tropics and subtropics.

benjamina L. ben-juh-*mee*-nuh. Weeping fig. From banyan, the name given to *F. benghalensis* after the traders (*banias*) that sat in its shade. SE Asia, to Pacific Is. and N Australia.

carica L. *ka*-ri-kuh. Common fig. Lat. of Caria (ancient reg. of SW Turkey). S Eur., N Africa, W and C Asia.

elastica Roxb. ex Hornem. ee-*las*-ti-kuh. Rubber plant. Lat. elastic (the milky sap has been used to make rubber). Himal., SE Asia.

lyrata Warb. lie-*rah*-tuh. Lyre-leaf fig. Lat. shaped like a lyre (the leaves). Trop. Africa.

pumila L. *pew*-mi-luh. Creeping fig. Lat. dwarf. China, Taiwan, Vietnam, Japan.

fiddleneck *Phacelia tanacetifolia* **fig** *Ficus*. **common** *F. carica*. **creeping** *F. pumila*. **lyre-leaf** *F. lyrata*. **weeping** *F. benjamina* **filbert** *Corylus maxima*

Filipendula Mill. (Rosaceae).fi-li-*pen*-dew-luh. From Lat. thread, hanging (the tubers 'hang' on thread-like roots). 15 spp. herbs. N temp. regs.
camtschatica (Pall.) Maxim. kamt-*shat*-i-kuh. Giant meadowsweet. Of Kamchatka. E Russia, Japan.
palmata (Pall.) Maxim. pahl-*mah*-tuh. Lat. hand-like (the leaves). E Russia, N China, N Korea.
×*purpurea* Maxim. pur-*pew*-ree-uh. Lat. purple (the flowers). *F. camtschatica* × *F*. sp. Cult.
rubra (Hill) B. L. Rob. *rue*-bruh. Queen-of-the-prairie. Lat. red (the flowers). E USA.
ulmaria (L.) Maxim. ul-*mair*-ree-uh. Meadowsweet. Eur. to China.
vulgaris Moench. vul-*gar*-ris. Dropwort. Lat. common. Eur., N Africa, W Asia.

finocchio *Foeniculum vulgare* Azoricum Group
fir *Abies*. **Algerian** *A. numidica*. **balsam** *A. balsamea*. **balm of Gilead** *A. balsamea*. **California red** *A. magnifica*. **Chinese** *Cunninghamia lanceolata*. **corkbark** *Abies lasiocarpa* var. *arizonica*. **Douglas** *Pseudotsuga menziesii*. **Fraser** *Abies fraseri*. **giant** *A. grandis*. **grand** *A. grandis*. **Greek** *A. cephalonica*. **Korean** *A. koreana*. **Nikko** *A. homolepis*. **noble** *A. procera*. **Nordmann** *A. nordmanniana*. **Pacific silver** *A. amabilis*. **red silver** *A. amabilis*. **silver** *A. alba*. **Spanish** *A. pinsapo*. **subalpine** *A. lasiocarpa*. **Veitch** *A. veitchii*. **white** *A. concolor*
fire on the mountain *Euphorbia cyathophora*
firecracker flower *Dichelostemma ida-maia*

firecracker plant *Cuphea ignea, Russelia equisetiformis*
firethorn *Pyracantha*

Fittonia Coem. (Acanthaceae). fit-*oh*-nee-uh. After sisters Elizabeth and Sarah Mary Fitton, 19th-cent. Irish botanical authors. 2 spp. evergreen perenn. herbs. S Am.
albivenis (Lindl. ex Veitch) Brummitt. al-bee-*ven*-is. Mosaic plant, nerve plant. Lat. white-veined (the leaves). **Argyroneura Group**. ar-gi-roh-*new*-ruh. Gk. with silver veins. **Verschaffeltii Group**. vair-shuh-*felt*-ee-ee. After Ambroise Verschaffelt (1825–1886), whose Belgian nursery introduced it to gardens.
argyroneura Coem. = *F. albivenis* Argyroneura Group
verschaffeltii (Lem.) Van Houtte = *F. albivenis* Verschaffeltii Group

fivespot *Nemophila maculata*
flamingo flower *Anthurium*
flannelbush *Fremontodendron*. **California** *F. californicum*
flax *Linum usitatissimum*. **blue** *L. perenne*. **bush** *Astelia nervosa*. **golden** *Linum flavum*. **mountain** *Phormium colensoi*. **New Zealand** *P. tenax*. **perennial** *Linum perenne*
flax lily *Dianella*. **blue** *D. caerulea*. **Tasman** *D. tasmanica*
fleabane, Mexican *Erigeron karvinskyanus*. **seaside** *E. glaucus*
flower of an hour *Hibiscus trionum*
foamflower *Tiarella cordifolia*

Foeniculum Mill. (Apiaceae).fee-*nik*-ew-loom. From Lat. hay. 1 sp., herb. S Eur., N Africa, W Asia.

vulgare Mill. vul-*gar*-ree. Fennel. Lat. common. **Azoricum Group**. uh-*zo*-ri-koom. Finocchio, Florence fennel. Of the Azores.

forget-me-not *Myosotis*. **Chatham Island** *Myosotidium hortensia*. **Chinese** *Cynoglossum amabile*. **Jamaican** *Browallia americana*. **water** *Myosotis scorpioides*. **wood** *M. sylvatica*

Forsythia Vahl (Oleaceae). for-*sieth*-ee-uh. After Scottish botanist William Forsyth (1737–1804), a founder member of the Royal Horticultural Society. 11 spp. shrubs, sometimes climbing. SE Eur., E Asia.
giraldiana Lingelsh. ji-ral-dee-*ah*-nuh. After Giuseppe Giraldi, Italian missionary and plant collector in China. China.
×***intermedia*** Zabel. in-ter-*mee*-dee-uh. Lat. intermediate (between the parents). *F. suspensa* × *F. viridissima*. Cult.
suspensa (Thunb.) Vahl. soos-*pen*-suh. Lat. hanging (the flowers). China.
viridissima Lindl. vi-ri-*dis*-i-muh. Lat. greenest (the dark leaves). China, Korea. **'Bronxensis'**. bronx-*en*-sis. Of the Bronx (it was raised at the Bronx Botanical Garden, New York, in 1939).

Fortunella japonica (Thunb.) Swingle = *Citrus japonica*

Fothergilla L. (Hamamelidaceae). fotH-uh-*gil*-uh. After John Fothergill (1712–1780), English physician and naturalist. 2 spp. shrubs. SE USA.
gardenii Murray. gar-*den*-ee-ee. Dwarf

witch alder. After Scottish physician and naturalist Alexander Garden (1730–1791), who worked in South Carolina and sent specimens of this and other plants to Linnaeus.
×***intermedia*** Ranney & Fantz. in-ter-*mee*-dee-uh. Lat. intermediate (between the parents). *F. gardenii* × *F. major*. Cult.
major Lodd. *may*-juh. Witch alder. Lat. large (compared to *F. gardenii*). **Monticola Group**. mon-*ti*-ko-luh. Lat. living in the mountains.
monticola Ashe = *F. major* Monticola Group

fountain plant *Russelia equisetiformis*
four o'clock plant *Mirabilis jalapa*
foxglove *Digitalis*. **Chinese** *Rehmannia elata*. **common** *Digitalis purpurea*. **fairy** *Erinus alpinus*. **Grecian** *Digitalis lanata*. **large yellow** *D. grandiflora*. **rusty** *D. ferruginea*. **straw** *D. lutea*
foxtail lily *Eremurus*

Fragaria L. (Rosaceae). fruh-*gah*-ree-uh. Strawberry. From Lat. scented, referring to the scent of the fruit. 20 spp. herbs. N hemisph., S Am.
×***ananassa*** Duchesne ex Rozier. an-uh-*nas*-uh. Garden strawberry. From *Ananas*, pineapple (it was originally known as the pineapple strawberry from the scent and flavour of the fruit). Cult.
chiloensis (L.) Mill. kee-loh-*en*-sis. Beach strawberry. Of Chiloé, Chile. W Canada, W USA, Argentina, Chile.
vesca L. *ves*-kuh. Woodland strawberry. Lat. small. Eur., W and C Asia to China, Canada, USA.

virginiana Mill. vir-jin-ee-*ah*-nuh.
Virginia strawberry. Of Virginia.
Canada, USA.

Francoa Cav. (Francoaceae).
fran-*koh*-uh. After Francisco Franco,
16th-cent. Spanish physician. 1 sp.,
herb. Chile.
appendiculata Cav. = *F. sonchifolia*
sonchifolia (Willd.) Cav. sonch-i-*foh*-
lee-uh. Bridal wreath. With leaves
like *Sonchus*.

Frangula Mill. (Rhamnaceae). *frang*-
ew-luh. The medieval name of *F.
alnus*, from Lat. to break, referring
to the brittle stems. 50 spp., shrubs,
trees. N Am., Eur., N Africa, Asia.
alnus Mill. *al*-noos. Alder buckthorn.
From the resemblance of the leaves to
those of *Alnus*. Eur., N Africa, W
and C Asia.
purshiana (DC.) J. G. Cooper. pursh-
ee-*ah*-nuh. Casacara buckthorn.
After German botanist Frederick
(Friedrich) Traugott Pursh (1774–
1820), who described it under
another name. SW Canada, W USA.

Franklinia Bartram ex Marshall
(Theaceae). frank-*lin*-ee-uh. After
American statesman Benjamin
Franklin (1706–1790), a family
friend of author Bartram who introduced it to cultivation. 1 sp., tree or
shrub. Georgia, USA (now extinct in
the wild).
alatamaha Marshall. uh-lah-tuh-
mah-huh. After the Altamaha River,
Georgia, USA, near where it used to
grow.

Fraxinus L. (Oleaceae). *frax*-i-noos.
Ashes. The Lat. name. 43 spp., trees,
shrubs. Temp. and subtrop. N
hemisph.
americana L. uh-me-ri-*kah*-nuh.
White ash. Of America. E N Am.
angustifolia Vahl. an-gus-ti-*foh*-
lee-uh. Narrow-leaved ash. Lat. with
narrow leaves (leaflets). S and E Eur.,
N Africa, W Asia. subsp. *oxycarpa*
(M. Bieb. ex Willd.) Franco & Rocha
Afonso. ox-ee-*kar*-puh. Gk. with
pointed fruit. E Eur., W Asia.
excelsior L. ex-*sel*-see-or. European
ash. Lat. taller. Eur., W Asia.
latifolia Benth. lat-i-*foh*-lee-uh.
Oregon ash. Lat. with broad leaves
(leaflets). W USA.
mandshurica Rupr. mand-*shoo*-ri-
kuh. Manchurian ash. Of Manchuria. E Russia, China, Korea, Japan.
mariesii Hook.f. = *F. sieboldiana*
nigra Marshall. *nie*-gruh. Black ash.
Lat. black, referring to the dark
wood. E N Am.
ornus L. *or*-noos. Manna ash. Lat.
name for mountain ash (*Sorbus aucuparia*). Eur., SW Asia.
pennsylvanica Marshall. pen-sil-*van*-
i-kuh. Green ash, red ash. Of Pennsylvania. E N Am.
quadrangulata Michx. kwod-rang-
ew-*lah*-tuh. Blue ash. Lat. four-
angled (the shoots). SE Canada,
E USA.
sieboldiana Blume. see-bold-ee-*ah*-
nuh. After German physician and
botanist Philip Franz von Siebold
(1796–1866), who studied the flora
and fauna of Japan. China, Korea,
Japan.
velutina Torr. vel-ew-*tee*-nuh, vel-*ue*-
ti-nuh. Arizona ash, velvet ash. Lat.

velvety (the leaf undersides and shoots, sometimes). SW USA, N Mex.

Freesia Ecklon ex Klatt (Iridaceae). *free*-zee-uh. After German physician and botanist Friedrich Heinrich Theodor Freese (1797–1876), a student of author Christian Friedrich Ecklon. 16 spp. cormous herbs. E and S Africa.
laxa (Thunb.) Goldblatt & J. C. Manning. *lax*-uh. Lat. open (the inflorescence). Kenya to S Africa.

Fremontodendron Cov. (Malvaceae). free-mont-oh-*den*-dron. Flannelbush. After American politician and explorer John Charles Frémont (1813–1890), and Gk. tree. Frémont collected the type specimen of *F. californicum* in 1846. 3 spp., trees, shrubs. SW USA, NW Mex.
californicum (Torr.) Cov. kal-i-*for*-ni-koom. California flannelbush. Of California.

friar's cowl *Arisarum vulgare*
fringe tree *Chionanthus virginicus.*
Chinese *C. retusus*

Fritillaria Tourn. ex L. (Liliaceae). fri-ti-*lair*-ree-uh. Fritillary. From Lat. dice box, referring to the checkered flowers of *F. meleagris*. 100 spp. bulbous herbs. Temp. N hemisph.
acmopetala Boiss. ak-moh-*pet*-uh-luh. Gk. with anvil-shaped petals. SW Asia.
affinis (Schult. & Schult.f.) Sealy. *af*-i-nis. Checker lily. Lat. related to (another species). W Canada, W USA.

aurea Schott. *aw*-ree-uh. Lat. golden (the flowers). Turkey.
biflora Lindl. bie-*flaw*-ruh. Chocolate lily, mission bells. Lat. two-flowered. Calif.
bithynica Baker. bi-*thin*-i-kuh. Lat. of Bithynia (ancient reg. of NW Turkey). Aegean Is., W Turkey.
camschatcensis (L.) Ker Gawl. kam-shat-*ken*-sis. Black sarana. Of Kamchatka. E Russia, Japan, NW N Am.
davisii Turrill. day-*vis*-ee-ee. After English botanist Peter Hadland Davis (1918–1992), who worked on the flora of Turkey and who collected the type specimen in 1940. S Greece.
imperialis L. im-peer-ree-*ah*-lis. Crown imperial. Lat. imperial. SE Turkey to W Himal.
meleagris L. mel-ee-*ag*-ris. Snake's head fritillary. Lat. spotted (the flowers). Eur., W Asia.
michailovskyi Fomin. mi-kiel-*of*-skee-ee. After S. J. Michailovsky, who collected the type specimen. E Turkey.
pallidiflora Schrenk. pa-li-di-*flaw*-ruh. Lat. with pale flowers. C Asia, NW China.
persica L. *per*-si-kuh. Lat. of Persia (Iran). SW Asia.
pontica Wahlenb. *pon*-ti-kuh. Lat. of Pontus (ancient reg. of NE Turkey). SE Eur., N Turkey.
pyrenaica L. pi-ruh-*nay*-i-kuh. Lat. of the Pyrenees. S France, N Spain.
uva-vulpis Rix. *ue*-vuh-*vul*-pis. Lat. fox grape, which the flowers resemble. SE Turkey, Iraq, NW Iran.
verticillata Willd. vur-ti-si-*lah*-tuh. Lat. whorled (the leaves). Siberia to Japan.

fritillary *Fritillaria*. **snake's head** *F. meleagris*

Fuchsia L. (Onagraceae). *few*-shuh, *fooks*-ee-uh. After German physician Leonhart Fuchs (1501–1566), who wrote on the med. use of herbs. 100 spp., shrubs, trees. Mex. to S Am., NZ, Tahiti.

arborescens Sims. ar-bor-*res*-uhnz. Lat. becoming tree-like. Mex.

×***bacillaris*** Lindl. bas-i-*lah*-ris. Lat. wand-like (the shoots). *F. microphylla* × *F. thymifolia*. Mex.

'Corallina'. ko-ruh-*leen*-uh. Lat. coral-red (the flowers).

glazioviana Taubert. gla-zee-ov-ee-*ah*-nuh. After French botanist and garden designer Auguste François Marie Glaziou (1828–1906), who collected the type specimen in 1888. Brazil.

hatschbachii P. E. Berry. hach-*bahk*-ee-ee. After Brazilian botanist Gert Guenther Hatschbach (b. 1923), manager of the Museu Botánico Municipal in Curitiba, who collected it in 1983. Brazil.

magellanica Lam. ma-juh-*lan*-i-kuh. Of the Magellan reg. Chile, Argentina. var. ***gracilis*** (Lindl.) Bailey. *gras*-i-lis. Lat. slender (the shoots). var. ***molinae*** Espinosa. mo-*leen*-ie. After Juan Ignacio Molina (1740–1829), Chilean priest and naturalist.

microphylla Kunth. mik-*rof*-i-luh. Gk. small-leaved. Mex., C Am.

paniculata Lindl. pan-ik-ew-*lah*-tuh. Lat. in panicles (the flowers). Mex., C Am.

procumbens R. Cunn. ex A. Cunn. proh-*kum*-buhnz. Lat. creeping. NZ (N.I.).

'Riccartonii'. rik-uh-*tohn*-ee-ee. After Riccarton, near Edinburgh, where it was raised.

splendens Zucc. *splen*-duhnz. Lat. splendid. S Mex., C Am.

Gaillardia Foug. (Asteraceae). gay-*lard*-ee-uh. Blanket flower. After Gaillard de Charrentonneau, 18th-cent. French patron of botany. 17 spp. herbs. Americas.

aristata Pursh. a-ris-*tah*-tuh. Lat. bristle-tipped (the pappus scales). W Canada, W USA.

×*grandiflora* Van Houtte. gran-di-*flaw*-ruh. Lat. large-flowered. *G. aristata* × *G. pulchella*. Cult.

pulchella Foug. pool-*kel*-uh. Lat. beautiful. USA, N Mex.

Galanthus L. (Amaryllidaceae). guh-*lanth*-oos. Snowdrops. From Gk. milk flower, referring to the white flowers. 19 spp. bulbous herbs. Eur. to N Iran.

'Atkinsii'. at-*kinz*-ee-ee. After English nurseryman James Atkins (1804–1884), who introduced it to cultivation.

elwesii Hook.f. el-*wez*-ee-ee. After English naturalist and plant collector Henry John Elwes (1846–1922), who introduced it to gardens in 1884 from near Smyrna (now Izmir), Turkey. SE Eur., W Asia. var. *monostictus* P. D. Sell. mon-oh-*stik*-toos. Gk. with one spot (on the petals). S Turkey.

ikariae Baker. i-*kah*-ree-ie. Lat. of Ikaria. Aegean Is.

nivalis L. ni-*vah*-lis. Common snowdrop. Lat. of the snow. Eur., Caucasus. 'Viridapice'. vi-rid-*ay*-pi-see. Lat. green at the tip (the petals).

plicatus M. Bieb. pli-*kah*-toos. Lat. folded (the leaves). E Eur., W Asia.

reginae-olgae Orph. re-*jee*-nie-*ol*-gie. After Queen Olga of Greece (1851–1926), grandmother of Prince Philip, Duke of Edinburgh. SE Eur.

woronowii Losinsk. vo-ro-*nov*-ee-ee. After Russian botanist Yuri Nikoláyevich Vóronov (1874–1931), who collected in the Caucasus. NE Turkey, Caucasus.

Galax Sims (Diapensiaceae). *ga*-lax. From Gk. milk, referring to the flower colour. 1 sp., herb. SE USA.

urceolata (Poir.) Brummitt. ur-kee-oh-*lah*-tuh. Beetleweed. Lat. like a small pitcher (the flowers).

Galega L. (Fabaceae). guh-*lee*-guh. From Gk. milk (*G. officinalis* has been used to increase milk production in goats and cattle). 6 spp. herbs. Eur., W Asia, N and E Africa.

×*hartlandii* Hartland. hart-*land*-ee-ee. After the Hartland nursery, Cork, Ireland, where it was raised. *G. officinalis* × *G. orientalis*. Cult.

officinalis L. o-fis-i-*nah*-lis. Goat's rue. Lat. sold as a med. herb. C and S Eur., N Africa, W Asia.

orientalis Lam. o-ree-en-*tah*-lis. Lat. eastern. Caucasus.

galingale *Cyperus longus*

Galium L. (Rubiaceae). *gal*-ee-oom. Bedstraws. From the Gk. name used by Dioscorides, who said that Gk. shepherds used *G. aparine* (cleavers) to strain milk, from Gk. milk. The flowers of *G. verum* were used to curdle milk. 400 spp. herbs. Widespread.
odoratum (L.) Scop. oh-do-*rah*-toom. Sweet woodruff. Lat. scented (the flowers and foliage). Eur., W and C Asia.
verum Scop. *veer*-oom. Lady's bedstraw. Lat. true. Eur., W Asia.

Galtonia candicans (Baker) Decne. = *Ornithogalum candicans*
viridiflora I. Verd. = *Ornithogalum viridiflorum*

gardener's garters *Phalaris arundinacea*

Gardenia J. Ellis (Rubiaceae). gar-*den*-ee-uh. After Alexander Garden (1730–1791), Scottish physician and naturalist who worked in South Carolina and sent specimens of other plants to the author, John Ellis. 140 spp., shrubs, trees. Old World tropics and subtropics.
augusta Merr. = *G. jasminoides*
jasminoides J. Ellis. jaz-min-*oy*-deez. Cape jasmine. Like jasmine (the flowers). SE Asia, S Japan.
thunbergia Thunb. thun-*berg*-ee-uh. From the genus *Thunbergia* (it was originally named *T. capensis*). S Africa.

garland flower *Daphne cneorum*
garlic *Allium sativum*. **keeled** *A. carinatum*. **Naples** *A. neapolitanum*. **round-headed** *A. sphaerocephalon*

Garrya Douglas ex Lindl. (Garryaceae). *ga*-ree-uh. After English-born Nicholas Garry (ca. 1782–1856), first secretary (later deputy governor) of the Hudson's Bay Co., who assisted David Douglas in his travels. 15 spp., shrubs, trees. W USA, Mex., C Am.
elliptica Douglas ex Lindl. ee-*lip*-ti-kuh. Lat. elliptic (the leaves). Calif., Oregon.
×*issaquahensis* Talbot de Malahide ex E. C. Nelson. is-uh-kwah-*en*-sis. Of Issaquah, Washington State, USA, where it was raised. *G. elliptica* × *G. fremontii*. Cult.

Gaultheria Kalm ex L. (Ericaceae). gawl-*theer*-ee-uh. After Jean François Gaultier (1708–1756), French-Canadian botanist and king's physician in Quebec, who acted as guide for Kalm when he visited Canada. 130 spp. shrubs. Americas, E Asia, Australia, NZ.
mucronata (L.f.) Hook. & Arn. mew-kron-*ah*-tuh. Lat. with a short point (the leaves). Chile, Argentina.
procumbens L. proh-*kum*-buhnz. Checkerberry, partridge berry, wintergreen. Lat. creeping. Canada, USA.
shallon Pursh. *sha*-lon. Salal. From the Native American name. SW Canada, W USA.
×*wisleyensis* Middleton. wiz-lee-*en*-sis. Of RHS Wisley, Surrey, England, where it was first raised. *G. mucronata* × *G. shallon*. Cult.

Gaura coccinea Pursh = *Oenothera suffrutescens*
lindheimeri Engelm. & A. Gray = *Oenothera lindheimeri*

gayfeather *Liatris*. **barrelhead** *L. cylindracea*. **dotted** *L. punctata*. **marsh** *L. spicata*. **northern** *L. scariosa*. **Northern Plains** *L. ligulistylis*. **prairie** *L. pycnostachya*. **rough** *L. aspera*. **smallhead** *L. microcephala*

Gazania Gaertn. (Asteraceae). guh-*zah*-nee-uh. After Theodorus Gaza (1398–1478), Gk. scholar who translated the works of Theophrastus from Greek into Latin. Alternatively Gk./Lat. (from Persian), royal treasure, riches. 16 spp. herbs. Trop. and S Africa.

rigens (L.) Gaertn. *ree*-guhnz. Lat. rigid (the leaves and spines). S Africa.

gean *Prunus avium*

Gelsemium Juss. (Gelsemiaceae). gel-*sem*-ee-oom. From the Italian word for jasmine. 3 spp. climbers. SE USA to C Am., China, SE Asia.

sempervirens (L.) J. St. Hil. sem-per-*vie*-ruhnz. Yellow jessamine. Lat. evergreen. SE USA, Mex., C Am.

Genista L. (Fabaceae). juh-*nis*-tuh. Broom. The Lat. name, possibly for Spanish broom (*Spartium junceum*). 90 spp., shrubs, trees. Eur., N Africa, W Asia.

aetnensis (Biv.) DC. et-*nen*-sis. Mount Etna broom. Lat. of Mount Etna (Lat. *Aetna*). Sicily, Sardinia.

hispanica L. his-*pan*-i-kuh. Spanish broom/gorse. Lat. of Spain (Lat. *Hispania*). SW Eur.

lydia Boiss. *lid*-ee-uh. Lat. of Lydia (ancient reg. of W Turkey). SE Eur., Turkey.

pilosa L. pi-*loh*-suh. Lat. with long hairs (the shoots and leaves). Eur.

tinctoria L. tink-*tor*-ree-uh. Dyers' greenweed. Lat. of dyers. Eur., W and C Asia.

gentian *Gentiana*. **bottle** *G. andrewsii*. **pale** *G. alba*. **spring** *G. verna*. **trumpet** *G. acaulis*. **willow** *G. asclepiadea*. **yellow** *G. lutea*

Gentiana L. (Gentianaceae). jent-shee-*ah*-nuh. Gentians. After Gentius, 2nd-cent. BCE king of Illyria (SE Eur.), who is said to have discovered their med. properties. 360 spp. herbs. Eur., Morocco, Asia, N and S Am., E Australia.

acaulis L. ay-*kaw*-lis. Trumpet gentian. Gk. stemless. C and S Eur.

alba Muhl. *al*-buh. Pale gentian. Lat. white (the flowers). E Canada, E and C USA.

andrewsii Griseb. an-*druez*-ee-ee. Bottle gentian. After English botanist and botanical artist Henry Charles Andrews (ca. 1770–1830), who illustrated it before it was named. Canada, E and C USA.

asclepiadea L. uh-sklee-pee-uh-*dee*-uh. Willow gentian. Like *Asclepias*. Eur., W Asia.

dahurica Fisch. dah-*hew*-ri-kuh. Of Dahuria. Siberia, China.

lutea L. *lue*-tee-uh. Yellow gentian. Lat. yellow (the flowers). Eur., Turkey.

septemfida Pall. sep-*tem*-fi-duh. Lat. divided into seven (the corolla). W Asia. var. *lagodechiana* Kusn. lag-oh-dek-ee-*ah*-nuh. Of Lagodekhi, Georgia.

sino-ornata Balf.f. *sie*-noh-or-*nah*-tuh.
The Chinese *G. ornata* (Himalayan
sp., from Lat. ornamental). W China.
tibetica King ex Hook.f. ti-*bet*-i-kuh.
Of Tibet. E Himal., Tibet.
verna L. *ver*-nuh. Spring gentian. Lat.
of spring (flowering). Eur., Morocco,
W Asia.

Geranium L. (Geraniaceae). juh-*ray*-
nee-oom. Cranesbills. Gk. name used
by Dioscorides, from Gk. crane, referring to the resemblance of the fruits
to a crane's head and beak. 260 spp.,
herbs, subshrubs. Widespread.
asphodeloides Burm.f. uhs-fod-uh-*loy*-
deez. Like *Asphodelus*. SE Eur., W
Asia.
×*cantabrigiense* Yeo. kant-uh-brig-ee-
en-see. Lat. of Cambridge, England
(whence it was described). *G. dalmaticum* × *G. macrorrhizum*. SE Eur.
cinereum Cav. sin-*e*-ree-oom. Lat. grey
(the leaves). France, Spain.
clarkei Yeo. *klark*-ee-ee. After English
botanist Charles Baron Clarke
(1832–1906), who collected the type
specimen. Kashmir.
dalmaticum (Beck) Rech.f. dal-*mat*-i-
koom. Of Dalmatia (now mostly in
Croatia). SE Eur.
endressii J. Gay. en-*dres*-ee-ee. After
German pharmacist Philipp Anton
Christoph Endress (1806–1831),
who collected the type specimen in
1831. Pyrenees.
himalayense Klotzsch. him-uh-lay-*en*-
see. Himalayan cranesbill. Of the
Himalaya. Afghanistan to Tibet.
macrorrhizum L. mak-roh-*rie*-zoom.
Gk. with a large root. S and C Eur.
maculatum L. mak-ew-*lah*-toom.
Spotted cranesbill. Lat. spotted (the

leaves, sometimes). SE Canada,
E USA.
×*magnificum* Hyl. mag-*ni*-fi-koom.
Lat. magnificent. *G. ibericum* × *G.
platypetalum*. Cult.
×*monacense* Harz. mon-uh-*ken*-see.
Of Munich (Lat. *Monachum*). *G.
phaeum* × *G. reflexum*. Cult.
orientalitibeticum R. Knuth. o-ree-
en-tah-lee-ti-*bet*-i-koom. Lat. of E
Tibet. W China.
×*oxonianum* Yeo. ox-oh-nee-*ah*-
noom. Lat. of Oxford (medieval Lat.
Oxonia), whence it was described.
G. endressii × *G. versicolor*. Cult.
palmatum Cav. pahl-*mah*-toom. Lat.
palmate (the leaves). Madeira.
phaeum L. *fee*-oom. Dusky cranesbill,
mourning widow. Gk. dark (the
flowers). Eur.
pratense L. pruh-*ten*-see. Meadow
cranesbill. Lat. of meadows. Eur.,
W and C Asia.
psilostemon Ledeb. see-*lo*-stem-on.
Armenian cranesbill. Gk. with glabrous stamens. W Asia.
renardii Trautv. re-*nard*-ee-ee. After
Karl Ivanovich (Charles Claude)
Renard (1809–1886), Russian physician and naturalist. Caucasus.
×*riversleanum* Yeo. riv-ers-lee-*ah*-
noom. Of the Riverslea nursery of
Maurice Prichard & Sons, Hampshire, England, where it was raised.
G. endressii × *G. traversii*. Cult.
sanguineum L. san-*gwin*-ee-oom.
Bloody cranesbill. Lat. blood-
coloured (the flowers). Eur., W Asia.
var. *lancastriense* (Mill.) Druce =
var. *striatum*. var. *striatum* Weston.
stree-*ah*-toom. Lat. marked with
lines (the petals). NW England.

sylvaticum L. sil-*vat*-i-koom. Wood cranesbill. Lat. of woods. Eur., W and C Asia.

wallichianum D. Don ex Sweet. wol-ik-ee-*ah*-noom. After Nathaniel Wallich (1786–1854), Danish botanist and surgeon with the East India Company, who collected plants in India and Nepal and sent seeds of this species from Nepal to England ca. 1820. Himal.

wlassovianum Fisch. ex Link. vla-sov-ee-*ah*-noom. After Vlassov, governor of Doroninsk, Russia, who collected the type specimen. E Russia, N China, Korea.

Gerbera L. (Asteraceae). *ger*-buh-ruh. After German physician and botanist Traugott Gerber (1710–1743). 35 spp. herbs. Africa, E Asia.

jamesonii Bolus ex Adlam. jaym-*son*-ee-ee. Barberton daisy. After Scottish-born businessman Robert Jameson (1832–1908), who collected specimens of it while exploring new goldfields. S Africa.

germander, shrubby *Teucrium fruticans*. **wall** *T. chamaedrys*. **wood** *T. scorodonia*

Geum L. (Rosaceae). *jee*-oom. Avens. The Lat. name, from Gk. taste, referring to the roots. 30 spp., herbs, subshrubs. Widespread.

chiloense hort. = *G. quellyon*

coccineum Sm. kok-*sin*-ee-oom. Lat. scarlet (the flowers). SE Eur., N Turkey.

macrophyllum Willd. mak-*rof*-i-loom. Gk. large-leaved. Japan, Canada, USA.

montanum L. mon-*tah*-noom. Alpine avens. Lat. of mountains. C and S Eur.

quellyon Sweet. *kel*-yon. From the Chilean name. Chile.

rivale L. ri-*vah*-lee. Water avens. Lat. of streams. Canada, USA, Eur., W and C Asia to Tibet.

triflorum Pursh. trie-*flaw*-room. Old man's whiskers. Lat. three-flowered (the inflorescence). Canada, USA.

urbanum L. ur-*bah*-noom. Herb Bennet. Lat. of towns. Eur., N Africa, W and C Asia.

gherkin *Cucumis sativus*

Gilia Ruiz & Pav. (Polemoniaceae). *gil*-ee-uh. After Italian naturalist Filippo Luigi Gilii (1756–1821), director of the Vatican Observatory, who wrote on South American cultivated plants. 40 spp. herbs. SW Canada to S Am.

aggregata (Pursh) Spreng. = *Ipomopsis aggregata*

capitata Sims. kap-i-*tah*-tuh. Blue thimble flower. Lat. in a head (the flowers). SW Canada, W USA, NW Mex. (B.C.).

rubra (L.) A. Heller = *Ipomopsis rubra*

tricolor Benth. *tri*-ko-lor. Bird's eyes. Lat. three-coloured (the flowers). Calif.

Gillenia Moench (Rosaceae). gil-*en*-ee-uh. After Arnold Gille (Lat. *Gillenius*), 17th-cent. German alchemist and physician. 2 spp. herbs. SE Canada, E USA.

trifoliata (L.) Moench. trie-foh-lee-*ah*-tuh. Indian physic. Lat. with three leaves (leaflets).

ginger, wild *Asarum canadense*
ginger lily *Alpinia, Hedychium.* **scarlet** *H. coccineum.* **yellow** *H. flavescens*

Ginkgo L. (Ginkgoaceae). *gink*-goh.
From the Chinese and Japanese
names, which mean silver apricot.
1 sp., tree. China.
biloba L. bie-*loh*-buh. Maidenhair
tree. Lat. two-lobed (the leaves).

Gladiolus L. (Iridaceae). glad-ee-*oh*-
loos. Lat. a small sword, referring to
the shape of the leaves. 270 spp.
cormous herbs. Eur., Africa, W and
C Asia.
byzantinus Mill. = *G. communis*
callianthus Marais = *G. murielae*
cardinalis Curtis. kar-di-*nah*-lis. Lat.
cardinal red (the flowers). S Africa.
carneus F. Delaroche. *kar*-nee-oos.
Lat. flesh-pink (the flowers). S Africa.
communis L. *kom*-ew-nis. Lat. common, or growing in colonies. Medit.
to Caucasus. var. ***byzantinus*** (Mill.)
O. Bolòs & Vigo = *G. communis*
dalenii Van Geel. duh-*len*-ee-ee. After
Cornelius Dalen (1766–1852),
Dutch botanist and director of the
Rotterdam Botanic Garden (it was
described from plants grown in the
Netherlands). SW Arabia to S
Africa.
flanaganii Baker. flan-uh-*gan*-ee-ee.
After South African citrus farmer
Henry George Flanagan (1861–
1919), who collected the type specimen in 1894. S Africa.
illyricus W. D. J. Koch. i-*li*-ri-koos.
Lat. of Illyria (ancient reg. of SE
Eur., now in Albania and Croatia).
Eur., Morocco, W Turkey.

italicus Mill. i-*tal*-i-koos. Lat. of Italy.
Medit., W and C Asia.
murielae Kelway. mew-ree-*el*-ie. After
Muriel Erskine, whose husband collected it in Ethiopia (it was described
from a plant he sent to the Kelway
Nursery). E Africa.
papilio Hook.f. puh-*pil*-ee-oh. Lat.
butterfly, moth (from the markings
inside the flower). S Africa.
tristis L. *tris*-tis. Lat. sad, gloomy (the
sombre flower colour). S Africa.

Glandularia J. Gmelin (Verbenaceae).
gland-ew-*lah*-ree-uh. From Lat.
gland, referring to the glandular
appearance of the stigma. 100 spp.
herbs. Americas.
bipinnatifida (Nutt.) Nutt. bie-pin-
at-i-*feed*-uh. Lat. twice pinnately cut
(the leaves). USA, Mex., Guatemala.
canadensis (L.) Nutt. kan-uh-*den*-sis.
Of Canada. USA.
gooddingii (Briq.) Solbrig. good-*ing*-
ee-ee. After American botanist Leslie
Newton Goodding (1880–1967),
who collected the type specimen in
Nevada in 1902. SW USA, NW
Mex.
×***hybrida*** (Groenl. & Rümpler) G. L.
Nesom & Pruski. *hib*-ri-duh. Garden
verbena. Lat. hybrid. Cult.
peruviana (L.) Small. puh-rue-vee-*ah*-
nuh. Of Peru. S Am.
pulchella (Sweet) Tronc. pool-*kel*-uh.
Lat. beautiful. S Am.

Glastonbury thorn *Crataegus
monogyna* 'Biflora'

Glaucidium Sieb. & Zucc. (Ranunculaceae). glaw-*kid*-ee-oom. From

Glaucium, referring to the similar foliage. 1 sp., herb. Japan.

palmatum Sieb. & Zucc. pahl-*mah*-toom. Lat. palmate (the leaves).

Glaucium Mill. (Papaveraceae). *glaw*-kee-oom. From Gk. blue-green, referring to the foliage. 23 spp. herbs. Eur., N Africa, W and C Asia.

flavum Crantz. *flah*-voom. Yellow horned poppy. Lat. yellow (the flowers). Eur., N Africa, W Asia.

Glebionis Cass. (Asteraceae). gleb-ee-*oh*-nis. Lat. characteristic of soil, referring to their occurrence on bare ground. 3 spp. herbs. S Eur., N Africa, W Asia.

carinata (Schousb.) Tzvelev. ka-ri-*nah*-tuh. Painted daisy. Lat. keeled (the bracts of the involucre). Morocco.

coronaria (L.) Cass. ex Spach. ko-ro-*nair*-ree-uh. Crown daisy. Lat. of garlands. Medit.

segetum (L.) Fourr. seg-*ee*-toom. Corn marigold. Lat. of cornfields. S Eur., N Africa, W Asia.

Gleditsia L. (Fabaceae). gle-*dits*-ee-uh. After Johann Gottlieb Gleditsch (1714–1786), German physician and botanist, director of the Berlin Botanical Garden. 16 spp., trees, shrubs. N and S Am., C and E Asia.

triacanthos L. trie-uh-*kanth*-os. Honey locust. Gk. three thorns, referring to the often three-branched spines. SE Canada, E and C USA.

globe amaranth *Gomphrena globosa*
globe flower *Trollius*
globe thistle *Echinops*

Globularia L. (Plantaginaceae). glob-ew-*lair*-ree-uh. Globe daisy. From Lat. a small globe (the flowerheads). 23 spp., herbs, subshrubs. Cape Verde Is., Canary Is., Eur., N Africa, SW Asia.

cordifolia L. kor-di-*foh*-lee-uh. Lat. with heart-shaped leaves. C and S Eur., Turkey.

meridionalis (Podp.) O. Schwarz. me-rid-ee-o-*nah*-lis. Lat. southern. SE Eur.

Gloriosa L. (Colchicaceae). glor-ree-*oh*-suh. Lat. glorious, from their striking flowers. 10 spp. climbing herbs. Trop. and S Africa, India, SE Asia.

modesta (Hook.) J. C. Manning & Vinn. mo-*des*-tuh. Lat. modest (its appearance) "in contrast with its very near ally the *Gloriosa superba*." Zimbabwe to S Africa.

superba L. sue-*per*-buh. Glory lily. Lat. superb. E and S Africa, S Asia.

'Rothschildiana'. roths-child-ee-*ah*-nuh. After English banker and zoologist Lionel Walter, 2nd Baron Rothschild (1868–1937); it was described from plants he grew at Tring Park.

glory flower *Clerodendrum bungei*

Gloxinia speciosa Lodd. = *Sinningia speciosa*

gloxinia *Sinningia speciosa*. **creeping** *Lophospermum erubescens*

Glyceria R. Br. (Poaceae). glie-*seer*-ree-uh. From Gk. sweet, referring to the sweet seeds of *G. fluitans*. 40 spp.

grasses. N temp. regs., S Am., Australia, NZ.

aquatica L. = *G. maxima*

canadensis (Michx.) Trin. kan-uh-*den*-sis. Rattlesnake grass. Lat. of Canada. Canada, E USA.

grandis S. Watson. *gran*-dis. American manna grass. Lat. large. Canada, USA.

maxima (Hartm.) Holmb. *max*-i-muh. Reed meadow grass. Lat. largest. Eur., W Asia.

Glycine Willd. (Fabaceae). glie-*seen*-ee. From Gk. sweet, referring to the edible tubers of *Apios americana*, which used to be included in the genus. 10 spp. herbs. E Asia.

max (L.) Merr. *max*. Soya bean. Lat. large (the pods and seeds). Cult.

Glycirrhiza L. (Fabaceae). glis-ee-*rie*-zuh. From Gk. sweet root. 20 spp. herbs. Eur., Asia, N and S Am., Australia.

glabra L. *glab*-ruh. Liquorice. Lat. glabrous (the leaves). Medit., SW Asia.

goat's beard *Aruncus dioicus*
goat's rue *Galega officinalis*
goatnut *Simmondsia chinensis*

Godetia Spach = *Clarkia*

golden club *Orontium aquaticum*
golden pothos *Epipremnum aureum*
golden ragwort *Packera aurea*
golden rain tree *Koelreuteria paniculata*, *Laburnum*
golden Spaniard *Aciphylla aurea*
golden trumpet *Allamanda cathartica*
goldeneye *Heliomeris*

goldenrod *Solidago*. prairie *S. ptarmicoides*
goldentop, common *Euthamia graminifolia*

Gomphrena L. (Amaranthaceae). gom-*free*-nuh. Gk. name for a species of *Amaranthus*. 100 spp. herbs. Widespread, warm temp. to trop. regs.

globosa L. glo-*boh*-suh. Globe amaranth. Lat. globose (the flowerheads). Tropics.

Goniolimon Boiss. (Plumbaginaceae). gon-ee-oh-*lee*-mon. From Gk. angled and *Limonium*, referring to the angled shoots. 20 spp. herbs. Eur., N Africa, W Asia to China.

tataricum (L.) Boiss. tuh-*ta*-ri-koom. Tatarian statice. From the reg. of C and E Asia once called Tartary. E Eur., N Africa, W Asia.

good King Henry *Chenopodium bonus-henricus*
gooseberry *Ribes uva-crispa*
goosefoot *Chenopodium album*
gorse *Ulex europaeus*. dwarf *U. gallii*. Spanish *Genista hispanica*
gourd, silver-seed *Cucurbita argyrosperma*. wax *Benincasa hispida*
goutweed *Aegopodium podagraria*
granadilla *Passiflora edulis*
grapefruit *Citrus* ×*aurantium*
grapevine *Vitis vinifera*
grass, African love *Eragrostis curvula*. alkali *Anticlea elegans*. American beach *Ammophila breviligulata*. American manna *Glyceria grandis*. autumn moor *Sesleria autumnalis*. Balkan moor *S. heufleriana*. bear *Xerophyllum tenax*. blue grama

Bouteloua gracilis. **blue moor** *Sesleria caerulea.* **blue oat** *Helictotrichon sempervirens.* **bottlebrush** *Elymus hystrix.* **buffalo** *Bouteloua dactyloides.* **Canary** *Phalaris canariensis.* **common quaking** *Briza media.* **creeping soft** *Holcus mollis.* **Elliott's love** *Eragrostis elliottii.* **false oat** *Arrhenatherum elatius.* **fountain** *Pennisetum setaceum.* **foxtail bristle** *Setaria italica.* **great quaking** *Briza maxima.* **holy** *Hierochloe odorata.* **Indian rice** *Achnatherum hymenoides.* **Kentucky blue** *Poa pratensis.* **love** *Eragrostis.* **Lyme** *Leymus arenarius.* **marram** *Ammophila arenaria.* **meadow** *Poa pratensis.* **millet** *Milium effusum.* **oat** *Arrhenatherum.* **pampas** *Cortaderia selloana.* **porcupine** *Hesperostipa spartea.* **poverty oat** *Danthonia spicata.* **prairie cord** *Spartina pectinata.* **purple fountain** *Pennisetum* ×*advena* 'Rubrum'. **purple love** *Eragrostis spectabilis.* **purple moor** *Molinia caerulea.* **quaking** *Briza.* **rattlesnake** *Glyceria canadensis.* **Ravenna** *Saccharum ravennae.* **reed canary** *Phalaris arundinacea.* **reed meadow** *Glyceria maxima.* **sideoats grama** *Bouteloua curtipendula.* **swamp meadow** *Poa palustris.* **sweet vernal** *Anthoxanthum odoratum.* **switch** *Panicum virgatum.* **tussock** *Deschampsia cespitosa.* **weeping love** *Eragrostis curvula.* **wood meadow** *Poa nemoralis.* **green and gold** *Chrysogonum virginianum*
green dragon *Arisaema dracontium*

Grevillea R. Br. ex Knight (Proteaceae). gruh-*vil*-ee-uh. After Charles Francis Greville (1749–1809),

English MP and collector of antiquities. 360 spp., shrubs, trees. Australia to Sulawesi.
alpina Lindl. al-*pie*-nuh. Lat. alpine. SE Australia.
juniperina R. Br. jue-ni-puh-*ree*-nuh. Lat. like *Juniperus* (the foliage). SE Australia (NSW). subsp. *sulphurea* (A. Cunn.) Makinson. sul-*few*-ree-uh. Lat. sulphur-yellow (the flowers).
lanigera A. Cunn. ex R. Br. luh-*ni*-juh-ruh. Lat. woolly (the foliage). SE Australia.
robusta A. Cunn. ex R. Br. roh-*bus*-tuh. Silky oak. Lat. robust. E Australia.
rosmarinifolia A. Cunn. roz-ma-ri-ni-*foh*-lee-uh. Lat. with leaves like *Rosmarinus*. SE Australia.
×*semperflorens* F. E. Briggs ex Mulligan. sem-per-*flaw*-ruhnz. Lat. always flowering. *G. juniperina* subsp. *sulphurea* × *G. thelmanniana*. Cult.
victoriae F. Muell. vik-*tor*-ree-ie. Royal grevillea. After Queen Victoria (1819–1901). SE Australia.

grevillea, royal *Grevillea victoriae*

Griselinia J. R. & G. Forst. (Griseliniaceae). griz-uh-*lin*-ee-uh. After Francesco Griselini (1717–1787), Italian botanist. 6 spp., trees, shrubs. NZ, S Am.
littoralis (Raoul) Raoul. li-to-*rah*-lis. Lat. of coasts. NZ.

ground elder *Aegopodium podagraria*
groundsel, tree *Baccharis halimifolia*
guava, pineapple *Acca sellowiana*
guavasteen *Acca sellowiana*
guelder rose *Viburnum opulus*

gum *Eucalyptus.* **alpine cider** *E. archeri.* **cider** *E. gunnii.* **lemon-scented** *Corymbia citriodora.* **mountain** *E. dalrympleana.* **snow** *E. pauciflora.* **spinning** *E. perriniana.* **Tasmanian blue** *E. globulus.* **Tasmanian snow** *E. coccifera.* **Tingiringi** *E. glaucescens*
gum cistus *Cistus ladanifer*

Gunnera L. (Gunneraceae). *gun*-uh-ruh. After Johan Ernst Gunner (1718–1773), Norwegian marine biologist and correspondent of Linnaeus. 50 spp. herbs. E and S Africa, S Am., Malaysia to Tasmania, NZ.
chilensis Lam. = *G. tinctoria*
hamiltonii Kirk. ham-il-*tohn*-ee-ee. After William Stewart Hamilton of Invercargill, who discovered it ca. 1884 and collected the type specimen. NZ (S.I.).
magellanica Lam. maj-uh-*lan*-i-kuh. Of the Magellan reg. S S Am., Falkland Is.
manicata Linden ex Delchev. man-i-*kah*-tuh. Lat. long-sleeved (the long leaf stalks). Brazil.
prorepens Hook.f. proh-*ree*-puhnz. Lat. creeping forward. NZ.
tinctoria (Molina) Mirb. tink-*tor*-ree-uh. Lat. of dyers (the roots give a black dye). Chile.

Gymnocarpium Newman (Woodsiaceae). jim-noh-*kar*-pee-oom. Gk. naked fruit (the sori are not covered). 8 spp. ferns. Temp. regs. of N Am., Eur., Asia.

dryopteris (L.) Newman. drie-*op*-te-ris. Oak fern. From Gk. oak fern.

Gymnocladus Lam. (Fabaceae). jim-noh-*klah*-doos. Gk. naked shoot (the type species is deciduous, producing its leaves late and losing them early). 4 spp. trees. USA, S Asia.
dioica (L.) K. Koch. die-*oy*-kuh. Kentucky coffee tree. Gk. dioecious. C USA.

Gynura Cass. (Asteraceae). gie-*new*-ruh. From Gk. female, tail, referring to the long style branches. 40 spp., herbs, subshrubs. Africa, Asia, Australia.
aurantiaca (Blume) DC. o-ran-tee-*ah*-kuh. Velvet plant. Lat. orange (the flowers). Indonesia.

Gypsophila L. (Caryophyllaceae). jip-*sof*-i-luh. From Gk. liking chalk or gypsum. 150 spp. herbs. Eur., Asia.
cerastioides D. Don. ke-ras-tee-*oy*-deez. Lat. like *Cerastium.* Himal.
elegans M. Bieb. *el*-i-ganz. Annual baby's breath. Lat. elegant. Ukraine, W Asia.
paniculata L. pan-ik-ew-*lah*-tuh. Baby's breath. Lat. in panicles (the flowers). C and E Eur., W and C Asia, W China.
repens L. *ree*-puhnz. Lat. creeping. C and S Eur.

gypsywort *Lycopus europaeus*

hackberry *Celtis*. **Chinese** *C. sinensis*. **common** *C. occidentalis*. **Mediterranean** *C. australis*. **netleaf** *C. reticulata*. **southern** *C. laevigata*

Hacquetia Necker ex DC. (Apiaceae). ha-*ket*-ee-uh. After Balthazar Hacquet (1739–1815), French-born Austrian physician, naturalist and geologist. 1 sp., herb. C Eur.
epipactis (Scop.) DC. e-pee-*pak*-tis. Gk. name for a plant used to curdle milk.

Hakonechloa Makino ex Honda (Poaceae). ha-kon-ee-*kloh*-uh. From Hakone (Japanese town) and Gk. grass. 1 sp., grass. Japan.
macra (Munro) Honda. *mak*-ruh. Lat. slender (it was originally named as a species of the much more robust *Phragmites*).

Halesia J. Ellis ex L. (Styracaceae). ha-*leez*-ee-uh, *hale*-zee-uh. After Stephen Hales (1677–1761), English clergyman, botanist and physiologist. 3 spp., shrubs, trees. E USA, China.
carolina L. ka-ro-*lee*-nuh. Silverbell, snowdrop tree. Lat. of the Carolinas. E USA. **Monticola Group**. mon-*ti*-

ko-luh. Lat. growing on mountains. **Vestita Group**. vest-*ee*-tuh. Lat. clothed (with hairs, the leaves).
diptera Ellis. *dip*-tuh-ruh. Two-wing silverbell. Gk. two-winged (the fruit). SE USA. **Magniflora Group**. mag-ni-*flaw*-ruh. Lat. large-flowered.
monticola (Rehder) Sarg. = *H. carolina* Monticola Group. var. **vestita** Sarg. = *H. carolina* Vestita Group
tetraptera Ellis = *H. carolina*

×**Halimiocistus** Janch. (Cistaceae). ha-lim-ee-oh-*sis*-toos. From the names of the parents (*Cistus* × *Halimium*). Shrubs. S France.
sahucii (Coste & Soulié) Janch. sa-*huek*-ee-ee. After French notary and archaeologist Joseph Sahuc (1863–1924), who collected plants with authors Hippolyte Jacques Coste and Joseph Auguste Soulié in the early 20th cent. *C. salviifolius* × *H. umbellatum*.
wintonensis O. & E. F. Warb. winton-*en*-sis. Of Winchester (old name Winton), where it was raised. Cult.

Halimium (Dunal) Spach (Cistaceae). ha-*lim*-ee-oom. From the resemblance of the leaves of some to *Atriplex halimus*. 9 spp. shrubs. Medit.
calycinum (L.) K. Koch. kal-i-*see*-noom. Lat. with a (conspicuous) calyx. Spain, Portugal, Morocco.
commutatum Pau = *H. calycinum*
formosum (Curtis) Willk. = *H. lasianthum*
lasianthum (Lam.) Spach. laz-ee-*anth*-oom. Gk. with woolly flowers (long hairs on the sepals). Spain, Portugal. subsp. *formosum* (Curtis) Heywood = *H. lasianthum*

ocymoides (Lam.) Willk. ok-i-*moy*-deez. Like *Ocimum*. Spain, Portugal, Morocco.
umbellatum (L.) Spach. um-buhl-*ah*-toom. Lat. in umbels (the flowers).

Halimodendron Fisch. ex DC. (Fabaceae). ha-lim-oh-*den*-dron. Gk. of the sea, tree (it grows in salty places). 1 sp., shrub. E Eur., W and C Asia.
halodendron (Pall.) Voss. ha-loh-*den*-dron. Salt tree. Gk. salt tree.

Hamamelis L. (Hamamelidaceae). ha-muh-*mel*-is. Witch hazels. Gk. name used by Hippocrates for *Mespilus germanica*. From Gk. apple, together (the fruits and flowers are borne at the same time). 5 spp., shrubs, trees. E Canada, E and C USA, NE Mex., China, Korea, Japan.
'Brevipetala'. brev-ee-*pet*-uh-luh. Lat. with short petals.
×*intermedia* Rehder. in-ter-*mee*-dee-uh. Lat. intermediate (between the parents). *H. japonica* × *H. mollis*. Cult.
japonica Sieb. & Zucc. juh-*pon*-i-kuh. Japanese witch hazel. Of Japan. Korea, Japan.
mollis Oliv. *mol*-is. Chinese witch hazel. Lat. soft (with hairs, the leaves). Korea, Japan.
vernalis Sarg. ver-*nah*-lis. Ozark witch hazel. Lat. of spring (flowering). C USA.
virginiana L. vir-jin-ee-*ah*-nuh. Lat. of Virginia. E Canada, E and C USA, NE Mex.

handkerchief tree *Davidia involucrata*

Hardenbergia Benth. (Fabaceae). har-duhn-*berg*-ee-uh. After Countess Franziska von Hardenberg (1794–1870). 3 spp. climbers. Australia.
violacea (Schneev.) Stearn. vie-o-*lay*-see-uh. Coral pea. Lat. violet (the flowers). SE Australia.

harebell *Campanula rotundifolia*
hare's ear *Bupleurum*. shrubby *B. fruticosum*
harlequin glorybower *Clerodendrum trichotomum*
Harry Lauder's walking stick *Corylus avellana* 'Contorta'

Hatiora Britton & Rose (Cactaceae). hat-ee-*or*-ruh. Anagram of *Hariota*, which it was originally called, a name that had already been used. After Thomas Harriot (Hariot) (1560–1621), English mathematician and astronomer. 5 spp. cacti. Brazil.
gaertneri (Regel) Barthlott. *gairt*-nuh-ree. Easter cactus. After Joseph Gaertner (1732–1791), German botanist.

haw, black *Viburnum prunifolium*. blue *V. cassinoides*
hawthorn *Crataegus*. Chinese *C. pinnatifida*. common *C. monogyna*. downy *C. mollis*. green *C. viridis*. Indian *Rhaphiolepis indica*. Midland *C. laevigata*. oriental *C. orientalis*. scarlet *C. coccinea*
hazel, American *Corylus americana*. beaked *C. cornuta*. California *C. cornuta* subsp. *californica*. common *C. avellana*. corkscrew *C. avellana* 'Contorta'. Turkish *C. colurna*
hearts on a string *Ceropegia linearis* subsp. *woodii*

heartsease *Viola tricolor*
heath *Erica*. **Cornish** *E. vagans*.
  cross-leaved *E. tetralix*. **Irish** *E. erigena*. **Spanish** *E. australis*. **St. Dabeoc's** *Daboecia cantabrica*. **tree** *Erica arborea*. **winter** *E. carnea*
heather *Calluna vulgaris*. **bell** *Erica cinerea*

Hebe albicans (Petrie) Cockayne = *Veronica albicans*
brachysiphon Summerh. = *Veronica brachysiphon*
buchananii (Hook.f.) Cockayne & Allan = *Veronica buchananii*
cupressoides (Hook.f.) Cockayne & Allan = *Veronica cupressoides*
×*franciscana* (Eastw.) Souster = *Veronica* ×*franciscana*
hulkeana (F. Muell.) Cockayne & Allan = *Veronica hulkeana*
macrantha (Hook.f.) Cockayne & Allan = *Veronica macrantha*
ochracea Ashwin = *Veronica ochracea*
odora (Hook.f.) Cockayne = *Veronica odora*
pimeleoides (Hook.f.) Cockayne & Allan = *Veronica pimeleoides*
pinguifolia (Hook.f.) Cockayne & Allan = *Veronica pinguifolia*
rakaiensis (J. B. Armstr.) Cockayne = *Veronica rakaiensis*
recurva G. Simpson & J. S. Thomson = *Veronica albicans* Recurva Group
salicifolia (G. Forst.) Penell = *Veronica salicifolia*
topiaria L. B. Moore = *Veronica topiaria*
vernicosa (Hook.f.) Cockayne & Allan = *Veronica vernicosa*
'Youngii' = *Veronica* 'Youngii'

Hedera L. (Araliaceae). *hed*-uh-ruh. Ivy. Lat. name for *H. helix*. 12 spp. climbers. Eur., N Africa, W Asia to Japan.
algeriensis Hibberd. al-jeer-ree-*en*-sis. Of Algeria. N Africa.
colchica K. Koch. *kol*-chi-kuh. Persian ivy. Lat. of Colchis on the Black Sea (now part of Georgia). Caucasus.
'Dentata Variegata'. den-*tah*-tuh va-ree-uh-*gah*-tuh. Lat. toothed, variegated (the leaves).
helix L. *hee*-lix. Common ivy. Gk. to turn. Eur., W Asia.
hibernica Bean. hie-*bern*-i-kuh. Irish ivy. Lat. of Ireland. W Eur.

Hedychium J. König (Zingiberaceae). he-*dik*-ee-oom. Ginger lily. From Gk. sweet snow, referring to the fragrant white flowers of the type species, *H. coronarium*. 88 spp. perenn, herbs. Himal., trop. Asia, Madagascar.
aurantiacum Roscoe = *H. coccineum* Aurantiacum Group
coccineum Buch.-Ham. ex Sm. kok-*sin*-ee-oom. Scarlet ginger lily. Himal., S China. **Aurantiacum Group**. o-ran-tee-*ah*-koom. Lat. orange (the flowers).
coronarium J. König. ko-ro-*nair*-ree-oom. Butterfly lily. Lat. of garlands (it has been used as a hair decoration in parts of Malaysia). E Himal., India, SE Asia.
densiflorum Wall. den-si-*flaw*-room. Lat. densely flowered (the inflorescence). Himal., Tibet.
flavescens Carey ex Roscoe. fluh-*ves*-uhnz. Yellow ginger lily. Lat. yellowish (the flowers). E Himal., SW China.

gardnerianum Sheppard ex Ker Gawl. gard-nuh-ree-*ah*-noom. After Edward Gardner (1784–1861), British political resident in Nepal. Himal., SE Asia.

greenii W. W. Sm. *green*-ee-ee. After Mr H. F. Green; it was described from plants that he collected in Bhutan and grew in his Darjeeling garden in the early 1900s. E Himal., Assam.

Hedysarum L. (Fabaceae). he-*dis*-uh-room. Gk. name for another plant, possibly fenugreek, from Gk. sweet. 160 spp., herbs, subshrubs. N temp. regs.

coronarium L. ko-ro-*nair*-ree-oom. French honeysuckle. Lat. of garlands. Spain, Italy, N Africa.

Helenium L. (Asteraceae). hel-*en*-ee-oom. Sneezeweed. Gk. name for elecampane (*Inula helenium*), after Helen of Troy of Gk. myth. 32 spp. herbs. Americas.

autumnale L. aw-toom-*nah*-lee. Common sneezeweed. Lat. of autumn (flowering). Canada, USA.

hoopesii A. Gray = *Hymenoxys hoopesii*

Helianthemum Mill. (Cistaceae). hel-ee-*anth*-uh-moom. Rock rose. Gk. sun, flower, from their love of sunny places. 100 spp. subshrubs. Eur., N Africa, W and C Asia, N and C Am.

nummularium (L.) Mill. num-ew-*lair*-ree-oom. Lat. coin-like (the leaves). Eur., W Asia.

Helianthus L. (Asteraceae). hel-ee-*anth*-oos. Sunflowers. From Gk. sun flower. 51 spp. herbs. N Am.

angustifolius L. an-gus-ti-*foh*-lee-oos. Swamp sunflower. Lat. narrow-leaved. E and C USA.

annuus L. *an*-ew-oos. Common sunflower. Lat. annual. Canada, USA, N Mex.

decapetalus L. dek-uh-*pet*-uh-loos. Thinleaf sunflower. Lat. with ten petals (ray florets). SE Canada, E and C USA.

divaricatus L. di-va-ri-*kah*-toos. Lat. wide-spreading (the branches). SE Canada, E and C USA.

giganteus L. jie-*gan*-tee-oos. Giant sunflower. Lat. very large. E N Am.

grosseserratus M. Martens. groh-suh-suh-*rah*-toos. Lat. with coarse teeth (the leaves). E and C USA.

×*laetiflorus* Pers. lie-ti-*flaw*-roos. Cheerful sunflower. Lat. with bright flowers. *H. pauciflorus* × *H. tuberosus*. E Canada, E and C USA.

maximilianii Schrad. max-i-mil-ee-*ah*-nee-ee. After Prince Alexander Philipp Maximilian of Wied-Neuwied (1782–1867), German explorer and naturalist who discovered it while studying the people and wildlife of the Great Plains area. S Canada to N Mex.

microcephalus Torr. & A. Gray. mik-roh-*kef*-uh-loos. Gk. with a small (flower) head. E USA.

mollis Lam. *mol*-is. Ashy sunflower. Lat. soft (with hairs, the leaves). E USA.

×*multiflorus* L. mul-ti-*flaw*-roos. Lat. many-flowered. *H. annuus* × *H. decapetalus*. Cult.

occidentalis Riddell. ok-si-den-*tah*-lis. Western sunflower. Lat. western. E and C USA.

salicifolius A. Dietr. sal-i-si-*foh*-lee-oos. Willow-leaved sunflower. Lat. willow-leaved. C USA.

strumosus L. stroom-*oh*-soos. Rough sunflower. Lat. with swellings (the swollen bases of the leaf hairs). SE Canada, E and C USA.

tuberosus L. tew-buh-*roh*-soos. Jerusalem artichoke. Lat. bearing tubers. Canada, USA.

Helichrysum Mill. (Asteraceae). hel-i-*krie*-soom. Gk. sun, golden, referring to the flowers. 600 spp., herbs, shrubs. Eur., Africa, Asia.

angustifolium (Lam.) DC. = *H. italicum*

bracteatum (Vent.) Andrews = *Xerochrysum bracteatum*

italicum (Roth) G. Don. i-*tal*-i-koom. Lat. of Italy. S Eur., N Africa. subsp. *microphyllum* (Willd.) Nyman = *H. microphyllum* (Willd.) Cambess. subsp. *serotinum* (Boiss.) P. Fourn. se-*rot*-i-noom. Curry plant. Lat. late (flowering). SW Eur., N Africa.

microphyllum hort. = *Plecostachys serpyllifolia*

microphyllum (Willd.) Cambess. mik-*rof*-i-loom. Gk. small-leaved. Balearic Is.

petiolare Hilliard & B. L. Burtt. pee-tee-oh-*lah*-ree. Liquorice plant. Lat. with a (conspicuous) petiole. S Africa.

splendidum (Thunb.) Less. *splen*-di-doom. Lat. splendid. S Africa.

Helictotrichon Besser (Poaceae). he-lik-toh-*trie*-kon. Gk. to turn, hair, referring to the twisted awns. 100 spp. grasses. Widespread.

sempervirens (Vill.) Pilg. sem-per-*vie*-ruhnz. Blue oat grass. Lat. evergreen. France, Italy.

Heliomeris Nutt. (Asteraceae). hel-ee-oh-*me*-ris. Goldeneye. Gk. sun, part, referring to the yellow flowers. 5 spp. ann. and perenn. herbs. SW USA, Mex.

multiflora Nutt. mul-ti-*flaw*-ruh. Lat. many-flowered.

Heliopsis Pers. (Asteraceae). hel-ee-*op*-sis. Gk. sun-like (the flowers). 18 spp. herbs. Canada to Bolivia.

helianthoides (L.) Sweet. hel-ee-anth-*oy*-deez. False sunflower. Like *Helianthus*. E Canada, E and C USA. var. *scabra* (Dunal) Fernald. *skay*-bruh. Lat. rough (the leaves).

heliotrope *Heliotropium arborescens*

Heliotropium L. (Boraginaceae). hel-ee-oh-*troh*-pee-oom. From Gk. sun, turn (the flowers and leaves turn toward the sun). 250 spp., herbs, shrubs. Widespread.

arborescens L. ar-bor-*res*-uhnz. Cherry pie, heliotrope. Lat. becoming tree-like. Peru.

hellebore *Helleborus*. **false** *Veratrum*. **green** *Helleborus viridis*. **stinking** *H. foetidus*

helleborine *Epipactis*. **giant** *E. gigantea*. **marsh** *E. palustris*

Helleborus L. (Ranunculaceae). he-*leb*-o-roos, hel-ee-*bor*-roos. Hellebores. Gk. name for a poisonous med. plant, perhaps *Veratrum*. 20 spp.

herbs. Eur., N Africa, W Asia, China.

argutifolius Viv. ar-gew-ti-*foh*-lee-oos. Lat. with sharply toothed leaves. Corsica, Sardinia.

×***ericsmithii*** B. Mathew. e-rik-*smith*-ee-ee. After English nurseryman and plant breeder Eric Smith (1917– 1986), who raised it. *H. niger* × *H.* ×*sternii*. Cult.

foetidus L. *fee*-tid-oos. Stinking hellebore. Lat. fetid. Eur., N Africa.

×***hybridus*** hort. ex Vilmorin. *hib*-ri-doos. Lat. hybrid. *H. orientalis* × *H.* sp. Cult.

lividus Aiton. *li*-vi-doos. Lat. lead-coloured (the leaves). Mallorca. subsp. ***corsicus*** (Willd.) Tutin = *H. argutifolius*

niger L. *nie*-ger. Christmas rose. Lat. black (the roots). C and SE Eur.

×***nigercors*** J. T. Wall. *nie*-ger-corz. From the names of the parents (*H. corsicus* is a synonym of *H. argutifolius*). *H. argutifolius* × *H. niger*. Cult.

orientalis Lam. o-ree-en-*tah*-lis. Lenten rose. Lat. eastern. N Greece, N Turkey, Caucasus.

purpurascens Waldst. & Kit. pur-pew-*ras*-uhns. Lat. purplish (the flowers). E Eur.

×***sternii*** Turrill. *stern*-ee-ee. After Sir Frederick Claude Stern (1884– 1967), English botanist and horticulturist in whose garden at Highdown it originated. *H. argutifolius* × *H. lividus*. Cult.

thibetanus Franch. ti-bet-*ah*-noos. Of Tibet. China.

torquatus Archer-Hind. tor-*kwah*-toos. Lat. adorned with a necklace (referring to the pale ring in the centre of the flower). Albania, Serbia.

viridis L. *vi*-ri-dis. Green hellebore. Lat. green (the flowers). C and W Eur.

Hemerocallis L. (Xanthorrhoeaceae). hem-uh-*rok*-uh-lis, hem-uh-roh-*kal*-is. Day lilies. From Gk. day, beauty (the attractive flowers last one day each). 18 spp. herbs. Eur. to Japan.

citrina Baroni. sit-*ree*-nuh. Lat. lemon-yellow (the flowers). China, Korea, Japan.

fulva (L.) L. *fool*-vuh. Lat. tawny, reddish yellow (the flowers). China, Taiwan, Korea, Japan.

lilioasphodelus L. lil-ee-oh-as-*fod*-uh-loos. Like *Lilium* and *Asphodelus* (the flowers). C Eur. to Korea.

middendorffii Trautv. & C. A. Mey. mid-uhn-*dorf*-ee-ee. After Alexander Theodor von Middendorff (1815– 1894), Russian naturalist and explorer who discovered it. E Russia, N China, Korea, Japan.

hemlock *Tsuga*. **eastern** *T. canadensis*. **mountain** *T. mertensiana*. **western** *T. heterophylla*

hemp agrimony *Eupatorium cannabinum*

Hepatica acutiloba DC. = *Anemone acutiloba*

americana (DC.) Ker Gawl. = *Anemone americana*

×***media*** Simonk. = *Anemone* ×*media*

nobilis Mill. = *Anemone hepatica*

transsilvanica Fuss = *Anemone transsilvanica*

Heptacodium Rehder (Caprifoliaceae). hep-tuh-*koh*-dee-oom. From Gk. seven, head (the flowers are borne in heads of seven). 1 sp., shrub, tree. China.

jasminoides Airy Shaw = *H. miconioides*

miconioides Rehder. mie-koh-nee-*oy*-deez. Seven son flower. Like *Miconia*; when E. H. Wilson collected the type specimen in 1907, he observed that "it resembles particularly *Miconia*."

Heracleum L. (Apiaceae). he-*rak*-lee-oom. After Hercules (Heracles of Gk. myth.), who is said to have used it medicinally. 65 spp. herbs. Eur., N Am., Asia, E Africa.

maximum Bartram. *max*-i-moom. American cow parsnip. Lat. largest. Canada, USA.

herb Bennet *Geum urbanum*
herb Paris *Paris quadrifolia*
Hercules' club *Aralia spinosa*

Hermodactylus tuberosus (L.) Mill. = *Iris tuberosa*

Hesperaloe Engelm. (Asparagaceae). hes-puh-*ra*-loh-ee. From Gk. western, *Aloe*. 7 spp. evergreen herbs. Texas, N Mex.

parviflora (Torr.) J. M. Coult. par-vi-*flaw*-ruh. Lat. small-flowered.

Hesperantha Ker Gawl. (Iridaceae). hes-puh-*ranth*-uh. Gk. evening flower. 84 spp. perenn. herbs. Africa.

coccinea (Backh. & Harv.) Goldblatt & J. C. Manning. kok-*sin*-ee-uh. Kaffir lily. Lat. scarlet (the flowers). S Africa.

Hesperis L. (Brassicaceae). *hes*-pe-ris. From Gk. evening (when the flowers are fragrant). 25 spp. herbs. Eur., W and C Asia, China.

matronalis L. mat-ron-*ah*-lis. Dame's violet. Lat. of matrons (referring to the Roman festival of matrons on March 1). Eur., W and C Asia.

Hesperostipa (M. K. Elias) Barkworth (Poaceae). hes-pe-roh-*steep*-uh. Gk. west, the related *Stipa* (from their distribution). 5 spp. grasses. N Am.

spartea (Trin.) Barkworth. *spart*-ee-uh. Porcupine grass. From Gk. cord.

Hesperoyucca (Engelm.) Trel. (Asparagaceae). hes-pe-roh-*yook*-uh. Gk. evening (signifying western, where the sun sets), *Yucca*. 3 spp. evergreen perenn. herbs. SW USA., N Mex.

whipplei (Torr.) Trel. *wi*-puh-lee. Our Lord's candle. After American army surveyor Amiel Weeks Whipple (1818–1863), who took part in the USA–Mexico boundary survey in S California in 1849, on which it was discovered. SW Calif., NW Mex. (B.C.).

Heuchera L. (Saxifragaceae). *hew*-kuh-ruh. Alum root. After Johann Heinrich von Heucher (1677–1746), Vienna-born physician. 37 spp. herbs. Canada, USA, N Mex.

americana L. uh-me-ri-*kah*-nuh. American alum root. Of America. SE Canada, E USA.

cylindrica Douglas. si-*lin*-dri-kuh. Poker alum root. Lat. cylindrical (the inflorescence). SW Canada, W USA.

micrantha Douglas ex Lind. mik-*ranth*-uh. Crevice alum root. Gk.

small-flowered. SW Canada, W
USA.
pulchella Wooton & Standl. pool-*kel*-
uh. Lat. beautiful. New Mexico.
richardsonii R. Br. rich-uhd-*sohn*-ee-
ee. After Scottish surgeon and
explorer Sir John Richardson (1787–
1865), who collected the type specimen in British Columbia in 1826.
Canada, USA.
sanguinea Engelm. san-*gwin*-ee-uh.
Coralbells. Lat. bloody (the flower
colour). SW USA, N Mex.
villosa Michx. vil-*oh*-suh. Hairy alum
root. Lat. with long hairs (on the
stems and leaves). E and C USA.

×***Heucherella*** Wehrh. (Saxifragaceae).
hew-kuh-*rel*-uh. From the names of
the parents (*Heuchera* × *Tiarella*).
Herbs. Cult.
alba (Lemoine) Stearn. *al*-buh. Lat.
white (the flowers). *H.* ×*brizoides* ×
T. wherryi.
tiarelloides (Lemoine) Wehrh. ex
Stearn. tee-uh-rel-*oy*-deez. Lat. like
Tiarella. H. ×*brizoides* × *T. cordifolia.*

Hexastylis arifolia (Michx.) Small =
Asarum arifolium
naniflora H. L. Blomq.= *Asarum
naniflorum*

Hibanobambusa Maruy. & H.
Okamura (Poaceae). hi-bah-noh-
bam-*bew*-suh. From Mount Hiba
(where it was found), *Bambusa.* 1 sp.,
bamboo. Japan.
tranquillans (Koidz.) Maruy. & H.
Okamura. *trank*-wil-anz. Lat. calm.

Hibiscus L. (Malvaceae). hi-*bis*-koos.
From a Gk. name used by Dioscorides

for a mallow. 200 spp., herbs, shrubs,
trees. Widespread in warm regs.
acetosella Welw. ex Hiern. uh-seet-oh-
sel-uh. African rosemallow. Lat. a little acid (the taste of the leaves). Trop.
Africa, Mauritius.
coccineus Walter. kok-*sin*-ee-oos.
Scarlet rosemallow. Lat. scarlet (the
flowers). SE USA.
huegelii Endl. = *Alyogyne huegelii*
laevis All. *lee*-vis. Halberdleaf rosemallow. Lat. smooth (the leaves). E
and C USA.
lasiocarpos Cav. = *H. moscheutos*
subsp. *lasiocarpos*
militaris Cav. = *H. laevis*
moscheutos L. mos-*kew*-tos.
Crimson-eyed rosemallow. Lat.
musk-scented (the flowers). E and C
USA. subsp. *lasiocarpos* (Cav.) O. J.
Blanchard. laz-ee-oh-*kar*-pos.
Woolly rosemallow. Gk. hairy fruit.
C and SW USA, N Mex.
mutabilis L. mew-*tab*-i-lis. Lat. changing (the flower colour). China, Taiwan, Japan.
palustris L. = *H. moscheutos*
rosa-sinensis L. *roh*-zuh-sin-*en*-sis.
Lat. rose of China. China.
sinosyriacus L. H. Bailey. sie-noh-si-
ree-*ah*-koos. The Chinese *H. syriacus.*
China.
syriacus L. si-ree-*ah*-koos. Rose of
Sharon. Lat. of Syria, where it was
thought to originate. China, Taiwan.
trionum L. trie-*oh*-noom. Flower of an
hour. Gk. name used by
Theophrastus for a related plant. E
Eur., Africa, W and C Asia.

hickory *Carya.* **big shellbark** *C.*
laciniosa. **shagbark** *C. ovata.* **shellbark** *C. ovata*

hierba mansa *Anemopsis californica*

Hierochloe R. Br. (Poaceae). hie-roh-*kloh*-ee. From Gk. sacred grass (*H. odorata* has been used in religious ceremonies). 33 spp. grasses. N temp. regs., trop. mts.
odorata (L.) P. Beauv. oh-do-*rah*-tuh. Holy grass. Lat. fragrant (the foliage). Canada, USA, Eur., temp. Asia.

Himalayacalamus Keng f. (Poaceae). him-uh-lay-uh-*kal*-uh-moos. From Himalaya, and Gk. reed. 8 spp. bamboos. Himal., Tibet, China.
falconeri (Munro) Keng f. fal-*koh*-nuh-ree. Candy stripe bamboo. After Scottish naturalist and surgeon Hugh Falconer (1808–1865), who worked in India. Himal., Tibet.
hookerianus (Munro) Stapleton. hook-uh-ree-*ah*-noos. Himalayan blue bamboo. After English botanist Joseph Dalton Hooker (1817–1911), son of William Joseph and director of RBG Kew, who collected the type specimen in Sikkim in 1848. Himal.

Hippeastrum Herb. (Amaryllidaceae). hip-ee-*as*-troom. From Gk. knight's star, from a supposed resemblance between the flowers and the star worn by knights. 55 spp. bulbous herbs. Mex. to S Am.

Hippocrepis L. (Fabaceae). hip-oh-*krep*-is. From Gk. horse shoe, referring to the shape of the seed pods. 34 spp., herbs, shrubs. Eur., N Africa, W Asia.
comosa L. ko-*moh*-suh. Horseshoe vetch. Lat. bearing tufts (the clustered flowers). Eur.

emerus (L.) Lassen. *em*-uh-roos. Scorpion senna. From an Italian name for vetch.

Hippophae L. (Elaeagnaceae). *hi*-po-fee, hi-*po*-fa-ee. The Gk. name, from Gk. horse, shining (it was fed to horses to improve their health and appearance). 5 spp., shrubs, trees. Eur., Asia.
rhamnoides L. ram-*noy*-deez. Sea buckthorn. Lat. like *Rhamnus*.

Hippuris L. (Plantaginaceae). hip-*ew*-ris. From Gk. horse tail. 1 sp., aquatic herb. Widespread.
vulgaris L. vul-*gar*-ris. Mare's tail. Lat. common.

hobblebush, Florida *Agarista populifolia*

Hoheria A. Cunn. (Malvaceae). hoh-*heer*-ree-uh. From the Maori name of *H. populnea*. 6 spp. trees. NZ.
glabrata Sprague & Summerh. glab-*rah*-tuh. Lat. becoming smooth (the leaves).
lyallii Hook.f. lie-*al*-ee-ee. After Scottish surgeon and naturalist David Lyall (1817–1895), who collected the type specimen.
populnea A. Cunn. po-*pool*-nee-uh. Lat. like *Populus* (the leaves).
sexstylosa Colenso. sex-stie-*loh*-suh. Lat. with six styles (the flowers).

Holboellia Wall. (Lardizabalaceae). hol-*bel*-ee-uh. After Danish botanist Frederik Ludvig Holbøll (1765–1829), superintendent of Copenhagen Botanical Garden. 20 spp. woody climbers. Himal., China, SE Asia.

coriacea Diels. ko-ree-*ay*-see-uh. Lat.
leathery (the leaves). C China.
latifolia Wall. lat-i-*foh*-lee-uh. Lat.
with broad leaves (leaflets). Himal.,
China.

Holcus L. (Poaceae). *hol*-koos. Gk./
Lat. name for a grain-producing
grass. 8 spp. grasses. Eur., N Africa,
W Asia.
mollis L. *mol*-is. Creeping soft grass.
Lat. soft (the foliage). Eur., W Asia.

holly *Ilex*. **American** *I. opaca*. **blue** *I.*
×*meserveae*. **Chilean** *Desfontainia
spinosa*. **common** *Ilex aquifolium*.
Highclere *I.* ×*altaclerensis*. **horned**
I. cornuta. **Japanese** *I. crenata*
hollyhock *Alcea rosea*

Holodiscus (K. Koch) Maxim. (Rosaceae). ho-loh-*disk*-oos. Gk. entire
disk, referring to the unlobed disk of
the flower. 6 spp. shrubs. SW Canada
to Colombia.
discolor (Pursh) Maxim. *dis*-ko-lor.
Ocean spray. Lat. two-coloured (the
upper and lower leaf surfaces). SW
Canada, W USA.

honesty *Lunaria annua*. **perennial** *L.
rediviva*
honeyflower *Melianthus major*
honeysuckle *Aquilegia canadensis,
Lonicera*. **Amur** *L. maackii*. **Cape**
Tecoma capensis. **common** *Lonicera
periclymenum*. **fly** *L. xylosteum*.
French *Hedysarum coronarium*.
Himalayan *Leycesteria formosa*.
Italian *Lonicera caprifolium*. **Japanese** *L. japonica*. **scarlet trumpet** *L.*
×*brownii*. **swamp** *Rhododendron*

viscosum. **Tatarian** *Lonicera tatarica*.
trumpet *L. sempervirens*
hop *Humulus lupulus*
hop bush *Dodonaea viscosa*
hop hornbeam *Ostrya carpinifolia*.
American *O. virginiana*
hop tree *Ptelea trifoliata*

Hordeum L. (Poaceae). *hor*-dee-oom.
Lat. name used by Pliny for barley.
32 spp. grasses. Eur., Africa, Asia,
Americas.
jubatum L. jue-*bah*-toom. Foxtail
barley. Lat. crested (the inflorescence). E Asia, Canada to N Mex.
vulgare L. vul-*gar*-ree. Barley. Lat.
common. SE Eur., N Africa, Asia.

Horminum L. (Lamiaceae). *hor*-min-
oom. Gk. name of a sage, possibly
Salvia horminum, from Gk. to excite
(it was believed to be an aphrodisiac).
1 sp., herb. S Eur.
pyrenaicum L. pi-ruh-*nay*-i-koom.
Pyrenean dead-nettle. Lat. of the
Pyrenees.

hornbeam *Carpinus*. **American** *C.
caroliniana*. **European** *C. betulus*.
Japanese *C. japonica*
hornwort *Ceratophyllum*
horse chestnut *Aesculus, A. hippocastanum*. **Indian** *A. indica*. **red** *A.*
×*carnea*
horsefly weed *Baptisia tinctoria*
horsemint *Monarda*
horseradish *Armoracia rusticana*
horsetail *Equisetum*

Hosta Tratt. (Asparagaceae). *hos*-tuh.
Plantain lily. After Nicolaus Thomas
Host (1771–1834), Austrian bota-

nist and physician. 45 spp. herbs.
China, Korea, E Russia, Japan.
clausa Nakai. *klaw*-suh. Lat. closed
(the flowers). Korea.
'Elegans'. *el*-i-ganz. Lat. elegant.
fortunei (Baker) L. H. Bailey.
for-*tewn*-ee-ee. After Robert Fortune
(1812–1880), Scottish botanist and
plant collector. Cult. 'Albopicta'.
al-boh-*pik*-tuh. Lat. painted white
(the foliage appears).
lancifolia Engl. lahn-si-*foh*-lee-uh.
Lat. with lance-shaped leaves. Cult.
plantaginea (Lam.) Asch. plan-tuh-
jin-ee-uh. Like *Plantago*. China.
sieboldiana (Hook.) Engl. see-bold-
ee-*ah*-nuh. After German physician
and botanist Philip Franz von
Siebold (1796–1866), who studied
the flora and fauna of Japan. Cult.
var. *elegans* Hyl. = *H.* 'Elegans'
'Undulata'. un-dew-*lah*-tuh. Lat.
undulate (the leaves).
'Undulata Univittata'. un-dew-*lah*-
tuh ew-nee-vi-*tah*-tuh. Lat. undulate
with one stripe (the leaves).
ventricosa Stearn. ven-tri-*koh*-suh.
Lat. with a swelling on one side (the
corolla). China.
venusta F. Maek. ven-*oos*-tuh. Lat.
handsome. Korea, Japan.
yingeri S. B. Jones. *ying*-uh-ree. After
American horticulturist Barry
Yinger, who, with others, collected
the type specimen and introduced it
in 1985. S Korea.

hot water plant *Achimenes*
Hottentot fig *Carpobrotus edulis*

Hottonia L. (Primulaceae). hot-*oh*-
nee-uh. After Petrus Hotton (1648–

1709), Dutch physician and botanist.
2 spp. aquatic herbs. USA, Eur.
palustris L. puh-*lus*-tris. Water violet.
Lat. of marshes. Eur.

hound's tongue *Cynoglossum*.
Chinese *C. amabile*. **Himalayan** *C.
nervosum*
houseleek *Sempervivum*. **cobweb** *S.
arachnoideum*

Houstonia L. (Rubiaceae). hew-*stoh*-
nee-uh. After William Houston
(1695–1733), Scottish botanist and
surgeon. 20 spp. herbs. N and C Am.
caerulea L. kie-*rue*-lee-uh. Bluets. Lat.
blue (the flowers). E N Am.

Houttuynia Thunb. (Saururaceae).
how-*tie*-nee-uh. After Maarten
Houttuyn (1720–1798), Dutch
naturalist and physician. 1 sp., herb.
E Asia.
cordata Thunb. kor-*dah*-tuh. Lat.
heart-shaped (the leaves).

Hoya R. Br. (Apocynaceae). *hoy*-uh.
After Thomas Hoy (ca. 1750–1822),
gardener to the Duke of Northumberland at Syon House. 200 spp.,
climbers, epiphytes. China, SE Asia,
Pacific Is., E Australia.
carnosa (L.f.) R. Br. kar-*noh*-suh. Wax
plant. Lat. fleshy (the leaves). S
China, SE Asia, E Australia.

huckleberry, California *Vaccinium
ovatum*. **red** *V. parvifolium*

Humulus L. (Cannabaceae).
hum-ew-loos. From *humela*, an old
German name for hops. 3 spp. herba-

ceous climbers. Eur., N Africa, Asia,
E N Am.
lupulus L. *lup*-ew-loos. Hop. Lat. a
small wolf (it is thought to be the
lupus salictarius, willow wolf, of Pliny
the Elder, as it climbs over willows).

hyacinth *Hyacinthus orientalis*. **grape**
Muscari. **Roman** *Bellevalia romana*.
summer *Ornithogalum candicans*.
tassel *Muscari comosum*

Hyacinthoides Heister ex Fabr.
(Asparagaceae). hie-uh-sinth-*oy*-deez.
Lat. like *Hyacinthus*. 8 spp. bulbous
herbs. W Eur., N Africa.
hispanica (Mill.) Rothm. his-*pan*-i-
kuh. Spanish bluebell. Lat. of Spain.
Spain, Portugal, N Africa.
non-scripta (L.) Chouard ex Rothm.
non-*skrip*-tuh. Bluebell. Lat. not
written upon (compared to the hyacinth of Gk. myth., which grew from
the blood of Hyacinthus after his
death and was marked by Apollo
with the word 'alas'). W Eur.

Hyacinthus Tourn. ex L. (Asparagaceae). hie-uh-*sinth*-oos. After Hyacinthus of Gk. myth. (see *Hyacinthoides
non-scripta*). 3 spp. bulbous herbs.
SW Asia.
orientalis L. o-ree-en-*tah*-lis. Hyacinth. Lat. eastern.

Hydrangea L. (Hydrangeaceae).
hie-*drane*-juh. From Gk. water vessel,
referring to the shape of the fruit. 35
spp., shrubs, trees, climbers. E Asia,
Americas.
anomala D. Don. uh-*nom*-uh-luh. Lat.
unusual (the climbing habit). Himal.,
China, Taiwan. subsp. *petiolaris*

(Sieb. & Zucc.) E. M. McClint. pee-
tee-o-*lah*-ris. Climbing hydrangea.
Lat. with a (conspicuous) petiole. E
Russia, Korea, Japan.
arborescens L. ar-bor-*res*-uhnz. Lat.
becoming tree-like. E USA.
aspera Buch.-Ham. ex D. Don.
as-puh-ruh. Lat. rough (the foliage).
Himal., China, SE Asia. subsp. *sargentiana* (Rehder) E. M. McClint.
sar-jen-tee-*ah*-nuh. After American
botanist Charles Sprague Sargent
(1841–1927), first director of the
Arnold Arboretum and colleague of
both E. H. Wilson, who collected the
type specimen in 1907, and Alfred
Rehder, who named it. China.
heteromalla D. Don. het-uh-roh-*mal*-
uh. Gk. variably hairy. Himal., N
Myanmar, China, N Vietnam.
involucrata Siebold. in-vo-lue-*krah*-
tuh. Lat. with an involucre (of bracts
around the flowerhead). Japan.
macrophylla (Thunb.) Ser. mak-ro-*fil*-
uh. Gk. large-leaved. E Asia.
paniculata Siebold. pan-ik-ew-*lah*-
tuh. Lat. in panicles (the flowers). E
Russia, China, Japan.
petiolaris Sieb. & Zucc. = *H. anomala*
subsp. *petiolaris*
quercifolia Bartram. kwurk-i-*foh*-lee-
uh. Oak-leaved hydrangea. Lat. with
leaves like *Quercus*. SE USA.
seemannii Riley. see-*man*-ee-ee. After
German botanist Berthold Carl
Seemann (1825–1871), who collected the type specimen in Durango
in 1849. Mex.
serrata (Thunb.) Ser. se-*rah*-tuh. Lat.
toothed (the leaves). S Korea, Japan.
serratifolia (Hook. & Arn.) F. Phil.
suh-rah-ti-*foh*-lee-uh. Lat. with
toothed leaves. Argentina, Chile.

hydrangea, climbing *Hydrangea anomala* subsp. *petiolaris*. **oak-leaved** *H. quercifolia*

Hydrocleys Rich. (Alismataceae). hid-*rok*-lee-is. From Gk. water, club-shaped, from the shape of the pistils. 5 spp. aquatic herbs. C and S Am.
nymphoides (Wiild.) Buchenau. nimf-*oy*-deez. Water poppy. Like *Nymphaea*.

Hymenoxys Cass. (Asteraceae). hie-muhn-*ox*-is. From Gk. membrane, sharp, referring to the pointed pappus scales. 25 spp. herbs. Americas.
hoopesii (A. Gray) Bierner. *hoops*-ee-ee. Owl's claws, orange sneezeweed. After Thomas Hoopes (1834–1925), American businessman, explorer and plant collector. It was described from plants grown from seed he collected in 1859. W USA.

Hypericum L. (Hypericaceae). hie-*pe*-ri-koom. St. John's wort. The Gk. name, from Gk. above, image (the plant was hung over religious icons to deter evil spirits). 450 spp., herbs, shrubs, trees. Widespread in temp. regs.
androsaemum L. an-dro-*see*-moom. Tutsan. Gk. name for a plant with red sap, from Gk. man, blood. Eur., N Africa, W Asia.
ascryon L. *as*-kree-on. From Gk. name of a species of *Hypericum*. C and E Asia, SE Canada, E USA.
calycinum L. kal-i-*see*-noom. Aaron's beard, rose of Sharon. Lat. with a (conspicuous) calyx. Bulgaria, Turkey.

frondosum Michx. frond-*oh*-soom. Golden St. John's wort. Lat. leafy. SE USA.
×*inodorum* Mill. in-oh-*dor*-room. Lat. unscented (compared to the goat-scented *H. hircinum*). *H. androsaemum* × *H. hircinum*. SW Eur.
kalmianum L. kal-mee-*ah*-noom. After Swedish botanist and student of Linnaeus Pehr Kalm (1716–1779), who collected the type specimen. SE Canada, NE USA.
kouytchense H. Lév. kuet-*chen*-see. Of Kweichow (now Guizhou). China.
lancasteri N. Robson. lang-*kas*-tuh-ree. After English plant collector and horticulturist Roy Lancaster (b. 1937), who, with Keith Rushforth, introduced it to cultivation in 1980. China (Yunnan, Sichuan).
×*moserianum* André. moh-zuh-ree-*ah*-noom. After Jean Jacques Moser (1846–1934), in whose Versailles nursery it was raised. *H. calycinum* × *H. patulum*. Cult.
olympicum L. o-*lim*-pi-koom. Of Mount Olympus, Greece. SE Eur., Turkey. f. *minus* Hausskn. *mie*-noos. Lat. smaller. Greece. **'Sulphureum'**. sul-*few*-ree-oom. Lat. sulphur-yellow (the flowers).
perforatum L. per-fo-*rah*-toom. Lat. perforated (referring to the black spots on the leaves). Eur., N Africa, temp. Asia.
prolificum L. proh-*lif*-i-koom. Broom-bush. Lat. prolific. SE Canada, E and C USA.

hyssop *Hyssopus officinalis*. **giant blue** *Agastache foeniculum*. **nettleleaf giant** *A. urticifolia*. **purple giant** *Agastache scrophulariifolia*. **rock**

Hyssopus officinalis subsp. *aristatus.*
yellow giant *Agastache nepetoides*

Hyssopus L. (Lamiaceae). his-*op*-oos.
Gk. name for another plant, probably
an origanum, from Gk. sprinkle, face
(it was used to sprinkle holy water).
2 spp., herbs, subshrubs. Eur., N
Africa, W and C Asia.

officinalis L. o-fis-i-*nah*-lis. Hyssop.
Lat. sold as a med. herb. Eur., N
Africa, W Asia. subsp. ***aristatus***
(Godr.) Briq. a-ris-*tah*-toos. Rock
hyssop. Lat. aristate (the bracts).
S Eur.

Hystrix patula Moench = *Elymus*
hystrix

Iberis L. (Brassicaceae). *ie*-buh-ris.
Candytuft. Gk. name used by
Dioscorides for a plant from Iberia
(Spain). 30 spp., herbs, subshrubs.
Eur., Medit.
sempervirens L. sem-per-*vie*-ruhnz.
Lat. evergreen. Medit.

ice plant *Sedum spectabile*

Ichtyoselmis Lidén & Fukuhara
(Papaveraceae). ik-tee-oh-*sel*-mis.
From Gk. fish, scaffold (or fishing
line, the flowers likened to fishes
hanging on a line). 1 sp., herb. China,
N Myanmar.
macrantha (Oliver) Lidén. mak-
ranth-uh. Gk. large-flowered.

Idesia Maxim. (Salicaceae). ie-*dee*-zee-
uh. After Eberhard Ysbrants Ides
(1657–1708), Dutch explorer. 1 sp.,
tree. China, Japan.
polycarpa Maxim. pol-ee-*karp*-uh.
Gk. with many fruits.

Ilex L. (Aquifoliaceae). *ie*-lex. Hollies.
Lat. name for holm oak (*Quercus
ilex*). 400 spp., trees, shrubs, climbers. Widespread.

×**altaclerensis** (hort. ex Loud.) Dalli-
more. al-tuh-kle-*ren*-sis. Highclere
holly. Of Highclere (Lat. *Alta Clera*),
Hampshire, UK, where it was raised.
I. aquifolium × *I. perado*. Cult.
'**Camelliifolia**'. kuh-mel-ee-i-*foh*-lee-
uh. Lat. with leaves like *Camellia*.
'**Hendersonii**'. hen-duh-*son*-ee-ee.
After Mr Henderson, friend of Mr
J. Shepherd, curator of Liverpool
Botanic Garden, who sent material
to the Handsworth nursery of Fisher
& Holmes. '**Hodginsii**'. hoj-*inz*-ee-
ee. After Irish nurseryman Thomas
Hodgins, who raised it before 1836.
'**Lawsoniana**'. law-son-ee-*ah*-nuh.
After the Lawson Nursery, Edinburgh, where it was raised before
1869.
aquifolium L. ak-wi-*foh*-lee-oom.
Common holly. The Lat. name. Eur.,
N Africa, W Asia.
×**attenuata** Ashe. uh-ten-ew-*ah*-tuh.
Lat. tapered (the leaves). *I. cassine* × *I.
opaca*. SE USA.
cornuta Lindl. & Paxton. kor-*new*-
tuh. Horned holly. Lat. horned
(referring to the often prominent leaf
spines). China, Korea.
crenata Thunb. kruh-*nah*-tuh. Japanese holly. Lat. with rounded teeth
(the leaves). E China, Korea, Taiwan,
Japan.
decidua Walter. de-*sid*-ew-uh. Possum
haw. Lat. deciduous. E and C USA,
N Mex.
glabra (L.) A. Gray. *glab*-ruh. Inkberry. Lat. glabrous (the leaves). E
Canada, E and C USA.
latifolia Thunb. lat-i-*foh*-lee-uh.
Tarajo. Lat. broad-leaved. E China,
Japan.

×*meserveae* S. Y. Hu. me-*ser*-vee-ie.
Blue holly. After Kathleen Kellogg
Meserve (1906–1999) of Long
Island, New York, who raised it.
I. aquifolium × *I. rugosa*. Cult.

opaca Aiton. oh-*pay*-kuh. American
holly. Lat. dull (the leaves, compared
to *I. aquifolium*). E and C USA.

pedunculosa Miq. pe-dunk-ew-*loh*-
suh. Lat. with a (long) stalk (the
fruit). China, Taiwan, Japan.

pernyi Franch. *per*-nee-ee. After Paul
Hubert Perny (1818–1907), French
missionary and plant collector who
discovered it. China.

verticillata (L.) A. Gray. vur-ti-si-*lah*-
tuh. Winterberry. Lat. whorled (the
flower clusters). E N Am.

vomitoria Sol. ex Aiton. vom-i-*tor*-ree-
uh. Yaupon. Lat. provoking vomiting
(it was used as an expectorant). E
USA, Mex.

Illicium L. (Schisandraceae). i-*lis*-ee-
oom. From Lat. to attract, referring
to the fragrant flowers. 40 spp., trees,
shrubs. E and SE Asia, N and C Am.

anisatum L. an-i-*sah*-toom. Japanese
star anise. Lat. anise-scented. Japan,
Korea, Taiwan.

floridanum Ellis. flo-ri-*dah*-noom.
Florida anise. Of Florida. SE USA,
NE Mex.

henryi Diels. *hen*-ree-ee. After
Scottish-born Irish plantsman
Augustine Henry (1857–1930), who
collected the type specimen in Hubei
in 1887. China.

parviflorum Michx. ex Vent. par-vi-
flaw-room. Swamp star anise. Lat.
small-flowered. SE USA (Florida,
Georgia).

Impatiens L. (Balsaminaceae).
im-*pat*-ee-uhnz, im-*pay*-shuhnz. Lat.
impatient (the fruits open explo-
sively). 690 spp., herbs, subshrubs.
Widespread.

arguta Hook.f. & Thomson. ar-*gew*-
tuh. Lat. sharply toothed (the leaves).
Himal., SW China.

balsamina L. bawl-suh-*mee*-nuh. Garden balsam. Lat. producing balsam.
SE Asia.

hawkeri W. Bull. *haw*-kuh-ree. After
Lt. Hawker R.N., who discovered
and collected it in 1884. Papua New
Guinea, Solomon Is.

niamniamensis Gilg. nee-am-nee-am-
en-sis. Of the Niam-Niam (now
Azande) tribe, who live where the
type specimen was collected. Trop.
Africa.

omeiana Hook.f. om-ay-*ah*-nuh.
Of Emei Shan (Mt. Omei). China
(Sichuan).

tinctoria A. Rich. tink-*tor*-ree-uh. Lat.
of dyers (the roots give a red dye).
Trop. Africa.

walleriana Hook.f. wol-er-ree-*ah*-
nuh. Busy lizzie. After English missionary Horace Waller (1833–1896),
who collected the type specimen in
the early 1860s when travelling on
the Zambezi River with Dr. David
Livingstone. E Africa.

Imperata Cirillo (Poaceae). im-pe-
rah-tuh. After Ferrante Imperato
(1550–1625), Naples apothecary.
11 spp. grasses. Widespread in warm
regs.

cylindrica (L.) P. Beauv. si-*lin*-dri-
kuh. Lat. cylindrical (the inflorescence). S Eur., Africa, Asia, Australia.

Incarvillea Juss. (Bignoniaceae). in-kar-*vil*-ee-uh. After French missionary and botanist Pierre Nicolas Le Chéron d'Incarville (1706–1757), who sent specimens of *I. sinensis* from China to Jussieu, the author, in Paris. 16 spp. ann. and perenn. herbs. Himal., C and E Asia.

delavayi Bureau & Franch. del-uh-*vay*-ee. After French missionary Jean Marie Delavay (1834–1895), who collected the type specimen in Yunnan in 1884. China (Sichuan, Yunnan).

mairei (H. Lév.) Grierson. *mair*-ree-ee. After French missionary Edouard-Ernest Maire (1848–1932), who collected the type specimen in Yunnan. Himal., China.

inchplant, creeping *Callisia repens*.
striped *C. gentlei* var. *elegans*
Indian bean tree *Catalpa bignonioides*
Indian paint *Chenopodium capitatum*
Indian physic *Gillenia trifoliata*
Indian pink *Spigelia marilandica*
Indian shot plant *Canna*
Indian tobacco *Lobelia inflata*
indigo, blue wild *Baptisia australis*.
false *Amorpha fruticosa*. **white wild** *Baptisia alba*. **yellow wild** *B. sphaerocarpa*

Indigofera L. (Fabaceae). in-di-*gof*-uh-ruh. Lat. bearing indigo (some species are used as a source of this dye). 750 spp., herbs, shrubs, small trees. Tropics and subtropics.

amblyantha Craib. am-blee-*anth*-uh. Gk. blunt flower. China.

heterantha Wall. ex Brandis. het-uh-*ranth*-uh. Gk. with different flowers. Himal., S Tibet.

pendula Franch. *pen*-dew-luh. Lat. pendulous (the inflorescence). China (Sichuan, Yunnan).

Indocalamus Nakai (Poaceae). in-doh-*kal*-uh-moos. Gk. Indian reed. 27 spp. shrubby bamboos. China.

tessellatus (Munro) P. C. Keng. tes-uh-*lah*-toos. Lat. tessellated (i.e., divided into small squares, the leaves by the veins). China (Hunan, Zhejiang).

inkberry *Ilex glabra*

Inula L. (Asteraceae). *in*-ew-luh. Lat. name for *I. helenium*, from Gk. to clean (from med. properties). 100 spp. ann. and perenn. herbs. Temp. regs. of the Old World.

ensifolia L. en-si-*foh*-lee-uh. Lat. with sword-shaped leaves. E Eur.

helenium L. hel-*en*-ee-oom. Elecampane. From the resemblance of the plant to a helenium. E Eur., W and C Asia.

hookeri C. B. Clarke. *hook*-uh-ree. After Joseph Dalton Hooker (1817–1911), English botanist and plant collector, son of William Joseph and director of RBG Kew, who sent seeds to Kew from Sikkim in 1849. Himal., W China.

orientalis Lam. o-ree-en-*tah*-lis. Lat. eastern. W Asia, Himal.

Ionactis Greene (Asteraceae). ie-on-*ak*-tis. From Gk. violet, ray, referring to the ray florets. 6 spp., herbs, subshrubs. N Am.

linariifolia (L.) Greene. li-nah-ree-i-*foh*-lee-uh. Flaxleaf white top aster. With leaves like *Linaria*. E N Am.

Ipheion uniflorum (Lindl.) Raf. =
Tristagma uniflorum

Ipomoea L. (Convolvulaceae). ip-o-
mee-uh. From Gk. like a worm, referring to the twining habit of many.
650 spp., herbs, shrubs, trees, climbers. Widespread, mainly tropics and
subtropics.
alba L. *al*-buh. Moonflower. Lat.
white (the flowers). Tropics.
batatas (L.) Lam. buh-*tah*-tuhs. Sweet
potato. From a Caribbean name.
Trop. Am.

Ipomopsis Michx. (Polemoniaceae).
ip-o-*mop*-sis. Gk. like *Ipomoea*. 30
spp. ann. and perenn. herbs. S Canada to S Am.
aggregata (Pursh) V. E. Grant. ag-ri-
gah-tuh. Lat. clustered (the flowers).
SW Canada to N Mex.
rubra (L.) Wherry. *rue*-bruh. Lat. red
(the flowers). SE USA.

Iresine P. Browne (Amaranthaceae).
ie-ri-*see*-nee. From Gk. a wreath or
staff wrapped with wool, referring to
the woolly hairs on the calyx. 70 spp.,
ann. and perenn. herbs, shrubs. S
Japan, W Africa, trop. and subtrop.
Am.
herbstii Hook. *herbst*-ee-ee. Beefsteak
plant. After Hermann Carl Gottlieb
Herbst (ca. 1830–1904), director of
the Botanic Gardens, Rio de Janeiro,
and of the Kew Nursery, Richmond,
who introduced it to cultivation in
Britain. Brazil.

Iris L. (Iridaceae). *ie*-ris. Gk. goddess
of the rainbow, referring to the
colourful flowers. 270 spp. rhizomatous or bulbous perenn. herbs. N
hemisph.
chrysographes Dykes. krie-so-*graf*-
eez. Gk. with golden lines (on the
perianth segments). China, N
Myanmar.
confusa Sealy. kon-*few*-suh. Lat. confused (with *I. wattii*). SW China.
domestica Goldblatt & Mabb.
dom-*es*-ti-kuh. Leopard lily. Lat. of
the home (it is commonly cultivated
in China). Himal., China, SE Asia.
ensata Thunb. en-*sah*-tuh. Japanese
water iris. Lat. sword-like (the leaves).
C and E Asia.
foetidissima L. fee-ti-*dis*-i-muh. Glad-
don iris. Lat. most fetid (the flowers).
Eur., N Africa.
forrestii Dykes. fo-*res*-tee-ee. After
Scottish botanist George Forrest
(1873–1932), who collected the type
specimen in Yunnan in 1906. SW
China, N Myanmar.
germanica L. ger-*man*-i-kuh. Lat.
German. Cult. **'Florentina'**. flo-ren-
tee-nuh. Lat. of Florence (Lat.
Florentia).
graminea L. gram-*in*-ee-uh. Lat. grass-
like (the leaves). Eur., Caucasus.
laevigata Fisch. lee-vi-*gah*-tuh. Lat.
smooth (the leaves). E Asia.
pallida Lam. *pa*-li-duh. Dalmatian
iris. Lat. pale (the flowers). SE Eur.
pseudacorus L. sued-*ak*-o-roos. Yellow
flag. Gk. false *Acorus*. Eur., N Africa,
W Asia.
setosa Pall. ex Link. see-*toh*-suh. Lat.
bristly (the tips of the petals). SW
Canada to Alaska, E Asia.
sibirica L. si-*bi*-ri-kuh. Lat. of Siberia.
Eur., W Asia, Siberia.
tuberosa L. tew-buh-*roh*-suh. Snake's
head iris. Lat. bearing tubers. S Eur.

unguicularis Poir. un-gwik-ew-*lah*-ris.
Algerian iris. Lat. clawed (the petals).
SE Eur., N Africa, SW Asia.
versicolor L. ver-*si*-ko-lor. Lat. variably
coloured (the flowers). Canada, USA.

iris, Algerian *Iris unguicularis.* **Cape**
Dietes iridioides. **Dalmatian** *Iris pallida.* **fairy** *Dietes grandiflora.* **Glad-
don** *Iris foetidissima.* **Japanese water**
I. ensata. **snake's head** *I. tuberosa*
iron cross begonia *Begonia masoniana*
ironweed *Vernonia*
ironwood *Carpinus caroliniana,
Ostrya virginiana*

Isatis L. (Brassicaceae). ie-*sah*-tis. The
Gk. name. 50 spp. ann. and perenn.
herbs. Medit., W and C Asia.
tinctoria L. tink-*tor*-ree-uh. Woad.
Lat. of dyers (the leaves give a blue
dye). SW Asia.

Isolepis R. Br. (Cyperaceae). ie-soh-
lep-is. Gk. with equal scales. 69 spp.
ann. and perenn. herbs. Widespread.
cernua (Vahl) Roem. & Schult.
sern-ew-uh. Lat. slightly drooping
(the foliage). Temp. regs.

Itea L. (Iteaceae). ie-*tee*-uh. Gk. name
for willow. 29 spp., shrubs, trees. E
Asia, E USA, Africa.
ilicifolia Oliv. i-lis-i-*foh*-lee-uh. Lat.
with leaves like *Ilex.* China.
virginica L. vir-*jin*-i-kuh. Virginia
sweetspire. Of Virginia. E USA.

ivory bells *Campanula alliariifolia*
ivy *Hedera.* **cape** *Senecio macroglossus.*
common *Hedera helix.* **devil's**
Epipremnum aureum. **Irish** *Hedera
hibernica.* **Persian** *H. colchica*

Jack in the pulpit *Arisaema triphyllum*

Jacobaea Mill. (Asteraceae). jak-o-*bee*-uh. After St. James (Lat. *Sanctus Jacobus*), referring to the flowering of the type species, *J. vulgaris* (*Senecio jacobaea*), on his feast day (July 25). 40 spp. ann., bienn. and perenn. herbs. Eur., N Africa, Asia.

maritima (L.) Pelser & Meijden. muh-*rit*-i-muh. Dusty miller. Lat. of the sea (it grows on coasts). S Eur., N Africa, W Turkey.

Jacob's ladder *Polemonium caeruleum*. **royal** *P. carneum*
jade plant *Crassula ovata*
Japanese angelica tree *Aralia elata*
Japanese knotweed *Fallopia japonica*
jasmine *Jasminum*. **Arabian** *J. sambac.* **Cape** *Gardenia jasminoides*. **Chilean** *Mandevilla laxa*. **common** *Jasminum officinale*. **Italian** *J. humile*. **primrose** *J. mesnyi*. **rock** *Androsace*. **winter** *Jasminum nudiflorum*

Jasminum L. (Oleaceae). *jaz*-min-oom. Jasmines. From the Persian name. 195 spp., shrubs, climbers.

Trop. and warm temp. regs. of the Old World.

beesianum Forrest & Diels. beez-ee-*ah*-noom. After Bees Nursery, Cheshire, founded by A. K. Bulley, sponsor of George Forrest, who collected the type specimen in Yunnan and introduced it to cultivation in 1906. China, SE Tibet.

humile L. *hew*-mi-lee. Italian jasmine. Lat. low (growing). Iran to China.

mesnyi Hance. *mez*-nee-ee. Primrose jasmine. After General William Mesny (1842–1919), Jersey-born explorer who spent many years in China, where he collected the type specimen in 1880. S China, Vietnam.

nudiflorum Lindl. new-di-*flaw*-room. Winter jasmine. Lat. naked flowers (it flowers when leafless). China, SE Tibet.

officinale L. of-is-i-*nah*-lee. Common jasmine. Lat. sold as a med. herb. W Asia to China.

parkeri Dunn. *par*-kuh-ree. After English botanist and forester Richard Neville Parker (1884–1958), who collected the type specimen in 1919 and later introduced it to gardens. W Himal.

polyanthum Franch. pol-ee-*anth*-oom. Gk. many-flowered. S China, Myanmar.

sambac (L.) Sol. *sam*-bak. Arabian jasmine. From an Arabian name. Himal., India.

×***stephanense*** É. Lemoine. stef-uhn-en-see. Of St. Etienne (Lat. *Sanctus Stephanus*), France, where it was raised, although found earlier in the wild. *J. beesianum* × *J. officinale*. China, Tibet.

Jeffersonia Barton (Berberidaceae). jef-er-*soh*-nee-uh. After Thomas Jefferson (1743–1826), third US president, in recognition of his knowledge of natural history. 2 spp. perenn. herbs. NE Asia, SE Canada, E USA.

diphylla (L.) Pers. die-*fil*-uh. Twinleaf. Gk. two-leaved (the leaves are deeply two-lobed). SE Canada, E USA.

dubia (Maxim.) Benth. & Hook.f. ex Baker & S. Moore. *dew*-bee-uh. Lat. doubtful. NE Asia.

Jimson weed *Datura stramonium*
Job's tears *Coix lacryma-jobi*
Joe Pye weed *Eutrochium.* **spotted** *E. maculatum.* **sweetscented** *E. purpureum*
jojoba *Simmondsia chinensis*
Joseph's coat *Amaranthus tricolor*
jostaberry *Ribes* ×*nidigrolaria*

Jovellana Ruiz & Pav. (Calceolariaceae). joh-vuh-*lah*-nuh. After Gaspar Melchor de Jovellanos (1744–1811), Spanish statesman and author. 4 spp. perenn. herbs and shrubs. NZ, Chile.

violacea (Cav.) G. Don. vie-o-*lay*-see-uh. Lat. violet (the flowers). Chile.

Jovibarba (DC.) Opiz (Crassulaceae). joh-vi-*bar*-buh. Lat. Jupiter's beard, referring to the fringed petals. 3 spp. succulent herbs. Eur., W Asia.

allionii (Jord. & Fourr.) D. A. Webb = *J. globifera* subsp. *allionii*

globifera (L.) J. Parn. glo-*bi*-fuh-ruh. Lat. bearing globes (the leaf rosettes). C and SE Eur. subsp. *allionii* (Jord. & Fourr.) J. Parn. al-ee-*oh*-nee-ee. After Carlo Allioni (1728–1804), Italian physician and botanist. Alps.

heufellii (Schott) A. & D. Löve. hoy-*fel*-ee-ee. After János (Johann) A. Heuffel (1800–1857), Hungarian botanist. SE Eur.

sobolifera (Sims) Opiz = *J. globifera*

joyweed *Alternanthera.* **Brazilian** *A. brasiliana*
Judas tree *Cercis siliquastrum*

Juglans L. (Juglandaceae). *jug*-luhnz. Walnuts. Lat. name for *J. regia*, meaning Jupiter's nut. 20 spp. trees. N and S Am., SE Eur., Asia.

ailantifolia Carrière. ie-lan-ti-*foh*-lee-uh. Japanese walnut. Lat. with leaves like *Ailanthus.* Japan. var. *cordiformis* (Makino) Rehder. kor-di-*form*-is. Lat. heart-shaped (the nuts).

cinerea L. sin-*e*-ree-uh. Butternut. Lat. grey (the bark). E Canada, E and C USA.

hindsii Jeps. ex R. E. Sm. *hiendz*-ee-ee. After its discoverer Richard Brinsley Hinds (1812–1847), English naval surgeon and naturalist on HMS *Sulphur*, who collected the first (but not the type) specimen in 1837. Calif.

nigra L. *nie*-gruh. Black walnut. Lat. black (the bark). SE Canada, E and C USA.

regia L. *ree*-jee-uh. Common walnut. Lat. royal. SE Eur. to China.

jumpseed *Persicaria virginiana*

Juncus L. (Juncaceae). *jung*-koos. Rush. Lat. name for a rush, from Lat. to join or bind (the stems were used for binding). 300 spp. herbs. Widespread.

balticus Willd. *ball*-ti-koos. Baltic rush. Lat. of the Baltic reg. Eur., N Am.

decipiens (Buchenau) Nakai. de-*sip-ee*-uhnz. Lat. misleading. E Asia.

dudleyi Wiegand. *dud*-lee-ee. Dudley's rush. After American botanist William Russell Dudley (1849–1911), who first described it. N Am.

effusus L. ee-*few*-soos. Soft rush. Lat. loose (the inflorescence). Eur., Africa, Asia, N and S Am.

ensifolius Wikstr. en-si-*foh*-lee-oos. Lat. with sword-shaped leaves. N Am., Japan, Kuriles.

tenuis Willd. *ten*-ew-is. Slender rush. Lat. slender (the stems). N and S Am.

torreyi Coville. *tor*-ee-ee. After American botanist John Torrey (1796–1873), who first described it under another name. N Am.

juniper *Juniperus*. Chinese *J. chinensis*. common *J. communis*. creeping *J. horizontalis*, *J. procumbens*. Irish *J. communis* 'Hibernica'. Rocky Mountain *J. scopulorum*. shore *J. rigida* subsp. *conferta*. Utah *J. osteosperma*

Juniperus L. (Cupressaceae). jue-*nip*-uh-roos. Junipers. The Lat. name, from Lat. producing youth (as they are evergreen). 50 spp., trees, shrubs. Widespread.

chinensis L. chin-*en*-sis. Chinese juniper. Of China. China, Korea, Japan. var. *sargentii* A. Henry. sar-*jent*-ee-ee. After American botanist Charles Sprague Sargent (1841–1927), first director of the Arnold Arboretum, who collected the type

specimen and introduced it to cultivation in 1892. NE Asia.

communis L. *kom*-ew-nis. Common juniper. Lat. common or growing in colonies. Eur., N Africa, Asia, Canada, USA. 'Hibernica'. hie-*bern*-i-kuh. Irish juniper. Lat. of Ireland.

conferta Parl. = *J. rigida* subsp. *conferta*

horizontalis Moench. ho-ri-zon-*tah*-lis. Creeping juniper. Lat. horizontal (the branches). Canada, N USA.

×*media* Melle = *J.* ×*pfitzeriana*

osteosperma (Torr.) Little. ost-ee-oh-*sperm*-uh. Utah juniper. Gk. with bony seeds. SW and C USA.

×*pfitzeriana* (Späth) P. A. Schmidt. fitz-uh-ree-*ah*-nuh. After Wilhelm Pfitzer, propagator with the Späth nursery, where it was first raised. *J. chinensis* × *J. sabina*. Cult. 'Armstrongii'. arm-*strong*-ee-ee. After the Armstrong Nursery, Calif., which first distributed it.

procumbens (Endl.) Miq. proh-*kum*-buhnz. Creeping juniper. Lat. creeping. Japan, Korea.

rigida Sieb. & Zucc. *ri*-ji-duh. Lat. rigid (the leaves). NE Asia. subsp. *conferta* (Parl.) Kitam. kon-*fer*-tuh. Shore juniper. Lat. closely pressed together (the leaves).

sabina L. suh-*bee*-nuh. Savin. The Lat. name. Eur., N Africa, W Asia. 'Tamariscifolia'. tam-uh-risk-i-*foh*-lee-uh. Lat. with leaves like *Tamarix*.

sargentii (A. Henry) Takeda ex Koidz. = *J. chinensis* var. *sargentii*

scopulorum Sarg. skop-ew-*lor*-room. Rocky Mountain juniper. Lat. of cliffs, rocky places. W Canada, W USA, N Mex.

squamata Buch.-Ham. ex G. Don.
skwo-*mah*-tuh. Lat. scaly (the bark).
Himal., China, N Myanmar.

virginiana L. vir-jin-ee-*ah*-nuh. Pencil
cedar. Of Virginia. SE Canada, E and
C USA.

Justicia L. (Acanthaceae). just-*is*-ee-
uh. After James Justice (1698–1763),
Scottish horticulturist. 600 spp.,
herbs, shrubs. Tropics.

brandegeeana Wassh. & L. B. Sm.
bran-di-gee-*ah*-nuh. Shrimp plant.
After American botanist Townshend
Stith Brandegee (1843–1925), who
first described it (as *Beloperone guttata*). Mex., C Am.

carnea Lindl. *kar*-nee-uh. Brazilian
plume. Lat. flesh-pink (the flowers).
Brazil, Argentina, Paraguay.

floribunda (K. Koch) Wassh. flo-ri-
bun-duh. Lat. profusely flowering.
Brazil, Paraguay, Argentina.

rizzinii Wassh. = *J. floribunda*

kaki *Diospyros kaki*

Kalanchoe Adans. (Crassulaceae). ka-lan-*koh*-ee. From the Chinese name of one species. 140 spp., ann. and perenn. herbs, succulent shrubs, climbers. S and E Africa, Asia.
beharensis Drake. bee-har-*ren*-sis. Of Behara. Madagascar.
blossfeldiana Poelln. blos-feld-ee-*ah*-nuh. After nurseryman and seed merchant Robert Blossfeld of Potsdam, Germany, who introduced it to cultivation ca. 1930. Madagascar.
daigremontiana Raym.-Hamet & H. Perrier. day-gri-mont-ee-*ah*-nuh. Devil's backbone. After M. & Mme Daigremont. Madagascar.
delagoensis Eckl. & Zeyh. de-lah-go-*en*-sis. Of Delagoa (now Maputo) Bay, Mozambique. Madagascar.
fedtschenkoi Raym.-Hamet & H. Perrier. fet-*shen*-koh-ee. After Boris Fedtschenko (1873–1947), Russian botanist. Madagascar.
pinnata (Lam.) Pers. pin-*ah*-tuh. Air plant. Lat. pinnate (some of the leaves). Madagascar.
tomentosa Baker. to-men-*toh*-suh. Lat. hairy (the leaves). Madagascar.

tubiflora (Harv.) Raym.-Hamet = *K. delagoensis*

kale *Brassica oleracea* Acephala Group.
sea *Crambe maritima*

Kalmia L. (Ericaceae). *kal*-mee-uh. After Pehr Kalm (1716–1779), Swedish botanist and student of Linnaeus, who collected in North America. 10 spp. evergreen shrubs. N Am., Cuba.
angustifolia L. an-gus-ti-*foh*-lee-uh. Sheep laurel. Lat. narrow-leaved. E N Am.
latifolia L. lat-i-*foh*-lee-uh. Calico bush, mountain laurel. Lat. broad-leaved. E USA.

Kalopanax Miq. (Araliaceae). kal-oh-*pan*-ax. From Gk. beautiful, and the related *Panax*. 1 sp., deciduous tree. NE Asia.
septemlobus (Thunb.) Koidz. sep-tem-*loh*-boos. Lat. seven-lobed (the leaves).

kangaroo vine *Cissus antarctica*
katsura tree *Cercidiphyllum japonicum*
Kentucky coffee tree *Gymnocladus dioica*
kerosene bush *Ozothamnus ledifolius*

Kerria DC. (Rosaceae). ke-*ree*-uh. After William Kerr (d. 1814), Scottish gardener and plant collector, who introduced the double form ('Pleniflora') to Kew in 1804. 1 sp., deciduous shrub. China, Japan.
japonica (L.) DC. juh-*pon*-i-kuh. Of Japan.

kingnut *Carya laciniosa*

Kirengeshoma Yatabe (Hydrangea-ceae). ki-reng-i-*shoh*-muh. From the Japanese name. 2 spp. perenn. herbs. China, Korea, Japan.
palmata Yatabe. pahl-*mah*-tuh. Lat. palmate (the leaves). E China, Japan.

kiwi fruit *Actinidia deliciosa*

Kleinia articulata (L.f.) Haw. = *Senecio articulatus*

knapweed *Centaurea*. **black** *C. nigra*. **giant** *C. macrocephala*. **greater** *C. scabiosa*. **lesser** *C. nigra*

Knautia L. (Dipsacaceae). *nawt*-ee-uh. After brothers Christian (1656–1716) and Christoph (1638–1694) Knaut, German physicians and botanists. 60 spp. perenn. herbs. Eur., Medit.
macedonica Griseb. mas-i-*don*-i-kuh. Lat. of Macedonia (reg. of SE Eur. distinct from the modern country). SE Eur.

Kniphofia Moench (Xanthorrhoeaceae). nie-*foh*-fee-uh. Red-hot poker. After Johann Hieronymus Kniphof (1704–1763), German physician. 65 spp. perenn. herbs. Arabia to S Africa.
caulescens Baker. kawl-*es*-uhnz. Lat. developing a stem. S Africa.
northiae Baker. *north*-ee-ie. After English botanical artist Marianne

North (1830–1890), who painted the type illustration of it in S Africa and introduced it to Kew in 1883. S Africa.
rooperi (T. Moore) Lem. *rue*-puh-ree. After Capt. Edward Rooper (1818–1854), who sent it to England. S Africa.
triangularis Kunth. trie-ang-ew-*lah*-ris. Lat. triangular (the leaves in cross section). S Africa.
uvaria (L.) Oken. ew-*vah*-ree-uh. Lat. like grapes (the flowers). S Africa.

Kochia scoparia (L.) Schrad. = *Bassia scoparia*

Koelreuteria Laxm. (Sapindaceae). kol-roy-*teer*-ree-uh. After Joseph Gottlieb Kölreuter (1733–1806), German botanist. 3 spp. deciduous trees. China, Taiwan, Japan.
paniculata Laxm. pan-ik-ew-*lah*-tuh. Golden rain tree, pride of India. Lat. in panicles (the flowers). China.

kohlrabi *Brassica oleracea* Gongylodes Group

Kolkwitzia Graebn. (Caprifoliaceae). kol-*kwitz*-ee-uh. After Richard Kolkwitz (1873–1956), German botanist. 1 sp., deciduous shrub. China.
amabilis Graebn. uh-*mah*-bi-lis. Beauty bush. Lat. beautiful.

kumquat *Citrus japonica*

Labrador tea *Rhododendron groen-landicum*

Laburnum Fabr. (Fabaceae). luh-*burn*-oom. Golden rain tree. The Lat. name. 2 spp. deciduous trees. C and S Eur.
anagyroides Medik. an-uh-gie-*roy*-deez. Lat. like *Anagyrus*, a related shrub.
×*watereri* (Wettst.) Dipp. *war*-tuh-ruh-ree. After the Waterer nursery, Knap Hill, Woking, Surrey, UK, where it was raised. *L. alpinum* × *L. anagyroides*. Cult.

Lactuca L. (Asteraceae). lak-*tue*-kuh. From Lat. milk, referring to the white sap. 75 spp. ann. and bienn. herbs. Eur., Africa, Asia, N and C Am.
sativa L. sa-*tee*-vuh. Lettuce. Lat. culti-vated. Cult.

lad's love *Artemisia abrotanum*
lady of the night *Cestrum nocturnum*
lady's fingers *Abelmoschus esculentus*, *Anthyllis vulneraria*
lady's mantle *Alchemilla*. **alpine** *A. alpina*
lady's slipper *Cypripedium*, *C. calceolus*. **Kentucky** *C. kentuckiense*. **large**

yellow *C. parviflorum* var. *pubescens*. **mountain** *C. montanum*. **showy** *C. reginae*. **small white** *C. candidum*. **small yellow** *C. parviflorum*. **stemless** *C. acaule*
lady's smock *Cardamine pratensis*

Lagerstroemia L. (Lythraceae). lag-uh-*strohm*-ee-uh. After Magnus von Lagerström (1696–1759), Swedish naturalist and merchant and a friend of Linnaeus. 55 spp., trees, shrubs. China, SE Asia to Australia.
indica L. *in*-di-kuh. Crape myrtle. Lat. of India or the Indies. China, SE Asia.

lamb's ears *Stachys byzantina*

Lamiastrum galeobdolon (L.) Ehrend. & Polatschek = *Lamium galeobdolon*

Lamium L. (Lamiaceae). *lay*-mee-oom. Dead-nettle. Lat. name used by Pliny for a non-stinging, nettle-like plant. 20 spp. ann. and perenn. herbs. Eur., N Africa, Asia.
galeobdolon (L.) Crantz. gal-ee-*ob*-do-lon. Yellow archangel. Lat. name used by Pliny for a nettle-like plant, from Gk. weasel, smell. Eur., W Asia.
maculatum L. mak-ew-*lah*-toom. Spotted dead-nettle. Lat. spotted (the leaves). Eur., N Africa.
orvala L. or-*vah*-luh. Lat. name for a sage. SC Eur.

Lamprocapnos Endl. (Papaveraceae). lamp-roh-*kap*-nos. From Gk. bright smoke, referring to the showy flowers and the fact that it was first described

in *Fumaria*. 1 sp., perenn. herb.
China, Korea.
spectabilis (L.) Fukuhara. spek-*tab*-i-
lis. Bleeding heart. Lat. spectacular.

lancewood *Pseudopanax crassifolius*.
toothed *P. ferox*
land cress *Barbarea verna*

Lantana L. (Verbenaceae). lan-*tah*-
nuh. Lat. name for a viburnum, from
the similar inflorescence. 150 spp.,
herbs, shrubs. Trop. Am., Africa.
camara L. kuh-*mah*-ruh. A native
S American name. Mex., C and N
S Am.
montevidensis (Spreng.) Briq. mon-
tee-vid-*en*-sis. Of Montevideo, Uruguay. S Am.

lantern tree *Crinodendron*
hookerianum

Lapageria Ruiz & Pav. (Philesiaceae).
lap-uh-*jeer*-ree-uh. After Marie
Josèphe Rose Tascher de La Pagerie
(1763–1814), first wife of Napoleon
Bonaparte. 1 sp., evergreen climber.
Chile, Argentina.
rosea Ruiz & Pav. *roh*-zee-uh. Chilean
bellflower. Lat. pink (the flowers).

larch *Larix*. **Dunkeld** *L.* ×*marsch-*
linsii. **European** *L. decidua*. **golden**
Pseudolarix amabilis. **Japanese**
Larix kaemferi

Larix Mill. (Pinaceae). *la*-rix. Larches.
The Lat. name. 10 spp. deciduous
trees. N hemisph.
decidua Mill. di-*sid*-ew-uh. European
larch. Lat. deciduous. Eur.

kaempferi (Lamb.) Carrière. *kemp*-
fuh-ree. Japanese larch. After German naturalist Engelbert Kaempfer
(1651–1716), one of the first European botanists to visit Japan. Japan.
×*marschlinsii* Coaz. marsh-*linz*-
ee-ee. Dunkeld larch. After Swiss
naturalist Carl Ulisses von Salis-
Marschlins (1762–1818), on whose
property it was found. *L. decidua* ×
L. kaempferi. Cult.

Lathyrus L. (Fabaceae). *lath*-i-roos.
Vetchling. Gk. name for pea. 150
spp. ann. and perenn. herbs, often
climbing. N hemisph., S Am., Africa.
aureus (Steven ex Fisch. & C. A. Mey.)
D. Brândza. *aw*-ree-oos. Lat. golden
(the flowers). E Eur., W and C Asia.
latifolius L. lat-i-*foh*-lee-oos. Perennial
pea. Lat. broad-leaved. Eur., N
Africa.
odoratus L. oh-do-*rah*-toos. Sweet
pea. Lat. fragrant (the flowers). S
Italy, Sicily.
vernus (L.) Bernh. *vern*-oos. Spring
vetch. Lat. of spring (flowering).
Eur., W and C Asia.

laurel, Alexandrian *Danae racemosa*.
bay *Laurus nobilis*. **California**
Umbellularia californica. **cherry**
Prunus laurocerasus. **mountain** *Kal-*
mia latifolia. **Portugal** *Prunus*
lusitanica. **sheep** *Kalmia angustifo-*
lia. **spurge** *Daphne laureola*

Laurus L. (Lauraceae). *lo*-roos. Lat.
name for *L. nobilis*. 2 spp. evergreen
trees. Medit., Macaronesia.
nobilis L. *noh*-bi-lis. Bay laurel, sweet
bay. Lat. renowned. Medit.

laurustinus *Viburnum tinus*
lavandin *Lavandula* ×*intermedia*

Lavandula L. (Lamiaceae). la-*van*-
dew-luh. Lavenders. From Lat. to
wash, from its use in soaps. 39 spp.,
herbs, shrubs. Medit., Macaronesia,
N Africa, India.
angustifolia Mill. an-gus-ti-*foh*-lee-
uh. Common lavender, English lavender. Lat. narrow-leaved. S Eur.
×***chaytoriae*** Upson & S. Andrews.
chay-*to*-ree-ie. After English botanist
Dorothy Chaytor (d. 2003), who
worked on the genus. *L. angustifolia*
× *L. lanata*. Cult.
×***christiana*** Gattef. & Maire. krist-ee-
ah-nuh. After Konrad Hermann
Heinrich Christ (1833–1933), Swiss
botanist. *L. canariensis* × *L. pinnata*.
Cult.
dentata L. den-*tah*-tuh. French lavender. Lat. toothed (the leaves). Spain,
N Africa.
×***intermedia*** Emeric ex Loisel. in-ter-
mee-dee-uh. Dutch lavender, lavandin. Lat. intermediate (between the
parents). *L. angustifolia* × *L. latifolia*. SW Eur.
pedunculata (Mill.) Cav. ped-unk-ew-
lah-tuh. Spanish lavender. Lat. with a
(conspicuous) peduncle (the inflorescence). SW Eur., Morocco, Turkey.
stoechas L. *stoy*-kuhs. French lavender.
From the Gk. name used by
Dioscorides, meaning from the
Stoechades (now Iles d'Hyères),
France. subsp. ***pedunculata*** (Mill.)
Samp. ex Rozeira = *L. pedunculata*

Lavatera arborea L. = *Malva dendromorpha*

×*clementii* Cheek = *Malva*
×*clementii*
maritima Gouan = *Malva wigandii*
olbia L. = *Malva olbia*
thuringiaca L. = *Malva thuringiaca*

lavender *Lavandula*. **common** *L.
angustifolia*. **Dutch** *L.* ×*intermedia*.
English *L. angustifolia*. **French** *L.
dentata*, *L. stoechas*. **Spanish** *L.
pedunculata*
lavender cotton *Santolina chamaecyparissus*
lead plant *Amorpha canescens*
leatherleaf *Chamaedaphne calyculata*
leatherwood *Eucryphia lucida*. **dwarf**
E. milliganii

Ledum groenlandicum Oeder = *Rhododendron groenlandicum*

leek, garden *Allium ampeloprasum*
Porrum Group. **three-cornered** *A.
triquetrum*. **wild** *A. ampeloprasum*

Legousia Durand (Campanulaceae).
luh-*gue*-see-uh. After French aristo-
crat and academic Bénigne Le Gouz
de Gerland (1695–1774), who
founded the botanic garden in Dijon.
6 spp. ann. herbs. Medit.
speculum-veneris (L.) Chaix.
spek-ew-loom-ven-*e*-ris. Venus's looking glass. Lat. mirror of Venus. C and
S Eur.

lemon *Citrus* ×*limon*
lemon balm *Melissa officinalis*
lemon verbena *Aloysia citrodora*
lemonwood *Pittosporum eugenioides*
Lenten rose *Helleborus orientalis*

Leonotis (Pers.) R. Br. (Lamiaceae). lee-on-*oh*-tis. From Gk. lion's ear, which the flowers have been said to resemble. 9 spp., perenn. herbs, subshrubs. Trop. and S Africa.
leonurus (L.) R. Br. lee-on-*ew*-roos. Lion's tail. Gk. a lion's tail (the inflorescence has been likened to one).

Leontopodium (Pers.) R. Br. (Asteraceae). lee-on-toh-*poh*-dee-oom. From Gk. lion's foot. 58 spp. perenn. herbs. Eur., Asia.
alpinum Cass. = *L. nivale* subsp. *alpinum*
nivale (Ten.) Hand.-Mazz. ni-*vah*-lee. Lat. of the snow. subsp. *alpinum* (Cass.) Greuter. al-*pie*-noom. Edelweiss. Lat. of the Alps. Mts. of Eur.

leopard's bane *Doronicum pardalianches*

Leptinella Cass. (Asteraceae). lep-tin-*el*-uh. Diminutive of Gk. slender. 33 spp. perenn. herbs. New Guinea, Australia, NZ, S S Am., Antarctic Is.
dendyi (Cockayne) D. G. Lloyd & C. J. Webb. *den*-dee-ee. After English zoologist and botanist Arthur Dendy (1865–1925), who was a friend of author Leonard Cockayne. NZ.
minor Hook.f. *mie*-nuh. Lat. small. NZ.
potentillina F. Muell. poh-ten-til-*ee*-nuh. Lat. like *Potentilla*. NZ (Chatham Is.).
squalida Hook.f. *skwo*-li-duh. Lat. dirty (the flower colour). NZ.

Leptospermum J. R. & G. Forst. (Myrtaceae). lep-toh-*sperm*-oom. Tea tree. Gk. slender-seeded. 85 spp., shrubs, trees. Australia and NZ to Malaysia.
lanigerum (Sol. ex Aiton) Sm. la-*nij*-uh-room. Woolly tea tree. Lat. woolly (the foliage). SE Australia, Tasmania.
scoparium J. R. & G. Forst. skoh-*pair*-ree-oom. Manuka, tea tree. Lat. broom-like. SE Australia, Tasmania, NZ. **'Chapmanii'**. chap-*man*-ee-ee. After Sir Frederick Revans Chapman (1849–1936), NZ judge, who discovered it. **'Keatleyi'**. *keet*-lee-ee. After Edward John Keatley (1875–1962), NZ sea captain, who discovered it.

Lespedeza Michx. (Fabaceae). les-ped-*ee*-zuh. After Vicente de Cespedes y Velasco (d. 1794), Spanish governor of West Florida 1784–90. 35 spp., herbs, shrubs. N and S Am., E Asia, Australia.
bicolor Turcz. *bi*-ko-lor. Lat. two-coloured (the flowers). E Asia.
thunbergii (DC.) Nakai. thun-*berg*-ee-ee. After Swedish botanist and physician Carl Peter Thunberg (1743–1828), who collected in Japan and S Africa. E Asia.

lettuce *Lactuca sativa*

Leucanthemopsis (Giroux) Heywood (Asteraceae). lue-kanth-uhm-*op*-sis. Gk. like *Leucanthemum*. 6 spp. perenn. herbs. Eur., N Africa.
alpina (L.) Heywood. al-*pie*-nuh. Alpine moon daisy. Lat. alpine. Eur.

Leucanthemum Mill. (Asteraceae). lue-*kanth*-uh-moom. Gk. white flower. 40 spp. perenn. herbs. Eur., Asia.

maximum (Ramond) DC. *max*-i-moom. Lat. largest. Pyrenees.

×*superbum* (Bergmans ex J. Ingram) D. H. Kent. sue-*per*-boom. Shasta daisy. Lat. superb. *L. maximum* × *L. vulgare*. Cult.

vulgare Lam. vul-*gar*-ree. Marguerite, ox-eye daisy. Lat. common.

Leucojum L. (Amaryllidaceae). lue-*koh*-joom. Gk. name of an early-flowering plant, from Gk. white violet. 2 spp. bulbous herbs. Eur., W Asia.

aestivum L. *ee*-stiv-oom. Summer snowflake. Lat. of summer. S Eur., W Asia.

autumnale L. = *Acis autumnalis*

vernum L. *ver*-noom. Spring snow-flake. Lat. of spring. C Eur.

Leucothoe D. Don (Ericaceae). lue-ko-*thoh*-ee. After Leucothoe of Gk. myth., who was changed into a shrub after being buried alive. 6 spp. shrubs. E Asia, N Am.

axillaris (Lam.) G. Don. ax-il-*ah*-ris. Coastal doghobble. Lat. in the (leaf) axils (the inflorescence). SE USA.

fontanesiana (Steud.) Sleumer. fon-tuh-nees-ee-*ah*-nuh. Mountain doghobble. After French botanist René Louiche Desfontaines (1750–1833), who called it *Andromeda lanceolata*, a name already used for an Asian species. SE USA.

populifolia (Lam.) Dippel = *Agarista populifolia*

Levisticum Hill (Apiaceae). le-*vis*-ti-koom. From Lat. to relieve, from med. properties and the similar

Ligusticum. 1 sp., perenn. herb. E Medit.

officinale W. D. J. Koch. of-is-i-*nah*-lee. Lovage. Lat. sold as a med. herb.

Lewisia Pursh (Portulacaceae). lue-*is*-ee-uh. After Meriwether Lewis (1774–1809), American explorer of the Lewis and Clark expedition (1804–06), during which the type specimen was collected. 16 spp. perenn. herbs. W N Am.

cotyledon (S. Watson) B. L. Rob. ko-ti-*lee*-don. Like *Cotyledon*. W USA.

nevadensis (A. Gray) B. L. Rob. nev-uh-*den*-sis. Of the Sierra Nevada. W USA.

pygmaea (A. Gray) B. L. Rob. *pig*-mee-uh. Lat. dwarf.

rediviva Pursh. re-di-*vee*-vuh. Bitter-root. Lat. coming back to life (a dried specimen from the Lewis herbarium grew after planting).

Leycesteria Wall. (Caprifoliaceae). les-*te*-ree-uh. After William Leycester, chief justice in Bengal ca. 1820, keen horticulturist and a friend of the author, Wallich. 6 spp. shrubs. Himal., China.

crocothyrsos Airy Shaw. kroh-koh-*thur*-sos. Gk. with saffron-coloured panicles (of flowers). NE India, N Myanmar, SE Tibet.

formosa Wall. for-*moh*-suh. Himalayan honeysuckle. Lat. beautiful. Himal., W China.

Leymus Hochst. (Poaceae). *lay*-moos. Anagram of *Elymus*. 50 spp. grasses. N temp. regs.

arenarius (L.) Hochst. a-ruhn-*ah*-ree-oos. Lyme grass. Lat. of sand (where it grows). Eur., Asia.

Liatris Gaertn. ex Schreb. (Asteraceae). lee-*ah*-tris. Blazing star, gayfeather. Deriv. obscure. 37 spp. perenn. herbs. N Am., W Indies.
aspera Michx. *as*-puh-ruh. Rough gayfeather. Lat. rough (the foliage). E USA.
cylindracea Michx. si-lin-*dray*-see-uh. Barrelhead gayfeather. Lat. cylindrical (the flowerheads). E USA.
ligulistylis (A. Nelson) K. Schum. lig-ew-li-*stie*-lis. Northern Plains gayfeather. Lat. with strap-shaped styles. C USA.
microcephala (Small) K. Schum. mik-roh-*kef*-uh-luh. Smallhead gayfeather. Gk. with small heads. SE USA.
punctata Hook. punk-*tah*-tuh. Dotted gayfeather. Lat. spotted (with glands, the leaves). C Canada, C USA, N Mex.
pycnostachya Michx. pik-noh-*stak*-ee-uh. Prairie gayfeather. Gk. with crowded spikes (of flowers). E USA.
scariosa (L.) Willd. ska-ree-*oh*-suh. Northern gayfeather. Lat. dry, membranous (the margins of the involucral bracts). E USA.
spicata (L.) Willd. spi-*kah*-tuh. Marsh gayfeather. Lat. in spikes (the flowers). SE Canada, E USA.
squarrosa (L.) Michx. skwo-*roh*-suh. Colicroot. Lat. with spreading tips (the involucral bracts). E and C USA.

Libertia Spreng. (Iridaceae). li-*bert*-ee-uh. After Marie-Anne Libert (1782–1865), Belgian botanist. 15 spp.

perenn. herbs. New Guinea, Australia, NZ, S Am.
caerulescens Kunth & C. D. Bouché = *L. sessiliflora*
ixioides (G. Forst.) Spreng. ix-ee-*oy*-deez. Like *Ixia*, a related genus. NZ.
perigrinans Cockayne & Allan. pe-ri-*green*-uhnz. Lat. travelling (it spreads by rhizomes). NZ.
sessiliflora (Poepp.) Skottsb. se-sil-i-*flaw*-ruh. Lat. with unstalked flowers. C Chile.

Ligularia Cass. (Asteraceae). lig-ew-*lair*-ree-uh. From Lat. strap, referring to the shape of the ray flowers. 125 spp. perenn. herbs. Eur., Asia.
dentata (A. Gray) H. Hara. den-*tah*-tuh. Lat. toothed (the leaves). China, Japan, Myanmar, Vietnam.
hodgsonii Hook.f. hoj-*son*-ee-ee. After Christopher Pemberton Hodgson (1821–1865), British consul in Hakodote, Japan, who sent it to Kew in 1859. Japan, E Russia, China.
japonica (Thunb.) Less. juh-*pon*-i-kuh. Of Japan. China, Korea, Japan.
przewalskii (Maxim.) Diels. shuh-*val*-skee-ee. After its discoverer, Nikolai Mikhaylovich Przhevalsky (1839–1888), Polish-born Russian explorer and naturalist. China.
tangutica (Maxim.) Bergm. = *Sinacalia tangutica*
veitchiana (Hemsl.) Greenm. veech-ee-*ah*-nuh. After Messrs Veitch & Sons, in whose Coombe Wood nursery it first flowered in 1905. China.
wilsoniana (Hemsl.) Greenm. wil-son-ee-*ah*-nuh. After English botanist Ernest Henry ('Chinese') Wilson (1876–1930), who collected prolifically in China for the Veitch

nursery and the Arnold Arboretum and introduced it to cultivation. China (Hubei, Sichuan).

×*yoshizoeana* (Makino) Kitam. yosh-ee-zoh-ee-*ah*-nuh. After Shiro Yoshizoe, of the Koishikawa Botanic Gardens, Imperial University of Tokyo, late 19th cent., where the type specimen was collected. *L. dentata* × *L. japonica*. Japan.

Ligusticum L. (Apiaceae). li-*gus*-ti-koom. Gk. name for a plant from Liguria, NE Italy, probably lovage (*Levisticum officinale*). 60 spp. perenn. herbs. Eur., Asia, N Am.
scoticum L. *skot*-i-koom. Scot's lovage. Lat. of Scotland. N Eur., E Asia, Canada, NE USA.

Ligustrum L. (Oleaceae). li-*gus*-troom. Privets. Lat. name for *L. vulgare*, from Lat. to tie, referring to the use of the shoots. 45 spp., shrubs, trees. Eur., Africa, Asia, Australia.
delavayanum Hariot. del-uh-vay-*ah*-noom. After French missionary Jean Marie Delavay (1834–1895), who collected the type specimen in 1889. SW China, N Myanmar.
japonicum Thunb. juh-*pon*-i-koom. Japanese privet. Of Japan. Japan, Korea, Taiwan.
lucidum W. T. Aiton. *lue*-sid-oom. Glossy privet. Lat. shiny (the leaves). China.
obtusifolium Sieb. & Zucc. ob-tews-i-*foh*-lee-oom. Border privet. Lat. blunt-leaved. China, Korea, Japan.
ovalifolium Hassk. oh-vahl-i-*foh*-lee-oom. Garden privet. Lat. oval-leaved. Japan, Korea.

quihoui Carrière. kee-*hue*-ee. After French horticulturist Antoine Quihou (1820–1889), from whose garden the type specimen was collected. China, Korea.
sinense Lour. sin-*en*-se. Chinese privet. Lat. of China. China, Taiwan, Laos, Vietnam.
vulgare L. vul-*gar*-ree. European privet. Lat. common. Eur., N Africa, W Asia.

lilac *Syringa*. **common** *S. vulgaris*. **Himalayan** *S. emodi*

Lilium L. (Liliaceae). *lil*-ee-oom. Lilies. The Lat. name, probably for *L. candidum*, from the Gk. name. 100 spp. bulbous perenn. herbs. N temp. regs., trop. mts.
candidum L. *kan*-did-oom. Madonna lily. Lat. white (the flowers). SE Eur., SW Asia.
cernuum Kom. *sern*-ew-oom. Nodding lily. Lat. nodding (the flowers). E Russia, NE China, Korea.
columbianum Leichtlin. ko-lum-bee-*ah*-noom. Columbia lily. Of the Columbia River. SW Canada, NW USA.
formosanum Wallace. for-moh-*sah*-noom. Formosa lily. Of Taiwan (Formosa). Taiwan.
henryi Baker. *hen*-ree-ee. After Scottish-born Irish plantsman Augustine Henry (1857–1930), who collected the type specimen in 1888. China.
lancifolium Thunb. lahn-si-*foh*-lee-oom. Tiger lily. Lat. with lance-shaped leaves. China, E Russia, Japan.

longiflorum Thunb. long-gi-*flaw*-room. Easter lily. Lat. with long flowers. Japan, Korea, Taiwan.

mackliniae Sealy. mak-*lin*-ee-ie. After Jean Macklin, who became Frank Kingdon-Ward's second wife a year after he discovered it in 1946. Assam.

martagon L. *mar*-tuh-gon. Martagon lily, Turk's cap lily. From a Turkish word for a type of turban, from the shape of the flowers. C and S Eur. to N China.

michiganense Farw. mish-i-guhn-*en*-see. Michigan lily. Of Michigan. SE Canada, E USA.

nepalense D. Don. nep-uh-*len*-see. Of Nepal. Himal. to Thailand.

pardalinum Kellogg. par-duh-*lee*-noom. Leopard lily. Lat. like a leopard (the spotted flowers). Calif., Oregon.

pumilum DC. *pew*-mi-loom. Lat. dwarf. E Asia.

regale E. H. Wilson. ree-*gah*-lee. Lat. royal. W China (Sichuan).

superbum L. sue-*per*-boom. American Turk's cap lily. Lat. superb. E USA.

lily *Lilium*. **American Turk's cap** *L. superbum*. **arum** *Zantedeschia aethiopica*. **belladonna** *Amaryllis belladonna*. **blueberry** *Dianella nigra*. **butterfly** *Hedychium coronarium*. **checker** *Fritillaria affinis*. **chocolate** *F. biflora*. **Columbia** *Lilium columbianum*. **day** *Hemerocallis*. **Easter** *Lilium longiflorum*. **Florida swamp** *Crinum americanum*. **Formosa** *Lilium formosanum*. **glory** *Gloriosa superba*. **Guernsey** *Nerine sarniensis*. **Ifafa** *Cyrtanthus mackenii*. **Jersey** *Amaryllis belladonna*. **Kaffir** *Clivia miniata*, *Hesperantha coccinea*.

leopard *Iris domestica*, *Lilium pardalinum*. **Madonna** *L. candidum*. **martagon** *L. martagon*. **Michigan** *L. michiganense*. **nodding** *L. cernuum*. **Paroo** *Dianella caerulea*. **pineapple** *Eucomis*. **rain** *Zephyranthes*. **Scarborough** *Cyrtanthus elatus*. **St. Bernard's** *Anthericum liliago*. **St. Bruno's** *Paradisea liliastrum*. **tiger** *Lilium lancifolium*. **toad** *Tricyrtis*. **Turk's cap** *Lilium martagon*. **voodoo** *Amorphophallus bulbifer*. **zephyr** *Zephyranthes*

lily of the valley *Convallaria majalis*. **American** *C. majalis* var. *montana*

lily of the valley tree *Clethra arborea*

lilyturf *Liriope, Ophiopogon*. **black** *O. planiscapus* 'Nigrescens'. **creeping** *Liriope spicata*. **dwarf** *Ophiopogon japonicus*. **giant** *O. jaburan*. **white** *O. jaburan*

lime *Citrus* ×*aurantiifolia*, *Tilia*. **American** *T. americana*. **broadleaved** *T. platyphyllos*. **common** *T.* ×*europaea*. **Kaffir** *Citrus hystrix*. **Mongolian** *Tilia mongolica*. **silver** *T. tomentosa*. **small-leaved** *T. cordata*. **weeping** *T. tomentosa* 'Petiolaris'

Limonium Mill. (Plumbaginaceae). li-*moh*-nee-oom. Gk./Lat. name of a plant growing in meadows, from Gk. meadow. 300 spp. herbs, mainly perenn. Widespread.

bellidifolium (Gouan) Dumart. bel-id-i-*foh*-lee-oom. Lat. with leaves like *Bellis*. Eur., N Africa, W Asia.

cosyrense (Guss.) Kuntze. kos-i-*ren*-see. Lat. of Pantelleria (Cosyra), a Medit. island. Sicily, Malta.

latifolium (Sm.) Kuntze = *L. platyphyllum*

platyphyllum Lincz. plat-ee-*fil*-oom.
Gk. broad-leaved. E Eur., W Asia.
sinuatum (L.) Mill. sin-ew-*ah*-toom.
Statice. Lat. wavy-edged (the leaves).
S Eur., N Africa, W Asia.
tataricum (L.) Mill. = *Goniolimon
tataricum*

Linaria Mill. (Plantaginaceae).
li-*nah*-ree-uh. Toadflax. Like *Linum*
(some have leaves similar to flax). 150
spp. ann. and perenn. herbs. Eur.,
Asia.
dalmatica (L.) Mill. dal-*mat*-i-kuh.
Balkan toadflax. Lat. of Dalmatia
(now mostly in Croatia). SE Eur.,
W Asia.
purpurea (L.) Mill. pur-*pew*-ree-uh.
Purple toadflax. Lat. purple (the
flowers). Italy.
triornithophora (L.) Willd. trie-or-ni-
tho-fo-ruh. Three birds flying. Gk.
bearing three birds (the flowers, in
threes, are likened to birds on the
stem). SW Eur.
vulgaris Mill. vul-*gar*-ris. Butter and
eggs, common toadflax. Lat. common. Eur., W Asia to China. var.
peloria (With.) Sm. pe-*lo*-ree-uh.
From Gk. monster.

linden *Tilia*

Lindera Thunb. (Lauraceae). *lin*-duh-
ruh. After Johan Linder (1676–
1724), Swedish botanist and physician. 100 spp., trees, shrubs. Temp.
and trop. Asia, E N Am.
benzoin (L.) Blume. ben-*zoh*-in. Spice
bush. From the Arabic name of the
aromatic resin of *Styrax benzoin*. SE
Canada, E USA.

obtusiloba Blume. ob-tew-si-*loh*-buh.
Lat. with blunt lobes (the leaves).
China, Korea, Japan.

ling *Calluna vulgaris*

Linnaea L. (Linnaeaceae). lin-*ay*-uh.
After Carl Linnaeus (1707–1778),
Swedish botanist and zoologist.
Often referred to as the father of
modern taxonomy, he is responsible
for the way we write plant names
today. It was his favourite plant. 1 sp.,
subshrub. Eur., Canada, USA.
borealis L. bo-ree-*ah*-lis. Twinflower.
Lat. northern.

Linum L. (Linaceae). *lie*-noom. Lat.
name for flax, from Gk. 200 spp.,
ann. and perenn. herbs, subshrubs.
Widespread in temp. and subtrop.
regs.
flavum L. *flah*-voom. Golden flax. Lat.
yellow (the flowers). C and SE Eur.,
W Asia.
perenne L. pe-*ren*-ee. Blue flax, perennial flax. Lat. perennial. Eur., W Asia.
usitatissimum L. ew-si-tat-*is*-i-moom.
Flax. Lat. most useful. Cult.

lion's tail *Leonotis leonurus*

Lippia citrodora Kunth = *Aloysia
citrodora*

Liquidambar L. (Altingiaceae).
lik-wid-*am*-buh. From Lat. liquid
amber, from the resin that flows from
the bark. 4 spp. trees. Turkey, E Asia,
USA to C Am.
acalycina Hung T. Chan. uh-kal-i-
seen-uh. Lat. without a calyx. China.

formosana Hance. for-moh-*sah*-nuh.
Of Taiwan (Formosa). China, Taiwan, Korea, Laos, Vietnam.
orientalis Mill. o-ree-en-*tah*-lis.
Oriental sweetgum. Lat. eastern.
SW Turkey.
styraciflua L. sti-rak-i-*flue*-uh. Sweetgum. Lat. flowing with storax (gum).
USA, Mex., C Am.

liquorice *Glycirrhiza glabra*
liquorice plant *Helichrysum petiolare*

Liriodendron L. (Magnoliaceae).
li-ree-oh-*den*-dron. Gk. lily tree.
2 spp. trees. SE Canada, E USA,
China.
chinense (Hemsl.) Sarg. chin-*en*-see.
Chinese tulip tree. Of China. China.
tulipifera L. tue-lip-*if*-uh-ruh. Tulip
tree. Lat. bearing tulips. SE Canada,
E USA.

Liriope Lour. (Asparagaceae). li-ree-
oh-pee. Lilyturf. After Liriope, a
nymph in Gk. myth., mother of Narcissus. 6 spp. perenn. herbs. E Asia.
muscari (Decne.) L. H. Bailey.
moos-*kah*-ree. Like *Muscari*. China,
Japan, Korea, Taiwan.
spicata Lour. spi-*kah*-tuh. Creeping
lilyturf. Lat. in spikes (the flowers).
China, Japan, Korea, Taiwan,
Vietnam.

Lithocarpus Blume (Fagaceae).
lith-oh-*kar*-poos. Gk. stone fruit
(from the hard shell of the nut). 300
spp. evergreen trees. E and SE Asia.
densiflorus (Hook. & Arn.) Rehder =
Notholithocarpus densiflorus
edulis (Makino) Nakai. *ed*-ew-lis. Lat.
edible (the nuts). Japan.

Lithodora Griseb. (Boraginaceae).
lith-oh-*dor*-ruh. Gk. stone gift (they
grow in rocky places). 7 spp. subshrubs. Eur., Medit., W Asia.
diffusa (Lag.) I. M. Johnst. di-*few*-suh.
Lat. wide-spreading. W Eur.

Lithops N. E. Br. (Aizoaceae). *lith*-ops.
Living stones, pebble plants. Gk.
resembling stones. 35 spp. succulent
perenn. herbs. S Africa.
karasmontana (Dinter & Schwantes)
N. E. Br. ka-ruhs-mon-*tah*-nuh. Of
the Karas Mts. Namibia.

Lithospermum diffusum Lag. =
Lithodora diffusa
purpurocaeruleum L. = *Buglossoides
purpurocaerulea*

littlebrownjug *Asarum arifolium*

Littonia modesta Hook. = *Gloriosa
modesta*

living stones *Lithops*

Lobelia L. (Campanulaceae). lo-*bee*-
lee-uh. After Mathias de L'Obel
(1538–1616), Flemish botanist. 300
spp., ann. and perenn. herbs, shrubs,
trees. Widespread.
bridgesii Hook. & Arn. brij-*es*-ee-ee.
After British explorer and plant collector Thomas Bridges (1807–1865),
who discovered it ca. 1832. Chile.
cardinalis L. kar-di-*nah*-lis. Cardinal
flower. Lat. red (the flowers). Canada
to Colombia.
erinus L. *e*-rin-oos. Edging lobelia.
Gk. name for an early-flowering
plant, from Gk. of spring. S Africa.

inflata L. in-*flay*-tuh. Indian tobacco. Lat. inflated (the fruit). E Canada, E and C USA.

laxiflora Kunth. lax-i-*flaw*-ruh. Lat. loosely flowered. SW USA to Colombia.

pedunculata R. Br. ped-un-kew-*lah*-tuh. Blue star creeper. Lat. peduncled (the flowers). SE Australia, NZ.

siphilitica L. si-fi-*li*-ti-kuh. Lat. of syphilis (which it was said to cure). Canada, USA.

×*speciosa* Sweet. spee-see-*oh*-suh. Lat. showy (the flowers). *L. cardinalis* × *L. siphilitica*. Cult.

tupa L. *tue*-puh. Chilean name for the plant. Chile.

lobelia, edging *Lobelia erinus*
lobster claw *Clianthus puniceus*

Lobularia Desv. (Brassicaceae). lob-ew-*lair*-ree-uh. From Gk./Lat. a small pod, referring to the fruit. 4 spp. ann. and perenn. herbs. Atlantic Is., Medit., SW Asia.

maritima (L.) Desv. muh-*rit*-i-muh. Sweet alyssum. Lat. of the sea. S Eur.

locust, black *Robinia pseudoacacia*.
bristly *R. hispida*. honey *Gleditsia triacanthos*
loganberry *Rubus* ×*loganobaccus*
lollipop plant *Pachystachys lutea*

Lomatia R. Br. (Proteaceae). loh-*mah*-tee-uh. From Gk. border (the seeds are edged with a papery wing). 12 spp., shrubs, trees. Australia, S Am.

ferruginea (Cav.) R. Br. fe-rue-*jin*-ee-uh. Lat. rusty (the hairs of the shoots and leaves). Chile, Argentina.

myricoides (C. F. Gaertn.) Domin. mi-ri-*koy*-deez. Lat. like *Myrica*. SE Australia.

tinctoria (Labil.) R. Br. tink-*tor*-ree-uh. Lat. of dyers (the fruit gives a red dye). Tasmania.

London pride *Saxifraga* ×*urbium*

Lonicera L. (Caprifoliaceae). lo-*nis*-uh-ruh, lo-ni-*se*-ruh. Honeysuckles. After Adam Lonitzer (Lat. *Lonicerus*) (1528–1586), German physician and botanist. 180 spp., shrubs, climbers. Eur., N Africa, Asia, N Am.

×*americana* (Mill.) K. Koch. uh-me-ri-*kah*-nuh. American (which it was thought to be). *L. etrusca* × *L. implexa*. Cult.

×*brownii* (Regel) Carrière. *brown*-ee-ee. Scarlet trumpet honeysuckle. After Brown. *L. hirsuta* × *L. sempervirens*. Cult.

caprifolium L. kap-ri-*foh*-lee-oom. Italian honeysuckle. Lat. goat leaf. Eur.

etrusca Santi. ee-*trus*-kuh. Lat. of Tuscany (Etruria). Medit.

fragrantissima Lindl. & Paxt. fray-gruhn-*tis*-i-muh. Lat. most fragrant (the flowers). E China.

×*heckrottii* Rehder. hek-*rot*-ee-ee. After Heckrott. *L.* ×*americana* × *L. sempervirens*. Cult.

henryi Hemsl. hen-*ree*-ee. After Scottish-born Irish plantsman Augustine Henry (1857–1930), who collected the type specimen in 1887. W China.

involucrata (Richardson) Spreng. in-vol-ue-*krah*-tuh. Twinberry. Lat. with an involucre (of conspicuous bracts). Canada, USA, N Mex.

×*italica* Tausch. i-*tal*-i-kuh. Lat. Italian. *L. caprifolium* × *L. etrusca*. Cult.

japonica Thunb. juh-*pon*-i-kuh. Japanese honeysuckle. Of Japan. E China, Japan, Korea. '**Halliana**'. hawl-ee-*ah*-nuh. After George Rogers Hall (1820–1899), American doctor and plant collector in Japan, who introduced it to gardens.

korolkowii Stapf. ko-rol-*kov*-ee-ee. After General Nicolai Iwanawitsch Korolkow (b. 1837), who introduced it to cultivation. W and C Asia.

maackii (Rupr.) Maxim. *mah*-kee-ee. Amur honeysuckle. After Russian explorer and naturalist Richard Otto (Karlovic) Maack (1825–1886), who collected the type specimen in 1855. E Asia.

nitida E. H. Wilson. *ni*-ti-duh. Lat. glossy (the leaves). W China.

periclymenum L. pe-ree-*klim*-uh-noom. Common honeysuckle, woodbine. Gk. name for honeysuckle, from Gk. twining around. Eur., N Africa. '**Belgica**'. *bel*-ji-kuh. Lat. of Belgium.

pileata Oliv. pil-ee-*ah*-tuh. Lat. with a cap (referring to the cap-like projection on the calyx). China.

×*purpusii* Rehder. pur-*poos*-ee-ee. After German botanist Carl Albert Purpus (1851–1941), who collected the type specimen from a plant grown at Darmstadt Botanic Garden ca. 1920. *L. fragrantissima* × *L. standishii*. Cult.

rupicola Hook.f. & Thomson. rue-*pik*-o-luh. Lat. growing on rocks. Himal., China. var. *syringantha* (Maxim.) Zabel. si-ring-*ganth*-uh. Gk. with flowers like *Syringa*.

sempervirens L. sem-per-*vie*-ruhnz. Trumpet honeysuckle. Lat. evergreen. E and S USA.

similis Hemsl. *sim*-i-lis. Lat. resembling (the leaves were likened to those of *L. macrantha*). W China, Myanmar. var. *delavayi* (Franch.) Rehder. del-uh-*vay*-ee. After French missionary Père Jean Marie Delavay (1834–1895), who, in the 1880s, collected several of the specimens from which it was described. W China.

standishii Jacques. stan-*dish*-ee-ee. After British nurseryman John Standish (1814–1875) of the Standish & Noble Nursery, Sunningdale, where it was grown. China.

syringantha Maxim. = *L. rupicola* var. *syringantha*

tatarica L. tuh-*ta*-ri-kuh. Tatarian honeysuckle. From the reg. of C and E Asia once called Tartary. E Eur. to C Asia.

tragophylla Hemsl. trah-goh-*fil*-uh. The Gk. equivalent of Lat. *caprifolium*, meaning goat leaf. China.

×*xylosteoides* Tausch. zie-los-tee-*oy*-deez. Lat. like *L. xylosteum*. *L. tatarica* × *L. xylosteum*. Cult.

xylosteum L. zie-*los*-tee-oom. Fly honeysuckle. A generic name that has been applied to *Lonicera*, from Gk. wood bone. Eur., W Asia.

loosestrife *Lysimachia*. **dotted** *L. punctata*. **fringed** *L. ciliata*. **gooseneck** *L. clethroides*. **purple** *Lythrum salicaria*

Lophomyrtus Burret (Myrtaceae). lof-oh-*mur*-toos. From Gk. crested, and the related *Myrtus* (referring to the

ribbon-like lobes of the placenta).
2 spp. shrubs. NZ.

bullata Burret. bool-*ah*-tuh. Lat.
puckered (the leaves).

×***ralphii*** (Hook.f.) Burret. *ralf*-ee-ee.
After Dr. Thomas Shearman Ralph
(1813–1891), who collected the type
specimen. *L. bullata* × *L. obcordata*.

Lophospermum D. Don ex R. Taylor
(Plantaginaceae). lof-oh-*sperm*-oom.
Gk. crested seed (referring to the
membranous crest on the seed). 10
spp. perenn. herbs. Mex., C Am.

erubescens D. Don. e-rue-*bes*-uhnz.
Creeping gloxinia. Lat. becoming
red, blushing (the flowers). Mex.

loquat *Eriobotrya japonica*
lords and ladies *Arum maculatum*

Loropetalum R. Br. ex Rchb. (Hamamelidaceae). lo-roh-*pet*-uh-loom.
Gk. with strap-shaped petals. 3 spp.,
shrubs, small trees. India, China,
Japan.

chinense (R. Br.) Oliv. chin-*en*-see.
Of China.

Lotus L. (Fabaceae). *loh*-toos. Gk.
name for several plants. 125 spp. ann.
and perenn. herbs. Widespread.

corniculatus L. kor-nik-ew-*lah*-toos.
Bird's foot trefoil. Lat. with a small
horn (referring to the fruit). Eur.,
Asia, N Africa.

hirsutus L. hir-*sue*-toos. Lat. hairy (the
foliage). S Eur., N Africa, SW Asia.

Louisiana canna *Canna glauca*
lovage *Levisticum officinale*. **Scot's**
Ligusticum scoticum
love-in-a-mist *Nigella damascena*

love-lies-bleeding *Amaranthus
caudatus*

Ludwigia L. (Onagraceae). lood-*wig*-
ee-uh. After Christian Gottlieb
Ludwig (1709–1773), German physician and botanist. 82 spp., herbs,
shrubs, often aquatic. Widespread.

alternifolia L. al-ter-ni-*foh*-lee-uh.
Rattlebox. Lat. with alternate leaves.
SE Canada, E and C USA.

sedoides (Bonpl.) H. Hara. sed-*oy*-
deez. Mosaic plant. Lat. like *Sedum*.
S Mex. to S Am.

Luma A. Gray (Myrtaceae). *lue*-muh.
Name used by the Mapuches in
Chile for the following. 2 spp., trees,
shrubs. S Am.

apiculata (DC.) Burret. uh-pik-ew-
lah-tuh. Lat. ending in a short,
abrupt point (the leaves). Argentina,
Chile.

Lunaria L. (Brassicaceae). lue-*nair*-
ree-uh. Lat. moon-like, referring to
the fruit. 3 spp. ann. and perenn.
herbs. Eur.

annua L. *an*-ew-uh. Honesty. Lat.
annual. SE Eur.

rediviva L. re-di-*vee*-vuh. Perennial
honesty. Lat. coming back to life (i.e.,
perennial).

lungwort *Pulmonaria*
lupin *Lupinus*. **Carolina** *Thermopsis
villosa*. **tree** *Lupinus arboreus*

Lupinus L. (Fabaceae). lue-*pie*-noos.
Lupins. The Lat. name, from Lat.
wolf. 220 spp., ann. and perenn.
herbs, shrubs. Americas, Eur., N
Africa, W Asia.

arboreus Sims. ar-*bor*-ree-oos. Tree lupin. Lat. tree-like. Calif.

argenteus Pursh. ar-*jen*-tee-oos. Lat. silvery (the foliage). W Canada, W and C USA.

chamissonis Eschsch. kam-i-*soh*-nis. After German botanist and poet Adelbert von Chamisso (1781–1838), who collected in California with the author Johann Friedrich Gustav von Eschscholtz. Calif.

perennis L. pe-*ren*-is. Lat. perennial. SE Canada, E USA.

polyphyllus Lindl. pol-ee-*fil*-oos. Gk. with many leaves (leaflets). W Canada, W USA.

sericeus Pursh. suh-*rik*-ee-oos. Lat. silky (the leaves). W Canada, W USA.

succulentus Douglas ex Lindl. suk-ew-*len*-toos. Lat. fleshy (the shoots). SW USA, NW Mex. (B.C.).

texensis Hook. tex-*en*-sis. Texas bluebonnet. Of Texas. Texas.

Luzula DC. (Juncaceae). *luz*-ew-luh. From Lat. a little light, from the way some species reflect light when covered in dew. 108 spp. perenn. herbs. Widespread in temp. and arctic regs. and trop. mts.

maxima (Reichard) DC. = *L. sylvatica*

nivea (Nathh.) DC. *niv*-ee-uh. Snow rush. Lat. snow-white (the flowers). Eur. (Pyrenees, Alps).

sylvatica (Huds.) Gaudin. sil-*vat*-i-kuh. Great wood rush. Lat. of woods. Eur., W Asia.

Lychnis coronaria (L.) Desr. = *Silene coronaria*

flos-cuculi L. = *Silene flos-cuculi*

flos-jovis (L.) Desr. = *Silene flos-jovis*

viscaria L. = *Silene viscaria*

Lycium L. (Solanaceae). *lie*-see-oom. Gk./Lat. name for a spiny shrub from Lycia (now in Turkey). 80 spp. shrubs. Widespread.

barbarum L. *bar*-buh-room. Duke of Argyll's tea tree. Lat. foreign. China.

Lycopersicum esculentum Mill. = *Solanum lycopersicum*

Lycopus L. (Lamiaceae). lie-*koh*-poos. From Gk. wolf's foot, from a supposed resemblance of the leaves. 14 spp. perenn. herbs. N Am., Eur., Asia, Australia.

americanus Muhl. ex W. P. C. Barton. uh-me-ri-*kah*-noos. American bugleweed. Of America. Canada, USA.

europaeus L. ew-roh-*pee*-oos. Gypsywort. European. Eur., Asia.

Lyonothamnus A. Gray (Rosaceae). lie-on-oh-*tham*-noos. After American forester and nurseryman William Scrugham Lyon (1851–1916), who discovered it, and Gk. shrub. 1 sp., evergreen tree or shrub. Calif. Is.

floribundus A. Gray. flo-ri-*bun*-doos. Catalina ironwood. Lat. flowering profusely. Santa Catalina Is. subsp.

asplenifolius (Greene) Raven. uh-splen-i-*foh*-lee-oos. Lat. with fern-like leaves.

Lysichiton Schott (Araceae). li-si-*kie*-ton. From Gk. dissolve, cloak, referring to the large spathe, which soon withers. 2 spp. perenn. herbs. NE Asia, W N Am.

americanus Hulten & H. St. John.
uh-me-ri-*kah*-noos. Skunk cabbage.
Of America. W Canada, W USA.
camtschatcensis (L.) Schott. kamt-
shat-*ken*-sis. Asian skunk cabbage.
Of Kamchatka. E Russia, Japan.

Lysimachia L. (Primulaceae).
li-si-*mak*-ee-uh. Loosestrife. After
Lysimachos (360–281 BCE), king of
Thrace, Macedonia and Asia Minor,
who is said to have used a piece of the
plant to calm a bull. 150 spp., herbs,
shrubs. Widespread.
atropurpurea L. at-roh-pur-*pew*-
ree-uh. Lat. dark purple (the flowers).
SE Eur.
ciliata L. sil-ee-*ah*-tuh. Fringed loosestrife. Lat. edged with long hairs (the
leaves). Canada, USA.
clethroides Duby. kleth-*roy*-deez.
Gooseneck loosestrife. Lat. like
Clethra (the inflorescence). E Asia.
ephemerum L. ef-*em*-uh-room. Lat./

Gk. lasting one day (i.e., short-lived).
S Eur., N Africa.
japonica Thunb. juh-*pon*-i-kuh. Of
Japan. E Asia. var. *minutissima*
Masam. min-ew-*tis*-i-muh. Dwarf
creeping Jenny. Lat. smallest. Japan.
nummularia L. num-ew-*lair*-ree-uh.
Creeping Jenny, moneywort. Lat.
coin-like (the leaves). S and E Eur.,
W Asia.
punctata L. punk-*tah*-tuh. Dotted
loosestrife. Lat. spotted (the leaf
undersides). Eur., W Asia.

Lythrum L. (Lythraceae). *lith*-room.
From Gk. blood, referring to the
flower colour. 35 spp., ann. and
perenn. herbs, shrubs. Widespread.
salicaria L. sal-i-*kair*-ree-uh. Purple
loosestrife. Lat. like *Salix* (the leaves).
Eur., N Africa, Asia, Australia.
virgatum L. vir-*gah*-toom. Lat.
twiggy. Eur., W and C Asia, N
China.

Maackia Rupr. (Fabaceae). *mah*-kee-uh. After Russian explorer and naturalist Richard Otto (Karlovic) Maack (1825–1886), who, together with Carl Maximowicz, collected the type specimen of *M. amurensis* in 1855. 12 spp. deciduous trees. E Asia.
amurensis Rupr. & Maxim. am-ew-*ren*-sis. Of the Amur River. NE Asia.

Machaeranthera Nees (Asteraceae). mak-uh-*ran*-thuh-ruh. Gk. with sword-like anthers. 2 spp. ann. and bienn. herbs. W USA, N Mex.
bigelovii (A. Gray) Greene = *Dieteria bigelovii*
coloradoensis (A. Gray) Osterh. = *Xanthisma coloradoense*
tanacetifolia (Kunth) Nees. tan-uh-see-ti-*foh*-lee-uh. Tansyaster. Lat. with leaves like *Tanacetum*.

Macleaya R. Br. (Papaveraceae). muh-*klay*-uh. After William Macleay (1767–1848), Scottish entomologist. 2 spp. perenn. herbs. China, Japan.
cordata (Willd.) R. Br. kor-*dah*-tuh. Plume poppy. Lat. heart-shaped (the leaves).
×*kewensis* Turrill. kew-*en*-sis. Of Kew (whence it was described). *M. cordata* × *M. microcarpa*. Cult.
microcarpa (Maxim) Fedde. mik-roh-*kar*-puh. Gk. small-fruited. China.

Maclura Nutt. (Moraceae). ma-*klue*-ruh. After William Maclure (1763–1840), Scottish-born American geologist. 12 spp., trees, shrubs, vines. Africa, Asia, USA, Australia.
pomifera (Raf.) C. K. Schneid. pom-*if*-uh-ruh. Osage orange. Lat. bearing apples. USA.

Madagascar periwinkle *Catharanthus roseus*
madrone, Pacific *Arbutus menziesii*
magic tree *Cantua buxifolia*

Magnolia L. (Magnoliaceae). mag-*noh*-lee-uh. After Pierre Magnol (1638–1715), French botanist. 235 spp. deciduous and evergreen trees and shrubs. E and SE Asia to New Guinea, SE Canada to S Am.
acuminata (L.) L. uh-kew-mi-*nah*-tuh. Cucumber tree. Lat. taper-pointed (the leaves). SE Canada, E USA.
×*brooklynensis* Kalmb. brook-lin-*en*-sis. Of Brooklyn (Botanic Garden), where it was first raised. *M. acuminata* × *M. liliiflora*. Cult.
campbellii Hook.f. & Thomson. kam-*bel*-ee-ee. After Archibald Campbell (1805–1874), Scottish political resident at Darjeeling, who travelled with Hooker in the Himalaya. E Himal. to S China.
denudata Desr. dee-new-*dah*-tuh. Lat. naked (it flowers before the leaves emerge). E and S China.

grandiflora L. gran-di-*flaw*-ruh. Bull bay. Lat. large-flowered. SE USA.

hypoleuca Sieb. & Zucc. = *M. obovata*

kobus DC. *koh*-boos. From the Japanese name. Japan, Korea.

liliiflora Desr. li-lee-i-*flaw*-ruh. Lat. with flowers like *Lilium*. China.

×*loebneri* Kache. *lobe*-nuh-ree. After German horticulturist Max Löbner, who raised it in the early 20th cent. *M. kobus* × *M. stellata*. Cult.

macrophylla Michx. mak-*rof*-i-luh. Gk. large-leaved. E USA.

obovata Thunb. ob-oh-*vah*-tuh. Lat. obovate (the leaves). Japan.

salicifolia (Sieb. & Zucc.) Maxim. sal-i-si-*foh*-lee-uh. Lat. with leaves like *Salix*. Japan.

sargentiana Rehder & E. H. Wilson. sar-jent-ee-*ah*-nuh. After American botanist Charles Sprague Sargent (1841–1927), first director of the Arnold Arboretum, to where it was introduced by Wilson in 1908. China (Sichuan, Yunnan).

sieboldii K. Koch. see-*bold*-ee-ee. After German physician and botanist Philip Franz von Siebold (1796–1866). China, Korea. subsp. *sinensis* (Rehder & E. H. Wilson) Spongberg. sin-*en*-sis. Lat. of China. China (Sichuan).

×*soulangeana* Soulange-Bodin. sue-lan-jee-*ah*-nuh. After French horticulturist Étienne Soulange-Bodin (1774–1846), who raised it. *M. denudata* × *M. liliiflora*. Cult. 'Lennei'. *len*-ee-ee. After German horticulturist Peter Joseph Lenné (1789–1866).

stellata (Sieb. & Zucc.) Maxim. stel-*ah*-tuh. Lat. star-like (the flowers). Japan.

tripetala (L.) L. trie-*pet*-uh-luh. Umbrella tree. Lat. with three petals (outer tepals). E USA.

virginiana L. vir-jin-ee-*ah*-nuh. Swamp bay, sweet bay. Of Virginia. E USA, Cuba.

×*wieseneri* Carrière. *veez*-nuh-ree. After Mr Wiesener, from whose garden it was described. *M. obovata* × *M. sieboldii*. Cult.

wilsonii Rehder. wil-*soh*-nee-ee. After English botanist Ernest Henry ('Chinese') Wilson (1876–1930), who collected the type specimen in Sichuan in 1904 and introduced it to cultivation in 1908. China.

×*Mahoberberis* C. K. Schneid. (Berberidaceae). mah-hoh-*ber*-buh-ris. From the names of the parents (*Berberis* × *Mahonia*). Shrubs. Cult.

aquisargentii Krüssm. ak-wi-sar-*jen*-tee-ee. From the names of the parents (*B. sargentii* × *M. aquifolium*).

Mahonia Nutt. (Berberidaceae). muh-*hoh*-nee-uh. After Bernard McMahon (1775–1816), Irish-born American horticulturist. 70 spp. evergreen shrubs. N and S Am., E Asia.

aquifolium (Pursh) Nutt. ak-wi-*foh*-lee-oom. Oregon grape. Lat. name for holly (*Ilex aquifolium*), from the similarity of the leaflets to holly leaves. SW Canada, W USA.

bealei (Fortune) Carrière. *beel*-ee-ee. After English merchant Thomas Chay Beale (1805–1857), who grew plants collected by Fortune in his Shanghai garden before they were sent to England. China.

japonica (Thunb.) DC. juh-*pon*-i-kuh.
Of Japan, where it is cultivated.
Taiwan. **'Bealei'** = *M. bealei*

lomariifolia Takeda. loh-ma-ree-i-*foh*-
lee-uh. Lat. with leaves like *Lomaria*.
SW China, Myanmar.

×*media* C. D. Brickell. *mee*-dee-uh.
Lat. intermediate (between the par-
ents). *M. japonica* × *M. lomariifolia*.
Cult.

nervosa (Pursh) Nutt. ner-*voh*-suh.
Lat. (prominently) veined (the leaflets). SW Canada, W USA.

repens (Lindl.) G. Don. *ree*-puhnz.
Lat. creeping. SW Canada, W USA.

Maianthemum F. H. Wigg. (Asparagaceae). mie-*anth*-uh-moom. Gk.
May flower, referring to their flowering time. 38 spp. perenn. herbs. N
temp. regs., Mex., C Am.

bifolium (L.) F. W. Schmidt. bie-*foh*-
lee-oom. Lat. two-leaved. Temp. Eur.
and Asia.

canadense Desf. kan-uh-*den*-see.
Canadian May-lily. Of Canada.
Canada, E and C USA.

racemosum (L.) Link. ras-i-*moh*-
soom. False spikenard. Lat. in
racemes (the flowers). Canada, USA,
N Mex.

stellatum (L.) Link. stel-*ah*-toom. Lat.
star-like (the flowers). Canada, USA,
N Mex.

maidenhair tree *Ginkgo biloba*
maize *Zea mays*
mallow *Malva*. **common** *M. sylvestris*.
  globe *Sphaeralcea*. **hemp marsh**
  Althaea cannabina. **marsh** *A. officinalis*. **musk** *Abelmoschus moschatus*,
  Malva moschata. **prairie** *Sidalcea
  candida*. **tree** *Malva dendromorpha*

Malus Mill. (Rosaceae). *ma*-loos.
Apples. Lat. name for apple. 40 spp.,
trees, shrubs. N temp. regs.

baccata (L.) Borkh. buh-*kah*-tuh.
Siberian crab. Lat. bearing berries
(the small fruits). E Asia.

coronaria (L.) Mill. ko-ro-*nair*-ree-uh.
Garland crab, sweet crab. Lat. of garlands. SE Canada, E and C USA.

domestica Borkh. = *M. pumila*

floribunda Siebold ex Van Houtte.
flo-ri-*bun*-duh. Japanese crab. Lat.
flowering profusely. Cult.

fusca (Raf.) C. K. Schneid. *foos*-kuh.
Oregon crab. Lat. dark brown. W
Canada, W USA.

hupehensis (Pamp.) Rehder. hew-pee-
hen-sis. Of Hubei (Hupeh). China,
Taiwan.

ioensis (Alph. Wood) Britton. ie-oh-
en-sis. Prairie crab. Of Iowa. C USA.

pumila Mill. *pew*-mi-luh. Orchard
apple. Lat. dwarf. C Asia.

×*purpurea* (Barbier) Rehder.
pur-*pew*-ree-uh. Lat. purple (the
leaves). Cult.

sargentii Rehder. sar-*jent*-ee-ee. After
American botanist Charles Sprague
Sargent (1841–1927), first director
of the Arnold Arboretum, who collected the type specimen in Hokkaido in 1892. Japan.

sylvestris (L.) Mill. sil-*ves*-tris. European crab. Lat. of woods. Eur.

transitoria (Batalin) C. K. Schneid.
tran-si-*tor*-ree-uh. Lat. short-lasting.
China.

trilobata (Poir.) C. K. Schneid.
trie-loh-*bah*-tuh. Lat. three-lobed
(the leaves). SE Eur., SW Asia.

tschonoskii (Maxim.) C. K. Schneid.
chon-*os*-kee-ee. After Sugawa
Tschonoski (Sukawa Chonosuke)

(1841–1925), who assisted Carl Maximowicz with collecting in Japan. Japan.

Malva L. (Malvaceae). *mal*-vuh. Mallow. Lat. name for mallow. 20 spp., herbs, subshrubs. Eur., Africa, Asia, Australia.
×**clementii** (Cheek) Stace. kle-*ment*-ee-ee. After English botanist Eric Clement (b. 1940), who first suggested its hybrid status. *M. olbia* × *M. thuringiaca*. Cult.
dendromorpha M. F. Ray. den-droh-*mor*-fuh. Tree mallow. Gk. tree-shaped. W Eur., Medit.
moschata L. mos-*kah*-tuh. Musk mallow. Lat. musk-scented (the flowers and foliage). Eur., N Africa.
olbia (L.) Alef. *ol*-bee-uh. Lat. of the Îsles d'Hyères (Lat. *Olbiam*), France. W Medit.
sylvestris L. sil-*ves*-tris. Common mallow. Lat. of woods. Eur., W and C Asia, N Africa.
thuringiaca (L.) Vis. thuh-ring-ee-*ah*-kuh. Of Thuringia, Germany. C and SE Eur.
wigandii (Alef.) M. F. Ray. vi-*gand*-ee-ee. After German botanist Julius Wilhelm Albert Wigand (1821–1886). SW Eur., N Africa.

Malvastrum lateritium (Hook.) G. Nicholson = *Modiolastrum lateritium*

mandarin *Citrus reticulata*

Mandevilla Lindl. (Apocynaceae). man-duh-*vil*-uh. After Henry John Mandeville (1773–1861), British diplomat in Buenos Aires, who intro-

duced *M. laxa* to cultivation in Britain. 130 spp., climbers, herbs, subshrubs. Trop. Am.
×**amabilis** (Backhouse) Dress. uh-*mah*-bi-lis. Lat. beautiful. Cult.
laxa (Ruiz & Pav.) Woodson. *lax*-uh. Chilean jasmine. Lat. loose, open (the inflorescence). Argentina, Bolivia.
suaveolens Lindl. = *M. laxa*

Manfreda Salisb. (Asparagaceae). man-*fray*-duh. After Manfredus de Monte Imperiale, 14th-cent. Italian medical scholar and author. 33 spp. perenn. herbs. C and E USA, Mex., C Am.
virginica (L.) Salisb. ex Rose. vir-*jin*-i-kuh. Of Virginia. E USA, NE Mex.

manuka *Leptospermum scoparium*
manzanita, hairy *Arctostaphylos columbiana*. **pinemat** *A. nevadensis*
maple *Acer*. **Amur** *A. tataricum* subsp. *ginnala*. **ash-leaved** *A. negundo*. **bigtooth** *A. saccharum* subsp. *grandidentatum*. **black** *A. saccharum* subsp. *nigrum*. **Cappadocian** *A. cappadocicum*. **Cretan** *A. sempervirens*. **David's** *A. davidii*. **field** *A. campestre*. **Forrest's** *A. forrestii*. **Freeman** *A.* ×*freemanii*. **fullmoon** *A. japonicum*. **hawthorn** *A. crataegifolium*. **hedge** *A. campestre*. **Honshu** *A. rufinerve*. **hornbeam** *A. carpinifolium*. **ivyleaf** *A. cissifolium*. **Japanese** *A. palmatum*. **Kyushu** *A. capillipes*. **Montpelier** *A. monspessulanum*. **mountain** *A. spicatum*. **Nikko** *A. maximowiczianum*. **Norway** *A. platanoides*. **Oregon** *A. macrophyllum*. **painted** *A. pictum*. **paperbark** *A. griseum*. **red** *A. rubrum*. **rock**

A. glabrum. **Shantung** *A. truncatum.*
silver *A. saccharinum.* **sugar** *A. saccharum.* **sycamore** *A. pseudoplatanus.*
Tatarian *A. tataricum.* **trident** *A. buergerianaum.* **vine** *A. circinatum*

Maranta Plum. ex L. (Marantaceae).
ma-*rant*-uh. After Bartolomea
Maranti, 16th-cent. Venetian botanist and physician. 41 spp. perenn.
herbs. C and S Am.
leuconeura E. Morren. lue-koh-*new*-
ruh. Prayer plant. Gk. white-veined
(the leaves). Brazil. **'Erythroneura'.**
e-rith-roh-*new*-ruh. Gk. red-veined
(the leaves). **'Kerchoveana'.** ker-
choh-vee-*ah*-nuh. After Belgian
naturalist Oswald de Kerchove de
Denterghem (1844–1906).

mare's tail *Hippuris vulgaris*
marguerite *Argyranthemum frutescens, Leucanthemum vulgare*
marigold *Tagetes.* **African** *T. erecta.*
corn *Glebionis segetum.* **French**
Tagetes erecta. **pot** *Calendula officinalis.* **sweet-scented** *Tagetes lucida*
mariposa lily, butterfly *Calochortus
venustus.* **goldenbowl** *C. concolor.*
splendid *C. splendens.* **yellow** *C.
luteus*
marjoram, pot *Origanum onites.*
sweet *O. majorana.* **wild** *O. vulgare*
marrow *Cucurbita pepo*
marsh marigold *Caltha palustris.*
white *C. leptosepala*
marvel of Peru *Mirabilis jalapa*
masterwort *Astrantia.* **greater** *A.
major.* **lesser** *A. minor*

Mathiasella Constance & C. Hitchc.
(Apiaceae). math-ee-uh-*sel*-uh. After
botanist Mildred Esther Mathias

(1906–1995), "an outstanding
American student of this difficult
but fascinating family." 1 sp., perenn.
herb. Mex.
bupleuroides Constance & C. Hitchc.
bew-plue-*roy*-deez. Like *Bupleurum.*

Matteuccia Tod. (Onocleaceae). ma-
tue-chee-uh. After Carlo Matteucci
(1811–1868), Italian physicist. 3 spp.
ferns. N temp. regs.
orientalis (Hook.) Trevis. o-ree-en-
tah-lis. Lat. eastern. E Asia.
struthiopteris (L.) Tod. strue-thee-*op*-
te-ris. Ostrich fern. Gk. ostrich fern.
Canada, USA, Eur., Asia.

Matthiola W. T. Aiton (Brassicaceae).
mat-ee-*oh*-luh. Stock. After Pietro
Andrea Matthioli (1500–1577), Italian botanist and physician. 50 spp.
ann., bienn. and perenn. herbs. Eur.,
Africa, W and C Asia.
bicornis (Sm.) DC. = *M. longipetala*
subsp. *bicornis*
incana (L.) R. Br. in-*kah*-nuh.
Brompton stock. Lat. grey (the foliage). S Eur.
longipetala (vent.) DC. long-gi-*pet*-
uh-luh. Lat. long-petalled. Greece,
SW Asia. subsp. *bicornis* (Sm.) P.
Ball. bie-*korn*-is. Night-scented
stock. Lat. two-horned (the fruit).

Maurandya Ortega (Plantaginaceae).
mor-*rand*-ee-uh. After Catalina
Pancracia Maurandy, 18th-cent.
Spanish botanist. 3 spp. climbing
herbs. USA, Mex.
erubescens (D. Don) A. Gray =
Lophospermum erubescens
scandens (Cav.) Pers. *skan*-duhnz. Lat.
climbing. Mex.

May apple *Podophyllum peltatum*
May-lily, Canadian *Maianthemum canadense*
mayhaw *Crataegus aestivalis*
maypop *Passiflora incarnata*
mayten *Maytenus boaria*

Maytenus Molina (Celastraceae). may-*ten*-oos. From the Chilean name of *M. boaria*. 200 spp., trees, shrubs. Tropics and subtropics.
boaria Molina. boh-*ah*-ree-uh. Mayten. Lat. of cattle (which eat the leaves). S Am.

Mazus Lour. (Phrymaceae). *may*-zoos. From Gk. nipple, referring to swellings in the corolla. 35 spp. ann. and perenn. herbs. E and SE Asia to Australia, NZ.
reptans N. E. Br. *rep*-tanz. Lat. creeping. Himal.

meadow rue *Thalictrum.* **lesser** *T. minus.* **yellow** *T. flavum*
meadowsweet *Filipendula ulmaria.* **giant** *F. camtschatica*

Meconopsis Viguier (Papaveraceae). mek-o-*nop*-sis. Gk. poppy-like. 54 spp. ann. and perenn. herbs. Himal., China, W Eur.
betonicifolia Franch. be-ton-i-ki-*foh*-lee-uh. Lat. with leaves like *Betonica* (*Stachys*). W China, N Myanmar.
cambrica (L.) Viguier. *kam*-bri-kuh. Welsh poppy. Lat. of Wales. W Eur.

medlar *Mespilus germanica*
meetinghouses *Aquilegia canadensis*

Melia L. (Meliaceae). *mel*-ee-uh. Gk. name for *Fraxinus ornus*, which exudes a sugary substance, from Gk. honey, from the similarity of the leaves. 3 spp., trees, shrubs. Asia to Australia.
azedarach L. uh-*zed*-uh-rak. Bead tree, Persian lilac. From the Persian name.

Melianthus L. (Melianthaceae). mel-ee-*anth*-oos. Gk. honey flower, from the profuse nectar. 8 spp. shrubs. S Africa.
major L. *may*-juh. Honeyflower. Lat. large.

Melica L. (Poaceae). *mel*-i-kuh. From Gk. name of a grass with sweet sap, from Gk. honey. 80 spp. grasses. Widespread in temp. regs.
altissima L. al-*tis*-i-muh. Siberian melic. Lat. tallest. C and E Eur., W and C Asia.

Melissa L. (Lamiaceae). mel-*is*-uh. Gk. honey bee (they are attracted to the flowers). 4 spp. perenn. herbs. Eur., N Africa, W and C Asia.
officinalis L. o-fis-i-*nah*-lis. Lemon balm. Lat. sold as a med. herb.

Melittis L. (Lamiaceae). mel-*it*-is. Gk. bearing honey. 1 sp., perenn. herb. Eur., W Asia.
melissophyllum L. mel-is-oh-*fil*-oom. Bastard balm. Gk. with leaves like *Melissa*.

melon *Cucumis melo.* **honeydew** *C. melo* Inodorus Group. **musk** *C. melo* Reticulatus Group

Mentha L. (Lamiaceae). *menth*-uh. Mint. The Lat. name, from Minthe of Gk. myth., a nymph who was turned into a mint plant. 20 spp. perenn. and ann. herbs. N temp. regs., Africa, Australia, NZ.

aquatica L. uh-*kwat*-i-kuh. Water mint. Lat. of water. Eur., Africa, W Asia.

arvensis L. ar-*ven*-sis. Corn mint, field mint. Lat. growing in fields. Eur., W and C Asia, Himal.

×*gracilis* Sole. *gras*-i-lis. Ginger mint. Lat. slender. *M. arvensis* × *M. spicata*. Cult.

longifolia (L.) Huds. long-gi-*foh*-lee-uh. Horse mint. Lat. long-leaved. Eur., Africa, W Asia.

×*piperita* L. pip-uh-*ree*-tuh. Peppermint. Lat. peppery. *M. aquatica* × *M. spicata*. Cult. 'Citrata'. sit-*rah*-tuh. Lemon mint. Lat. like *Citrus* (the scent).

pulegium L. pue-*lee*-gee-oom. Pennyroyal. The Lat. name, from Lat. flea (it was used as a repellant). Eur., N Africa, W and C Asia.

requienii Benth. rek-wee-*en*-ee-ee. Corsican mint. After French naturalist Esprit Requien (1788–1851), who described it as a species of *Thymus*. Corsica, Sardinia.

spicata L. spi-*kah*-tuh. Spearmint. Lat. in spikes (the flowers). SE Eur., Egypt, SW Asia.

suaveolens Ehrh. sway-vee-*oh*-luhnz. Apple mint. Lat. sweet-smelling. Eur., N Africa, W Turkey.

×*villosa* Huds. vil-*oh*-suh. Lat. with long hairs. *M. spicata* × *M. suaveolens*. Eur.

Mentzelia L. (Loasaceae). ment-*zee*-lee-uh. Blazing star. After Christian Mentzel (1622–1701), German bota-

nist and physician. 80 spp., herbs, shrubs, trees. SW Canada, W and S USA to S Am.

laevicaulis (Douglas) Torr. & A. Gray. lee-vi-*kaw*-lis. Lat. smooth-stemmed. SW Canada, W USA.

lindleyi Torr. & A. Gray. *lind*-lee-ee. After English botanist John Lindley (1799–1865), who described it as *Bartonia aurea*. SW USA.

Menyanthes L. (Menyanthaceae). men-ee-*anth*-eez. Name used by Theophrastus for an aquatic plant, from Gk. moon flower. 1 sp., aquatic herb. Circumboreal.

trifoliata L. trie-foh-lee-*ah*-tuh. Bogbean. Lat. with three leaves (leaflets).

Menziesia Sm. (Ericaceae). men-*zeez*-ee-uh. After Archibald Menzies (1754–1842), Scottish surgeon and naturalist with the Royal Navy, who collected the type specimen of *M. ferruginea* in 1788. 10 spp. deciduous shrubs. Canada, USA, NE Asia.

ciliicalyx Maxim. sil-ee-i-*kay*-lix. Lat. with a fringed calyx. Japan.

Mertensia Roth (Boraginaceae). mer-*tenz*-ee-uh. After Frank Carl Mertens (1764–1831), German botanist. 45 spp. perenn. herbs. N Am., Eur., Asia.

maritima (L.) A. Gray. muh-*rit*-i-muh. Oyster plant. Lat. of the sea (it grows on coasts). Circumpolar.

virginica (L.) Pers. ex Link. vir-*jin*-i-kuh. Virginia bluebells. Of Virginia. SE Canada, E USA.

mescal bean *Calia secundiflora*

Mespilus L. (Rosaceae). *mes*-pil-oos. Lat. name of the medlar. 1 sp., deciduous shrub or tree. SE Eur., W and C Asia.
germanica L. jer-*man*-i-kuh. Medlar. Lat. of Germany.

Metasequoia Miki ex Hu & W. C. Cheng (Cupressaceae). me-tuh-see-*kwoy*-uh. From Gk. changed, and the related *Sequoia*. 1 sp., deciduous conifer. C China.
glyptostroboides Hu & W. C. Cheng. glip-toh-strob-*oy*-deez. Dawn redwood. Like the related *Glyptostrobus*.

Meum Mill. (Apiaceae). *mee*-oom. Gk. name for *M. athamanticum*. 3 spp. perenn. herbs. Eur., N Africa.
athamanticum Jacq. ath-uh-*man*-ti-koom. Baldmoney. Of Mount Athamas. Sicily.

Mexican hat *Ratibida columnifera*
Mexican orange blossom *Choisya ternata*
Mexican tea *Dysphania ambrosioides*
mezereon *Daphne mezereum*

Microbiota Komarov (Cupressaceae). mik-roh-bie-*oh*-tuh. Gk. small, *Biota* (*Thuja*). 1 sp., shrubby conifer. E Siberia.
decussata Komarov. dee-kus-*ah*-tuh. Lat. with leaves arranged in adjacent pairs, at right angles.

mile-a-minute *Fallopia baldschuanica*

Milium L. (Poaceae). *mil*-ee-oom. The Lat. (from Gk.) name for millet. 5 spp. grasses. Eur., temp. Asia, N Am.

effusum L. ee-*few*-soom. Millet grass. Lat. open, spread out (the inflorescence).

milkweed *Asclepias*. **butterfly** *A. tuberosa*. **common** *A. syriaca*. **poke** *A. exaltata*. **prairie** *A. sullivantii*. **purple** *A. purpurascens*. **showy** *A. speciosa*. **spider** *A. asperula*. **swamp** *A. incarnata*. **whorled** *A. verticillata*
milkwort *Polygala*

Mimosa L. (Fabaceae). mi-*moh*-suh. From Gk. mimic, referring to the sensitive leaves. 500 spp., trees, shrubs, herbs, climbers. Mostly trop. Am.
pudica L. *pew*-di-kuh. Sensitive plant. Lat. shy (it shrinks away when touched). Trop. Am.

mimosa *Acacia dealbata*. **prairie** *Desmanthus illinoensis*

Mimulus L. (Phrymaceae). *mim*-ew-loos. Monkey flower. Lat. mimic (the flowers have been likened to a monkey's face). 91 spp., ann. and perenn. herbs, shrubs. W N Am. to S Am., Africa, Asia.
aurantiacus Curtis. o-ran-tee-*ah*-koos. Lat. orange (the flowers). W USA, NW Mex.
cardinalis Douglas ex Benth. kar-di-*nah*-lis. Cardinal monkey flower. Lat. scarlet (the flowers). W USA, N Mex.
guttatus Fisch. ex DC. gu-*tah*-toos. Lat. spotted (the flowers). SW Canada, W USA, N Mex.
luteus L. *lue*-tee-oos. Yellow monkey flower. Lat. yellow (the flowers). Chile.

ringens L. *ring*-uhnz. Allegheny monkey flower. Lat. wide open (the flowers). Canada, USA.

mind-your-own-business *Soleirolia soleirolii*
miniature grape ivy *Cissus striata*
mint *Mentha.* **apple** *M. suaveolens.* **corn** *M. arvensis.* **Corsican** *M. requienii.* **field** *M. arvensis.* **ginger** *M.* ×*gracilis.* **horse** *M. longifolia.* **lemon** *M.* ×*piperita* 'Citrata'. **water** *M. aquatica*

Mirabilis L. (Nyctaginaceae). mi-*ra*-bi-lis. Lat. wonderful. 60 spp. perenn. herbs. N and S Am.
jalapa L. huh-*lah*-puh. Four o'clock plant, marvel of Peru. An old generic name applied to a herb grown near Jalapa (Xalapa). Mex.
multiflora (Torr.) A. Gray. mul-ti-*flaw*-ruh. Lat. many-flowered. W USA, N Mex.

Miscanthus Anderss. (Poaceae). mis-*kanth*-oos. From Gk. stalk, flower, referring to the stalked spikelets. 15 spp. grasses. SE Asia, S Africa.
×***giganteus*** J. M. Greef & Deuter ex Hodk. & Renvoize. jie-*gan*-tee-oos. Lat. very large. *M. sinensis* × *M. sacchariflorus.* Cult.
nepalensis (Trin.) Hack. nep-uh-*len*-sis. Of Nepal. Himal., W China.
sacchariflorus (Maxim.) Hack. sak-uh-ri-*flaw*-roos. Lat. with flowers like *Saccharum.* E Asia.
sinensis Anderss. si-*nen*-sis. Lat. of China. China, Taiwan, Japan, Korea. subsp. ***condensatus*** (Hack.) T. Koyama. kon-den-*sah*-toos. Lat. dense (the panicles).

transmorrisonensis Hayata = *M. sinensis*

mission bells *Fritillaria biflora*

Mitchella L. (Rubiaceae). mi-*chel*-uh. After John Mitchell (1711–1768), American botanist, physician and geographer, who first described it under another name. 2 spp. perenn. herbs. N Am., Guatemala, Japan.
repens L. *ree*-puhnz. Partridge berry. Lat. creeping. E Canada, E and C USA, Mex., Guatemala.

Mitella L. (Saxifragaceae). mie-*tel*-uh. Mitrewort. Lat. a small headband or turban, referring to the cap-shaped fruit. 20 spp. perenn. herbs. Canada, USA, E Asia.
breweri A. Gray. *brue*-uh-ree. After American botanist William Henry Brewer (1828–1910), who collected the type specimen in 1863 during the Geological Survey of California. SW Canada, W USA.
diphylla L. die-*fil*-uh. Gk. two-leaved (each flowering stem). SE Canada, E USA.

Mitraria Cav. (Gesneriaceae). mie-*trair*-ree-uh. From Gk. turban or cap, referring to the fruit. 1 sp., evergreen climber. Chile, Argentina.
coccinea Cav. kok-*sin*-ee-uh. Lat. scarlet (the flowers).

mitrewort *Mitella*
moccasin flower *Cypripedium*
mock orange *Philadelphus, P. coronarius.* **desert** *P. microphyllus*

Modiolastrum K. Schum. (Malvaceae). mod-ee-oh-*las*-troom. Lat. somewhat like *Modiola*, a related genus (from Lat. hub of a wheel, referring to the fruit). 7 spp. herbs. S Am.
lateritium (Hook.) Krapov. lat-uh-*rit*-ee-oom. Lat. brick-coloured (the flowers). Argentina, Brazil, Paraguay, Uruguay.

Molinia Schrank (Poaceae). mo-*lin*-ee-uh. After Juan Ignacio Molina (1740–1829), Chilean priest and botanist. 2 spp. grasses, Eur., N. Africa, Asia.
caerulea (L.) Moench. kie-*rue*-lee-uh. Purple moor grass. Lat. blue. Eur., N Africa, W and C Asia. subsp. *arundinacea* (Schrank) K. Richt. uh-run-di-*nay*-see-uh. Lat. reed-like.

Moluccella L. (Lamiaceae). mol-ue-*kel*-uh. Diminutive of Molucca (*M. spinosa* was thought to originate in the Moluccas). 2 spp. ann. or perenn. herbs. S and E Eur., N Africa, W and C Asia.
laevis L. *lee*-vis. Bells of Ireland. Lat. smooth (the shoots and leaves). E Eur., W and C Asia.

Monarda L. (Lamiaceae). mon-*ar*-duh. Bee balm, horsemint. After Nicolás Bautista Monardes (1493–1588), Spanish physician and botanist. 16 spp. ann. and perenn. herbs. N Am.
bradburyana L. C. Beck. brad-buh-ree-*ah*-nuh. After Scottish botanist John Bradbury (1768–1823), who had recently died, as "a tribute to the memory of a highly valued friend and distinguished botanist." C and SE USA.

citriodora Cerv. ex Lag. sit-ree-oh-*dor*-ruh. Lemon bee balm. Lat. lemon-scented. E and C USA, Mex.
didyma L. *did*-i-muh. Oswego tea. Lat. in pairs (the stamens). E USA.
fistulosa L. fist-ew-*loh*-suh. Lat. with hollow stems. Canada, USA, N Mex.
punctata L. punk-*tah*-tuh. Spotted bee balm. Lat. spotted (the corolla). E USA, NE Mex.

mondograss *Ophiopogon japonicus*
moneywort *Lysimachia nummularia*
monkey flower *Mimulus*. **Allegheny** *M. ringens*. **cardinal** *M. cardinalis*. **yellow** *M. luteus*
monkey puzzle *Araucaria araucana*
montbretia *Crocosmia*

Monstera Adans. (Araceae). mon-*ste*-ruh. From Lat. strange, monstrous (the often perforated leaves). 40 spp. evergreen climbers. S Mex. to S Am.
deliciosa Liebm. del-is-ee-*oh*-suh. Swiss cheese plant. Lat. delicious (the fruit). S Mex. to Panama.

moonflower *Ipomoea alba*

Morella Lour. (Myricaceae). mo-*rel*-uh. Diminutive of *Morus* (the fruits were likened to a small mulberry). 46 spp., trees, shrubs. Widespread.
cerifera (L.) Small. se-*ri*-fuh-ruh. Southern bayberry. Lat. bearing wax (candle wax can be obtained from the fruits). E USA to Panama.
pensylvanica (Mirb.) Kartesz. pen-sil-*van*-i-kuh. Northern bayberry. Of Pennsylvania. E N Am.

Morina L. (Caprifoliaceae). mo-*ree*-nuh. After Louis Morin (1635–

1715), French botanist and physician. 10 spp. perenn. herbs. SE Eur. to W China.

longifolia Wall. ex DC. long-gi-*foh*-lee-uh. Lat. long-leaved. Himal., S Tibet.

Morus L. (Moraceae). *mo*-roos. Mulberries. Lat. name for *M. nigra*. 12 spp., trees, shrubs. N and S Am., Eur., Africa, Asia.

alba L. *al*-buh. White mulberry. Lat. white (the fruits, sometimes). China.

nigra L. *nie*-gruh. Black mulberry. Lat. black (the fruit). SW Asia.

mosaic plant *Fittonia albivenis, Ludwigia sedoides*
mosquito plant *Agastache cana*
mother-in-law's tongue *Sansevieria trifasciata*
mother of thousands *Saxifraga stolonifera*
mountain ash *Sorbus aucuparia*. **American** *S. americana*
mountain cottonwood *Ozothamnus leptophyllus*
mountain pepper *Tasmannia lanceolata*
mountain whitethorn *Ceanothus cordulatus*
mourning widow *Geranium phaeum*
mouse-ear chickweed *Cerastium*. **alpine** *C. alpinum*
mouse plant *Arisarum vulgare*
Mrs Robb's bonnet *Euphorbia amygdaloides* subsp. *robbiae*

Muehlenbeckia Meissn. (Polygonaceae). mue-luhn-*bek*-ee-uh. After Henri (Heinrich) Gustav Muehlenbeck (1798–1845), French physician and botanist. 22 spp. climbing and creeping shrubs. C and S Am., New Guinea, Australia, NZ.

complexa (A. Cunn.) Meissn. kom-*plex*-uh. Lat. embracing (the tepals enlarge to surround the fruit). NZ.

mugwort *Artemisia vulgaris*

Mukdenia Koidz. (Saxifragaceae). mook-*den*-ee-uh. Of Shenyang (Mukden). 1 sp., perenn. herb. NE China, Korea.

rossii (Oliv.) Koidz. *ros*-ee-ee. After Scottish missionary John Ross (1842–1915), who collected the type specimen in NE China.

mulberry *Morus*. **black** *M. nigra*. **paper** *Broussonetia papyrifera*. **white** *Morus alba*
mullein *Verbascum*. **common** *V. thapsus*. **nettle-leaved** *V. chaixii*. **purple** *V. phoeniceum*

Muscari Mill. (Asparagaceae). moos-*kah*-ree. Grape hyacinth. The Turkish name. 42 spp. bulbous herbs. N Africa, Eur., Medit., W and C Asia.

armeniacum Leichtlin ex Baker. ar-men-ee-*ah*-koom. Of Armenia. SE Eur., Caucasus.

azureum Fenzl. uh-*zew*-ree-oom. Lat. blue (the flowers). Turkey.

botryoides (L.) Mill. bot-ree-*oy*-deez. Lat. like a bunch of grapes (the clustered flowers). Eur.

comosum (L.) Parl. ko-*moh*-soom. Tassel hyacinth. Lat. in tufts (the flowers). N Africa, S and E Eur., W Asia.

latifolium J. Kirk. lat-i-*foh*-lee-oom. Lat. broad-leaved. Turkey.

mustard, black *Brassica nigra*. **Chinese** *B. juncea*. **white** *B. hirta*

Myosotidium Hook. (Boraginaceae). mie-oh-soh-*tid*-ee-oom. Gk. diminutive of *Myosotis*. 1 sp., perenn. herb. Chatham Is. (NZ).
hortensia (Decne.) Baill. hor-*ten*-see-uh. Chatham Island forget-me-not. Lat. of gardens (it was originally described from cultivated plants).

Myosotis L. (Boraginaceae). mie-oh-*soh*-tis. Forget-me-nots. Gk. mouse ear, from the shape of the leaves. 50 spp. ann. and perenn. herbs. N Am., Eur., Asia, Africa, Australia.
palustris Hill = *M. scorpioides*
scorpioides L. skor-pee-*oy*-deez. Water forget-me-not. Lat. curled like a scorpion's tail (the inflorescence). Eur. to E Siberia.
sylvatica Hoffm. sil-*vat*-i-kuh. Wood forget-me-not. Lat. of woods. Eur., W Asia, Himal.

Myrica L. (Myricaceae). *mi*-ri-kuh. Gk. name for *Tamarix*. 2 spp. shrubs. N temp. regs.
cerifera L. = *Morella cerifera*
gale L. *gah*-lee. Bog myrtle. From the Old English name. Canada, USA, Eur., E Asia.

pensylvanica Mirb. = *Morella pensylvanica*

Myriophyllum L. (Haloragaceae). mi-ree-*of*-i-loom. Water milfoil. Gk. many leaves, the leaves are finely divided. 40 spp. aquatic herbs. Widespread.
aquaticum (Vell.) Verdc. uh-*kwat*-i-koom. Parrot's feather. Lat. of water. S Am.

myrobalan *Prunus cerasifera*

Myrrhis Mill. (Apiaceae). *mi*-ris. The Gk. name, used by Dioscorides. 1 sp., perenn. herb. C and S Eur.
odorata (L.) Scop. oh-do-*rah*-tuh. Sweet Cicely. Lat. fragrant.

myrtle *Myrtus communis*. **sea** *Baccharis halimifolia*. **Tarentum** *Myrtus communis* 'Tarentina'

Myrtus L. (Myrtaceae). *mur*-toos. The Lat. (from Gk.) name for *M. communis*. 2 spp. shrubs. Medit.
communis L. *kom*-ew-nis. Myrtle. Lat. common. '**Tarentina**'. ta-ren-*tee*-nuh. Tarentum myrtle. Lat. of Tarento, S Italy.
ugni Molina = *Ugni molinae*

Nandina Thunb. (Berberidaceae). nan-*deen*-uh. From the Japanese name. 1 sp., evergreen shrub. China, Japan.
domestica Thunb. do-*mest*-i-kuh. Heavenly bamboo, sacred bamboo. Lat. of the home (i.e., cultivated).

Narcissus L. (Amaryllidaceae). nar-*sis*-oos. Daffodils. After Narcissus of Gk. myth. A plant appeared where he died after gazing at his own reflection in a pool. 57 spp. bulbous herbs. Eur., Medit., N Africa, W Asia.
bulbocodium L. bul-boh-*koh*-dee-oom. Hoop-petticoat daffodil. Gk. with a woolly bulb. SW Eur., NW Africa.
obvallaris Salisb. ob-vuh-*lah*-ris. Tenby daffodil. Lat. surrounded by ramparts (referring to the lobed corona). S Wales.
papyraceus Ker Gawl. pap-i-*ray*-see-oos. Paper white daffodil. Lat. papery (the white flowers). Medit.
poeticus L. poh-*et*-i-koos. Poet's daffodil. Lat. of poets. S and E Eur.
pseudonarcissus L. sue-doh-nar-*sis*-oos. Wild daffodil. Gk. false *Narcissus*. W Eur.

romieuxii Braun-Blanq. & Maire. rom-*ew*-ee-ee. After Swiss botanist Henri Auguste Romieux (1857–1937), who grew it in his Geneva garden. Algeria, Morocco.

Nassella (Trin.) E. Desv. (Poaceae). nas-*el*-uh. Possibly from Lat. name for a narrow-necked basket used for catching fish, from the appearance of the spikelets. 116 spp. grasses. Mostly S Am.
tenuissima (Trin.) Barkworth. ten-ew-*is*-i-muh. Lat. most slender. SW USA, N Mex.

Nasturtium R. Br. (Brassicaceae). nuh-*stur*-shum. From Lat. twisted nose, referring to the scent. 5 spp. perenn. herbs. USA to C Am., Eur., N Africa, W and C Asia.
officinale W. T. Aiton. of-is-i-*nah*-lee. Watercress. Lat. sold as a med. herb. Eur., N Africa, W and C Asia.

nasturtium *Tropaeolum majus*
navelwort *Umbilicus rupestris*
nectarine *Prunus persica*

Nectaroscordum bulgaricum Janka = *Allium siculum* subsp. *dioscoridis*
siculum (Ucria) Lindl. = *Allium siculum*

Neillia D. Don (Rosaceae). *neel*-ee-uh. After Patrick Neill (1776–1851), Scottish botanist and friend of the author, David Don. 15 spp. shrubs. C and E Asia.
affinis Hemsl. *af*-i-nis. Lat. related to (*N. gracilis*). China.
incisa (Thunb.) S. Oh. in-*sie*-suh. Lat. sharply cut (the leaves). Japan.

tanakae Franch. & Sav. ta-*nah*-kie. After Japanese botanist Yoshio Tanaka (1838–1916). Japan.
thibetica Bureau & Franch. ti-*bet*-i-kuh. Of Tibet. W China.

Nemesia Vent. (Scrophulariaceae). nem-*ee*-see-uh. Gk. name used by Dioscorides for a similar plant. 70 spp., ann. and perenn. herbs, subshrubs. Trop. and S Africa.
denticulata (Benth.) Grant ex Fourc. den-tik-ew-*lah*-tuh. Lat. with small teeth (the leaves). S Africa.

Nemophila Nutt. (Boraginaceae). nem-*of*-i-luh. Gk. glade-loving (they grow in shady woods). 11 spp. ann. herbs. W N Am.
maculata Benth. ex Lindl. mak-ew-*lah*-tuh. Fivespot. Lat. spotted (the corolla). SW USA.
menziesii Hook. & Arn. men-*zeez*-ee-ee. Baby blue-eyes. After Scottish surgeon and naturalist Archibald Menzies (1754–1842), who collected it. W USA, NW Mex.

Nepeta L. (Lamiaceae). ne-*pee*-tuh, *ne*-pi-tuh. Catmint. The Lat. name, from Nepi (Nepete), Tuscany. 250 spp., ann. and perenn. herbs, subshrubs. Eur., Asia, N and trop. Africa.
cataria L. ka-*tah*-ree-uh. Catmint, catnip. Lat. of cats (which like it). Eur., W and C Asia, Himal.
×*faassenii* Bergm. ex Stearn. fah-*sen*-ee-ee. After Johannes Hubertus Faassen (1892–1963), in whose Dutch nursery it was raised. *N. mussinii* × *N. nepetella*. Cult.
govaniana (Wall. ex Benth.) Benth. guv-an-ee-*ah*-nuh. After George

Govan (1787–1865), correspondent of author Wallich and first superintendent of the Saharanpur Botanical Garden, N India. Himal.
grandiflora M. Bieb. gran-di-*flaw*-ruh. Lat. large-flowered. W Asia.
nervosa Royle ex Benth. ner-*voh*-suh. Lat. (prominently) veined (the leaves). Himal.
nuda L. *new*-duh. Lat. naked (without hairs). Eur., W and C Asia.
racemosa Lam. ras-i-*moh*-suh. Lat. with flowers in racemes. W Asia.
sibirica L. si-*bi*-ri-kuh. Lat. of Siberia. N China, E Siberia.
subsessilis Maxim. sub-*ses*-i-lis. Lat. almost unstalked (the leaves). Japan.

Nephrolepis Schott (Lomariopsidaceae). nef-roh-*lep*-is. Gk. with kidney-shaped scales (covering the spore-producing bodies). 25 spp. ferns. Widespread in warm regs.
exaltata (L.) Schott. ex-al-*tah*-tuh. Lat. very high (grows on trees as an epiphyte). Trop. Am. **'Bostoniensis'**. bos-toh-nee-*en*-sis. Boston fern. Of Boston, to where it was introduced.

Nerine Herb. (Amaryllidaceae). ne-*ree*-nee. After Nerine, a sea nymph of Gk. myth. 25 spp. bulbous herbs. S Africa.
bowdenii W. Watson. bow-*den*-ee-ee. After Athelstan Hall Cornish-Bowden (1871–1942), English-born surveyor general of the Cape Colony, who sent plants to England from S Africa in 1902.
sarniensis (L.) Herb. sarn-ee-*en*-sis. Guernsey lily. Lat. of Guernsey (Lat. *Sarnia*), where it was thought to have established as a result of a shipwreck.

undulata (L.) Herb. un-dew-*lah*-tuh. Lat. wavy (the perianth lobes).

Nerium L. (Apocynaceae). *ne*-ree-oom. Gk. name for *N. oleander*. 1 sp., evergreen shrub. Medit. to Japan.
oleander L. ol-ee-*an*-der. Oleander. From the Italian name, referring to the resemblance of the foliage to that of the olive (*Olea*).

Nertera Banks & Sol. ex Gaertn. (Rubiaceae). *ner*-tuh-ruh. From Gk. low, referring to their habit. 15 spp. perenn. herbs. Taiwan to New Guinea, Australia, NZ, Mex. to S Am.
depressa Banks & Sol. ex Gaertn. = *N. granadensis*
granadensis (Mutis ex L.f.) Druce. gran-uh-*den*-sis. Bead plant. Of (New) Granada (now Colombia), whence it was described.

nerve plant *Fittonia albivenis*
nettle tree *Celtis*
New Jersey tea *Ceanothus americanus*

Nicandra Adans. (Solanaceae). nik-*an*-druh. After Nicander, poet of Colophon, Turkey, who wrote about plants ca. 100 BCE. 1 sp., ann. herb. Peru.
physalodes (L.) Gaertn. fie-suh-*loh*-deez. Apple of Peru. Like *Physalis*.

Nicotiana L. (Solanaceae). ni-kot-ee-*ah*-nuh. After Jean Nicot (1530–1600), French diplomat and ambassador to Portugal, from where he introduced tobacco to France. 75 spp., ann. and perenn. herbs, shrubs. Trop. Am., SW Africa, Australia.

glauca Graham. *glaw*-kuh. Tree tobacco. Lat. bluish white (the leaves). S Am.
langsdorffii Weinm. langz-*dorf*-ee-ee. After German-born Georg Heinrich (Grigori Ivanovitch) von Langsdorff (1774–1852), who sent seeds to Europe while Russian consul in Rio de Janeiro. Brazil.
rustica L. *rust*-i-kuh. Wild tobacco. Lat. of the country (i.e., wild). Bolivia, Ecuador, Peru.
sylvestris Speg. & Comes. sil-*ves*-tris. Lat. of woods. Bolivia, Argentina.
tabacum L. tab-*ak*-oom. Tobacco. From a Caribbean name of a pipe used to smoke this and other material. Cult.

Nierembergia Ruiz & Pav. (Solanaceae). near-ruhm-*berg*-ee-uh. After Juan Eusebio Nieremberg (1595–1658), Spanish priest and naturalist. 20 spp., ann. and perenn. herbs, subshrubs. Mex. to S Am.
linariifolia Graham. lin-ah-ree-i-*foh*-lee-uh. Cup flower. Lat. with leaves like *Linaria*. S Am.

Nigella L. (Ranunculaceae). ni-*jel*-uh. Diminutive of Lat. black, referring to the seeds. 20 spp. ann. herbs. Eur., N Africa, W and C Asia.
damascena L. dam-uh-*seen*-uh. Love-in-a-mist. Lat. of Damascus. Eur., W Asia.
hispanica L. his-*pan*-i-kuh. Fennel flower. Lat. of Spain. SW Eur., N Africa.
sativa L. sa-*tee*-vuh. Black cumin. Lat. cultivated. W Asia.

ninebark *Physocarpus opulifolius.*
Pacific *P. capitatus*

Nipponanthemum Kitam. (Asteraceae). ni-pon-*anth*-uh-moom. From Nippon (Japanese for Japan), and Gk. flower. 1 sp., subshrub. Japan.
nipponicum (Maxim.) Kitam. ni-*pon*-i-koom. Of Japan.

Nolina recurvata (Lem.) Hemsl. = *Beaucarnea recurvata*

Nothofagus Blume (Nothofagaceae). noth-oh-*fay*-goos. Southern beeches. Gk. false *Fagus.* 34 spp., trees, shrubs. New Guinea to Australia, NZ, S Am.
alpina (Poepp. & Endl.) Oerst. al-*pie*-nuh. Lat. alpine. Chile, Argentina.
antarctica (G. Forst.) Oerst. an-*tark*-ti-kuh. Antarctic beech. Of Antarctic regs. Chile.
dombeyi (Mirbel) Blume. *dom*-bee-ee. After French botanist Joseph Dombey (1742–1794), who collected the type specimen in Chile. Chile, Argentina.
obliqua (Mirbel) Blume. o-*bleek*-wuh. Roble beech. Lat. oblique (the leaf base). Chile, Argentina.
procera (Poepp. & Endl.) Oerst. = *N. alpina*

Notholithocarpus Manos, Cannon & S. H. Oh (Fagaceae). noth-oh-lith-oh-*kar*-poos. Gk. false *Lithocarpus.* 1 sp., evergreen tree or shrub. Calif., Oregon.
densiflorus Manos, Cannon & S. H. Oh. dens-i-*flaw*-roos. Tanbark oak. Lat. densely flowered.

Notospartium carmichaeliae Hook.f. = *Carmichaelia carmichaeliae*
glabrescens Petrie = *Carmichaelia glabrescens*

Nymphaea L. (Nymphaeaceae). *nimf*-ee-uh. Waterlilies. From Gk. nymph. 40 spp. aquatic herbs. Widespread.
alba L. *al*-buh. European waterlily. Lat. white (the flowers). Eur., N Africa, W Asia.
odorata Aiton. oh-do-*rah*-tuh. Fragrant waterlily. Lat. fragrant (the flowers). Americas.

Nyssa L. (Cornaceae). *nis*-uh. Name of a water nymph in Gk. myth. The first species named, *N. aquatica*, grows in swamps. 8 spp. trees. SE Canada, USA, Mex., E Asia.
sinensis Oliv. sin-*en*-sis. Lat. of China. China, Myanmar.
sylvatica Marshall. sil-*vat*-i-kuh. Sour gum, tupelo. Lat. of woods. SE Canada to Mex.

oak *Quercus*. **Algerian** *Q. canariensis*.
black *Q. velutina*. **bur** *Q. macro-carpa*. **chestnut** *Q. montana*. **chest-nut-leaved** *Q. castaneifolia*. **cork** *Q. suber*. **Daimio** *Q. dentata*. **English** *Q. robur*. **Gambel** *Q. gambelii*. **holm** *Q. ilex*. **Hungarian** *Q. frainetto*. **Jerusalem** *Dysphania botrys*. **live** *Quercus virginiana*. **loquat** *Q. ryso-phylla*. **Nuttall's** *Q. texana*. **Oregon** *Q. garryana*. **overcup** *Q. lyrata*. **pin** *Q. palustris*. **red** *Q. rubra*. **sawtooth** *Q. acutissima*. **scarlet** *Q. coccinea*. **sessile** *Q. petraea*. **shingle** *Q. imbri-caria*. **southern red** *Q. falcata*. **swamp red** *Q. shumardii*. **swamp Spanish** *Q. pagoda*. **swamp white** *Q. bicolor*. **tanbark** *Notholithocarpus densiflorus*. **turkey** *Quercus cerris*. **valley** *Q. lobata*. **water** *Q. nigra*. **white** *Q. alba*. **willow** *Q. phellos*. **yellow chestnut** *Q. muehlenbergii*
oats *Avena sativa*
obedient plant *Physostegia virginiana*
ocean spray *Holodiscus discolor*

Ocimum L. (Lamiaceae). *o*-ki-moom. Gk. name used by Theophrastus for an aromatic herb. 100 spp., herbs, shrubs. Widespread in warm and trop. regs.

americanum L. uh-me-ri-*kah*-noom. African basil, American basil. Of America, where it was thought to be native, though introduced. Africa, trop. Asia.
basilicum L. buh-*sil*-i-koom. Basil. From Gk. royal, of kings. Trop. Asia.
tenuiflorum L. ten-ew-i-*flaw*-room. Lat. with slender flowers. Trop. Asia to N Australia.

Oemleria Rchb. (Rosaceae). urm-*le*-ree-uh. After German naturalist Augustus Gottlieb Oemler (1773–1852), who lived in Georgia, USA, and sent American plants to Reichenbach. 1 sp., deciduous shrub. SW Canada, W USA.
cerasiformis (Torr. & A. Gray ex Hook. & Arn.) J. W. Landon. ke-ruh-si-*form*-is. Osoberry. Lat. cherry-shaped (the fruit).

Oenothera L. (Onagraceae). ee-*noth*-uh-ruh. Gk. name for another plant, possibly *Nerium oleander*, from Gk. donkey catcher. 145 spp., ann., bienn. and perenn. herbs, subshrubs. N and S Am. and other regions from hybrid origin.
biennis L. bie-*en*-is. Evening primrose. Lat. biennial. Canada, USA.
fruticosa L. frue-ti-*koh*-suh. Sundrops. Lat. shrubby. E N Am. subsp. *glauca* (Michx.) Straley. *glaw*-kuh. Lat. blu-ish white (the leaves).
glazioviana Micheli. glaz-ee-ov-ee-*ah*-nuh. After French botanist Auguste François Marie Glaziou (1828–1906), who collected the type specimen in Brazil in 1868. Cult.
lindheimeri (Engelm. & A. Gray) W. L. Wagner & Hoch. lind-*hie*-

muh-ree. After German-Texan botanist Ferdinand Jacob Lindheimer
(1801–1879), who collected the type
specimen in Texas in 1842. S USA.
macrocarpa Nutt. mak-roh-*kar*-puh.
Gk. large-fruited. C USA, N Mex.
serrulata Nutt. se-rue-*lah*-tuh. Lat.
finely toothed (the leaves). Canada,
USA, N Mex.
speciosa Nutt. spee-see-*oh*-suh. White
evening primrose. Lat. showy (the
flowers). E and C USA, N Mex.
stricta Ledeb. ex Link. *strik*-tuh. Lat.
upright (the stems). Argentina,
Chile.
suffrutescens (Ser.) W. L. Wagner &
Hoch. suh-frue-*tes*-uhnz. Lat. subshrubby. W Canada, W and C USA,
Mex.

okra *Abelmoschus esculentus*. **musk**
A. moschatus
old man's beard *Clematis vitalba*
old man's whiskers *Geum triflorum*

Olea L. (Oleaceae). *oh*-lee-uh. Lat.
name of the olive. 33 spp., evergreen
shrubs, trees. Medit. to China and
SE Asia, Africa.
europaea L. ew-roh-*pee*-uh. Olive. Of
Europe. Medit. to China, S Africa.

oleander *Nerium oleander*

Olearia Moench (Asteraceae). o-lee-
ah-ree-uh, oh-*leer*-ree-uh. Daisy
bushes. After Adam Ölschläger (Lat.
Olearius) (1603–1671), German
scholar. 190 spp., shrubs, trees. Australia, New Guinea, NZ.
avicenniifolia (Raoul) Hook.f. av-i-
sen-ee-i-*foh*-lee-uh. With leaves like
Avicennia (mangrove). NZ.

cheesemanii Cockayne & Allan.
cheez-*man*-ee-ee. After English-born
NZ botanist Thomas Frederick
Cheeseman (1846–1923), who collected the type specimen in 1897.
NZ.
macrodonta Baker. mak-roh-*don*-tuh.
Gk. with large teeth (the leaves). NZ.
nummularifolia (Hook.f.) Hook.f.
num-ew-lah-ri-*foh*-lee-uh. Lat. with
coin-shaped leaves. NZ.
phlogopappa (Labill.) DC. flog-oh-
pap-uh. Gk. with a *Phlox*- or flame-
like pappus (the hairs attached to the
seeds). SE Australia.
×*scilloniensis* Dorrien-Smith. sil-oh-
nee-*en*-sis. Of the Isles of Scilly, UK,
where it was raised. *O. lirata* × *O.
phlogopappa*. Cult.
stellulata DC. stel-ew-*lah*-tuh. Lat.
with small stars (the flowers).
Tasmania.
traversii (F. Muell.) Hook.f. = *O.
traversiorum*
traversiorum (F. Muell.) Hook.f.
tra-vurs-ee-*or*-room. After Irish-born
NZ lawyer and naturalist William
Thomas Locke Travers (1819–1903)
and his son, Henry Hammersley
Travers (1844–1928). Chatham Is.
(NZ).
virgata (Hook.f.) Hook.f. vir-*gah*-tuh.
Lat. twiggy. NZ.
'**Waikariensis**'. wie-kah-ree-*en*-sis. Of
Waikari, NZ.

Oligoneuron album (Nutt.) G. L.
Nesom = *Solidago ptarmicoides*

olive *Olea europaea*

Omphalodes Mill. (Boraginaceae).
omf-uh-*loh*-deez. Gk. navel-like,

referring to the seeds. 30 spp. ann., bienn. and perenn. herbs. Eur., W Asia, N Africa, Mex.

cappadocica (Willd.) DC. kap-uh-*doh*-si-kuh. Lat. of Cappadocia (now part of Turkey). NE Turkey, Georgia.

verna Moench. *ver*-nuh. Blue-eyed Mary. Lat. of spring (flowering). C and SE Eur.

onion *Allium cepa*. **tree** *A.* ×*proliferum*. **tumbleweed** *A. schubertii*. **Welsh** *A. fistulosum*

Onoclea L. (Onocleaceae). on-*ok*-lee-uh. Gk. name used by Dioscorides for another plant, from Gk. closed cup (the sori are enclosed by the revolute leaf margins). 1 sp., fern. Canada, USA, E Asia.

sensibilis L. sen-*si*-bi-lis. Sensitive fern. Lat. sensitive (to early frosts).

Onopordum L. (Asteraceae). on-oh-*por*-doom. From the Gk. name, from Gk. donkey flatulence, according to Pliny's report of the effects of eating them. 40 spp. bienn. herbs. Eur. and Medit. to C Asia.

acanthium L. uh-*kanth*-ee-oom. Cotton thistle. Gk. name for a thistle or similar plant, from Gk. spiny.

Ophiopogon Ker Gawl. (Asparagaceae). of-ee-oh-*poh*-gon. Lilyturf. Gk. snake's beard (from the Japanese name). 67 spp. perenn. herbs. E Asia.

jaburan (Siebold) Lodd. *jab*-ue-ran. Giant lilyturf, white lilyturf. From the Japanese name. Japan, Korea.

japonicus (Thunb.) Ker Gawl. juh-*pon*-i-koos. Dwarf lilyturf, mondo-

grass. Of Japan. China, Korea, Japan, SE Asia.

planiscapus Nakai. plan-i-*skay*-poos. Lat. with a flat scape (inflorescence stalk). Japan. **'Nigrescens'**. nig-*res*-uhnz. Black lilyturf. Lat. blackish (the foliage).

Opuntia Mill. (Cactaceae). o-*poon*-tee-uh. Prickly pears. Gk. of Opus. The name was used by Theophrastus for a plant that grew near that ancient Greek city. 200 spp. cacti. Americas.

humifusa (Raf.) Raf. hew-mi-*few*-suh. Creeping prickly pear. Lat. low spreading (its habit). SE Canada, E and C USA.

polyacantha Haw. pol-ee-uh-*kanth*-uh. Gk. with many spines. W Canada, W and C USA, N Mex.

orache *Atriplex hortensis*. **sea** *A. halimus*

orange *Citrus* ×*aurantium*

orchid, broad-leaved marsh *Dactylorhiza majalis*. **common spotted** *D. fuchsii*. **heath spotted** *D. maculata*. **lion's moustache** *Angraecum leonis*. **Madeiran** *Dactylorhiza foliosa*. **northern marsh** *D. purpurella*. **robust marsh** *D. elata*. **southern marsh** *D. praetermissa*. **star of Bethlehem** *Angraecum sesquipedale*

oregano *Origanum vulgare*. **Cuban** *Plectranthus amboinicus*

Oregon grape *Mahonia aquifolium*

Origanum L. (Lamiaceae). o-ri-*gah*-noom. From Gk. name of an aromatic plant, from Gk. mountain bright. 20 spp., herbs, small shrubs. Eur. and Medit. to China, Taiwan.

amanum Post. uh-*mah*-noom. Of the Amanus Mts. S Turkey.

dictamnus L. dik-*tam*-noos. Cretan dittany. From the Gk. name. Crete.

laevigatum Boiss. lee-vi-*gah*-toom. Lat. smooth (the leaves). Turkey, Cyprus.

majorana L. mah-jo-*rah*-nuh. Sweet marjoram. From Gk./Lat. name of an aromatic herb. Turkey, Cyprus.

onites L. oh-*nie*-teez. Pot marjoram. Gk. of donkeys (which eat it). SE Eur., Turkey.

vulgare L. vul-*gar*-ree. Oregano, wild marjoram. Lat. common. subsp. *hirtum* (Link) Ietsw. *hir*-toom. Lat. hairy (the leaves). SE Eur., Turkey, Cyprus.

Ornithogalum L. (Asparagaceae). or-ni-*tho*-guh-loom. From Gk. bird's milk, a term used by the Romans for something wonderful. 180 spp. bulbous herbs. Eur., N Africa, W and C Asia, E and S Africa.

candicans (Baker) J. C. Manning & Goldblatt. *kan*-di-kanz. Summer hyacinth. Lat. white (the flowers). S Africa.

nutans L. *new*-tanz. Lat. nodding (the flowers). SE Eur., Turkey.

umbellatum L. um-buhl-*ah*-toom. Star of Bethlehem. Lat. in umbels (the flowers). Eur., SW Asia.

viridiflorum (I. Verd.) J. C. Manning & Goldblatt. vi-ri-di-*flaw*-room. Lat. green-flowered. S Africa.

Orontium L. (Araceae). o-*ron*-tee-oom. Gk. name of an aquatic plant on the River Orontes (Lebanon, Syria, Turkey). 1 sp., aquatic herb. E USA.

aquaticum L. uh-*kwat*-i-koom. Golden club. Lat. of water.

Oryzopsis hymenoides (Roem. & Schult.) Ricker ex Piper = *Achnatherum hymenoides*

miliacea (L.) Benth. & Hook.f. ex Asch. & Schweinf. = *Piptatherum miliaceum*

Osage orange *Maclura pomifera*
osier, common *Salix viminalis*. **purple** *S. purpurea*

Osmanthus Lour. (Oleaceae). oz-*manth*-oos. From Gk. fragrant flower. 30 spp., evergreen trees, shrubs. Asia, SE USA, Mex.

americanus (L.) Benth. & Hook.f. ex A. Gray. uh-me-ri-*kah*-noos. Devilwood. Of America. SE USA, Mex.

×*burkwoodii* (Burkw. & Skipw.) P. S. Green. burk-*wood*-ee-ee. Of the Burkwood & Skipwith nursery, where it was raised. *O. decorus* × *O. delavayi*. Cult.

decorus (Boiss. & Bal.) Kasapl. *dek*-o-roos. Lat. ornamental. Turkey, Armenia, Georgia.

delavayi Franch. del-uh-*vay*-ee. After French missionary Jean Marie Delavay (1834–1895), who collected the type specimen in Yunnan in 1883. SW China.

×*fortunei* Carrière. for-*tewn*-ee-ee. After Robert Fortune (1812–1880), Scottish botanist and plant collector who introduced it to gardens in 1862. *O. fragrans* × *O. heterophyllus*. Cult.

fragrans Lour. *fray*-gruhns. Lat. fragrant (the flowers). Himal., China, Japan, Thailand.

heterophyllus (G. Don) P. S. Green. het-uh-roh-*fil*-oos. Gk. with varied leaves (entire and toothed on the same plant). Japan, Taiwan.

Osmunda L. (Osmundaceae). oz-*moon*-duh. Medieval Lat. name for another fern, possibly after Osmunder, Saxon name for the Norse god Thor. 10 spp. ferns. Widespread.

cinnamomea L. = *Osmundastrum cinnamomeum*

claytoniana L. klay-ton-ee-*ah*-nuh. Interrupted fern. After John Clayton (1694–1773), English-born botanist who moved to Virginia, and from whose specimens Linnaeus named it. E Canada, NE USA, E Asia.

regalis L. ree-*gah*-lis. Royal fern. Lat. royal.

Osmundastrum C. Presl (Osmundaceae). oz-moond-*ast*-room. Lat. somewhat like *Osmunda*. 1 sp., fern. E N Am. to S Am., E Asia.

cinnamomeum (L.) C. Presl. sin-uh-*mohm*-ee-oom. Cinnamon fern. Cinnamon-coloured (the fronds).

osoberry *Oemleria cerasiformis*

Osteospermum L. (Asteraceae). ost-ee-oh-*sperm*-oom. From Gk. bony seed, referring to the hard seed coat. 70 spp., ann. and perenn. herbs, shrubs. S Africa to Arabia.

ecklonii (DC.) Norl. ek-*lon*-ee-ee. After Danish apothecary Christian Friedrich Ecklon (1795–1868), one of the early botanical explorers of the Cape, who collected the type specimen. S Africa.

jucundum (E. Phillips) Norl. ju-*kun*-doom. Lat. delightful, pleasing. S Africa.

Ostrya Scop. (Betulaceae). *os*-tree-uh. Lat. name of a tree, from Gk. scale, referring to the scaly fruit clusters. 9 spp., trees, shrubs. N and C Am., Eur., temp. Asia.

carpinifolia Scop. kar-pie-ni-*foh*-lee-uh. Hop hornbeam. Lat. with leaves like *Carpinus*. S Eur., W Asia.

virginiana (Mill.) K. Koch. vir-jin-ee-*ah*-nuh. American hop hornbeam, ironwood. Of Virginia. Canada to C Am.

Oswego tea *Monarda didyma*

Othonna L. (Asteraceae). oth-*on*-uh. From Gk. linen, from the white hairs covering the leaves of some species. 150 spp., herbs, small shrubs. Africa.

cheirifolia L. kie-ri-*foh*-lee-uh. Gk. with wallflower-like leaves. S Africa.

our Lord's candle *Hesperoyucca whipplei*

owl's claws *Hymenoxys hoopesii*

Oxalis L. (Oxalidaceae). ox-*ah*-lis. Sorrel. From Gk. sharp, referring to the sour taste of the leaves. 700 spp., ann. and perenn., often bulbous, herbs, shrubs. Widespread.

acetosella L. uh-see-toh-*sel*-uh. Wood sorrel. Diminutive of Lat. vinegar (from the acidic taste). Eur., Asia.

adenophylla Gillies ex Hook. & Arn. uh-den-oh-*fil*-uh. Gk. glandular-leaved (from the dark leaflet stalks, which were originally thought to be glandular). Chile, Argentina.

bowiei Herb. ex Lindl. *boh*-ee-ee.
After Kew gardener James Bowie (ca.
1789–1869), who collected plants in
S Africa. S Africa.

enneaphylla Cav. en-ee-uh-*fil*-uh. Gk.
with nine leaves (leaflets). Patagonia,
Falklands.

magellanica G. Forst. ma-juh-*lan*-i-
kuh. Of the Magellan reg. Patagonia,
SE Australia.

oregana Nutt. o-ri-*gah*-nuh. Redwood
sorrel. Of Oregon. W USA.

regnellii Miq. = *O. triangularis*

triangularis A. St. Hil. trie-ang-ew-
lah-ris. Lat. triangular (the leaflets).
S Am. subsp. ***papilionacea***
(Hoffmanns. ex Zucc.) Lourteig.
pa-pil-ee-on-*ay*-see-uh. Lat. butterfly-
like (the leaves).

versicolor L. ver-*si*-ko-lor. Lat. variably
coloured (the flowers). S Africa.

ox-eye *Buphthalmum*
oxlip *Primula elatior*

Oxydendrum DC. (Ericaceae). ox-ee-
den-droom. From Gk. sharp tree,
from the acidic taste of the leaves.
1 sp., deciduous tree. E USA.

arboreum (L.) DC. ar-*bor*-ree-oom.
Sorrel tree, sourwood. Lat. tree-like.

oyster plant *Mertensia maritima*

Ozothamnus R. Br. (Asteraceae).
oz-oh-*tham*-noos. From Gk. scented
shrub, referring to the often aromatic
foliage. 50 spp., evergreen shrubs,
trees. New Caledonia, Australia, NZ.

ledifolius (DC.) Hook.f. led-i-*foh*-lee-
oos. Kerosene bush. Lat. with leaves
like *Ledum*. Tasmania.

leptophyllus (G. Forst.) Breitw. &
J. M. Ward. lep-toh-*fil*-oos. Mountain cottonwood. Gk. with slender
leaves. NZ.

rosmarinifolius (Labill.) DC.
roz-ma-ri-ni-*foh*-lee-oos. Lat. with
leaves like *Rosmarinus*. SE Australia.

Pachyphragma (DC.) Rchb. (Brassicaceae). pak-ee-*frag*-muh. From Gk. thick partition, referring to the relatively thick septum that divides the fruit. 1 sp., perenn. herb. Caucasus.
macrophyllum (Hoffm.) Busch. mak-*rof*-i-loom. Gk. large-leaved (compared to species of *Thlaspi*, in which it was originally included).

Pachysandra Michx. (Buxaceae). pak-is-*an*-druh. From Gk. thick male, referring to the thick filaments of the stamens. 3 spp. subshrubs. SE USA, China, Taiwan, Japan.
procumbens Michx. proh-*kum*-buhnz. Allegheny spurge. Lat. creeping. SE USA.
terminalis Sieb. & Zucc. ter-min-*ah*-lis. Lat. terminal (the inflorescence, unlike the other two species). China, Japan.

Pachystachys Nees (Acanthaceae). pak-ee-*stak*-is. Gk. thick spike, referring to the stout inflorescence. 12 spp. evergreen shrubs. Trop. Am.
lutea Nees. lue-tee-uh. Lollipop plant. Lat. yellow (the bracts). Ecuador, Peru.

Packera Á. Löve & D. Löve (Asteraceae). *pak*-uh-ruh. After Canadian botanist John G. Packer (b. 1929), who worked on this group. 64 spp. ann., bienn. and perenn. herbs. N Am., Siberia.
aurea (L.) Á. Löve & D. Löve. *aw*-ree-uh. Golden ragwort. Lat. golden (the flowers). E Canada, E and C USA.

Paeonia L. (Paeoniaceae). pee-*oh*-nee-uh. Peonies. Gk. name used by Dioscorides, meaning of Paeon, in Gk. myth. physician to the gods., from the med. properties. 30 spp., perenn. herbs, shrubs. Eur., N Africa, temp. Asia, W USA, NW Mex.
cambessedesii (Willk.) Willk. = *P. corsica*
corsica Sieber ex Tausch. *kor*-si-kuh. Lat. of Corsica. Balearic Is., Corsica, Sardinia.
delavayi Franch. del-uh-*vay*-ee. After French missionary Jean Marie Delavay (1834–1895), who collected the type specimen in Yunnan in 1888. China. **Lutea Group**. *lue*-tee-uh. Lat. yellow (the flowers).
lactiflora Pall. lak-ti-*flaw*-ruh. Lat. with milky-coloured flowers. NE Asia.
×*lemoinei* Rehder. luh-*mwun*-ee-ee. After French plant breeder Victor Lemoine (1823–1911), in whose nursery it was raised. *P. delavayi* × *P. suffruticosa*. Cult.
ludlowii (Stern & Taylor) D. Y. Hong. lud-*loh*-ee-ee. After English army officer and botanist Frank Ludlow (1885–1972), who, with George Sherriff and George Taylor, collected the type specimen in Tibet in 1951. Tibet.

lutea Delavay ex Franch. = *P. delavayi*
Lutea Group. var. *ludlowii* Stern &
Taylor = *P. ludlowii*
mlokosewitschii Lomakin. mlo-kos-
uh-*vich*-ee-ee. After Polish naturalist
Ludwik Franciszek Mlokosewitsch
(1831–1909), who collected the type
specimen in Georgia in 1901.
Caucasus.
officinalis L. o-fis-i-*nah*-lis. Lat. sold
as a med. herb. Eur.
suffruticosa Andrews. suh-frue-ti-
koh-sa. Lat. subshrubby. China.
tenuifolia L. ten-ew-i-*foh*-lee-uh. Lat.
with slender leaves. E Eur., Caucasus.
veitchii Lynch. *veech*-ee-ee. After the
nursery of James Veitch & Sons. The
type specimen was taken from a
plant grown from seed that E. H.
Wilson collected for them. China.

pagoda tree *Styphnolobium japonicum*
palm, bamboo *Chamaedorea seifrizii*.
California fan *Washingtonia filifera*.
Canary Island *Phoenix canariensis*.
cardboard *Zamia furfuracea*. **date**
Phoenix dactylifera. **dwarf fan**
Chamaerops humilis. **lady** *Rhapis*.
metallic *Chamaedorea metallica*.
Mexican fan *Washingtonia robusta*.
parlour *Chamaedorea elegans*.
pygmy date *Phoenix roebelenii*. **reed**
Chamaedorea seifrizii. **windmill**
Trachycarpus fortunei

Pandorea (Endl.) Spach (Bignoniaceae). pan-*dor*-ree-uh. After Pandora
of Gk. myth. 6 spp. climbers. SE Asia
to Australia.
jasminoides (Lindl.) K. Schum. jaz-
min-*oy*-deez. Bower plant. Lat. like
Jasminum. E Australia.

Panicum L. (Poaceae). *pan*-i-koom.
Lat. name for a kind of millet, from
Lat. bread. 500 spp. grasses. Tropics,
temp. N Am.
virgatum L. vir-*gah*-toom. Switch
grass. Lat. twiggy. Canada to C Am.,
Cuba.

pansy *Viola* ×*wittrockiana*

Papaver L. (Papaveraceae). puh-*pah*-
vuh. Poppies. Lat. name for poppy.
80 spp. ann. and perenn. herbs. Eur.,
N Africa, Asia, W N Am.
alpinum L. al-*pie*-noom. Alpine
poppy. Lat. alpine. Eur.
nudicaule L. new-di-*kaw*-lee. Arctic
poppy, Icelandic poppy. Lat. with a
bare stem (all the leaves are basal).
N Am (Alaska, Yukon), C and
NE Asia.
orientale L. o-ree-en-*tah*-lee. Oriental
poppy. Lat. eastern. W Asia.
rhoeas L. *ree*-uhs. Corn poppy. The
Gk. name, from Gk. red. Eur., N
Africa, W Asia.
rupifragum Boiss. & Reut. rue-pi-
frah-goom. Spanish poppy. Lat.
breaking rocks (it grows in crevices).
Spain, Morocco.
somniferum L. som-*nif*-uh-room.
Opium poppy. Lat. bearing sleep. S
Eur., N Africa.

papyrus *Cyperus papyrus*
para-cress *Acmella oleracea*

Paradisea Mazzuc. (Asparagaceae).
pa-ruh-*diz*-ee-uh. After Giovanni
Paradisi (1760–1820), Italian botanist and senator. 2 spp. perenn. herbs.
C and SW Eur.

liliastrum (L.) Bertol. lil-ee-*as*-troom. St. Bruno's lily. Lat. somewhat like *Lilium*.
lusitanica (Cout.) Samp. lue-si-*tan*-i-kuh. Lat. of Portugal. Spain, N Portugal.

Parahebe catarractae (G. Forst.) W. R. B. Oliv. = *Veronica catarractae*
lyallii (Hook.f.) W. R. B. Oliv. = *Veronica lyallii*
perfoliata (R. Br.) B. G. Briggs & Ehrend. = *Veronica perfoliata*

parasol whitetop *Doellingeria umbellata*

Paris L. (Melanthiaceae). *pa*-ris. From Lat. equal, referring to the four symmetrically arranged leaves. 26 spp. perenn. herbs. Eur., Asia.
polyphylla Sm. pol-ee-*fil*-uh. Gk. many-leaved. Himal., China, SE Asia.
quadrifolia L. kwod-ri-*foh*-lee-uh. Herb Paris. Lat. with four leaves. Eur., Siberia, N China.

Parrotia C. A. Mey. (Hamamelidaceae). puh-*rot*-ee-uh. After Johann Jacob Friedrich Wilhelm Parrot (1792–1841), German physician and naturalist. 2 spp., deciduous trees, shrubs. W Asia, China.
persica (DC.) C. A. Mey. *per*-si-kuh. Persian ironwood. Lat. of Persia (Iran). N Iran, Azerbaijan.

parrot's bill *Clianthus puniceus*
parrot's feather *Myriophyllum aquaticum*
parsley *Petroselinum crispum*
parsnip *Pastinaca sativa*

Parthenium L. (Asteraceae). par-*then*-ee-oom. From the Gk. name of a related plant, from Gk. virgin. 16 spp., ann. and perenn. herbs, shrubs. USA to S Am.
integrifolium L. in-teg-ri-*foh*-lee-oom. American feverfew. Lat. with untoothed leaves. E and C USA.

Parthenocissus Planch. (Vitaceae). par-then-oh-*sis*-oos. Gk. virgin ivy, from Virginia creeper, the common name of *P. quinquefolia*. 12 spp. woody climbers. N and C Am., E Asia.
henryana (Hemsl.) Diels & Gilg. After Augustine Henry (1857–1930), Scottish-born Irish plantsman who collected the type specimen ca. 1885. China.
himalayana (Royle) Planch. him-uh-lay-*ah*-nuh. Of the Himalaya. Himal.
quinquefolia (L.) Planch. kwink-wi-*foh*-lee-uh. Virginia creeper. Gk. with five leaves (leaflets). SE Canada, E and C USA, Mex., Guatemala.
tricuspidata (Sieb. & Zucc.) Planch. trie-kus-pi-*dah*-tuh. Boston ivy. Lat. with three points (the leaves). China, Taiwan, Korea, Japan. **'Lowii'**. *loh*-ee-ee. After Messrs Low & Sons, nurserymen, who raised it. **'Veitchii'**. *veech*-ee-ee. After British plant collector and nurseryman John Gould Veitch (1839–1870), who introduced the species ca. 1862.

partridge berry *Gaultheria procumbens, Mitchella repens*
pasque flower *Anemone pulsatilla*

Passiflora L. (Passifloraceae). pas-i-*flaw*-ruh. Passion flowers. Lat.

passion flower, from a likening of parts of the flower to objects related to the Passion. 530 spp., woody and herbaceous climbers, shrubs, trees. Warm and trop. Am., SE Asia, Australia, Pacific Is.
caerulea L. kie-*rue*-lee-uh. Blue passion flower. Lat. blue. Argentina, Brazil, Paraguay, Uruguay.
edulis Sims. *ed*-ew-lis. Granadilla. Lat. edible (the fruit). Argentina, Brazil, Paraguay.
incarnata L. in-kar-*nah*-tuh. Maypop. Lat. flesh-coloured (the flowers). E and C USA.

passion flower *Passiflora*. blue *P. caerulea*

Pastinaca L. (Apiaceae). pas-ti-*na*-kuh. Lat. name for parsnip and carrot. 14 spp. bienn. and perenn. herbs. Eur., Asia.
sativa L. sa-*tee*-vuh. Parsnip. Lat. cultivated. Eur., W Asia.

Patrinia Juss. (Valerianaceae). puh-*trin*-ee-uh. After French naturalist Eugène Louis Melchior Patrin (1742–1815), who collected plants in Siberia. 20 spp. bienn. and perenn. herbs. C and E Asia.
scabiosifolia Fisch. ex Link. skay-bee-oh-si-*foh*-lee-uh. Lat. with leaves like *Scabiosa*. E Asia.
triloba Miq. trie-*loh*-buh. Lat. three-lobed (the leaves). Japan.

Paulownia Sieb. & Zucc. (Paulowniaceae). paw-*loh*-nee-uh. After Grand Duchess Anna Pavlovna (Paulowna) of Russia (1795–1865), daughter of Czar Paul I. 7 spp. trees. China, SE Asia.
elongata S. Y. Hu. ee-long-*ah*-tuh. Lat. elongated (the inflorescence). China.
fortunei (Seem.) Hemsl. for-*tewn*-ee-ee. After Scottish botanist Robert Fortune (1812–1880), who collected the type specimen in China. China, Taiwan, Laos, Vietnam.
tomentosa (Thunb.) Steud. to-men-*toh*-suh. Empress tree. Lat. hairy (the leaves). China.

pawpaw *Asimina triloba*

Paxistima Raf. (Celastraceae). pax-i-*steem*-uh. From Gk. thick stigma. 2 spp. evergreen shrubs. Canada to N Mex.
canbyi A. Gray. *kan*-bee-ee. After American businessman William Marriott Canby (1831–1904), who collected the type specimen ca. 1868. E USA.
myrsinites (Pursh) Raf. mur-sin-*ie*-teez. Gk. like myrtle (*Myrtus communis*). SW Canada, W USA, N Mex.

pea *Pisum sativum*. perennial *Lathyrus latifolius*. sweet *L. odoratus*
pea tree *Caragana arborescens*
peace lily *Spathiphyllum*
peach *Prunus persica*
peacock flower *Dietes bicolor, Tigridia pavonia*
pear *Pyrus*. Asian *P. pyrifolia*. Callery *P. calleryana*. common *P. communis*. sand *P. pyrifolia*. Ussurian *P. ussuriensis*. willow-leaved *P. salicifolia*
pearlbush *Exochorda racemosa*
pearlwort *Sagina subulata*

pebble plants *Lithops*
pecan *Carya illinoinensis*

Pelargonium L'Hér. (Geraniaceae).
pel-ar-*goh*-nee-oom. From Gk. stork,
referring to the similarity of the fruit
to a stork's beak. 280 spp., ann. and
perenn. herbs, subshrubs. Africa, SW
Asia, Australia.

Pennisetum Rich. (Poaceae). pen-i-*see*-
toom. Gk. feather bristle, referring to
the inflorescence. 80 spp. grasses.
Widespread, trop. to warm temp.
regs.
×*advena* Wipff & Veldkamp ad-*veen*-
uh. Lat. stranger, foreigner (from its
mistaken identity and unknown origin). *P. macrostachyum* × *P. setaceum*.
Cult. '**Rubrum**'. *rue*-broom. Purple
fountain grass. Lat. red (the foliage).
alopecuroides (L.) Spreng. al-oh-pek-
ew-*roy*-deez. Lat. like *Alopecurus*. E
and SE Asia, Australia.
macrourum Trin. mak-roh-*ew*-room.
Gk. large tail (the long inflorescence).
S Africa.
orientale Rich. o-ree-en-*tah*-lee. Lat.
eastern. N Africa, W and C Asia,
Himal.
setaceum (Forssk.) Chiov. see-*tay*-see-
oom. Fountain grass. Lat. bristly (the
inflorescence). Africa, SW Asia.
'**Rubrum**' = *P.* ×*advena* 'Rubrum'
villosum R. Br. ex Fresen. vil-*oh*-soom.
Feathertop. Lat. softly hairy (the
inflorescence). NE Africa, Yemen.

pennyroyal *Mentha pulegium*
pennywort *Umbilicus rupestris*

Penstemon Schmidel (Plantaginaceae). pen-*stem*-uhn. Gk. five stamens
(present in each flower, one of which
is sterile). 250 spp., herbs, shrubs. N
and C Am.
barbatus (Cav.) Roth. bar-*bah*-toos.
Lat. bearded (the lower lip of the
corolla). SW USA, NW Mex.
campanulatus (Cav.) Willd. kam-
pan-ew-*lah*-toos. Lat. bell-shaped
(the flowers). Mex.
cobaea Nutt. *koh*-bee-uh. From the
resemblance of the flowers to those of
Cobaea. C USA.
cyananthus Hook. sie-uhn-*anth*-oos.
Gk. blue-flowered. W USA.
digitalis Nutt. ex Sims. dij-i-*tah*-lis.
Lat. like a foxglove (*Digitalis*). E
Canada, E and C USA.
eatonii A. Gray. ee-*ton*-ee-ee. After
American botanist Daniel Cady
Eaton (1834–1895), who was with
Sereno Watson when he collected
the type specimen in Utah in 1869.
W USA.
fruticosus (Pursh) Greene. frue-ti-*koh*-
soos. Lat. shrubby. SW Canada,
NW USA.
glaber Pursh. *glay*-ber. Lat. glabrous
(the foliage). C USA.
grandiflorus Nutt. gran-di-*flaw*-roos.
Lat. large-flowered. C and NW
USA.
heterophyllus Lindl. het-uh-roh-*fil*-
oos. Lat. with variable leaves (the
upper leaves are much narrower than
the lower). Calif.
hirsutus (L.) Willd. hir-*sue*-toos. Lat.
hairy (the stems). SE Canada, E
USA. '**Pygmaeus**'. *pig*-mee-oos. Lat.
dwarf.
palmeri A. Gray. *palm*-uh-ree. After
English-born botanist and archaeologist Edward Palmer (1829–1911),
who collected the type specimen

with Elliott Coues in Arizona in 1866. SW USA.

pinifolius Greene. pin-i-*foh*-lee-oos. Lat. with leaves like *Pinus*. SW USA, N Mex.

procerus Douglas ex Graham. *pros*-uh-ruhs. Lat. tall. W Canada, W USA.

rydbergii A. Nelson. rid-*berg*-ee-ee. After Swedish-born American botanist Per Axel Rydberg (1860–1931), for his generous assistance to the author, Aven Nelson. W USA.

smallii A. Heller. *smawl*-ee-ee. After American botanist John Kunkel Small (1869–1938), who collected the type specimen with author Amos Arthur Heller in North Carolina in 1890. SE USA.

strictus Benth. *strik*-toos. Lat. upright. W USA.

whippleanus A. Gray. wip-uhl-ee-*ah*-noos. After Amiel Weeks Whipple (1818–1863), American army surveyor on whose expedition to find a rail route to the Pacific in 1853 John Bigelow collected the type specimen in New Mexico. W USA.

peony *Paeonia*

Peperomia Ruiz & Pav. (Piperaceae). pe-puh-*roh*-mee-uh. Gk. like pepper. 1600 spp. herbs. Widespread, trop. and subtrop. regs.

argyreia (Miq.) E. Morren. ar-gi-*ree*-uh. Lat. silvery (the foliage). Brazil.

caperata Yunck. cap-uh-*rah*-tuh. Lat. wrinkled (the leaves). Brazil?

maculosa (L.) Hook. mak-ew-*loh*-suh. Lat. spotted (the stems). Mex. to S Am.

obtusifolia (L.) A. Dietr. ob-tew-si-*foh*-lee-uh. Lat. blunt-leaved. Florida to S Am.

pepper, bell *Capsicum annuum* Grossum Group. **bird** *C. frutescens*. **Cayenne** *C. annuum* Longum Group. **cherry** *C. annuum* Cerasiforme Group. **chili** *C. annuum* Longum Group. **cone** *C. annuum* Conoides Group. **red chili** *C. frutescens*. **red cone** *C. annuum* Fasciculatum Group

pepper tree *Pseudowintera colorata*

peppermint *Mentha* ×*piperita*. **narrow-leaved black** *Eucalyptus nicholii*

Pericallis D. Don (Asteraceae). pe-ree-*kal*-is. Gk. around beauty (the showy flowerheads). 14 spp., herbs, shrubs. Macaronesia.

×***hybrida*** (Regel) B. Nord. *hib*-ri-duh. Cineraria. Lat. hybrid. Cult.

lanata (L'Hér.) B. Nord. luh-*nah*-tuh. Lat. woolly (the leaves and stems). Tenerife.

Peritoma DC. (Cleomaceae). pe-ri-*toh*-muh. Gk. cut around, referring to the base of the calyx. 6 spp., ann. and perenn. herbs, shrubs. S Canada, USA, Mex.

serrulata (Pursh) DC. se-rue-*lah*-tuh. Rocky Mountain bee plant. Lat. finely toothed (the leaves). S Canada, USA.

periwinkle, greater *Vinca major*. **lesser** *V. minor*

Perovskia Kar. (Lamiaceae). pe-*rov*-skee-uh. After Vasily Alekseevich Perovsky (1794–1857), Russian general. 7 spp. subshrubs. SW Asia to China.

atriplicifolia Benth. a-tri-plis-i-*foh*-lee-uh. Lat. with leaves like *Atriplex*. Afghanistan to NW China.

Persea Mill. (Lauraceae). *per*-see-uh. Gk. name used by Dioscorides and Theophrastus for an evergreen tree with edible fruit, thought to be *Mimusops laurifolia*. 150 spp., trees, shrubs. New World trop. and subtrop. regs.
americana Mill. uh-me-ri-*kah*-nuh. Avocado. Of America. S Mex., C Am.

Persian ironwood *Parrotia persica*
Persian lilac *Melia azedarach*
Persian shield *Strobilanthes dyeriana*

Persicaria (L.) Mill. (Polygonaceae). per-si-*kair*-ree-uh. Lat./Gk. peach-like (Lat. *persica*), referring to the leaves of some species. 100 spp. ann. and perenn. herbs. Widespread.
affinis (D. Don) Ronse Decr. af-i-nis. Lat. related to (*P. vivipara*). Himal., Tibet.
alpina (All.) H. Gross. al-*pie*-nuh. Lat. alpine. Eur. to China.
amplexicaulis (D. Don) Ronse Decr. am-plex-i-*kawl*-is. Lat. clasping the stem (the leaf bases). Afghanistan to China.
bistorta (L.) Samp. bis-*tort*-uh. Bistort. Lat. twice twisted (the rhizomes). Eur., Morocco, W Asia to Japan.
campanulata (Hook.f.) Ronse Decr. kam-pan-ew-*lah*-tuh. Lat. bell-shaped (the flowers). Himal., W China.
capitata (Buch.-Ham. ex D. Don) H. Gross. kap-i-*tah*-tuh. Lat. in a head (the flowers). Himal., China, SE Asia.

microcephala D. Don. mik-roh-*kef*-uh-luh. Gk. small-headed (the inflorescence). Himal., China.
orientalis (L.) Spach. o-ree-en-*tah*-lis. Prince's feather. Lat. eastern. Iran to Japan, SE Asia, Australia.
tenuicaulis (Bisset & S. Moore) Cubey. ten-ew-i-*kaw*-lis. Lat. with slender stems. Japan.
vacciniifolia (Wall. ex Meisn.) Ronse Decr. vak-sin-ee-i-*foh*-lee-uh. Lat. with leaves like *Vaccinium*. Himal., Tibet.
virginiana (L.) Gaertn. vir-jin-ee-*ah*-nuh. Jumpseed. Of Virginia. SE Canada, E and C USA, Mex.

persimmon, American *Diospyros virginiana*. **Japanese** *D. kaki*

Petasites Mill. (Asteraceae). pet-uh-*sie*-teez. Butterbur. From Gk. a wide-brimmed hat, referring to the large leaves. 18 spp. perenn. herbs. Canada, USA, Eur., Asia.
japonicus (Sieb. & Zucc.) Maxim. juh-*pon*-i-koos. Of Japan. China, Korea, Japan. subsp. *giganteus* Kitam. jie-*gant*-ee-oos. Lat. very large. Japan.

Petroselinum Hill (Apiaceae). pet-roh-sel-*ee*-noom. Gk. name for parsley, from Gk. rock and name of a related plant. 2 spp. bienn. herbs. Eur., W Asia.
crispum (Mill.) Fuss. *kris*-poom. Parsley. Lat. curled (the leaves).

Petunia Juss. (Solanaceae). puh-*tew*-nee-uh. From an old French name (of S Am. origin) for the related tobacco. 3 spp. ann. and perenn. herbs. S Am.

×*hybrida* (Hook.) Vilm. *hib*-ri-duh.
Lat. hybrid. *P. axillaris* × *P. integrifolia*. Cult.

petunia, seaside *Calibrachoa parviflora*

Peucedanum L. (Apiaceae). pew-*sed*-
uh-noom. Gk. name for one of the
species. 100 spp. perenn. herbs. Eur.,
Africa, Asia.
verticillare (L.) K. Koch ex DC.
vur-ti-si-*lah*-ree. Lat. in whorls (the
inflorescence branches). E Eur.

Phacelia Juss. (Boraginaceae).
fuh-*kee*-lee-uh. From Gk. bundle,
referring to the clustered flowers. 100
spp. ann., bienn. and perenn. herbs.
Americas.
campanularia A. Gray. kam-pan-ew-
lair-ree-uh. California bluebell. Lat.
bell-like (the flowers). Calif.
tanacetifolia Benth. tan-uh-see-ti-*foh*-
lee-uh. Fiddleneck. Lat. with leaves
like *Tanacetum*. SW USA, NW Mex.

Phalaris L. (Poaceae). fuh-*lah*-ris. Gk.
name of a grass. 18 spp. ann. and
perenn. grasses. Eur., Africa, Asia,
N Am.
arundinacea L. uh-run-di-*nay*-see-uh.
Gardener's garters, reed canary grass.
Lat. reed-like. Eur., N Africa, Asia,
Canada, USA. **'Picta'**. *pik*-tuh. Lat.
painted (the leaves).
canariensis L. kuh-nair-ree-*en*-sis.
Canary grass. Lat. of the Canary Is.
Madeira, Canary Is., N Africa.

Phaseolus L. (Fabaceae). fay-zee-*oh*-
loos. Beans. Gk. name of a kind of

bean. 50 spp. ann. and perenn., often
climbing herbs. Warm and trop. Am.
coccineus L. kok-*sin*-ee-oos. Runner
bean. Lat. scarlet (the flowers). Mex.
to S Am.
lunatus L. lue-*nah*-toos. Butter bean,
Lima bean. Lat. moon-shaped (the
pods). Mex. to S Am.
vulgaris L. vul-*gar*-ris. Dwarf bean,
French bean. Lat. common. Mex. to
S Am.

pheasant's eye *Adonis annua*

Phegopteris (C. Presl) Fée (Thelypteridaceae). feg-*op*-te-ris. From Gk.
beech fern. 4 spp. ferns. Canada,
USA, Eur., Asia.
connectilis (Michx.) Watt. kon-*ek*-ti-
lis. Beech fern. Lat. joined (the sori).
decursive-pinnata (H. C. Hall) Fée.
dee-*kur*-si-vee-pi-*nah*-tuh. Lat. with
pinnae extending along the rachis.
E and SE Asia.

Phellodendron Rupr. (Rutaceae).
fel-oh-*den*-dron. Cork trees. Gk.
cork tree, referring to the bark. 2 spp.
deciduous trees. E Asia.
amurense Rupr. am-ew-*ren*-see. Amur
cork tree. Of the Amur River. E Russia, NE China.

Philadelphus L. (Hydrangeaceae).
fil-uh-*delf*-oos. Mock oranges. Gk.
name of a plant, from Gk. brotherly
love, or for Ptolemy Philadelphus
(309–246 BCE), king of Egypt. 70
spp. shrubs. Temp. N hemisph.
coronarius L. ko-ro-*nair*-ree-oos.
Mock orange. Lat. of garlands. Eur.,
W Asia.

lewisii Pursh. lue-*is*-ee-ee. After Meriwether Lewis (1774–1809), American explorer of the Lewis and Clark expedition (1804–06), who collected the type specimen in Idaho in 1806. SW Canada, W USA.

microphyllus A. Gray. mik-*rof*-i-loos. Desert mock orange. Gk. small-leaved. W USA, NW Mex.

Phillyrea L. (Oleaceae). fil-i-*ree*-uh. The Gk. name, from Gk. leaf. 2 spp. evergreen shrubs, trees. Medit. to W Asia.

angustifolia L. an-gus-ti-*foh*-lee-uh. Lat. narrow-leaved. S Eur., N Africa.

latifolia L. lat-i-*foh*-lee-uh. Lat. broad-leaved.

Philodendron Schott (Araceae). fil-oh-*den*-dron. Gk. tree-loving (they are normally epiphytic). 700 spp. evergreen climbers. Trop. Am.

bipinnatifidum Scott ex Endl. bie-pin-at-i-*fid*-oom. Lat. twice pinnate (the leaves). S Am.

hederaceum (Jacq.) Schott. hed-uh-*ray*-see-oom. Lat. like *Hedera*. Mex. to S Am.

scandens K. Koch & Sello = *P. hederaceum*

Phlomis L. (Lamiaceae). *floh*-mis. From Gk. flame (the leaves of some were used as lamp wicks). 75 spp., perenn. herbs, shrubs. Medit. to China.

fruticosa L. frue-ti-*koh*-suh. Jerusalem sage. Lat. shrubby. Medit.

italica L. i-*tal*-i-kuh. Lat. of Italy, where it was thought to originate. Balearic Is.

purpurea L. pur-*pew*-ree-uh. Lat. purple (the flowers). SW Eur.

russeliana (Sims) Lag. ex Benth. rus-el-ee-*ah*-nuh. After English physician and naturalist Alexander Russell (1715–1768), who illustrated it in his *Natural History of Aleppo*. Syria.

samia L. *sah*-mee-uh. Lat. of Samos (Aegean Is.). SE Eur., Turkey.

tuberosa L. tew-buh-*roh*-suh. Lat. bearing tubers. Eur., W Asia to China.

Phlox L. (Polemoniaceae). *flox*. From Gk. flame, referring to the flowers. 70 spp. ann. and perenn. herbs. Canada, USA, N Mex.

×*arendsii* hort. uh-*rendz*-ee-ee. After German nurseryman Georg Arends (1863–1952), who raised it. *P. divaricata* × *P. paniculata*. Cult.

carolina L. ka-ro-*lie*-nuh. Of the Carolinas (whence it was described). SE USA.

divaricata L. di-va-ri-*kah*-tuh. Lat. wide-spreading (the branches). SE Canada, E USA. subsp. *laphamii* (Alph. Wood) Wherry. la-*fam*-ee-ee. After American naturalist Increase Lapham (1811–1875), who collected the type specimen in Wisconsin. E and C USA.

douglasii Hook. dug-*las*-ee-ee. After Scottish botanist David Douglas (1799–1834), who collected the type specimen in Oregon in 1826. W USA.

drummondii Hook. drum-*ond*-ee-ee. After Scottish naturalist Thomas Drummond (1793–1835). It was named from plants grown from seed he sent to Kew just before his death. Texas.

maculata L. mak-ew-*lah*-tuh. Lat. spotted (the stems). E USA.

paniculata L. pan-ik-ew-*lah*-tuh. Lat. in panicles (the flowers). E USA.

pilosa L. pi-*loh*-suh. Lat. hairy (the stems and leaves). SE Canada, E and C USA.

stolonifera L. stoh-lon-*if*-uh-ruh. Lat. bearing stolons. E USA.

subulata L. sub-ew-*lah*-tuh. Lat. awl-shaped (the leaves). SE Canada, E USA.

Phoenix L. (Arecaceae). *fee*-nix. Gk. name for date palm. 14 spp. palms. Africa to SE Asia.

canariensis Chabaud. kuh-nair-ree-*en*-sis. Lat. of the Canary Is. Canary Island palm. Canary Is.

dactylifera L. dak-ti-*lif*-uh-ruh. Date palm. Lat. bearing fingers (i.e., the dates). SW Asia to Pakistan.

roebelenii O'Brien. roh-buh-*len*-ee-ee. Pygmy date palm. After German orchid collector Carl Roebelen (1855–1927), who collected the type specimen in Laos. SW China, SE Asia.

Phormium J. R. & G. Forst. (Xanthorrhoeaceae). *form*-ee-oom. From Gk. a small basket (many products were woven from the leaf fibres). 2 spp. evergreen herbs. NZ.

colensoi Hook.f. kol-en-*zo*-ee. Mountain flax. After William Colenso (1811–1899), English-born NZ botanist.

cookianum Le Jol = *P. colensoi*

tenax J. R. & G. Forst. *ten*-ax. New Zealand flax. Lat. tough (the leaves).

Photinia Lindl. (Rosaceae). foh-*tin*-ee-uh. From Gk. shining, referring to the glossy foliage of some. 65 spp., evergreen and deciduous trees, shrubs. Himal., E Asia, Mex.

davidiana (Decne.) Cardot. da-vid-ee-*ah*-nuh. After French missionary, botanist and zoologist Armand David (1826–1900), who collected the type specimen in 1869. China, SE Asia.

×*fraseri* Dress. *fray*-zuh-ree. After Ollie W. Fraser, in whose Birmingham, Alabama, nursery it was first raised. *P. glabra* × *P. serratifolia*. Cult.

serratifolia (Desf.) Kalkman. suh-rah-ti-*foh*-lee-uh. Lat. with toothed leaves. E Asia.

villosa (Thunb.) DC. vil-*oh*-suh. Lat. with long hairs (on the shoots). China, Korea, Japan.

Phragmites Adans. (Poaceae). frag-*mie*-teez. From Gk. hedge reed. 4 spp. grasses. Widespread.

australis (Cav.) Steud. os-*trah*-lis. Common reed. Lat. southern.

Phuopsis (Griseb.) Hook.f. (Rubiaceae). fue-*op*-sis. From Gk. like a valerian. 1 sp., perenn. herb. W Asia.

stylosa (Trin.) B. D. Jackson. stie-*loh*-suh. Lat. with a (conspicuous) style.

Phygelius E. Meyer ex Benth. (Scrophulariaceae). fie-*jee*-lee-oos. Gk. fleeing from the sun (they tend to grow in shade). 2 spp. shrubs. S Africa.

aequalis Harv. ex Hiern. ee-*kwah*-lis. Lat. equal (the corolla lobes).

capensis E. Meyer ex Benth. kuh-*pen*-sis. Of the Cape.

×*rectus* Coombes. *rek*-toos. Lat. straight (the corolla tube). Cult.

Phyllostachys Sieb. & Zucc. (Poaceae). fil-oh-*stak*-is. Gk. leaf spike, referring to the inflorescence. 50 spp. bamboos. China.

aurea (Carrière) Rivière & C. Rivière. *aw*-ree-uh. Lat. golden (the culms).

aureosulcata McClure. aw-ree-oh-sul-*kah*-tuh. Lat. with golden grooves (the culms). '*Aureocaulis*'. aw-ree-oh-*kaw*-lis. Lat. golden-stemmed.

bambusoides Sieb. & Zucc. = *P. reticulata*

bissetii McClure. bi-*set*-ee-ee. After David Bisset, superintendent of the USDA Plant Introduction Station, Savannah, Georgia, 1924–57, to where it was introduced from China in 1941.

dulcis McClure. *dul*-sis. Lat. sweet (the edible shoots).

edulis (Carrière) J. Houz. *ed*-ew-lis. Lat. edible (the shoots).

nigra (Lodd.) Munro. *nie*-gruh. Black bamboo. Lat. black (the culms of some forms). '*Boryana*'. bo-ree-*ah*-nuh. Possibly for French naturalist Jean Baptiste Bory de Saint-Vincent (1778–1846). '*Henonis*'. hen-*oh*-nis. After Dr. Hénon, who introduced it to cultivation in France from Japan.

nuda McClure. *new*-duh. Lat. naked (referring to the lack of auricles and bristles on the leaf sheaths).

reticulata (Rupr.) K. Koch. re-tik-ew-*lah*-tuh. Lat. net-veined (the leaves).

viridiglaucescens (Carrière) Rivière & C. Rivière. vi-ri-dee-glaw-*kes*-uhnz. Lat. green becoming bluish white (the leaves).

vivax McClure. *vee*-vax. Lat. vigorous.

Physalis L. (Solanaceae). *fis*-uh-lis. From Gk. bladder, from the appearance of the fruit. 75 spp. ann. and perenn. herbs. Widespread, mainly warm and trop. Am.

alkekengi L. al-kuh-*ken*-jee. Chinese lantern. Gk. name used by Dioscorides from a related plant, originally from Persian via Arabic. Eur. to China. var. *franchetii* (Masters) Mak. fran-*shet*-ee-ee. After French botanist Adrien René Franchet (1834–1900).

ixocarpa Brot. ex Hornem. = *P. philadelphica*

philadelphica Lam. fil-uh-*delf*-i-kuh. Of Philadelphia. Mex., C Am.

Physocarpus (Cambess.) Raf. (Rosaceae). fie-soh-*karp*-oos. Gk. bladder fruit, referring to the inflated fruit. 20 spp. deciduous shrubs. Canada, USA, N Mex., China, NE Asia.

capitatus (Pursh) Kuntze. kap-i-*tah*-toos. Pacific ninebark. Lat. in a head (the flowers). SW Canada, W USA.

opulifolius (L.) Maxim. op-ew-li-*foh*-lee-oos. Ninebark. Lat. with leaves like *Viburnum opulus*. SE Canada, E and C USA.

Physostegia Benth. (Lamiaceae). fie-soh-*stee*-jee-uh. Gk. bladder covering, referring to the inflated calyx that covers the fruit. 12 spp. perenn. herbs. N Am.

virginiana (L.) Benth. vir-jin-ee-*ah*-nuh. Obedient plant. Of Virginia. Canada, E and C USA, N Mex.

Phytolacca L. (Phytolaccaceae). fie-toh-*lak*-uh. From Gk. plant, and Medieval Lat. (from Persian), a red dye, referring to the dye obtained from the fruit. 25 spp., perenn. herbs, shrubs, trees. N and S Am., Eur., Asia, Australia.
americana L. uh-me-ri-*kah*-nuh. Pokeweed. Of America. Canada, USA.

Picea A. Dietr. (Pinaceae). *pie*-see-uh. Spruces. Lat. name for a pine that produces pitch, from Lat. pitch. 35 spp. evergreen conifers. N Am., Eur., temp. Asia.
abies (L.) Karst. *ab*-ee-ayz. Norway spruce. Lat. name for fir (*Abies*). Eur. **'Clanbrassiliana'**. klan-bruh-sil-ee-*ah*-nuh. After James Hamilton (1730–1798), 2nd Earl of Clanbrassil, who discovered it. **'Nidiformis'**. nid-i-*form*-is. Lat. nest-shaped.
breweriana S. Watson. brew-uh-ree-*ah*-nuh. Brewer spruce. After American botanist William Henry Brewer (1828–1910), who discovered it in 1863. Oregon, Calif.
engelmannii Parry ex Engelm. eng-uhl-*man*-ee-ee. After George Engelmann (1809–1884), German-born botanist who worked on the flora of the W USA and described it under another name. SW Canada, W USA, N Mex.
glauca (Moench) Voss. *glaw*-kuh. White spruce. Lat. bluish white (the foliage). Canada, N USA. var. *albertiana* (S. Br.) Sarg. al-bert-ee-*ah*-nuh. Alberta white spruce. Of Alberta (Canada).
mariana (Mill.) Britton et al. ma-ree-*ah*-nuh. Black spruce. Of Maryland. Canada, N USA.

omorika (Pančić) Purk. o-*mo*-ri-kuh. Serbian spruce. From the native name. Serbia, Bosnia and Herzegovina.
orientalis (L.) Link. o-ree-en-*tah*-lis. Oriental spruce. Lat. eastern. Turkey, Georgia.
pungens Engelm. *pung*-uhnz. Blue spruce. Lat. sharp-pointed (the leaves). W USA.
purpurea Mast. pur-*pew*-ree-uh. Lat. purple (the young cones). W China.
sitchensis (Bong.) Carrière. sit-*chen*-sis. Sitka spruce. Of Sitka (Alaska). SW Canada, W USA.

pickaback plant *Tolmiea menziesii*
pickerel weed *Pontederia cordata*

Pieris D. Don (Ericaceae). *peer*-ris, pee-*e*-ris. From Pieria, the home of the Muses of Gk. myth. 7 spp., shrubs, trees. SE USA, Cuba, E Asia.
formosa (Wall.) D. Don. for-*moh*-suh. Lat. beautiful. Himal., China, SE Asia. **Forrestii Group**. fo-*rest*-ee-ee. After Scottish botanist and plant collector George Forrest (1873–1932), who introduced it to gardens. It was described (as *P. forrestii*) from plants grown from seed he collected in China ca. 1905.
japonica (Thunb.) D. Don ex G. Don. juh-*pon*-i-kuh. Of Japan. China, Taiwan, Japan.

pignut *Carya glabra*

Pilea Lindl. (Urticaceae). pie-*lee*-uh. From Lat. cap, from the appearance of the calyx. 400 spp., ann. and perenn. herbs, shrubs. Widespread in warm regs. except Australasia.

cadierei Gagnep. & Guillaumin. kad-ee-*e*-ree-ee. Aluminium plant. After R.P. (Révérend Père) Léopold Michel Cadière (1869–1955), French missionary. It was described from plants grown from his introduction from Vietnam. SW China, Vietnam.

microphylla (L.) Liebm. mik-*rof*-i-luh. Artillery plant. Gk. small-leaved. SE USA to S Am.

peperomioides Diels. pep-uh-roh-mee-oy-deez. Lat. like *Peperomia* (the leaves). China (Sichuan, Yunnan).

Pileostegia Hook.f. & Thomson. (Hydrangeaceae). pil-ee-oh-*stee*-gee-uh. Gk. cap covering, referring to the cap-like corolla. 3 spp. evergreen climbers. India, China, Japan.

viburnoides Hook.f. & Thomson. vie-burn-*oy*-deez. Lat. like *Viburnum* (the flowerheads). NE India, China, Japan.

pimpernel, blue *Anagallis monelli.* **bog** *A. tenella.* **scarlet** *A. arvensis*
pine *Pinus.* **arolla** *P. cembra.* **Austrian** *P. nigra.* **big-cone** *P. coulteri.* **black** *P. thunbergii.* **blue** *P. wallichiana.* **Bosnian** *P. heldreichii.* **bristlecone** *P. aristata.* **Corsican** *P. nigra* subsp. *laricio.* **dwarf Siberian** *P. pumila.* **eastern white** *P. strobus.* **Jack** *P. banksiana.* **Japanese red** *P. densiflora.* **Japanese white** *P. parviflora.* **Jeffrey** *P. jeffreyi.* **Kauri** *Agathis australis.* **King William** *Athrotaxis selaginoides.* **Korean** *Pinus koraiensis.* **lacebark** *P. bungeana.* **limber** *P. flexilis.* **loblolly** *P. taeda.* **lodgepole** *P. contorta* var. *latifolia.* **longleaf** *P. palustris.* **Macedonian** *P. peuce.* **maritime** *P. pinaster.* **Monterey** *P.*

radiata. **mountain** *P. mugo.* **New Caledonia** *Araucaria columnaris.* **Norfolk Island** *A. heterophylla.* **pitch** *Pinus rigida.* **red** *Dacrydium cupressinum, Pinus resinosa.* **Scots** *P. sylvestris.* **scrub** *P. virginiana.* **shore** *P. contorta.* **stone** *P. pinea.* **Tasmanian pencil** *Athrotaxis cupressoides.* **umbrella** *Pinus pinea, Sciadopitys verticillata.* **western white** *Pinus monticola.* **western yellow** *P. ponderosa.* **Weymouth** *P. strobus.* **Wollemi** *Wollemia nobilis*
pineapple *Ananas comosus*
pink *Dianthus.* **Carthusian** *D. carthusianorum.* **Cheddar** *D. gratianopolitanus.* **clove** *D. caryophyllus.* **maiden** *D. deltoides*
pink siris *Albizia julibrissin*

Pinus L. (Pinaceae). pie-noos. Pines. The Lat. name. 100 spp. evergreen conifers. N and C Am., Eur., N Africa, Asia.

aristata Engelm. a-ris-*tah*-tuh. Bristlecone pine. Lat. finely pointed (the cone scales). SW USA.

ayacahuite Ehrenb. ex Schltdl. ie-yak-uh-*weet*-ay. The native name. C Mex. to C Am.

banksiana Lamb. bank-see-*ah*-nuh. Jack pine. After English botanist and explorer Sir Joseph Banks (1743–1820), who informed the author, Aylmer Bourke Lambert, of the existence of the tree growing at Pains Hill, Surrey, from which it was described. Canada, NE USA.

bungeana Zucc. ex Lindl. bunj-ee-*ah*-nuh. Lacebark pine. After Russian botanist Alexander Georg von Bunge (1803–1890), who found it near Beijing in 1831. China.

cembra L. *sem*-bruh. Arolla pine. An Italian name for *Pinus pinea*. C and S Eur.

contorta Douglas ex Loudon. kon-*tor*-tuh. Shore pine. Lat. twisted (the stems of trees growing on the coast). W Canada, W USA. var. *latifolia* Engelm. lat-i-*foh*-lee-uh. Lodgepole pine. Lat. broad-leaved.

coulteri D. Don. *kool*-tuh-ree. Big-cone pine. After Irish physician and botanist Thomas Coulter (1793–1843), who collected plants in Mexico and SW USA; he collected the type specimen ca. 1832. Calif., NW Mex.

densiflora Sieb. & Zucc. dens-i-*flaw*-ruh. Japanese red pine. Lat. densely flowered. NE Russia, NE China, Korea, Japan.

edulis Engelm. *ed*-ew-lis. Colorado pinyon. Lat. edible (the seeds). W and C USA, N Mex.

flexilis E. James. *flex*-i-lis. Limber pine. Lat. flexible (the shoots). SW Canada, W and C USA.

heldreichii H. Christ. hel-*driek*-ee-ee. Bosnian pine. After German botanist Theodor Heinrich Hermann von Heldreich (1822–1902), who collected the type specimen in 1863. SE Eur. '**Schmidtii**'. *shmit*-ee-ee. After Eugen Schmidt, who discovered it near Sarajevo in 1926.

jeffreyi Balf. *jef*-ree-ee. Jeffrey pine. After Scottish botanist John Jeffrey (1826–1854), who collected the type specimen in California in 1852. W USA, NW Mex.

koraiensis Sieb. & Zucc. ko-ray-*en*-sis. Korean pine. Of Korea. NE Russia, NE China, Korea, Japan.

monticola Douglas ex D. Don. mon-*ti*-ko-luh. Western white pine. Lat.

living on mountains. SW Canada, W USA.

mugo Turra. *mew*-goh. Mountain pine. A name used in 18th-cent. Italy for this species. C and E Eur.

nigra J. F. Arnold. *nie*-gruh. Austrian pine. Lat. black (the bark). C and SE Eur. subsp. *laricio* Maire. la-*ris*-ee-oh. Corsican pine. Italian name for larch trees. Italy, Corsica.

palustris Mill. puh-*lus*-tris. Longleaf pine. Lat. of marshes. SE USA.

parviflora Sieb. & Zucc. par-vi-*flaw*-ruh. Japanese white pine. Lat. small-flowered. Japan, South Korea.

patula Schiede ex Schltdl. & Cham. *pat*-ew-luh. Lat. wide-spreading (the branches). Mex.

peuce Griseb. *pew*-see. Macedonian pine. Gk. name for pine and fir trees. SE Eur.

pinaster Aiton. pin-*as*-ter. Maritime pine. The Lat. name, probably of *P. sylvestris*, meaning similar but inferior (for eating) to the pine (*P. pinea*). S Eur., Morocco.

pinea L. pie-*nee*-uh. Stone pine, umbrella pine. Lat. of pines (the edible seeds were called *nux pinea*). S Eur., SW Asia.

ponderosa P. & C. Lawson. pon-duh-*roh*-suh. Western yellow pine. Lat. heavy (the wood). SW Canada, W USA.

pumila (Pall.) Regel. *pew*-mi-luh. Dwarf Siberian pine. Lat. dwarf. Siberia to Japan.

radiata D. Don. ray-dee-*ah*-tuh. Monterey pine. Lat. radiating (cracks on the cone scales). Calif., NW Mex.

resinosa Aiton. re-zi-*noh*-suh. Red pine. Lat. resinous (it produces large amounts of resin when cut). Canada, NE USA.

rigida Mill. *ri*-ji-duh. Pitch pine. Lat. rigid (the cone scales). SE Canada, E USA.

strobus L. *stroh*-boos. Eastern white pine, Weymouth pine. Gk. cone, or the name of a resinous tree. Canada, E USA.

sylvestris L. sil-*ves*-tris. Scots pine. Lat. of woods. Eur. to N China.

'Watereri'. *war*-tuh-ruh-ree. After English nurseryman and plant breeder Anthony Waterer (1822–1896), who discovered it.

taeda L. tie-*ee*-duh. Loblolly pine. Lat. name of a pitch-producing tree (the wood is resinous). E USA.

thunbergii Parl. thun-*berg*-ee-ee. Black pine. After Swedish botanist and physician Carl Peter Thunberg (1743–1828), plant collector in Japan and S Africa, who described it as *P. sylvestris*. Japan, S Korea.

virginiana Mill. vir-jin-ee-*ah*-nuh. Scrub pine. Of Virginia. E USA.

wallichiana A. B. Jacks. wol-ik-ee-*ah*-nuh. Blue pine. After Nathaniel Wallich (1786–1854), Danish botanist and surgeon with the East India Company, who collected plants in India and Nepal. Himal., W China.

pinyon, Colorado *Pinus edulis*
pipevine *Aristolochia macrophylla*

Piptanthus Sweet (Fabaceae). pip-*tanth*-oos. From Gk. to fall, flower (the corolla, calyx and stamens fall together). 2 spp. shrubs. Himal., W China.

laburnifolius (D. Don) Stapf = *P. nepalensis*

nepalensis (Hook.) Sweet. nep-uh-*len*-sis. Of Nepal.

Piptatherum P. Beauv. (Poaceae). pip-*tath*-uh-room. From Gk. to fall, bristle, referring to the deciduous awns. 30 spp. grasses. Eur. to China, N Am.

miliaceum (L.) Coss. mil-ee-*ay*-see-oom. Rice millet. Lat. like *Milium*. S Eur., N Africa, W Asia.

pistachio *Pistacia vera*. **Chinese** *P. chinensis*

Pistacia L. (Anacardiaceae). pi-*stas*-ee-uh. From Gk. name of the pistachio (*P. vera*). 12 spp., deciduous and evergreen trees, shrubs. Medit. and E Africa to China, SE Asia, Texas, Mex., C Am.

chinensis Bunge. chin-*en*-sis. Chinese pistachio. Of China. China, Taiwan, Philippines.

vera L. *veer*-ruh. Pistachio. Lat. true. W and C Asia.

Pistia L. (Araceae). *pis*-tee-uh. From Gk. water, where it grows. 1 sp., aquatic herb. Africa, Asia, N and S Am., Australia.

stratiotes L. strat-ee-*oh*-teez. Water lettuce. Gk. soldier, from Gk. name of a water plant.

Pisum L. (Fabaceae). *pee*-soom. Lat. name for pea. 2 spp. ann. herbs. S and E Eur., N Africa, W Asia.

sativum L. sa-*tee*-voom. Pea. Lat. cultivated. Cult.

pitcher plant *Sarracenia*

Pittosporum Banks ex Gaertn. (Pittosporaceae). pit-*os*-po-room. From Gk. pitch, seed, referring to the sticky coating on the seeds. 150 spp., evergreen trees, shrubs. Madeira, SE Asia to Australia, NZ, Pacific and Indian Ocean Is.

crassifolium Banks & Sol. ex A. Cunn. kras-i-*foh*-lee-oom. Lat. thick-leaved. NZ.

eugenioides A. Cunn. ew-jeen-ee-*oy*-deez. Lemonwood. Lat. like *Eugenia*. NZ.

'Garnettii'. gar-*net*-ee-ee. After Arthur Garnett, who found it in a NZ nursery.

ralphii Kirk. *ralf*-ee-ee. After surgeon and botanist Thomas Shearman Ralph (1813–1891), who collected the type specimen ca. 1870. NZ.

tenuifolium Gaertn. ten-ew-i-*foh*-lee-oom. Lat. thin-leaved. NZ.

tobira (Thunb.) W. T. Aiton. to-*bie*-ruh. From the Japanese name. E China, Taiwan, S Korea, Japan.

plane *Platanus*. **American** *P. occidentalis*. **London** *P.* ×*hispanica*. **oriental** *P. orientalis*

Plantago L. (Plantaginaceae). plan-*tah*-goh. Plantains. From Lat. sole of the foot, referring to the way the leaves of the type species, *P. major*, often lie flat against the ground. 200 spp., ann. and perenn. herbs, shrubs. Widespread.

major L. *may*-juh. Common plantain. Lat. larger (than other species). Eur., Asia.

plantain *Plantago*. **common** *P. major*. **Indian** *Arnoglossum*. **pale Indian**

A. atriplicifolium. **water** *Alisma, A. plantago-aquatica*
plantain lily *Hosta*

Platanus L. (Platanaceae). *plat*-uh-noos. Planes. Gk. name for *P. orientalis*. 8 spp. trees. SE Canada, USA, Mex., SE Eur., Turkey, SE Asia.

×*hispanica* Mill. ex Münchh. London plane. Lat. of Spain. *P. occidentalis* × *P. orientalis*. Cult.

occidentalis L. ok-si-den-*tah*-lis. American plane/sycamore. Lat. western. SE Canada, USA, N Mex.

orientalis L. o-ree-en-*tah*-lis. Chenar tree, oriental plane. Lat. eastern. SE Eur., Turkey. f. **digitata** (Gordon) Jankó. di-ji-*tah*-tuh. Lat. with finger-like divisions (the leaf lobes).

Platycladus Spach (Cupressaceae). plat-ee-*klay*-doos. Gk. with broad or flattened shoots. 1 sp., conifer. China, Korea.

orientalis (L.) Franco. o-ree-en-*tah*-lis. Chinese arborvitae. Lat. eastern. **'Rosedalis'**. rohz-*dah*-lis. Of the Rosedale Nursery, Texas, where it originated.

Platycodon A. DC. (Campanulaceae). plat-ee-*koh*-don. Gk. a wide bell, referring to the flower shape. 1 sp., perenn. herb. China, Korea, Japan, E Russia.

grandiflorus (Jacq.) A. DC. gran-di-*flaw*-roos. Balloon flower. Lat. large-flowered.

Plecostachys Hilliard & B. L. Burtt (Asteraceae). plek-oh-*stak*-is. Gk. plaited spike, referring to the

intricately branched habit. 2 spp.
shrubs. S Africa.
serpyllifolia (Berg.) Hilliard & B. L.
Burtt. ser-pil-i-*foh*-lee-uh. Lat. with
thyme-like leaves.

Plectranthus L'Hér. (Lamiaceae).
plek-*tranth*-oos. Gk. spur flower,
referring to the spur on the corolla
of the type species. 200 spp., perenn.
herbs, subshrubs. Old World tropics
and subtropics.
amboinicus (Lour.) Spreng.am-boh-
in-i-koos. Cuban oregano. Of
Amboina Is. (Indonesia). E and S
Africa.
argentatus S. T. Blake. ar-jen-*tah*-toos.
Silver spurflower. Lat. silvery (the
foliage). Australia.
scutellarioides (L.) R. Br. skue-tuh-
lah-ree-*oy*-deez. Lat. like *Scutellaria*.
SE Asia to Australia.

Pleioblastus Nakai (Poaceae). plie-oh-
blast-oos. Gk. many buds, referring
to the many buds at each node, lead-
ing to clustered branches. 40 spp.
bamboos. China, Vietnam, Japan.
pygmaeus (Miq.) Nakai. *pig*-mee-oos.
Lat. dwarf. Japan.
simonii (Carrière) Nakai. si-*mohn*-
ee-ee. After Gabriel Eugène Simon
(b. 1829), consul in Shanghai, who
introduced it to cultivation in France
in 1862. Japan.
variegatus (Siebold ex Miq.) Makino.
va-ree-uh-*gah*-toos. Lat. variegated
(the leaves). Japan.
viridistriatus (Regel) Makino. vi-ri-
dee-stree-*ah*-toos. Lat. green-striped
(the leaves). Japan.

Pleione D. Don (Orchidaceae). plie-
oh-nee. After Pleione of Gk. myth.
20 spp. orchids. Himal. to SE Asia.
formosana Hayata. for-moh-*sah*-nuh.
Of Taiwan (Formosa). China,
Taiwan.

Pleomele sanderiana (Sander) N. E.
Br. = *Dracaena braunii* 'Sanderiana'

plover eggs *Adromischus cooperi*
plum *Prunus domestica*. **American**
P. americana. **beach** *P. maritima*.
cherry *P. cerasifera*
plum yew *Cephalotaxus*. **Chinese** *C.
fortunei*. **Japanese** *C. harringtonii*

Plumbago L. (Plumbaginaceae).
plum-*bay*-goh. Lat. lead, name used
by Pliny for a plant believed to cure
lead poisoning. 20 spp., herbs,
shrubs, sometimes climbing. Widespread, warm and trop. regs.
auriculata Lam. o-rik-ew-*lah*-tuh.
Cape leadwort. Lat. with small, ear-
like lobes (at the base of the petiole).
S Africa.

plume flower *Celosia argentea* Plumosa Group

Poa L. (Poaceae). *poh*-uh. Gk. grass or
meadow. 500 spp. grasses. Widespread.
labillardierei Steud. la-bil-ar-dee-*e*-
ree-ee. After French botanist Jacques
de Labillardière (1755–1834), who
explored southern Australia in the
late 1700s and collected the type
specimen. E Australia.
nemoralis L. nem-o-*rah*-lis. Wood
meadow grass. Lat. of woods. Eur.,
N Africa, W Asia to Japan.

palustris L. puh-*lus*-tris. Swamp meadow grass. Lat. of marshes. N temp. regs.
pratensis L. pruh-*ten*-sis. Kentucky blue grass, meadow grass. Lat. of meadows. N temp. regs.

Podocarpus L'Hér. ex Pers. (Podocarpaceae). pod-oh-*karp*-oos. Gk. foot fruit, referring to the stalked fruit. 100 spp., evergreen trees, shrubs. Tropics and subtropics, temp. S hemisph.
lawrencei Hook.f. lo-*rents*-ee-ee. After English botanist Robert William Lawrence (1807–1833), who collected the type specimen in Tasmania in 1826. SE Australia.
macrophyllus (Thunb.) Sweet. mak-*rof*-i-loos. Gk. large-leaved (compared to other *Taxus* species, in which genus it was first named). Japan, Taiwan.
nivalis Hook. ni-*vah*-lis. Alpine totara. Lat. of snow (it grows on high mountains). NZ.
salignus D. Don. suh-*lig*-noos. Lat. willow-like (the leaves). Chile.
totara G. Benn ex D. Don. toh-*tah*-ruh. Totara. The native name. NZ.

Podophyllum L. (Berberidaceae). pod-oh-*fil*-oom. Gk. foot leaf (the leaf has been likened to a duck's foot). 1 sp., perenn. herb. SE Canada, E USA.
delavayi Franch. = *Dysosma delavayi*
emodi Wall. ex Hook.f. & Thomson = *Sinopodophyllum hexandrum* var. *emodi*
hexandrum Royle = *Sinopodophyllum hexandrum*
peltatum L. pel-*tah*-toom. May apple. Lat. peltate (the leaves).

versipelle Hance = *Dysosma versipellis*

poinsettia *Euphorbia pulcherrima*
pokeweed *Phytolacca americana*

Polemonium L. (Polemoniaceae). pol-ee-*moh*-nee-oom. From Gk. name of a med. herb. 20 spp., mainly perenn. herbs. Temp. N hemisph., S Am.
caeruleum L. kie-*rue*-lee-oom. Jacob's ladder. Lat. blue (the flowers). Eur. to Japan, W Canada, Alaska.
carneum A. Gray. *kar*-nee-oom. Royal Jacob's ladder. Lat. flesh-pink (the flowers). W USA.
pulcherrimum Hook. pool-*ke*-ri-moom. Lat. very beautiful. W Canada, W USA.
reptans L. *rep*-tanz. Lat. creeping. E and C USA.
yezoense (Miyabe & Kudô) Kitam. ye-zo-*en*-see. Of Hokkaido (Yezo). Japan. var. *hidakanum* Koji Ito. hid-uh-*kah*-noom. Of the Hidaka Mts. Japan (Hokkaido).

Polianthes L. (Asparagaceae). pol-ee-*anth*-eez. From Gk. grey flower. 17 spp. perenn. herbs. Mex.
tuberosa L. tew-buh-*roh*-suh. Tuberose. Lat. bearing tubers.

polyanthus *Primula* ×*polyantha*

Polygala L. (Polygalaceae). po-*lig*-uh-luh. Milkworts. The Gk. name, from Gk. much milk (they were believed to increase milk production in cattle). 500 spp., ann. and perenn. herbs, shrubs, trees. Widespread.
chamaebuxus L. kam-ee-*bux*-oos. Gk. dwarf, *Buxus*. C and S Eur.

×*dalmaisiana* L. H. Bailey. dal-may-see-*ah*-nuh. After M. Dalmais, the French gardener who raised it in 1839. *P. fruticosa* × *P. myrtifolia.* Cult.

Polygonatum Mill. (Asparagaceae). po-lig-o-*nah*-toom. Solomon's seals. Gk. name used by Dioscorides for this or a similar plant, from Gk. many knees, referring to the many-jointed rhizome. 53 spp. rhizomatous herbs. Temp. N hemisph.

biflorum (Walter) Elliott. bie-*flaw*-room. Lat. two-flowered (the inflorescence, sometimes). S Canada, E and C USA, NE Mex.

canaliculatum (Willd.) Pursh = *P. biflorum*

cirrhifolium (Wall.) Royle. si-ri-*foh*-lee-oom. Lat. tendril leaf (the leaves often end in tendrils). Himal., S China.

commutatum (Schult. & Schult.f.) A. Dietr. = *P. biflorum*

curvistylum Hua. curv-i-*stie*-loom. Lat. with a curved style. Nepal, SW China.

humile Fisch. ex Maxim. *hew*-mi-lee. Lat. low (growing). C Asia to Japan.

×*hybridum* Brügger. *hib*-ri-doom. Lat. hybrid. *P. multiflorum* × *P. odoratum.* Eur.

multiflorum (L.) All. mul-ti-*flaw*-room. Lat. many-flowered. Eur., W and C Asia, W Himal.

odoratum (Mill.) Druce. oh-do-*rah*-toom. Lat. fragrant (the flowers). Eur. to E Asia.

verticillatum (L.) All. vur-ti-si-*lah*-toom. Lat. whorled (the leaves). Eur. to China.

Polypodium L. (Polypodiaceae). pol-ee-*poh*-dee-oom. Gk. many feet, referring to the branched rhizome. 100 spp. ferns. Widespread.

cambricum L. *kam*-brik-oom. Welsh polypody. Lat. Welsh. Eur., Turkey.

vulgare L. vul-*gar*-ree. Common polypody. Lat. common. Eur., Africa, Asia, Greenland.

polypody, common *Polypodium vulgare.* **Welsh** *P. cambricum*

Polystichum Roth (Dryopteridaceae). pol-*is*-ti-koom. Gk. many rows, referring to the rows of sori on the pinnae. 180 spp. ferns. Widespread.

acrostichoides (Michx.) Schott. uh-kros-ti-*koy*-deez. Christmas fern. Lat. like *Acrostichum* (another genus of ferns). SE Canada, E USA.

aculeatum (L.) Roth. uh-kew-lee-*ah*-toom. Hard shield fern. Lat. spiny (the pinnule lobes). Eur., N Africa, W Asia to China.

makinoi (Tagawa) Tagawa. mak-i-*noh*-ee. After Japanese botanist Tomitaro Makino (1862–1957). Japan.

munitum (Kaulf.) C. Presl. mew-*nee*-toom. Sword fern. Lat. armed (with spiny teeth). SW Canada, W USA, NW Mex.

polyblepharum (Roem. ex Kunze) C. Presl. pol-ee-*blef*-uh-room. Tassel fern. Gk. many eyelashes (the bristly scales on the rachis). S Korea, Japan.

rigens Tagawa. *ree*-guhnz. Rigid holly fern. Lat. rigid (the foliage). China, Japan.

setiferum (Forssk.) Woyn. see-*tif*-uh-room. Soft shield fern. Lat. bristly (the foliage). Azores, Eur., Turkey.

tsussimense (Hook.) J. Sm. tsue-shim-en-see. Korean rock fern. Of Tsushima (Tsus-sima) Is., between S Korea and Japan. E and SE Asia.

pomegranate *Punica granatum*
pomelo *Citrus maxima*

Poncirus trifoliata (L.) Raf. = *Citrus trifoliata*

Pontederia L. (Pontederiaceae). pon-te-*de*-ree-uh. After Giulio Pontedera (1688–1757), Italian botanist. 6 spp. aquatic herbs. Americas.
cordata L. kor-*dah*-tuh. Pickerel weed. Lat. heart-shaped (the leaves).

poplar *Populus*. **balsam** *P. balsamifera*. **black** *P. nigra*. **Chinese necklace** *P. lasiocarpa*. **Lombardy** *P. nigra* 'Italica'. **white** *P. alba*
poppy *Papaver*. **alpine** *P. alpinum*. **arctic** *P. nudicaule*. **California** *Eschscholzia californica*. **corn** *Papaver rhoeas*. **crested prickly** *Argemone polyanthemos*. **dawn** *Eomecon chionantha*. **Icelandic** *Papaver nudicaule*. **Matilija** *Romneya coulteri*. **opium** *Papaver somniferum*. **oriental** *P. orientale*. **plume** *Macleaya cordata*. **prickly** *Argemone*. **snow** *Eomecon chionantha*. **Spanish** *Papaver rupifragum*. **tree** *Romneya coulteri*. **Welsh** *Meconopsis cambrica*. **yellow horned** *Glaucium flavum*
poppy mallow *Callirhoe*. **clustered** *C. triangulata*. **purple** *C. involucrata*

Populus L. (Salicaceae). *pop*-ew-loos. Cottonwoods, poplars. From the Lat. name *arbor populi* (tree of the people). 30 spp. trees. Mostly N hemisph.

×*acuminata* Rydb. uh-kew-min-*ah*-tuh. Lat. taper-pointed (the leaves). *P. angustifolia* × *P. deltoides*. W USA.
alba L. *al*-buh. White poplar. Lat. white (the leaf undersides). Eur., N Africa, W Asia to China.
angustifolia E. James. an-gus-ti-*foh*-lee-uh. Narrowleaf cottonwood. Lat. narrow-leaved. SC Canada, W and C USA.
balsamifera L. bawl-suhm-*i*-fuh-ruh. Balsam poplar. Lat. bearing balsam. Canada, N USA.
×*canadensis* Moench. kan-uh-*den*-sis. Of Canada, where it was thought to be native. *P. deltoides* × *P. nigra*. Cult.
deltoides Bartram ex Marshall. del-*toy*-deez. Eastern cottonwood. Shaped like the Gk. letter delta (i.e., triangular, the leaves). S Canada, USA.
euramericana Guinier = *P.* ×*canadensis*
grandidentata Michx. gran-di-den-*tah*-tuh. Bigtooth aspen. Lat. with large teeth (the leaves). Canada, E USA.
lasiocarpa Oliv. laz-ee-oh-*kar*-puh. Chinese necklace poplar. Gk. woolly-fruited. China.
nigra L. *nie*-gruh. Black poplar. Lat. black (the bark). Eur., N Africa, W Asia to W China. 'Italica'. i-*tal*-i-kuh. Lombardy poplar. Lat. Italian.
tremula L. *trem*-ew-luh. Aspen. Lat. trembling (the leaves). Eur., N Africa, temp. Asia.
tremuloides Michx. trem-ew-*loy*-deez. Quaking aspen. Lat. like *P. tremula*. Canada, USA, Mex.
trichocarpa Torr. & A. Gray. trik-oh-*kar*-puh. Black cottonwood. Gk.

hairy-fruited. SW Canada, W USA, NW Mex.

possum haw *Ilex decidua*
potato *Solanum tuberosum*
potato bean *Apios americana*

Potentilla L. (Rosaceae). poh-tuhn-*til*-uh. Diminutive of Lat. powerful, referring to med. properties. 500 spp., perenn. herbs, shrubs. Mainly N hemisph.
alba L. *al*-buh. Lat. white (the flowers). Eur.
argyrophylla Wall. ex Lehm. = *P. atrosanguinea* var. *argyrophylla*
atrosanguinea Lodd. et al. at-roh-san-*gwin*-ee-uh. Lat. dark red (the flowers). Himal. var. *argyrophylla* (Wall. ex Lehm.) Grierson & D. G. Long. ar-gi-roh-*fil*-uh. Gk. silver-leaved.
aurea L. *aw*-ree-uh. Lat. golden (the flowers). Alps, Pyrenees.
fruticosa L. frue-ti-*koh*-suh. Lat. shrubby. N Am., Eur., Asia.
×*hopwoodiana* Sweet. hop-wood-ee-*ah*-nuh. After Mr E. Hopwood, in whose Twickenham nursery it was raised before 1830. *P. nepalensis* × *P. recta*. Cult.
megalantha Takeda. meg-uh-*lanth*-uh. Gk. large-flowered. E Russia, Japan (Hokkaido).
nepalensis Hook. nep-uh-*len*-sis. Of Nepal. Himal.
neumanniana Rchb. noy-man-ee-*ah*-nuh. After Joseph Henri François Neumann (1800–1858), French botanist. N Eur.
recta L. *rek*-tuh. Lat. upright. Eur., W Asia to W China.
rupestris L. rue-*pest*-ris. Lat. growing on rocks. Eur. to N China.

thurberi A. Gray. *thur*-buh-ree. After American pharmacist and botanist George Thurber (1821–1890), who collected the type specimen in New Mexico in 1851. SW USA.

Poterium sanguisorba L. = *Sanguisorba minor*
Pratia pedunculata (R. Br.) Benth. = *Lobelia pedunculata*

prayer plant *Maranta leuconeura*
prickleweed *Desmanthus illinoensis*
prickly Moses *Acacia verticillata*
prickly pear *Opuntia*. **creeping** *O. humifusa*
pride of Barbados *Caesalpinia pulcherrima*
pride of India *Koelreuteria paniculata*
primrose *Primula vulgaris*. **cape** *Streptocarpus* ×*hybridus*

Primula L. (Primulaceae). *prim*-ew-luh. Diminutive of Lat. first, referring to the early flowers. 500 spp., mainly perenn. herbs. N temp. regs.
allionii Loisel. al-ee-*ohn*-ee-ee. After Carlo Ludovico Allioni (1728–1804), Italian physician and botanist. N Italy, S France.
alpicola (W. W. Sm.) Stapf. al-*pik*-o-luh. Lat. growing in alpine regs. Bhutan, Tibet.
auricula L. o-*rik*-ew-luh. Auricula. Lat. a little ear (from the shape of the leaves). C Eur.
beesiana Forrest. beez-ee-*ah*-nuh. After Bees Nursery, Cheshire, founded by A. K. Bulley, sponsor of George Forrest, who introduced it to cultivation. SW China, N Myanmar.
×*bulleesiana* Janson. bool-eez-ee-*ah*-

nuh. From the names of the parents, *P. beesiana* × *P. bulleyana*. Cult.

bulleyana Forrest. bool-ee-*ah*-nuh. After Liverpool cotton merchant Arthur Kiplin Bulley (1861–1942), founder of Bees Nursery and sponsor of George Forrest, who introduced it to cultivation. SW China (Sichuan, Yunnan).

capitata Hook. kap-i-*tah*-tuh. Lat. in a head (the flowers). Himal., W China.

chionantha Balf.f. & Forrest. kee-on-*anth*-uh. Gk. snow flower. George Forrest, who collected the type specimen in Yunnan in 1913, described the flowers as "pure snow white." SW China.

chungensis Balf.f. & Kingdon-Ward. chung-*en*-sis. Of the Chung Valley, NW Yunnan. SW China.

cockburniana Hemsl. koh-burn-ee-*ah*-nuh. After H. Cockburn of HM Consular Service, Chungking (now Chongqing), and Rev. G. Cockburn of the Church of Scotland mission in China, for their assistance to Antwerp Pratt, who collected the type specimen. China (Sichuan).

denticulata Sm. den-tik-ew-*lah*-tuh. Lat. finely toothed (the leaves). Himal., Tibet.

elatior Hill. ee-*lay*-tee-or. Oxlip. Lat. taller. Eur., W Asia.

florindae Kingdon-Ward. flo-*rin*-die. After Florinda, first wife of Frank Kingdon-Ward. He collected the type specimen in Tibet in 1924. Tibet.

japonica A. Gray. juh-*pon*-i-kuh. Of Japan. Japan.

jeffreyi (hort. ex Van Houtte) A. R. Mast & Reveal. *jef*-ree-ee. Sierra shooting star. After Scottish plant collector John Jeffrey (1826–1854), who discovered it. SW Canada, W USA.

marginata Curtis. mar-ji-*nah*-tuh. Lat. margined (with white, the leaves). S France, N Italy.

meadia (L.) A. R. Mast & Reveal. *meed*-ee-uh. Shooting star. After Richard Mead (1630–1699), physician to George II and patron of Mark Catesby, who illustrated it. E and C USA.

pauciflora (Greene) A. R. Mast & Reveal. paw-si-*flaw*-ruh. Pretty shooting star. Lat. few-flowered (the inflorescence, sometimes). W Canada, W USA.

poissonii Franch. pwah-*son*-ee-ee. After Jules Poisson (1833–1919), French botanist. China (Sichuan, Yunnan).

×*polyantha* Mill. pol-ee-*anth*-uh. Polyanthus. Gk. many-flowered. *P. veris* × *P. vulgaris*. Eur.

prolifera Wall. proh-*lif*-uh-ruh. Lat. proliferous, producing offshoots. Himal. to Indonesia.

×*pubescens* Wulfen. pew-*bes*-uhnz. Lat. hairy (the leaves). *P. auricula* × *P. hirsuta*. Cult.

pulverulenta Duthie. pul-ve-rue-*len*-tuh. Lat. dusty (the flower stems). China (Sichuan).

rosea Royle. *roh*-zee-uh. Lat. pink (the flowers). N India, N Pakistan.

secundiflora Franch. se-kun-di-*flaw*-ruh. Lat. with flowers facing in one direction. W China.

sieboldii E. Morren. see-*bold*-ee-ee. After German physician and botanist Philip Franz von Siebold (1796–1866), who introduced it to cultivation. E Asia.

sikkimensis Hook. si-kim-*en*-sis. Of
Sikkim. Himal., China.
veris L. *ve*-ris. Cowslip. Lat. of spring.
Eur., W Asia.
vialii Delavay ex Franch. vee-*al*-ee-ee.
After Paul Vial (1855–1917), French
missionary in Yunnan. China (Sich-
uan, Yunnan).
vulgaris Huds. vul-*gar*-ris. Primrose.
Lat. common. Eur., N Africa, W
Asia. subsp. *sibthorpii* (Hoffmanns.)
W. W. Sm. & Forrest. sib-*thorp*-ee-ee.
After English botanist John Sibthorp
(1758–1796), who, with artist
Ferdinand Bauer, discovered it on a
journey to Greece and Turkey. SE
Eur., Turkey.

prince's feather *Amaranthus cruentus,
A. hypochondriacus, Persicaria
orientalis*

Prinsepia Royle (Rosaceae). prin-*sep*-
ee-uh. After James Prinsep (1799–
1840), English scholar of philology
and numismatics in India. 5 spp.
deciduous shrubs. Himal., E Asia.
sinensis (Oliv.) Oliv. ex Bean. sin-*en*-
sis. Lat. of China. E Russia, N China,
Korea.

privet *Ligustrum.* **border** *L. obtusifolium.* **Chinese** *L. sinense.* **European**
L. vulgare. **garden** *L. ovalifolium.*
glossy *L. lucidum.* **Japanese** *L.
japonicum*

Prosartes D. Don (Liliaceae). proh--
sar-teez. Fairy bells. From Gk. to
hang upon, referring to the sus-
pended ovules. 5 spp. perenn. herbs.
Canada, USA.

hookeri Torr. *hook*-uh-ree. After Sir
William Jackson Hooker (1785–
1865), English botanist and first
director of RBG Kew, who first
described it as a form of *Uvularia
lanuginosa.* SW Canada, W USA.
smithii (Hook.) Utech, Shinwari &
Kawano. *smith*-ee-ee. After English
botanist James Edward Smith (1759–
1828), founder and first president of
the Linnaean Society, who originally
named it *Uvularia puberula.* W USA.

Prostanthera Labill. (Lamiaceae).
prost-*anth*-uh-ruh. Gk. appendage,
anther, referring to the spur-like
anther appendages. 100 spp., shrubs,
sometimes trees. Australia.
lasianthos Labill. laz-ee-*anth*-os. Gk.
with woolly flowers. E Australia.
rotundifolia R. Br. roh-tun-di-*foh*-lee-
uh. Lat. round-leaved. SE Australia.

Prunella L. (Lamiaceae). prue-*nel*-uh.
From German for quinsy, which it
was said to cure. 7 spp. perenn. herbs.
N hemisph.
grandiflora (L.) Scholler. gran-di-
flaw-ruh. Lat. large-flowered. Eur.
vulgaris L. vul-*gar*-ris. Self-heal. Lat.
common. Eur., N Africa, Asia,
N Am.

Prunus L. (Rosaceae). *prue*-noos. Lat.
name for plum. 300 spp., trees,
shrubs. N hemisph., Africa, SE Asia
to New Guinea, S Am.
americana Marshall. uh-me-ri-*kah*-
nuh. American plum. Of America.
Canada, USA, N Mex.
armeniaca L. ar-men-ee-*ah*-kuh.
Apricot. Of Armenia. N China.

avium (L.) L. *ay*-vee-oom. Gean, sweet cherry. Lat. of birds (which eat the fruit). Eur., W Asia.

×*blireana* André. bli-ree-*ah*-nuh. Of Bléré, France, where it was found. *P. cerasifera* × *P. mume*. Cult.

caroliniana (Mill.) Aiton. ka-ro-lin-ee-*ah*-nuh. Carolina laurel cherry. Of the Carolinas. SE USA.

cerasifera Ehrh. ke-ruh-*si*-fuh-ruh. Cherry plum, myrobalan. Lat. bearing cherries. SE Eur., W and C Asia. **'Pissardii'**. pis-*ard*-ee-ee. After M Pissard, French gardener to the Shah of Persia, who found it ca. 1880 and introduced it to Europe.

cerasus L. *suh*-ray-soos. Sour cherry. Lat. name for cherry. Cult.

×*cistena* (N. E. Hansen) Koehne. sis-*teen*-uh. Sioux Indian name for baby (from the dwarf habit). *P. cerasifera* × *P. pumila*. Cult.

domestica L. do-*mes*-ti-kuh. Plum. Lat. of the home. Cult. subsp. *insititia* (L.) C. K. Schneid. in-si-*tish*-ee-uh. Damson. Lat. grafted.

dulcis (Mill.) D. A. Webb. *dul*-sis. Almond. Lat. sweet. SW Asia.

glandulosa Thunb. gland-ew-*loh*-suh. Lat. glandular (the sepals). China.

incisa Thunb. in-*sie*-suh. Fuji cherry. Lat. cut (into teeth, the leaf margin). Japan.

insititia L. = *P. domestica* subsp. *insititia*

laurocerasus L. lo-roh-suh-*ray*-soos. Cherry laurel. Lat. laurel cherry. SE Eur., W Asia.

lusitanica L. lue-si-*tan*-i-kuh. Portugal laurel. Lat. of Portugal. SW Eur., Morocco.

maackii Rupr. *mahk*-ee-ee. Manchurian cherry. After its discoverer, Russian explorer and naturalist Richard Otto (Karlovic) Maack (1825–1886). E Russia, NE China, Korea.

maritima Marshall. muh-*rit*-i-muh. Beach plum. Lat. of the sea (it grows on coasts). E N Am.

mume Sieb. & Zucc. *mue*-mee. Japanese apricot. From the Japanese name. China, Taiwan.

padus L. *pad*-oos. Bird cherry. Gk. name used by Theophrastus for a cherry. Eur., Morocco, Asia.

pensylvanica L.f. pen-sil-*van*-i-kuh. Pin cherry. Of Pennsylvania. Canada, USA.

persica (L.) Batsch. *per*-si-kuh. Peach, nectarine. Lat. of Persia (Iran). Cult.

pumila L. *pew*-mi-luh. Sand cherry. Lat. dwarf. SE Canada, NE USA. var. *besseyi* (L. H. Bailey) Gleason. *bes*-ee-ee. Western sand cherry. After American botanist Charles Edwin Bessey (1845–1915), who extolled its virtues and introduced it to gardens. It was described from one of his introductions. W Canada, C USA.

sargentii Rehder. sar-*jent*-ee-ee. After American botanist Charles Sprague Sargent (1841–1927), first director of the Arnold Arboretum, who confused it with another species. E Russia, Japan, Korea.

serotina Ehrh. se-*ro*-ti-nuh, se-ro-*teen*-uh. Black cherry, rum cherry. Lat. late (flowering, compared to other species). E Canada to Guatemala.

serrula Franch. *se*-rue-luh. Lat. finely toothed (the leaves). China.

spinosa L. spi-*noh*-suh. Blackthorn, sloe. Lat. spiny (the shoots). Eur., W Asia.

×*subhirtella* Miq. sub-hir-*tel*-uh. Lat. somewhat hairy. *P. incisa* × *P.*

pendula. Cult. **'Autumnalis'**. aw-toom-*nah*-lis. Lat. of autumn (flowering).
tenella Batsch. ten-*el*-uh. Dwarf Russian almond. Lat. delicate. C and E Eur., C Asia.
tomentosa Thunb. to-men-*toh*-suh. Downy cherry. Lat. hairy (the shoots and leaves). China, Korea.
triloba Lindl. trie-*loh*-buh. Lat. three-lobed (the leaves). China, Korea.
virginiana L. vir-jin-ee-*ah*-nuh. Choke cherry. Of Virginia. Canada, E and C USA. var. *melanocarpa* (A. Nelson) Sarg. me-lan-oh-*kar*-puh. Western choke cherry. Gk. black-fruited. W Canada, W and C USA.
×*yedoensis* Matsum. yed-oh-*en*-sis. Of Yedo (old name for Tokyo). *P. speciosa* × *P.* ×*subhirtella*. Cult.

Pseudofumaria Medik. (Papaveraceae). sue-doh-few-*mair*-ree-uh. Gk. false *Fumaria*. 2 spp. perenn. herbs. Eur.
alba (Mill.) Lidén. *al*-buh. Lat. white (the flowers). SE Eur.
lutea (L.) Borkh. *lue*-tee-uh. Lat. yellow (the flowers). Italy, Switzerland.

Pseudolarix Gordon (Pinaceae). sue-doh-*la*-rix. Gk. false *Larix*. 1 sp., deciduous conifer. China.
amabilis (J. Nelson) Rehder. uh-*mah*-bi-lis. Golden larch. Lat. beautiful.

Pseudopanax K. Koch (Araliaceae). sue-doh-*pan*-ax. Gk. false *Panax*. 7 spp., evergreen trees, shrubs. NZ.
crassifolius (Sol. ex A. Cunn.) K. Koch. kras-i-*foh*-lee-oos. Lancewood. Lat. thick-leaved.

ferox Kirk. *fe*-rox. Toothed lancewood. Lat. spiny (the leaves).
lessonii (DC.) K. Koch. les-*ohn*-ee-ee. After French botanist Adolphe Pierre Primivère Lesson (1805–1888), who collected it on a voyage to New Zealand in the 1820s.

Pseudosasa Makino ex Nakai (Poaceae). sue-doh-*sah*-suh. Gk. false *Sasa*. 19 spp. bamboos. China, Japan, Korea.
japonica (Sieb. & Zucc. ex Steud.) Makino ex Nakai. juh-*pon*-i-kuh. Of Japan.

Pseudotsuga Carrière (Pinaceae). sue-doh-*tsue*-guh. Gk. false *Tsuga*. 5 spp. coniferous trees. China, Taiwan, Japan, W Canada, W USA, Mex.
menziesii (Mirb.) Franco. men-*zeez*-ee-ee. Douglas fir. After Archibald Menzies (1754–1842), Scottish surgeon and naturalist, who discovered it in 1793 on a voyage to the Pacific Northwest. SW Canada, W USA, Mex.

Pseudowintera Dandy (Winteraceae). sue-doh-*win*-tuh-ruh. Gk. false *Wintera*. 3 spp., evergreen shrubs, trees. NZ.
colorata (Raoul) Dandy. kol-o-*rah*-tuh. Pepper tree. Lat. coloured (the leaves).

Ptelea L. (Rutaceae). *tee*-lee-uh. Gk. name for elm, from the similar fruit. 3 spp., shrubs, trees. Canada, USA, Mex.
trifoliata L. trie-foh-lee-*ah*-tuh. Hop tree. Lat. with three leaves (leaflets). SE Canada, E and C USA, Mex.

Pteris L. (Pteridaceae). *te*-ris. Gk. name of a fern, from Gk. feather. 300 spp. ferns. Widespread in warm and trop. regs.

cretica L. *kret*-i-kuh. Cretan brake. Lat. of Crete. S Eur., trop. and subtrop. Africa and Asia.

Pterocarya Kunth (Juglandaceae). te-roh-*ka*-ree-uh. Wingnuts. Gk. wing nut, referring to the winged fruit. 6 spp. deciduous trees. Caucasus, E Asia.

fraxinifolia (Lam.) Spach. frax-in-i-*foh*-lee-uh. Caucasian wingnut. Lat. with leaves like *Fraxinus*. Caucasus.

×*rehderiana* C. K. Schneid. ray-duh-ree-*ah*-nuh. After Alfred Rehder (1863–1949), American botanist of the Arnold Arboretum, who raised it in 1879. *P. fraxinifolia* × *P. stenoptera*. Cult.

stenoptera C. DC. sten-*op*-tuh-ruh. Chinese wingnut. Lat. narrow wing (on the rachis). China, Taiwan, Korea.

Pterostyrax Sieb. & Zucc. (Styracaceae). te-roh-*stie*-rax. Gk. wing, and the related *Styrax*, referring to the winged fruit of the type species, *P. corymbosus*. 4 spp. deciduous trees. E Asia.

corymbosus Sieb. & Zucc. ko-rim-*boh*-soos. Lat. in corymbs (the flowers). China, Japan.

hispidus Sieb. & Zucc. *his*-pi-doos. Lat. bristly (the fruit). Japan.

Pulmonaria L. (Boraginaceae). pul-mon-*ah*-ree-uh. Lungwort. From Lat. lungs, referring to the appearance of the spotted leaves and sup-posed med. properties. 16 spp. med. herbs. Eur., W and C Asia to W China.

angustifolia L. an-gus-ti-*foh*-lee-uh. Lat. narrow-leaved. Eur.

longifolia (T. Bastard) Boreau. long-gi-*foh*-lee-uh. Lat. long-leaved. W Eur.

officinalis L. o-fis-i-*nah*-lis. Lat. sold as a med. herb. Eur.

rubra Schott. *rue*-bruh. Lat. red (the flowers). E Eur.

saccharata Mill. sak-uh-*rah*-tuh. Lat. sprinkled with sugar (the spotted leaves). Italy, France.

Pulsatilla vulgaris Mill. = *Anemone pulsatilla*

pumpkin *Cucurbita maxima, C. moschata, C. pepo*

Punica L. (Lythraceae). *pew*-ni-kuh. From the Lat. name, which meant apple of Carthage. 2 spp., trees, shrubs. W and C Asia.

granatum L. gruh-*nah*-toom. Pomegranate. Lat. containing grain (seeds).

purple amaranth *Amaranthus cruentus*
purple gromwell *Buglossoides purpurocaerulea*
purple top *Verbena bonariensis*

Purshia DC. ex Poir. (Rosaceae). *pursh*-ee-uh. After German botanist Frederick (Friedrich) Traugott Pursh (1774–1820), who described the type species, *P. tridentata*, in another genus. 6 spp. shrubs. SW Canada, W USA, N Mex.

mexicana (D. Don) S. L. Welsh.
mex-i-*kah*-nuh. Cliff rose. Of Mexico. W USA, NW Mex.
tridentata (Pursh) DC. trie-den-*tah*-
tuh. Bitterbrush. Lat. three-toothed
(the leaves). SW Canada, W USA.

Puschkinia Adams (Asparagaceae).
poosh-*kin*-ee-uh. After Count
Apollos Apollosovich Mussin-
Pushkin (1760–1805), Russian plant
collector and chemist. 2 spp. bulbous
herbs. SW Asia.
libanotica Zucc. = *P. scilloides*
scilloides Adams. sil-*oy*-deez. Like
Scilla.

pussy toes *Antennaria*

Puya Molina (Bromeliaceae). *pue*-yuh.
The Chilean name of *P. chilensis*. 190
spp. evergreen herbs. S Am.
alpestris (Poepp.) Gay. al-*pes*-tris. Lat.
alpine. Chile, Argentina.

Pyracantha M. Roem. (Rosaceae). pie-
ruh-*kanth*-uh. Firethorns. Gk. fire
thorn, referring to the spiny shoots
and red berries. 10 spp., evergreen
shrubs, trees. SE Eur., W Asia,
Himal., China, Taiwan.
coccinea M. Roem. kok-*sin*-ee-uh. Lat.
scarlet (the fruit). SE Eur., W Asia.
koidzumii (Hayata) Rehder. koyd-
zuem-ee-ee. After Japanese botanist

Gen-Iti Koidzumi (1883–1953).
Taiwan.
rogersiana (A. B. Jacks.) Chitt.
ro-jerz-ee-*ah*-nuh. After Charles
Coltman-Rogers (1854–1929), of
Stanage Park, Wales, who grew and
exhibited it from the original introduction. China.

pyrethrum *Tanacetum cinerariifolium*

Pyrus L. (Rosaceae). *pie*-roos. Pears.
Lat. name for pear. 25 spp., deciduous trees, shrubs. Eur., N Africa,
Asia.
calleryana Decne. kal-uh-ree-*ah*-nuh.
Callery pear. After French missionary Joseph Callery, who collected the
type specimen in 1858. China, Taiwan, Korea, Vietnam.
communis L. *kom*-ew-nis. Common
pear. Lat. common. Cult.
pyrifolia (Burm.f.) Nakai. pi-ri-*foh*-
lee-uh. Asian pear, sand pear. Lat.
with leaves like *Pyrus* (it was originally described as a species of *Ficus*).
China, Laos, Vietnam.
salicifolia Pall. sal-i-si-*foh*-lee-uh.
Willow-leaved pear. Lat. with leaves
like *Salix*. W Asia.
ussuriensis Maxim. oo-soo-ree-*en*-sis.
Ussurian pear. Of the Ussuri River.
E Russia, N China, Korea, Japan.

quailbush *Atriplex lentiformis*
Queen Anne's lace *Anthriscus
sylvestris*
queen-of-the-prairie *Filipendula
rubra*

Quercus L. (Fagaceae). *kwer*-koos.
Oaks. Lat. name of an oak. 450 spp.,
trees, shrubs. Canada to Colombia,
Eur., N Africa, Asia.
acutissima Carruth. ak-ew-*tis*-i-muh.
Sawtooth oak. Lat. sharpest (the leaf
teeth). Himal., E and SE Asia.
alba L. *al*-buh. White oak. Lat. white
(the bark). SE Canada, E USA.
bicolor Willd. *bi*-ko-lor. Swamp white
oak. Lat. two-coloured (the contrast-
ing upper and lower leaf surfaces). SE
Canada, E USA.
canariensis Willd. kuh-nair-ree-*en*-sis.
Algerian oak. Lat. of the Canary Is.,
where it was thought to originate. S
Spain, S Portugal, N Africa.
castaneifolia C. A. Mey. kas-tan-ee-i-
foh-lee-uh. Chestnut-leaved oak. Lat.
with leaves like *Castanea*. W Asia.
cerris L. *se*-ris. Turkey oak. The Lat.
name. Eur., W Asia.
coccinea Münchh. kok-*sin*-ee-uh.
Scarlet oak. Lat. scarlet (the autumn
colour). E USA.

dentata Thunb. den-*tah*-tuh. Daimio
oak. Lat. toothed (the leaves). E Asia.
falcata Michx. fawl-*kah*-tuh. Southern red oak. Lat. sickle-shaped (the
leaf lobes). E USA.
frainetto Ten. fray-*net*-oh. Hungarian
oak. From a misspelling of the Italian
name, *farnetto*. E Eur., NW Turkey.
gambelii Nutt. Gambel oak. gam-*bel*-
ee-ee. After William Gambel (1821–
1849), American explorer, physician
and naturalist who collected the type
specimen in New Mexico in 1841.
SW USA, N Mex.
garryana Douglas ex Hook. ga-ree-*ah*-
nuh. Oregon oak. After Nicholas
Garry (ca. 1782–1856), English-born
deputy governor of the Hudson's Bay
Co., friend and benefactor of David
Douglas. SW Canada, W USA.
×*hispanica* Lam. his-*pan*-i-kuh. Lat.
of Spain. *Q. cerris* × *Q. suber*. S Eur.
ilex L. *ie*-lex. Holm oak. The Lat.
name. S Eur., N Africa, W Asia.
imbricaria Michx. im-bri-*kair*-ree-uh.
Shingle oak. Lat. tile-like (the wood
was used to make roof tiles). E USA.
lobata Née. loh-*bah*-tuh. Valley oak.
Lat. lobed (the leaves). Calif.
lyrata Walter. lie-*rah*-tuh. Overcup
oak. Lat. lyre-shaped (the leaves).
E USA.
macrocarpa Michx. mak-roh-*kar*-puh.
Bur oak. Gk. large-fruited. S Canada,
E and C USA.
montana Willd. mon-*tah*-nuh. Chestnut oak. Lat. of mountains. E USA.
muehlenbergii Engelm. mue-luhn-
berg-ee-ee. Yellow chestnut oak.
After American botanist Gotthilf
Henry Ernst Muhlenberg (1753–
1815), who first described it as *Q. castanea*. SE Canada, E USA, N Mex.

nigra L. *nie*-gruh. Water oak. Lat. black (the bark). SE USA.

nuttallii E. J. Palmer = *Q. texana*

pagoda Raf. puh-*goh*-duh. Swamp Spanish oak. Like a pagoda (the leaf shape). SE USA.

palustris Münchh. puh-*lus*-tris. Pin oak. Lat. of marshes. SE Canada, E USA.

petraea (Matt.) Liebl. pe-*tree*-uh. Sessile oak. Lat. of rocky places. Eur., W Asia.

phellos L. *fel*-os. Willow oak. Gk. cork (referring to the bark of old trees). E USA.

robur L. *roh*-buh. English oak. Lat. name of an oak with very hard wood. Eur., W Asia.

rubra L. *rue*-bruh. Red oak. Lat. red (the leaf veins). SE Canada, E USA.

rysophylla Weath. ris-*o*-fil-uh. Loquat oak. Gk. with wrinkled leaves. E Mex.

shumardii Buckley. shue-*mard*-ee-ee. Swamp red oak. After Benjamin Franklin Shumard (1820–1869), American geologist and physician. E USA.

suber L. *sue*-buh. Cork oak. Lat. name for cork and the cork oak. SW Eur., N Africa.

texana Buckley. tex-*ah*-nuh. Nuttall's oak. Of Texas. S USA.

velutina Lam. vel-ew-*teen*-uh, vel-*ue*-ti-nuh. Black oak. Lat. velvety (the leaf underside). SE Canada, E USA.

virginiana Mill. vir-jin-ee-*ah*-nuh. Live oak. Of Virginia. SE USA.

quince *Cydonia oblonga*. **flowering** *Chaenomeles*

rabbit berry *Shepherdia canadensis*
radish *Raphanus sativus*
ragged robin *Silene flos-cuculi*

Ramonda Rich. (Gesneriaceae).
ruh-*mon*-duh. After French botanist
Louis François Ramond de
Carbonnière (1755–1827), who
explored the Pyrenees. 3 spp. perenn.
herbs. S Eur.
myconi (L.) Rchb. mie-*koh*-nee. After
Francisco Micó (1528–1592), Spanish physician and botanist. Pyrenees.

Ranunculus L. (Ranunculaceae). ruh-
nunk-ew-loos. Buttercups. Lat. a little frog (many grow in water). 300
spp. ann. and perenn. herbs. Widespread.
aconitifolius L. ak-o-nie-ti-*foh*-lee-
oos. With leaves like *Aconitum*. C
and S Eur.
acris L. *ak*-ris. Meadow buttercup.
Lat. sharp (referring to the taste).
Canada, USA, Eur., W Asia.
asiaticus L. ay-see-*at*-i-koos. Lat.
Asian. SE Eur., N Africa, W Asia.
ficaria L. = *Ficaria verna*
gramineus L. gram-*in*-ee-oos. Lat.
grass-like (the leaves). C and S Eur.
lingua L. *ling*-wuh. Greater spearwort.

Lat. tongue-like (the leaves). Eur.,
W and C Asia.
repens L. *ree*-puhnz. Creeping buttercup. Lat. creeping. Eur., N Africa,
Asia.

rape *Brassica napus*

Raphanus L. (Brassicaceae). *raf*-uh-
noos. Lat. name for radish. 3 spp.
bienn. and perenn. herbs. Eur., N
Africa, W and C Asia.
sativus L. sa-*tee*-voos. Radish. Lat. cultivated. Cult.

raspberry *Rubus idaeus*

Ratibida Raf. (Asteraceae). rat-i-*beed*-
uh. Deriv. obscure. 7 spp. perenn.
herbs. Canada, USA, Mex.
columnaris (Sims) D. Don = *R.
columnifera*
columnifera (Nutt.) Wooton &
Standl. ko-loom-*nif*-uh-ruh. Mexican hat, prairie coneflower. Lat.
bearing columns (referring to the
shape of the receptacle). S Canada,
USA, Mex.
pinnata (Vent.) Barnhart. pin-*ah*-tuh.
Drooping prairie coneflower. Lat.
pinnate (the leaves). SE Canada, E
and C USA.

rattlebox *Ludwigia alternifolia*
red cardinal *Erythrina herbacea*
red-hot cat tail *Acalypha hispida*
red-hot poker *Kniphofia*
redbud *Cercis canadensis*. **California**
C. occidentalis. **Chinese** *C. chinensis*.
Texas *C. canadensis* var. *texana*.
western *C. occidentalis*
redmaids *Calandrinia*. **fringed** *C.
ciliata*

redwood, California *Sequoia semper-virens.* **coast** *S. sempervirens.* **giant** *Sequoiadendron giganteum*
reed, common *Phragmites australis.* **giant** *Arundo donax*
reedmace *Typha*

Rehmannia Libosch. ex Fisch. & C. A. Mey. (Orobanchaceae). ray-*man*-ee-uh. After Joseph Rehmann (1799–1831), physician of St. Petersburg. 6 spp. perenn. herbs. China.
elata N. E. Br. ex Prain. ee-*lah*-tuh. Chinese foxglove. Lat. tall.

Reineckea Kunth (Asparagaceae). rie-*nek*-ee-uh. After H. J. Reinecke (1798–1871), German grower of tropical plants. 1 sp., perenn. herb. China, Japan.
carnea (Andrews) Kunth. *kar*-nee-uh. Lat. flesh-pink (the flowers).

rex begonia vine *Cissus discolor*

Rhamnus L. (Rhamnaceae). *ram*-noos. Gk. name of a spiny shrub. 100 spp., shrubs, trees. N and S Am., Eur., Africa, Asia.
alaternus L. al-uh-*tern*-oos. Italian buckthorn. The Lat. name. S Eur., N Africa, SW Asia.
cathartica L. kuh-*thart*-i-kuh. Buckthorn. Gk. purging (it has been used as a laxative). Eur., N Africa, W and C Asia.
frangula L. = *Frangula alnus*
purshiana DC. = *Frangula purshiana*

Rhaphiolepis Lindl. (Rosaceae). raf-ee-oh-*lep*-is. Gk. needle scale, referring to the slender flower bracts. 15 spp., evergreen shrubs, trees. E Asia.

×*delacourii* André. del-uh-*kur*-ree-ee. After Delacour, French gardener who raised it near Cannes in the late 19th cent. *R. indica* × *R. umbellata.* Cult.
indica (L.) Lindl. ex Ker Gawl. *in*-di-kuh. Indian hawthorn. Lat. of India or the Indies. China, Taiwan, SE Asia.
umbellata (Thunb.) Makino. um-buhl-*ah*-tuh. Lat. in umbels (the flowers appear to be). E China, Taiwan, Japan.

Rhapis L.f. ex Aiton (Arecaceae). *rah*-pis. Lady palms. Gk. rod, referring to the rod-like stems. 8 spp. palms. S China, Japan, SE Asia.
excelsa (Thunb.) A. Henry. ex-*sel*-suh. Lat. tall. S China, Japan.
humilis Blume. *hew*-mi-lis. Lat. low (growing). S China, S Japan.

Rhazya orientalis (Decne.) A. DC. = *Amsonia orientalis*

Rheum L. (Polygonaceae). *ree*-oom. From the Gk. name. 60 spp. perenn. herbs. Eur., Asia.
×*hybridum* Murray. *hib*-ri-doom. Garden rhubarb. Lat. hybrid. *R. palmatum* × *R. rhaponticum.* Cult.
palmatum L. pahl-*mah*-toom. Ornamental rhubarb. Lat. palmate (the leaves). China.

Rhodanthe Lindl. (Asteraceae). roh-*danth*-ee. Gk. rose flower. 45 spp. ann. herbs. Australia.
chlorocephala (Turcz.) Paul G. Wilson. klo-roh-*kef*-uh-luh. Gk. green-headed, referring to the green involucral bracts. SW Australia. subsp. *rosea* (Hook.) Paul G. Wilson.

roh-zee-uh. Pink and white everlasting. Lat. pink (the bracts).

Rhodanthemum (Vogt) B. H. Wilcox et al. (Asteraceae). roh-*danth*-e-moom. Gk. rose flower. 15 spp., perenn. herbs, subshrubs. SW Eur., N Africa.
hosmariense (Ball) B. H. Wilcox et al. hos-mah-ree-*en*-see. Of the Beni Hosmar Mts. (near Tétouan, where the type specimen was collected). Morocco.

Rhodiola L. (Crassulaceae). roh-dee-*oh*-luh. From Gk. rose, referring to the fragrant roots of *R. rosea*. 90 spp. perenn. herbs. Alpine regs. of N hemisph.
pachyclados (Aitch. & Hemsl.) H. Ohba. pak-ee-*klay*-dos. Gk. with thick shoots. Afghanistan, Pakistan.
rosea L. *roh*-zee-uh. Roseroot. Lat. rose (from the fragrant roots). Eur., Asia, N Am.

Rhodochiton Zucc. ex Otto & Dietr. (Plantaginaceae). roh-doh-*kie*-ton. Gk. rose, or red, and cloak, referring to the large red calyx. 3 spp. semi-woody climbers. Mex., C Am.
atrosanguineum (Zucc.) Rothm. at-roh-san-*gwin*-ee-oom. Lat. dark red (the calyx). Mex.

Rhododendron L. (Ericaceae). roh-doh-*den*-dron. Gk. name for *Nerium oleander*, from Gk. rose tree. 1000 spp., shrubs, trees. N Am., Eur., Asia, Australia.
arborescens (Pursh) Torr. ar-bor-*res*-uhnz. Lat. becoming tree-like. E USA.

arboreum Sm. ar-*bor*-ree-oom. Lat. tree-like. Himal., China.
atlanticum (Ashe) Rehder. at-*lant*-i-koom. Of the Atlantic (states). E USA.
canescens (Michx.) Sweet. ka-*nes*-uhnz. Lat. greyish (the foliage). E USA.
'Cilpinense'. sil-pin-*en*-see. From the names of the parents, *R. ciliatum* × *R. moupinense*.
cinnabarinum Hook.f. sin-uh-buh-*reen*-oom. Lat. cinnabar red (the flowers). Himal., Tibet.
falconeri Hook.f. fal-*koh*-nuh-ree. After Scottish geologist and botanist Hugh Falconer (1808–1865), who travelled with author J. D. Hooker to India. Himal.
groenlandicum (Oeder) Kron & Judd. grurn-*land*-i-koom. Labrador tea. Of Greenland. Canada, Greenland, N USA.
impeditum Balf.f. & W. W. Sm. im-ped-*ee*-toom. Lat. intricate, tangled (the habit). China (Sichuan, Yunnan).
lutescens Franch. lue-*tes*-uhnz. Lat. yellowish (the flowers). China (Sichuan).
maccabeanum G. Watt ex Balf.f. muh-kay-bee-*ah*-noom. After Robert Blair McCabe (ca. 1854–1897), deputy commissioner in Manipur, who organised the expedition on which the first specimens were collected. NE India.
macrophyllum D. Don ex G. Don. mak-*rof*-i-loom. California rosebay. Gk. large-leaved. SW Canada, W USA.
maximum L. *max*-i-moom. Lat. large. SE Canada, E USA.

mucronulatum Turcz. mew-kron-ew-*lah*-toom. Lat. ending in a small point (the leaves). NE Asia.

occidentale (Torr. & A. Gray) A. Gray. ok-si-den-*tah*-lee. Lat. western. Calif., Oregon.

periclymenoides (Michx.) Shinners. pe-ree-klim-uhn-*oy*-deez. Lat. like *Periclymenum* (honeysuckle), referring to the flowers. E USA.

ponticum L. *pon*-ti-koom. Lat. of Pontus (now NE Turkey). Portugal, Spain, Bulgaria, W Asia.

'**Praecox**'. *prie*-kox. Lat. early (the flowers).

prinophyllum (Small) Millais. pree-*nof*-i-loom. Lat. with leaves like *Prinos* (deciduous species of *Ilex*). SE Canada, E USA.

prunifolium (Small) Millais. prue-ni-*foh*-lee-oom. Lat. with leaves like *Prunus*. SE USA.

schlippenbachii Maxim. shlip-uhn-*bahk*-ee-ee. After Russian baron and naval officer Alexander Egorovich von Schlippenbach (b. 1828), who discovered it in Manchuria in 1854. E Russia, Korea.

sinogrande Balf.f. & W. W. Sm. sie-noh-*grand*-ee. The Chinese *R. grande*. W China, N Myanmar.

vaseyi A. Gray. *vay*-zee-ee. After English-born American botanist George Vasey (1822–1893), who discovered it in 1878. SE USA (North Carolina).

viscosum (L.) Torr. vis-*koh*-soom. Swamp honeysuckle. Lat. sticky (the corolla glands). E USA.

williamsianum Rehder & E. H. Wilson. wil-yamz-ee-*ah*-noom. After John Charles (J. C.) Williams (1861–1939) of Caerhays Castle, Cornwall,

"the first amateur to appreciate the value of the Rhododendrons of western China." China (Sichuan).

yakushimanum Nakai. ya-kue-shi-*mah*-noom. Of Yahushima Is. Japan (Yakushima).

yedoense Maxim. yed-oh-*en*-see. Of Yedo (old name for Tokyo). Korea, Japan. var. *poukhanense* (H. Lév.) Nakai. pue-kan-*en*-see. Of Mount Bukhansan (Poukhan), S Korea. Korea.

yunnanense Franch. yue-nan-*en*-see. Of Yunnan. SW China, NW Myanmar.

Rhodohypoxis Nel (Hypoxidaceae). roh-doh-hie-*pox*-is. Gk. rose, and the related *Hypoxis*, referring to the flower colour. 6 spp. perenn. herbs. S Africa.

baurii (Baker) Nel. *bow*-ree-ee. After German pharmacist and missionary Leopold Richard Baur (1825–1889), who collected the type specimen in 1885.

milloides Hilliard & B. L. Burtt. mil-*oy*-deez. Lat. like *Milla*.

Rhodotypos Sieb. & Zucc. (Rosaceae). roh-doh-*tie*-pos. Gk. rose type, from the rose-like flowers. 1 sp., deciduous shrub. China, Japan, Korea.

scandens (Thunb.) Makino. *skan*-duhnz. Lat. climbing.

×**Rhodoxys** B. Mathew (Hypoxidaceae). roh-*dox*-is. From the names of the parents (*Hypoxis* × *Rhodohypoxis*). Cult.

hybrida B. Mathew. *hib*-ri-duh. Lat. hybrid.

rhubarb, garden *Rheum* ×*hybridum.*
ornamental *R. palmatum*

Rhus L. (Anacardiaceae). *roos.* Gk.
name for *R. coriaria.* 250 spp., trees,
shrubs, climbers. Widespread in
temp. and subtrop. regs.
aromatica Aiton. a-ro-*mat*-i-kuh. Fragrant sumach. Lat. aromatic (the foliage). Canada, USA, N Mex.
copallinum L. ko-puh-*leen*-oom.
Shining sumach. Like gum copal
(Nahuatl word for resin), from the
resemblance of the resin to that produced by a different tree. SE Canada,
E USA, Cuba.
glabra L. *glab*-ruh. Smooth sumach.
Lat. glabrous (the shoots). Canada,
USA, N Mex.
×*pulvinata* Greene. pool-vin-*ah*-tuh.
Lat. cushion-like (the fruit). *R. glabra* × *R. typhina.* Canada, USA.
trilobata Nutt. ex Torr. & A. Gray.
trie-loh-*bah*-tuh. Skunkbush. Lat.
three-lobed (the leaves). SW Canada,
W USA, Mex.
typhina L. tie-*feen*-uh. Stag's horn
sumach. Lat. like *Typha* (the velvety
shoots). E Canada, E and C USA.

Ribes L. (Grossulariaceae). *rie*-beez.
From Arabic acidic, referring to the
fruit. 160 spp. shrubs. Eur., N Africa,
Asia, Americas.
alpinum L. al-*pie*-noom. Alpine currant. Lat. of the Alps. Eur., N Africa,
W Asia.
aureum Pursh. *aw*-ree-oom. Golden
currant. Lat. golden (the flowers).
SW Canada, W and C USA. var. *villosum* DC. vil-*oh*-soom. Buffalo currant, clove currant. Lat. with long
hairs (on the shoots). C USA.

cereum Douglas. *seer*-ree-oom. Wax
currant. Lat. waxy (the foliage). SW
Canada, W USA.
×*culverwellii* Macfarl. kul-vuh-*wel*-
ee-ee. After W. Culverwell of York-
shire, who raised it in 1883. *R.
nigrum* × *R. uva-crispa.* Cult.
×*gordonianum* Lem. gor-doh-nee-*ah*-
noom. After William Gordon
(1794–1836) of Haffield, Hereford-
shire, whose gardener Donald Bea-
ton raised it in 1837. *R. odoratum* ×
R. sanguineum. Cult.
laurifolium Jancz. lo-ri-*foh*-lee-oom.
Lat. with leaves like *Laurus.* SW
China.
×*nidigrolaria* Rud. Bauer & A. Bauer.
ni-di-groh-*lair*-ree-uh. Jostaberry.
From the names of the parents, *R.
divaricatum* × *R. nigrum* × *R. uva-
crispa* (*Grossularia* is an old name for
the gooseberry). Cult.
nigrum L. *nie*-groom. Black currant.
Lat. black (the fruit). Eur., W and C
Asia, N China.
odoratum H. Wendl. = *R. aureum*
var. *villosum*
rubrum L. *rue*-broom. Red currant.
Lat. red (the fruit). Eur.
sanguineum Pursh. san-*gwin*-ee-oom.
Flowering currant. Lat. blood-red
(the flowers). SW Canada, W USA.
'Brocklebankii'. brok-uhl-*bank*-ee-
ee. After Ralph Brocklebank of
Haughton Hall, Cheshire, whose
head gardener, Thomas Winkworth,
raised it before 1914.
speciosum Pursh. spee-see-*oh*-soom.
Lat. showy (the flowers). Calif., N W
Mex.
uva-crispa L. *ue*-vuh-*kris*-puh. Gooseberry. Old name for gooseberry, from

Lat. crisp grape. Eur., N Africa, W Asia.

rice millet *Piptatherum miliaceum*
rice paper plant *Tetrapanax papyrifer*

Ricinus L. (Euphorbiaceae). *ris*-i-noos. Lat. tick, from the appearance of the seeds. 1 sp., shrub. NE trop. Africa.
communis L. *kom*-ew-nis. Castor oil plant. Lat. common.

Robinia L. (Fabaceae). rob-*in*-ee-uh. After Jean Robin (1550–1629), French botanist and physician, who grew plants from E North America, including *R. pseudoacacia*. 4 spp., trees, shrubs. USA, N Mex.
×***ambigua*** Poir. am-*big*-ew-uh. Lat. ambiguous, going two ways (i.e., with characters of two species). *R. pseudoacacia* × *R. viscosa*. Cult.
hispida L. *his*-pid-uh. Bristly locust. Lat. bristly (the shoots). SE USA.
×***margaretta*** Ashe. mar-guh-*ret*-uh. After Margaret Henry Wilcox, who married the author, William Willard Ashe, in 1906. *R. hispida* × *R. pseudoacacia*. SE USA.
pseudoacacia L. sue-doh-uh-*kay*-see-uh. Black locust. Gk. false *Acacia*. E and C USA.

rock purslane *Calandrinia umbellata*
rock rose *Helianthemum*
rockcress *Arabis*. **rose** *A. blepharophylla*
rocket *Eruca vesicaria* subsp. *sativa*. **yellow** *Barbarea vulgaris*
Rocky Mountain bee plant *Peritoma serrulata*

Rodgersia A. Gray (Saxifragaceae). ro-*jerz*-ee-uh. After US Navy commander John Rodgers (1812–1882), for his interest in "the naturalists in his squadron" and who, with others, collected the type specimen of *R. podophylla* from Hokkaido, Japan, in 1855. 5 spp. perenn. herbs. Himal., E Asia.
aesculifolia Batalin. ees-kew-li-*foh*-lee-uh. Lat. with leaves like *Aesculus*. China.
pinnata Franch. pin-*ah*-tuh. Lat. pinnate (the leaves). China.
podophylla A. Gray. pod-oh-*fil*-uh. Gk. foot leaf (from the resemblance of the leaves to a duck's foot). E China, Korea, Japan.
sambucifolia Hemsl. sam-bew-si-*foh*-lee-uh. Lat. with leaves like *Sambucus*. China.

Rohdea Roth (Asparagaceae). *roh*-dee-uh. After Michael Rohde (1782–1812), German physician and botanist. 4 spp. perenn. herbs. Himal. to Japan.
japonica (Thunb.) Roth. juh-*pon*-i-kuh. Of Japan. China, Korea, Japan.

Romneya Harv. (Papaveraceae). *rom*-nee-uh. After Irish astronomer and physicist Thomas Romney Robinson (1792–1882), to honour "Dr. Coulter's memory through his friend" (*Coulteria* had already been used for another genus). 1 sp., perenn. herb or subshrub. Calif., NW Mex.
coulteri Harv. *kool*-tuh-ree. Matilija poppy, tree poppy. After Irish physician and botanist Thomas Coulter (1793–1843), who collected the type specimen in California in 1832.

Rorippa nasturtium-aquaticum (L.)
Rendle & Britten = *Nasturtium*
officinale

Rosa L. (Rosaceae). *roh*-zuh. Roses.
Lat. name for the rose. 200 spp.,
shrubs, climbers. Eur., N Am., N and
E Africa, Asia.
acicularis Lindl. uh-sik-ew-*lah*-ris.
Prickly rose. Lat. prickly (the shoots).
Eur., Asia, Canada, USA.
arkansana Porter. ar-kuhn-*sah*-nuh.
Prairie rose. Of Arkansas. Canada,
E and C USA.
banksiae W. T. Aiton. *banks*-ee-ie.
After Lady Dorothea Banks (1758–
1820), wife of Sir Joseph Banks.
China.
blanda Aiton. *bland*-uh. Lat. smooth
(the prickles are sparse). E Canada,
NE and C USA.
brunonii Lindl. brue-*non*-ee-ee.
Himalayan musk rose. After Robert
Brown (1773–1858), botanist with
the Horticultural Society. Himal.,
China.
canina L. ka-*neen*-uh. Dog rose. From
the Gk. name (it was believed to cure
the bite of a mad dog). Eur., N Africa,
W and C Asia.
carolina L. ka-ro-*leen*-uh. Carolina
rose. Of the Carolinas. SE and C USA.
filipes Rehder & E. H. Wilson. *fil*-i-
peez. Lat. slender-stalked (the fruit).
China.
foetida Herrm. *feet*-i-duh. Austrian
briar. Lat. fetid (the flowers). W and
C Asia. **'Bicolor'**. *bi*-ko-lor. Austrian
copper briar. Lat. two-coloured (the
flowers). **'Persiana'**. pursh-ee-*ah*-nuh.
Persian yellow rose. Lat. of Persia
(Iran).
gallica L. *gal*-i-kuh. Red rose. Lat. of

France. Eur., W Asia. **'Officinalis'**.
o-fis-i-*nah*-lis. Apothecaries' rose.
Lat. sold as a med. herb.
glauca Pourr. *glaw*-kuh. Lat. bluish
white (the foliage). C and S Eur.
hugonis Hemsl. = *R. xanthina* f.
hugonis
moyesii Hemsl. & E. H. Wilson. moy-
eez-ee-ee. After Rev. James Moyes
(1876–1930), of the China Inland
Mission, stationed at Tatien-lu, for
his "hospitality, assistance, and com-
panionship [to author Wilson] . . . in
Eastern Tibet." China.
nutkana C. Presl. noot-*kah*-nuh.
Nootka rose. Of the Nootka Sound
reg., British Columbia. SW Canada,
W USA.
×*odorata* (Andrews) Sweet. oh-do-
rah-tuh. Lat. fragrant (the flowers).
R. chinensis × *R. gigantea*. Cult.
'Mutabilis'. mew-*tab*-i-lis. Lat.
changing (the flower colour).
palustris Marshall. puh-*lus*-tris.
Swamp rose. Lat. of marshes.
E N Am.
pimpinellifolia L. = *R. spinosissima*
rubiginosa L. rue-bij-i-*noh*-suh. Sweet
briar. Lat. rusty red (the foliage). Eur.,
W Asia.
rugosa Thunb. rue-*goh*-suh. Lat.
rough, wrinkled (the leaves). E Russia, E China, Korea, Japan.
sericea Lindl. suh-*rik*-ee-uh. Lat. silky
(the leaves). Himal., China. subsp.
omeiensis (Rolfe) A. V. Roberts. om-
ay-*en*-sis. Of Emei Shan (Mt. Omei).
China. f. *pteracantha* Franch. te-ruh-
kanth-uh. Gk. wing spine (referring
to the broad spines). China.
setigera Michx. see-*tij*-uh-ruh. Prairie
rose. Lat. bristly (the shoots). E and
C USA.

spinosissima L. spin-oh-*sis*-i-muh. Burnet rose. Lat. most spiny (the shoots). Eur., W and C Asia.

virginiana Mill. vir-jin-ee-*ah*-nuh. Of Virginia. E N Am.

wichurana Crép. wich-ue-*rah*-nuh. After German lawyer and plant collector Max Ernst Wichura (1817–1866), who collected the type specimen ca. 1860. E Asia.

woodsii Lindl. *woodz*-ee-ee. After English architect and botanist Joseph Woods (1776–1864), who studied roses. Canada, USA, N Mex.

xanthina Lindl. zanth-*een*-uh. Gk. yellow (the flowers). China. f. *hugonis* (Hemsl.) A. V. Roberts. hew-*goh*-nis. After Father Hugh (Lat. *Hugo*) Scallon, Welsh missionary in W China, who sent specimens to the British Museum. Seed from one of these was sent to Kew in 1899, from which it was raised and described.

Roscoea Sm. (Zingiberaceae). ros-*koh*-ee-uh. After William Roscoe (1753–1831), lawyer, politician and writer of Liverpool, UK. 22 spp. perenn. herbs. Pakistan, Himal., China.

alpina Royle. al-*pie*-nuh. Lat. alpine. N Pakistan, Himal.

auriculata K. Schum. o-rik-ew-*lah*-tuh. Lat. with small, ear-like lobes (at the leaf bases). Himal., Tibet.

cautleyoides Gagnep. kawt-lee-*oy*-deez. Lat. like *Cautleya*. China (Sichuan, Yunnan).

humeana Balf.f. & W. W. Sm. hewm-ee-*ah*-nuh. After Private David Hume of the Royal Scots, a young gardener at RBG Edinburgh, where it was grown, who was killed in

action in France in 1914. China (Sichuan, Yunnan).

purpurea Sm. pur-*pew*-ree-uh. Lat. purple (the flowers). Himal.

scillifolia (Gagnep.) Cowley. sil-i-*foh*-lee-uh. Lat. with leaves like *Scilla*. China (Yunnan).

rose *Rosa*. **apothecaries'** *R. gallica* 'Officinalis'. **burnet** *R. spinosissima*. **Carolina** *R. carolina*. **dog** *R. canina*. **Himalayan musk** *R. brunonii*. **Nootka** *R. nutkana*. **Persian yellow** *R. foetida* 'Persiana'. **prairie** *R. arkansana, R. setigera*. **prickly** *R. acicularis*. **red** *R. gallica*. **swamp** *R. palustris*

rose-bay willow herb *Chamerion angustifolium*

rose of Sharon *Hibiscus syriacus, Hypericum calycinum*

rosemallow, African *Hibiscus acetosella*. **crimson-eyed** *H. moscheutos*. **halberdleaf** *H. laevis*. **scarlet** *H. coccineus*. **woolly** *H. moscheutos* subsp. *lasiocarpos*

rosemary *Rosmarinus officinalis*. **bog** *Andromeda polifolia*

roseroot *Rhodiola rosea*

Rosmarinus L. (Lamiaceae). roz-*ma*-rin-oos. The Lat. name, from Lat. sea dew. 3 spp. shrubs. Medit.

officinalis L. o-fis-i-*nah*-lis. Rosemary. Lat. sold as a med. herb.

rowan *Sorbus aucuparia*

rubber plant *Ficus elastica*

Rubus L. (Rosaceae). *rue*-boos. The Lat. name. 250 spp., shrubs, herbs. Widespread.

cockburnianus Hemsl. koh-burn-ee-*ah*-noos. After H. Cockburn of HM Consular Service, Chungking (now Chongqing), and Rev. G. Cockburn of the Church of Scotland mission in China, for their assistance to Antwerp Pratt, who collected the type specimen. China.

fruticosus L. frue-ti-*koh*-soos. Blackberry, bramble. Lat. shrubby. Eur.

idaeus L. i-*dee*-oos. Raspberry. Lat. of Mount Ida. Eur. to Japan.

lineatus Reinw. ex Blume. lin-ee-*ah*-toos. Lat. lined (referring to the conspicuous leaf veins). Himal., W China, SE Asia.

×*loganobaccus* L. H. Bailey. loh-gahn-oh-*bak*-oos. Loganberry. After American judge and horticulturist James Harvey Logan (1841–1928), who raised it, and Lat. berry. Cult.

odoratus L. oh-do-*rah*-toos. Thimbleberry. Lat. fragrant (the flowers). E N Am.

parviflorus Nutt. par-vi-*flaw*-roos. Salmonberry, thimbleberry. Lat. small-flowered. Canada, USA, N Mex.

phoenicolasius Maxim. feen-i-ko-*lay*-see-oos. Japanese wineberry. Gk. purple-haired (the shoots). China, Korea, Japan.

spectabilis Pursh. spek-*tab*-i-lis. Salmonberry. Lat. spectacular. SW Canada, W USA.

thibetanus Franch. ti-bet-*ah*-noos. Of Tibet. China.

tricolor Focke. *tri*-ko-lor. Lat. three-coloured. China (Sichuan, Yunnan).

Rudbeckia L. (Asteraceae). rood-*bek*-ee-uh. Coneflowers. For Olaus (Olof) Johannes Rudbeck (1630–1702) and Olaus (Olof) Olai Rudbeck (1660–1740), father and son, professors at Uppsala University, Sweden. 23 spp. ann., bienn. and perenn. herbs. N Am.

amplexicaulis Vahl. am-plex-i-*kawl*-is. Lat. with leaves clasping the stem. C and SE USA.

fulgida Aiton. *fool*-ji-duh. Orange coneflower. Lat. shining. E USA. var. *deamii* (S. F. Blake) Perdue. *deem*-ee-ee. After American forester Charles Clemon Deam (1865–1953), who collected the type specimen in Indiana in 1916. USA (Indiana, Ohio). var. *speciosa* (Wenderoth) Perdue. spee-see-*oh*-suh. Showy coneflower. Lat. showy. var. *sullivantii* (C. L. Boynton & Beadle) Cronquist. sul-i-*vant*-ee-ee. After American surveyor William Starling Sullivant (1803–1873), who collected the type specimen in Ohio in 1840.

hirta L. *hirt*-uh. Black-eyed Susan. Lat. hairy (the leaves and stems). E USA.

laciniata L. luh-sin-ee-*ah*-tuh. Cutleaf coneflower. Lat. deeply cut (the leaves). S Canada, E and C USA.

maxima Nutt. *max*-i-muh. Great coneflower. Lat. largest. SE USA.

occidentalis Nutt. ok-si-den-*tah*-lis. Western coneflower. Lat. western. W USA.

subtomentosa Pursh. sub-to-men-*toh*-suh. Sweet coneflower. Lat. somewhat hairy. E USA.

triloba L. trie-*loh*-buh. Brown-eyed Susan. Lat. three-lobed (the leaves). E and C USA.

rue *Ruta graveolens*

Rumex L. (Polygonaceae). *rue*-mex. Docks. Possibly from Lat. to suck (the leaves were sucked to quench thirst). 200 spp. ann. and perenn. herbs. Widespread, mainly temp. regs.

acetosa L. a-see-*toh*-suh. Garden sorrel. Lat. acid (the taste of the leaves). Eur. to Japan, N Africa.

sanguineus L. san-*gwin*-ee-oos. Bloody dock. Lat. bloody (the leaf veins). Eur., W Asia.

scutatus L. skue-*tah*-toos. French sorrel. Lat. shield-shaped (the leaves). Eur., W Asia.

Ruscus L. (Asparagaceae). *rus*-koos. From the Lat. name. 6 spp. evergreen shrubs. Macaronesia to W Asia.

aculeatus L. uh-kew-lee-*ah*-toos. Butcher's broom. Lat. prickly (the foliage). Medit., W Asia.

rush *Juncus.* **Baltic** *J. balticus.* **Dudley's** *J. dudleyi.* **flowering** *Butomus umbellatus.* **great wood**

Luzula sylvatica. **slender** *Juncus tenuis.* **snow** *Luzula nivea.* **soft** *Juncus effusus*

Russelia Jacq. (Plantaginaceae). rus-*el*-ee-uh. After Alexander Russell (1715–1768), English physician and naturalist. 50 spp. shrubs. Mex. to Colombia.

equisetiformis Schltdl. & Cham. ee-kwiz-i-tee-*form*-is. Firecracker plant, fountain plant. Lat. like *Equisetum.* Mex.

Russian olive *Elaeagnus angustifolia* **Russian vine** *Fallopia baldschuanica*

Ruta L. (Rutaceae). *rue*-tuh. From the Gk. name. 7 spp., herbs, shrubs. Macaronesia to SW Asia.

graveolens L. grav-ee-*oh*-luhnz. Rue. Lat. strongly scented (the foliage). S Eur.

Saccharum L. (Poaceae). *sak*-uh-room. From Gk. sugar, which is produced from some species. 40 spp. grasses. Old World trop. and subtrop. regs.
ravennae (L.) L. ra-*ven*-ie. Ravenna grass. Lat. of Ravenna, Italy. S Eur., N Africa, W and C Asia.

saffron *Crocus sativus*
sage *Salvia officinalis*. **blue** *S. azurea*. **Jerusalem** *Phlomis fruticosa*. **mealy** *Salvia farinacea*. **scarlet** *S. coccinea*. **silver** *S. argentea*. **white** *S. apiana*
sagebrush, big *Artemisia tridentata*. **black** *A. nova*. **sand** *A. filifolia*. **white** *A. ludoviciana*
sagewort, prairie *Artemisia frigida*

Sagina L. (Caryophyllaceae). suh-*geen*-uh. From Lat. fodder (sheep were fed on a related plant). 20 spp. ann. and perenn. herbs. N temp. regs., trop. mts.
subulata (Sw.) C. Presl. sub-ew-*lah*-tuh. Pearlwort. Lat. awl-shaped (the leaves). Eur.

Sagittaria Rupp. ex L. (Alismataceae). sag-i-*tah*-ree-uh. Arrowhead. From Lat. arrow, referring to the leaf shape. 40 spp. aquatic herbs. Widespread.

latifolia Willd. lat-i-*foh*-lee-uh. Lat. broad-leaved. S Canada to Ecuador.
sagittifolia L. sag-i-ti-*foh*-lee-uh. Lat. with arrow-shaped leaves. Eur., W Asia.

Saintpaulia H. Wendl. (Gesneriaceae). saint-*pawl*-ee-uh. After Baron Walter von Saint Paul-Illaire (1860–1910), German governor of a province of Tanganyika (now in Tanzania), who discovered *S. ionantha* and sent seeds to his father, which gave the plants from which it was described. 6 spp. perenn. herbs. E Africa.
ionantha H. Wendl. ie-on-*anth*-uh. African violet. Gk. with violet flowers. Tanzania.

salal *Gaultheria shallon*

Salix L. (Salicaceae). *sa*-lix. Willows. The Lat. name. 450 spp., trees, shrubs. Americas, Eur., Africa, Asia.
acutifolia Willd. uh-kew-ti-*foh*-lee-uh. Lat. with sharp-pointed leaves. E Eur., W and C Asia.
alba L. *al*-buh. White willow. Lat. white (the leaves). Eur. to China, N Africa. **'Britzensis'**. britz-*en*-sis. Scarlet willow. Of Britz, near Berlin, where it was raised at the Späth nursery. var. **caerulea** (Sm.) W. D. J. Koch. kie-*rue*-lee-uh. Cricket bat willow. Lat. blue (the foliage). var. **sericea** Gaudin. suh-*rik*-ee-uh. Lat. silky (the leaves). var. **vitellina** (L.) Stokes. vi-tuh-*leen*-uh. Golden willow. Lat. egg-yolk yellow (the shoots).
amygdaloides Anderss. uh-mig-duh-*loy*-deez. Peach-leaf willow. Lat.

almond-like (the leaves). Canada, USA, N Mex.

arenaria L. = *S. repens* subsp. *arenaria*

babylonica L. bab-i-*lon*-i-kuh. Weeping willow. Lat. of Babylon. It was thought to be the willow of Babylon mentioned in the Bible, now known to be *Populus euphratica*. China. var. *pekinensis* Henry. pee-kin-*en*-sis. Peking willow. Of Peking (Beijing). NE China, Korea.

bebbiana Sarg. beb-ee-*ah*-nuh. After American botanist Michael Schuck Bebb (1833–1895), who studied willows. Canada, USA, NE Russia.

caprea L. ka-*pree*-uh. Goat willow, pussy willow. Lat. of goats. Eur. to E Russia, N China.

chaenomeloides Kimura. kie-nom-uh-*loy*-deez. Lat. like *Chaenomeles* (the leaves). China, Korea, Japan.

cinerea L. sin-*e*-ree-uh. Grey willow, pussy willow. Lat. ash-grey (the foliage). Eur., W and C Asia.

daphnoides Vill. daf-*noy*-deez. Violet willow. Lat. laurel-like (the foliage). Eur.

discolor Muhl. *dis*-ko-lor. American pussy willow. Lat. two-coloured (the leaves). Canada, USA.

eleagnos Scop. el-ee-*ag*-nos. Hoary willow. Gk. olive-like. Eur., Turkey. 'Erythroflexuosa'. e-rith-roh-flex-ew-*oh*-suh. Gk. red, twisted (the shoots).

euxina I. V. Belyaeva. ewx-*een*-uh. Crack willow. Gk. of the Baltic. Eur., W Asia.

exigua Nutt. ex-*ig*-ew-uh. Coyote willow. Lat. small. Canada, USA, N Mex.

fargesii Burkill. far-*jee*-zee-ee. After French missionary Paul Guillaume Farges (1844–1912), who collected

one of the specimens from which it was described in Sichuan. China.

×*fragilis* L. *fraj*-i-lis. Lat. fragile (the shoots). *S. alba* × *S. euxina*. Eur.

fragilis auct. = *S. euxina*

gracilistyla Miq. gras-i-li-*stie*-luh. Lat. with a slender style. China, Japan, Korea. 'Melanostachys'. me-lan-oh-*stak*-is. Gk. with black spikes (the catkins).

hastata L. has-*tah*-tuh. Halberd willow. Lat. spear-shaped (the leaves). Eur. to NE Russia, NW Canada, Alaska. 'Wehrhahnii'. vair-*hahn*-ee-ee. After German horticultural writer H. R. Wehrhahn (1887–1940).

helvetica Vill. hel-*vet*-i-kuh. Swiss willow. Lat. of Switzerland (Lat. *Helvetia*). C and S Eur.

hookeriana Barratt ex Hook. hook-uh-ree-*ah*-nuh. After Sir William Jackson Hooker (1785–1865), English botanist and first director of RBG Kew. The name was published in his *Flora Boreali-Americana*. SW Canada, W USA.

integra Thunb. in-*teg*-ruh. Lat. entire, untoothed (the leaves). E Russia, Korea, Japan.

lanata L. lan-*ah*-tuh. Woolly willow. Lat. woolly (the leaves). N Eur., Siberia.

magnifica Hemsl. mag-*ni*-fi-kuh. Lat. magnificent. China (Sichuan).

matsudana Koidz. = *S. babylonica* var. *pekinensis*

nigra Marshall. *nie*-gruh. Black willow. Lat. black (the bark). E Canada. E and C USA.

×*pendulina* Wender. pen-dew-*leen*-uh. Lat. weeping (the branches). *S. babylonica* × *S. euxina*. Cult.

pentandra L. pent-*an*-druh. Bay willow. Gk. with five stamens. Eur. to E Russia, China.

purpurea L. pur-*pew*-ree-uh. Purple osier. Lat. purple (the shoots). Eur., N Africa.

repens L. *ree*-puhnz. Creeping willow. Lat. creeping. Eur. var. *argentea* (Sm.) Wimm. & Grab. = subsp. *arenaria*. subsp. *arenaria* (L.) Hiitonen. a-ruh-*nah*-ree-uh. Lat. growing on sand.

×*rubens* Schrank = *S.* ×*fragilis*

scouleriana Barratt ex Hook. skuel-uh-ree-*ah*-nuh. After Scottish physician and naturalist John Scouler (1804–1871), who collected the type specimen in 1825. W Canada, W USA, N Mex.

×*sepulcralis* Simonk. sep-ool-*krah*-lis. Lat. of graveyards. *S. alba* × *S. babylonica*. Cult. 'Chrysocoma'. krie-soh-*kohm*-uh. Golden weeping willow. Gk. with a golden head of hair (referring to the shoots).

sericea Marshall. suh-*rik*-ee-uh. Silky willow. Lat. silky (the leaves). E N Am.

udensis Trautv. & C. A. Mey. ue-*den*-sis. Of the Uda River. E Russia, N China, Japan.

viminalis L. vim-i-*nah*-lis. Common osier. Lat. with long, slender shoots. Eur. to N China, E Russia.

salmonberry *Rubus parviflorus, R. spectabilis*

salt tree *Halimodendron halodendron*

saltbush, big *Atriplex lentiformis.* **cattle** *A. polycarpa.* **four-wing** *A. canescens.* **Gardner's** *A. gardneri.* **spiny** *A. confertifolia*

Salvia L. (Lamiaceae). *sal*-vee-uh. Lat. name for sage, from Lat. to heal, referring to its med. properties. 900 spp., herbs, shrubs. Eur., Africa, Asia, Americas.

apiana Jeps. ap-ee-*ah*-nuh. White sage. Lat. of bees (which are attracted to it). Calif., NW Mex. (B.C.).

argentea L. ar-*jent*-ee-uh. Silver sage. Lat. silvery (the foliage). Medit.

aurea L. *aw*-ree-uh. Lat. golden (the flowers). S Africa.

azurea Lam. uh-*zew*-ree-uh. Blue sage. Lat. blue (the flowers). SE and C USA. var. *grandiflora* Benth. grandi-*flaw*-ruh. Lat. large-flowered.

blepharophylla Brandegee. blef-uh-roh-*fil*-uh. Gk. with fringed leaves. Mex.

buchananii Hedge. bew-kan-*an*-ee-ee. After Sir Charles Buchanan, who grew it from Mexican seed. Cult.

cacaliifolia Benth. kuh-kah-lee-i-*foh*-lee-uh. Lat. with leaves like *Cacalia*. Mex., Guatemala.

candelabrum Boiss. kan-duh-*lab*-room. Lat. like a candelabra (the inflorescence). S Spain.

chamaedryoides Cav. kam-ee-dree-*oy*-deez. Lat. like a dwarf oak (the leaves). Mex.

clevelandii (A. Gray) Greene. kleev-*land*-ee-ee. After American lawyer and naturalist Daniel Cleveland (1839–1929), who collected the type specimen in 1875. Calif., NW Mex. (B.C.).

coccinea Buc'hoz ex Etl. kok-*sin*-ee-uh. Scarlet sage. Lat. scarlet (the flowers). S USA to Brazil.

discolor Kunth. *dis*-ko-lor. Lat. two-coloured (the leaves). Peru.

elegans Vahl. *el*-i-ganz. Lat. elegant. Mex., Guatemala.

farinacea Benth. fa-ri-*nay*-see-uh. Mealy sage. Lat. mealy (the stems). S USA, Mex.

forsskaolii L. for-*shohl*-ee-ee. After Finnish botanist Pehr Forsskål (1732–1753), a student of Linnaeus. SE Eur., Turkey.

fulgens Cav. *fool*-juhnz. Lat. shining (the flowers). Mex.

glutinosa L. glue-ti-*noh*-suh. Lat. sticky (the leaves and shoots). Eur., W Asia.

greggii A. Gray. *greg*-ee-ee. After American naturalist Josiah Gregg (1806–1850), who collected the type specimen in Mexico ca. 1848. Texas, Mex.

guaranitica A. St.-Hil. ex Benth. ga-ra-*nit*-i-kuh. Of Guara, Brazil. S Am.

involucrata Cav. in-vol-ue-*krah*-tuh. Lat. with an involucre (of bracts). Mex. **'Bethellii'**. beth-*el*-ee-ee. After Mr Bethell, who raised it before 1880.

×*jamensis* J. Compton. hahm-*en*-sis. Of Jame, Coahuila, where it was discovered in 1991. *S. greggii* × *S. microphylla*. Mex.

lavandulifolia Vahl. la-van-dew-li-*foh*-li-uh. Lat. with leaves like *Lavandula*. SW Eur., N Africa.

leucantha Cav. lue-*kanth*-uh. Gk. white-flowered. Mex., C Am.

lyrata L. lie-*rah*-tuh. Lat. with lyre-shaped leaves. E USA.

microphylla Kunth. mik-*rof*-i-luh. Gk. small-leaved. Mex.

nemorosa L. nem-o-*roh*-suh. Lat. of woods. Eur., W and C Asia. subsp.

tesquicola (Klokov & Pobed.) Soó. tes-*kee*-ko-luh. Lat. of the steppe.

officinalis L. o-fis-i-*nah*-lis. Sage. Lat. sold as a med. herb. SE Eur.

patens Cav. *pay*-tuhnz. Lat. spreading (the flowers). Mex.

pratensis L. pruh-*ten*-sis. Meadow clary. Lat. of meadows. Eur.

sclarea L. *sklair*-ree-uh. Clary. An old name, from Lat. clear; clary from clear eye, from med. properties. S Eur., W and C Asia.

splendens Sellow ex Schult. *splen*-duhnz. Lat. splendid. Brazil.

×*superba* Stapf. sue-*per*-buh. Lat. superb. Cult.

×*sylvestris* L. sil-*ves*-tris. Lat. of woods. C Asia.

uliginosa Benth. ew-lij-i-*noh*-suh. Lat. of marshes. S Am.

verticillata L. vur-ti-si-*lah*-tuh. Whorled clary. Lat. whorled (the flowers). Eur., W Asia.

viridis L. *vi*-ri-dis. Annual clary. Lat. green (the bracts, sometimes). Eur., N Africa, W and C Asia.

Sambucus L. (Adoxaceae). sam-*bew*-koos. The Lat. name. 9 spp., trees, shrubs, herbs. Temp. and trop. regs.

canadensis L. = *S. nigra* subsp. *canadensis*

nigra L. *nie*-gruh. Elder. Lat. black (the fruit). Eur., N Africa, W Asia. subsp. *canadensis* (L.) R. Bolli. kan-uh-*den*-sis. American elder. Of Canada. Canada, USA, Mex.

racemosa L. ras-i-*moh*-suh. Red-berried elder. Lat. in racemes (the flowers). Eur., Asia, N Am.

sandwort *Arenaria*

Sanguinaria L. (Papaveraceae). san-gwin-*air*-ree-uh. From Lat. blood, referring to the red sap. 1 sp., perenn. herb. SE Canada, E USA.
canadensis L. kan-uh-*den*-sis. Blood-root. Of Canada.

Sanguisorba L. (Rosaceae). san-gwi-*sorb*-uh. From Lat. blood, to absorb (it was said to stop bleeding). 30 spp. perenn. herbs. Eur., N Africa, Asia, N Am.
albiflora (Makino) Makino. al-bi-*flaw*-ruh. Lat. white-flowered. Japan.
canadensis L. kan-uh-*den*-sis. Cana-dian burnet. Of Canada. Canada, USA.
hakusanensis Makino. hak-ue-san-*en*-sis. Of Mount Hakusan, Japan. Japan, Korea.
menziesii Rydb. men-*zeez*-ee-ee. After Archibald Menzies (1754–1842), Scottish surgeon and naturalist. W Canada, NW USA.
minor Scop. *mie*-nuh. Salad burnet. Lat. small. Eur., N Africa, W Asia.
obtusa Maxim. ob-*tew*-suh. Lat. blunt (the leaflets). Japan.
officinalis L. o-fis-i-*nah*-lis. Great bur-net. Lat. sold as a med. herb. Eur., Asia, Canada, USA.
tenuifolia Fisch. ex Link. ten-ew-i-*foh*-lee-uh. Lat. with slender leaves (leaf-lets). NE Asia.

Sansevieria Thunb. (Asparagaceae). san-sev-ee-*e*-ree-uh. After Italian scientist Raimondo di Sangro (1710–1771), prince of Sansevero. 65 spp. evergreen herbs. Africa, Arabia, S Asia.
trifasciata Prain. trie-fas-ee-*ah*-tuh. Mother-in-law's tongue. Lat. in clus-ters of three (the flowers). Trop. Africa. **'Laurentii'**. lo-*rent*-ee-ee. After French plant collector Émile Laurent (1861–1904), who intro-duced it to gardens from Zaire.

Santolina L. (Asteraceae). sant-o-*lee*-nuh. From Lat. holy flax (*sanctum linum*). 5 spp. shrubs. Medit.
chamaecyparissus L. kam-ee-sip-uh-*ris*-oos. Lavender cotton. Gk. dwarf cypress. S Eur.
pinnata Viv. pin-*ah*-tuh. Lat. pinnate (the leaves). Italy. subsp. *neapolitana* (Jord. & Fourr.) Guinea. nee-uh-pol-i-*tah*-nuh. Lat. of Naples (Lat. *Neapoli*).
rosmarinifolia L. roz-ma-ri-ni-*foh*-lee-uh. Lat. with leaves like *Rosmarinus*. SW Eur.

Saponaria L. (Caryophyllaceae). sa-pon-*ah*-ree-uh. From Lat. soap, which can be made from *S. officina-lis*. 30 spp. ann. and perenn. herbs. Medit. to China.
×*lempergii* hort. lem-*perg*-ee-ee. After Austrian botanist Fritz Lemperg, who raised it. *S. cypria* × *S. haussknechtii*. Cult.
ocymoides L. ok-i-*moy*-deez. Rock soapwort. Lat. like *Ocimum*. C and S Eur.
officinalis L. o-fis-i-*nah*-lis. Bouncing Bet, soapwort. Lat. sold as a med. herb. Madeira, Eur., W Asia, Siberia.

sapphire flower *Browallia speciosa*

Sarcococca Lindl. (Buxaceae). sar-koh-*kok*-uh. Christmas box, sweet box. Gk. fleshy berry, referring to the fruit. 20 spp. evergreen shrubs. China, Taiwan, Mex., C Am.

confusa Sealy. kon-*few*-suh. Lat. confused (with other species in gardens). Cult.

hookeriana Baill. hook-uh-ree-*ah*-nuh. After English botanist Joseph Dalton Hooker (1817–1911), who collected it in the Himalaya. Himal., China. var. *digyna* Franch. die-*gie*-nuh. Gk. with two styles.

orientalis C. Y. Wu ex M. Cheng. o-ree-en-*tah*-lis. Lat. eastern. China.

ruscifolia Stapf. rus-ki-*foh*-lee-uh. Lat. with leaves like *Ruscus*. China. var. *chinensis* (Franch.) Rehder & E. H. Wilson. chin-*en*-sis. Of China.

Sarracenia L. (Sarraceniaceae).sa-ruh-*seen*-ee-uh. Pitcher plants. After Michel Sarrazin (Sarrasin) (1659–1734), Canadian surgeon and botanist. 11 spp. perenn. herbs. N Am.

alata (Alph. Wood) Alph. Wood. uh-*lah*-tuh. Lat. winged (the pitchers). SE USA.

leucophylla Raf. lue-koh-*fil*-uh. Gk. white-leaved (the pitchers). SE USA.

oreophila W herry. o-ree-oh-*fil*-uh. Gk. mountain-loving. SE USA.

purpurea L. pur-*pew*-ree-uh. Lat. purple (the flowers). SE USA.

rubra Walter. *rue*-bruh. Lat. red (the flowers and pitchers). SE USA.

Sasa Makino & Shibata (Poaceae). *sah*-suh. The Japanese name. 50 spp. bamboos. China, Japan, Korea, E Russia.

kurilensis (Rupr.) Makino & Shibata. koo-ril-*en*-sis. Of the Kuril Is. E Russia (Sakhalin), Japan, Korea.

palmata (hort. ex Burb.) E. G. Camus. pahl-*mah*-tuh. Lat. hand-like (the arrangement of the leaves). E Russia, Japan. f. *nebulosa* (Makino) Suzuki. neb-ew-*loh*-suh. Lat. like a little cloud (the blotched stems).

tessellata (Munro) Makino & Shibata = *Indocalamus tessellatus*

tsuboiana Makino. tsue-boh-ee-*ah*-nuh. After Japanese bamboo grower Isuke Tsuboi. Japan.

veitchii (Carrière) Rehder. veech-ee-ee. After British plant collector and nurseryman John Gould Veitch (1839–1870), who introduced it to England ca. 1861. Japan.

Sasaella Makino (Poaceae). sah-suh-*el*-uh. Diminutive of *Sasa*. 11 spp. bamboos. Japan.

masamuneana (Makino) Hatus. & Muroi ex Sugim. mas-uh-mewn-ee-*ah*-nuh. After Japanese botanist Genkei Masamune (1899–1993), who collected the type specimen in 1928.

ramosa (Makino) Makino. ra-*moh*-suh. Lat. branched.

Sassafras Nees & Eberm. (Lauraceae). *sas*-uh-fras. From the French and Spanish name, possibly derived from a Native American name. 3 spp. trees. SE Canada, E USA, China, Taiwan.

albidum (Nutt.) Nees. *al*-bi-doom. Sassafras. Lat. white (the lower leaf surface). SE Canada, E USA.

satin flower *Clarkia amoena*
satsuma *Citrus reticulata*

Satureja L. (Lamiaceae). sat-ew-*ree*-uh. Lat. (from Arabic) name of a

herb. 38 spp., herbs, shrubs. Medit., W Asia.
hortensis L. hor-*ten*-sis. Summer savoury. Lat. of gardens. S Eur., Turkey.
montana L. mon-*tah*-nuh. Winter savoury. Lat. of mountains. S Eur., W Asia.
spicigera (K. Koch) Boiss. spi-*si*-juh-ruh. Lat. bearing spikes (of flowers). W Asia.

savin *Juniperus sabina*
savoury, summer *Satureja hortensis.* **winter** *S. montana*
sawwort *Serratula*

Saxegothaea Lindl. (Podocarpaceae). sax-i-*goth*-ee-uh. After Prince Albert of Saxe-Coburg-Gotha (1818–1861), husband of Queen Victoria. 1 sp., conifer. Chile, Argentina.
conspicua Lindl. kon-*spik*-ew-uh. Prince Albert's yew. Lat. conspicuous.

Saxifraga L. (Saxifragaceae). sax-i-*frah*-guh. Saxifrages. Lat. stone, break (they often grow in crevices). 450 spp., mainly perenn. herbs. Eur., Asia, N and S Am.
cuneifolia L. kew-nee-i-*foh*-lee-uh. Lat. with wedge-shaped leaves. C Eur.
fortunei Hook.f. for-*tewn*-ee-ee. After Robert Fortune (1812–1880), Scottish botanist and plant collector. It was described from his introduction. E Asia.
hirsuta L. hir-*sue*-tuh. Kidney saxifrage. Lat. hairy (the leaves). W Eur.
oppositifolia L. o-po-si-ti-*foh*-lee-uh. Purple saxifrage. Lat. with opposite leaves. Canada, USA, Eur., temp. Asia.

paniculata Mill. pan-ik-ew-*lah*-tuh. Lat. in panicles (the flowers). C and S Eur., W Asia.
stolonifera Curtis. stoh-lon-*if*-uh-ruh. Mother of thousands. Lat. bearing stolons. China, Taiwan, Korea, Japan.
umbrosa L. um-*broh*-suh. Lat. growing in shade. Pyrenees.
×***urbium*** D. A. Webb. *urb*-ee-oom. London pride. Lat. of towns. *S. hirsuta* × *S. umbrosa*. Cult.

saxifrage *Saxifraga.* **kidney** *S. hirsuta.* **purple** *S. oppositifolia*

Scabiosa L. (Dipsacaceae). ska-bee-*oh*-suh. Scabious. Lat. itch, from med. properties. 80 spp., herbs, shrubs. Eur., Africa, Asia.
atropurpurea L. at-roh-pur-*pew*-ree-uh. Sweet scabious. Lat. dark purple (the flowers).
caucasica M. Bieb. kaw-*kas*-i-kuh. Lat. of the Caucasus. W Asia.
columbaria L. ko-loom-*bah*-ree-uh. Lat. dove-like. Eur., N Africa, W and C Asia.
ochroleuca L. ok-roh-*lue*-kuh. Gk. yellowish white (the flowers). Eur. to N China.

scabious *Scabiosa.* **alpine** *Cephalaria alpina.* **devil's bit** *Succisa pratensis.* **giant** *Cephalaria gigantea.* **sweet** *Scabiosa atropurpurea*

Scaevola L. (Goodeniaceae). skie-*voh*-luh. Lat. left-handed, from the appearance of the corolla. 80 spp., herbs, shrubs, trees. SE Asia to Australia.

aemula R. Br. *eem*-ew-luh. Fairy fan flower. Lat. emulating. SE Australia.

Schefflera J. R. & G. Forst. (Araliaceae). *shef*-luh-ruh. After Jacob Christoph Scheffler (1698–1742), German botanist and physician. 600 spp., shrubs, trees, climbers. Tropics and subtropics.
actinophylla (Endl.) Harms. ak-tin-oh-*fil*-uh. Gk. ray leaf (from the arrangement of the leaflets). New Guinea, NE Australia.
arboricola (Hayata) Merr. ar-bo-*ri*-ko-luh. Lat. living on trees (it is epiphytic). Taiwan.
elegantissima (Masters) Lowry & Frodin. el-i-gan-*tis*-i-muh. Lat. most elegant. New Caledonia.

Schisandra Michx. (Schisandraceae). ski-*san*-druh. From Gk. divided man, referring to the separated anther cells. 22 spp. woody climbers. E and SE Asia.
chinensis (Turcz.) Baill. chin-*en*-sis. Of China. China, E Russia, Korea, Japan.
grandiflora (Wall.) Hook.f. & Thomson. gran-di-*flaw*-ruh. Lat. large-flowered. Himal., Tibet.
rubriflora Rehder & E. H. Wilson. rue-bri-*flaw*-ruh. Lat. red-flowered. Assam to SW China.

Schizachyrium Nees (Poaceae). skits-uh-*ki*-ree-oom. Gk. split chaff, referring to the divided lemma. 60 spp. grasses. Widespread, mainly warm and trop. regs.
scoparium (Michx.) Nash. skoh-*pair*-ree-oom. Little bluestem. Lat. broom-like. Canada, USA, N Mex.

Schizophragma Sieb. & Zucc. (Hydrangeaceae). skits-oh-*frag*-muh. Gk. divided wall, referring to the split walls of the fruit. 10 spp. woody climbers. China, Korea, Japan.
hydrangeoides Sieb. & Zucc. hie-drayn-jee-*oy*-deez. Lat. like *Hydrangea*. Japan.
integrifolium Oliv. in-teg-ri-*foh*-lee-oom. Lat. with untoothed leaves. China.

Schizostylis coccinea Backh. & Harvey = *Hesperantha coccinea*

Schlumbergera Lem. (Cactaceae). shloom-*burg*-uh-ruh. After French cactus collector Frédéric Schlumberger (1823–1893). 6 spp. cacti. Brazil.
×*buckleyi* (T. Moore) Tjaden. *buk*-lee-ee. Christmas cactus. After William Buckley, who raised it in the 1840s. *S. russelliana* × *S. truncata*. Cult.
truncata (Haw.) Moran. trun-*kah*-tuh. Thanksgiving cactus. Lat. abruptly cut off (the stem segments).

Schoenoplectus (Rchb.) Palla (Cyperaceae). skeen-oh-*plek*-toos. Bulrushes. Gk. reed, plaited (the stems are used for making objects). 77 spp. ann. and perenn. herbs. Widespread.
acutus (Muhl. ex Bigelow) Á. Löve & D. Löve. uh-*kew*-toos. Lat. sharp-pointed (the spikelets). Canada, USA.
lacustris (L.) Palla. luh-*kus*-tris. Lat. of lakes. Eur., Asia, Africa.
pungens (Vahl) Palla. *pung*-uhnz. Lat. sharp-pointed (the flower scales).
tabernaemontani (C. C. Gmel.) Palla. tab-er-nie-mon-*tah*-nee. After German physician and botanist

Jacob Theodore Mueller von Bergzabern (Lat. *Tabernaemontanus*) (1522–1590). '**Zebrinus**'. zeb-reen-oos. Zebra-like (the striped shoots).

validus Vahl = *S. tabernaemontani*

Sciadopitys Sieb. & Zucc. (Sciadopityaceae). skee-uh-*do*-pi-tis. Gk. umbrella pine, from the arrangement of the leaves. 1 sp., conifer. Japan.
verticillata (Thunb.) Sieb. & Zucc. vur-ti-si-*lah*-tuh. Umbrella pine. Lat. whorled (the leaves).

Scilla L. (Asparagaceae). *sil*-uh. Gk. name for *Urginea maritima* (sea squill). 80 spp. bulbous herbs. Eur., Africa, W Asia.
autumnalis L. aw-toom-*nah*-lis. Autumn squill. Lat. of autumn (flowering). Eur., N Africa, W Asia.
bifolia L. bie-*foh*-lee-uh. Lat. two-leaved. Eur., W Asia.
forbesii (Baker) Speta. *forbz*-ee-ee. After Manx naturalist Edward Forbes (1815–1854), who collected the type specimen ca. 1842. Turkey.
litardierei Breistr. li-tard-ee-*e*-ree. After René Verriet de Litardière (1888–1957), French botanist. Croatia.
luciliae (Boiss.) Speta. lue-*sil*-ee-ie. After Lucile Françoise Butini (1822–1849), wife of author Pierre Edmund Boissier. He collected the type specimen in 1842 and named it *Chionodoxa luciliae*. W Turkey.
mischtschenkoana Grossh. mish-chen-koh-*ah*-nuh. After Pavel Ivanovich Misczenko (1869–1938), Russian botanist. Caucasus, N Iran.
peruviana L. pe-rue-vee-*ah*-nuh. Of Peru, where it was thought to originate. SW Eur., N Africa.
sardensis (Whittall ex Barr & Sayden) Speta. sard-*en*-sis. Lat. of Sart (Sardes), Turkey. W Turkey.
siberica Haw. si-*be*-ri-kuh. Lat. of Siberia. W Asia.

Scindapsus aureus (Linden & André) Engl. = *Epipremnum aureum*

Scirpus L. (Cyperaceae). *skirp*-oos. Bulrushes. Lat. name for a kind of rush. 35 spp. perenn. herbs. N Am., Eur., Asia, Australia.
acutus Muhl. ex Bigelow = *Schoenoplectus acutus*
atrovirens Willd. at-roh-*vie*-ruhnz. Lat. dark green. Canada, USA.
cernuus Vahl = *Isolepis cernua*
cyperinus (L.) Kunth. si-puh-*reen*-oos. Lat. sedge-like. Canada, USA, Mex.
fluviatilis (Torr.) A. Gray = *Bolboschoenus fluviatilis*
maritimus L. = *Bolboschoenus maritimus*
pungens Vahl = *Schoenoplectus pungens*
sylvaticus L. sil-*vat*-i-koos. Lat. of woods. Eur., W and C Asia.
tabernaemontani C. C. Gmel. = *Schoenoplectus tabernaemontani*

Scopolia Jacq. (Solanaceae). skoh-*pol*-ee-uh. After Italian physician and naturalist Giovanni Antonio Scopoli (1723–1788), who first collected it. 2 spp. perenn. herbs. Eur., W Asia, Japan, Korea.
carniolica Jacq. kar-nee-*ol*-i-kuh. Lat. of Carniola (now part of Slovenia), where Scopoli collected it. C and E Eur., Caucasus.

scorpion senna *Hippocrepis emerus*
scouring rush *Equisetum hyemale*.
  dwarf *E. scirpoides*

Scrophularia L. (Scrophulariaceae).
skrof-ew-*lah*-ree-uh. From scrofula,
referring to med. properties, from
Middle English for a breeding sow,
which were believed to be susceptible
to the disease. 200 spp., mainly
perenn. herbs, subshrubs. Eur., Asia,
N Am.
auriculata L. o-rik-ew-*lah*-tuh. Water
figwort. Lat. with small, ear-like lobes
(at the leaf bases). Eur., N Africa.

Scutellaria L. (Lamiaceae). skue-tuh-
lah-ree-uh. Skullcaps. From Lat. a
small dish, referring to the appearance of the calyx in fruit. 350 spp.,
herbs, subshrubs. Widespread.
baicalensis Georgi. bie-kuhl-*en*-sis.
Of Lake Baikal, Siberia. E Russia,
China, Korea.
incana Biehler. in-*kah*-nuh. Lat. grey
(the stems). E USA.
lateriflora L. la-tuh-ri-*flaw*-ruh. Lat.
with flowers on one side (of the inflorescence). Canada, USA.
scordiifolia Fisch. ex Schrank.
skor-dee-i-*foh*-lee-uh. Lat. with leaves
like *Scordium* (*Teucrium*). Siberia to
China.

sea buckthorn *Hippophae rhamnoides*
sea holly *Eryngium maritimum*
sedge *Carex*. **awlfruit** *C. stipata*.
  Bebb's *C. bebbii*. **Bicknell's** *C.
  bicknellii*. **broom** *C. scoparia*.
  Buchanan's *C. buchananii*. **fox** *C.
  vulpinoidea*. **fringed** *C. crinita*.
  glaucous *C. flacca*. **Gray's** *C. grayi*.
  greater brown *C. brunnea*. **hairy** *C.

lacustris. **hop** *C. lupulina*. **long hair**
C. comosa. **Muskingum** *C. muskingumensis*. **muttonbird** *C. trifida*.
orange *C. testacea*. **pendulous** *C.
pendula*. **Pennsylvania** *C. pensylvanica*. **plantainleaf** *C. plantaginea*.
slender tufted *C. acuta*. **tufted** *C.
elata*. **umbrella** *Cyperus involucratus*. **upright** *Carex stricta*. **water** *C.
aquatilis*

Sedum L. (Crassulaceae). *see*-doom.
From the Lat. name, possibly for
Sempervivum and/or *Sedum*, from
Lat. to sit, referring to their habit, or
to assuage, from med. properties. 500
spp., ann. and perenn. herbs, subshrubs. N and C Am., Eur., Africa,
Asia.
acre L. *ak*-ree. Stonecrop. Lat. sharp-
tasting (the leaves). Eur., N Africa,
W Asia.
aizoon L. ie-*zoh*-on. Gk. always alive.
E Russia, China, Korea, Japan.
album L. *al*-boom. White stonecrop.
Lat. white (the flowers). Eur., N
Africa, W Asia.
cauticola Praeger. kaw-*ti*-ko-luh. Lat.
growing on cliffs. Japan (Hokkaido).
dasyphyllum L. das-ee-*fil*-oom. Gk.
thick-leaved. Eur., N Africa, Turkey.
ellocombianum Praeger. el-uh-koom-
bee-*ah*-noom. After English clergyman and horticulturist Henry
Nicholson Ellacombe (1822–1916),
who urged Praeger to revise the cultivated sedums. Japan.
erythrostictum (Miq.) H. Ohba.
e-rith-roh-*stik*-toom. Gk. red-spot-
ted. China, E Russia, Korea, Japan.
ewersii Ledeb. ew-*erz*-ee-ee. After
German historian Johann Philipp
Gustav von Ewers (1779–1830),

friend of author Carl Friedrich von Ledebour. N India, C Asia.

floriferum Praeger. flo-*rif*-uh-room. Lat. bearing (many) flowers. China (Shandong).

kamtschaticum Fisch. kamt-*shat*-i-koom. Of Kamchatka. E Russia, China, Japan (Hokkaido).

lydium Boiss. *lid*-ee-oom. Lat. of Lydia (ancient reg. of W Turkey). Turkey.

middendorffianum Maxim. mid-uhn-dorf-ee-*ah*-noom. After Russian physician and naturalist Alexander Theodorowitsch Middendorff (1815–1894), who collected it in Siberia. E Russia, N China, Korea.

morganianum E. Walther. mor-gan-ee-*ah*-noom. Burro's tail. After San Francisco optometrist and plant collector Meredith Morgan, who first flowered it. Mex.

oreganum Nutt. o-ri-*gah*-noom. Of Oregon. SW Canada, W USA.

reflexum L. = *S. rupestre*

rupestre L. rue-*pes*-tree. Lat. growing on rocks. Eur., Caucasus.

sexangulare L. sex-ang-ew-*lah*-ree. Lat. six-angled (the leafy shoots). Eur.

spathulifolium Hook. spath-ew-li-*foh*-lee-oom. Lat. with spatula-shaped leaves. SW Canada, W USA.

spectabile Boreau. spek-*tab*-i-lee. Ice plant. Lat. spectacular. China, Korea.

spurium M. Bieb. *spoo*-ree-oom. Lat. false. W Asia.

telephium L. te-*lef*-ee-oom. Gk. name of a plant. Eur. subsp. ***ruprechtii*** Jalas. rue-*prekt*-ee-ee. After Franz Joseph Ruprecht (1814–1870), who

described it under another name. NE Eur.

self-heal *Prunella vulgaris*

Selinum L. (Apiaceae). se-*leen*-oom. Gk. name of a related plant. 8 spp. perenn. herbs. Eur., Asia.

wallichianum (DC.) Raizada & H. O. Saxena. wol-ik-ee-*ah*-noom. After Nathaniel Wallich (1786–1854), Danish botanist and surgeon with the East India Company, who collected it in the Himalaya. Himal., Tibet.

Semiaquilegia ecalcarata (Maxim.) Sprague & Hutch. = *Aquilegia ecalcarata*

Semiarundinaria Makino ex Nakai (Poaceae). sem-ee-uh-run-di-*nah*-ree-uh. Lat. half, the related *Arundinaria*. 10 spp. bamboos. E China, Japan.

fastuosa (Lat.-Marl. ex Mitford) Makino ex Nakai. fas-tew-*oh*-suh. Lat. proud. Japan.

yashadake (Makino) Makino. yash-uh-*dah*-kee. The Japanese name. Japan.

Sempervivum L. (Crassulaceae). sem-per-*vie*-voom. Houseleeks. Lat. always alive. 40 spp. succulents. Eur., N Africa, W Asia.

arachnoideum L. a-rak-*noyd*-ee-oom. Cobweb houseleek. Gk. cobweb-like (the hairs). C and S Eur.

atlanticum (Ball) Ball. at-*lan*-ti-koom. Of the Atlas Mts. Morocco.

calcareum Jord. kal-*kair*-ree-oom. Lat. growing on chalk or limestone. France, Italy.

cantabricum Huber. kan-*tab*-ri-koom. Of Cantabria (reg. of N Spain). N and C Spain.

ciliosum Craib. sil-ee-*oh*-soom. Lat. fringed with hairs (the leaves). SE Eur.

marmoreum Griseb. mar-*mor*-ree-oom. Lat. marbled. E Eur.

montanum L. mon-*tah*-noom. Lat. of mountains. C and S Eur.

tectorum L. tek-*tor*-room. Lat. growing on roofs. C and S Eur., Morocco.

Senecio L. (Asteraceae). se-*nek*-ee-oh. From Lat. an old man, referring to the grey-white hairs of the fruit. 1000 spp., ann. and perenn. herbs, climbers, shrubs. Widespread.

articulatus (L.f.) Sch. Bip. ar-tik-ew-*lah*-toos. Candle plant. Lat. jointed (the shoots). S Africa.

aureus L. = *Packera aurea*

cineraria DC. = *Jacobaea maritima*

compactus Kirk. = *Brachyglottis compacta*

macroglossus DC. mak-roh-*glos*-oos. Cape ivy. Gk. with a large tongue, referring to the ray flowers. S Africa.

monroi Hook.f. = *Brachyglottis monroi*

polyodon DC. pol-ee-*oh*-don. Gk. with many teeth (the leaves). S Africa.

Senna Mill. (Fabaceae). *sen*-uh. The Arabic name. 260 spp., herbs, shrubs, trees. Widespread, mainly trop. regs.

hebecarpa (Fernald) H. S. Irwin & Barneby. hee-bee-*karp*-uh. Gk. with hairy fruit. SE Canada, E USA.

marilandica (L.) Link. ma-ri-*land*-i-kuh. Of Maryland. E and C USA.

sensitive plant *Mimosa pudica*

Sequoia Endl. (Cupressaceae). see-*kwoy*-uh. After Native American silversmith Sequoyah (ca. 1767–1843), who created a syllabary for the Cherokee language. 1 sp., conifer. Calif., Oregon.

sempervirens (D. Don) Endl. sem-per-*vie*-ruhnz. California redwood, coast redwood. Lat. evergreen.

Sequoiadendron J. Buchholz (Cupressaceae). see-kwoy-uh-*den*-dron. From *Sequoia* and Gk. tree. 1 sp., conifer. Calif.

giganteum (Lindl.) J. Buchholz. jie-*gant*-ee-oom. Giant redwood, Wellingtonia. Lat. very large.

Serratula L. (Asteraceae). se-ruh-*tew*-luh. Sawwort. Lat. a little saw, referring to the toothed leaves. 70 spp. perenn. herbs. Eur., N Africa, Asia.

seoanei Willk. say-oh-*ahn*-ee-ee. After Víctor López Seoane y Pardo-Montenegro (1832–1900), Spanish naturalist. SW Eur., N Africa.

service tree *Sorbus domestica*. **wild** *S. torminalis*

Sesleria Scop. (Poaceae). sez-*le*-ree-uh. After Leonard Sesler (d. 1785), Italian physician and botanist. 30 spp. grasses. Eur., W Asia.

autumnalis (Scop.) F. W. Schulz. aw-toom-*nah*-lis. Autumn moor grass. Lat. of autumn (flowering). SE Eur.

caerulea (L.) Ard. kie-*rue*-lee-uh. Blue moor grass. Lat. blue (the leaves). Eur.

heufleriana Schur. hoyf-luh-ree-*ah*-nuh. Balkan moor grass. After Ludwig Samuel Joseph David

Alexander Heufler zu Rasen (1817–1885), Austrian botanist. E Eur., Caucasus.

nitida Ten. *nit*-i-duh. Lat. glossy (the foliage). Italy, Sicily.

Setaria P. Beauv. (Poaceae). see-*tair*-ree-uh. From Lat. bristle, referring to the bristly inflorescence. 110 spp. grasses. Widespread in warm temp. and trop. regs.

italica (L.) P. Beauv. i-*tal*-i-kuh. Lat. of Italy. Foxtail bristle grass. Eur., N Africa, Asia.

seven son flower *Heptacodium miconioides*
shallot *Allium cepa* Aggregatum Group
sheepberry *Viburnum lentago*
shell ginger *Alpinia zerumbet*

Shepherdia Nutt. (Elaeagnaceae). shep-*erd*-ee-uh. After John Shepherd (1764–1836), English botanist and friend of the author, Thomas Nuttall. 3 spp. shrubs. Canada, USA.

argentea (Pursh) Nutt. ar-*jen*-tee-uh. Buffalo berry. Lat. silvery (the foliage). W Canada, W and C USA.

canadensis (L.) Nutt. kan-uh-*den*-sis. Rabbit berry. Of Canada.

Shibataea Makino ex Nakai (Poaceae). shib-uh-*tay*-uh. After Keita Shibata (1877–1949), Japanese botanist. 7 spp. bamboos. China.

kumasaca (Steud.) Nakai. kue-muh-*sah*-kuh. Japanese name of a bamboo. E China.

shooting star *Primula meadia*. **pretty** *P. pauciflora*. **sierra** *P. jeffreyi*

shrimp plant *Justicia brandegeeana*
Siberian melic *Melica altissima*

Sidalcea A. Gray (Malvaceae). sid-*al*-see-uh. From *Sida* and *Alcea*, two related genera. 20 spp. ann. and perenn. herbs. W N Am.

candida A. Gray. *kan*-di-duh. Prairie mallow. Lat. white (the flowers). W USA.

Silene L. (Caryophyllaceae). sie-*leen*-ee. Campions. Gk. name for one of the species, probably after Silenus of Gk. myth. 700 spp. ann. and perenn. herbs. N hemisph.

acaulis (L.) Jacq. ay-*kawl*-is. Moss campion. Lat. stemless. Eur., Canada, USA, Greenland, E Russia.

alba (Mill.) E. H. L. Krause = *S. latifolia* subsp. *alba*

armeria L. ar-*meer*-ree-uh. Lat. name for a species of *Dianthus*. Eur., Turkey.

caroliniana Walter. ka-ro-lin-ee-*ah*-nuh. Of the Carolinas. E USA.

coronaria (L.) Clairv. ko-ro-*nair*-ree-uh. Dusty miller, rose campion. Lat. of garlands. Eur., W and C Asia.

dioica (L.) Clairv. die-*oy*-kuh. Red campion. Gk. dioecious. Eur., Morocco.

fimbriata Sims. fim-bree-*ah*-tuh. Lat. fringed (the petals). Caucasus.

flos-cuculi (L.) Greuter & Burdet. *flos*-kook-ew-lee. Ragged robin. Lat. cuckoo flower (from the flowering time). Eur. to Siberia.

flos-jovis (L.) Greuter & Burdet. *flos*-joh-vis. Lat. flower of Jupiter. S Eur.

latifolia Poir. lat-i-*foh*-lee-uh. White campion. Lat. broad-leaved. Eur.,

N Africa, temp. Asia. subsp. *alba.*
(Mill.) Greuter & Burdet. *al*-buh.
Lat. white (the flowers).
regia Sims. *ree*-jee-uh. Lat. royal.
E USA.
schafta J. G. Gmel. ex Hohen.
shaf-tuh. The native name. Caucasus.
uniflora Roth. ew-ni-*flaw*-ruh. Sea
campion. Lat. one-flowered. N and
W Eur.
virginica L. vir-*jin*-i-kuh. Of Virginia.
E USA.
viscaria (L.) Jess. vis-*kair*-ree-uh. Lat.
sticky (the stems). Eur., W Asia.

silk tree *Albizia julibrissin*
silky oak *Grevillea robusta*

Silphium L. (Asteraceae). *sil*-fee-oom.
Gk. name of a plant. 12 spp. perenn.
herbs. N Am.
integrifolium Michx. in-teg-ri-*foh*-lee-
oom. Lat. with untoothed leaves. S
Canada, C USA.
laciniatum L. luh-sin-ee-*ah*-toom.
Compass plant. Lat. deeply cut (the
leaves). E and C USA.
perfoliatum L. per-foh-lee-*ah*-toom.
Cup plant. Lat. with the leaf base
encircling the stem. E and C USA.
terebinthinaceum Jacq. te-re-binth-
in-*ay*-see-oom. Prairie dock. Lat. tur-
pentine-scented (the leaves). E USA.

silver berry *Elaeagnus commutata*
silver spurflower *Plectranthus
argentatus*
silver vine *Actinidia polygama*
silverbell *Halesia carolina*. **two-wing**
H. diptera

Silybum Vaill. (Asteraceae). *sil*-i-
boom. Gk. name of a thistle-like

plant. 2 spp. ann. and bienn. herbs.
Medit.
marianum (L.) Gaertn. ma-ree-*ah*-
noom. Holy thistle, our lady's milk
thistle. Lat. of Mary.

Simmondsia Nutt. (Simmondsia-
ceae). sim-*ondz*-ee-uh. After Thomas
William Simmonds (1767–1804),
English physician and botanist. 1 sp.,
evergreen shrub. SW USA, NW
Mex.
chinensis (Link) C. K. Schneid. chin-
en-sis. Goatnut, jojoba. Of China,
where it was thought to originate
when it was named *Buxus chinensis.*

Sinacalia H. Rob. & Brettell (Asteraceae). sie-nuh-*kal*-ee-uh. From Lat./
Gk. China, and the related *Cacalia.*
4 spp. perenn. herbs. China.
tangutica (Maxim.) R. Nord.
tan-*gew*-ti-kuh. Of Gansu.

Sinningia Nees (Gesneriaceae).
sin-*ing*-ee-uh. After William
Sinning, gardener at the University
of Bonn, where the type species was
raised from Brazilian seed before
1825. 60 spp., herbs, shrubs. Trop.
Am.
speciosa (Lodd. et al.) Hiern.
spee-see-*oh*-suh. Gloxinia. Lat.
showy. Brazil.

Sinocalycanthus chinensis (Cheng &
Chang) Cheng & Chang = *Calycanthus chinensis*

Sinopodophyllum T. S. Ying (Berberi-
daceae). sie-noh-pod-oh-*fil*-oom.
Lat./Gk. China, and the related
Podophyllum, in which it was once

included. 1 sp., perenn. herb. Himal., China.

hexandrum (Royle) T. S. Ying. hex-*an*-droom. Gk. with six stamens. var. ***chinense*** (Sprague) Stearn ex J. M. H. Shaw & Cubey. chin-*en*-see. Of China. var. ***emodi*** (Wall. ex Hook.f. & Thomson) J. M. H. Shaw. em-*oh*-dee. Lat. of the Himalaya.

Sisyrinchium L. (Iridaceae). sis-i-*rink*-ee-oom. Gk. name of a plant, possibly from Gk. a shaggy coat, referring to the covering on the corm. 140 spp. perenn. or ann. herbs. Americas.

angustifolium Mill. an-gus-ti-*foh*-lee-oom. Lat. narrow-leaved. E Canada, E and C USA.

bellum S. Watson. *bel*-oom. Lat. beautiful. W USA, NW Mex. (B.C.).

bermudiana L. ber-mew-dee-*ah*-nuh. Blue-eyed grass. Of Bermuda. Bermuda.

californicum (Ker Gawl.) Dryand. kal-i-*for*-ni-koom. Of California. SW Canada, W USA.

campestre E. P. Bicknell. kam-*pes*-tree. Lat. of fields. Canada, E and C USA.

idahoense E. P. Bicknell. ie-duh-hoh-*en*-see. Of Idaho. W Canada, W and C USA.

palmifolium L. pahl-mi-*foh*-lee-um. Lat. with palm-like leaves. S Am.

striatum Sm. stree-*ah*-toom. Lat. striped (the flowers). Chile, Argentina.

Skimmia Thunb. (Rutaceae). *skim*-ee-uh. From the Japanese name. 4 spp., evergreen shrubs, trees. Himal., E Asia.

×***confusa*** N. P. Taylor. kon-*few*-suh.

Lat. confused (with another species). *S. anquetilia* × *S. japonica*. Cult.

japonica Thunb. juh-*pon*-i-kuh. Of Japan. Japan. subsp. ***reevesiana*** (Fortune) N. P. Taylor & Airy Shaw. reevz-ee-*ah*-nuh. After John Reeves (1774–1856), a tea inspector with the East India Company. China, SE Asia.

skullcap *Scutellaria*
skunk cabbage *Lysichiton americanus*. **Asian** *L. camtschatkensis*
skunkbush *Rhus trilobata*
sloe *Prunus spinosa*

Smilax L. (Smilacaceae). *smie*-lax. Gk. name of a plant. 350 spp., herbs, woody climbers. Widespread from trop. to warm temp. regs.

aspera L. *as*-puh-ruh. Lat. rough (the prickly shoots). Medit., S Asia, trop. Africa.

smoke tree *Cotinus coggygria*. **American** *C. obovatus*

Smyrnium L. (Apiaceae). *smir*-nee-oom. Gk. myrrh-scented. 7 spp. bienn. herbs. Eur., Medit.

olusatrum L. ol-ew-*sat*-room. Alexanders. From Lat. pot herb, black (the seeds). W and S Eur., Medit.

perfoliatum L. per-foh-lee-*ah*-toom. Lat. with the leaf base encircling the stem. S and C Eur.

snakeroot, black *Actaea racemosa*. **white** *Ageratina altissima*
snapdragon *Antirrhinum majus*
sneezeweed *Helenium*. **common** *H. autumnale*. **orange** *Hymenoxys hoopesii*

sneezewort *Achillea ptarmica*
snow-in-summer *Cerastium tomentosum*
snow on the mountain *Euphorbia marginata*
snowball, Chinese *Viburnum macrocephalum*. **Japanese** *V. plicatum*
snowbell, American *Styrax americanus*. **Japanese** *S. japonicus*
snowberry *Symphoricarpos albus*. **mountain** *S. oreophilus*. **western** *S. occidentalis*
snowbrush *Ceanothus velutinus*
snowdrop *Galanthus*. **common** *G. nivalis*
snowdrop tree *Halesia carolina*
snowflake, autumn *Acis autumnalis*. **spring** *Leucojum vernum*. **summer** *L. aestivum*
soapwort *Saponaria officinalis*. **rock** *S. ocymoides*

Solanum L. (Solanaceae). so-*lah*-noom. Lat. name used by Pliny for a nightshade. 1200 spp., ann. and perenn. herbs, climbers, shrubs, trees. Mainly trop. and subtrop. regs.
crispum Ruiz & Pav. *kris*-poom. Lat. wavy-edged (the leaves). Argentina, Chile.
jasminoides Paxton = *S. laxum*
laxum Spreng. *lax*-oom. Lat. open (the inflorescence). S Am.
lycopersicum L. lie-koh-*pers*-i-koom. Tomato. Gk. wolf apple. S Am.
melongena L. me-lon-*jeen*-uh. Aubergine. Gk. apple-bearing. Cult.
pseudocapsicum L. sue-do-*kap*-si-koom. Jerusalem cherry. Gk. false *Capsicum*. Mex. to S Am.
tuberosum L. tew-buh-*roh*-soom. Potato. Lat. bearing tubers. Cult.

Soleirolia Gaudich. (Urticaceae). so-lay-*rol*-ee-uh. After French naturalist Joseph Francis Soleirol (1781–1863), who collected it in Corsica. 1 sp., perenn. herb. W Medit.
soleirolii (Req.) Dandy. so-lay-*rol*-ee-ee. Baby's tears, mind-your-own-business. Deriv. as for genus.

Solidago L. (Asteraceae). so-lid-*ah*-goh. Goldenrods. From Lat. to make whole, referring to med. properties. 100 spp. perenn. herbs. Americas, Eur., N Africa, Asia.
caesia L. *seez*-ee-uh. Lat. grey-blue (the stems). SE Canada, E USA.
canadensis L. kan-uh-*den*-sis. Of Canada. SE Canada, NE USA.
flexicaulis L. flex-i-*kawl*-is. Lat. with bending stems. SE Canada, E USA.
graminifolia (L.) Salisb. = *Euthamia graminifolia*
juncea Aiton. *jun*-see-uh. Lat. rush-like. SE Canada, E USA.
nemoralis Aiton. nem-o-*rah*-lis. Lat. of woods. SE Canada, E USA.
ohioensis Riddell. oh-hie-oh-*en*-sis. Of Ohio. SE Canada, NE USA.
ptarmicoides (Torr. & A. Gray) B. Boivin. tar-mik-*oy*-deez. Prairie goldenrod. Lat. like *Achillea ptarmica*. S Canada, E and C USA.
riddellii Frank. ri-*del*-ee-ee. After American physician and botanist John Leonard Riddell (1807–1865), who collected the type specimen in Ohio. SE Canada, NE USA.
rigida L. *rij*-i-duh. Lat. rigid (the stems). SE Canada, E and C USA.
speciosa Nutt. spee-see-*oh*-suh. Lat. showy. E and C USA.

ulmifolia Muhl. ex Willd. ul-mi-*foh*-lee-uh. Lat. with leaves like *Ulmus*. SE Canada, E and C USA.

virgaurea L. virg-*aw*-ree-uh. Lat. golden rod. Eur., N Africa, Asia.

Sollya heterophylla Lindl. = *Billardiera heterophylla*

Solomon's seal *Polygonatum*

Sophora L. (Fabaceae). *sof*-o-ruh. From the Arabic name of a related tree. 50 spp., herbs, shrubs, trees. Widespread.

davidii (Franch.) Skeels. da-*vid*-ee-ee. After French missionary, botanist and zoologist Armand David (1826–1900), who collected it in China. SW China.

japonica L. = *Styphnolobium japonicum*

microphylla Aiton. mik-*rof*-i-luh. Gk. small-leaved. NZ.

tetraptera J. F. Mill. tet-*rap*-tuh-ruh. Gk. four-winged (the fruit). NZ.

Sorbaria (Ser. ex DC.) A. Braun (Rosaceae). sor-*bair*-ree-uh. Lat. like *Sorbus* (the foliage). 4 spp. shrubs. Asia.

sorbifolia (L.) A. Braun. sorb-i-*foh*-lee-uh. Lat. with leaves like *Sorbus*. Siberia to Japan.

tomentosa (Lindl.) Rehder. to-men-*toh*-suh. Lat. hairy (the shoots and leaves). Himal. var. *angustifolia* (Wenz.) Rahn. an-gus-ti-*foh*-lee-uh. Lat. with narrow leaves (leaflets). Afghanistan, Pakistan.

Sorbus L. (Rosaceae). *sor*-boos. Lat. name for *S. aucuparia*. 120 spp.,

trees, shrubs. Eur., N Africa, Asia, N Am.

alnifolia (Sieb. & Zucc.) K. Koch. al-ni-*foh*-lee-uh. Lat. with leaves like *Alnus*. E Asia.

americana Marshall. uh-me-ri-*kah*-nuh. American mountain ash. Of America. E Canada, E and C USA.

aria (L.) Crantz. *ah*-ree-uh. Whitebeam. Gk. name for this or a related plant. Eur., N Africa, W Asia.

aucuparia L. aw-kew-*pair*-ree-uh. Mountain ash, rowan. Lat. bird-catching (the fruit was used as bait to catch birds). Eur., Asia.

commixta Hedl. kom-*ix*-tuh. Lat. mixed together. E Russia, Japan, Korea.

domestica L. do-*mes*-ti-kuh. Service tree. Lat. of the home. Eur., N Africa, W Asia.

glabriuscula McAll. glab-ree-*usk*-ew-luh. Lat. somewhat glabrous. China.

hupehensis hort. = *S. glabriuscula*

intermedia (Ehrh.) Pers. in-ter-*mee*-dee-uh. Swedish whitebeam. Lat. intermediate (between two species). Eur.

reducta Diels. re-*duk*-tuh. Lat. reduced (in size). SW China, N Myanmar.

scalaris Koehne. skuh-*lah*-ris. Lat. ladder-like (the leaves). SW China.

scopulina Greene. skop-ew-*leen*-uh. Lat. twiggy. W Canada, W USA.

thibetica (Cardot) Hand.-Mazz. ti-*bet*-i-kuh. Of Tibet. W China, Himal.

×*thuringiaca* (Nyman) Schonach. thoo-ring-ee-*ah*-kuh. Of Thuringia, Germany. *S. aria* × *S. aucuparia*. Eur.

torminalis (L.) Crantz. tor-mi-*nah*-lis. Chequer tree, wild service tree. Lat.

of colic, referring to med. properties. Eur., N Africa, W Asia.

vilmorinii C. K. Schneid. vil-mo-*rin*-ee-ee. After French nurseryman Maurice Lévêque de Vilmorin (1849–1918), to whom the first seeds were sent in 1889. SW China.

sorrel *Oxalis.* **French** *Rumex scutatus.* **garden** *R. acetosa.* **redwood** *Oxalis oregana.* **wood** *O. acetosella*
sorrel tree *Oxydendrum arboreum*
sour gum *Nyssa sylvatica*
sourwood *Oxydendrum arboreum*
southernwood *Artemisia abrotanum*
sow thistle, mountain *Cicerbita plumieri*
soya bean *Glycine max*

Sparganium L. (Sparganiaceae). spar-*gan*-ee-oom. Bur reeds. From Gk. swaddling band, for the strap-shaped leaves. 14 spp. aquatic herbs. N temp. regs., Mex., NZ, Australia.

erectum L. ee-*rek*-toom. Lat. upright. Eur., N Africa, Asia.

eurycarpum Engelm. ew-ree-*karp*-oom. Gk. broad fruit. Canada, USA, Mex., E Asia.

Spartina Schreb. (Poaceae). spar-*tee*-nuh. From Gk. cord (it has been used for binding). 17 spp. grasses. Widespread.

pectinata Link. pek-ti-*nah*-tuh. Prairie cord grass. Lat. comb-like (the inflorescence). Canada, USA.

Spartium L. (Fabaceae). *spart*-ee-oom. From Gk. cord (it has been used for binding). 1 sp., shrub. Medit.

junceum L. *jun*-see-oom. Spanish broom. Lat. rush-like (the shoots).

Spathiphyllum Schott (Araceae). spath-i-*fil*-oom. Peace lilies. Gk. spathe leaf, referring to the showy, leaf-like spathe. 50 spp. evergreen herbs. Trop. Am., Malesia, Pacific Is.

wallisii Regel. wol-*is*-ee-ee. After German botanist Gustav Wallis (1830–1878), who collected the type specimen in Colombia. Colombia, Venezuela.

spearmint *Mentha spicata*
spearwort, greater *Ranunculus lingua*
speedwell *Veronica.* **digger's** *V. perfoliata*

Speirantha Baker (Asparagaceae). spay-*ranth*-uh. Gk. twisted flower. 1 sp., perenn. herb. SE China.

convallarioides Baker = *S. gardenii*

gardenii (Hook.) Baill. gar-*den*-ee-ee. After Captain Garden, who was mistakenly believed to have introduced it from S Africa.

Sphaeralcea A. St.-Hil. (Malvaceae). sfair-*al*-see-uh. Globe mallows. Gk. globe, and the related *Alcea*, referring to the spherical fruit. 40 spp., ann. and perenn. herbs, subshrubs. N and S Am.

ambigua A. Gray. am-*big*-ew-uh. Lat. doubtful. SW USA, N Mex.

coccinea (Nutt.) Rydb. kok-*sin*-ee-uh. Lat. scarlet (the flowers). W Canada, W and C USA, N Mex.

munroana (Douglas ex Lindl.) Spach ex A. Gray. mun-roh-*ah*-nuh. After Mr Munro, gardener to the Horticultural Society, from which garden it was first illustrated. SW Canada, W USA.

spice bush *Lindera benzoin*
spider plant *Chlorophytum comosum,
Tarenaya hassleriana*
spiderflower, showy *Cleoserrata
speciosa*

Spigelia L. (Loganiaceae). spi-*gel*-
ee-uh. After Flemish anatomist and
botanist Adriaan van den Spiegel
(Spigelius) (1578–1625), the first to
publish instructions on how to prepare herbarium specimens. 60 spp.,
ann. and perenn. herbs, subshrubs. N
and trop. Am.
marilandica (L.) L. ma-ri-*land*-i-kuh.
Indian pink. Of Maryland. E USA.

spikenard, American *Aralia racemosa*. **California** *A. californica*. **false**
Maianthemum racemosum

Spilanthes oleracea L. = *Acmella
oleracea*

spinach *Spinacia oleracea*. **New Zealand** *Tetragonia tetragoniodes*

Spinacia L. (Amaranthaceae). spin-*ay*-
see-uh. From the Arabic or Persian
name. 3 spp. ann. herbs. N Africa,
SW Asia.
oleracea L. ol-uh-*ray*-see-uh. Spinach.
Lat. vegetable-like. Cult.

spindle tree *Euonymus europaeus*

Spiraea L. (Rosaceae). spie-*ree*-uh. Gk.
name of a plant used in garlands. 80
spp. shrubs. N Am., Eur., Asia.
'**Arguta**'. ar-*gew*-tuh. Lat. sharp-
toothed (the leaves). *S. multiflora* ×
S. thunbergii.
douglasii Hook. dug-*las*-ee-ee.

Steeplebush. After Scottish botanist
and plant collector David Douglas
(1799–1834), who discovered it ca.
1827 and sent seed to Glasgow
Botanic Garden. SW Canada, W
USA.
fritschiana C. K. Schneid. frich-ee-*ah*-
nuh. After Austrian botanist Karl
Fritsch (1864–1934). China.
japonica L.f. juh-*pon*-i-kuh. Of Japan.
China, Japan, Korea.
nipponica Maxim. ni-*pon*-i-kuh. Of
Japan. Japan.
prunifolia Sieb. & Zucc. prue-ni-*foh*-
lee-uh. Lat. with leaves like *Prunus*.
China, Taiwan, Korea.
thunbergii Siebold ex Blume. thun-
berg-ee-ee. After Swedish botanist
and physician Carl Peter Thunberg
(1743–1828), who collected in Japan
and S Africa.
tomentosa L. to-men-*toh*-suh. Steeplebush. Lat. hairy (the shoots and
leaves). Canada, E USA.
×*vanhouttei* (Briot) Zabel. van-*huet*-
ee-ee. After Belgian nurseryman
Louis van Houtte (1810–1876). *S.
trilobata* × *S. cantoniensis*. Cult.

spleenwort *Asplenium*. **ebony** *A.
platyneuron*. **maidenhair** *A.
trichomanes*

Sporobolus R. Br. (Poaceae). spo-ro-
bo-loos. Gk. seed casting, referring to
how the seeds are dispersed. 160 spp.
grasses. Widespread.
airoides (Torr.) Torr. air-*roy*-deez. Lat.
like *Aira*, another grass genus. SW
Canada, USA, Mex.
cryptandrus (Torr.) A. Gray. kript-
and-roos. Gk. with hidden stamens.
Canada, USA, Mex., Argentina.

heterolepis (A. Gray) A. Gray. he-tuh-roh-*lep*-is. Gk. with unequal scales (the flower). Canada, USA.

spruce *Picea*. **Alberta white** *P. glauca* var. *albertiana*. **black** *P. mariana*. **blue** *P. pungens*. **Brewer** *P. breweriana*. **Norway** *P. abies*. **oriental** *P. orientalis*. **Serbian** *P. omorika*. **Sitka** *P. sitchensis*. **white** *P. glauca*

spurge *Euphorbia*. **Allegheny** *Pachysandra procumbens*. **caper** *Euphorbia lathyris*. **cypress** *E. cyparissias*. **honey** *E. mellifera*. **horned** *E. cornigera*. **sweet** *E. dulcis*. **wood** *E. amygdaloides*

squash *Cucurbita maxima, C. moschata*

squawcarpet *Ceanothus prostratus*

squill, autumn *Scilla autumnalis*

squirrel corn *Dicentra canadensis*

St. John's wort *Hypericum*. **golden** *H. frondosum*

Stachys L. (Lamiaceae). *stak*-is. Gk. name of a related plant, from Gk. spike, referring to the flower arrangement. 450 spp., herbs, subshrubs. Widespread.

byzantina K. Koch. biz-uhn-*teen*-uh. Lamb's ears. Lat. of Byzantium (Istanbul). W Asia.

macrantha (K. Koch) Stearn. mak-*ranth*-uh. Gk. large-flowered. W Asia.

officinalis (L.) Trevis. o-fis-i-*nah*-lis. Betony. Lat. sold as a med. herb. Eur., N Africa, W Asia.

Stachyurus Sieb. & Zucc. (Stachyuraceae). stak-ee-*ew*-roos. Gk. spike tail, referring to the slender inflorescence. 8 spp., shrubs, trees. E Asia.

chinensis Franch. chin-*en*-sis. Of China. China.

praecox Sieb. & Zucc. *prie*-koks. Lat. early (flowering). Japan.

Staphylea L. (Staphyleaceae). stuh-*fil*-ee-uh. Bladdernuts. Gk. cluster, referring to the arrangement of the flowers. 13 spp., shrubs, trees. Eur., Asia, N Am.

colchica Steven. *kol*-chi-kuh. Lat. of Colchis on the Black Sea (now part of Georgia). Georgia.

pinnata L. pin-*ah*-tuh. Lat. pinnate (the leaves). Eur., Turkey.

trifolia L. trie-*foh*-lee-uh. American bladdernut. Lat. with three leaves (leaflets). SE Canada, E USA.

star of Bethlehem *Ornithogalum umbellatum*

starfruit *Averrhoa carambola*

statice *Limonium sinuatum*. **Tatarian** *Goniolimon tataricum*

Stauntonia DC. (Lardizabalaceae). stawn-*toh*-nee-uh. After Sir George Leonard Staunton (1737–1801), Irish physician and diplomat. 25 spp. woody climbers. E Asia.

hexaphylla Decne. hex-uh-*fil*-uh. Gk. with six leaves (leaflets). Korea, Japan.

steeplebush *Spiraea douglasii, S. tomentosa*

Stephanandra incisa Thunb. = *Neillia incisa*

tanakae (Franch. & Sav.) Franch. & Sav. = *Neillia tanakae*

Sternbergia Waldst. & Kit. (Amaryllidaceae). stern-*berg*-ee-uh. After Kaspar Maria von Sternberg (1761–1838), Bohemian entomologist and botanist. 8 spp. bulbous herbs. S Eur. to C Asia.

lutea (L.) Ker Gawl. ex Spreng. *lue*-tee-uh. Lat. yellow (the flowers). S Eur., W Asia.

Stewartia L. (Theaceae). stew-*art*-ee-uh. After John Stuart, 3rd Earl of Bute (1713–1792). 20 spp., shrubs, trees. E N Am., E Asia.

pseudocamellia Maxim. sue-do-kuh-*mel*-ee-uh. Gk. false *Camellia*. Japan, S Korea.

serrata Maxim. se-*rah*-tuh. Lat. toothed (the leaves). Japan.

sinensis Rehder & E. H. Wilson. sin-*en*-sis. Lat. of China. China.

Stipa L. (Poaceae). *steep*-uh. Gk. tow (the inflorescence was used for making fibres). 150 spp. grasses. Eur., N Africa, Asia.

arundinacea (Hook.f.) Benth. = *Anemanthele lessoniana*

barbata Desf. bar-*bah*-tuh. Lat. bearded (the inflorescence). S Eur., N Africa, W and C Asia.

calamagrostis (L.) Wahlenb. = *Achnatherum calamagrostis*

gigantea Link = *Celtica gigantea*

spartea Trin. = *Hesperostipa spartea*

tenuissima Trin. = *Nassella tenuissima*

stock *Matthiola*. **Brompton** *M. incana*. **night-scented** *M. longipetala* subsp. *bicornis*

Stokesia L'Hér. (Asteraceae). *stohks*-ee-uh. After Jonathan Stokes (1755–1831), English botanist and physician. 1 sp., perenn. herb. SE USA.

laevis (Hill) Greene. *lee*-vis. Lat. smooth.

stonecrop *Sedum acre*. **white** *S. album*

stork's bill *Erodium*

strawberry *Fragaria*. **beach** *F. chiloensis*. **garden** *F.* ×*ananassa*. **Virginia** *F. virginiana*. **woodland** *F. vesca*

strawberry blite *Chenopodium capitatum*

strawberry bush *Euonymus americanus*

strawberry tree *Arbutus unedo*

Strelitzia Banks (Strelitziaceae). stre-*lits*-ee-uh. After Charlotte of Mecklenburg-Strelitz (1744–1818), wife of King George III. 5 spp. perenn. herbs. S Africa.

reginae Banks. re-*jeen*-ie. Bird of paradise flower. Lat. of the queen (deriv. as for genus).

Streptocarpus Lindl. (Gesneriaceae). strep-toh-*karp*-oos. Gk. twisted fruit (the fruits twist when ripe to release the seeds). 50 spp. ann. and perenn. herbs. Trop. and S Africa.

×*hybridus* Voss. *hib*-ri-doos. Cape primrose. Lat. hybrid. Cult.

Strobilanthes Blume (Acanthaceae). stro-bil-*anth*-eez. Gk. cone flower (the conical flower clusters). 400 spp., herbs, shrubs. Trop. Asia.

attenuata Nees. uh-ten-ew-*ah*-tuh. Lat. with a drawn-out point (the leaves). Himal.

dyeriana Mast. die-uh-ree-*ah*-nuh. Persian shield. After William Turner Thiselton-Dyer (1843–1928), English botanist and director of RBG Kew, where it was grown. Myanmar.

wallichii Nees. wol-*ik*-ee-ee. After Nathaniel Wallich (1786–1854), Danish botanist and surgeon with the East India Company, who studied plants in India and Nepal and collected the type specimen in 1821. Himal.

Sturt's desert pea *Swainsona formosa*

Styphnolobium Schott (Fabaceae). stif-noh-*loh*-bee-oom. Gk. contracted pod (the fruits are contracted between the seeds). 9 spp., trees, shrubs. S USA to C Am., China, Korea.

japonicum (L.) Schott. juh-*pon*-i-koom. Pagoda tree. Of Japan, where it is cultivated. China, Korea.

Styrax L. (Styracaceae). *stie*-rax. Gk. name, from Arabic, for *S. officinalis* and the resin it produces. 130 spp., trees, shrubs. USA to S Am., SE Eur., W and E Asia.

americanus Lam. uh-me-ri-*kah*-noos. American snowbell. Of America. E and C USA.

hemsleyanus Diels. hemz-lee-*ah*-noos. After William Botting Hemsley (1843–1924), who worked on Chinese plants at Kew. China.

japonicus Sieb. & Zucc. juh-*pon*-i-koos. Japanese snowbell. Of Japan. E and SE Asia.

obassia Sieb. & Zucc. oh-*bas*-ee-uh. The Japanese name. China, Korea, Japan.

Succisa Haller (Dipsacaceae). suk-*sie*-suh. Gk. cut off (the base of the rhizome is cut off in autumn; also the origin of the common name). 1 sp., perenn. herb. Eur., W Asia.

pratensis Moench. pra-*ten*-sis. Devil's bit scabious. Lat. of meadows.

sugarbeet *Beta vulgaris*
sugarberry *Celtis laevigata*
sumach, fragrant *Rhus aromatica*. **shining** *R. copallinum*. **smooth** *R. glabra*. **stag's horn** *R. typhina*
summersweet *Clethra alnifolia*
sundrops *Oenothera fruticosa*
sunflower *Helianthus*. **ashy** *H. mollis*. **cheerful** *H. ×laetiflorus*. **common** *H. annuus*. **false** *Heliopsis helianthoides*. **giant** *Helianthus giganteus*. **rough** *H. strumosus*. **swamp** *H. angustifolius*. **thinleaf** *H. decapetalus*. **western** *H. occidentalis*. **willowleaved** *H. salicifolius*
sunset hibiscus *Abelmoschus manihot*

Sutera cordata (Thunb.) Kuntze = *Chaenostoma cordatum*

Swainsona Salisb. (Fabaceae). swayn-*soh*-nuh. After English physician and horticulturist Isaac Swainson (1746–1812), who had a botanical garden at Twickenham, London. 70 spp., herbs, subshrubs. Australia.

formosa (G. Don) Joy Thomps. for-*moh*-suh. Sturt's desert pea. Lat. beautiful.

swallowwort *Asclepias curassavica, Chelidonium majus*
swede *Brassica napus* Napobrassica Group
sweet alyssum *Lobularia maritima*

sweet cicely *Myrrhis odorata*
sweet flag *Acorus calamus*
sweet Nancy *Achillea ageratum*
sweet pepperbush *Clethra alnifolia.*
downy *C. tomentosa.* mountain *C.
acuminata*
sweet potato *Ipomoea batatas*
sweet sultan *Amberboa moschata*
sweet William *Dianthus barbatus*
sweet woodruff *Galium odoratum*
sweetfern *Comptonia peregrina*
sweetgum *Liquidambar styraciflua.*
oriental *L. orientalis*
sweetheart vine *Ceropegia linearis*
subsp. *woodii*
Swiss cheese plant *Monstera deliciosa*
sycamore *Acer pseudoplatanus.* American *Platanus occidentalis*

Sycopsis Oliv. (Hamamelidaceae). sie-
kop-sis. Gk. like a fig (the leaves).
3 spp., trees, shrubs. India (Assam),
China.
sinensis Oliv. sin-*en*-sis. Lat. of China.
China.

Symphoricarpos Duhamel (Caprifoliaceae). sim-fo-ree-*karp*-os. Gk.
together, fruit, referring to the clustered fruit. 17 spp. deciduous shrubs.
N Am., China.
albus (L.) S. F. Blake. *al*-boos. Snowberry. Lat. white (the fruit). Canada,
USA. var. *laevigatus* (Fernald) S. F.
Blake. lee-vi-*gah*-toos. Lat. smooth
(the shoots). W Canada, W USA.
×*chenaultii* Rehder. shuh-*nawlt*-ee-
ee. Of the Chenault nursery,
Orleans, France, where it was raised.
S. microphyllus × *S. orbiculatus.* Cult.
occidentalis Hook. ok-si-den-*tah*-lis.
Western snowberry. Lat. western. W
Canada, W and C USA.

orbiculatus Moench. or-bik-ew-*lah*-
toos. Coralberry. Lat. orbicular (the
fruit). E and C USA, N Mex.
oreophilus A. Gray. o-ree-oh-*fil*-oos.
Mountain snowberry. Gk.
mountain-loving. SW Canada, W
USA, N Mex.

Symphyotrichum Nees (Asteraceae).
sim-fee-*ot*-ri-koom. Gk. union, hair,
referring to the joined pappus bristles
of the type species. 90 spp. ann. and
perenn. herbs. Americas, E Asia.
carolinianum (Walter) Wunderlin &
B. F. Hansen. ka-ro-lin-ee-*ah*-noom.
Climbing aster. Of the Carolinas.
SE USA.
chilense (Nees) G. L. Nesom. chi-*len*-
see. Pacific aster. Of Chile, where it
was mistakenly thought to originate.
W USA, SW Canada.
cordifolium (L.) G. L. Nesom. kor-di-
foh-lee-oom. Common blue wood
aster. Lat. with heart-shaped leaves.
E USA, SE Canada.
drummondii (Lindl.) G. L. Nesom.
drum-*on*-dee-ee. Drummond's aster.
After Scottish naturalist Thomas
Drummond (1793–1835), who collected the type specimen. E USA.
dumosum (L.) G. L. Nesom. dew-
moh-soom. Rice button aster. Lat.
bushy. E USA, SE Canada.
ericoides (L.) G. L. Nesom. e-ri-*koy*-
deez. White heath aster. Lat. heath-
like. Canada, USA, N Mex.
laeve (L.) Á. Löve & D. Löve. *lee*-vee.
Smooth blue aster. Lat. smooth (the
leaves). SE Canada, E and C USA.
lanceolatum (Willd.) G. L. Nesom.
lahn-see-oh-*lah*-toom. White panicle
aster. Lat. lance-shaped (the leaves).
Canada, USA.

lateriflorum (L.) Á. Löve & D. Löve. la-tuh-ri-*flaw*-room. Calico aster. Lat. with flowers on one side (of the inflorescence). var. *horizontale* (Desf.) G. L. Nesom. ho-ri-zon-*tah*-lee. Lat. spreading horizontally.

novae-angliae (L.) G. L. Nesom. *noh*-vie-*ang*-lee-ie. New England aster. Of New England. S Canada, USA.

novi-belgii (L.) G. L. Nesom. *noh*-vee-*belg*-ee-ee. Michaelmas daisy, New York aster. Lat. of Nova Belgica (New Belgium, 16th-cent. name for a reg. of coastal NE USA including present-day New York). E N Am.

oblongifolium (Nutt.) G. L. Nesom. ob-long-gi-*foh*-lee-oom. Aromatic aster. Lat. with oblong leaves. E and C USA, N Mex.

oolentangiense (Riddell) G. L. Nesom. ue-luhn-tan-jee-*en*-see. Sky blue aster. Of the Olentangy River, Ohio. SE Canada, E and C USA, N Mex.

pilosum (Willd.) G. L. Nesom. pil-*oh*-soom. Oldfield aster. Lat. hairy (the shoots). SE Canada, E USA. var. *pringlei* (A. Gray) G. L. Nesom. *pring*-uhl-ee. Pringle's aster. After American horticulturist Cyrus Guernsey Pringle (1838–1911), who collected specimens in Vermont ca. 1880 from which it was described.

prenanthoides (Muhl. ex Willd.) G. L. Nesom. pree-nanth-*oy*-deez. Crooked stem aster. Lat. like *Prenanthes*, a related genus. SE Canada, NE USA.

puniceum (L.) Á. Löve & D. Löve. pew-*nis*-ee-oom. Purplestem aster. Lat. crimson (the stems). Canada, E and C USA.

sericeum (Vent.) G. L. Nesom. suh-*rik*-ee-oom. Silky aster. Lat. silky (the leaves). SC Canada, E and C USA, W Indies.

shortii (Lindl.) G. L. Nesom. *short*-ee-ee. Short's aster. After American physician and botanist Charles Wilkins Short (1794–1863), who collected the type specimen in Kentucky in 1832. SE Canada, E USA.

tradescantii (L.) G. L. Nesom. trad-es-*kant*-ee-ee. Shore aster. After English botanist and horticulturist John Tradescant (1608–1662), who introduced it from Virginia. SE Canada, NE USA.

Symphytum L. (Boraginaceae). *sim*-fit-oom. The Gk. name, from Gk. grow together, plant (they were used to heal broken bones). 20 spp. perenn. herbs. Eur., Asia.

caucasicum M. Bieb. kaw-*kas*-i-koom. Lat. of the Caucasus. Caucasus, Iran.

grandiflorum A. DC. gran-di-*flaw*-room. Lat. large-flowered. Caucasus.

ibericum Steven. i-*be*-ri-koom. Lat. of Iberia (Roman name for a reg. of the Caucasus, now in Georgia). NE Turkey, Georgia.

officinale L. o-fis-i-*nah*-lee. Comfrey. Lat. sold as a med. herb. Eur., W and C Asia.

tuberosum L. tew-buh-*roh*-soom. Lat. bearing tubers. Eur., Turkey.

×*uplandicum* Nyman. up-*land*-i-koom. Of Uppland (reg. of E Sweden). *S. asperum* × *S. officinale*. Cult.

Syringa L. (Oleaceae). si-*ring*-guh. Lilacs. From Gk. pipe, referring to the hollow stems. 20 spp., shrubs, trees. SE Eur. to Japan.

emodi Wall. ex G. Don. em-*oh*-dee. Himalayan lilac. Lat. of the Himalaya. Himal.

×*hyacinthiflora* Rehder. hie-uh-sinth-i-*flaw*-ruh. Lat. with flowers like *Hyacinthus*. *S. oblata* × *S. vulgaris*. Cult.

×*josiflexa* I. Preston ex J. S. Pringle. joh-si-*flex*-uh. From the names of the parents, *S. josikaea* × *S. komarovii* subsp. *reflexa*. Cult.

×*laciniata* Mill. luh-sin-ee-*ah*-tuh. Lat. deeply cut (the leaves). *S. protolaciniata* × *S. vulgaris*. Cult.

meyeri C. K. Schneid. *may*-uh-ree. After Frank Nicholas Meyer (1875–1918), Dutch-born USDA plant collector, who introduced it to the Arnold Arboretum. N China.

microphylla Diels = *S. pubescens* subsp. *microphylla*

×*persica* L. *pers*-i-kuh. Persian lilac. Lat. of Persia (Iran), where it was cultivated. Cult.

×*prestoniae* McKelvey. prest-*oh*-nee-ie. After English-born hybridist Isabella Preston (1881–1965), who raised it at the Government Experiment Station, Ottawa, Canada, in the 1920s. *S. komarovii* subsp. *reflexa* × *S. villosa*. Cult.

pubescens Turcz. pew-*bes*-uhnz. Lat. hairy (the shoots and leaves). China. subsp. *microphylla* (Diels) M. C. Chang & X. L. Chen. mik-*rof*-i-luh. Gk. small-leaved.

reticulata (Blume) H. Hara. re-tik-ew-*lah*-tuh. Lat. net-veined (the leaves). E Asia. subsp. *pekinensis* (Rupr.) P. S. Green & M. C. Chang. pee-kin-*en*-sis. Of Peking (Beijing). China.

vulgaris L. vul-*gar*-ris. Common lilac. Lat. common. SE Eur.

Tagetes L. (Asteraceae). tag-*ee*-teez. Marigolds. After Tages, an Etruscan deity, son of Jupiter, who sprang from the ploughed earth, as do many of the species. 40 spp., ann. and perenn. herbs, shrubs. Warm and trop. Am.

erecta L. ee-*rek*-tuh. African marigold, French marigold. Lat. upright. USA, Mex.

lucida Cav. *lue*-si-duh. Sweet-scented marigold. Lat. shining (the leaves). Mex., C Am.

patula L. = *T. erecta*

tamarisk *Tamarix*

Tamarix L. (Tamaricaceae). *tam*-uh-rix. Tamarisks. The Lat. name. 90 spp., shrubs, trees. Eur., N Africa, Asia.

ramosissima Ledeb. ram-oh-*sis*-i-muh. Lat. most branched. E Eur. to China.

tetrandra Pall. ex M. Bieb. tet-*rand*-ruh. Lat. with four stamens. E Eur., W Asia.

Tanacetum L. (Asteraceae). tan-uh-*seet*-oom. From Medieval Lat. immortality (wreaths of *T. vulgare* were placed on the dead at funerals).

160 spp. ann. and perenn. herbs. Eur., N Africa, Asia, N Am.

balsamita L. bawl-suhm-*eet*-uh. Alecost. An old name for this plant meaning balsam (referring to the fragrance). W Asia.

cinerariifolium (Trevir.) Sch. Bip. sin-uh-rah-ree-i-*foh*-lee-oom. Pyrethrum. Lat. with leaves like *Cineraria*. SE Eur.

coccineum (Willd.) Grierson. kok-*sin*-ee-oom. Lat. scarlet (the flowers). W Asia.

parthenium (L.) Sch. Bip. par-*then*-ee-oom. Feverfew. Gk. name for this or similar plants, from Gk. virgin. SE Eur.

vulgare L. vul-*gar*-ree. Tansy. Lat. common. Eur. to Japan.

tangerine *Citrus reticulata*
tansy *Tanacetum vulgare*
tansy-leaved thorn *Crataegus tanacetifolia*
tansyaster *Machaeranthera tanacetifolia*. **Colorado** *Xanthisma coloradoense*
tarajo *Ilex latifolia*

Tarenaya Raf. (Cleomaceae). ta-ruh-*nie*-uh. A Brazilian name for *T. spinosa*. 33 spp. ann. herbs. S Am.

hassleriana (Chodat) H. H. Iltis. has-luh-ree-*ah*-nuh. Spider plant. After Swiss botanist and surgeon Émile Hassler (1861–1937), who collected the type specimen in Paraguay in the late 19th cent. Argentina, Brazil, Paraguay.

taro *Colocasia esculenta*
tarragon *Artemisia dracunculus*

Tasmannia R. Br. ex DC. (Wintera-ceae). taz-*man*-ee-uh. After Dutch explorer Abel Janszoon Tasman (1603–1659), the first European to reach Tasmania. 50 spp., trees, shrubs. SE Asia to Australia.
lanceolata (Poir.) A. C. Sm. lahn-see-oh-*lah*-tuh. Mountain pepper. Lat. lance-shaped (the leaves). SE Australia.

Taxodium Rich. (Cupressaceae). tax-*oh*-dee-oom. Gk. resembling *Taxus*. 2 spp. conifers. USA, Mex.
ascendens Brongn. = *T. distichum* var. *imbricarium*
distichum (L.) Rich. *dis*-tik-oom. Bald cypress, swamp cypress. Lat. arranged in two rows (the leaves). SE USA. var. *imbricarium* (Nutt.) Croom. im-bri-*kah*-ree-oom. Pond cypress. Lat. overlapping (the leaves).

Taxus L. (Taxaceae). *tax*-oos. Yews. Lat. name of the yew. 9 spp. ever-green trees. Eur., N Africa, N Am., Asia.
baccata L. buh-*kah*-tuh. English yew. Lat. bearing berries. Eur., N Africa, W Asia.
cuspidata Sieb. & Zucc. kus-pi-*dah*-tuh. Japanese yew. Lat. ending in a short point (the leaves). E Russia, NE China, Japan.
×*media* Rehder. *mee*-dee-uh. Lat. intermediate (between the parents). *T. baccata* × *T. cuspidata*. Cult.

tea plant *Camellia sinensis*
tea tree *Leptospermum*, *L. scoparium*.
  woolly *L. lanigerum*
teasel *Dipsacus fullonum*

Tecoma Juss. (Bignoniaceae). te-*koh*-muh. From the Nahuatl (Mexican) name, meaning a flower resembling an earthenware vessel. 15 spp., trees, shrubs, climbers. S USA to S Am., S Africa.
capensis (Thunb.) Lindl. kuh-*pen*-sis. Cape honeysuckle. Of the Cape. S Africa.

Tecophilaea Bertero ex Colla (Tecophilaeaceae). tek-oh-*fil*-ee-uh. After Tecophila Billoti, 18th-cent. botanical artist and daughter of Luigi Colla, who published the name. 2 spp. cormous herbs. Chile, Peru.
cyanocrocus Leyb. sie-an-oh-*kroh*-koos. Gk. blue *Crocus*. Chile.

Telekia Baumg. (Asteraceae). te-lee-kee-uh. After Count Sámuel Teleki de Szék (1739–1822), chancellor of Transylvania. 1 sp., perenn. herb. C and E Eur., W Asia.
speciosa (Schreb.) Baumg. spee-see-*oh*-suh. Lat. showy.

Tellima R. Br. (Saxifragaceae). tel-*ee*-muh. Anagram of the related *Mitella*. 1 sp., perenn. herb. SW Canada, W USA.
grandiflora (Pursh) Douglas ex Lindl. gran-di-*flaw*-ruh. Lat. large-flowered.

Telopea R. Br. (Proteaceae). tel-*oh*-pee-uh. From Gk. seen from afar, refer-ring to the showy flowers. 5 spp., evergreen shrubs, small trees. SE Australia.
truncata (Labill.) R. Br. trung-*kah*-tuh. Lat. abruptly cut off (the leaf tips). Tasmania.

Tetradium Lour. (Rutaceae). tet-*ray*-dee-oom. From Gk. four (the parts of the flowers are in fours). 9 spp., trees, shrubs. E and SE Asia.

daniellii (Benn.) T. G. Hartley.dan-*yel*-ee-ee. After British army surgeon and botanist William Freeman Daniell (1818–1865), who collected it in China. China, Korea.

Tetragonia L. (Aizoaceae). tet-ruh-*goh*-nee-uh. Gk. four-angled (the fruit). 60 spp., ann. and perenn. herbs, subshrubs. Africa, E Asia, NZ, Australia, S Am.

tetragonioides (Pall.) Kuntze. tet-ruh-goh-nee-*oy*-deez. New Zealand spinach. Lat. like *Tetragonia* (it was originally described in another genus). NZ.

Tetrapanax (K. Koch) K. Koch (Araliaceae). tet-ruh-*pan*-ax. Gk. four, and *Panax*. The parts of the flowers are usually in fours (fives in the related *Panax*). 1 sp., shrub, tree. S China, Taiwan.

papyrifer (Hook.) K. Koch. pa-*pi*-ri-fer. Rice paper plant. Lat. bearing paper (the pith is used to make rice paper).

Teucrium L. (Lamiaceae). *tewk*-ree-oom. The Gk. name, possibly from Teucer, king of Troy, who is said to have used it medicinally. 260 spp., herbs, subshrubs. Widespread.

chamaedrys L. kam-*ee*-dris. Wall germander. Gk. like a dwarf oak (the leaves). Eur., N Africa, W and C Asia.

fruticans L. *frue*-ti-kanz. Shrubby germander. Lat. shrubby. S Eur., N Africa.

hircanicum L. hir-*kan*-i-koom. Lat. of Hyrcania (ancient reg. now in N Iran and Turkmenistan). W Asia.

×***lucidrys*** Boom. lue-*sid*-ris. From the names of the parents, *T. chamaedrys* × *T. lucidum*. Cult.

scorodonia L. sko-ro-*doh*-nee-uh. Wood germander. An old name applied to this plant, from Gk. onion. Eur., N Africa.

Texas bluebonnet *Lupinus texensis*

Thalia L. (Marantaceae). *thal*-ee-uh. After Johannes Thal (1542–1583), German physician and botanist. 6 spp. aquatic perenn. herbs. USA to S Am., W Africa.

dealbata Fraser ex Roscoe. dee-al-*bah*-tuh. Lat. whitened (the floral bracts). SE and C USA.

Thalictrum L. (Ranunculaceae). thuh-*lik*-troom. Meadow rues. Gk. name used by Dioscorides for a plant. 150 spp. perenn. herbs. Widespread.

aquilegiifolium L. ak-wi-lee-jee-i-*foh*-lee-oom. Lat. with leaves like *Aquilegia*. Eur. to Japan.

dasycarpum Fisch. ex Avé-Lall.das-ee-*karp*-oom. Gk. thick-fruited. Canada, USA.

delavayi Franch. del-uh-*vay*-ee. After French missionary Jean Marie Delavay (1834–1895), who collected the type specimen in Yunnan in 1887. SW China.

flavum L. *flah*-voom. Yellow meadow rue. Lat. yellow (the flowers). Eur., N Africa, Asia. subsp. ***glaucum*** (Desf.) Batt. *glaw*-koom. Lat. bluish white (the leaves).

isopyroides C. A. Mey. ie-soh-pie-*roy*-deez. Lat. like the related *Isopyrum*. C and SW Asia.

kiusianum Nakai. kee-ue-zee-*ah*-noom. Of Kyushu. Japan.

lucidum L. *lue*-sid-oom. Lat. shining (the foliage). Eur., Turkey.

minus L. *mie*-noos. Lesser meadow rue. Lat. small. Eur. to Japan, N Africa.

rochebruneanum Franch. & Sav. rosh-broon-ee-*ah*-noom. After French botanist and zoologist Alphonse Trémeau de Rochebrune (1836–1912), a colleague of author Adrien Franchet. Japan.

thalictroides (L.) A. J. Eames & B. Boivin. tha-lik-*troy*-deez. Rue anemone. Lat. like *Thalictrum* (it was originally described as a species of *Anemone*). SE Canada, E and C USA.

Thamnocalamus Munro (Poaceae). tham-no-*kal*-uh-moos. Gk. shrubby reed. 2 spp. bamboos. Himal., China.

crassinodus (T. P. Yi) Demoly = *T. spathiflorus* var. *crassinodus*

spathiflorus (Trin.) Munro. spath-i-*flaw*-roos. Lat. spathe flower, referring to the spathe-like bracts that subtend the inflorescence. Himal., S Tibet. var. *crassinodus* (T. P. Yi) Stapleton. kras-i-*noh*-doos. Lat. with thick nodes.

Thelypteris Schmidel (Thelypteridaceae). thel-*ip*-te-ris. Gk. female fern. 875 spp. ferns. Widespread.

decursive-pinnata = *Phegopteris decursive-pinnata*

noveboracensis (L.) Nieuwl. noh-vee-bo-ruh-*ken*-sis. New York fern. Of New York, from Lat. new, and

Eboracum, Roman city where present-day York, UK, is. E N Am.

palustris Schott. puh-*lus*-tris. Marsh fern. Lat. of marshes. Eur., Asia.

Thermopsis R. Br. (Fabaceae). ther-*mop*-sis. Gk. lupin-like. 25 spp. perenn. herbs. N Am., C and E Asia.

montana Nutt. mon-*tah*-nuh. Lat. of mountains. W USA.

rhombifolia (Pursh) Richardson. rom-bi-*foh*-lee-uh. Lat. with diamond-shaped leaves. W Canada, W and C USA.

villosa (Walter) Fernald & B. G. Schub. vil-*oh*-suh. Carolina lupin. Lat. with long hairs (the pods). SE USA.

thimbleberry *Rubus odoratus*, *R. parviflorus*

thistle, cotton *Onopordum acanthium*. **holy** *Silybum marianum*. **our lady's milk** *S. marianum*

thorow wax *Bupleurum*

three birds flying *Linaria triornithophora*

thrift *Armeria maritima*

throatwort *Campanula trachelium*

Thuja L. (Cupressaceae). *thue*-yuh. Arborvitae. Gk. name of a juniper or similar tree. 5 spp. conifers. N Am., E Asia.

occidentalis L. ok-si-den-*tah*-lis. American arborvitae. Lat. western. E N Am.

orientalis L. = *Platycladus orientalis*

plicata Donn ex D. Don. pli-*kah*-tuh. Western red cedar. Lat. folded together (the leaves). W Canada, W USA.

Thujopsis Sieb. & Zucc. ex Endl.
(Cupressaceae). thue-*yop*-sis. Gk. like
Thuja. 1 sp., conifer. Japan.
dolabrata (Thunb. ex L.f.) Sieb. &
Zucc. dol-uh-*brah*-tuh. Lat. axe-
shaped (the leaves).

Thunbergia Retz. (Acanthaceae).
thun-*berg*-ee-uh. After Carl Peter
Thunberg (1743–1828), Swedish botanist and physician, who collected in
Japan and S Africa. 100 spp., shrubs,
ann. and perenn. herbs, often climbing. Trop. and S Africa, trop. Asia.
alata Bojer ex Sims. uh-*lah*-tuh.
Black-eyed Susan. Lat. winged (the
leaf stalks). Trop. and S Africa.

thyme *Thymus*. caraway *T. herba-barona*. garden *T. vulgaris*. wild *T.
serpyllum*

Thymus L. (Lamiaceae). tie-moos.
Thyme. The Gk. name, from Gk. to
make a burnt offering (it was burned
as incense to the gods). 300 spp.,
perenn. herbs, subshrubs. Eur., N
Africa, temp. Asia.
caespititius Brot. ses-pi-*tit*-ee-oos. Lat.
mat-forming. SW Eur.
camphoratus Hoffmanns. & Link.
kam-fo-*rah*-toos. Lat. camphor-
scented. SW Portugal.
herba-barona Loisel. *herb*-uh-buh-
roh-nuh. Caraway thyme. From its
use in seasoning baron of beef. Corsica, Sardinia.
pseudolanuginosus Ronniger.
sue-doh-luh-nue-ji-*noh*-soos. Gk.
false *T. lanuginosus*. Cult.
pulegioides L. pue-lee-jee-*oy*-deez. Lat.
like *Mentha pulegium*. Eur.

serpyllum L. ser-*pil*-oom. Wild thyme.
Lat. thyme-like. Eur., W Asia.
vulgaris L. vul-*gar*-ris. Garden thyme.
Lat. common. S Eur., N Africa.

Tiarella L. (Saxifragaceae). tee-uh-*rel*-
uh. Diminutive of Gk./Lat. turban,
referring to the shape of the fruit.
3 spp. perenn. herbs. N Am., E Asia.
cordifolia L. kord-i-*foh*-lee-uh. Foamflower. Lat. with heart-shaped leaves.
SE Canada, E USA.
wherryi Lakela = *T. cordifolia*

tick trefoil *Desmodium*. **Canadian**
D. canadense
tickseed *Coreopsis*. **golden** *C. tinctoria*. **goldenmane** *C. basalis*. **lanceleaf** *C. lanceolata*. **large flower** *C.
grandiflora*. **lobed** *C. auriculata*.
pink *C. rosea*. **stiff** *C. palmata*. **tall**
C. tripteris. **whorled** *C. verticillata*

Tigridia Juss. (Iridaceae). ti-*grid*-
ee-uh. From Lat. tiger, referring to
the patterned flowers. 50 spp. bulbous herbs. Mex. to S Am.
pavonia (L.f.) DC. puh-*voh*-nee-uh.
Peacock flower. Lat. peacock, from
the showy flowers. Mex., C Am.

Tilia L. (Malvaceae). *ti*-lee-uh. Limes,
lindens. The Lat. name. 23 spp.
deciduous trees. N Am., Eur., Asia.
americana L. uh-me-ri-*kah*-nuh.
American lime, basswood. Of America. Canada, E and C USA, Mex.
cordata Mill. kor-*dah*-tuh. Small-
leaved lime/linden. Lat. heart-shaped
(the leaves). Eur., W Asia.
dasystyla Steven. das-i-*stie*-luh. Lat.
with a thick style. E Eur.

×*euchlora* K. Koch. ew-*klor*-ruh. Gk. good green (the leaf colour). *T. cordata* × *T. dasystyla*. Cult.

×*europaea* L. ew-roh-*pee*-uh. Common lime/linden. Lat. of Europe. *T. cordata* × *T. platyphyllos*. Eur.

henryana Szyszyl. hen-ree-*ah*-nuh. After Scottish-born Irish plantsman Augustine Henry (1857–1930), who collected the type specimen in Hubei in 1888. China.

mongolica Maxim. mon-*gol*-i-kuh. Mongolian lime. Of Mongolia. N China.

platyphyllos Scop. plat-ee-*fil*-os. Broad-leaved lime/linden. Gk. broad-leaved. Eur., Turkey.

tomentosa Moench. to-men-*toh*-suh. Silver lime/linden. Lat. hairy (the shoots and leaf undersides). E Eur., Turkey. '**Petiolaris**'. pee-tee-oh-*lah*-ris. Weeping lime/linden. Lat. with a (conspicuous) petiole.

toadflax *Linaria*. **Balkan** *L. dalmatica*. **common** *L. vulgaris*. **ivy-leaved** *Cymbalaria muralis*. **purple** *Linaria purpurea*
tobacco *Nicotiana tabacum*. **tree** *N. glauca*. **wild** *N. rustica*

Tolmiea Torr. & A. Gray (Saxifragaceae). *tol*-mee-uh. After William Fraser Tolmie (1812–1886), Scottish surgeon with the Hudson's Bay Co. at Puget Sound. 1 sp., perenn. herb. SW Canada, NW USA.

menziesii (Pursh) Torr. & A. Gray. men-*zeez*-ee-ee. Pickaback plant. After Scottish surgeon and naturalist Archibald Menzies (1754–1842), who collected the type specimen "on the north-west coast."

tomato *Solanum lycopersicum*

Toona (Endl.) M. Roem. (Meliaceae). *tue*-nuh. From the Indian name for *T. ciliata*. 5 spp. trees. China to Australia.

sinensis (A. Juss) M. Roem. sin-*en*-sis. Lat. of China. Himal., China, SE Asia.

totara *Podocarpus totara*. **alpine** *P. nivalis*

Trachelospermum Lem. (Apocynaceae). trak-uh-loh-*sperm*-oom. Gk. neck seed, referring to the shape of the seeds. 15 spp. woody climbers. E Asia, SE USA.

asiaticum (Sieb. & Zucc.) Nakai. ay-zee-*at*-i-koom. Lat. of Asia. China, Korea, Japan, Thailand.

jasminoides (Lindl.) Lem. jaz-min-*oy*-deez. Lat. like *Jasminum* (the flowers). China, Korea, Japan, Vietnam.

Trachycarpus H. Wendl. (Arecaceae). trak-ee-*karp*-oos. Gk. rough fruit, referring to their irregular shape. 9 spp. palms. Himal., China, SE Asia.

fortunei (Hook.) H. Wendl. for-*tewn*-ee-ee. Windmill palm. After Scottish botanist Robert Fortune (1812–1880), who introduced it to Kew in 1849. S China, N Myanmar.

wagnerianus Becc. = *T. fortunei*

Trachystemon D. Don (Boraginaceae). trak-ee-*stem*-on. Gk. rough stamen, referring to the hairy filaments of the following. 2 spp. perenn. herbs. SE Eur., W Asia.

orientalis (L.) G. Don. o-ree-en-*tah*-lis. Lat. eastern.

Tradescantia Ruppius ex L. (Commelinaceae). trad-es-*kant*-ee-uh. After John Tradescant (ca. 1570–1638), English naturalist and gardener to King Charles I, and his son John (1608–1662), who collected plants in North America. 70 spp. perenn. herbs. Americas.

Andersoniana Group. an-der-soh-nee-*ah*-nuh. After American botanist Edgar Shannon Anderson (1897–1969), who worked on hybridisation in the genus.

bracteata Small. brak-tee-*ah*-tuh. Lat. with (conspicuous) bracts. C USA.

ohioensis Raf. oh-hie-oh-*en*-sis. Of Ohio. SE Canada, E and C USA.

pallida (Rose) D. R. Hunt. *pa*-li-duh. Lat. pale (the flowers). Mex.

spathacea Sw. spath-*ay*-see-uh. Lat. with a (conspicuous) spathe. S Mex., C Am.

virginiana L. vir-jin-ee-*ah*-nuh. Of Virginia. SE Canada, E USA.

zebrina hort. ex Bosse. ze-*breen*-uh. Wandering Jew. Zebra-like (the striped leaves). Trop. Am.

traveller's joy *Clematis vitalba*
tree anemone *Carpenteria californica*
tree of heaven *Ailanthus altissima*
tree poppy *Dendromecon rigida*

Tricyrtis Wall. (Liliaceae). trie-*kurt*-is. Toad lily. Gk. three swellings, referring to the three sac-like nectaries at the base of the outer tepals. 23 spp. perenn. herbs. Himal. to E and SE Asia.

formosana Baker. for-moh-*sah*-nuh. Of Taiwan (Formosa). Taiwan.

hirta (Thunb.) Hook. *hirt*-uh. Lat. with long hairs (the stems). Japan.

latifolia Maxim. lat-i-*foh*-lee-uh. Lat. broad-leaved. China, Japan.

Trifolium L. (Fabaceae). trie-*foh*-lee-oom. Clovers. The Lat. name, from Lat. three leaves (the leaves have three leaflets). 240 spp. ann. and perenn. herbs. Widespread.

incarnatum L. in-kar-*nah*-toom. Crimson clover. Lat. flesh-coloured (the flowers). Eur., Turkey.

ochroleucum Huds. ok-roh-*lue*-koom. Sulphur clover. Gk. yellowish white (the flowers). Eur., N Africa, W Asia.

pratense L. pruh-*ten*-see. Red clover. Lat. of meadows. Eur., N Africa, W and C Asia.

repens L. *ree*-puhnz. White clover. Lat. creeping. Eur., N Africa, W and C Asia.

Trillium L. (Melanthiaceae). *tril*-ee-oom. Wake robins. From Gk. three, and *Lilium*. The leaves and parts of the flowers are in threes. 43 spp. perenn. herbs. N Am., Himal., E Asia.

albidum J. D. Freeman. *al*-bid-oom. Lat. white (the flowers). Calif., Oregon.

catesbaei Elliott. *kates*-bee-ee. After English naturalist Mark Catesby (1682–1749), who illustrated it. SE USA.

chloropetalum (Torr.) Howell. klo-roh-*pet*-uh-loom. Gk. with green petals. Calif.

cuneatum Raf. kew-nee-*ah*-toom. Lat. wedge-shaped (the petals). SE USA.

erectum L. ee-*rek*-toom. Lat. upright. E N Am.

flexipes Raf. *flex*-i-peez. Lat. with a flexible stalk (the flowers). SE Canada, NE USA.

grandiflorum (Michx.) Salisb. gran-di-*flaw*-room. Lat. large-flowered. SE Canada, NE USA.

kurabayashii J. D. Freeman. koo-ruh-bie-*ash*-ee-ee. After Japanese botanist Masataka Kurabayashi, the first to suggest this was a distinct species. Calif., Oregon.

luteum (Muhl.) Harb. *lue*-tee-oom. Lat. yellow (the flowers). SE USA.

recurvatum L. C. Beck. ree-kur-*vah*-toom. Lat. recurved (the sepals). EC USA.

sessile L. *ses*-i-lee. Lat. unstalked (the flowers). NE and C USA.

sulcatum T. S. Patrick. sul-*kah*-toom. Lat. grooved (the sepals). SE USA.

vaseyi Harb. *vayz*-ee-ee. After English-born American botanist George Vasey (1822–1893), who collected the type specimen in North Carolina in 1878. SE USA.

Tristagma Poepp. (Amaryllidaceae). trie-*stag*-muh. Gk. three drops, referring to the three nectaries. 30 spp. bulbous herbs. S Am.

uniflorum (Lindl.) Traub. ew-ni-*flaw*-room. Lat. one-flowered. Argentina, Uruguay.

Triteleia Douglas ex Lindl. (Asparagaceae). tri-tel-*ay*-uh. Gk. three, perfect, complete (the parts of the flower are in threes). 15 spp. cormous herbs. SW Canada, W USA.

laxa Benth. *lax*-uh. Lat. lax, open (the inflorescence). Calif.

Tritonia Ker Gawl. (Iridaceae). trie-*toh*-nee-uh. From Lat. weather vane, referring to the variable orientation of the stamens. 26 spp. cormous herbs. Trop. and S Africa.

crocata (L.) Ker Gawl. kroh-*kah*-tuh. Lat. saffron-yellow (the colour of the flowers on the dried specimen from which it was described; they are orange-red when fresh). S Africa.

disticha (Klatt) Baker. *dis*-tik-uh. Lat. arranged in two rows (the leaves). S Africa.

Trochodendron Sieb. & Zucc. (Trochodendraceae). trok-oh-*den*-dron. Gk. wheel tree, the spreading stamens likened to the spokes of a wheel. 1 sp., evergreen tree. Taiwan, Korea, Japan.

aralioides Sieb. & Zucc. uh-rah-lee-*oy*-deez. Lat. like *Aralia*.

Trollius L. (Ranunculaceae). *trol*-ee-oos. Globeflowers. From German globe flower. 30 spp. perenn. herbs. N temp. and arctic N Am., Eur., Asia.

chinensis Bunge. chin-*en*-sis. Of China. China.

×*cultorum* Bergmans. kul-*tor*-room. Lat. of gardeners. Cult.

europaeus L. ew-roh-*pee*-oos. Lat. of Europe. Eur., W Asia.

pumilus D. Don. *pew*-mi-loos. Lat. dwarf. Himal., W China.

Tropaeolum L. (Tropaeolaceae). troh-pee-*oh*-loom. From Gk. trophy. Linnaeus likened the leaves of *T. majus* to shields and the flowers to helmets; those of the enemy were fixed to a tree after victory. 90 spp. ann. and perenn. herbs. Mex. to S Am.

majus L. *may*-joos. Nasturtium. Lat. larger. Cult.

peregrinum L. pe-ri-*green*-oom. Canary creeper. Lat. travelling, spreading (the vigorous shoots). Peru.

polyphyllum Cav. pol-ee-*fil*-oom. Gk. with many leaves (leaf lobes). Argentina, Chile.

speciosum Poepp. & Endl. spee-see-*oh*-soom. Lat. showy (the flowers). Chile.

tuberosum Ruiz & Pav. tew-buh-*roh*-soom. Lat. bearing tubers. S Am.

trout lily *Erythronium*. **yellow** *E. americanum*

trumpet creeper *Campsis radicans*. **Chinese** *C. grandiflora*

Tsuga (Endl.) Carrière (Pinaceae). *tsue*-guh. Hemlocks. The Japanese name. 10 spp. conifers. N Am., E Asia.

canadensis (L.) Carrière. kan-uh-*den*-sis. Eastern hemlock. SE Canada, E USA.

heterophylla (Raf.) Sarg. het-uh-*rof*-i-luh. Western hemlock. Gk. with variable leaves. W Canada, NW USA.

mertensiana (Bong.) Carrière. mer-tenz-ee-*ah*-nuh. Mountain hemlock. After German naturalist and physician Karl Heinrich Mertens (1796–1830), who collected the type specimen at Sitka, Alaska, in 1827. SW Canada, W USA.

tuberose *Polianthes tuberosa*

Tulbaghia L. (Amaryllidaceae). tool-*bahg*-ee-uh. After Ryk Tulbagh (1699–1771), Dutch governor of the Cape Colony from 1751 until his death in the year the genus was

named. 26 spp. perenn., often bulbous, herbs. Trop. and S Africa.

violacea Harv. vie-o-*lay*-see-uh. Lat. violet (the flowers). S Africa.

tulip *Tulipa*

tulip tree *Liriodendron tulipifera*. **Chinese** *L. chinense*

Tulipa L. (Liliaceae). *tew*-lip-uh. Tulips. From Turkish turban (the shape of the flowers). 150 spp. bulbous herbs. Eur., N Africa, Asia.

acuminata Vahl ex Hornem. = *T. gesneriana*

altaica Pall. ex Spreng. al-*tie*-i-kuh. Of the Altai reg. C Asia.

biflora Pall. bie-*flaw*-ruh. Lat. two-flowered (the flowers are sometimes in pairs). SE Eur., W and C Asia, NW China.

clusiana DC. klue-zee-*ah*-nuh. After Flemish botanist and physician Charles d'Écluse (Lat. *Carolus Clusius*), whose 16th-cent. planting of tulips in Holland is thought to have inspired the mania for growing tulips there. W Asia to W Himal.

gesneriana L. ges-ne-ree-*ah*-nuh. After Swiss naturalist and physician Conrad Gesner (1516–1565), who described and illustrated cultivated tulips. N Turkey, Caucasus.

humilis Herb. *hew*-mi-lis. Lat. low (growing). W Asia.

kolpakowskiana Regel = *T. altaica*

linifolia Regel. li-ni-*foh*-lee-uh. Lat. with leaves like *Linum* (flax). C Asia.

praestans H. B. May. *prie*-stans. Lat. outstanding. C Asia.

saxatilis Sieber ex Spreng. sax-*at*-i-lis. Lat. growing in rocky places. S Greece, W Turkey.

sprengeri Baker. *spreng*-uh-ree. After German botanist and plant breeder Carl Ludwig Sprenger (1846–1917), the first to grow it, in his nursery in Naples. Turkey.

sylvestris L. sil-*vest*-ris. Lat. of woods. Eur., Caucasus.

tarda Stapf. *tard*-uh. Lat. late (flowering). NW Iran, C Asia.

turkestanica (Regel) Regel. tur-kes-*tan*-i-kuh. Of Turkestan. C Asia.

tupelo *Nyssa sylvatica*
turkey corn *Dicentra eximia*
turnip *Brassica rapa* Rapifera Group
turtlehead *Chelone*. **pink** *C. lyonii*. **red** *C. obliqua*. **white** *C. glabra*
tutsan *Hypericum androsaemum*
twinberry *Lonicera involucrata*
twinflower *Linnaea borealis*

twinleaf *Jeffersonia diphylla*
twinspur *Diascia*

Typha L. (Typhaceae). *tie*-fuh. Reedmaces. The Gk. name, from Gk. marsh, referring to the habitat. 16 spp. perenn. aquatic herbs. Widespread.

angustifolia L. an-gus-ti-*foh*-lee-uh. Lat. narrow-leaved. N temp. regs.

latifolia L. lat-i-*foh*-lee-uh. Lat. broadleaved. N and S Am., Eur., Asia.

laxmannii Lepech. lax-*man*-ee-ee. After Swedish explorer Erik Gustavovich Laxmann (1737–1796), who collected the type specimen in Dahuria, Russia. E Eur. to China.

minima Funck ex Hoppe. *min*-i-muh. Lat. smallest. Eur. to China.

Ugni Turcz. (Myrtaceae). *oog*-nee. From the native name in Chile (pronounced *oon*-yee). 4 spp. shrubs. S Mex. to S Am.
molinae Turcz. mo-*leen*-ie. After Chilean priest and naturalist Juan Ignacio Molina (1740–1829), who first described it (as *Myrtus ugni*). Chile, Argentina.

Ulex L. (Fabaceae). *ew*-lex. Lat. name used by Pliny for this or a similar shrub. 20 spp. spiny shrubs. W Eur., N Africa.
europaeus L. ew-roh-*pee*-oos. Gorse. Lat. of Europe. W Eur.
gallii Planch. *gal*-ee-ee. Dwarf gorse. Lat. of France (Lat. *Gallia*). W Eur.

ulmo *Eucryphia cordifolia*

Ulmus L. (Ulmaceae). *ool*-moos. Elms. The Lat. name. 40 spp., trees, shrubs. Eur., N Africa, Asia, N Am.
americana L. uh-me-ri-*kah*-nuh. American elm. Of America. Canada, E and C USA.
carpinifolia Gled. = *U. minor*
glabra Huds. *glab*-ruh. Wych elm, Scotch elm. Lat. smooth (the bark). Eur., W Asia.

×**hollandica** Mill. hol-*and*-i-kuh. Dutch elm. Lat. of Holland, where it was thought to originate. Eur., W Asia.
minor Mill. *mie*-nuh. Field elm. Lat. smaller. Eur., N Africa, W Asia.
parvifolia Jacq. par-vi-*foh*-lee-uh. Chinese elm. Lat. small-leaved. China, Korea, Taiwan, Japan.
pumila L. *pew*-mi-luh. Siberian elm. Lat. dwarf. C and E Asia.
rubra Muhl. *rue*-bruh. Red elm, slippery elm. Lat. red (the shoots). SE Canada, E and C USA.

Umbellularia (Nees) Nutt. (Lauraceae). um-bel-ew-*lair*-ree-uh. Lat. in little umbels, referring to the inflorescence. 1 sp., evergreen tree. Calif., Oregon.
californica (Hook. & Arn.) Nutt. kal-i-*for*-ni-kuh. California bay/laurel. Of California.

Umbilicus DC. (Crassulaceae). um-*bil*-i-koos. Lat. navel, from the appearance of the leaves. 14 spp. succulent perenn. herbs. Eur., W Asia.
oppositifolius (Ledeb.) Ledeb. o-pos-i-ti-*foh*-lee-oos. Lat. with opposite leaves. Caucasus.
rupestris (Salisb.) Dandy. rue-*pes*-tris. Navelwort, pennywort. Lat. growing on rocks. Eur., W Asia.

umbrella plant *Darmera peltata*
umbrella tree *Magnolia tripetala*

Uncinia Pers. (Cyperaceae). un-*sin*-ee-uh. From Lat. hook, referring to the conspicuously hooked tip of the rachilla. 70 spp. perenn. herbs. SE Asia to NZ, Pacific Is., Mex. to S Am.

egmontiana Hamlin. eg-mont-ee-*ah*-nuh. Of Mount Egmont, where the type specimen was collected in 1955. NZ.

uncinata (L.f.) Kük. un-sin-*ah*-tuh. Lat. hooked (deriv. as for genus). NZ, Hawaii.

Uvularia L. (Colchicaceae). ue-vew-*lair*-ree-uh. Bellworts. From Lat. uvula, from a supposed resemblance of the flowers to that pendulous part of the mouth palate. 5 spp. perenn. herbs. E N Am.

grandiflora Sm. gran-di-*flaw*-ruh. Lat. large-flowered. SE and SC Canada, E and C USA.

perfoliata L. per-foh-lee-*ah*-tuh. Lat. with the leaf base encircling the stem. SE Canada, E USA.

sessilifolia L. ses-i-li-*foh*-lee-uh. Lat. with unstalked leaves. SE and SC Canada, E and C USA.

Vaccinium L. (Ericaceae). vak-*sin*-ee-oom. Lat. name, possibly for *V. myrtillus* (bilberry). 450 spp., shrubs, trees. N hemisph., Africa, S Am.

angustifolium Aiton. an-gust-i-*foh*-lee-oom. Lowbush blueberry. Lat. narrow-leaved. E N Am.

corymbosum L. ko-rim-*boh*-soom. Blueberry. Lat. with flowers in corymbs. E Canada, E and C USA.

glaucoalbum Hook.f. ex C. B. Clarke. glaw-koh-*al*-boom. Lat. bluish white, white (the leaf undersides). Himal., W China.

macrocarpon Aiton. mak-roh-*karp*-on. Cranberry. Gk. large-fruited. E N Am.

ovatum Pursh. oh-*vah*-toom. California huckleberry. Lat. ovate (the leaves). SW Canada, W USA.

oxycoccus L. ox-ee-*kok*-oos. European cranberry. Gk. sharp berry (the taste). Canada, USA, Eur., Asia.

parvifolium Sm. par-vi-*foh*-lee-oom. Red huckleberry. Lat. small-leaved. SW Canada, W USA.

vitis-idaea L. *vie*-tis-ee-*die*-uh. Cowberry. Gk. grape of Mount Ida. Canada, USA, Eur., Asia.

valerian *Valeriana*. **common** *V. officinalis*. **red** *Centranthus ruber*

Valeriana L. (Valerianaceae). vuh-le-ree-*ah*-nuh. Valerians. 200 spp. perenn. herbs. Widespread.

officinalis L. o-fis-i-*nah*-lis. Common valerian. Lat. sold as a med. herb. Eur., Asia.

phu L. *fue*. Gk. with an unpleasant scent (the roots). Eur., Caucasus.

pyrenaica L. pi-ruh-*nay*-i-kuh. Lat. of the Pyrenees. Pyrenees.

Vallota speciosa (L.f.) T. Durand & Schinz = *Cyrtanthus elatus*

Vancouveria C. Morren & Decne. (Berberidaceae). van-kue-*ve*-ree-uh. After George Vancouver (1757–1758), British Royal Navy captain who explored the Pacific Northwest. 3 spp. perenn. herbs. W USA.

hexandra (Hook.) C. Morren & Decne. hex-*an*-druh. Gk. with six stamens (normal for this genus but originally named as an epimedium, which have four stamens).

vanilla leaf *Achlys triphylla*
velvet plant *Gynura aurantiaca*
Venus's fly trap *Dionaea muscipula*
Venus's looking glass *Legousia speculum-veneris*

Veratrum L. (Melanthiaceae). ver-*raht*-room. False hellebores. Lat. true black, referring to the roots. 30 spp. perenn. herbs. N hemisph.

album L. *al*-boom. Lat. white (the flowers). Eur., Asia, Alaska.

californicum Durand. kal-i-*for*-ni-koom. Of California. W USA.

nigrum L. *nie*-groom. Lat. black (the dark flowers). Eur., Asia.

Verbascum L. (Scrophulariaceae). ver-*bas*-koom. Mulleins. From the Lat. name, from Lat. bearded, referring to the hairy filaments. 300 spp. ann., bienn. and perenn. herbs. Eur., N Africa, Asia.

bombyciferum Boiss. bom-bi-*si*-fuh-room. Lat. silk-bearing (silky hairs cover the plant). SW Asia.

chaixii Vill. *shayz*-ee-ee. Nettle-leaved mullein. After French amateur botanist Abbé Dominique Chaix (1730–1799), whose student, Dominique Villars, named it for him. Eur.

olympicum Boiss. o-*limp*-i-koom. Lat. of Mount Olympus. Turkey.

phoeniceum L. fee-*nis*-ee-oom. Purple mullein. Gk. red-purple (the flowers). Eur., C Asia.

thapsus L. *thap*-soos. Aaron's rod, common mullein. Gk. name of a plant from Thapsos, a settlement near Syracuse, Sicily. Eur. to China.

Verbena L. (Verbenaceae). ver-*been*-uh. Lat. name for sacred boughs of olive, myrtle and other plants carried in processions. 200 spp., ann. and perenn. herbs, shrubs. Mainly N and S Am, also Eur., Africa, Asia.

bonariensis L. bon-ah-ree-*en*-sis. Purple top. Of Buenos Aires, Argentina (named for Our Lady of Bonaria, patroness of Cagliari, Sardinia). S Am.

canadensis (L.) Britton = *Glandularia canadensis*

hastata L. has-*tah*-tuh. American vervain. Lat. spear-shaped (the leaves). Canada, USA.

officinalis L. o-fis-i-*nah*-lis. Common vervain. Lat. sold as a med. herb. Eur., Africa, Asia, N Am.

rigida Spreng. *rij*-i-duh. Lat. rigid (the shoots). S Am.

stricta Vent. *strik*-tuh. Hoary vervain. Lat. upright. SE Canada, USA.

tenuisecta auct. = *Glandularia pulchella*

verbena, garden *Glandularia* ×*hybrida*

Verbesina L. (Asteraceae). ver-bes-*een*-uh. Lat. like *Verbena*. 200 spp., ann. and perenn. herbs, shrubs, trees. N to S Am.

alternifolia (L.) Britton ex Kearney. al-ter-ni-*foh*-lee-uh. Lat. with alternate leaves. SE Canada, E and C USA.

Vernonia Schreb. (Asteraceae). ver-*noh*-nee-uh. Ironweeds. After English naturalist William Vernon (ca. 1666–1715), who collected in Maryland in 1697–98. 20 spp. perenn. herbs. SC Canada, USA, N Mex.

arkansana DC. ar-kuhn-*sah*-nuh. Of Arkansas. SC USA.

fasciculata Michx. fa-sik-ew-*lah*-tuh. Lat. clustered (the flowerheads). SC Canada, C USA.

gigantea (Walter) Trel. ex Branner & Coville. jie-*gan*-tee-uh. Lat. very large. SE Canada, E and C USA.

noveboracensis (L.) Michx. noh-vee-bo-ruh-*ken*-sis. Of New York, from Lat. new and Eboracum, Roman city where present-day York, UK, is. E USA.

Veronica L. (Plantaginaceae). vuh-*ron*-i-kuh. Speedwells. After St. Veronica. 450 spp., herbs, shrubs, trees. Widespread.

albicans Petrie. *al*-bi-kanz. Lat. whitish (the leaves). NZ (S.I.). **Recurva Group**. ree-*kurv*-uh. Lat. recurved (the leaves).

austriaca L. os-tree-*ah*-kuh. Of Austria. C and E Eur., W Asia. subsp. **teucrium** (L.) D. A. Webb. *tewk*-ree-oom. Like *Teucrium*. Eur. to China.

beccabunga L. bek-uh-*bung*-guh. Brooklime. From the German name. Eur., N Africa, W and C Asia, China.

brachysiphon (Summerh.) Bean. brak-ee-*sie*-fon. Gk. with a short tube (the flowers). NZ (S.I.).

buchananii Hook.f. bew-kan-*an*-ee-ee. After Scottish-born NZ botanist and artist John Buchanan (1819–1898), who, with James Hector, collected the type specimen. NZ (S.I.).

catarractae G. Forst. kat-uh-*rak*-tie. Lat. of waterfalls. NZ.

cupressoides Hook. kew-pres-*oy*-deez. Lat. like *Cupressus* (the foliage). NZ (S.I.).

×**franciscana** Eastw. fran-sis-*kah*-nuh. Of San Francisco (whence it was described). *V. elliptica* × *V. speciosa*. Cult.

gentianoides Vahl. jent-shee-uhn-*oy*-deez. Lat. like *Gentiana*. E Eur., W Asia.

grandis Fisch. ex Spreng. *gran*-dis. Lat. large. C and NE Asia.

hulkeana F. Muell. hulk-ee-*ah*-nuh. After Thomas H. Hulke, who collected the type specimen. NZ.

liwanensis K. Koch. li-van-*en*-sis. Of Livana (now Artvin), NE Turkey (whence it was described). NE Turkey.

longifolia L. long-gi-*foh*-lee-uh. Lat. long-leaved. Eur. to China.

lyallii Hook.f. lie-*al*-ee-ee. After Scottish explorer David Lyall (1817–1895), who collected the type specimen. NZ.

macrantha Hook.f. mak-*ranth*-uh. Gk. large-flowered. NZ (S.I.).

ochracea (Ashwin) Garn-Jones. ok-*ray*-see-uh. Gk. ochre-yellow (the foliage). NZ (S.I.).

odora Hook.f. oh-*dor*-ruh. Lat. fragrant (the flowers). NZ.

perfoliata R. Br. per-foh-lee-*ah*-tuh. Digger's speedwell. Lat. with the leaf base encircling the stem. SE Australia.

pimeleoides Hook.f. pie-mee-lee-*oy*-deez. Lat. like *Pimelea*. NZ (S.I.).

pinguifolia Hook.f. ping-gwi-*foh*-lee-uh. Lat. with waxy leaves. NZ (S.I.). 'Pagei'. *pay*-jee-ee. After Edward Page, foreman of Dunedin Botanical Garden, NZ.

prostrata L. pro-*strah*-tuh. Lat. prostrate. Eur., W Asia.

rakaiensis J. B. Armstr. rak-ie-*en*-sis. Of the Rakaia Valley, where the type specimen was collected. NZ (S.I.).

salicifolia G. Forst. sal-i-si-*foh*-lee-uh. Lat. with leaves like *Salix*. NZ, S Chile.

spicata L. spi-*kah*-tuh. Lat. in spikes (the flowers). Eur. to N China. subsp. **incana** (L.) Walters. in-*kah*-nuh. Lat. grey (the foliage).

topiaria (L. B. Moore) Garn.-Jones. toh-pee-*ah*-ree-uh. Lat. used in ornamental gardening. NZ (S.I.).

umbrosa M. Bieb. um-*broh*-suh. Lat. growing in shade. E Eur., Caucasus.

vernicosa Hook.f. vern-i-*koh*-suh. Lat. varnished (the leaves appear). NZ (S.I.).

'Youngii'. *yung*-ee-ee. After James

Young (1862–1934), curator of Christchurch Botanic Garden, where it was first grown in the 1920s.

Veronicastrum Heist. ex Fabr. (Plantaginaceae). vuh-ron-i-*kas*-troom. Lat. somewhat like *Veronica*. 20 spp. perenn. herbs. N Am., E Asia.
virginicum (L.) Farw. vir-*jin*-i-koom. Culver's root. Of Virginia. S Canada, E and C USA.

vervain, American *Verbena hastata*. **common** *V. officinalis*. **hoary** *V. stricta*

Vesalea M. Martens & Galeotti (Linnaeaceae). ves-*ah*-lee-uh. After Andreas van Wessel (Lat. *Vesalius*) (1514–1564), Flemish anatomist. 2 spp. shrubs. Mex.
floribunda M. Martens & Galeotti. flo-ri-*bun*-duh. Lat. flowering profusely.

Vestia Willd. (Solanaceae). *vest*-ee-uh. After Lorenz Chrysanth von Vest (1776–1840), Austrian scientist and physician. 1 sp., shrub. Chile.
foetida (Ruiz & Pav.) Hoffmanns. *feet*-i-duh. Lat. fetid (the leaves).
lycioides Willd. = *V. foetida*

vetch, horseshoe *Hippocrepis comosa*. **kidney** *Anthyllis vulneraria*. **spring** *Lathyrus vernus*
vetchling *Lathyrus*

Viburnum L. (Adoxaceae). vie-*burn*-oom. Lat. name for *V. lantana*. 200 spp., shrubs, trees. Eur., N Africa, Asia, N and S Am.
acerifolium L. ay-suh-ri-*foh*-lee-oom.

Dockmackie. Lat. maple-leaved. SE Canada, E USA.
awabuki K. Koch = *V. odoratissimum* var. *awabuki*
×***bodnantense*** Aberc. ex Stearn. bod-nuhn-*ten*-see. Of Bodnant Garden, N Wales, where it was raised (not for the first time). *V. farreri* × *V. grandiflorum*. Cult.
×***burkwoodii*** Burkwood & Skipwith. After the Burkwood & Skipwith nursery, where it was raised. *V. carlesii* × *V. utile*. Cult.
×***carlcephalum*** Burkwood ex R. B. Pike. karl-*kef*-uh-loom. From the names of the parents, *V. carlesii* × *V. macrocephalum*. Cult.
carlesii Hemsl. karl-*ee*-zee-ee. After William Richard Carles (1848–1929), English diplomat in Korea, who collected one of the specimens from which it was described. Japan, Korea.
cassinoides L. kas-i-*noy*-deez. Blue haw. Lat. like *Cassine* (the leaves). E N Am.
cinnamomifolium Rehder. sin-uh-mohm-i-*foh*-lee-oom. Lat. with leaves like *Cinnamomum*. W China.
cylindricum Buch. Ham. ex D. Don. si-*lin*-dri-koom. Lat. cylindrical (the flowers). Himal., China, SE Asia.
davidii Franch. da-*vid*-ee-ee. After French missionary, botanist and zoologist Armand David (1826–1900), who collected the type specimen in 1869. W China.
dentatum L. den-*tah*-toom. Arrowwood. Lat. toothed (the leaves). E Canada, E and C USA.
dilatatum Thunb. di-luh-*tah*-toom. Lat. enlarged, expanded. China, Japan, Korea.

farreri Stearn. *fa*-ruh-ree. After English plant collector and author Reginald John Farrer (1880–1920), who sent seeds of it to the Royal Horticultural Society from China. China.

×*globosum* Coombes. glo-*boh*-soom. Lat. globose (the habit). *V. calvum* × *V. davidii*. China.

×*hillieri* Stearn. *hil*-ee-uh-ree. After Hillier Nurseries, UK, where it was raised. *V. erubescens* × *V. henryi*. Cult.

×*juddii* Rehder. *jud*-ee-ee. After William Henry Judd (1888–1946), propagator at the Arnold Arboretum, who raised it in 1920. *V. bitchiuense* × *V. carlesii*. Cult.

lantana L. lan-*tah*-nuh. Wayfaring tree. Lat. name for *Viburnum*. Eur., N Africa, W Asia.

lentago L. len-*tah*-goh. Sheepberry. Lat. flexible (the shoots). Canada, USA.

macrocephalum Fortune. mak-roh-*kef*-uh-loom. Chinese snowball. Gk. with a large head (of flowers). China.

odoratissimum Ker Gawl. oh-do-ruh-*tis*-i-moom. Lat. most fragrant. E and SE Asia. var. *awabuki* (K. Koch) Zabel. ah-wuh-*bue*-kee. The Japanese name. Japan, Taiwan.

opulus L. *op*-ew-loos. Guelder rose. Lat. name for a kind of maple. Eur., C Asia. var. *americanum* Aiton. uh-me-ri-*kah*-noom. Of America. Canada, USA. var. *sargentii* (Koehne) Takeda. sar-*jent*-ee-ee. After American botanist Charles Sprague Sargent (1841–1927), first director of the Arnold Arboretum, who introduced it to Europe. E Asia.

plicatum Thunb. pli-*kah*-toom. Japanese snowball. Lat. folded together (the leaves). China, Taiwan, Korea, Japan.

'**Pragense**'. prahg-*en*-see. Of Prague, where it was raised. *V. rhytidophyllum* × *V. utile*.

prunifolium L. prue-ni-*foh*-lee-oom. Black haw. Lat. with leaves like *Prunus*. E and C USA.

rhytidophyllum Hemsl. ri-ti-*dof*-i-loom. Gk. with wrinkled leaves. China.

sargentii Koehne = *V. opulus* var. *sargentii*

sieboldii Miq. see-*bold*-ee-ee. After Philip Franz von Siebold (1796–1866), who studied the flora and fauna of Japan. Japan.

tinus L. *teen*-oos. Laurustinus. The Lat. name. Medit.

trilobum Marshall = *V. opulus* var. *americanum*

Vicia L. (Fabaceae). *vis*-ee-uh. The Lat. name, from Lat. to bind, referring to the tendrils. 160 spp. ann. and perenn. herbs. N temp. regs., Africa, S Am.

faba L. *fah*-buh. Broad bean. The Lat. name. Cult.

Viguiera multiflora (Nutt.) S. F. Blake = *Heliomeris multiflora*

Vinca L. (Apocynaceae). *ving*-kuh. From the Lat. name, from Lat. to wind about (*pervincire*, hence periwinkle; it was used in wreaths). 5 spp., perenn. herbs, subshrubs. Eur., N Africa, W and C Asia.

difformis Pourr. di-*form*-is. From Lat. misshapen (the flowers). Portugal.

major L. *may*-juh. Greater periwinkle. Lat. larger. S Eur. '**Oxyloba**'. ox-ee-*loh*-buh. Gk. with pointed lobes (the corolla).

minor L. *mie*-nuh. Lesser periwinkle. Lat. smaller. Eur.

rosea L. = *Catharanthus roseus*

Viola L. (Violaceae). vie-*oh*-luh, *vie*-o-luh. Violets. Lat. name for several plants with fragrant flowers. 500 spp., ann. and perenn. herbs, subshrubs. Widespread, mainly N hemisph.

canadensis L. kan-uh-*den*-sis. Canada violet. Of Canada. Canada, USA, N Mex.

cornuta L. kor-*newt*-uh. Horned violet. Lat. horned (the long spur on the corolla). Pyrenees, Spain.

labradorica Schrank. lab-ruh-*do*-ri-kuh. Labrador violet. Of Labrador. Canada, Greenland, N and E USA.

odorata L. oh-do-*rah*-tuh. Sweet violet. Lat. fragrant. Eur., N Africa, W Asia.

pedata L. ped-*ah*-tuh. Bird's foot violet. Lat. deeply divided into cut lobes (the leaves). SE Canada, E and C USA.

pedatifida G. Don. ped-at-i-*feed*-uh. Lat. pedately (as above) cut (the leaves). Canada, E and C USA.

pubescens Aiton. pew-*bes*-uhnz. Lat. hairy (the leaves). Canada, E and C USA.

riviniana Rchb. ri-vin-ee-*ah*-nuh. After German physician and botanist Augustus Quirinus Rivinus (1652–1723). Eur., N Africa, W Asia.

sororia Willd. so-*ro*-ree-uh. Lat. a sister to (a related species). Canada, USA.

tricolor L. *tri*-ko-lor. Heartsease. Lat. three-coloured (the flowers). Eur., W Asia.

×*wittrockiana* Gams. wit-rok-ee-*ah*-nuh. Pansy. After Swedish botanist Veit Brecher Wittrock (1839–1914),

who wrote a history of garden pansies. Cult.

violet *Viola*. **bird's foot** *V. pedata*. **Canada** *V. canadensis*. **horned** *V. cornuta*. **Labrador** *V. labradorica*. **sweet** *V. odorata*

viper's bugloss *Echium vulgare*

virgin's bower *Clematis virginiana*

Virginia bluebells *Mertensia virginica*

Virginia creeper *Parthenocissus quinquefolia*

Virginia sweetspire *Itea virginica*

Vitaliana primuliflora Bertol. = *Androsace vitaliana*

Vitex L. (Lamiaceae). *vie*-tex. Lat. name for this or another tree, possibly from Lat. to plait (the flexible shoots were used to make fences and baskets). 250 spp., trees, shrubs. Widespread in trop. and temp. regs.

agnus-castus L. *an*-yoos-*kast*-oos. Chaste tree. Lat. chaste lamb, from the Gk. name. S Eur., N Africa, W and C Asia.

Vitis L. (Vitaceae). *vie*-tis. Lat. name for grapevine. 60 spp. woody climbers. N temp. regs., subtropics.

coignetiae Pulliat ex Planch. koin-*yet*-ee-ie. After the wife of Jean Francisque Coignet (1835–1902), French mining engineer in Japan. It was described from plants raised from seeds she sent to France. E Russia (Sakhalin), Japan.

riparia Michx. ri-*pah*-ree-uh. Lat. of riverbanks. Canada, E and C USA.

vinifera L. vin-*if*-uh-ruh. Grapevine. Lat. wine-producing. Eur., N Africa, W and C Asia.

wake robin *Trillium*

Waldsteinia Willd. (Rosaceae). wold-
stien-ee-uh. After Franz de Paula
Adam von Waldstein (1759–1823),
Austrian botanist and soldier. 6 spp.
perenn. herbs. N temp. regs.
ternata (Stephan) Fritsch. ter-*nah*-
tuh. Lat. divided into three (the
leaves). C and E Eur., E Asia.

wallflower *Erysimum cheiri*
walnut *Juglans*. black *J. nigra*. common *J. regia*. Japanese *J. ailantifolia*
wandering Jew *Tradescantia zebrina*
wandflower *Dierama*
Washington thorn *Crataegus phaenopyrum*

Washingtonia H. Wendl. (Arecaceae).
wosh-ing-*toh*-nee-uh. After George
Washington (1732–1799), first US
president. 2 spp. palms. SW USA,
NW Mex.
filifera (Linden ex André) H. Wendl.
fi-*li*-fuh-ruh. California fan palm.
Lat. bearing threads (the frayed edges
of the leaf divisions). SW USA, NW
Mex. (B.C.).
robusta H. Wendl. roh-*bus*-tuh.
Mexican fan palm. Lat. robust

(though less robust than *W. filifera*).
NW Mex.

water figwort *Scrophularia aquatica*
water lettuce *Pistia stratiotes*
water milfoil *Myriophyllum*
water poppy *Hydrocleys nymphoides*
water violet *Hottonia palustris*
watercress *Nasturtium officinale*
waterlily *Nymphaea*. European *N.
alba*. fragrant *N. odorata*
watermelon *Citrullus lanatus*

Watsonia Mill. (Iridaceae). wot-*soh*-
nee-uh. After English physician and
naturalist Sir William Watson
(1715–1787), friend of the author,
Philip Miller. 52 spp. cormous herbs.
S Africa.
aletroides (Burm.f.) Ker Gawl. a-let-
roy-deez. Like *Aletris*, referring to the
flowers.
borbonica (Pourr.) Goldblatt. bor-
bon-i-kuh. Of Île Bourbon (now
Réunion), where it was thought to
originate.
pillansii L. Bolus. pi-*lanz*-ee-ee. After
South African botanist Neville
Stuart Pillans (1884–1964), who
collected the type specimen in 1919.

wattle *Acacia*. black *A. melanoxylon*.
hedge *A. paradoxa*. kangaroo *A.
paradoxa*. knife-leaf *A. cultriformis*.
Ovens *A. pravissima*. sallow *A. longifolia*. silver *A. dealbata*. swamp *A.
retinodes*. Sydney golden *A. longifolia*. Wally's *A. pataczekii*
wax plant *Hoya carnosa*
wayfaring tree *Viburnum lantana*

Weigela Thunb. (Diervillaceae). wie-
geel-uh, *vie*-guh-luh. After Christian

Ehrenfried von Weigel (1748–1831), German scientist. 10 spp. deciduous shrubs. NE Asia.

florida (Bunge) A. DC. *flo*-ri-duh. Lat. flowering. China, Japan, Korea.

middendorffiana (Carrière) K. Koch. mid-uhn-dorf-ee-*ah*-nuh. After Alexander Theodor von Middendorff (1815–1894), Russian naturalist and explorer. E Russia, Japan.

praecox (Lemoine) L. H: Bailey. *prie*-koks. Lat. early (flowering). E Russia, N Korea.

Wellingtonia *Sequoiadendron giganteum*

white forsythia *Abeliophyllum distichum*

whitebeam *Sorbus aria.* **Swedish** *S. intermedia*

whiteweed, flat-top *Ageratum corymbosum*

willow *Salix.* **American pussy** *S. discolor.* **bay** *S. pentandra.* **black** *S. nigra.* **coyote** *S. exigua.* **crack** *S. euxina.* **creeping** *S. repens.* **cricket bat** *S. alba* var. *caerulea.* **goat** *S. caprea.* **golden** *S. alba* var. *vitellina.* **golden weeping** *S.* ×*sepulcralis* 'Chrysocoma'. **grey** *S. cinerea.* **halberd** *S. hastata.* **hoary** *S. eleagnos.* **peachleaf** *S. amygdaloides.* **Peking** *S. babylonica* var. *pekinensis.* **pussy** *S. caprea, S. cinerea.* **scarlet** *S. alba* 'Britzensis'. **silky** *S. sericea.* **Swiss** *S. helvetica.* **violet** *S. daphnoides.* **weeping** *S. babylonica.* **white** *S. alba.* **woolly** *S. lanata*

windflower, snowdrop *Anemone sylvestris*

wineberry, Japanese *Rubus phoenicolasius*

winecup *Callirhoe digitata*

wingnut *Pterocarya.* **Caucasian** *P. fraxinifolia.* **Chinese** *P. stenoptera*

winter aconite *Eranthis hyemalis*

Winter's bark *Drimys winteri*

winterberry *Ilex verticillata*

wintergreen *Gaultheria procumbens*

wintersweet *Chimonanthus praecox*

Wisteria Nutt. (Fabaceae). wist-*e*-ree-uh. After Caspar Wistar (1761–1818), American physician and anatomist. The spelling may have been chosen deliberately to avoid the pronunciation wist-*air*-ree-uh. 5 spp. woody climbers. China, Japan, USA.

brachybotrys Sieb. & Zucc. brak-ee-*bot*-ris. Gk. with short clusters (of flowers). Japan.

floribunda (Willd.) DC. flo-ri-*bun*-duh. Lat. flowering profusely. Japan.

frutescens (L.) Poir. frue-*tes*-uhnz. Lat. somewhat shrubby. SE USA. var.

macrostachya Torr. & A. Gray. mak-roh-*stak*-ee-uh. Gk. with large spikes (of flowers). E and C USA.

macrostachya (Torr. & A. Gray) Nutt. ex B. L. Rob. & Fernald = *W. frutescens* var. *macrostachya*

sinensis (Sims) DC. sin-*en*-sis. Lat. of China. China.

venusta Rehder & E. H. Wilson = *W. brachybotrys*

witch alder *Fothergilla major.* **dwarf** *F. gardenii*

witch hazel *Hamamelis.* **Chinese** *H. mollis.* **Japanese** *H. japonica.* **Ozark** *H. vernalis*

woad *Isatis tinctoria*

wolfsbane *Aconitum lycoctonum*

Wollemia W. G. Jones, K. D. Hill & J. M. Allen (Araucariaceae).

wol-*em*-ee-uh. After Wollemi National Park, NSW, where it was discovered in 1994. 1 sp., conifer. NSW, Australia.

nobilis W. G. Jones, K. D. Hill & J. M. Allen. Wollemi pine. After David Noble (b. 1965), English-born explorer and NSW park ranger, who discovered it.

wood vamp *Decumaria barbara*
woodbine *Lonicera periclymenum*

Woodsia R. Br. (Dryopteridaceae). *woodz*-ee-uh. After Joseph Woods (1776–1864), English botanist and geologist. 30 spp. ferns. N temp. regs., trop. mts.

obtusa (Spreng.) Torr. ob-*tew*-suh. Lat. blunt (the frond lobes). SE Canada, E and C USA.

Woodwardia Sm. (Blechnaceae). wood-*ward*-ee-uh. After Thomas Jenkinson Woodward (1745–1820), English botanist. 14 spp. ferns. N and C Am., Eur., N Africa, E Asia.

fimbriata Sm. fim-bree-*ah*-tuh. Giant chain fern. Lat. fringed. SW Canada, W USA, NW Mex. (B.C.).

radicans (L.) Sm. *rad*-i-kanz. Chain fern. Lat. producing roots (the plant-lets on the fronds). SW Eur., N Africa.

unigemmata (Makino) Nakai. ew-nee-gem-*ah*-tuh. Lat. with one bud (below the frond apex). China, Japan, SE Asia.

wormwood, beach *Artemisia stelleriana*. **Roman** *A. pontica*. **sweet** *A. annua*

Xanthisma DC. (Asteraceae). zanth-*iz*-muh. Gk. yellow quality, referring to the flowers. 17 spp., ann. and perenn. herbs, shrubs. SW Canada, W USA, Mex.
coloradoense (A. Gray) D. R. Morgan & R. L. Hartman. ko-lo-rah-doh-*en*-see. Colorado tansyaster. Of Colorado. USA (Colorado, Wyoming).

Xanthoceras Bunge (Sapindaceae). zanth-oh-*se*-ruhs. Gk. yellow horn, referring to the yellow horn-like glands between the petals. 1 sp., deciduous shrub or tree. N China, Korea.
sorbifolium Bunge. sorb-i-*foh*-lee-oom. Lat. with leaves like *Sorbus*.

Xanthocyparis Farjon & Hiep (Cupressaceae). zanth-oh-*sip*-uh-ris.

Gk. yellow cypress (from the colour of the wood of *X. vietnamensis*). 2 spp. conifers. SW Canada, NW USA, Vietnam.
nootkatensis (D. Don) Farjon & D. K. Harder. nuet-kuh-*ten*-sis. Nootka cypress. Of the Nootka Sound reg., British Columbia. SW Canada, NW USA.

Xanthorhiza Marshall (Ranunculaceae). zanth-oh-*rie*-zuh. Gk. yellow root. 1 sp., shrub. E USA.
simplicissima Marshall. sim-pli-*sis*-i-muh. Yellowroot. Lat. most simple (the unbranched stems).

Xerochrysum Tzvelev (Asteraceae). zeer-ro-*krie*-soom. Gk. dry, golden (the showy dry bracts of the flowerhead). 6 spp. ann. and perenn. herbs. Australia.
bracteatum (Vent.) Tzvelev. brak-tee-*ah*-toom. Golden everlasting. Lat. bearing bracts (the flowerhead).

Xerophyllum Michx. (Melanthiaceae). zeer-*rof*-i-loom. 2 spp. perenn. herbs. SW Canada, E and NW USA.
tenax (Pursh) Nutt. *ten*-ax. Bear grass. Lat. tough (the leaves). SW Canada, NW USA.

yarrow *Achillea*. **common** *A. mille-folium*. **Greek** *A. ageratifolia*

yaupon *Ilex vomitoria*

yellow archangel *Lamium galeob-dolon*

yellow flag *Iris pseudacorus*

yellow jessamine *Gelsemium sempervirens*

yellow tuft *Alyssum murale*

yellowroot *Xanthorhiza simplicissima*

yellowwood *Cladrastis kentukea*. **Chinese** *C. delavayi*

yesterday, today and tomorrow *Brunfelsia pauciflora*

yew *Taxus*. **English** *T. baccata*. **Japanese** *T. cuspidata*. **Prince Albert's** *Saxegothaea conspicua*

Yucca L. (Asparagaceae). *yook*-uh. Caribbean name for *Manihot esculenta* (cassava), incorrectly applied to this genus. 50 spp. evergreen herbs, often shrubby or tree-like. N and C Am.

aloifolia L. a-loh-i-*foh*-lee-uh. Lat. with leaves like *Aloe*. SE USA, Mex., Caribb.

baccata Torr. ba-*kah*-tuh. Lat. bearing berries (the fruit). SW USA, N Mex.

elephantipes Regel ex Trel. = *Y. gigantea*

filamentosa L. fil-uh-men-*toh*-suh. Lat. bearing threads (the leaf margin). SE USA.

flaccida Haw. *flak*-si-duh. Lat. drooping (the leaves). SE Canada, E USA.

gigantea Lem. jie-*gant*-ee-uh. Lat. very large. Mex., C Am.

glauca Nutt. *glaw*-kuh. Lat. bluish white (the leaves). SC Canada, C USA.

gloriosa L. glor-ree-*oh*-suh. Lat. glorious. SE USA.

rostrata Engelm. ex Trel. ros-*trah*-tuh. Lat. beaked (the fruit). Tex., N Mex.

whipplei Torr. = *Hesperoyucca whipplei*

Yushania P. C. Keng (Poaceae). yue-*shan*-ee-uh. Of Yushan (Mount Morrison), Taiwan, where the type specimen was collected in 1905. 80 spp. bamboos. Africa, E Asia.

anceps (Mitford) W. C. Lin. *an*-seps. Lat. doubtful (the country of origin). Himal.

Zabelia (Rehder) Makino (Linnaeaceae). za-*bel*-ee-uh. After German botanist Hermann Zabel (1832–1912), the first to divide *Abelia* into sections. 6 spp. deciduous shrubs. Afghanistan to E Asia.
mosanensis (Chung ex Nakai) Hisauti & Hara. moh-san-*en*-sis. Fragrant abelia. Lat. of Mosan, N Korea. Korea.
triflora (R. Br. ex Wall.) Makino. trie-*flaw*-ruh. Lat. with (up to) three flowers (in each cluster). Himal., W China.

Zaluzianskya F. W. Schmidt (Scrophulariaceae). za-lue-zee-*an*-skee-uh. After Bohemian botanist Adam Zaluziansky von Zaluzian (1558–1613). 55 spp. ann. and perenn. herbs. S Africa.
capensis (L.) Walp. kuh-*pen*-sis. Of the Cape.
ovata (Benth.) Walp. oh-*vah*-tuh. Lat. ovate (the leaves).

Zamioculcas Schott (Araceae). zah-mee-oh-*kool*-kuhs. From *Zamia* (which the foliage resembles) and culcas, the Arabic name for *Colocasia*

antiquorum, which has a similar rhizome. 1 sp., perenn. herb. E Africa.
zamiifolia (Lodd.) Engl. zah-mee-i-*foh*-lee-uh. Lat. with leaves like *Zamia*.

Zamia L. (Zamiaceae). *zah*-mee-uh. From Lat. name used by Pliny for a pine cone, from Gk. dried up. 53 spp. cycads. SE USA to S Am.
furfuracea L.f. fur-few-*ray*-see-uh. Cardboard palm. Lat. scurfy (referring to the short brown hairs on the leaves). Mex. (Veracruz).

Zantedeschia Spreng. (Araceae). zan-te-*desk*-ee-uh. After Giovanni Zantedeschi (1773–1846), Italian botanist and physician. 8 spp. perenn. herbs. C and S Africa.
aethiopica (L.) Spreng. ee-thee-*op*-i-kuh. Arum lily. Lat. of Africa. S Africa.

Zauschneria californica C. Presl = *Epilobium canum*
cana Greene = *Epilobium canum*

Zea L. (Poaceae). *zee*-uh. Gk. name for another cereal grass. 6 spp. grasses. Mex., C Am.
mays L. *mayz*. Corn, maize. From a Caribbean name. Cult. with subspecies in Mex. and C Am.

zebra plant *Aphelandra squarrosa*

Zebrina pendula Schnizl. = *Tradescantia zebrina*

Zelkova Spach (Ulmaceae). zel-*koh*-vuh. From the Georgian name of

Z. carpinifolia, from Georgian bar
rock, referring to the use of the hard
wood in building. 6 spp., deciduous
trees, shrubs. Sicily, Crete, W and
E Asia.

carpinifolia (Pall.) K. Koch. kar-pie-
ni-*foh*-lee-uh. Caucasian elm. Lat.
with leaves like *Carpinus*. W Asia.

serrata (Thunb.) Makino. se-*rah*-tuh.
Lat. toothed (the leaves). E Russia,
Korea, Japan, Taiwan.

Zenobia D. Don (Ericaceae). ze-*noh*-
bee-uh. After Septimia Zenobia, 3rd-
cent. queen of Palmyra, Syria. 1 sp.,
shrub. SE USA.

pulverulenta (Bartr. ex Willd.)
Pollard. pul-ve-rue-*lent*-uh. Lat. pow-
dery (a white bloom usually covers
the leaves).

Zephyranthes Herb. (Amaryllidaceae). zef-i-*ranth*-eez. Rain lilies,
zephyr lilies. Gk. flower of the west
wind, referring to their origin. 70
spp. bulbous herbs. SE USA to S Am.

candida (Lindl.) Herb. *kan*-di-duh.
Lat. white (the flowers). S Am.

Zigadenus elegans Pursh = *Anticlea
elegans*

Zinnia L. (Asteraceae). *zin*-ee-uh.
After Johann Gottfried Zinn (1727–
1759), German botanist and ophthal-
mologist. 17 spp., ann. and perenn.
herbs, subshrubs. USA to S Am.

elegans Jacq. *el*-i-ganz. Lat. elegant.
Mex.

zucchini *Cucurbita pepo*

Selected bibliography

Books

Coombes, A. J. 1985. *The Collingridge Dictionary of Plant Names.* Collingridge.

Coombes, A. J. (ed.), W. Ehrhardt, E. Götz, N. Bödeker, and S. Seybold. 2009. *The Timber Press Dictionary of Plant Names.* Timber Press.

Gledhill, D. 2008. *The Names of Plants.* Cambridge University Press.

Griffiths, M. 1994. *Index of Garden Plants.* The Royal Horticultural Society.

Lewis, C. T. 1963. *Elementary Latin Dictionary.* Oxford University Press.

Liddell, H. G., and R. Scott. 1891. *Greek-English Lexicon.* Oxford University Press.

Lord, T. (ed.). 2009. *RHS Plant Finder.* Dorling Kindersley.

Mabberley, D. J. 2008. *Mabberley's Plant Book.* Cambridge University Press.

Stearn, W. T. 1973. *Botanical Latin.* David & Charles.

Websites

California Plant Names. http://www.calflora.net/botanicalnames/

Flora of China. http://hua.huh.harvard.edu/china/index.html

Flora of North America Editorial Committee, eds. 1993–. Flora of North America North of Mexico. www.fna.org

Plant Information Online. Andersen Horticultural Library, University of Minnesota. http://plantinfo.umn.edu/

Stevens, P. F. 2001–. Angiosperm Phylogeny Website. Version 9, June 2008. http://www.mobot.org/MOBOT/research/APweb/.

The International Plant Names Index. http://www.ipni.org

Tropicos.org. Missouri Botanical Garden. http://www.tropicos.org

World Checklist of Selected Plant Families. The Board of Trustees of the Royal Botanic Gardens, Kew. Published on the Internet; http://www.kew.org/wcsp/

USDA, ARS, National Genetic Resources Program. Germplasm Resources Information Network (GRIN) [Online Database]. National Germplasm Resources Laboratory, Beltsville, Maryland. http://www.ars-grin.gov/cgi-bin/npgs/html/tax_search.pl